Christ, the Life of the Soul

BOOKS BY

Blessed Columba Marmion

Christ in His Mysteries

Christ, the Ideal of the Monk

Christ, the Ideal of the Priest

The English Letters of Abbot Marmion

Union with God

Words of Life

Sponsa Verbi

BOOKS BY

Alan Bancroft

Collected Poems of St Thérèse of Lisieux
(translations into English verse)

Barb of Fire: Twenty Poems of Blessed Elizabeth
of the Trinity, with selected passages from
Blessed Columba Marmion

BLESSED COLUMBA MARMION

CHRIST, THE LIFE of the SOUL

Translated by
Alan Bancroft

ZACCHEUS PRESS
Bethesda

Nihil Obstat: Father Ian G. Kelly, M. Phil.

Imprimatur: Monsignor Mark Davies
Vicar General, Diocese of Salford
November 2, 2005

The text is set in Sabon.

Library of Congress Cataloging-in-Publication Data

Marmion, Columba, Abbot, 1858-1923.
   [Christ, vie de l'ame. English]
   Christ, the life of the soul / by Columba Marmion ; translated by Alan Bancroft.
     p. cm.
   Summary: "A guide to the Christian spiritual life, with an emphasis on Jesus Christ as the source of all grace and holiness"—Provided by publisher.
   ISBN-13: 978-0-9725981-4-9 (hardback : alk. paper)
   ISBN-10: 0-9725981-4-6 (hardback : alk. paper)
   ISBN-13: 978-0-9725981-5-6 (pbk. : alk. paper)
   ISBN-10: 0-9725981-5-4 (pbk. : alk. paper)
   1. Meditations. 2. Jesus Christ—Meditations. 3. Spiritual life—Catholic Church.
I. Title.
   BX2183.M2913 2005
   248.4'82—dc22

                                2005015615

10 9 8 7 6 5 4 3 2 1

To learn more about Blessed Columba Marmion, please visit our webpage:

www.zaccheuspress.com

Contents

Book One
The Divine Designs

Book Two
The Christian Life

Book Two
The Christian Life (*cont.*)

APPENDICES

FOREWORD

by

Father Benedict J. Groeschel, CFR

As someone who read and reread the works of Abbot Marmion over a half century ago, when I was in a Capuchin seminary, I was delighted to receive an invitation to write a Foreword to this fine translation of what might well be considered the greatest of his works. Marmion enthusiasts have waited for years for a new edition of his works that would present the flurry of Scripture quotations in the vernacular and clarify some imprecisions in the original translation. Certainly the original English translation done by a nun of Tyburn Convent was not deficient, but in almost one hundred years since the book appeared, certain turns of phrase and theological concepts have come to be nuanced and expressed in slightly different ways. In the present translation Alan Bancroft, who has had a long career as a lawyer and who more recently has turned to the translation of spiritual writings from French, shows that he is well suited to this task.

Dom Mark Tierney, OSB, Vice-Postulator of Blessed Columba's cause for canonization, shares my enthusiasm for Mr. Bancroft's accomplishment. The Marmion scholars, a group I hope will grow as his possible canonization approaches, will find the extensive footnotes a rich source of research and the beginning of a new scholarship about this great and original spiritual writer.

Rather than trying to anticipate such scholarship, I would prefer to share with you my thoughts on Marmion as a most effective spiritual author. Dom Bernard Capelle, OSB, in an excellent treatment of Marmion's place in the history of spirituality,[1] focused on two important characteristics of Marmion. The first is his complete and emphatic Christocentrism, which has echoes, as he points out, in Saints Paul, Ignatius of Antioch, and Augustine, as well as many other great Christian writers. A second hallmark of Marmion is his thorough theological examination of the idea of divine adoption. In the vast literature of Christian spirituality Dom Bernard could have found many other emphases, ascetical and mystical. Perhaps no writer other than Marmion has so clearly developed the idea that we are adopted children of God and that our filiation is profoundly related to the divine exemplar of the relationship of Father and Son. However, as Dom Bernard notes:

> It is not in attaching importance to the fact of our filial adoption that Dom Marmion's doctrine is original; many had done so before him. But it would be difficult to find another who had given the mystery such preeminence, making it, as he does, the beginning and the end of the spiritual life. And with Dom Marmion it is not so much a theory or a system, as a living truth that acts directly on the soul.

It is especially important today to recognize that among writings on the spiritual life Marmion's work is a timely and much-needed antidote to several less than healthy trends noticeable during the past decade. First of all, Marmion's profound Christology, based on rocksolid scriptural and patristic sources, is an antidote to the many confusing christologies of our time, which range, sadly enough, from excessive humanism to thinly disguised adoptionism and Unitarianism.

[1] Dom Bernard Capelle, "Marmion's Place in the History of Spirituality," in *Abbot Marmion: An Irish Tribute*, edited by the Monks of Glenstal (Westminster: The Newman Press, 1948).

Marmion delivers us effectively from the mere superhuman Christ, a concept dangerously attractive in a superficial time, and from far worse trends that have emerged as a kind of Catholic unitarianism. One theologian observed to me that some who call themselves Catholic have left Arius far behind. I ascribe the fact that I was never tempted in these directions to my lifelong familiarity with Augustine and Marmion.

One name that should be mentioned in a summary of Abbot Marmion is that of Archbishop Alban Goodier, SJ, who carried on a long correspondence with the abbot. They shared the stage of popular Catholic spiritual writers at the time, although they were quite different. Marmion's approach was profoundly theological, while Goodier's presentation of Christ engaged the psychological needs, desires, and aspirations of the Catholic reading public, who were becoming more and more introspective as a result of the impact of modern psychology. A remarkable photograph exists showing the two fervent Christ-centered writers conversing, although they actually never met. They were so similar in their goals that the photographer used a composite photo to put them apparently in the same physical venue. This custom of another time may strike us as amusing, but symbolically, it illustrates how close they were in recognizing that Jesus Christ is indeed the life of the soul.

The doctrine of divine adoption of the human being who is a disciple of Christ and the potential adoption of all who may be touched and saved by His grace needs much more examination and application in our confused age. Popular piety is clamoring for such an emphasis in preaching and pastoral work. Our conception of human nature has been badly distorted by the negative view of Freudian psychoanalysis and other more popular psychologies emerging from it. On the other hand, psychologies that are filled with a denial of the very real dysfunction and aberration of human nature have come to appear superficial to many people. This overly positive view is in fact a new form of Pelagianism, which has affected Christian piety across the board.

Christian education desperately needs to be informed and reoriented to Christ as He is proclaimed by the evangelists and other writers of the New Testament and as He is presented by the Church Fathers and mystics. The idea of divine adoption for those who follow Christ's teaching answers the desperate human need for salvation and focuses on Christ as the single and unique source of our redemption.

This new edition of *Christ, the Life of the Soul* is an invitation to laity, religious, and clergy to return to the pure waters of life and leave behind the murky creeks and polluted rivers that have engulfed us for much of the last half century.

INTRODUCTION

by

Dom Mark Tierney, OSB

*Vice-Postulator for the Cause of Canonization
of Blessed Columba Marmion*

It is with great pleasure that I hail this new English translation of *Christ, the Life of the Soul*. Alan Bancroft has achieved what might have been thought impossible, namely to present Marmion to the people of the twenty-first century in a language easily understood and eminently readable. The first English translation—by a nun of Tyburn convent, London—was a great success, and went through many editions, but it eventually became somewhat "dated." This new translation allows Marmion's words to shine out anew. Mr. Bancroft remains faithful to the original, and beautifully captures the "atmosphere" and even the rhythm of Marmion's style, while at the same time crafting a text that reads as graceful, modern English.

Ever since the Beatification of Dom Columba Marmion in 2000, there has been a renewed interest in his writings and in his spiritual message. During the ceremony of the Beatification, Pope John Paul II spoke of the importance of Marmion in the history of Catholic spirituality, and praised him for re-stating the *centrality of Christ* in his writings. He expressed the hope that Marmion's books would continue to be read by the faithful, as they contained a message of great spiritual value.

However, it is a fact that all Marmion's books in English are now out of print and unobtainable, except in an expensive one-volume edition, *The Spiritual Writings of Dom Columba Marmion* (P. Leth-ielleux, Maredsous Abbey, 2000). Something had to be done to bring Marmion back into popular circulation, and that is what Mr. Bancroft has achieved. It is to be hoped that this will be the first of Marmion's books to be given such treatment, and that the rest of the trilogy[1] will soon be available in new translations. Due credit must be given to the publishers on both sides of the Atlantic (Zaccheus Press and Gracewing) for giving their support to the present venture.

Marmion was born in Dublin, Ireland, in 1858. English was his mother-tongue—despite the fact that his mother was French! However, he spent most of his adult life in Belgium, in the abbey of Maredsous, where French was the spoken language. He became Abbot of this monastery in 1909, and held office up to his death in 1923. His books were compiled from notes of Conferences and Retreats which he had given, in French, over a large number of years. Dom Raymond Thibaut, the monk of Maredsous who edited the trilogy knew no English. Thus it was that the original versions of Marmion's writings appeared in French. Mr. Bancroft now offers us an authentic English version of Marmion's spiritual message, which is addressed, not to an elite audience but to everyone.

It is true that, in our computer/television age, people do not read as much as in times gone by. Spiritual reading, especially, seems to have fallen by the wayside, although the Bible continues to be a best-seller. The problem for writers, as for publishers, is to revive people's interest in reading what may be called "serious" books, and Marmion would surely come into this category. Reading a book is always an *adventure*, a jump into the unknown. Spiritual reading is a special kind of adventure, a searching for God and for ourselves in God.

---

[1] *Christ, the Life of the Soul, Christ in His Mysteries,* and *Christ, the Ideal of the Monk.*

So, why read Marmion today? What message has he for the twenty-first century? Human nature does not change, despite the passage of time. We are all searching for the Truth, for the meaning of Life. We want to find some element of certainty or sanity in our world. And that is exactly what Marmion offers us. Perhaps his world was somewhat more God-centered than ours, but that should not deter us from seeking God in the same measure as he did.

The great Belgian Cardinal Mercier—a contemporary of Marmion—when asked what was the secret of the success of Marmion's books, replied with these words: "He makes you *touch God*." Marmion had a special charism, which he proffered with a gentle touch, to bring people close to God. Furthermore, he believed that spiritual reading can, in itself, be a prayer, as it lifts the mind up to heavenly things. This fits in with his general definition of prayer, which he declares to be nothing else than "spending time with God." *Christ, the Life of the Soul* is permeated, through and through, with God-moments. It is a book to be read slowly, and not more than a few pages at a time. It is a book born out of prayer, the fruit of Marmion's own personal contact with God. It should be read in the same prayerful way. Time spent reading this book is *time spent with God*.

If one were to pinpoint the central theme of all Marmion's teaching, it could be summed up in the two words *Divine adoption*. Over and over again he takes up the Pauline idea: "We are by Adoption what Christ is by Nature." God has adopted us as His children, called us to be brothers and sisters of Christ, destined for the eternal life in heaven. Taking his cue from Sacred Scripture, he reminds us that in the beginning, according to the Book of Genesis, God created each human person in His own image. Even after the Fall, God did not abandon the human race, but sent His only Son as our Savior. As followers of the Savior, Jesus Christ, we are called *Christians*, i.e. *other Christs*. Marmion goes further than most spiritual writers, in that he tells us we are called to be "deified," to become like God, even in this life. This *deification* begins with our Baptism and continues throughout our lives. As you read *Christ, the Life of the Soul*, you will discover the deeper meaning of this—our divine destiny! Marmion offers us the fruits of his own meditation on the Sacred Mysteries, and provides us with a wonderful synthesis of Scripture and all that is best in Theology and the Church's liturgical experience.

Marmion had the mind and heart of an apostle, and he exercised his apostolate first through the spoken word, and then in his spiritual writings. He spent his life bringing people to God, and God to people. He continues to do so today through his books.

He had, at the same time, a very human side to him, which is more evident in his extensive correspondence than in his spiritual writings. He constantly emphasizes the spiritual side of our human condition, and the human side of our spiritual condition. A selection of his Letters has been published in two books: *Union with God* and *The English Letters of Abbot Marmion*, which are both out-of-print. A new, definitive edition of the complete *Marmion Correspondence* is in preparation and should be available in the near future.

What Marmion offers us in *Christ, the Life of the Soul* is a practical road to holiness. He points out this road with a sure and steady hand. He has no time for those who wish to travel on their own, and who base their journeying on purely human ideas. For such people, he says, "their life becomes a toil, subject to incessant difficulty, a toil without an opening-up to full flower." He often told the story about his own spiritual director in Clonliffe College, Dublin, who maintained that there was only one road to holiness: *Practice the virtues, and keep on practicing them*, until in the end—after many long years—you come to love God. Marmion had no sympathy with such an approach, which, he said, was in fact *difficult and impossible*. He proposed a more God-centered way: "Begin by loving God, and in time—very soon, in fact—you will be led to practice and relish the virtues." Speaking from his own experience, he maintained that this way was *easy and agreeable*.

Marmion is not offering anything new to his readers. Rather, he is following in a long line of spiritual masters, such as St. Francis de Sales, whose book *The Love of God* he especially recommends. Within the covers of *Christ, the Life of the Soul* you will find a synthesis of spiritual wisdom, which draws on Sacred Scripture, the Liturgy, and the vast treasures of the Church's ascetical and mystical experience. Marmion breaks the bread of divine life for us, in a way that is comprehensible and attractive. He takes up some of the more difficult points of our Faith, such as Grace, and gives us new insights into them. "Grace," he says, "is nothing else than *the life of Christ in the soul.*" Hence the title of the book: *Christ, the Life of the Soul.*

Marmion's final message to his readers of today, is that we should make Christ the center of our lives. Christ should be our All in all. In his own special way, Marmion offers us a challenge as well as an invitation. The *challenge* is one that calls for courage, determination and perseverance: we are challenged to plunge ourselves into the supernatural, with faith and hope. The *invitation* is equally insistent: to seek union with God, through love and service. According to Marmion, our path through life is a gradual progress towards the supernatural. Christ *is* the Life of our Soul. We could not find a more sure way to achieve that than in this spiritual classic, *Christ, the Life of the Soul.*

Glenstal Abbey
Murroe, Co. Limerick
Ireland

TRANSLATOR'S INTRODUCTORY NOTE

MARMION'S WORDS, which make up *Le Christ, Vie de l'âme*, were originally delivered orally—hence the conversational tone and the references to "talks."

The book was first published in 1917. This translation is from the edition of 1920 and is the first full translation into English since that of the "Nun of Tyburn" in 1922. It is rather extraordinary that there should be an English translation at all, since the native language of Marmion, an Irishman, was English. But, as the abbot of a Belgian monastery, he gave his spiritual talks in French.

Typography, and truths that are deep

The capital initials used in this translation for the pronouns "He" and "Him," referring to Christ, are making a continuous point—or rather, they emphasize what is precisely Marmion's central point. Christ's *divinity* is at the very heart of what Marmion is saying. We have, he writes, to "pierce the veil of the humanity of Christ and reach the depths of His divinity." "In the face of the world which denies Him and disowns Him," we are adjured to repeat like St. Peter: 'You are Christ, the Son of the Living God'" (*Christ, the Ideal of the Priest*, ch. III).

But in Marmion's exposition that central point is allied with another, no less central, namely that Christ is God *made man*. The fact that Christ is man, as well as God, has to be remembered at all times.

At the Incarnation—when "the Word was made flesh, and dwelt among us" (John 1:14)—the Eternal Word, that is to say, the Eternal Son of the Father, "united Himself to a human nature within the sphere of time; but in so close a way that this (human) nature, while being perfect in itself, belongs entirely to the Divine Person to whom it is united" (Marmion, pages 7-8 of the present book). The Eternal Son incarnate is the one Person only, but He has two *natures,* hypostatically united: the nature of God and the nature of man, both. In the words of the Nicene Creed, He—Christ, born of the Virgin—is "true God and true man." Fail to remember this, and much of what Marmion is saying will not be understood in its true depth or at all.

In *Christ, the Life of the Soul,* Marmion's descriptions appropriately begin with what literally had no beginning—the existence of the uncreated Son in eternity: "...begotten, not made; of one Being with the Father": "I and the Father are one," said Christ (John 10:30). Then, in Marmion's words, the "Divine Hymn, a living Hymn, who sings the praise of the Father by expressing the plenitude of the Father's perfections" (this is the Son from all eternity)—that "living Hymn," after the Incarnation, "takes on a human expression, human accents." Being man, He is therefore able to give to His Father *adoration,* something which He, "the Word, equal to the Father, could not *as* the Word, render to Him" (page 392).

"The Father is greater than I" (John 14:28) was said by the Son made man. But my point in giving the above quotation from Marmion is that it emphasizes, at the same time, that the Son's *loving reverence* for His Father—what Marmion calls *piété*—is something eternal and of the essence of the equal Son's love for the Father and did not only begin when the Son became incarnate as Christ.

Along with our adoption in Christ, the mutual and eternal love within the Trinity is a recurrent theme in the present book.

Marmion frequently quotes Psalm 2:7: "You are my Son, this day have I begotten you." What does "this day" mean? Is it a prophetic reference to the day of the Incarnation, when God the Second Person of the Trinity became incarnate as an event in the sphere of time? The *eternal* Sonship of the Second Person had no "yesterday," no beginning. For God, eternity has no beginning, as well as no end. Marmion, like other distinguished commentators, relates the phrase to the Father's eternal generation of the Son, the Son's eternal Sonship: "You are my Son; today—*that is, in an eternal present,* interpolates Marmion—have I begotten you" (*Christ, the Ideal of the Priest,* ch. II). Another scriptural phrase Marmion quotes: "...before the day-star I begot you" (Ps. 109 (110):3) also refers to that eternal Sonship—always existent, existent before anything of creation came to be.

We creatures, who each had a beginning, find it hard to grasp the concept of the Son's taking His being from the Father and yet taking it thus *eternally,* having existed always as the Father has always existed. But that is how it in fact is (except that the past tense—"having existed"—strictly has no application to the Father, the Son and the Holy Spirit). Marmion writes: "The Word"—the Son—"by essence belongs entirely to the Father; He has everything from Him, *without on that account being less than the Father.* But ... He makes everything relate back to His Father: 'I draw life from the Father' (John 6:57); His essence is to live by the Father" (page 385, my italics).

Sometimes when one uses the word "God" on its own, it is clear from the context that one indeed means God *the Father.* Many examples of this usage are to be found in Marmion's writings. When the "He" of one's human language is not intended to refer to the Father in particular (and even when it is) one must remember that God is one God in three Persons. See further, on the inadequacy of our human language, pages 10-11.

If the reader shares my experience, he or she will find new insights on practically every one of Marmion's pages. Yet Marmion is not presenting us with ideas that are novel and speculative. Scriptural quotations as authority are everywhere. And, as his citations of Aquinas,

Augustine and others indicate, his commentaries derive from rich nuggets out of deep theological mines, polished and made to shine.

A final thought, a vital one, prompted by his words. We shall be utterly wide of the mark if in reading this book we (so to say) make God in our own image: ourselves in a bigger, even an immensely bigger, size. As one example: the Eternal Father and the Eternal Son, and the Third Person of the Trinity whose eternal origin is the mutual love of the Father and the Son, are *spirit*—not spirit and body (it was only at the Incarnation that the Son took to Himself a human body and soul, which He retains, glorious, in heaven). And God—the Trinity of Persons—is Infinite Love *transcending all our preconceptions and analogies.* "God is a spirit, and those who worship Him must worship Him in spirit and in truth" (John 4:24). We, who have been made in God's image, have the ability to comprehend, albeit dimly, that God—this transcendent God—is not impersonal but Personal. The revelation of the existence of the Trinity brings this home to us.

The trouble is that we subconsciously assume there to be no personality, no personhood, outside the narrow scope of ourselves and those around us. We see ourselves as the fire, but in terms of personhood we are only sparks and there is a Fire, a Threefold Fire. That is a point which will surface at intervals throughout this book, when our attention is drawn to things that God can say about God, but we cannot say about ourselves.

Reader, in thinking about the Trinity (and He has credibility, this unique man, yet infinitely more than a man, who spoke to us of the Father and Himself and the Spirit and then died and rose from the dead) do not for a moment doubt the possibility and fact of ineffable Personhood that is not based on the model—and does not have the limitations—of yourself and myself. I venture a second example of the point that we should not make God in our own image. If, in rightly concentrating on the Personhood of God, we ask ourselves: "How can even a Divine Person, how can the Holy Spirit, possibly guide the myriads of faithful souls towards their homeland individually as Marmion says?" that is because we are still fixated with the analogy of *human* personhood. Enmeshed in that thought, we imagine God's immensity to be less immense than it is. But God has no limits, is not limited. The Divine cognizance extends not only to the rolling aeons of time, but also to that microscopic flake of plaster on the wall, to that sparrow, and to *you,* who are "of much more value than many sparrows."

At the beginning, this book is tough going. Persevere with it, though, for later it gets lyrical.

Scriptural versions in English

The vernacular scriptural version with which Marmion would have been familiar during his Irish education is the Douai-Rheims (Douai, Old Testament; Rheims, New Testament). In this translation, whenever I give a direct (in inverted commas) quotation from the New Testament *without further attribution*, and without the word "See" in the relevant footnote, the quotation is from: "A revision of the Challenor-Rheims version, edited by Catholic scholars under the patronage of the Episcopal Committee of the Confraternity of Christian Doctrine" (St. Anthony Guild Press, Paterson, New Jersey, 1941)—the "Confraternity version," or "Cfy" for short. One can think of it as a revised and, to some extent, modernized Rheims. I am very grateful to Dom Placid Murray, OSB, of Glenstal Abbey, Co. Limerick, for his suggestion of the use of this version.

Whenever I give a direct quotation from the Old Testament without further attribution, the quotation is from the Douai. (More precisely, it is from an early nineteenth century edition I have of the Douai-Rheims.)

In a relatively small number of instances I have used other versions where this assists the onward flow, as also where I deem them particularly familiar or felicitous or, more important, helpfully close either to Marmion's own words or to the (French) wording of his quotations.

Those other versions are: *For the New Testament:* The old Rheims version, unrevised (indicated in the footnotes by "Rheims").

For the Old Testament: The Holy Bible, St. Paul Edition, translated by members of the Catholic Biblical Association of America, 1959 (indicated by "St P.").

For both New and Old Testaments: The Jerusalem Bible (Darton, Longman & Todd, London, 1966); The Holy Bible, Knox version (Burns & Oates, London, 1955); and The Holy Bible, Revised Standard Version, Catholic Edition (Ignatius Press, San Francisco, 1966) — indicated respectively by "Jerus.", "Knox" and "RSV, Cath."

I have confined myself to the versions stated above.

Where, in a footnote, I give a scriptural reference preceded by "See," this signals that the direct quotation in the text to which the note refers is a translation of the words Marmion uses in giving the quotation, and not a *precisely* verbatim quotation from any of the versions mentioned above. It does *not* of itself imply any substantial difference. Unless, conceivably, taken from some particular French translation he had in mind, a number of the quotations in Marmion's talks are from the many that were "in his ear," so to speak, rather than from a book open before him or consulted. Whilst being clear and accurate on their substantial meaning, he may have misremembered the precise wording of some of the texts he quoted (sometimes he telescopes two texts into one), and sometimes it might be truer to say that he *paraphrases* — his paraphrases being illuminating or at least interesting.

In giving the scriptural quotations I have changed "*he*," "*him*," "*his*" to "*He*," "*Him*," "*His*," where they refer to Christ or to the Father or the Holy Spirit. Had I not done so, that very readability which is the motive for the small initials in the various scriptural versions would have been hampered by the momentary jolts resulting from juxtaposition with the large initials in the main text of the book. In this respect, both in the text and in the scriptural quotations, I am in line with the stylistic practice of Dom Matthew Dillon, OSB, in his translation of *Christ, the Ideal of the Priest* (1952, but recently re-issued by Ignatius Press). He indeed went even further, using capital initials even for "*Who*," "*You*" and "*Your*," and "*Me*" and "*My*," as in her translations the "Nun of Tyburn" also did. In another respect besides this I have differed from them both. Seeking readability to the modern eye and ear, I have in the scriptural quotations allowed myself the liberty of changing (without the signal of a "See") "thou" and "thee" to "you," "thy" to "your," "thine" to "yours"; as also intrusive forms like "hath," "hast," "do thou," etc., to their present-day equivalents.

It remains to add that Marmion often gave scriptural quotations in the Latin of the Vulgate, as well as or instead of French. I have here used English versions throughout.

In translating generally, I have not gone out of my way to use "inclusive language"; to do so would often have been clumsy. To those who are offended by the use (in relation to one of us human beings) of "he" or other masculine words on their own, I apologize. However, they may be assured that Marmion—who lived in an age of less self-sensitivity than ours—does mean "he" to include "she." It would not have occurred to him to think otherwise.

The explanatory footnotes, as distinct from those simply giving the scriptural and other references, are Marmion's whenever there is no indication to the contrary. When an explanatory footnote is my own, and this is not obvious from its content, I have indicated the fact by (*Translator's note*) or (*Translator's quotation*). In general I only *state* that an explanatory footnote is Marmion's where it is juxtaposed with a "Translator's note" and therefore might otherwise be taken for one of mine.

I surmise that it may have been Marmion's editor and "collaborator," Dom Raymond Thibaut, who under Marmion's general surveillance provided the scriptural references in the notes (to which references I have added a few more). It may very possibly have been he who gave some of the quotations like those from Aquinas. I suppose it may be said in general that when one speaks of "Marmion" in relation to some point of detail or other, one may really be speaking of Thibaut.

Wishing to avoid puzzlement, the publisher of this American edition has asked me to explain my usage of what in Britain are called "square brackets" within Marmion's text. These simply indicate that the wording within them has been interpolated and is not part of the text itself. Sometimes the interpolation is mine; sometimes Marmion himself has interpolated words in a quotation from someone else.

Acknowledgments

My foremost gratitude is due to Dom Mark Tierney, OSB, of Glenstal Abbey, Co. Limerick. In his gentle and charming way, he has encouraged, suggested and guided, while wholly respecting my freedom as a translator. He has been an inspiration and a rock of support.

I am also grateful to his fellow European Vice-Postulator, Dom R-Frederick Poswick, OSB, of Maredsous, for valuable insights. Dom Placid Murray, OSB, of Glenstal, has helped me by answering numerous questions I put to him. My gratitude goes also to my friend Peter Dunne, a Classical scholar with great sensitivity to English words, who assessed and corrected my frequently halting translations of non-scriptural Latin passages.

I much appreciate the moral and practical support given to me by Fr. Ian G. Kelly in some fraught weeks and days before publication. He was a real facilitator, as, through specific and helpful advice he gave, was Fr. Aidan Nichols, OP. Dom Hugh Gilbert, OSB, Abbot of Pluscarden, greatly helped me concerning particular, but important, points which arose in those last days, and I warmly thank him also.

Finally, I thank John O'Leary, of Zaccheus Press, for his phenomenal patience and constructive co-operation, and for his pursuit and capture of such typographical elegance for Marmion.

Alan Bancroft
Manchester, England

LIST OF ABBREVIATIONS

Acts	The Acts of the Apostles
The Apoc.	Apocalypse (Revelation)
CCC	Catechism of the Catholic Church (1994)
Cfy	"Confraternity" version of the New Testament: "A revision of the Challoner-Rheims version, edited by Catholic scholars under the patronage of the Episcopal Committee of the Confraternity of Christian Doctrine"
Col.	St. Paul's Epistle to the Colossians
1 Cor.	St. Paul's First Epistle to the Corinthians
2 Cor.	St. Paul's Second Epistle to the Corinthians
Deut.	Deuteronomy
Douai	The Douai version of the Old Testament
Enarr. in Ps.	Commentaries [by St. Augustine] on the Psalms
Eph.	St. Paul's Epistle to the Ephesians
Exod.	Exodus
ff.	and what follows the numerical reference given
Gal.	St. Paul's Epistle to the Galatians
Gen.	Genesis
Habac.	Habacuc (Habakkuk)
Hebr.	St. Paul's Epistle to the Hebrews
Hos.	Hosea (Osee)
Ibid.	*Ibidem*, the same place
Isa.	Isaiah (Isaias)
James	The Epistle of St. James
Jerem.	Jeremiah (Jeremias)
Jerus.	The Jerusalem Bible
John	The Gospel of St. John
1 John	St. John's First Epistle
1 Kings	First Book of Kings (otherwise known as First Book of Samuel)

4 Kings	Fourth Book of Kings (otherwise known as Second Book of Kings)
Knox	The Holy Bible, Knox version
Lam.	Lamentations
Levit.	Leviticus
Luke	The Gospel of St. Luke
2 Mach.	Second Book of Maccabees
Mark	Gospel of St. Mark
Matt.	Gospel of St. Matthew
Num.	Numbers
St P.	The Holy Bible, St. Paul Edition, translated by members of the Catholic Biblical Association of America
1 Peter	St. Peter's First Epistle
2 Peter	St. Peter's Second Epistle
Phil.	St. Paul's Epistle to the Philippians
Philem.	St. Paul's Epistle to Philemon
Prov.	Proverbs
Ps.	The Psalms
Rheims	The Rheims version of the New Testament
Rom.	St. Paul's First Epistle to the Romans
RSV, Cath.	The Holy Bible, Revised Standard Version, Catholic edition
1 Thess.	St. Paul's First Epistle to the Thessalonians
St Thomas	St. Thomas Aquinas (*Summa Theologica*, unless otherwise stated)
1 Tim.	St. Paul's First Epistle to Timothy
2 Tim.	St. Paul's Second Epistle to Timothy
Titus	St. Paul's Epistle to Titus
Tob.	Tobias (Tobit)
Tract. in Johann.	*Tractatus in evangelium Johannis*, Treatise [by St. Augustine] on St. John's Gospel
Vatican II	The Second Vatican Council
vv.	verses
Zach.	Zachariah (Zacharias)

It is with Christ that we travel, and we walk in His steps. It is He who is our Guide, and the burning torch that lights up our way. Pioneer of salvation, it is He who leads us to heaven, to the Father; He who promises success in this to those who seek in faith. What He is, in glory, we shall be one day, if, through faithful imitation of His example, we become true Christians, "other Christs."

St. Cyprian, *De idolorum vanitate*, c. XV.

BOOK ONE

WHAT GOD HAS DISPOSED:
THE DIVINE DESIGNS

CHAPTER ONE

The Divine Plan of Our Adoptive Predestination in Jesus Christy

Introduction: *Importance*, **for the spiritual life, of knowledge of the Divine plan.**

It is *in Christ* —"in Him"— that "the God and Father of our Lord Jesus Christ" chose us "before the foundation of the world, that we should be holy and without blemish" in His, the Father's, sight. In His love, "according to the purpose of His will," He predestined us to be His adopted sons, through Jesus Christ, "unto the praise of the glory of His grace," by which He has made us pleasing to His eyes, "in His beloved Son."[1]

It is in those terms that the apostle St. Paul, who had been "caught up to the third heaven"[2] and who among us was, as Paul himself says, the one chosen by God to bring to light the "dispensation of the mystery which has been hidden from eternity in God";[3] it is in those terms that Paul indicates the Divine plan concerning us. We see the great apostle labor without respite to make known this eternal plan, established by God Himself for the purpose of achieving the holiness of our souls. Why do all the Apostle's efforts (as Paul takes care to say) aim at enlightening all men about the dispensation of the Divine designs?

Because only God, author of our salvation and primary source of our holiness, could make known to us what He wants of us in order that we may reach Him.

[1] Eph. 1:3-6. [2] 2 Cor. 12:3.
[3] Eph. 3:8-9: "Yes, to me ... there was given this grace, to announce...."

Among the souls who seek God, you find those who only succeed in coming to Him with great difficulty.

Some have no precise idea of what holiness is. Unaware of, or setting aside, the plan traced by Eternal Wisdom, they make holiness consist of this or that conception stemming from their own mind; they wish to find their way entirely on their own. Attached to purely human ideas which they have worked out for themselves, they wander from the path. If they take great strides, it is outside the true way traced by God; they are victims of those illusions against which St. Paul was already putting the first Christians on their guard.[1]

Others have clear notions on points of detail but lack a view of the whole. Losing themselves in minutiae, not having any synthesis of view, often they merely lift one foot after the other on the place where they were before. Their life becomes a real toil, subject to incessant difficulties; a toil without *élan*, without an opening-out to flower; and, often, without much result—because these souls accord their acts a greater importance, or give them a lesser value, than those acts ought to have in the full picture.

It is therefore an extremely important thing to run the race, as St. Paul says, "not without a purpose," but in such a manner as to attain the sought object—"So run as to obtain it."[2] It is important to know as perfectly as possible the Divine idea of holiness; to scrutinize with the greatest care, so that we may adapt ourselves to it, the plan traced by God Himself for making us arrive at Him. It is only at that price, indeed, that our salvation and our holiness will be achieved.

In a matter so grave, in a question so vital, we ought to look at and weigh things as God looks at and weighs them. God judges all things in daylight, and His judgment is the final norm of all truth. "We must not judge things according to our own taste," says St. Francis de Sales, "but according to God's—that is the great thing to be said. If we are holy pursuant to our own will, we shall never be truly so; we have to

---

[1] Col. 2:8.   [2] 1 Cor. 9:24-26.

be holy according to God's will."[1] Divine Wisdom is infinitely above human wisdom; God's thought contains fertile riches that no created thought possesses. This is why the plan established by God is of one of such wisdom that it can never fail to reach its goal because of intrinsic insufficiency; only through our own fault. If we let the Divine Idea have complete power to operate in us, if we adapt ourselves to it with love and fidelity, it becomes extremely fruitful and can bring us to the most sublime holiness.

Let us then, in the light of Revelation, contemplate God's plan for us. That contemplation will be for our souls a source of light, strength and joy.

To begin with, I am going to give you a quite general idea of the Divine plan. We shall afterwards return to a detailed account of it by following the words of St. Paul quoted at the beginning of this talk.

1. *General idea* of this plan: the holiness to which God calls us through super-natural adoption is a participation in the Divine life brought by Christ Jesus.

HUMAN REASON can demonstrate that there exists a Supreme Being, First Cause of every created being; this world's Providence, Sovereign Rewarder, Last End of all things. From this rational knowledge, and from its manifestation to us of the relationship between created beings and God, there flow for us certain duties towards God and towards our neighbor, duties which together are the foundation of what is called the natural law, duties the observance of which constitutes natural religion.

But, powerful though it may be, our reason has been able to discover nothing, with certainty, of the inner life of the Supreme Being.

---

[1] Letter to President Brulart, mid-September 1606, *Œuvres* (Edition of the Visitation Nuns of Anneçy, vol. XIII, p. 213).

The Divine life appears to it infinitely distant, in impenetrable solitude: "Who … dwells in light inaccessible."[1]

Revelation has come, bringing us its light.

It teaches us that there is, in God, an ineffable Paternity. God is a *Father*: that is the fundamental dogma which all the others presuppose, a magnificent dogma which leaves the reason confounded, but delights faith and enraptures souls who are holy.

God is a Father. Eternally, before ever created light rose upon the world, God begets[2] a Son to whom He communicates His nature, His perfections, His beatitude, His life—for to beget is to communicate[3] being and life: "You are my Son";[4] "from the womb before the day-star I begot you."[5] Thus, life is in God, life communicated by the Father and received by the Son. This Son, in all things like to the Father, is unique: "*the only-begotten Son of God.*"[6] He is unique because He has,[7] with the Father, one and the same, one indivisible, Divine nature; and the two, though distinct from each other (by reason of their personal properties

---

[1] 1 Tim. 6:16.

[2] See Translator's Note, "*Human language inadequate,*" on pages 10-11.

[3] By the gift of a nature like the giver's.

[4] Ps. 2:7; Hebr. 1:5; 5:5.   [5] Ps. 109 (110):3.

[6] See John 1:18. [*Translator's note*: Giving the Latin of that verse of John in a footnote, Marmion quotes more of it than I give above: he adds "*qui est in sinu Patris.*" The Rheims translation of that expression from St. John is: "who is in the bosom of the Father"—"in sinu Patris," "au sein du Père" in the French. Fashions of expression change, however, and nowadays the translation "in the bosom of" will strike many as odd, if not risible. The Jerusalem version takes an established secular meaning of classical Latin's "*in sinu meo*" ("my darling," "very dear to my heart") and has the fresh and lovely translation "*nearest to the Father's heart.*" I have used a not dissimilar phrase, "*in the heart's-embrace of the Father,*" when translating "in sinu Patris"/ "au sein du Père," wherever it appears in the book. But in relation to the Trinity all human language (including "heart," especially if imagined as physical, rather than as the seat of love) is analogous only, and inadequate.]

[7] Speaking more strictly, one would say that He *is* with the Father and the Holy Spirit one and the same Divine nature. The lips of us creatures stammer when it is a question of such mysteries.

"of being Father" and "of being Son") are united in a strong and substantial embrace of love, whence proceeds that Third Person whom Revelation calls by a mysterious name: the Holy Spirit.

Such, so far as faith is able to know it, is the secret of the inner life of God. The fullness and fruitfulness of that life is the source of the immeasurable bliss possessed by the ineffable fellowship of the three Divine Persons.

And see how God, not in order to add to His plenitude but to enrich other beings by it, will extend, so to speak, His Paternity. This Divine life, so transcendent that only God has the right to live it, this eternal life communicated by the Father to the only Son, and, by them, to the Spirit common to them—this life, God decrees creatures shall be called to share. By a transport of love which has its source in the fullness of the Being and the Goodness that is God, this life will overflow from the heart of Divinity to reach and beatify—by elevating them above their nature—beings drawn from nothingness. God will ennoble these purely created beings and make them hear the sweet name of "children." By nature, God has only one Son. By love, He will have a multitude of them, without number. This is *the grace of super-natural adoption.*[1]

Realized in Adam from the dawn of creation, then cut across by the sin of the head of humankind who drew the whole of his race with him into his disgrace, this Decree of love would be restored through a marvelous devising of justice and mercy, of wisdom and goodness. See how the only Son (who lives in the eternal heart's-embrace of the Father) unites Himself to a human nature within the sphere of time; but in so close a way that this nature, while being perfect in itself,

---

[1] [*Translator's note*: Throughout the present translation the word "super-natural" is given in hyphenated form, so as to bring out Marmion's meaning. "Super" is the Latin for "above"; and "super-natural" as he uses the word means "above the natural." "Super-natural life," for example, means a life that is above a merely natural life.]

belongs entirely to the Divine Person to whom it is united. The Divine life, communicated in its fullness to this humanity, makes it the Son of God's own humanity: this is the admirable work of *the Incarnation*. It is true to say of this man, called Jesus Christ, that He is God's own Son.

But this Son who, by nature, is the only Son of the eternal Father—"only-begotten" Son of God[1]—appears here below simply so as to become the firstborn of all those who would receive Him, after having been ransomed by Him: "the firstborn among many brethren."[2] Only-begotten of the Father in the eternal splendors, only Son by right, He is constituted the head of a multitude of brethren, to whom, by His work of redemption, He will restore the grace of divine life.

And this, in such a way that the same divine life which flows from the Father into the Son, which streams from the Son into the humanity of Jesus, will circulate, through Christ, into all those who are willing to accept Him. It will draw them up to the beatifying heart of the Father, where Christ has gone before us[3] after having paid—by His blood, for us here below—the price of such a gift.

All holiness from then on will consist of receiving the divine life from Christ and through Christ, who possesses the fullness of it and who is established as our only Mediator; of preserving it, of increasing it constantly by an adhesion ever more perfect, a union ever more close, to Him who is its source.

Holiness, then, is a *mystery of divine life communicated and received*—communicated, in God, from the Father to the Son, by an indescribable "generation";[4] communicated, outside God, by the Son to the humanity to which He unites Himself personally in the Incarnation; then, through that humanity, restored to souls and received by

---

[1] See John 1:18; 3:16.   [2] Rom. 8:29.
[3] "I ascend to my Father and your Father"; "In my Father's house there are many mansions.... I go to prepare a place for you": John 20:17; 14:2.   [4] Isa. 53:8.

each of them in the measure of their particular predestination:[1] "according to the measure of Christ's bestowal";[2] in such a way that Christ is truly the life of the soul, because He is its source and its dispenser.

Communication of it to men will be carried out in the Church,[3] right up to the day fixed by the eternal decrees for the completion of the Divine work on earth. On that day, the number of children of God, of brethren of Jesus, will have attained its perfection. Presented by Christ to His Father,[4] the innumerable throng of these predestined[5] will surround the throne of God, to draw from living springs an endless beatitude, to exalt the splendors of the Divine goodness and glory. Union will be eternally complete and God will be "all in all."[6]

---

[1] [*Translator's note*: "Predestination": It is important to keep in mind throughout the book that this word as used by Marmion has not the slightest overtone of anything inconsistent with free will, nor is there in it any suggestion that God offers the eternal inheritance to some and not all. Indeed, Marmion stresses in many places that the inheritance is offered to all. Since humanity's redemption by Christ the Savior, everyone coming into existence has the pre-existent *destiny*, desired by God, of being happy with God after the person's life on earth has ended. Whether that eternal destiny eventuates in an individual case, however, depends on the individual's use of free will on earth—on his or her response to grace—and, crucially, on the presence or absence of a state of sanctifying grace at the moment of death. The attaining of one's destiny is not automatic. In a way, this inheritance is comparable to a human legacy subject to some condition being fulfilled. As to the separate point of the *measure* of the inheritance, the "measure of Christ's bestowal" in St. Paul's phrase, Marmion speaks of this aspect briefly on page 123; and it is perhaps useful to remember the point made by St. Teresa of Avila in relation to eternal happiness: that a little pot and a large pot, filled each to the brim, are both "full."]

[2] Eph. 4:7.

[3] [*Translator's note*: As to "those who, through no fault of their own, do not know and accept Christ and the Church" (*Lumen Gentium*, 16), see further note on pages 115-117 of the present book.]

[4] 1 Cor. 15:24-28.

[5] [*Translator's note*: God, being outside time, always has foreknowledge of what our individual response to Him will be. Our response, however, is not otherwise than free on that account.]   [6] 1 Cor. 15:28.

Such, in altogether general outline, is the Divine plan. Such, expressed very briefly, is the graph the super-natural work describes.

When, in prayer, the soul considers this munificence, and these attentions of which it is the object gratuitously on the part of God, it feels a need to lose itself in adoration and to sing praises—a hymn of thanksgiving—to the Infinite Being who abases Himself before that soul to give it the name of "child." "O Lord, how great are your works! your thoughts are exceeding deep."[1] "Lord, who is like to you?"[2] "You have multiplied your wonderful works, O Lord, my God," your designs in our favor, "and in your thoughts there is no one like to you."[3] "For you have given me, O Lord, a delight in your doings: and in the work of your hands I shall rejoice."[4] "I will sing to the Lord as long as I live: I will sing praise to my God while I have my being."[5] "Let my mouth be filled with praise, that I may sing your glory; your greatness all the day long."[6]

[1] Ps. 91 (92):6.   [2] Ps. 34 (35):10.   [3] Ps. 39 (40):6.
[4] Ps. 91 (92):5.   [5] Ps. 103 (104):33.   [6] Ps. 70 (71):8.

—⁂—

TRANSLATOR'S NOTE: HUMAN LANGUAGE INADEQUATE[1]

Marmion very appositely says that human beings can "only stammer" when speaking of the Trinity.

Using our human language, which is the only language we have, we say "He," singular, when speaking of God (except in a context referring to and distinguishing between the three Divine Persons as Persons, when we might say "they"). "He," a singular pronoun for the Triune God, is the best our human language can do. In one sense, indeed, it carries the right overtones, for God is *one* God. But God is one God *in three Persons*. Yet if "He" is

[1] This note substantially appeared in the translator's *Barb of Fire* (Gracewing, 2001).

inadequate, "they" is linguistically impossible: *"not three Gods, but only one God"* (Athanasian Creed).

Of course, as has been stated earlier, a context sometimes shows that the speaker or writer is referring to God the Father, as distinct from the other two Divine Persons, when saying "God" or "He."

In thinking about the Trinity one must beware of taking expressions in the sense they would bear if used of human beings. For example, "begets a son," if used of a human being, would imply that there was a time when the son did not exist, and that he then came into being. But the time continuum does not apply to God: God simply IS. God the Son is *"eternally* begotten of the Father" (Nicene Creed) — "eternally" connoting no beginning as well as no end. "Beginning" and "end" have no application to God. Though the Son "proceeds from" the Father, the Son is eternal God, as the Father is.

Father and Son, though each is eternal and distinct from the other, are, with the Holy Spirit, One. "God from God, Light from Light," says the Nicene Creed, of the eternally-begotten Son. (As to the mode of the eternal "begetting," the words of St. Gregory Nazianzen are apt. "Let the doctrine be honored silently; it is a great thing for you to know the fact; the mode, we cannot admit that even angels understand....") And the Holy Spirit, a Divine Person distinct from the Father and the Son, has (in Marmion's words) "His exclusive source of [eternal] origin in the love of the Father and the Son": *Christ, the Ideal of the Priest*, ch. I.

Louismet, commentating on Trinitarian doctrine, uses the helpful language of eternal *circularity*: "The whole Divine life proceeds from God the Father to His Divine Son and returns to Him through their Holy Spirit: proceeds from Him without going out of Him: returns to Him without having been separated from Him." It is, says the same writer, like a "fountain which ever springs and ever flows within its own Divine Self."

That Life is, as it were, extended by "adoption." A sharing in that Life is offered *to human beings*, through the coming of Christ.

—ovo—

2. *God wishes* to make us share in His own life so as to *render us holy* and fill us with beatitude. What is *holiness* in God.

LET US NOW CONTINUE with the account in detail, by guiding ourselves according to the words of the Apostle. This account will inevitably occasion some repetitions, but I trust that your charity will bear them by reason of the elevation and the importance of these questions, so vital are they. We cannot really glimpse the grandeur of these dogmas and their fruitfulness for our souls unless we prolong the contemplation somewhat.

In every science, as you know, there are first principles, fundamental points that one must know at the very beginning because upon them rest all the later developments and the final conclusions. These primary elements need going into more deeply, and they demand more attention, in proportion as their consequences are more important and more extensive. Our minds, it is true, are so made as to be easily put off in the analysis or meditation of fundamental notions. Every initiation to a science, like mathematics; to an art, like music; to a doctrine, like that of the interior life, calls for an attention that our mind readily shirks. In its natural impatience, it would like to run ahead at once to the developments so as to admire their ordered arrangement, to the applications so as to gather and taste their fruits. But it is much to be feared that if it does not fathom the principles with care, it will merely lack solidity in the developments it can afterwards draw from them, however brilliant those developments may appear. The conclusions will often be unstable and the applications hazardous.

This is why I do not hesitate to go back over these fundamental truths with you, at the risk of repeating myself a little. Besides, do you not yourselves feel that it is only by remaining at the heart of the dogma that one will be able to draw forth from it life, fruitfulness and the joy of our souls?

According to the thought of St. Paul, whose words I quoted to you at the beginning, this plan can be reduced to three great features. *It is His holiness that God wishes to communicate to us*; He chose us in Christ "that we should be holy and without blemish."[1] This holiness consists in a *life of adoptive sons*, a life of which *grace* is the mainspring, and the character *super-natural*: God has predestined us "to be his adopted children."[2] Finally, and above all, this ineffable mystery will only become reality "*through Jesus Christ.*"[3]

God wants us to be holy: this is His eternal will; it is for this that He has chosen us: "He chose us ... *that* we should be holy and without blemish in His sight." "For this is the will of God, your sanctification," as St. Paul again puts it.[4]

God desires, with an infinite will, that we should be holy; He wishes it because He is holy Himself,[5] because He has placed in that sanctification the glory He expects from us,[6] and the joy with which He desires to satisfy us.[7]

But what is "being holy"? We are creatures, our holiness exists only through a participation in the holiness of God. Therefore, in order to understand it, we have to go back all the way up to God. He alone is holy by essence, or rather He is holiness itself.

Holiness is the Divine perfection that is the object of the eternal contemplation of the angels. Open the book of the Scriptures. You will note that, twice only, heaven has half-opened before two great prophets, one of the Old Covenant, the other of the New: Isaiah and St. John. And what did they see? What did they hear? Both saw God in His glory, both saw the heavenly spirits surround His throne, both heard them sing without ceasing, not of the beauty of

---

[1] Eph. 1:4. [2] Eph. 1:5 (Knox). [3] *Ibid.* [4] 1 Thess. 4:3.
[5] Levit. 11:44; 1 Peter 1:16. [6] John 15:8. [7] John 16:22.

God, nor of His mercy, nor of His justice, nor of His greatness—
but of His *holiness*:

> *Holy, Holy, Holy,*
>   *Lord God of Hosts;*
> *Heaven and earth are*
>   *full of your glory.*[1]

Now, in what does this holiness in God consist?

In God, everything is simple; His perfections are, in Him, really
identical with Himself. Furthermore, the notion of holiness can only be
applied to Him in a way that is absolutely transcendent; we have no
proper term that renders the reality of this Divine perfection with
commensurate aptness, and yet the employment of human language is
permitted us. What, then, is holiness in God?

According to our manner of speaking, it seems to us that it consists
of two elements: in the first place, an infinite distance from everything
that is imperfection, of everything that is "creature," of everything that
is not God Himself.

That is only a "negative" aspect; there is another element, which
consists in this: that *God adheres—by an act immutable and always
present, an act of His will—to infinite good* (which is no other than
Himself) in such a way as to conform—infinitely to conform[2]—to all this
infinite good is. God knows Himself perfectly; His All-Wisdom shows
Him His own essence as the supreme norm of all activity. God cannot
will, do or approve anything that is not governed, through His sovereign
wisdom, by this latter norm of all-good which is the Divine essence.

This immutable adhesion, this supreme conformity of the Divine
will to the infinite, Divine, essence considered as ultimate norm of activity,
could not be more *perfect*, because in God the will is really identical
with the essence.

[1] *Sanctus* of the Mass, taken from Isa. 6:3; Apoc. 4:8.

[2] [*Translator's note*: This is a free translation of Marmion's adverb "*adéquatement*,"
"adequate" being used in the philosophic sense of "equal in magnitude."]

The Divine holiness, then, comes down to the very perfect love and the sovereignly immutable fidelity with which God loves Himself infinitely.[1]

And as His supreme Wisdom shows to God that he is All-Perfection, the sole necessary Being, it makes Him relate everything to Himself and to His own glory. This is why the Sacred Books make us hear the song of the angels: "Holy, holy, holy ... heaven and earth are full of your glory." It is as if the angels were saying: "You are the Most High, O God, you are Holiness itself, because, with sovereign wisdom, you glorify yourself worthily and perfectly."

From this it follows that the Divine holiness serves as first foundation, as universal example and as unique source of every created holiness. Because (you understand) necessarily loving Himself with an infinite perfection, God also necessarily wishes every creature to exist for the manifestation of His glory[2] and, inhabiting his rank of creature, to act only in conformity with the relations of dependence and of end which Eternal Wisdom finds in the Divine essence.

[1] Cf. D.L. Janssens, *Praelectiones de Deo Uno*, vol. 2, p. 238 and 366 ff.

[*Translator's note*: With us, "self-love" has a pejorative sense, but that is because, by adhering to *our*selves rather than to God, WE adhere to what is staggeringly short of the glorious and ineffable essence of Almighty God, the Uncreated. The difference between what one might term our "is-ness" and God's "is-ness" is simply a matter of fact or (as St. Teresa of Avila said) "truth." There is no usurpation in God's "measuring all things by the glory He receives from them" (page 343), as there would be if *we* had such a standard of measure. "God's sanctity," wrote Marmion in *Christ, the Ideal of the Priest*, ch. II, "consists in the love which He bears His own essence, His own goodness. This adherence of love is wise and supremely justified, *for it is in conformity with the absolute excellence of the Divine nature*.... When man recognizes his absolute dependence in regard to the Creator, he is acting in complete conformity with the law of *his* nature, and God approves this submission ... just as, for the same reason, God must necessarily disapprove of any attitude of insubordination or revolt, and condemn sin. This is not from egoism or from pride, but on account of His sanctity which desires that all things should be accomplished in accordance with rectitude, wisdom *and truth*" (my italics). Furthermore, God being the Trinity, Love radiates between the three Divine Persons, and out to us, God's creatures.]

[2] See page 33, n. 1.

Therefore the more there is in us of dependence of love in regard to God, of conformity of our free will to our primordial end which is the manifestation of the Divine glory, the more we *adhere to God* (something which can only be achieved through detachment from everything that is not God), the more, finally, that this dependence, this conformity, this adhesion, this detachment is *firm and stable*—the higher will be our holiness.[1]

3. Holiness *in the Trinity*; fullness of the life for which God destines us.

HUMAN REASON can succeed in establishing the existence of this holiness of the supreme Being, holiness which is an attribute, a perfection of the Divine nature considered in itself.

But Revelation has brought us a new light.

Here we should lift up the eyes of our soul with reverence, all the way to the sanctuary of the Adorable Trinity; we should listen to what Christ Jesus—as much to nourish our loving reverence as to exercise our faith—has willed either to reveal to us Himself, or to propound to us through His Church, about the inner life of God.

You know that in God there are three distinct Persons, the Father, the Son and the Holy Spirit, yet all three having but one and the same unique nature or Divine essence. Infinite understanding, the Father has perfect knowledge of His perfections. He expresses this knowledge in one unique Utterance: it is "the Word,"[2] the living substantial utterance,

---

[1] St. Thomas Aquinas (*Summa Theologica*, II-II, q. LXXXI, a. 8, in c) demands as elements of holiness in us: *purity* (distancing of oneself from every sin, every imperfection; detachment from everything created) and *stability* in adhesion to God. To these two elements correspond, in God, *the all-perfection* of His infinite *transcendent* Being, and the *immutability* of His will in adhesion to Himself.

[2] John 1:1: "In the beginning was the Word...." [*Translator's note*: When the creation of things began, the Son (who, like the Father and the Holy Spirit, has no beginning) already was, or rather *is*.]

the commensurately infinite expression, of who the Father is. By utter-
ing this Word, the Father begets His Son, to whom He communicates
all His essence, His nature, His perfections, His life: "For as the Father
has life in Himself; so He has given to the Son also to have life in
Himself."[1] Likewise, the Son is entirely His Father's, is entirely given
up to Him by a total donation which stems from His nature as Son. And
from this mutual donation of only one and the same love proceeds, as
from one unique source, the Holy Spirit who seals the union of the
Father and the Son, in being their substantial and living love.

This mutual communication of the three Persons, this adherence —
infinite and full of love — of the Divine Persons between themselves,
assuredly constitutes a new revelation of holiness in God: it is the
union of God with Himself in the unity of His nature and the Trinity
of the Persons.[2]

In this inexpressibly one and fruitful life God finds all His essential
beatitude. To exist, God has need only of Himself and His perfections.

---

[1] John 5:26 (Rheims).

[2] Let us state, for minds more initiated in theological matters, that each of the
Persons of the Trinity is *identical with the Divine essence*, and consequently is holy, of
a substantial holiness, because each Person acts only in conformity with this essence
considered as supreme norm of life and activity. One may add that the Persons are
holy because each of them gives Himself and is the Other's in an act of infinite
adhesion. Finally, the Third Person is particularly called holy because He proceeds
from the other two *through love*: love is the principal act by which the will tends to
and is united with its desired end; it designates the highest act of adhesion to the
norm of all goodness — that is to say, of holiness; and this is why the Spirit who, in
God, proceeds through love bears par excellence the name of *Holy*. The following is
the passage of St. Thomas which expounds to us this beautiful and profound doctrine: "Since the good that one loves has relation to the end one seeks (according to
which sought end, moreover, the will is rendered good or bad), the love by which
one loves the absolute good, which is God, necessarily has a certain goodness above
all else, *which is denoted holiness*.... Therefore the Spirit who instills in us the love with
which God loves Himself is called the Holy Spirit": *Opuscula selecta*, vol. III, c. XLVII.
From all this, one sees that consideration of the Trinity of Persons gives one a
deeper conception of the Divine holiness.

Finding all bliss in the perfections of His nature and in the ineffable society of His Persons, He has no need of any creature. It is to Himself —in Himself, in His Trinity—that He relates the glory welling forth from His infinite perfections.

As you know, God has decreed that we enter into a sharing of this inner life that belongs to Him alone; He wishes to communicate to us this unfathomable beatitude that has its source in the plenitude of Infinite Being.

That being so—and this is the first point in St. Paul's account of the Divine plan—our holiness will be *to adhere to God known and loved*, not any longer simply as the author of creation but *as He knows and loves Himself* in the bliss of His Trinity. To be united with God to the point of sharing His inner life—that is what it will be. In what marvelous manner God achieves His design, we are going to see soon. Let us at this stage pause a moment to consider the greatness of the gift He makes to us. We shall have some idea of it if we glance at what happens in the natural order.

Look at minerals: they do not live. Within them there is no interior principle that can be a source of activity. Minerals possess a share of being, with certain properties, but their mode of being is very inferior. Take plants: they live, they move harmoniously, in a constant manner and following fixed laws, towards the perfection of their being; but this life is of the lowest grade, for plants lack consciousness. Though superior to that of plants, the life of animals is nevertheless limited to having senses and to the necessities of instinct. With man, we rise to a higher sphere: reason and free will characterize the life peculiar to a human being; but man is also matter. Above man are the angels, pure spirits whose life marks the highest degree of all in the domain of creation. Infinitely surpassing all these created lives, which are received by way of participation, there is the Divine life—life uncreated, life absolutely transcendent, fully autonomous and independent, above the

strength of every creature; life necessary, subsistent in itself. God, limitless Understanding, grasps — by an eternal act of apprehending — infinity
and all the beings whose prototype is to be found in Him. Sovereign
Will, He attaches Himself, without any shadow of failure, to supreme
Good, which is no other than Himself. In this Divine life, which shines
forth in all fullness, are to be found the source of all perfection and the
wellspring of all bliss.

It is this life that God wants to communicate to us; participation
in this life constitutes our holiness. And as, for us, there are degrees
of this participation, the more the participation extends, the higher
is our holiness.

And let us not forget that it is solely through love that God has
resolved[1] to give Himself in this way. There is no necessity in God —
other than the ineffable communications of the Divine Persons between themselves:[2] these mutual relations belong to the very essence of
God; this is God's life. Every other communication of Himself that
God makes is the fruit of a love that is sovereignly free. But as this
love is Divine, the gift he gives is Divine also. God loves Divinely; He
gives Himself. We are called to receive, in ineffable measure, this
Divine communication. God means not only to give Himself to us as
Supreme Beauty, object of contemplation, but to unite Himself to us,
so as to make Himself, so far as is possible, but one with us.

"O Father," said Christ Jesus at the Last Supper, "may my disciples
be one in us, as you and I are one, in order that they find in this union
the unending joy of our own beatitude":[3] "that they may have my joy
made full in themselves."[4]

---

[1] See Rom. 3:25.
[2] Necessary in the sense that they cannot not be. Cf. St Thomas, I, q. XLI, a. 2, ad 5.
[3] See John 17:11.   [4] John 17:13; cf. 15:11.

4. Effecting of this decree through *Divine adoption* by means of grace. *Super-natural* character of the spiritual life.

HOW DOES GOD effect this magnificent design by which He wishes us to have part in this life which exceeds the dimensions of our nature, which surpasses our nature's own rights and energies, which is not called for by any of its demands, but which, without destroying that nature, showers on it a bliss undreamt-of by the human heart? How will God make us have ineffable "fellowship with"[1] His Divine life so as to make us sharers of the eternal beatitude?

By adopting us as His children.

Through a will infinitely free, but full of love, "according to the purpose of His will,"[2] God predestines us to be, no longer simply His creatures but His children; He has predestined us "to be His adopted children,"[3] to participate in this way in His own Divine nature: "partakers of the Divine nature."[4] God adopts us as His children. What does St. Paul mean by this? What is *human* adoption?

It is the admission of a stranger into a family. By adoption, the stranger becomes a member of the family, he takes its name, he receives its title, he has the right of inheritance of possessions. But to be able to be adopted, one must be of the same race; to be adopted by men, one must be a member of the human race. Now, we who are not of the race of God, who are poor creatures, who are, by nature, further from God than animals are from men, who are infinitely distant from God, "strangers and foreigners"[5]—how can we be adopted by God?

It is here we find the marvel of the Divine wisdom, power and goodness. God gives us a mysterious sharing of His nature that we call "*grace*"; "that ... you may be made partakers of the Divine nature."[6]

---

[1] 1 John 1:3.   [2] Eph. 1:5.   [3] Eph. 1:5 (Knox).   [4] 2 Peter 1:4.   [5] Eph. 2:19.

[6] 2 Peter 1:4 (Rheims). St. Peter does not say that we become partakers of the Divine *essence*, but of the Divine *nature*; that is to say, of that activity which constitutes the life of God and which consists in the knowledge and the fruitful and beatifying love of the Divine Persons.

Grace is an *interior quality* produced in us by God, inhering in the soul, adorning the soul and making it pleasing to God—just as, in the natural domain, beauty and strength are qualities of the body; genius and learning, qualities of the mind; loyalty and courage, qualities of the heart.

According to St. Thomas Aquinas, this grace is a "likeness to the Divine nature, by participation": *participata similitudo divinae naturae.*[1] Grace, in a manner the uttermost depths of which elude us, makes us sharers of God's nature. By grace, we are raised above our nature, we become, in a way, gods. We become, not equal to, but *like* God; that is why Our Lord said to the Jews: "Is it not written in your law: 'I said, you are gods'?"[2]

For us, then, participation in this Divine life is effected through grace, in virtue of which our soul becomes capable of knowing God as God knows Himself; of loving God as God loves Himself; of joying in God as God is filled with His own beatitude, and thus of living the life of God Himself.

Such is the ineffable mystery of our Divine adoption. But there is a profound difference between Divine adoption and human adoption. The latter is only exterior, a fiction: it is established by a legal document no doubt, but it does not penetrate the nature of the one who is adopted. In adopting us, in giving us grace, God, on the contrary, penetrates the depths of our nature. Without changing what is essential in the order of this nature, He elevates it interiorly by this grace, to the point that we are truly children of God. This act of adoption has so much efficacy that we really, through grace, become sharers of the Divine nature. And as participation in the Divine life constitutes our holiness, this grace is called *sanctifying*.

The consequence of this Divine decree of our adoption, of this predestination by which God wants to make us His children—a

---

[1] III, q. LXII, a. 1. That is why it is said in theology that grace is *deiform*, to indicate the divine resemblance it produces in us.   [2] John 10:34 (Rheims).

predestination so full of love!—is to give our holiness a special character. And what is this character?

That our holiness is *super-natural.*

In relation to us, as in relation to every [human] creature, the life to which God raises us is super-natural, that is to say, exceeding the dimensions and the strength, the rights and the exigencies of our nature. That being so, it is no longer as simply human creatures that we must be holy; but *as children of God, by acts inspired and animated by grace.* Grace becomes in us the mainspring of a divine life. What is *to live?* For us, to live is to move by virtue of an inner mainspring that is the source of actions which tend to the perfection of our being. Upon our natural life is grafted, so to speak, another life of which the basis is grace. Grace becomes in us the cause of actions and operations that are super-natural and tend towards a divine end, namely possessing God one day and joying in Him, as He knows Himself and joys in His perfections.

This point is of capital importance, and I want you never to lose sight of it. God might have contented Himself with accepting from us the homage of a natural religion. The latter would have been the source of a morality that was human, natural; of a union with God in conformity with our nature as reasonable beings, based on our relationship as creatures to our Creator and our relationship with those like us.

But God has not willed to restrict Himself to this natural religion. We have all met men who are not baptized, and who nevertheless are upright, loyal, who are men of integrity, equitable and just, compassionate; but there can be only a natural decency in that.[1] Without His rejecting it (on the contrary!), God is not content with it. Because He has decided to make us share in His infinite life, in His own beatitude—which is for us a super-natural end; because He has given us His grace, God asks that our union with Him be a union, a super-natural holiness, that has this grace as its mainspring.

---

[1] One must however add that, because of the bad propensities which result from original sin, this purely natural decency is rarely perfect.

Outside this plan, there is nothing for us but eternal loss.[1] God is master of His gifts, and He has decreed, from all eternity, that we shall only be *holy* in His sight *by living, through grace, as children of God.*

O heavenly Father, grant me to safeguard in my soul the grace that makes me your child! Preserve me from all evil that could separate me from you!

[1] [*Translator's note*: But see further on this the Note below.]

—◁ΰ/ΰ▷—

TRANSLATOR'S NOTE: THOSE NOT BAPTIZED BY WATER

The full balanced position of the Catholic Church on this matter needs to be understood by reference to her modern documents. As Marmion himself says indeed (page 90): "Christ, being God, is absolute master of His gifts and of the way in which He distributes them." Under the heading "The Necessity of Baptism," the recent *Catechism of the Catholic Church* first says this: "The Lord Himself affirms that Baptism is necessary for salvation (cf. John 3:5). He also commands His disciples to proclaim the Gospel to all nations and to baptize them. Baptism is necessary for salvation for those to whom the Gospel has been proclaimed and who have had the possibility of asking for this sacrament. The Church does not know of any means other than Baptism that assures entry into eternal beatitude; this is why she takes care not to neglect the mission she has received from the Lord to see that all who can be baptized are 'reborn of water and the Spirit'" (CCC, para. 1257; Council of Trent (1547); Vatican II, *Lumen Gentium*, 14).

That said, the Catechism in the very next sentence emphasizes that though "God has bound salvation to the sacrament of Baptism, *He Himself is not bound by His sacrament.*" (Ibid.) Over the centuries the Church has taught that there are circumstances in which "the fruits [effects] of Baptism" are received without actual Baptism by water. "Those who suffer death for the sake of the faith without having received Baptism are baptized by their death for and with Christ"; this is *Baptism of blood* (CCC, para. 1258). Similarly, *desire* for Baptism "brings about the fruits of Baptism." Moreover, "Baptism of desire" (which brings about the fruits of Baptism) is something wider than explicit desire for baptism. Every person who "is ignorant of the Gospel of Christ and of his Church, but seeks the truth and does the will of God in accordance with (that person's) understanding of it, can be saved. It can be supposed that such persons would have *desired Baptism explicitly* if they had known its necessity" (CCC, paras. 1258, 1260; *Lumen Gentium*, 16).

—⁕—

5. The Divine plan, cut across by sin, re-established by the *Incarnation.*

AS YOU KNOW, it was as far back as the creation of the first man that God effected His design: Adam received, for him and for his [the human] race, the grace that made him a child of God. But, by his fault, he lost that Divine gift—for himself, and for his race too. Ever since his revolt, we are all born sinners, deprived of that grace which would make us children of God. We are, on the contrary, *Filii irae*, enemies of God and "by nature children of wrath."[1] Sin has cut across God's plan.

But God, the Church tells us, has shown Himself even more wonderful in the restoration of His designs than He had been at the creation: "O God who, in creating human nature, wonderfully dignified it, and has *still more wonderfully* renewed it."[2] How is that? What is this Divine marvel?

This mystery is *the Incarnation.*

It is through the Word Incarnate that God will restore everything. Such is "the mystery which has been hidden from eternity"[3] in the

---

[1] Eph. 2:3. [*Translator's note*: Sanctifying grace being equated with "the friendship of God," the absence of sanctifying grace is equated with its opposite. Marmion, like St. Augustine, takes St. Paul's above-quoted words as directly referring to our being born in original sin. "Original sin," it should be remembered, is not our individual personal sin but an *absence* due to the Fall—an absence for the remedy of which Christ came.]

[2] Offertory of the Mass.   [3] Eph. 3:9.

thoughts of God, and which St. Paul comes to reveal to us. Christ, the Man-God, will be our Mediator; He it is who will reconcile us and give us back grace. And as this great design has been anticipated from all eternity, it is with good reason that St. Paul speaks of it to us as an ever-present mystery. It is the last great feature by which the Apostle completes his disclosing of the Divine plan to us.

Let us listen to him with faith, for we touch here the very heart of the Divine work.

The Divine thought is to constitute Christ head of all the redeemed, "above every name that is named, not only in this world, but also in that which is to come":[1] in order that by Him, with Him and in Him we may all arrive at union with God, that we may achieve the supernatural holiness God requires of us.

No thought could be clearer in the letters of St. Paul; none of which he could be more convinced; none he puts in higher relief. Read all his epistles, and you will see that he constantly returns to it, to the extent of making it almost the one ground of his doctrine. Look: in that passage from the Epistle to the Ephesians[2] that I quoted to you at the beginning, what is he saying to us? It is *"in Christ"* that God has chosen us, so that we might be holy; He has predestined us to be His adopted sons *"through Jesus Christ"*; we are acceptable in His eyes *"in His beloved Son."* It is in His Son Jesus that God has resolved to "re-establish all things";[3] or, better, according to the Greek text, to "bring all things back under" Christ, as under one and only head. Christ is always uppermost in the Divine thoughts.

How is that effected?

"The Word"—whose eternal generation, in the heart's-embrace of the Father, we adore—"was made flesh."[4] The Most Holy Trinity created a

---

[1] Eph. 1:21.   [2] Eph. 1:3-6.   [3] Eph. 1:10.   [4] John 1:14.

humanity like our humanity, and from the first instant of its creation united it, in an ineffable and indissoluble manner, to the Person of the Word, of the Son, of the Second Person of the Blessed Trinity. This God-Man is Jesus Christ. This union is so close that there is only one single Person, that of the Word. Perfect God by His Divine nature, the Word becomes, by His incarnation, perfect man. In making Himself man, He remains God. "That which He has been, He has remained; that which He was not, He has taken to Himself":[1] the fact of having taken a human nature, so as to unite it to Himself, has not lessened the divinity.

In the Word Incarnate, Christ Jesus, the two natures are united, without mixture or confusion. They remain distinct, united though they are in the unity of the Person. Because of the personal character of this union, Christ is God's own Son, He possesses the life of God: "For as the Father has life in Himself; so He has given to the Son also to have life in Himself."[2] It is the same Divine life that subsists in God and fills the humanity of Jesus. The Father communicates His life to the Word, to the Son; and the Word communicates it to the humanity that He has united to Himself personally. That is why, in looking at Our Lord, the Eternal Father recognizes Him as His true Son; "You are my Son; this day have I begotten you."[3] And because He is His Son, because this humanity is the humanity of His Son, it possesses a full and entire communication of all the Divine perfections. The soul of Christ is *full* of all the treasures of the knowledge and wisdom of God: "Christ Jesus, in whom are hidden *all the treasures* of wisdom and knowledge."[4] In Christ, says St. Paul, "dwells *all the fullness* of the Godhead bodily";[5] the sacred humanity is "full of grace and of truth."[6]

The Word-made-flesh is therefore adorable in His humanity as in His divinity, because beneath this humanity is veiled the Divine life. O Christ Jesus, Word Incarnate, I prostrate myself before you, because

---

[1] Antiphon of the Office of the Feast of the Circumcision.   [2] John 5:26 (Rheims).
[3] Ps. 2:7; Hebr. 5:5. [For Marmion's exegesis, see Translator's Introduction.]
[4] Col. 2:3.   .   [5] Col. 2:9.   [6] John 1:14.

you are the Son of God, equal to your Father. You are truly the Son of God, *God from God, Light from Light, true God from true God.*[1] You are the beloved Son of the Father, the One in whom He is well pleased.[2] I love you and adore you. *Venite adoremus!*

But—and here is a wonderful revelation that fills us with joy—this fullness of Divine life which is in Jesus Christ is meant to overflow from Him to us, to the whole of humankind.

The Divine Sonship which is in Christ by nature and makes Him God's own and only Son, the only-begotten Son, in the heart's-embrace of the Father[3]—that Sonship is meant to extend all the way to us through grace, in such a way that Christ, in the Divine thought, is but the firstborn of a multitude of brethren who are, through grace as He is by nature, sons of God. He has predestined us to "become conformed to the image of His Son, that He should be the firstborn among many brethren."[4]

We are here at the central point of the Divine plan: *the Divine adoption. It is from Jesus Christ, it is through Jesus Christ, that we receive it.* It was to confer adoption on us, says St. Paul, that God sent His Son: "God sent his Son, born of a woman ... to enable us to be adopted as sons."[5] The grace of Christ, Son of God, is communicated to us to become in us the wellspring of adoption; it is upon the fullness of the Divine life and grace of Christ Jesus that we all have to draw. St. Paul, after having said that the fullness of the Divinity dwells bodily in Christ, adds immediately by way of conclusion: "and in Him who is the head of every Principality and Power[6] you have received of that fullness"[7]— see, in Him you have everything fully, because He is your head. And St. John says the same, after having shown us the Word made flesh, full of grace and truth: "And of His fullness we have all received."[8]

---

[1] Nicene Creed.
[2] Matt. 3:17, 17:5; Luke 3:22.
[3] *"In sinu Patris"*; cf. John 1:18 (Jerus.)
[4] Rom. 8:29.
[5] Gal. 4:4-5 (Jerus.)
[6] [*Translator's note*: angels.]
[7] Col. 2:10: "Him who is the head, Christ," Eph. 4:15.
[8] John 1:16.

So, it is not simply that the Father has from all eternity chosen us: note also the expression "in Him," Christ. The Father "chose us *in Him* before the foundation of the world."[1] It is in His Christ that He has chosen us; everything that is outside Christ does not exist, so to speak, in the Divine thought. But *grace*, as well—the means of the adoption He has destined for us; it is through Jesus Christ that we receive it. The Father predestined us to be "adopted ... *through Jesus Christ*."[2] We are sons, like Jesus—we by title of grace, He by nature. "He is Son, and we are sons: He, His own Son, and we, adopted sons. But He saves, and we are saved."[3] It is through Christ that we enter the family of God; it is from Him and through Him that grace comes to us, and consequently divine life: "I am ... the life";[4] "I came that they may have life, and have it more abundantly."[5]

Such is the very source of our holiness. Just as the whole of Christ Jesus can be summed up by His Divine Sonship, so the whole of a Christian can be summed up by participation in this Sonship, through Jesus Christ, in Jesus Christ. *Our holiness is nothing other than that. The more we participate in the Divine life through the communication Christ Jesus makes to us of the grace of which He ever possesses the plenitude, the higher is the degree of our holiness.* Christ is not only holy in Himself, He is *our holiness.* All the holiness that God has destined for souls has been deposited in the humanity of Christ, and this is the source at which we must draw.

"O Christ Jesus," let us sing with the Church in the *Gloria* of the Mass, "you alone are holy." Alone holy, because you possess the plenitude of Divine life; alone holy, because we wait upon you alone for our holiness. You have, as your great apostle says, "become FOR US God-given wisdom, and justice, and sanctification";[6] *our* wisdom, *our* justice, *our* redemption, *our* holiness. In you we find everything. In receiving you, we receive everything; for in giving you to us, your Father—who,

---

[1] Eph. 1:4.
[4] John 14:6.

[2] Eph. 1:5.
[5] John 10:10.

[3] P.L. Migne, LXVII, 701.
[6] 1 Cor. 1:30.

as you yourself have said,[1] is *our* Father—has given us everything: "how can He fail to grant us also all things with Him?"[2] All the graces of salvation and pardon, all the riches, all the super-natural fruitfulness with which the world of souls overflows, come from you alone: "In Him we have redemption ... according to the riches of His grace. This grace has abounded beyond measure in us."[3] Let all praise, then, be rendered you, O Christ! And through you, let all praise rise up to your Father for the "inexpressible gift"[4] He has made us, of you!

6. *Universality* of the Divine adoption; the *ineffable love* it manifests.

IT IS each and every one of us who ought to participate in the holiness of Jesus. Christ has excluded no one from the life that He brought, and by which He makes us God's children: "Christ died for all";[5] it is for the whole of humanity that Christ has re-opened the doors of eternal life.[6] As St. Paul says, He is the firstborn, but of a multitude of brethren.[7] The eternal Father wills that Christ, His Son, be constituted leader of a kingdom, of the kingdom of His children. The Divine plan would not be complete if Christ were on His own. It is His glory, as it is the glory of the Father—"unto the praise of the glory of His grace"[8]—that He be at the head of an assembly without number, as if it were His "completion" (*pleroma* in Greek) and without which He would not, so to speak, be perfect.

---

[1] John 20:17.   [2] Rom. 8:32.   [3] Eph. 1:7-8.
[4] 2 Cor. 9:15 (Jerus.)   [5] 2 Cor. 5:15.

[6] [*Translator's note*: This is in no way inconsistent with Marmion's speaking, in later sections, of the state of grace and the right use of free will, and bluntly warning about hell. I illustrate that by a quotation the terminology of which is not dissimilar to Marmion's. James Archer, one of Challoner's missionary priests in late 18th century London, put the point in striking words. In a sermon, he spoke of "a blissful inheritance in a better life, which none can take from (a person); which is his, *as long as he chooses to retain his title to it.*" Thus he and Marmion, both men of deep traditional faith, speak of "title" or "entitlement" to an "inheritance," but an inheritance dependent on the individual's soul-state at the moment of death.]

[7] Rom. 8:29.   [8] Eph. 1:6.

St. Paul says it so clearly in his letter to the Ephesians, where he traces the Divine plan. The Father has set Christ "at His right hand in heaven above every Principality and Power and Virtue and Domination — in short, above every name that is named, not only in this world, but also in that which is to come. And all things He made subject under His feet; and Him He gave as head over all the Church, which indeed is His body."[1] It is this assembly, this Church, that Christ has won for Himself, according to the words of the same apostle, in order that she might at the last day be without "spot or wrinkle, or any such thing, but ... holy and without blemish."[2] This Church, this Kingdom, is growing to its maturity from here below on earth. One enters it by baptism; on earth one lives in it through grace, in faith, hope and charity: but the day will come when we shall behold its perfect completion in heaven. This will be the kingdom of glory, in the bright light of vision, in the joy of possession and union without end. That is why St. Paul said that the grace of God is "life everlasting in Christ Jesus our Lord,"[3] everlasting life itself, brought to the world by Jesus Christ.

There it is, the great mystery of the Divine thoughts. "If you only knew what God is offering!"[4] A gift ineffable in itself; ineffable, above all, in its source which is *love*.

It is because He loves us that God wishes to make us share His own beatitude, as His children: "Behold what manner of love the Father has bestowed on us, that we should be called children of God; and such we are."[5] The love is infinite which makes us such a gift, for, as St. Leo says: "The gift surpassing all gifts is that God calls a man His child, and that a man calls God his Father."[6] Each one of us can say of himself or herself, in all truth: "It is by an individual act of love and kindness that God has created me and has called me, by baptism, to Divine

---

[1] Eph. 1:20-23.   [2] Eph. 5:27.   [3] Rom. 6:23.
[4] John 4:10 (Jerus.)   [5] 1 John 3:1.   [6] *Sermo* VI on the Nativity.

adoption. For, in His plenitude and His infinite richness, God has no need of any creature: "*Of His own will* He has begotten us by the word of truth."[1] By a special act of loving-kindness and fondness, God has chosen me—*elegit nos*, has chosen us—to be raised infinitely above my natural condition, to enjoy eternally His own beatitude, to be the realization of one of His Divine thoughts, to be one voice in the concert of the elect, to be one of those brethren who are like Jesus, and who share, without end, His celestial inheritance.

This love shows itself with especial radiance in the mode of effecting the Divine plan: "in Christ Jesus."[2]

God has revealed His love for us, by sending His only-begotten Son into the world so that "*we may live through Him*."[3] Yes, God loves us so much that, to show us this love, He gave us His only-begotten Son[4]—so that His Son might become our brother and that we might one day be His Son's co-heirs, that we might have part in the riches of His grace and of His glory: "That He might show ... *the overflowing riches* of His grace, *in kindness towards us* in Christ Jesus."[5]

Such, then, in its majestic breadth of sail, its simplicity of mercy, is God's plan for us. *God wants our holiness*, He wants it because He loves us infinitely, and we ought to want it with Him. God's wish is to render us holy, *by making us share in His very life*; and, for that, He *adopts us as His children* and heirs of His infinite glory and His eternal beatitude. *Grace* is the wellspring of this holiness, *super-natural* in its source, in its acts, in its fruits. But God does not give us this adoption other than *through His Son, Christ Jesus*: it is in Him, through Him, that God wishes to unite Himself with us and wishes us to unite ourselves with Him: "*No one* comes to the Father but through me."[6] Christ is the way, and the sole way, to lead us to God. "Without me," said

---

[1] James 1:18.   [2] Eph. 2:7.   [3] 1 John 4:9.
[4] John 3:16.   [5] Eph. 2:7.   [6] John 14:16.

Christ, "you can do *nothing*."[1] "For other foundation no one can lay, but that which has been laid, which is Christ Jesus."[2]

Thus it is that God communicates the plenitude of His Divine life to the humanity of Christ—and, through that humanity, to every soul "according to the measure of Christ's bestowal."[3]

Let us understand that we shall only be holy in the same measure as the life of Christ is in us. It is this holiness alone that God asks of us, there is no other holiness than that. We shall be holy only in Jesus Christ, or we shall not be holy at all. In that which is created is found not one atom of this holiness. Holiness derives from God by a sovereignly free act of His Almighty Will, and that is why it is super-natural.

St. Paul brings up, more than once, both the gratuitousness of the Divine gift of adoption, and the eternity of ineffable love that has resolved that we share in that gift, and the wonderful means of effecting it through the grace of Christ Jesus. "Remember," he wrote to his disciple Timothy, "that God has called us with a holy calling, not according to our works, but according to His own purpose and the grace which was granted to us in Christ Jesus before this world existed."[4] It is by grace that you are saved and sanctified, he wrote to the faithful of Ephesus: "By grace you are saved through faith, and that not of yourselves"— not by your own strength, "for it is the gift of God, not [the outcome of] works, that no man may glory."[5]

---

[1] John 15:5.   [2] 1 Cor. 3:11.   [3] Eph. 4:7.
[4] See 2 Tim. 1:9: Marmion has: "God has chosen us through a holy calling...."
[5] Eph. 2:8-9 (Rheims). [*Translator's note*: "That no man may glory": Cfy has "lest anyone may boast."]

7. Primordial *object* of the Divine plan: *the glory of Christ Jesus and of His Father* in the unity of their Spirit.

It is God, indeed, to whom all glory has to return. This glory is the fundamental object of the Divine work.[1] St. Paul shows us this in ending his account of the Divine plan with the words "unto the praise of the glory of His grace."

If God adopts us as His children, if He brings about this adoption through grace the plenitude of which is in His Son, Jesus Christ, if He wishes to give us part in the beatitude of the eternal inheritance of Christ—it is for the exaltation of His glory.

Notice with what insistence St. Paul presses this point in expounding to us the Divine plan in the words I quoted to you at the beginning: God chose us "*unto the praise of the glory of His grace.*"[2] He returns to that twice, further on: God has predestined us "*to contribute to the praise of His glory*"; "our inheritance ... *unto the praise of His glory.*"[3]

---

[1] The [First] Vatican Council defined that "it is not in order to increase His beatitude, nor to put the seal on His perfection, but to manifest this perfection with the aid of the benefits He showers on His creatures, that God has freely drawn each creature out of nothing by an act both of His goodness and of His almightiness." (Dogmatic constitution, *De fide catholica*). In the 4th canon, the Council anathematizes "those who shall deny that the world has been created for the glory of God." These passages bring out that God created the world for His glory; that this glory consists in the manifestation of His perfections by the gifts He lavishes on His creatures; that the motive that freely determines Him to glorify Himself in this way is His goodness (or in the formal expression of theologians, love of His goodness). God, then, unites the creature's happiness with His glory; to glorify God becomes our beatitude. "The gifts of God," says D.L. Janssens, "have no other source, and no other goal, than the supreme goodness of which His glory is the best expression as synthesis." Now, the gift par excellence, whence all the others flow for us, is that of the hypostatic union in Christ. "God so loved the world that He *gave* His only-begotten Son" (John 3:16). "How can He fail to *grant* us also *all things*"; all things "*with Him*" (Rom. 8:32).

[2] Eph. 1:6; note the use, in the Greek text, of the preposition *eis*, which indicates the end towards which one aims in an active manner.

[3] Eph. 1, vv. 12, 14. Cf. Phil. 1:10-11: "that you may be upright and without offense unto the day of Christ, filled with the fruit of justice, through Jesus Christ, *to the glory and praise of God.*"

The Apostle's first expression is particularly remarkable. He does not say "unto the praise of His grace," but "unto the praise of *the glory of His grace*"—his meaning being that this grace will be surrounded with the splendor which attaches to triumphs. Why does St. Paul speak in that way? It is because Christ, in order to give Divine adoption back to us, has had to triumph over the obstacles created by sin; but these obstacles have only served to make the Divine marvels in the work of our super-natural restoration shine forth more to the eyes of the whole world: "O God, who in creating human nature didst wonderfully dignify it, *and has still more wonderfully renewed it....*"[1] Every one of the elect is the fruit of the blood of Jesus and of the wonderful operations of His grace; all the elect are so many trophies won by that Divine blood, and that is why they are like a glorious praise to Christ and to His Father: "unto the praise of" His glory.

I was telling you, when I began, that the Divine perfection the angels sing of particularly is holiness: "*Sanctus, Sanctus, Sanctus,*" "Holy, Holy, Holy." But what is the thunder of praise which, in heaven, rises from the choir of the elect? What is the continuous hymn of that immense throng which constitutes the kingdom whose head is Christ? "O Lamb that was slain, you have redeemed us, you have restored to us title to an inheritance, you have made us have part in it. To you, and to Him who sits on the throne, praise, honor, glory and dominion!"[2] This is the hymn of praise resounding from heaven to exalt the triumphs of the grace of Jesus: "Unto the praise of the *glory* of His grace."

To unite ourselves with this hymn while yet here below is therefore to enter into thoughts eternal. Look at St. Paul: when writing that wonderful epistle to the Ephesians he is a prisoner; but at this moment when he prepares to reveal to them the mystery hidden throughout the ages, he is ravished with such delight at the greatness of this mystery of Divine adoption in Jesus Christ, he is so dazzled by the "unfathomable

---

[1] Offertory of the Mass.   [2] See Apoc. 5:9; 5:13.

riches"[1] brought by Christ, that despite his privations he cannot prevent himself giving forth a cry of praise and of thanksgiving, at the very start of his letter: "Blessed be the God and Father of our Lord Jesus Christ, who has blessed us"—blessed us "in Christ"—"with every spiritual blessing."[2] Yes, blessed be the Eternal Father who from all eternity has called us to Himself to make us His children and to cause us to share in His own life and His own beatitude; who, to effect His designs, has given us in Christ all benefits, all riches, all treasures, such that in Him we lack nothing: "that you lack no grace."[3]

This is the Divine plan.

Our entire holiness consists in deepening, in the light of faith, this "mystery which has been hidden from eternity in God,"[4] God's private idea; in entering into the Divine thought; in bringing about within us the Eternal disposings.[5]

He who wishes to save us, to make us holy, has traced the plan of it with a wisdom equalled only by His goodness. Let us adapt ourselves to this Divine thought that wishes us to find our holiness in our conformity with Christ Jesus. There is (to say it again) no other way. We shall be pleasing to the eternal Father—and is not the very basis of holiness "to be pleasing to God"?—only if He recognizes in us the features of His Son. Through grace and our virtues, we ought to be so identified with Christ, that the Father, gazing on our souls, may recognize us as His true children, may take pleasure in that, as He did in contemplating Christ Jesus on earth. Christ is His beloved Son, and it is in Him that all the blessings leading us to the fullness of our adoption in the beatitude of heaven will be showered upon us.

[1] Eph. 3:8.　　[2] Eph. 1:3.　　[3] 1 Cor. 1:7.　　[4] Eph. 3:9; Col. 1:26.
[5] [*Translator's note*: "Disposings": Marmion uses the word *économie*, "*l'économie éternelle.*" In the present translation the Divine "*économie*" is rendered as "the Divine disposings" or a similar phrase.]

How good it is, now, in the light of these truths (so high and beneficial are they) to repeat the prayer that Jesus Himself, the beloved Son of the Father, has placed on our lips and which, coming from Him, is par excellence the prayer of a child of God:

O Father,
Holy One who art in heaven,
we are your children, seeing that you
wish to be called our Father!

Hallowed, honored, glorified
be your name.

May your perfections be praised and
exalted more and more on earth: may
we, by our works, manifest in ourselves
the splendor of your grace.

Widen, then, your reign; may it constantly
increase, this Kingdom—which is also
that of your Son, in that you have
constituted Him as its head.

May your Son be truly the King of our souls.
May we express this kingship in us by the
perfect accomplishment of your will;
may we seek constantly, like Him,
to adhere to you by carrying out
your good pleasure,[1] your Eternal thought
concerning us, so that in all things
we may be like your Son Jesus,
and be, through Him,
children worthy
of your love![2]

[1] "I do always the things that are pleasing to Him": John 8:29.
[2] For the Lord's Prayer, see Matt. 6:9-13; Luke 11:2-4.

CHAPTER TWO

CHRIST, THE ONE AND ONLY MODEL OF ALL PERFECTION: *CAUSA EXEMPLARIS*

INTRODUCTION: Fruitfulness and diverse aspects of the mystery of Christ.

WHEN ONE READS the Epistles that St. Paul addressed to the Christians of his time, one is struck by the insistence with which he speaks of Our Lord Jesus Christ. He constantly returns to this subject—with which, moreover, he is so filled that for him Christ is his life: "For me to live is Christ."[1] Therefore He spends himself for Christ and His members, not counting the cost: "I will most gladly spend and be spent myself for your souls."[2]

Chosen and instructed by Jesus Himself to be the herald of His mystery throughout the whole world,[3] he has penetrated so far into the depths and the grandeurs of this mystery, that his one desire is to reveal it, to make the adorable person of Christ known and loved. He writes to the Colossians that what fills him with joy in the midst of his tribulations is the thought that he has been able to announce "the mystery which has been hidden from ages and generations" but is now manifested to the faithful—for it is to them that God has willed to make known "the riches of the glory of this mystery ... which is Christ."[4]

---

[1] Phil. 1:21.
[3] Eph. 3:8-9.

[2] 2 Cor. 12:15.
[4] Col. 1:26-27 (Rheims).

37

Look how, when in prison, he is told that other people than he are preaching Christ. Some are doing it out of a spirit of contention, in opposition to him, Paul; others with good intentions.[1] Does he feel pain or jealousy at this? Quite the contrary. Provided Christ is preached, what matters it to him? However it be done, he says, whether it be with ulterior motives or sincerely, "I rejoice, yes and I shall rejoice."[2] To that extent does he make all his knowledge, all his preaching, all his love, all his life, come down to Jesus Christ. "For I determined not to know anything among you, except Jesus Christ."[3] In the labors and the struggles of his apostolate, one of his joys is to think that he is "giving birth"—it is his own expression—to Christ in souls.[4]

The Christians of the first ages understood the doctrine the great apostle expounded to them. They understood that God has given us His only Son, Christ Jesus, that He may be everything for us, our "wisdom, and justice, and sanctification, and redemption."[5] They understood the Divine plan: that God has given the fullness of grace to Christ so that in Christ we might find everything. They lived by that doctrine, "Christ ... who is your life,"[6] and that is why their spiritual life was at once so simple and so fruitful.

Now, let us rightly say to ourselves that in our day the heart of God is not less loving, nor His arm less powerful. God is ready to lavish on us graces, I do not say as extraordinary in character, but as abundant and as useful as upon the first Christians. His love for us is not less than it was for them. All the means of sanctification they had, we possess: and we have in addition, to encourage us, the example of the saints who have followed Christ. But we are too often like the leper, come to consult the prophet and beg from him a cure: he almost failed to obtain it because he found the remedy too simple.[7]

---

[1] Phil. 1:12 ff.   [2] Phil. 1:18.   [3] 1 Cor. 2:2.
[4] See Gal. 4:19.   [5] 1 Cor. 1:30.   [6] Col. 3:4 (Rheims).
[7] 4 Kings, 5:1 ff. Our Lord alluded to this fact Himself (Luke 4:27). Naaman, commander-in-chief of the armies of Syria, was stricken with a leprosy that entirely

This is the case with a number of those who embark on the spiritual life. You find some minds which are so attached to their way of seeing things, that they are scandalized at the simplicity of the Divine plan. And this scandal is not harmless. These souls who have not understood the mystery of Christ lose themselves in a multiplicity of details and often tire themselves out in joyless labor. Why is that? Because everything that our human ingenuity is able to create for our interior life serves for nothing if we do not base our edifice on Christ: "For other foundation no one can lay, but that which has been laid, which is Christ Jesus."[1]

That explains the change sometimes brought about in certain souls. For years they have lived as if cramped; often depressed, almost never contented, constantly finding new difficulties in the spiritual life. Then, one day, God has given them the grace to understand that Christ is our All, that He is the "*Alpha* and the *Omega*,"[2] that outside of Him we have nothing; that in Him we have everything, that everything is embodied in Him. From that moment all is, so to speak, changed for these souls; their difficulties have vanished like the shades of night before the rising sun. As soon as Our Lord, true Sun of our life, "the Sun of

---

disfigured him. Having learned of the wonders the prophet Elisha was working in Samaria, he betakes himself near him, to ask for a cure. Elisha sends word to him: "Go and wash seven times in the Jordan, and you will be cured." This response annoys Naaman. "I imagined," he says to his followers, "that the prophet would have presented himself in person to me, that he would have cured me by invoking Jehovah on my behalf. Does he then think, this prophet, that the rivers of Syria are not the equal of all the waters of Israel? Why could I not immerse myself *there* to recover health?" And, filled with disappointment and anger, he prepares to retake the road back to his own country. But his servants approach him: "Master," they say to him, "what if the prophet is right after all? If he had asked of you something more difficult, would you not have done it? That being so, how much more ought you to obey him, now that he commands so simple a thing of you?" Naaman bows to this suggestion that is so full of sense; he goes to immerse himself seven times in the Jordan, and, in accordance with the words of the man of God, he recovers his health.

[1] 1 Cor. 3:11.   [2] Apoc. 22:13.

justice,"[1] fully lights up these souls, it gives them fertility; and they unfold, they rise upwards, and bear numerous fruits of holiness.

Trials will doubtless not be absent from the life of such souls; often trials are the very condition of interior progress. Collaboration with divine grace will remain quite as attentive and generous—but everything that narrows the heart, puts a stop to *élan* and brings discouragement has vanished. The soul lives in the light, it "dilates": "I have run the way of your commandments, when you enlarged my heart";[2] its life is simplified. The soul understands the poverty of those means which it has itself created, which it has constantly renewed, asking them to shore up its own spiritual edifice. It grasps the truth of these words: "Unless the Lord build the house, they labor in vain that build it"[3]—"If you yourself, O Lord, do not build your dwelling in us, we cannot succeed in constructing for you a habitation that is worthy of you." It is in Christ, and no longer in itself, that the soul seeks the source of its holiness. It knows that this holiness is super-natural in its mainspring, its nature and the end it seeks, and that the treasures of sanctification are only to be found amassed there in Jesus in order that we may share in them. It understands that it is only with the riches of Christ that it is rich.

These riches, according to the words of St. Paul, are unsoundable: "the unfathomable riches of Christ."[4] We shall never exhaust them; and, even, everything we say about them will fall short always of the praise they deserve.

There are, however, three aspects of the mystery of Christ that we should contemplate when we speak of Our Lord as the source of our sanctification. We borrow the idea of this from St. Thomas, prince of theologians, in his teaching on the sanctifying causality of Christ.[5]

---

[1] Malachi (Malachias) 4:2.　　　　　　　　[2] Ps. 118 (119):32.
[3] Ps. 126 (127):1.　　　　　　　　　　　　[4] Eph. 3:8.
[5] III, q. XXIV, a. 3 and 4; q. XLVIII, a. 6; q. L, a. 6; q. LVI, a. 1, ad 3 and 4.

Christ is at one and the same time the exemplary cause, the meritorious cause, the efficient cause[1] of all our holiness. Christ is the *one model of our perfection; the author of our redemption and the infinite treasury of our graces; the efficient cause of our sanctification.*

Those three points sum up perfectly what we have got to say of *Christ* Himself as *the Life of our souls.* Grace is, indeed, the cause of that super-natural life of children of God that constitutes the foundation and the substance of all holiness. Well, this grace in its fullness is met with in Christ, and all the works we accomplish through grace have their pattern in Jesus. And further, Christ has merited this grace for us by the satisfactions[2] of His life, Passion and death. Finally, Christ Himself produces this grace in us, through the sacraments and through the contact we have with Him in faith.

But so rich are these truths, that we should contemplate each one separately. In this talk, we shall consider Our Lord as our Divine model in all things, as the exemplar of the holiness at which we should aim. The first thing to consider is the goal we have to attain. Once this goal is well understood, the application of the appropriate means to attain it will come quite naturally.

---

[1] [*Translator's note*: Marmion uses "efficient cause" to mean strictly the "cause which effects," the cause which produces the effect.]

[2] [*Translator's note*: For the meaning of this word, see note on page 60.]

1. Necessity of *knowing God* in order to be united to Him. God *reveals Himself* to us *in His Son Jesus*: whoever sees Him, sees His Father.

As I HAVE SHOWN YOU, our holiness is but a participation in the Divine holiness: we are holy if we are children of God and if we live as true children of the heavenly Father, worthy of our super-natural adoption. "Be, therefore," said St. Paul, "imitators of God, as very dear children."[1] Jesus Himself said to us: "Be therefore perfect"—it is all His followers whom Our Lord is addressing. And not just any perfection, but "as your heavenly Father is perfect."[2] And why is that? Because *noblesse oblige*: God has adopted us as His children, and children should in their lives resemble their father.

But to imitate God one must know Him, and how are we able to know God? He "dwells in light inaccessible," says St. Paul.[3] "No one," says St. John, "has ever seen God."[4] How, then, shall we be able to reproduce and imitate the perfections of Him whom we do not see?

Some words of St. Paul give us the answer. He "has shone ... in the face of Christ."[5] God is revealed to us by His Son and in His Son, Jesus Christ. Christ Jesus is "the brightness of His (the Father's) glory,"[6] "the image of the invisible God";[7] perfectly like His Father; able to reveal Him to men, for He knows Him as He Himself is known by Him. "No one," said Jesus, "knows the Father except the Son, and those to whom the Son wills to reveal Him."[8] Christ Jesus, who is always in the heart's-embrace of the Father, tells us: "I know my Father":[9] but He knows Him in order to reveal Him to us: "It is the only Son ... who has made Him known."[10] Christ is the revelation of the Father.

And how does the Son reveal the Father to us? By becoming incarnate. The Word, the Son, has become incarnate, is made man; and in Him, through Him, we know God. Christ is God put within our reach,

---

[1] Eph. 5:1.   [2] See Matt. 5:48.   [3] 1 Tim. 6:16.   [4] 1 John 4:12.
[5] 2 Cor. 4:6 (RSV, Cath.)   [6] Hebr. 1:3.   [7] Col. 1:15.   [8] See Matt. 11:27.
[9] See John 10:15.   [10] John 1:18 (Jerus.)

in human manifestation: it is Divine perfection revealing itself to us under earthly forms; it is holiness itself, appearing in perceptible form to our eyes for thirty-three years, to make itself tangible and imitable.[1] We can never think too much about this. Christ is God making Himself man, living among men, so as to make them learn, by His words and above all by His life, how men should live in order to imitate God and be pleasing to Him. Thus to live as children of God we have, first of all, only to open our eyes, with faith and love, and, in seeing Jesus, to contemplate God.

There is in the Gospel an episode that is very simple, and yet magnificent. You are familiar with it, but this is the place at which to recall it. It was the eve of Jesus's Passion. Our Lord, as only He could, had spoken of His Father to His apostles; and they, quite transported, desired to see and know the Father. The apostle Philip cries out: "Lord, show us the Father and we shall ask for nothing more." And Christ Jesus, in reply, says: "Have I been so long a time with you, and you still do not know me? Philip, he who sees me sees also the Father."[2] Yes, Christ is the revelation of God, of His Father. As God, He is but one with Him; and whoever contemplates Him sees the revelation of God.

When you contemplate Christ abasing Himself in the poverty of the crib, recall those words: "He who sees me sees also the Father." When you see the adolescent of Nazareth working, full of obedience, in the humble workshop up to the age of thirty, say again those words: "Whoever sees Him sees also his Father," whoever contemplates Him contemplates God. When you see Christ making His way through the small Galilean towns and everywhere doing good, healing the sick, announcing the good tidings; when you see the tortured victim of the cross dying for love of men, an object of derision to his executioners, listen: it is He who says to you: "Whoever sees me sees also the Father;

---

[1] To be a model and to be imitable are the two characteristics that are to be met with in an exemplary cause.   [2] See John 14:8-9.

whoever sees me sees God Himself." There you have so many manifestations of God, so many revelations of the Divine perfections.

God's perfections are in themselves as incomprehensible as the Divine nature. Who among us, for example, could understand what Divine Love is? It is an abyss that surpasses all we can conceive of it. But when we see Christ, who, as God, is one with His Father, "I and the Father are one";[1] who has in Him the same Divine life as the Father[2]—when we see Christ instruct men, die upon a cross, give His life for love of us; when we see Him institute the Eucharist, we understand then the greatness of God's love.

So it is with each of the attributes of God, with each of His perfections. Christ reveals them to us; and to the extent that we advance in love of Him, He makes us penetrate further forward into His mystery: "He who loves me will be loved of my Father, and I will love him and manifest myself to him."[3] Which comes down to saying: "If someone loves me, receives me in my humanity, he will be loved by my Father, and I also will love him and will manifest myself to him in my divinity; I will disclose its secrets to him."

"The Life," writes St. John, "was made known and we have seen," and this is why we "testify and announce to you the Life Eternal which was with the Father, and has appeared to us"[4]—has been made visible here below, in Christ Jesus. So much so, that in order to know and imitate God we have only to know and imitate His Son Jesus, who is the expression, at once human and divine, of the infinite perfections of His Father: "He who sees me sees also the Father."

---

[1] John 10:30.
[2] "For as the Father has life in Himself; so He has given to the Son also to have life in Himself" (John 5:26, Rheims).   [3] John 14:21.   [4] 1 John 1:2.

2. **Christ our model** *in His person*: **perfect God, perfect man.
Grace, the fundamental sign of** *likeness to Jesus,* **considered** *in
His state* **of Son of God.**

BUT how and in what is the Word Incarnate, Christ, our model, our
exemplar?

Our model—Christ is doubly this: in His person and in His works;
in His *state* of Son of God and in His human *activity*; for He is both
Son of God and Son of Man; perfect God and perfect man.

Christ is God, perfect God: *Perfectus Deus.*

Let us transport ourselves to Judea, at the time of Christ. He has
already fulfilled one part of His mission, travelling through Palestine,
teaching and performing "the works of God."[1] See Him, after a day of
apostolic journeys, having drawn apart from the crowd, surrounded by
only His disciples. He asks them: "Who do men say the Son of Man
is?" The disciples echo all the rumors widespread among the people.
"Master, some say that you are John the Baptist, or Elijah, or Jeremiah,
or one of the other prophets." "But you," says Jesus, "who do *you* say I
am?" Then Peter spoke, and said to Him: "You are the Christ, the Son
of the living God." And Our Lord, confirming the testimony of His
apostle, answers him: "Blessed are you, for it is not flesh and blood that
has revealed this to you"—not through natural intuition that you have
learnt who I am; "it is my Father who has made this revelation to you."[2]

Christ, then, is the Son of God, "God from God, Light from Light,
true God from true God," as our Creed[3] expresses it. Christ, says St. Paul,
did not think it a usurpation to call Himself the equal of the Father.[4]

---

[1] See John 9:4; "the works of Him who sent me."   [2] See Matt. 16:13-17.
[3] Nicene Creed.

[4] Phil. 2:6. [*Translator's note*: Marmion's words accord with the Rheims version:
Christ "thought it not robbery to be equal to God"—not a usurpation. Other scriptural translations interpret the meaning as: "Though He was by nature God, [He]
did not consider being equal to God a thing to be clung to" (Cfy); Christ's humility
in becoming man allowed His divinity to seem to have been robbed from Him.]

Three times, moreover, the voice of the Eternal Father has made itself heard, and each time it was to glorify Christ by proclaiming Him to be His Son, the Son in whom He delights, the living Voice of His words to us: "This is my beloved Son, in whom I am well pleased: hear Him."[1] Let us prostrate ourselves, like the disciples who on Tabor heard this voice of the Father. With Peter, inspired as he was from on high, let us repeat to Jesus: "Yes, you are the Christ, the Word Incarnate, true God, equal to your Father, perfect God, possessing all the Divine attributes. You, O Jesus—like your Father and with the Holy Spirit—are the Almighty; you are the Eternal; you are Infinite Love. I believe in you, and I adore you—you, my Lord and my God!"

Son of God, Christ is also Son of Man, perfect man: *Perfectus homo.*
The Son of God is made flesh; He remains what He is—perfect God; but He unites Himself to a human nature, complete like ours, entire in its essence, with all its native properties. Christ, like all of us, is "born of a woman,"[2] He belongs authentically to our race. Often in the Gospel He calls Himself "the Son of Man." Eyes of flesh have seen Him, human hands have touched Him;[3] even on the morrow of His glorious resurrection He makes the unbelieving apostle take note of the reality of His human nature: "Feel, handle me and see: for a spirit does not have flesh and bones as you see I have."[4] Like each of us, He has a soul, created directly by God; a body formed in the womb of the Virgin; an intellect that knows, a will that loves and chooses, all the faculties that we have, memory, imagination. He has passions in the philosophic, elevated and noble sense of the word—a sense excluding all disorder and all weakness. Passions, but in Him these passions are perfectly subjected to reason and come into play only by an act of His will.[5] His human nature, then, is in all things like ours, like that of His

---

[1] Matt. 17:5; Matt. 3:17, John 12:28.   [2] Gal. 4:4.   [3] 1 John 1:1.   [4] See Luke 24:39.
[5] Theology calls them *propassions*, in order to indicate by this special term their character of transcendence and of purity.

brother-humans: "It was right," says St. Paul, "that he should in all things be made like unto His brethren,"[1] "in all things except sin."[2] Jesus has known neither sin nor what is the source or consequence of sin: ignorance, error, disease, all things unworthy of His perfection, of His wisdom, of His dignity, of His divinity.

But our Divine Savior wished greatly to bear our infirmities during His mortal life, all the infirmities compatible with His holiness. The Gospel shows us that clearly. There is nothing in man's nature that Jesus cannot have sanctified: our labors, our sufferings, our tears—He made them all His own. See Him at Nazareth; for thirty years He spent His life in the lowly labor of a workman, so much so that when He begins His preaching, His compatriots are astonished at His doing so, for they have only known Him up to then as the son of the carpenter: "Is not this the carpenter's son? ... Then where did he get all this?"[3] Like us, Our Lord felt hunger; after having fasted in the desert "He was hungry."[4] He suffered thirst; did He not ask the Samaritan woman: "Give me to drink"?[5] And on the cross did He not cry out "I thirst"?[6] Like us, He experienced tiredness; the long journeys across Palestine fatigued His limbs. When, at Jacob's well, He asked for water to quench His thirst, St. John tells us that He was tired; it was the noon-day hour; after having walked a long time He sat down, wearied, on the coping-stone of the well.[7] And thus, as St. Augustine remarked in the admirable commentary he has given us of this beautiful scene in the Gospel: "He who is the very Strength of God is overcome by weariness": *Fatigatur Virtus Dei*.[8] Sleep closed His eyelids; "He was asleep" in the small boat when the storm arose.[9] He was truly asleep; and so His apostles, who feared to be engulfed by the fury of the waves, had to wake Him up.

---

[1] Hebr. 2:17.
[4] Matt. 4:2.
[7] John 4:6.
[2] Hebr. 4:15.
[5] John 4:7.
[8] *Tract. in Johann.*, XV.
[3] Matt. 13:55-56.
[6] John 19:28.
[9] Matt. 8:24.

He wept over Jerusalem, His home city, which He loved despite its ingratitude: the thought of the disasters that, after His death, were going to fall upon it forced out of Him tears, and accents full of affliction. "If you had known ... the things that are for your peace!"[1] He "wept over it."[2] He wept at the death of His friend Lazarus, as we shed tears over those we hold dear, to the extent that the Jews, witnessing this spectacle, said to themselves: "See how he loved him."[3] Christ shed tears, not because that was the thing to do, but because He had a heart that was touched—He mourned him who was His friend; it was from the depths of His heart that His tears poured out. Likewise, it is said of Him several times in the Gospel that His heart was touched with compassion.[4]

What else? He experienced feelings of sadness, worry, fear: "And He began to fear, and to be heavy";[5] "He began to grow sorrowful and to be sad."[6] In His agony in the Garden of Olives, His soul was overwhelmed with sorrow: "My soul is sorrowful even unto death";[7] anguish penetrated His soul to the extent that it wrung loud cries from Him.[8] All the revilings, all the affronts which swamped Him during His Passion—His being buffeted, spat upon—made Him suffer immensely: the mockery, the insults, did not leave Him feeling nothing. Very much the opposite; His nature being more perfect, His sensibility was greater, more delicate. He was plunged deep in suffering. Finally, having taken upon Himself all our infirmities, after being shown to be truly a man, like us in all things, He willed to endure death like all the sons of Adam: "And, bowing His head, He gave up His spirit."[9]

---

[1] Luke 19:42.   [2] Luke 19:41.   [3] John 11:36.
[4] Luke 7:13; Mark 8:2; Matt. 15:32.   [5] Mark 14:33 (Rheims).
[6] Matt. 26:37 (Rheims).   [7] Matt. 26:38 (Rheims).
[8] "Jesus, in the days of His earthly life, with a loud cry and tears, offered up prayers and supplications to Him who was able to save Him from death...." (Hebr. 5:7).   [9] John 19:30.

It is therefore as Son of God and as Son of Man, both together, that Our Lord is our model: but He is our model first of all as Son of God. This *state* of Son of God is, strictly speaking, what is basic, fundamental, in Christ, and it is through this that we ought to resemble Him first of all.

And how is one to resemble Him in that?

The Divine Sonship of Christ is the type of our super-natural sonship. His condition, His "being" of Son of God is the pattern of that state in which sanctifying grace should establish us first of all. Christ is the Son of God by nature and by right, by virtue of the union of the Eternal Word with the human nature.[1] We are this by adoption and by grace, but we are really this, and by a very true title. Christ has, in addition, sanctifying grace; He possesses its fullness. It flows down into us from that fullness, more or less abundantly; but in its substance it is the same grace that fills the created soul of Jesus and that deifies us. St. Thomas says that our divine sonship is a likeness to the eternal Sonship.[2]

Such is the primordial and pre-eminent way in which Christ is first the pattern for us to follow. In the Incarnation He is constituted, by right, Son of God; we have to become this by participation in the grace which derives from Him and which, deifying the substance of our soul, constitutes us in the *state* of child of God. That is the primary and basic feature of resemblance we should have to Christ Jesus, the one on which all our super-natural activity depends. If we do not, first and above all, possess within us this *sanctifying grace* which is the *fundamental sign of resemblance to Jesus*, the eternal Father will not recognize us as His own; and all we do, in the whole of our life, without

---

[1] This is what one calls in theology the "Grace of union," by virtue of which a human nature has been chosen to be *united*, in an ineffable way, to a Divine Person, the Word, and to make it the humanity of one who is God. This grace is unique and is met with only in Jesus Christ.   [2] I, q. XXII, a. 3.

this grace is of no merit for making us share in the eternal inheritance. We shall only be co-heirs of Christ if we are His brothers by grace.[1]

3. Christ our *model in His works* and *His virtues.*

CHRIST is our model *in His works* too.

We have seen how true it is that He *was* man. One must, also, say how true it is that He *acted* as man.

In this again Our Lord is for us a consummate, and yet an accessible, model of all holiness. He practiced to an incomparable degree all the virtues that can adorn human nature, all those at least which were compatible with His Divine nature.

Along with sanctifying grace, as you know, there was given to the soul of Christ a magnificent procession of the virtues and gifts of the Holy Spirit. These virtues flowed from grace, like water from a spring. In the course of Jesus's life they were given expression in all their perfection.

Admittedly, He did not have Faith; this theological virtue exists only in a soul that does not yet enjoy the vision of God. The soul of Christ gazed upon God face to face, it could not "believe" in this God whom it *saw*; but it had that submission of the will which is necessary for the perfection of Faith, that reverence, that adoration of God, first and infallible Truth. This disposition was in the soul of Christ to a very high degree.

No more than that did Christ Jesus have the virtue of Hope, properly speaking. It is no longer possible to hope for what one already possesses. The theological virtue of Hope makes us desire the possession of God, while giving us the confidence of receiving the graces necessary to attain it. The soul of Christ, through its union with the

---

[1] "Oh, if you had only come to understand the grace of God through Jesus Christ, our Lord, and His incarnation itself, by which He received the soul and body of a man, you would have been able to perceive the highest example of grace!" (St. Augustine, *The City of God*, X, 29).

Word, was filled with the Divinity. It therefore could not have Hope; this virtue only existed in Christ in the sense that He was able to desire, and indeed desired, the glorification of His sacred humanity, the accidental glory that was to return to Him after His resurrection: "And now, Father, glorify me."[1] That glory, He possessed in Himself from the time of His incarnation, its source and root. He let it flower forth for a moment when He was transfigured on Tabor, but His mission here below among men obliged Him to veil its splendor, right up to His death. There were also certain graces that Christ asked of His Father; for example, at the raising of Lazarus we see that He addresses Himself to His Father with the most absolute confidence: "Father, I give you thanks that you have heard me. Yet I knew that you always hear me."[2]

As for Charity, He practiced it to the supreme degree. The heart of Christ is an immense furnace of love. Christ's great love is the love He bears for His Father; the whole of His life can be summed up in these words: "I seek only what is pleasing to my Father."[3]

Let us meditate upon these words in prayer; it is only in prayer that we can penetrate their secret a little. This unutterable love, this inclination of the soul of Christ Jesus towards His Father, is the necessary consequence of His hypostatic union. The Son is altogether orientated towards His Father—*Ad Patrem*, as the theologians say. There, if I may so express it, is His essence: the sacred humanity is carried along in this Divine current. Having, through the Incarnation, become the Son of God's own humanity, it belongs to the Father entirely. It is necessarily the case that the fundamental disposition, the first and habitual sentiment, of the soul of Christ shall be: I live for my Father, "I love the Father."[4] It is because He loves His Father that Jesus gives Himself up to His Father's every will. His first act on coming into this world is an act of love towards Him: "Behold, I come to do your will, O God."[5]

---

[1] John 17:5.   [2] John 11:41-42.   [3] See John 8:29.   [4] John 14:31.   [5] Hebr. 10:9.

One can say that the whole of His existence on earth was to be but the continued expression of that initial act. Throughout His life He loves to repeat that His "food" is to do the will of His Father;[1] that is why He always does what is pleasing to His Father: "I do always the things that are pleasing to Him."[2] Everything His Father had determined for Him, He carried out to the last jot and tittle,[3] that is to say, to the last detail. Finally, it was for love of His Father that He became "obedient unto death, even to death on a cross":[4] "that the world may know that I love the Father: and as the Father has given me commandment, so do I."[5] Let us not forget this: that if Christ was able to say that "greater love than this no man has, that a man lay down his life for his friends,"[6] if it is of faith that He died "for us and for our salvation,"[7] it remains true that it was above all through love of His Father that Our Lord laid down His life. In loving us, it is His Father that He loves. He sees us, He finds us, in His Father: "I pray for them ... because they are yours"[8]—we have there His own words. Yes, Christ loves us: because we are the children of His Father, because we belong to His Father. He loves us with an ineffable love, one that surpasses all we can imagine, to the extent that each of us can say with St. Paul: He "loved me, and gave Himself up for me."[9] He gave Himself up for me because He loved me.

Our Lord possessed all the other virtues as well. Gentleness and humility: "Learn from me, for I am meek and humble of heart."[10] He, the Lord before whom every knee bends in heaven and on earth—He kneels before His disciples to wash their feet. Obedience: He is submissive to His mother and St. Joseph; a phrase in the Gospel sums up His hidden life at Nazareth: "and was subject to them."[11] He obeys the

---

[1] John 4:34.
[2] John 8:29.
[3] Matt. 5:18.
[4] Phil. 2:8.
[5] John 14:31 (Rheims).
[6] John 15:13 (Rheims).
[7] Nicene Creed.
[8] John 17:9.
[9] Gal. 2:20.
[10] Matt. 11:29.
[11] Luke 2:51.

Mosaic law, He goes assiduously to the assemblies in the temple. He subjects Himself to the legitimately established powers, declaring that one must "render to Caesar the things that are Caesar's";[1] He Himself pays the tribute money. Patience: how many testimonies of this has He not given, above all during His sorrowful Passion! His infinite mercy towards sinners: He welcomes with kindness the Samaritan woman, and Mary Magdalene. The "good shepherd,"[2] He runs in search of the strayed flock and brings them back to the fold. He is filled with an ardent zeal for the glory and interests of His Father; it is that zeal which makes Him drive out the sellers from the temple and hurl anathemas at the hypocrisy of the Pharisees. His prayer is continual: He "continued all night in prayer to God."[3] Who can say what was this conversation of the Incarnate Word, heart-to-heart with His Father thus, or the spirit binding Him to His Father, the spirit of adoration that animated Him?

In Him, then, all the virtues blossom in their due season, for the glory of His Father and for our salvation.

You know that the ancient patriarchs, before leaving the earth, used to give their eldest son a solemn blessing, one which was like a pledge of heavenly prosperity for their descendants. Well, we read in the Book of Genesis that the patriarch Isaac, before giving this solemn blessing to his son Jacob, embraced him, and, breathing in the perfume that escaped from his garments, cried out in an access of joy: "Behold, the smell of my son is as the smell of a plentiful field, which the Lord has blessed." And straightaway, completely transported, he called down upon his son's head the richest of blessings from on high: "God give you of the dew of heaven, and of the fatness of the earth, abundance of corn and wine. And let peoples serve you, and tribes worship you: be lord of your brethren.... Cursed be he that curses you: and let him that blesses you be filled with blessings."[4]

---

[1] See Matt. 22:21.   [2] John 10:14.   [3] Luke 6:12.   [4] Gen. 27:27-29.

That scene is an image of the rapture the Father feels in contemplating the humanity of His Son Jesus, and of the spiritual blessings He lavishes on those who are united to His Son. Like a field bedecked with flowers, the soul of Christ is adorned with all the virtues that embellish human nature. God is infinite, as such He has infinite demands; and yet, the least of the actions of Jesus was the object of His Father's pleasure. When Christ Jesus labored in the humble workshop at Nazareth, when He conversed with men or took His meals with His disciples—all apparently quite simple things—His Father looked on Him and said: "This is my beloved Son, in whom I am well pleased."[1] And He added: "Hear Him"[2]—that is to say, contemplate Him so as to imitate Him: He is your model, follow Him; He is the way, and no one comes to me except by Him, no one partakes of my blessings except in Him,[3] for I have given Him the fullness of them, exactly in the way that I have destined the nations of the earth to be His inheritance.[4] Why did the Heavenly Father take this infinite pleasure in Jesus? Because Christ accomplished all perfectly and because His acts were the expression of the most sublime virtues; but especially because all Christ's actions, while being in themselves human actions, were Divine in their mainspring.

O Christ Jesus, full of grace and model of every virtue, beloved Son in whom the Father has set all His delight, be the one object of my contemplation and of my love. May I regard every passing thing "as so much rubbish"[5] so as to place my joy in but you alone. May I seek to imitate you so as to be, through you and with you, pleasing to your Father in all things!

---

[1] Matt. 17:5.   [2] *Ibid.*
[3] "... the God and Father of our Lord Jesus Christ, who has blessed us with every spiritual blessing ... in Christ": Eph. 1:3.   [4] Ps. 2:8.   [5] Phil. 3:8 (Jerus.)

4. *Our imitation* of Christ is achieved *through grace*; and then, through this *basic disposition* of referring everything *to the glory of His Father.* "THE CHRISTIAN IS ANOTHER CHRIST."

WHEN ONE GOES THROUGH the Gospel of St. John, one notices the insistence Christ places on repeating: "My teaching is not my own,"[1] "The Son can do nothing of himself,"[2] "Of myself I can do nothing."[3] "Of myself I do nothing."[4]

Does that mean that Christ had no human intellect, no human will, no human activity? Not at all, it would be a heresy to think that: but (the humanity of Jesus being united hypostatically[5] to the Word) there was not within Christ any human person to which His faculties could have been attached. In Him was but one single Person, that of the Word who does everything in union with the Father. Everything was in the most absolute dependence on the divinity; all Christ's activity emanated from the single Person who was in Him, that of the Word. This activity, even though it was carried out by the human nature directly, was Divine in its root, in its mainspring; and that is why the eternal Father received from it an infinite glory and found there so much pleasure.

Are we able to imitate this? Yes! since, by sanctifying grace, we share in the Divine Sonship of Jesus. Through this grace, our activity is raised higher and is as though divinized in its mainspring. It goes without saying that, in the order of *being*, we always keep our personality; we always stay, by nature, purely human creatures. Our union with God through grace, close and intimate as it may be, remains an accidental union, not a substantial one; but it becomes greater to the extent that the autonomy of our personality, in the order of *activity*, effaces itself further before Divinity.

If we want nothing to interpose between ourselves and God, nothing to hinder our union with Him, if we want the Divine blessings to

---

[1] John 7:16.   [2] John 5:19.   [3] John 5:30.   [4] John 8:28.
[5] "Hypostatically," from a Greek word that means: "by a *personal* union."

flood into our soul, we have not only to renounce sin and imperfection but, also, to strip ourselves of our personality *in so far as it constitutes an obstacle to perfect union with God*. It places such an obstacle when our own judgement, our self-will, our self-love, our susceptibilities, make us think and act otherwise than in accordance with the desires of our Heavenly Father. Believe me, our faults of weakness, our miseries, our human servitudes, hinder our union with God infinitely less than does that habitual attitude of the soul which wants, so to speak, to keep in all things the proprietorship of its activity. We should, then, not annihilate our personality—that is neither possible nor wished by God—but rather bring it (if I may use the phrase) to a complete capitulation before God. We should deposit it at the feet of God and ask God to be, through His Spirit, the driving-force of all our thoughts, all our feelings, all our words, all our actions, all our life—in the same way as for the humanity of Christ.[1]

When a soul succeeds in stripping itself of every sin, of every attachment to itself and to creatures;[2] succeeds in destroying in itself, as far as possible, all purely natural and human motivations so as to deliver itself up completely to the Divine action; succeeds in living in absolute dependence on God, on His will, on His commandments, on the spirit of the Gospel, succeeds in making everything relate to the Heavenly Father, then it is able to say: "The Lord rules me,"[3] the Lord directs me; everything in me comes from Him, I am in His hands. That soul has arrived at perfect imitation of Christ, to the point that its life is the very reproduction of that of Christ: "I live, *now not I*; but Christ lives in me."[4] God rules it, directs it; everything in it moves under Divine impetus: this is holiness, the most perfect imitation of Jesus Christ in

---

[1] "Let all our thought and understanding, and all our words and all our acts, truly breathe self-negation; or rather, a testimony and confession of Christ": Origen, Homily 2 on Matt. 16.

[2] [*Translator's note*: In this context, "creatures" (*la créature*) includes, besides persons, *things*, such as goods or riches.]   [3] Ps. 22 (23):1.   [4] Gal. 2:20 (Rheims).

His *being*, in His *state* of Son of God, as also in His primordial disposition of being entirely His Father's; in His person and in His *activity*.

Let us not think it may be a presumption on our part to want to turn into reality an ideal so sublime. No, this is the very desire of God; it is His eternal thought with regard to us: He "predestined" us to "become conformed to the image of His Son."[1] The more we are conformed to His Son, the more the Father loves us because we are more united to Him.[2] When He sees a soul fully transformed into His Son, He surrounds that soul with His altogether special protection, with the most attentive care of His providence; He showers on it His blessings, He sets no bounds on the communication of His graces: that is the secret of the largesses of God.

Oh, let us thank our Heavenly Father for having given us His Son, Christ Jesus as our model, in such wise that we have but to look at Him to know what we have to do: "Hear Him."[3] Christ has said to us: "I have given you an example, that as I have done to you, so you also should do."[4] He has left us His example, so that we might walk in His footsteps.[5] He is the only way we must follow: "I am the way."[6] One who follows that way does not walk in darkness but comes to the light of life. This is the model that faith reveals to us, a model transcendent yet accessible: "Look and make it according to the pattern."[7]

The soul of Our Lord, at every moment, contemplated the Divine essence. In that same gaze His soul saw the ideal conceived by God for humanity, and each one of His actions was the expression of that ideal. Let us, then, lift up our eyes, let us love to know Christ Jesus more and more, to study His life in the Gospels, to follow His mysteries in the admirable order established by the Church herself in her liturgical cycle,

---

[1] Rom. 8:29.

[2] "If you would show yourself to be an imitator of Christ, you have approached Christ, and, through Christ, God": St. Ambrose, *Sermo* XXII, on Psalm 118.

[3] Matt. 17:5.   [4] John 13:15.   [5] 1 Peter 2:21.   [6] John 14:6.   [7] Exod. 25:40.

from Advent to Pentecost; let us open the eyes of our faith, and live in such a way as to reproduce in us the features of this Exemplar, to conform our lives to His words and His acts. This model is Divine and visible; He shows us God acting in the midst of us and sanctifying, in His humanity, all our actions, even the most ordinary; all our feelings, even the most intimate; all our sufferings, even the deepest of them.

Let us contemplate Him, this model, but with faith. We are sometimes tempted to envy the contemporaries of Jesus who were able to see Him, to follow Him, to listen to Him. But faith makes Him present to us also, in a presence no less efficacious for our souls. Christ has Himself said it to us: "*Blessed* are they who have not seen, and yet have believed."[1] This is to make us understand that it is no less advantageous for us to stay in contact with Jesus by faith than to have seen Him in the flesh. He whom we see living and acting when we read the Gospels, or when we celebrate His mysteries, is God's own Son. We have said everything when we have said of Christ: "You are the Son of the living God";[2] and there we have the fundamental aspect of the Divine Model of our souls.

Let us contemplate Him, not with a contemplation that is abstract, exterior, theoretical, cold, but with a contemplation full of love, attentive to seize upon the smallest features of this model to reproduce them in our own lives, but above all that basic and primordial disposition of Christ, of living for His Father. The whole of His life can be said to come down to that feature; all the virtues of Christ are the effect of this orientation of His soul towards the Father; and this orientation is itself but the product of that ineffable union by which, in Jesus, the whole of humanity is drawn into that Divine impetus which carries the Son towards His Father.

It is this that properly constitutes a Christian—in the first place, to share, *through sanctifying grace*, in the Divine Sonship of Christ. That

---

[1] John 20:29.   [2] See Matt. 16:16.

is imitation of Jesus in *His state* of Son of God. Next, to reproduce, *by our virtues*, the traits of this unique archetype of perfection. That is imitation of Jesus in *His works*. St. Paul indicates as much when he tells us that Christ should be "formed" in us:[1] "Put on the Lord Jesus Christ,"[2] bear a resemblance to Christ—bear "the likeness of the heavenly."[3]

Christianus, alter Christus, "the Christian is another Christ." This is the true definition of a Christian given by the whole of tradition, if not in those actual terms, at least by the use of equivalent expressions. "Another Christ," because a Christian is first of all, through grace, a child of the Heavenly Father and one of the brethren of Christ here below, so as to be His co-heir on high. "Another Christ," because all his, the Christian's, activity—thoughts, desires, actions—puts down its roots in this grace, in order that he behave in practice according to the thoughts, desires, feelings of Jesus, and in conformity with Jesus's actions: "Have this mind in you which was also in Christ Jesus."[4]

[1] Gal. 4:19; cf. Eph. 4:13.   [2] Rom. 13:14.   [3] 1 Cor. 15:49.   [4] Phil. 2:5.

CHRIST, AUTHOR OF OUR REDEMPTION AND INFINITE TREASURY OF OUR GRACES: *CAUSA SATISFACTORIA ET MERITORIA*

INTRODUCTION: Christ, by His satisfactions, merits for us the grace of divine sonship.

THE IMITATION of Christ Jesus, in His being—His being of grace—and in His virtues, constitutes the substance of our holiness. That is what I strove to show you in the preceding talk. To make you know better this one whom we should imitate, I sought to put before the eyes of your souls our Divine model: Christ Jesus, true God and true man. There is no doubt at all that the contemplation of Our Lord, so adorable in His person, so admirable in His life and in His works, will have kindled in your hearts an ardent desire to be able to resemble Him and to unite yourselves to Him.

But can created beings aspire to reproduce in themselves the traits of the Incarnate Word, to share His life? Can they find the strength to follow this unique Way that leads to the Father? Yes; Revelation tells us that we find that strength in the grace which has been merited for us by the satisfactions[1] of Christ.

Our God does all things with wisdom; nay more, He *is* Infinite

---

[1] [*Translator's note*: Throughout, Marmion uses "satisfactions" in the sense of atonement or reparation. His adjective "satisfactory" means "making satisfaction" in that sense.]

Wisdom. As His eternal thought is to make us be conformed to the image of His Son, we may be sure that He has put means of infallible power at the service of the end sought by this ineffable design. Not only can we aspire to the realization of the Divine ideal in us, but God Himself invites us to do so—He "has predestined" us "to become conformed to the image of His Son."[1] He wants us to reproduce in ourselves—even though we can do this in limited measure only—His beloved Son's features. To desire to reproduce this ideal is neither pride nor presumption, but a response to God's own desire: "Hear Him." All we have to do is to employ the means He Himself has determined.

Christ, we have seen, is not only the one and universal Exemplar of every perfection; He is also, as I have told you, the Satisfactory and Meritorious Cause, the Efficient Cause, of our sanctification. Christ is, for us, the source of grace, because, having paid all our debts to Divine Justice by His life, His Passion and His death, He has merited to distribute every grace to us: *Causa satisfactoria et meritoria.*

Let us examine this truth that is so beneficial. We shall, in the next talk, see how Christ is the efficient cause of our holiness.

1. **Impossibility for the human race, issue of *sinful Adam*, to win back the eternal inheritance. Only one who is *God*-made-*Man* is able to give a *fully sufficient satisfaction*.**

WHAT IS TO BE understood when we say that Christ is the satisfactory and meritorious cause of our salvation and of our sanctification?

As you know, God in creating the first man established him in justice and in grace; in so doing He made him His child and heir. But the Divine plan was cut across by sin; Adam, constituted head of his race, betrayed the trust. At a stroke he lost, for himself and his descendants, all right to divine life and divine inheritance. All the children of

---

[1] Eph. 1:5.

Adam, captives of the devil as they had become,[1] shared in his disgrace. That is why they are born, as St. Paul says, "enemies" of God,[2] objects of "wrath,"[3] and, for that reason, excluded from the eternal beatitude.[4]

Would not anyone be found, among the sons of Adam, to ransom his brothers and lift the curse that weighed upon them all? No one — for all had sinned in Adam. No one, either for himself or for the others, would be able to give an adequate satisfaction.

Sin is an insult given to God, an insult that has to be expiated. Man, being simply a creature, is by himself incapable of paying off properly the debt contracted against Divine Majesty by a wrongdoing the malice of which is infinite. A satisfaction, to be adequate, must be offered by someone of a dignity equivalent to that of the one offended. The gravity of an insult is proportionate to the dignity of the person offended; the same insult given to a prince takes on a greater gravity because of his rank than if it had been given to a peasant.[5] For satisfaction, one must reverse the principle. The greatness of a reparation is governed by the dignity, not of the one who receives it, but of the one who gives it. The same king receives the homage of a peasant and of a prince: it is quite obvious that the prince's homage outweighs that of the peasant.

Now, between us and God there is an infinity. Ought humanity to have despaired, then? Would there never be reparation for the outrage done to God? Would man never re-enter into possession of the eternal benefits? God alone was able to answer us, God alone was able to give to this anguishing problem a solution.

---

[1] Acts 26:18; John 12:31; Col. 1:13.   [2] Rom. 5:10, 11:28.
[3] 1 Thess. 1:10; Rom. 2, vv. 5, 8; Eph. 2:3.   [4] Rom. 2:2; 5:15-18.
[5] "Sin committed against God has an infinite quality because of the infinity of the Divine majesty, for an offense is greater to the extent that the one transgressed against is greater": St Thomas, III, q. 1, a. 2, ad 2; cf. I-II, q. LXXXVII, a. 4.

You know what God's answer has been, the solution He brought, which was at once full of mercy and of justice. In His unfathomable designs, He decreed that the ransom of humanity would only be brought about by a satisfaction equal to the rights of His infinite justice, and that this satisfaction would be given by the bloody sacrifice of a victim who would substitute Himself freely, voluntarily, for sinful humanity. Who would this victim be? Who would be this Savior? "Are you he who is to come?"[1] It was on the morrow of Adam's sin that God promised a Savior, but thousands of years would pass before He came; thousands of years during which the human race lifted up their hands from the bottom of a nameless abyss, from which they were powerless to raise themselves; thousands of years during which they piled up sacrifice on sacrifice, holocaust on holocaust, to free themselves from their servitude.

But when "the fullness of time" came,[2] God sent the promised Savior, the Savior who was to ransom creation, destroy sin[3] and reconcile men with God. Who was it who would come? It was to be the Son of God made man.

Being man, issued from the race of Adam, He would be able to substitute himself voluntarily for all His brethren and, so to speak, show solidarity with their sin. Freely accepting to suffer and to expiate in His flesh which was susceptible of suffering, He would be capable of meriting. Being God, His merit would have an infinite value, the satisfaction would be commensurate, the reparation would be complete. There is nowise, said St. Thomas, a *fully* sufficient satisfaction outside

---

[1] Matt. 11:3.   [2] Gal. 4:4.

[3] [*Translator's note*: "destroy sin." Marmion is not, of course, saying that sin and the tendency to sin no longer exist—he says the very opposite of that later. Here he is referring to the removal, by the Redemption, of the bar which formerly existed, as the result of original sin, to our being united with God in heaven. Or, put positively, the return of grace to humanity. See his words two paragraphs further on, and those on page 441: "Christ has closed the gap that separates man from God."]

of an operation fully infinite in value—that is to say, an operation that only God was able to carry out.[1] In the same way that the order of justice requires that the penalty fits the fault, it seems to require also, said St. Thomas, that he should satisfy for the sin who has committed the sin, and that is why it was necessary to have from *within* the nature corrupted by the fault the one who was to be offered in satisfaction for the whole of this nature.[2]

Such is the solution God Himself brought. He could have brought others, but this is the one that it pleased His Wisdom, His Power, His Goodness to give us; this is the one that therefore we should contemplate and praise. For this solution is a wonderful one. "The humanity of Christ," says St. Gregory, "permitted Him to die and to satisfy for men: His divinity gave Him the power to restore to us the grace that sanctifies."[3] Death had come from a human nature soiled by sin. From a human nature united to one who is God, would spring forth the source of grace and of life: "That out of that from which death arose, life might rise again."[4]

2. *Jesus, Savior. Infinite value of all the actions* of the Word Incarnate. However, *the Redemption* was only brought about, in actual fact, *by the Sacrifice of the cross.*

WHEN THE FULLNESS of the time fixed by the heavenly decrees had come, said St. Paul, "God sent His Son, born of a woman, born a subject of the Law, to redeem the subjects of the Law and to enable us to be adopted as sons."[5] To ransom humanity from sin and, through grace, to restore Divine adoption to it—such, in fact, is the basic mission of the Word Incarnate, the work Christ came here below to accomplish.

---

[1] III, q. 1, a. 2, ad 2.   [2] *Ibid.*, q. IV, a. 6.   [3] *Moralia*, XVII, c. 30, n. 46.
[4] Preface of the Mass for Passiontide.   [5] Gal. 4:4-5 (Jerus.)

His name, the name "Jesus," given to Him by God Himself, is not without import, not without significance: "Jesus does not bear a name that is empty or vain."[1] This name, meaning *Savior*, signifies His special mission of salvation, and points to the work that is His: the world's Redemption. "And you shall call His name Jesus," said the angel sent to St. Joseph, "for He shall *save* His people from their sins."[2]

And see Him come.

Let us contemplate Him at this solemn moment, unique in the history of humanity. What does He say? What does He do? "And this is what He said, on coming into the world: 'You, who wanted no sacrifice or oblation, prepared a body for me. You took no pleasure in holocausts or sacrifices for sin; then I said... *Here I am.*'"[3] These words, taken from St. Paul, reveal to us the very first movement of Christ's heart at the time of His Incarnation. And having made this initial act in statement of total oblation, He "has rejoiced as a giant to run the way" that opened before Him.[4]

A giant indeed, for this is a Man-God; and all His actions, all His works, are those of one who is God, and, in consequence, are worthy of God to whom He thereby did homage.

According to the language of philosophy, "acts belong to the person": *Actiones sunt suppositorum*. The different actions we perform have their source in human nature and in the faculties which derive from that nature; but, in the last analysis, we attribute them to the person who possesses that nature and makes use of his faculties. Thus, it is with the intellect that I think, with the eye that I see, with the hearing that I hear. Hearing, seeing and thinking are actions of human nature; but we relate them finally to the person; it is *I*, the same "I," who hear, see and think. Even though each of these actions may have

---

[1] St. Bernard, *Sermo* I on the Circumcision.   [2] Matt. 1:21.
[3] Hebr. 10:5-7 (Jerus.); cf. Ps. 39 (40):7-8.   [4] Ps. 18 (19):6.

for immediate source a different faculty, they come back to the one and same person who possesses the nature endowed with these faculties.

Now, in Jesus Christ, the human nature, perfect and whole in itself, is united to the Person of the Word, of the Son of God. Many actions, in Christ, are only able to be performed in His human nature. If He works, if He walks, if He sleeps, if He eats, if He teaches, if He suffers, if He dies, it is in His humanity, it is through His human nature: but all His actions belong to the Divine Person to whom this humanity is united. It is a Divine Person *who* acts and operates *through* the human nature.

The result of this is that all the actions performed through the humanity of Jesus Christ—however tiny, however ordinary, however simple, however limited they may be in their physical reality and their earthly duration—are attributed to the Divine Person to whom this humanity is united; they are the actions of one who is God.[1] On this account, they possess a beauty and a glory that are transcendent; they acquire, from the moral point of view, an inestimable worth, an infinite value, an inexhaustible efficacy. The moral value of the human actions of Christ is measured by the infinite dignity of the Divine Person in whom the human nature subsists and acts.

If that is true of the smallest actions of Christ, how much more true it is of those that properly constitute or are related to His mission here below: His voluntarily substituting Himself for us as a victim without stain so as to pay off our debt and restore divine life to us by His expiation and the satisfactions He made.

For such was the mission He had to fulfill, the course He had to run. "The Lord has laid on Him"—a man like us, of the race of Adam; a just man nevertheless, innocent and without sin—"the iniquity of us all."[2] Because He has, so to speak, become bound up with our nature

---

[1] Theology calls them *theandric*, from two Greek words meaning *God* and *man*.
[2] Isa. 53:6.

and with our sin, Christ has merited to make us be bound up with His justice and His holiness. According to St. Paul's expression (and how vigorous it is!) God, "by sending His own Son in the likeness of sinful flesh as a sin-offering, has condemned sin in the flesh";[1] and, with a vigor more astonishing still: "For our sake God made the sinless one into sin."[2] What vigor there is in that expression: "made into sin"! The Apostle does not say "a sinner," but actually "sin."

Christ, for His part, accepted the taking of all our sins upon Himself, to the extent of His becoming upon the cross, in a way, universal sin, living sin. He voluntarily put Himself in our place, and for that reason would be stricken by death: our ransom He "has purchased with His own blood."[3] Humanity would be redeemed, "not with perishable things, with silver or gold, but with the precious blood of Christ, as of a lamb without blemish and without spot," one who was "foreknown indeed before the foundation of the world."[4]

Oh! let us not forget that we have been "bought at a great price."[5] Christ Jesus has poured out, for us, the very last drop of His blood. It is true to say that one single drop of this Divine blood would have sufficed to redeem us; the least suffering, the lightest humiliation of Christ, even a single desire coming from His heart, would have sufficed to expiate all the sins, all the crimes that could be committed. For each one of the actions of Christ, being the action of a Divine Person, constitutes a satisfaction of infinite worth. But, to make the immense love His Son bears for Him shine out more to the eyes of the whole world: "that the world may know that I love the Father";[6] and also the ineffable charity this same Son has in *our* regard: "Greater love than this no man has....";[7] and so that we may have a keener touch of our finger-tips on how infinite is the Divine holiness and how deep the malice of sin; and for other reasons still that we are not able to

---

[1] See Rom. 8:3.   [2] 2 Cor. 5:21 (Jerus.)   [3] Acts 20:28.   [4] 1 Peter 1:18-20.
[5] 1 Cor. 6:20.   [6] John 14:31.   [7] John 15:13 (Rheims).

discover,[1] God the Eternal Father has asked as expiation for the crimes of humanity all the sufferings, the Passion and the death, of His Divine Son. Thus, in point of fact, the satisfaction was only complete when, from the height of the cross, Jesus with His dying voice pronounced the *Consummatum est*, "All is accomplished."[2] Only then was His personal mission of Redemption here below fulfilled, only then was His work of salvation achieved.

3. Christ *merits* not only for Himself, but *for us*. This merit is founded on the grace of Christ *constituted head of humankind*; on the *sovereign liberty* and the *ineffable love* with which Christ underwent His Passion *for all men*.

BY THE SATISFACTIONS He has made, as moreover by all the acts of His life, Christ Jesus has *merited* for us every grace of pardon, of salvation and of sanctification.

What indeed is merit?

It is a *right* to reward.[3] When we say that the works of Christ are meritorious *for us*, we say that, through them, Christ has title of right to the eternal life, and all the graces leading or attaching to that life, which may be given to us. That is in fact what St. Paul tells us. We are "justified" (rendered just in the eyes of God, that is) not by our own works but "freely by His grace"—by a gratuitous gift of God, namely grace, which comes to us "through the redemption which is in Christ Jesus"; by means of the redemption effected by Jesus Christ.[4] Thus, the apostle makes us understand that the Passion of Jesus, which com-

---

[1] The Redemption is a mystery of faith; we can know its wonderful points of appropriateness after it has been revealed to us, but fundamentally it remains hidden to us. This is what St. Paul calls "the mystery which has been hidden from eternity in God": Eph. 3:9; see also Col. 1:26; Eph. 1:9, 3:3.   [2] See John 19:30.

[3] We are speaking of merit properly so called, of a strict and rigorous right, which is called in theology *meritum de condigno*.   [4] Rom. 3:24.

pletes and crowns all the works of His life on earth, is the source from which eternal life for us flows. Christ is the *meritorious cause* of our sanctification.

And what is the profound reason for this merit? For all merit is personal. When we are in a state of grace, we are able to merit for ourselves an increase of that grace, but this merit is restricted to our own person. We cannot merit grace for others; we can at the very most implore it, beg it, from God. How, then, can Christ merit for us? What is the fundamental reason why Christ can not only merit for Himself the glorification of His humanity, for example, but can, as well as this, merit life eternal for others, for us, for all humankind?

Merit, the fruit and property of grace, has—if we may put it like this—the same range as the grace upon which it is based. Christ Jesus is filled with sanctifying grace, by virtue of which He can personally merit for Himself. But this grace in Jesus does not stop at Him alone; it does not possess only a personal character, it enjoys a privilege of universality. Christ has been predestined to become our head, the chief one of us, our representative. The eternal Father wills to make Him "the firstborn of every creature."[1] As a result of this eternal predestination to be head of all the elect, the grace of Christ (who is of our race through the Incarnation) takes on a character of pre-eminence and universality, the object of which is more than to sanctify the human soul of Jesus. Its object is to make Him, in the domain of eternal life, head of all humanity.[2] Hence the social character that is attached to every one of the acts of Jesus when they are considered in relation to humankind. Everything Christ does, He carries out not only *for* us, but in our name. That is why St. Paul tells us that "as by the disobedience of the one man, the many were constituted sinners"; as the disobedience of

[1] Col. 1:15.
[2] This is called in theology *Gratia capitis*, "the Grace of the head" (cf. St Thomas, III, q. XLVIII, a. 1).

one man, Adam, dragged us into sin and death, so also the obedience
—and what obedience!—of another man (but a man who, as well as
being man, is God) sufficed to put us all back into the order of grace.[1]
Thus, Christ Jesus in His capacity of head, of chief one of us, has
merited for all of us—just as by substituting Himself for us He has
satisfied for us. And since, in this case, the one who merits is one who
is *God*, His merits have an infinite value and an inexhaustible efficacy.[2]

What completes the giving of all beauty and fullness to the satisfactions and merits of Christ is that He accepted His sufferings voluntarily and from love. Liberty is an essential element of merit, for an act is
only deserving of praise if the one who carries it out is responsible:
"Where liberty is not, neither is merit," says St. Bernard.[3]

This liberty envelops the whole redemptive mission of Jesus. God-
Man, Christ sovereignly accepted to suffer in His flesh, a flesh capable of
suffering, susceptible of pain. When, on His entry into this world, He
said to His Father "Here I am; I come to do your will,"[4] He foresaw all
the humiliations, all the pains of His Passion and death; and, freely, from
the depths of His heart, for love of His Father and of us, He accepted
them all: "I have desired it, and your law in the midst of my heart."[5]

This will, Christ kept intact throughout the whole of his life. The
hour of His sacrifice is always present to Him; He awaits it with impatience, He calls it "his hour,"[6] as if that were the only one that counted
for Him during His life. He foretells His death to His disciples, He
traces its details in advance to them, in terms so clear that they cannot

---

[1] Rom. 5:19.

[2] It goes without saying that Christ's merits have to be applied to us in order that
we may experience their efficacy. Baptism inaugurates this application of them to
us. By baptism we are incorporated into Christ, we become living members of His
mystical body; a bond is established between the head and the members. Once
justified by baptism, we can merit in our turn.

[3] *Sermo* I on the Song of Songs.

[4] See Hebr. 10:9; Ps. 39 (40):8-9.

[5] Ps. 39 (40):9.

[6] John 13:1.

mistake them. Therefore when St. Peter, wholly overcome at the thought of seeing his Master die, wishes to oppose the coming to pass of His sufferings, Jesus repulses him: "You savor not the things that are of God."[1] As for Christ Himself, He knows His Father. For love of His Father and in charity for us, He reaches forth towards His Passion with all the ardor of His sacred soul, but also with a sovereign liberty that is fully master of itself. If this loving will is so strong that in Him it is like a furnace — "I have come to cast fire upon the earth"; if He burned to have a baptism of blood: "I have a baptism to be baptized with,"[2] nevertheless no one will have the power to take His life from Him, it is of His own accord that He will leave it.[3] See how He makes the truth of His words shine out. One day, the inhabitants of Nazareth want to cast Him down from a rocky height; Jesus withdraws from the midst of them, with a wonderful tranquility.[4] Another time, at Jerusalem, the Jews want to stone Him because He affirms that He is Divine. He hides Himself and goes out of the temple:[5] His hour had not yet come.

But, when it has arrived, He delivers Himself up. Look at Him in the Garden of Olives, on the eve of His death. The armed bands advance towards Him to take Him and get Him condemned. "Whom do you seek?" He asks of them. To their response, "Jesus of Nazareth," He says to them simply, "I am he."[6] Coming from His lips, this answer on its own is enough to make His enemies fall back. He would have been able to hold them prostrate upon the ground; He would have been able, as He Himself said, to ask His Father, and He "would promptly send more than twelve legions of angels to my defense."[7] He recalls, at this precise moment, that every day He has been in the temple and that no one has been able to lay a hand on His person; the hour had not then come; that is why He did not give them license to seize Him. Now the hour had sounded when, for the salvation of the

---

[1] Mark 8:31-33 (Rheims).   [2] Luke 12:49-50.   [3] John 10:18.
[4] Luke 4:30.   [5] John 8:59.   [6] John 18:4-5.   [7] Matt. 26:53 (Jerus.)

world, He had to deliver Himself up to His executioners, who but acted as instruments of the power of hell: "This is your hour, and the power of darkness."[1] The rabble of soldiery take Him from tribunal to tribunal; He lets them do it. However, in His appearance before the Sanhedrin, the supreme tribunal of the Jews, He proclaims His rights as Son of God; then He abandons Himself to the fury of His enemies, right up to the moment when He consummates His sacrifice upon the cross.

It is truly because He willed it that He was delivered up to death: "He was offered *because* it was *His own* will."[2] In this voluntary, and love-filled, handing over of His entire self on the cross; by this death of the Man-God; by this immolation of a Victim without stain, who offers Himself from love and with a sovereign liberty—by this, an infinite satisfaction is given for us to Divine Justice,[3] an inexhaustible merit is won for us by Christ, while life eternal is restored to humanity. "And being consummated, He became, to all that obey Him, the cause of eternal salvation."[4] Because He consummated the work of His mediation, Christ has become, for all those who follow Him, *the meritorious cause of eternal salvation*. Thus St. Paul was right to say that by this His will "we are sanctified by the oblation of the body of Jesus Christ once,"[5] that is: by virtue of this will, we are sanctified by the oblation Jesus Christ has made, once and for all, of His own body.

For it is for us, for each one of us, that Our Lord died: "Christ died for all."[6] "And He is the propitiation for our sins: and not for ours only, but also for those of the whole world,"[7] in such wise that He is the "one Mediator between God and men, Himself man, Christ Jesus."[8]

When one studies the Divine plan, especially in the light of St. Paul's letters, one sees that God wills that we seek our salvation and

---

[1] Luke 22:53.   [2] Isa. 53:7.

[3] "In the death of Christ is consummation of those things which were required for satisfaction": St Thomas, 3 *Sent.*, dist. XXI. q. 2, a. 1, ad 3 and 4.

[4] Hebr. 5:9 (Rheims).   [5] Hebr. 10:10 (Rheims).   [6] 2 Cor. 5:15.

[7] 1 John 2:2 (Rheims).   [8] 1 Tim. 2:5.

sanctity only in the blood of His Son; there is no other Redeemer, "there is no other name under heaven given to men by which we must be saved";[1] since His death is sovereignly efficacious. "For by one offering *He has perfected forever* those who are sanctified."[2] The Father's will is that His Son Jesus, having substituted Himself for the whole of humanity in the sorrowful Passion, be constituted head of all the elect whom He has saved by His sacrifice and death.

That is why the hymn that a ransomed humanity makes heard in heaven is a hymn of praise and thanksgiving to Christ: "You ... have redeemed us for God with your blood, out of every tribe and tongue and people and nation."[3] When we are in the Blest Eternity, united with the choir of the saints, we shall gaze on Our Lord and say to Him:

It is you who have redeemed us
by your precious blood;
it is thanks to you, to your Passion,
to your Sacrifice on the cross,
to the satisfactions you made,
to your merits,
that we have been saved from death
and eternal damnation;

O Christ Jesus,
Lamb that was slain,
to you be praise, honor, glory
and blessing for ever![4]

---

[1] Acts 4:12.   [2] Hebr. 10:14.   [3] Apoc. 5:9.   [4] See Apoc. 5:11-13.

4. *Infinite efficacy* of Christ's satisfactions and merits. *Unlimited confidence* to which they give rise.

IT IS ABOVE ALL in their *fruits* that the Passion and death of our Divine Savior reveal their efficacy.

St. Paul never tires of enumerating the good things that the infinite merits won by the Man-God, in His life and sufferings, have earned for us. When he speaks of them, the great apostle exults. To express his thoughts he finds no other terms than those of *abundance, superabundance*; *riches* that he declares to be *beyond our imagining*.[1] Christ's death "buys us back,"[2] brings us close again to God, "reconciles" us with Him,[3] "justifies" us,[4] brings us holiness and the new life of Christ.[5] To sum it up, the Apostle compares Christ to Adam, whose work He came here to mend. Adam brought us sin, condemnation, death. Christ, the second Adam, restores to us justice, grace, life:[6] "we have passed from death to life";[7] the redemption has been abundant—"and with Him plentiful redemption."[8] For as regards the free gift (grace), it is not as it was with the fault. "If by reason of one man's offense death reigned through the one man, much more will they who receive the abundance of the grace ... reign in life through the one Jesus Christ":[9] there "where sin abounded, grace did more abound."[10] That is why there is no longer any condemnation for those who will to live united to Christ Jesus.[11]

Our Lord, by offering to His Father a satisfaction of infinite value in our name, has destroyed the barrier that existed between man and God: the Eternal Father looks now with love on the human race, redeemed by the blood of His Son; because of His Son, He has showered

---

[1] Rom. 5:17 ff.; 1 Cor. 1:5-7; Eph. 1, vv. 7-8, 18-19; Eph. 2:7; Eph. 3:18; Col. 1:27; 2:2; Phil. 4:19; 1 Tim. 1:14; Titus 3:6.   [2] See 1 Cor. 6:20.
[3] See Eph. 2:11-18; Col. 1:14.   [4] Rom. 3:24-26.   [5] Titus 2:14; Eph. 5:27.
[6] 1 Cor. 15:22.   [7] 1 John 3:14.   [8] Ps. 129 (130):7
[9] Rom. 5:17; the whole passage [vv. 15-21] should be read. [Marmion's note.]
[10] Rom. 5:20 (Rheims).   [11] Rom. 8:1.

on it all the graces it needs to be united to Him, to "live for"[1] Him with the very life of God: "to serve the *living* God."[2]

In this way, every super-natural good that is given us, all the lights God is so prodigal in according us, all the helps with which He envelops our spiritual life, are bestowed on us by virtue of the life, Passion and death of Christ. All the graces of pardon, of justification, of persever-ance that God gives, and will ever give to souls at all times, have their one and only source in the cross.

Ah! truly, if "God so loved the world that He gave His only-begotten Son";[3] if He has rescued us from the power of darkness, and "trans-ferred us into the kingdom of His beloved Son," in whom "we have our redemption … the remission of our sins";[4] if (as St. Paul further says) Christ has "loved us and delivered Himself up for us"[5]—each one of us —to witness to the love He bears His brethren; if He "gave Himself for us that He might redeem us from all iniquity and cleanse for Himself an acceptable people,"[6] a people that would belong to Him, why still hesitate in our faith and our trust in Christ Jesus? He has expiated everything, paid off everything, merited everything; and His merits are ours. Just look at us—"made rich" in every good, so much so that, if we will it, we lack nothing at all for our holiness: "You are made rich in Him … so that *nothing is wanting* to you in *any* grace."[7]

Why, then, does one find pusillanimous souls who say that holiness is not for them, that perfection is not within their reach? who say, as soon as one speaks to them about perfection: "This is not for me, I wouldn't know how to arrive at holiness"? Do you know what makes them talk like that? Their lack of faith in the efficacy of the merits of Christ. For it is God's will that all be sanctified: "What God wants is for you all to be holy";[8] it is the Lord's precept:[9] "Be therefore perfect,

---

[1] Rom. 14:8 (Jerus.)   [2] Hebr. 9:14.   [3] John 3:16.   [4] Col. 1:13-14.
[5] Eph. 5:2.   [6] Titus 2:14.   [7] 1 Cor. 1:5-7 (Rheims).
[8] 1 Thess. 4:3 (Jerus.)   [9] [*Translator's note*: "Precept" has the meaning of a command, something more than a mere counsel.]

as also your heavenly Father is perfect."[1] But too often we forget the Divine plan; we forget that our holiness is a super-natural holiness, the source of which is only in Christ Jesus, chief of us all and our head; we slight the infinite merits and inexhaustible satisfactions of Christ. There is no doubt that, by ourselves, we are able to do nothing upon the path of grace and perfection. Our Lord said to us categorically: "Without me you can do nothing";[2] and St. Augustine, commenting on this text, adds: "Nothing, whether of little or great account, can happen without Him, without whom nothing can happen."[3] That is so true! Whether it is a question of big things or little, we are able to do nothing without Christ. But, by dying for us, Christ has given us free and confident access to the Father,[4] and through Him, there is no grace we may not hope for.

Souls of little faith, why do we doubt God, *our* God?

5. **At this very time,** *Christ pleads* **incessantly** *for us* **before His Father.** *Our weakness, the title to* **heavenly** *mercies.* **How** *we glorify God* **by calling upon the satisfactions of His Son.**

AT THIS TIME, it is true, Christ does not merit any longer (merit being possible only up to the moment of death), but His merits stay won for us and His satisfactions remain for us. For this High Priest, "because He remains *for ever*, can never lose His Priesthood. It follows, then, that His power to save is utterly certain, since He is living for ever to intercede for all who come to God through Him."[5]

St. Paul provides particular authority to show that Christ, in heaven, intercedes now for us, in His capacity of High Priest, Bridge of

---

[1] Matt. 5:48 (Rheims).   [2] John 15:5.   [3] *Tract. in Johann.*, LXXXI, 3.
[4] Eph. 2:18; 3:12.   [5] Hebr. 7:24-25 (Jerus.)

man to God.[1] Jesus ascended to heaven *"for us,"* as "our forerunner";[2] if He is seated at the right hand of the Father, it was so that He might thenceforth plead there for us, "that He may appear *now* in the presence of God *for us*,"[3] *"always living* to make intercession *for us*."[4]

Unremittingly, because He is our head, Christ shows to His Father, for us, the scars He still has of His wounds; He turns His merits to our account, for us, and because He is ever worthy to be heard by His Father, His prayer is endlessly granted: "Father ... I knew that you always hear me."[5] What unlimited trust should we not have in such a High Priest, who is the beloved Son of His Father and who is constituted by Him the chief one of us and our head, who gives us to share in all His merits, in all His satisfactions![6]

---

[1] [*Translator's note*: "High priest, Bridge of man to God" translates Marmion's single word *"pontife."* Thus I have expanded one French word to seven English ones, and an explanation for this seems due. When Marmion, later in the book, speaks of the Jewish high priest of the Old Testament, he refers to him by the expression *"le grand prêtre."* Why the different term, *"pontife,"* when he refers to Christ's high-priesthood? Because that word and the Latin *"pontifex"* from which it derives, has an express etymological element of *"bridge"* (Latin *pons*, French *pont*). "Pontife" is often—and rightly—translated simply as "high priest"; but two Marmion scholars, the European vice-postulators of his Canonization Cause, have told me they have no doubt that, when using this word in relation to Christ, Marmion had at the forefront of his mind that etymological allusion to a bridge. So, urged to it by these two experts on Marmion, I have sought to bring out the nuance in this free manner wherever that can be done without disturbing the flow of the translation. The Latin word "pontifex" is generally taken to be from *pons* ("bridge") and *facio* ("make"); and indeed Christ, the Word Incarnate, is by His Sacrifice on the cross both Bridge-maker and Bridge between man and God.]

[2] Hebr. 6:20.   [3] Hebr. 9:24 (Rheims).

[4] Hebr. 7:25 (Rheims). St. Paul employs the same expression in his letter to the Romans, and this was so that we might at once conclude from it that our trust ought to be boundless, "God having granted us all things in giving us his Son" [see Rom. 8:32].

[5] John 11:42.

[6] "The head and the members are as it were one mystical person, and therefore the satisfaction of Christ extends to all the faithful as to His members": St Thomas, III, q. XLVIII, a. 2, ad 1.

It sometimes happens, when we groan beneath the weight of our weaknesses, our miseries and our sins, that we say with the Apostle, "Unhappy man that I am! I feel in me two laws: the law of concupiscence which draws me towards evil, and the law of God which urges me towards good; who will deliver me from this struggle, who will give me victory?"[1] Listen to St. Paul's reply: "The grace of God, through Jesus Christ our Lord"[2]—the grace of God, merited for us and given us by Jesus Christ our Lord. We find in Christ Jesus everything we need to be victorious here below while we await the final triumph in glory.

Would that we could have a deep conviction that we are powerless without Christ, and that in Him we have everything! How has the Father not "with Him," Christ, given us *all things*"?[3] Of ourselves, we are weak, very weak. In the world of souls there are failures of every kind, but that is no reason for us to be discouraged: these miseries, when they are not willed, are rather things that give us title to Christ's mercy. Look at those unfortunates who wish to excite the pity of people from whom they are begging alms. Far from hiding their poverty, they display their rags, they show their sores; these are their title to the compassion and charity of passers-by. For us too, as for the sick who were brought to Him when He lived in Judea, it is our misery —recognized, avowed, displayed to the eyes of Christ, that draws to us His mercy. St. Paul tells us that Christ Jesus willed to experience our infirmities—sin excepted—so as to learn to be affected with compassion for us, and in point of fact we read several times in the Gospels that Jesus was "moved with pity" at the sight of the sufferings He witnessed.[4] St. Paul expressly adds that Christ in His glory retains this feeling of compassion; and he immediately concludes from that: "Let

---

[1] See Rom. 7:22-24.   [2] Rom. 7:25.   [3] Rom. 8:32 (Rheims).
[4] E.g. Luke 7:13; Mark 8:2; cf. Matt. 15:32.

us therefore draw near *with confidence* to the throne of grace"—the throne of Him who is the source of grace—for, if we do so with these dispositions, we shall "obtain mercy."[1]

Besides, to act in this way is to glorify God, it is to render to Him a very pleasing homage. Why so? Because the Divine thought is that we should find *everything* in Christ; and when we humbly acknowledge our weakness and lean on the strength of Christ, the Father looks upon us with benevolence, with joy, because by so doing we declare that His Son Jesus is the one Mediator He has willed to give to the world.

See how convinced of this truth the great apostle was. In one of his letters, after having proclaimed how wretched he is, what struggles he has to bear within his soul, he cries out: "Gladly ... I will glory in my infirmities."[2] Instead of complaining of his infirmities, his weaknesses, his struggles, he "glories" in them. That seems strange, does it not? But he gives a profound reason for this. What is that reason? "That the strength of Christ may dwell in me."[3] So that it may be, not *my* strength but the strength of Christ, the grace of Christ who dwells in me, that shall make me triumph: and that all glory may be returned to Him alone.

And see, too, the lengths to which St. Paul goes in speaking of our weakness. "Not that we are sufficient of ourselves to think anything of ourselves, as from ourselves":[4] he goes so far as to say that we cannot even have a good thought, a thought that avails us for heaven, by ourselves, "as from ourselves"—and he was inspired by God when he wrote those words. We are incapable of drawing forth a good thought from ourselves as its source. Everything that is good, everything there is of good in ourselves, everything that is meritorious for life eternal, comes from God through Christ; "our sufficiency is from God."[5] It is

[1] Hebr. 4:14-16.   [2] 2 Cor. 12:9.   [3] *Ibid.*   [4] 2 Cor. 3:5.   [5] *Ibid.*

God who gives us the power, not only to act but even to will super-naturally: "For it is God who of His good pleasure works in you both the will and the performance."[1] We ourselves, then, can super-naturally neither will, nor have a good thought, nor act, nor pray; we can do nothing: "Without me you can do *nothing*."[2]

Is that something for us to complain about? Not in the least. St. Paul, after having gone into detail about our weakness, adds: "I can do all things in Him who strengthens me"[3]—I can do *all things*, not by myself, but "in Him who strengthens me," so that all glory may be returned to Christ, who for us has merited all, and in whom we have all. There is no obstacle I cannot surmount, no difficulty I cannot endure, no trial I cannot undergo, no temptation I cannot resist, through the grace which Christ Jesus has merited for me. In Him, through Him, I can do all things, because His triumph is to render strong what is weak: "My grace is sufficient for you, for strength is made perfect in weakness."[4] God wills thereby that all glory shall return upwards to Him through Christ, whose grace triumphs over our weaknesses: "Unto the praise of the *glory* of His grace."[5]

At the Last Day, when we appear before God, we shall not be able to say to Him: "My God, I have had to surmount difficulties that were too great; triumphing over them was impossible, my numerous faults disheartened me." For God would reply to us: "That would have been true if you had found yourself to be on your own; but I have given you my Son Jesus; He has expiated everything, He has paid off everything. In His Sacrifice were all the satisfactions I was entitled to demand for all the sins of the world; He has merited everything for you by His death; He has been your redemption and He has merited to be your justification, your wisdom, your holiness. It is on Him that you should

[1] Phil 2:13.   [2] John 15:5.   [3] Phil. 4:13.
[4] 2 Cor. 12:9.   [5] Eph. 1:6.

have been leaning for support. In my Divine thought He is not only your salvation, He is the source of your strength. For all His satisfactions, all His merits, all His riches—and they are infinite—have been yours from the time of your baptism; and, ever since He has been seated at my right hand, He has been offering me, for you, the fruits of His sacrifice ceaselessly. It is on Him that you ought to have been leaning, for in Him I would have given you superabundantly the strength to conquer every evil, as He Himself asked of me: 'I pray you to keep them from evil';[1] that you be showered with every good thing, because it is for you, and not for Himself, that He is 'living for ever to intercede' with me."[2]

Oh! if we knew the infinite value of the gift of God!—"If you only knew what God is offering."[3] If, above all, we had faith in the immense merits of Jesus, a lively and practical faith that would fill us with an invincible confidence in prayer, fill us with *abandon* to God in all our soul's needs! In company with the Church who in her liturgy repeats this phrase each time she addresses a prayer to God, we should ask for nothing except in His name. For this Mediator, ever living, reigns as God, with the Father and the Holy Spirit: "*Through our Lord Jesus Christ, who with Thee and the Holy Spirit lives and reigns....*" Through Him, we are sure of obtaining everything by way of grace. When St. Paul expounds the Divine plan, he says that it is in Christ that "we have redemption through His blood, the remission of sins, according to the riches of His grace, which has superabounded in us."[4] We have at our disposal all those riches won by Jesus: through baptism they have become ours, we have only to draw upon Him to be like that spouse "that cometh up from the desert," the desert of her poverty, but "flowing with delights" because she is "leaning upon her beloved."[5]

---

[1] See John 17:15.   [2] Hebr. 7:25 (Jerus.)   [3] John 4:10 (Jerus.)
[4] Eph. 1:7 (Rheims).   [5] Song of Songs 8:5.

If only we lived by these truths! Our life would then be a continual hymn of praise, of thanksgiving to God for the inestimable gift He has made us of His Son, Christ Jesus: "Thanks be to God for His inexpressible gift."[1] We would in that way enter fully—for the greatest good and the liveliest joy of our souls—into the thoughts of God whose will is that we find everything in Jesus, and that, receiving everything from Him, we should render to Jesus and to His Father, in the unity of the Spirit common to both, all "blessing and honor, and glory and dominion, forever and ever."[2]

[1] 2 Cor. 9:15 (Jerus.)   [2] Apoc. 5:13.

CHAPTER FOUR

CHRIST, EFFICIENT CAUSE OF ALL GRACE:
CAUSA EFFICIENS

INTRODUCTION.

IT IS STILL of the adorable person of Our Lord that we are going to speak. Never tire of hearing Him talked of, never weary of it. No subject ought to be dearer to us, and none can be of such use to us. In Christ we have everything, and outside of Him neither salvation nor sanctification are possible.[1] The more you study the Divine plan as in the Sacred Scriptures, the more do you see one great thought stand out and dominate everything. It is that Christ Jesus, true God and true man, is the center of creation and of redemption; that all things relate to Him; that through Him all grace is given to us and all glory rendered to His Father.

Contemplation of Our Lord is not only holy; it makes us holy. Doing no more than thinking of Him, gazing on Him with faith and love, sanctifies us. For certain souls, the life of Christ Jesus is one subject of meditation among many others; this is not enough. Christ is not *one* of the means of spiritual life; He is *all* our spiritual life. The Father sees all in His Word, in His Christ, finds all in Him. Infinite as His require-

---

[1] [*Translator's note*: A later note (pages 115-117), whilst holding firmly to this statement of Marmion's, clarifies it so that it will not be misunderstood.]

ments of glory and praise may be, He finds them in His Son, in the least actions of His Son. Christ is His beloved Son, in whom He is well pleased. Why should Christ not equally be *our* all, our model, the one who satisfies for us, our hope, the one who substitutes for us, our light, our strength, our joy? This truth is of such capital importance that I wish to insist on it.

The spiritual life consists above all in contemplating Christ in order to reproduce in us His state of Son of God and His virtues. Souls who constantly keep their eyes fixed on Christ see, in His light, the things within themselves that are opposed to the flowering of the divine life. They then seek in Jesus the strength to remove the obstacles, in order to please Him; they ask Him to be the support of their weakness, to put within them, and ceaselessly to increase in them, this radical disposition—to which all holiness comes down—of seeking always what is pleasing to His Father.

These souls enter fully into the Divine plan; they advance rapidly and surely in the way of perfection and holiness. They have neither the temptation to be disheartened at outbreaks of their weakness—they know too well that of themselves they can do nothing: "Without me you can do nothing"[1]—nor are they tempted to derive the least bit of vanity from their progress, because they are convinced that, though their personal efforts are necessary to correspond with grace, it is nevertheless to Christ, who inhabits them and lives and works within them, that they owe their perfection. If they bear much fruit, it is not only because they dwell in Christ by grace and the fidelity of their love, but also because Christ dwells in them: "He who abides in me, and I in him, he bears much fruit."[2]

Christ, indeed, is not only a model like the one a painter contemplates when he does a portrait. Nor, any more than to that, can we compare imitation of Him to the imitation certain mediocre minds

---

[1] John 15:5.   [2] *Ibid.*

achieve when they copy the actions and gestures of a great man they admire. An imitation of that kind is all pose, all surface; it does not penetrate to the interior of the soul.

It is quite otherwise with our imitation of Christ. Christ is *more* than a model, more than a High Priest who has obtained for us the grace of imitating Him. He is Himself the one who, through His Spirit, acts in the intimacy of the soul, to help us imitate Him. Why is that? Because, as I told you in expounding the Divine plan, our holiness is of an order essentially *super-natural*. God, having resolved to make us His children, does not and never will content Himself with a natural morality or a natural religion; He wishes us to act as children of divine race. But it is through His Son, it is in His Son, through the grace His Son Christ Jesus has merited for us, that He gives us the ability to achieve this holiness. All of the holiness He purposes all souls to have, God has deposited in Christ, and it is from Christ's plenitude that all of us have to receive the graces that make us holy: "Christ Jesus, who has become for us God-given wisdom, and justice, and sanctification, and redemption."[1]

If Christ possesses "all the treasures of wisdom and knowledge,"[2] and of holiness, it is so as to make us share in them. He came in order that we might have divine life, and have it in abundance.[3] By His Passion and death, He has re-opened its source for all: but never forget that this source is in Him and not outside of Him; it is still He who sheds it upon us. Grace, the fount of super-natural life, comes only through Him. That is why St. John writes that one who is united to the Son possesses life, one who is not united to the Son has not life: "Anyone who has the Son has life: anyone who does not have the Son, does not have life."[4]

---

[1] 1 Cor. 1:30.   [2] Col. 2:3.   [3] John 10:10.   [4] 1 John 5:12 (Jerus.)

1. How during Christ's earthly existence His *humanity* was, as *instrument of the Word,* the *source of grace* and of life.

LET US CONTEMPLATE Jesus during His earthly existence; we shall see how He is the efficient cause[1] of all grace and the source of life. This contemplation is beneficial, because it shows how we can expect everything from Our Lord.

We see His sacred humanity become the instrument of which the divinity makes use in order to shed around it all grace and all life.

Bodily life or health, to begin with.

A leper presents himself to Jesus, asking to be cured; Christ puts forth His hand, touches him and says: "I will; be made clean," and immediately the leprosy disappears.[2] Two blind men are brought to Him: Jesus touches their eyes with His hand, saying: "Let it be done to you according to your faith," and their eyes are opened to the light.[3] Another day, a deaf and dumb man is brought in before Him; he is asking Christ to lay His hands upon him. Then Jesus, drawing him away from the crowd, puts His finger in his ears, touches his tongue with spittle, and raising His eyes to heaven, sighs and says: "Be opened." Immediately this man hears, his tongue is loosed and he starts to speak distinctly.[4] Again, look at Jesus at the tomb of Lazarus: it is by His words that Christ calls the dead man back to life.[5]

In all these things He does, we see the sacred humanity serve as an organ of the divinity. It is the Divine Person of the Word who cures and raises from the dead: but to work these marvels, the Word makes use of the human nature that is united to Him, it is through His human nature that Christ speaks the words and, with His hands, touches the sick. Thus, life derived from the divinity and reached bodies and souls through the humanity.[6] We can understand the words of the Gospel,

---

[1] [*Translator's note*: For the meaning of "efficient cause" see note 2 on page 41.]
[2] Matt. 8:2-3.   [3] Matt. 9:27-30.   [4] Mark 7:32-35.   [5] John 11:43.
[6] To employ the theological term, the humanity served as source of life inasmuch as it was "an instrument united to the Word": *ut instrumentum conjunctum.*

which tells us that "all the crowd were trying to touch Him, for power went forth from Him and healed all."[1] Power went forth from Him.

Christ keeps the same process in the super-natural domain of grace. It is by an action, word or gesture, of the human nature which is united to Him, that the Word remits sins and justifies sinners.

Look at Mary Magdalene coming, in the middle of a feast, to bedew Christ's feet with tears. Jesus says to her: "Your sins are for-given you.... Your faith has made you safe, go in peace."[2] It is Christ's divinity that forgives sins, it alone can do so, but it is through words that Jesus pronounces this forgiveness: His humanity became the instrument of grace.

Another scene in the Gospel is still more explicit. A paralytic, lying on a pallet-bed, is one day presented to Jesus. "Your sins are forgiven you," Jesus says. But the Pharisees, who hear Him and do not believe in Christ's divinity, murmur: "Who is this man who claims to forgive sins? Only God can forgive sins." And Our Lord, wishing to show them that He is God, replies to them: "Which is easier, to say 'Your sins are forgiven you'; or to say 'Arise and walk'? But that you may know that the Son of Man"—note the expression *Son of Man*; Our Lord uses it on purpose instead of the term *Son of God*—"has power on earth to forgive sins, I tell you (here he speaks to the paralytic): 'Arise, take up your pallet and return to your house.' And immediately this man, rising in front of the crowd, took up the bed on which he had been brought in, and went back to his house, glorifying God."[3]

In this way Christ works miracles, remits sins and distributes grace, with sovereign liberty and power, because, being God, He is the source of all grace and all life; but He does it by making use of His humanity. The humanity of Christ is "life-giving" because of its union with the Divine Word.[4]

---

[1] Luke 6:19.   [2] Luke 7:48-50 (Rheims).   [3] See Luke 5:18-25.

[4] "We call the flesh of the Lord life-giving because it has been made the Word's own flesh, the Word mighty to give life to all things": Council of Ephesus, can. 11.

It is the same with what is effected by the Passion and death of Jesus. It is in His human nature that Jesus suffers, expiates and merits: His humanity becomes the instrument of the Word, and these sufferings of the sacred humanity *bring about* our salvation, are the *cause* of our redemption and restore life to us.[1] We were dead in sin, but God has restored us to life with Christ, because of Christ, in forgiving us all our sins.[2] St. Thomas tells us this clearly.[3] At that time when Christ, for love of His Father and love of us, was about to deliver Himself up so as to restore divine life to all men, He asked His Father to "glorify your Son" since "you have given Him power over all flesh," in order that He may (He adds) *"give eternal life* to all whom you have given Him."[4] Jesus asks His Father to effect—already; at the beginning—His eternal plan. The Father has established Christ as head of humanity; it is in Christ alone that He wishes all humanity to find its salvation, and Our Lord asks that this may be so since, through His Passion and death, He is about to expiate all the crimes of humanity and to merit for humanity all grace of salvation and of life by substituting Himself for us.

The prayer of Our Lord has been granted. Because He has brought about the salvation of humankind by His sufferings and His merits, Christ is established as universal dispenser of all grace. He "emptied Himself," and this is *why*—*"for which cause,"* on the day of the Ascension, His Father "has exalted Him, and has given Him a name which is above all names,"[5] has established His Son as "heir of all things."[6] Because Christ has bought them by His blood, His Father has given

---

[1] "The actions of the humanity by virtue of the divinity were for us life-giving, as being *causers* of grace in us, both by merit and *by a certain efficacy"* (St Thomas, III, q. VIII, a. 1, ad 1).   [2] Col. 2:13.

[3] Let us quote this beautiful proposition of the Angelic Doctor: "The Word, in that He "was in the beginning with God" (John 1:1), gives life to souls as one acting primarily. However, His flesh and the mysteries accomplished therein work instrumentally towards the life of the soul": III, q. LXII, a. 5, ad 1. Cf. III, q. XLVIII, a. 6; q. XLIX, a. 1; q. XXVII de Veritate, a. 4.   [4] John 17:1-2 (Rheims).

[5] Phil. 2, vv. 7, 9 (Rheims).   [6] Heb. 1:2.

Him the nations as an inheritance: "Ask of me and I will give you the nations for an inheritance."[1] For them, "all power" of grace and of life has been given to Christ, in heaven and on earth: "All power in heaven and on earth has been given to me."[2] Because He loves His Son, the Father has put everything into His hands: "The Father loves the Son, and has given *all things* into His hand."[3]

Thus, this unique model, Christ Jesus—supreme High Priest, Redeemer of the world and universal Mediator—is in addition established as *dispenser of all grace*. The effusion of grace into us, says St. Thomas, belongs only to Christ; and this sanctifying causality results from the intimate union existing in Christ between the divinity and the humanity.[4] The soul of Christ, he says again, has received grace in the supremest degree of plenitude. In consequence of this plenitude that He has received, it is befitting for Christ to make souls partakers of it, and it is thus that He fulfills His role as chief one of us and head of the Church. That is why the grace which adorns the soul of Christ is, in its essence, the same as that which purifies us.[5]

2. How, since His Ascension, Christ brings about this effecting of grace and life. Official means: *the Sacraments. They produce grace* of themselves, but by virtue of the merits of Christ.

BUT, you will ask me: now that Christ has ascended into heaven, now that men no longer see Him here below, no longer hear Him, no longer touch Him, how is this power of grace made present? How is the action of Our Lord exercised upon us, in us? How is He, now, the efficient cause of our holiness, and how does He produce grace, the source of life, in us?

---

[1] Ps. 2:8 (St P.)   [2] Matt. 28:18.   [3] John 3:35.   [4] III, q. VIII, a. 6.   [5] III, q. VIII, a. 5.

Christ, being God, is absolute master of His gifts and of the way in which He distributes them; we can no more determine all His modes of action than we can limit His power. Christ Jesus can, when it seems good to Him, cause grace to flow into a soul directly, without intermediary. The lives of the saints are full of such examples of Divine liberty and Divine liberality.

Nevertheless, in the existent Divine disposings,[1] the normal and official way by which the grace of Christ comes to us consists, above all, of the sacraments He instituted. He could sanctify us otherwise than as He does; but from the time that He, who is God, Himself established these means of salvation—means which He alone had the right to determine because He alone is the Author of the super-natural order— it is to these authentic means that we are first to have recourse. All the ascetical practices we can devise in order to maintain and increase the divine life within us have value only in measure as they help us to profit more abundantly from these sources of life. In the sacraments one indeed has springs that are real and pure, and at the same time inexhaustible, where we shall infallibly find the Divine life with which Christ Jesus is filled and of which He wants us to partake: "I am come, that they may have life."[2]

Let us, then, see what these means are. I shall not give you here all the theology of the sacraments; but I hope to say enough to show you how the goodness and wisdom of our Divine Savior shines forth in what He has devised.

What, then, is a sacrament?

The holy Council of Trent (to which we should always have recourse in this matter, because it defined the doctrine with admirable precision) tells us that a sacrament is a perceptible sign that signifies and produces an invisible grace; it is a symbol which contains and con-

---

[1] [*Translator's note*: "existent" Divine disposings, i.e. now that Christ has ascended into heaven.]   [2] John 10:10 (Rheims).

fers divine grace. It is a sign that is perceptible, outward, tangible. We are at the same time matter and spirit, both, and Christ has willed to make use of matter—water, oil, wheat, wine, words, the imposition of hands—in order to indicate the grace He wills to produce in our souls. Christ, Eternal Wisdom, has adapted to our nature, which is material and spiritual, the perceptible means of communicating His grace to us.[1]

I say "communicate," for the outward signs do more than merely signify or symbolize grace; they contain it and confer it. By the will and the institution of Christ Jesus, to whom the Father has given all power and who with the Father and the Holy Spirit is God, these signs and these rites are efficacious, truly producing grace. The effect of the sacraments is grace, brought about in our inmost soul.

Let us listen to our Divine Savior. He teaches us that the water of baptism cleanses us of our sins, causes us be born to the life of grace, makes us children of God and heirs to His kingdom: "Unless a man is born again of water and the Holy Spirit, he cannot enter the kingdom of God."[2] Again, He teaches us that the words of His priest when absolving us wipe out our sins: "Whose sins you shall forgive, they are forgiven them";[3] that under the appearances of bread and wine are truly contained His body and blood[4] which one must eat and drink in order to have life.[5] He declares to us on the subject of marriage that no man can separate those whom God has united.[6] Tradition, echoing the teaching of Jesus, repeats to us that the imposition of hands confers on those who receive it the Holy Spirit and His gifts.[7]

---

[1] "If you had been incorporeal, He would have given you gifts that were purely incorporeal also; but because the soul is joined to a body, understanding through the senses is better for you" (St. John Chrysostom, Homily 82 on Matthew, and Homily 60 to the people of Antioch).

[2] See John 3:5. [See translator's note on pages 23-24.]

[3] John 20:23.

[4] Matt. 26:26-28; Mark 14:22-24; Luke 22:19-20; 1 Cor. 11:23-25.

[5] John 6:54-59.   [6] Matt. 19:6; Mark 10:9.

[7] As for the question of knowing whether all the sacraments were instituted *directly, in all their details,* by Christ Himself—this matters little. Several sacraments

One of the features marking the condescension of our Divine Savior in instituting the sacraments is that these signs which contain grace produce it of themselves: *Ex opere operato*. It is the sacramental act itself, the deed performed—solely the proper application of the symbols and rites to the soul—that gives grace; and this independently, not of intention, but of the personal worth of the one who administers it. The unworthiness of an heretical or sacrilegious minister cannot prevent the effect of the sacrament, as long as this minister conforms to the intention of the Church and means to carry out what the Church does in such a case. The baptism given by an heretical minister is valid. Why is that? Because Christ, Man-God, has wished to place the communication of graces above every consideration of the merit or virtue of those who serve Him as instruments. The value of the sacrament does not depend on human worthiness or human holiness; it derives from the sacrament's having been instituted by Christ, and this gives rise in the faithful soul to an infinite confidence in these helps from God.[1]

Is that to say that we should make use of these means without any disposing of ourselves to do so; that we can approach them without its being necessary to make the least preparation? Very much the opposite. What, then, is required?

In the first place a general disposition, which has regard to the very production of grace, namely, that the one who receives the sacraments places no obstacles to their action, to their operation, to their energy. Oppose a barrage to the waters of a torrent, and the waters stop. Destroy the barrage, remove the obstacle, and at once the waters, now free,

---

present that character, but we do not read in the Gospels that it may have been thus for all of them. But if Christ left to His Apostles the determination of certain details, even important ones, it is no less true that it was He who attached to all these symbols the grace of which He alone is the Author and unique Source.

[1] "The Church, sure in her wisdom, does not place her hope in man—but places her hope in Christ, who thus accepts the likeness of a servant, that she may not lose the likeness of God" (St. Augustine, *Epistola*, LXXXIX, 5).

will rush forward and sweep across the plain. So it is with the grace of
the sacraments: there is in a sacrament everything needed for it to act;
but it is still necessary that grace does not encounter any obstacle in
ourselves. What obstacle? It varies in nature according to the character
of the signs and the grace they confer. Thus, we can only receive the
grace of a sacrament if we consent to doing so; the adult on whom
baptism is conferred cannot receive the grace if his will is opposed to
the reception of the sacrament. In the same way, lack of contrition is
an obstacle to reception of the grace of the Sacrament of Penance. So
also, mortal sin constitutes an obstacle that prevents us from receiving
the grace of the Eucharist. Remove the obstacle, and the grace comes
down into you immediately the sacrament is conferred on you.

But I will add: enlarge the capacity of your souls, by faith, trust and
love, and grace will abound in you. For, if the grace of the sacraments
is substantially the same for all, it varies in degree, in intensity, according to the dispositions of those who receive it after having cleared
away the obstacle. It is in proportion—not indeed in its entity, but in
its fruitfulness and its scope of action—to the dispositions of the soul.
Then, let us open the avenues of our souls to Divine grace, open them
up wide; bring to them every desirable charity and purity, so that
Christ may make His Divine life superabound in us.

For it is He, Christ, the Incarnate Word, who—inasmuch as He is
God—is the efficient cause, the first and principal cause, of the grace
produced by the sacraments. Why is that? Because He alone can produce
grace who is its Author and its Source. The sacraments, signs charged
with transmitting this grace to the soul, act only in the capacity of
instruments. They are a cause of grace, a real and efficient cause, but
an instrumental one only.

Observe an artist in his studio: with his chisel he works at and
delves into the marble, to realize the ideal that haunts his genius. When
the masterpiece is finished, it will be correct to say that the artist is
author of it; but the chisel has been the instrument charged with trans-

mission of the artist's idea. The work is due to the chisel, but to the chisel guided and given life by the master's hand, itself directed by the genius who has conceived the work to be produced.

So is it with the sacraments. They are the signs that produce the grace, not as principal cause—it is Christ alone who pours down sanctifying grace, as from His one and only spring—but as instruments, by virtue of the propulsion they receive from Christ's humanity which is united to the Word and filled with the Divine life.[1] In the person of the priest, it is Christ Himself who baptizes, who absolves. "Peter baptizes?," says St. Augustine, "It is Christ who is baptizing. Judas baptizes? It is Christ who is doing so."[2] Whoever the priest is, he here acts only in virtue of Christ.[3] These are Christ's merits that are applied to us; these are His satisfactions that are given to us to share in. It is the life of Christ which, through these channels, flows down into our souls.

All the efficacy of the sacraments in communicating divine life to us comes, then, from Christ, who, by His life and His sacrifice on the cross, has merited for us every grace, and has instituted these signs so as to make the grace come to us. If only we had faith, if understood that these are Divine means—doubly Divine: in their first and primordial source and in the ultimate objective at which they aim, with what fervor and frequency would we make use of these means—means multiplied along our road by the goodness of our Savior!

[1] "The sacraments relating to the body, by their own operation which they exercise with regard to the body they touch, effect by reason of the Divine power an instrumental operation with regard to the soul—as the water of baptism, for example, in washing the body according to the water's own power, washes the soul, inasmuch as the water is an instrument of the Divine power; for of soul and body has one thing been made. And this is why St. Augustine says that 'it touches the body, and washes the heart'" (St Thomas, III, q. LXII, a. 1, ad 2). "Spiritual strength is in the sacraments to the extent that it has been ordained by God for a spiritual effect" (III, q. LXVII, a. 4, ad 1). Cf. q. LXIV, a. 4.   [2] *Tract. in Johann.*, VI.

[3] Commenting on the words "The Lord baptized more people than John, even though Jesus Himself did not baptize; only His disciples did," St. Augustine writes: "It was He Himself and yet not He Himself—He Himself by His power, they by their ministering. They acted as servants in the work of baptizing, but the power of baptizing remained with Christ" (*Tract. in Johann.*, V, 1).

3. *Universality* of the sacraments: they extend to the whole of our
   super-natural life. The limitless confidence we ought to have in
   these *authentic wellsprings.*

INDEED, what completes the shining-forth of the wonderful wisdom of
the Incarnate Word in this domain is that the sacraments envelop the
whole of our life with sanctifying influences.

There is, says St. Thomas, an analogy between natural life and
super-natural life.[1] We are born to super-natural life by Baptism. This
life must grow strong; that is the work of Confirmation. Being born,
coming to manhood—these happen only once: that is why those two
sacraments are not repeated. Like the body, the soul has to be nourished: the soul's food is the Eucharist, which can become a nourishment
daily. When we succumb to sin, the Sacrament of Penance restores
grace to us, as many times as this is necessary, by cleansing us of our
sins. Does illness strike us down, to the point of threatening us with
death? Extreme Unction will prepare us for our passage to eternity,
and sometimes, if such is God's design, even restore bodily health to
us. All these sacraments, various as they are, create, nourish,
strengthen, give assurance, put right; make the divine life grow and
blossom in the soul of each of us.

And as man is not simply an isolated individual but is a member of
society as well, the sacrament of Matrimony sanctifies the family and
blesses the propagation of the human race, while the sacrament of Holy
Orders perpetuates, through the priesthood, the power of spiritual
paternity.

All these sacraments, without exception, confer grace—that is,
communicate to or increase within the soul Christ's life: sanctifying
grace, infused virtues, gifts of the Holy Spirit—that wonderful totality
which under the name "state of grace" adorns the substance of our soul
and super-naturally renders its faculties fruitful, in order that it may resemble Christ Jesus and be made worthy of the gaze of the Eternal Father.

[1] III, q. LXV, a. 1.

In each sacrament, we receive sanctifying grace or an increase of that grace; but in the different sacraments this grace takes on a modality of its own—contains special energies, produces particular, determined, effects in conformity with the end for which the sacrament has been instituted and which we have just been indicating. And, as you know also, Baptism, Confirmation and Holy Orders imprint an ineffaceable character on the soul, like a seal: the character of Christian, of soldier of Christ, of priest of the Most High.

What we should especially keep in mind from this analogy (an analogy we ought not to push to its extreme limit),[1] is that the life of a Christian is sanctified at its principal periods and that Christ has provided for all our super-natural needs. At whatever stage of our existence, then—however small the importance of that stage may be—grace is there under a particular form of timeliness and beneficence. It is throughout the whole of our pilgrimage here below that Christ Jesus accompanies us; He is with us "all along the line."

Let us, then, have faith—let us have a lively and practical faith—in these means of sanctification. Christ has willed and has merited that they be of sovereign efficacy, their excellence transcendent, their fruitfulness inexhaustible: these are signs charged with divine life. Christ has willed to gather up in them all His merits and His satisfactions so that these may be communicated to us. Nothing either can or should replace them. In the existent Divine disposings of Redemption, they are necessary for salvation.[2]

That needs repeating; because experience shows how much, in the long run—even among souls who seek God—is sometimes left to be desired in the estimation *in practice* of these means of salvation. The

---

[1] Notably for the Sacrament of Penance when it restores divine life to the soul. In the natural life, one dies only once.

[2] Though one may need to add that this necessity is not the same for all the sacraments. For example, Baptism is absolutely necessary for everyone, but the same is not true—in what concerns men taken individually—of Holy Orders and Matrimony. [*Translator's note*: For clarification of "the necessity of baptism," see note on pages 23-24.]

sacraments, along with the doctrine given by the Church, are the official channels authentically created by Christ to make us attain to His Father. Not to appreciate their value, their riches, their fruitfulness, is to wrong Christ; whereas He is glorified when we draw upon these treasures acquired by His merits. We thereby acknowledge that everything we have is from Him; and to do that is to render to Him a very pleasing homage.

There are some souls who have only a mediocre faith in these sacred signs and who, in practice, only make use of them parsimoniously; whose attention is not much riveted by the grace the sacraments produce in them; who only prepare for the sacraments listlessly, or who fix their preferences on extraordinary means. Admittedly, as I have said to you, Christ Jesus always remains absolute master of His gifts; He distributes them when He thinks fit, and to whom He pleases. We see in the saints marvels of Divine generosity, starting with the charisms that made illustrious the lives of the first Christians, right up to the unparalleled favors which, in our days still, abound among so many souls: "God is wonderful in His saints."[1] But in this matter, Christ has made no promises to anyone. He has not indicated these means as the regular way either of salvation or even of holiness; whereas He did institute the sacraments, with their particular energies and their efficacious power. From that time on, they constitute, in their harmonious variety, an assemblage of means of salvation that are singularly sure. As regards them, no illusion is possible—and we know how dangerous are illusions, created by the devil, in the matter of piety and holiness!

God *wants* our sanctification: "For this is the will of God, your sanctification."[2] Christ repeats it: "Be therefore perfect, as also your heavenly Father is perfect."[3] Thus, in what He there says He is talking not simply of salvation but of *perfection*, of holiness. Now, it is not in

---

[1] Ps. 67 (68):36 (Septuagint reading in Douai).   [2] 1 Thess. 4:3.   [3] Matt. 5:48 (Rheims).

extraordinary means, raptures, ecstasies, that Our Lord has normally placed the life He wants to communicate to us in order to make us perfect, make us holy, make us pleasing to His Father: it is first and foremost in the sacraments. That He should have willed this is sufficient to make our souls, eager for holiness, abandon themselves to that will in all faith, in all confidence. There, in the sacraments, are the true wellsprings of life and of sanctification, springs ample and abundant. Were we to go and draw water elsewhere, it would be in vain: we would be forsaking "the fountain of living water" in order (as the strong words of Scripture have it) to dig "leaky cisterns that hold no water."[1] The whole of our spiritual activity ought to have no other raison d'être, no other object, than that we apply ourselves to draw ever more abundantly, more largely, with more faith and purity, from those Divine wellsprings; to bring to flower with more ease and liberty, with more vigor and strength, the grace proper to each sacrament.

Oh! come with joy to draw upon these wellsprings of salvation: "You shall draw waters with joy out of the Savior's fountains."[2] Draw from these salutary waters; enlarge the capacity of your souls, through repentance, humility, trust, and above all through love, in order that the action of the sacrament may be made both deeper and vaster and more enduring. Each time that we approach them, let us renew our faith in the riches of Christ. In a soul frequenting those springs, such faith prevents routine creeping in. Draw from them frequently—the Eucharist above all, the Sacrament of Life par excellence; these are the founts the Savior has made spring forth, through His infinite merits, from the foot of the cross or, better, from the depths of His sacred heart.

Commenting upon a Gospel text about the death of Christ: "One of the soldiers opened His side with a lance,"[3] St. Augustine writes these remarkable words: "The Evangelist makes use of an expression chosen designedly; he does not say (in speaking of the lance-thrust given by

---

[1] Jerem. 2:13 (Jerus.)   [2] Isa. 12:3.   [3] John 19:34.

the soldier to Jesus on the cross) that he *struck* or he *wounded* His side, or anything like that, but rather that he *opened* His side—to teach us that by doing this he was opening for us the gate of life, whence have issued forth the sacraments, without which one cannot have access to true life."[1] All these founts spring forth from the cross, from Christ's love. All of them apply to us the fruits of the Savior's death through the power of Jesus's blood.

If, then, we wish to live in a Christian way, if we seek perfection, if we aim at holiness, let us draw from there with joy. *With joy*, for these are the wellsprings of life here below, of glory above. "If anyone thirst, let him come to me and drink."[2] For one "who drinks of the water that I will give him shall never thirst," and "the water that I will give him shall become in him a fountain of water, springing up into life everlasting."[3] "Come, my beloved ones," the Savior seems to say to us, "come, and be quenched"—"drink, and be inebriated, my dearly beloved";[4] come and drink at these founts by which, under the veil of faith, I communicate my own life to you here below—until that day when, all symbols having disappeared, I will myself intoxicate you from the torrent of my beatitude, in the eternal splendor of my light: "You shall make them drink of the torrent of your pleasure."[5]

4. *Power of sanctification* the humanity of Jesus has, outside the sacraments, by the spiritual *contact of faith*. Capital importance of this truth.

THE RICHES OF GRACE Christ communicates to us are so great—St. Paul declares them "unfathomable"[6]—that the sacraments do not exhaust them. Outside the sacraments, Christ yet acts and works in us. How so? By the contact we have with Him in faith.

---

[1] *Tract. in Johann.*, CXX. [2] John 7:37. [3] John 4:13-14.
[4] Song of Songs 5:1. [5] Ps. 35 (36):9. [6] Eph. 3:8.

To understand this, let us read over again an incident as related by St. Luke. Our Divine Savior, in one of His apostolic journeys, is surrounded and pressed in by the crowd. A sick woman, desiring to be healed, approaches Him and, full of trust, touches the hem of His garment. Immediately, Our Lord asks those around Him: "Who touched me?" And Peter, in reply, says: "Master, the crowd presses upon you from every side, and you ask who touched you?" But Jesus insists: "Someone touched me, for I felt that a power had gone out from me."[1] And at that very moment, indeed, this woman had been cured; and she had been cured because of her faith: "Your faith has made you whole."[2]

Something analogous takes place for us too. Every time that, outside the sacraments, we approach Christ, a strength, a Divine virtue, will go out of Him and penetrate our souls to give them light, to help them.

You know the means of approaching Him. It is faith. By faith, we touch Christ, and at this Divine contact, bit by bit, our soul is transformed.

As I have told you, Christ came among us to give us a share in all His riches, in all the perfection of His virtues. For everything He has belongs to us; everything is for us. Each one of Our Lord's actions is not only a model for us but a wellspring of grace. In practicing all the virtues, He has merited for us the grace of being able to practice the same virtues as those we behold in Him: and each one of His mysteries contains a special grace of which He wills to give us a real share.

It is certain that those who were living in Judea with Christ, and had faith in Him, received an abundant share of these graces that He merited for all men. We can see this in the Gospels. Christ, as I have shown you, had not only the power of curing bodily infirmities; He had the power of sanctifying souls as well. Look, for example, at how He sanctified the Samaritan woman who, after having conversed with Him, believed Him to be the Messiah;[3] how He purified Mary Magda-

---

[1] See Luke 8:42-46.   [2] Luke 8:48 (Rheims).   [3] John 4:7 ff.

lene who, considering Him to be a prophet, believing Him to be sent from God, came and spread her perfumes on His sacred feet.[1]

For souls who have faith in Him, contact with the Son of God becomes the source of life: "Your faith has made you whole."[2] See how during His Passion, by one look, He gives Peter the grace to repent; Peter who had denied Him. Look at the good thief, at the time of Jesus's death: he recognizes Jesus as the Son of God, since he asks Him for a place in His kingdom; and immediately the Savior, on the point of expiring, grants him forgiveness of his crimes: "This day you shall be with me in paradise."[3]

We know all this; we are so convinced of it that sometimes we say to ourselves: "Oh! if only it had been given to me to be living in Judea with Our Lord, to have followed Him like the Apostles, to have approached Him during His life and been present at His death—how surely would I then have been sanctified!" And yet, listen to what Jesus says: "*Blessed* are they who have not seen, and yet have believed."[4]

Does that not teach us that contact with Him by faith alone is still more efficacious, and more advantageous to us? Let us then believe in that saying of our Divine Master; His words are "spirit and life."[5] Let us be fully persuaded that the power and virtue of His sacred humanity are the same for us as for His contemporaries. For Christ is living always: "Jesus Christ yesterday, and *today*: and the same for ever."[6]

I cannot repeat often enough how eminently useful it is to your souls to remain united to Our Lord through the contact of faith. You know that, at the time of their journeying through the desert, the Israelites murmured against Moses. To punish them, God sent them serpents whose bites caused them great suffering. Then, touched by their repentance, God ordered Moses to raise high a bronze serpent, the simple sight of which was enough to heal the bite-wounds of the children of

---

[1] Luke 7:37 ff.   [2] Mark 5:34 (Rheims); Luke 8:48; 17:19.   [3] Luke 23:43.
[4] John 20:29.   [5] John 6:64.   [6] Hebr. 13:8 (Rheims).

Israel.[1] Now, according to Our Lord's own words,[2] this bronze serpent prefigured Christ, raised high on the cross. And Our Lord said: "And I, if I be lifted up from the earth, will draw all things to myself."[3] Because He has merited for us all grace by His Sacrifice on the cross, Christ Jesus has become for us the source of all light and all strength. And that is why a soul's humble and loving gaze upon the sacred humanity of Jesus is so fruitful and so efficacious.

We do not think enough about this power of sanctification which Christ's humanity possesses, even outside the sacraments.[4]

The means of putting ourselves into contact with Christ is faith in His divinity, in His omnipotence, in the infinite value of His satisfactions, in the inexhaustible efficacy of His merits. In one of his sermons to the people of Hippo, St. Augustine asks how we can "touch Christ" now that He is ascended into heaven. He answers: "*By faith*: he touches Christ who believes in Christ." And the Holy Doctor recalls the faith of that woman who touched Jesus to obtain her cure: "It was by faith that she touched, and healing followed." There are, he says, many carnal men who have seen in Jesus Christ only a man, and have not understood the divinity that was veiled by His humanity. They have not known how to touch Him, because their faith has not been what it ought to have been. "You wish really to touch Jesus Christ—to touch Him fruitfully? Then, discern the divinity which, as the Word of God, He shares from all eternity with the Father—and you have touched Him."[5]

Believing in the divinity of Jesus Christ is, then, the means that puts us in contact with Christ, the source of all grace and all life. When,

---

[1] Num. 21:9.   [2] John 3:14.   [3] John 12:32.

[4] Read on this subject the *Spiritual Retreat* by Msgr. Hedley, OSB, Bishop of Newport, who died recently [in 1915]. In Chapter XII, *Looking upon Jesus*, one finds expounded by one of the best English ascetical writers this power of "almost miraculous efficacy of transformation," which the sacred humanity has upon souls who contemplate it in faith.

[5] *Sermo* CCXLIII, 2. Cf. *Sermones* LXII, 3; CCXLIV, 3, and CCXLV, 3; *Tract. in Johann.*, XXVI, 3.

therefore, in reading the Gospels, we go over in our minds the words and actions of Our Lord; when, in prayer, in meditation, we contemplate His virtues; when, above all, we join together with the Church in the celebration of His mysteries (as I shall show you later); when we unite ourselves to Him in each of our actions, be it that we are eating, or working, or doing some act of a seemly nature in union with the similar actions He Himself carried out when He was living here below —when we do that with faith and love, with humility and trust, there is then a strength, a power, a Divine virtue which comes forth from Christ, so as to enlighten us, so as to help us clear away the obstacles to His Divine working in us, so as to produce grace in our souls.

You will perhaps say to me: "But I do not feel that." It is not necessary to feel it. Our Lord said Himself that His reign in souls eludes the experience of the senses.[1] The super-natural life is not based on sentimentality. If God makes us experience a sweetness in serving Him, one extending to our faculties of feeling, we ought to thank Him for it, to use this lesser gift as a ladder to go up higher, as a means of increasing our fidelity—but not to be attached to the sweetness, and, above all, not to found our interior life upon this devotion of the feelings; that is too unstable a base. We can be as much in error in thinking we are advanced in the way of perfection because our feelings of devotion are very intense, as in imagining that we are not making any progress because our soul is in spiritual dryness.

What, then, is the true foundation of our super-natural life? It is faith, and faith is a virtue that is exercised by our higher faculties: intellect and will. Now, what does faith tell us? That Jesus is God as well as man; that His humanity is the humanity of one who is God, the humanity of the Being who is Infinite Wisdom, Love itself, and Omnipotence. How can we doubt, then, that when we approach Him, even outside the sacraments, *by faith*, with humility and trust, a Divine

---

[1] Luke 17:20 ff.

power flows out from Him to enlighten us, to strengthen us, to help us, to succor us? No one has ever approached Christ Jesus with faith and has not been affected by the beneficent rays that issue ceaselessly from that hearth of warmth and light: "Power went forth from him...."[1]

Thus, Christ Jesus—who is ever-living and whose humanity remains indissolubly united to the Divine Word—becomes in this way, and that in the measure of our faith, of the liveliness of our desire to imitate Him, a light and a source of life for us. And, bit by bit, if we are faithful in contemplating Him in this fashion, He will imprint on us a resemblance to Himself, by revealing Himself more intimately to us, by making us share the sentiments[2] of His Divine Heart, and by giving us the strength to make our conduct accord with those sentiments. "It is a thing quite evident to me," said St. Teresa of Avila, "that in order to please God, in order to receive great graces from Him, it is necessary—and this is His will—that they pass through the hands of this sacred humanity (of Christ) in which He has declared Himself well-pleased. I have experienced it an endless number of times, and Our Lord Himself has said it to me. I have seen clearly that this is the gate through which we must enter if we wish Our Sovereign Majesty to reveal high secrets to us.... One walks with confidence along that road."[3]

We then understand the truth of those words of Jesus: "I am the vine, you are the branches. He who abides in me, and I in him, he bears much fruit";[4] "I am the true vine; and it is my Father who tends it."[5] According to the fine remark of St. Augustine, it is as man that Christ is the vine. As God, one with His Father, He is the vine-*dresser*, who works, not as vine-dressers do here below, on the outside; He works in the intimacy of the soul, to give it increase of grace and of life. For, adds the great Doctor, after St. Paul:[6] he who plants does not

---

[1] Luke 6:19; 8:46; Mark 5:30.

[2] Here, the word "sentiment" is to be taken in its spiritual sense of affection of *the will*.

[3] *Life of St. Teresa*, written by herself, Ch. XXII, 8-9.   [4] John 15:5.

[5] John 15:1 (Knox); Cfy and Jerusalem have: "is the vinedresser."

[6] 1 Cor. 3:6: "I have planted, Apollos watered, but God has given the growth."

amount to much, any more than he who waters does. It is God who gives the increase."[1]

From the vine, who is Jesus, the sap of grace rises into the vine-shoots, which are our souls—as long, however, as we *abide* in, remain united to the vine. How?

Through the sacraments—and especially that of the Eucharist, the Sacrament of Union itself: "He who eats my flesh, and drinks my blood, *abides* in me and I in him."[2] Next, through faith. St. Paul says to us: "That Christ may *dwell by faith* in your hearts...."[3] By a faith vivified by love (that is to say, the perfect faith that accompanies the state of grace), Christ *dwells* in us; and each time we come into contact with Jesus through this faith, Christ exercises over us His sanctifying power.[4]

For that, though, it is necessary for us to clear away all the obstacles to His action—sin, imperfections fully willed, attachment to creatures[5] and to ourselves. Necessary, too, that we have an ardent desire to resemble Him; that our faith be a lively and practical one. A lively faith—that is to say, an unshakable faith in the infinite treasures of holiness contained in Christ who is our *All*. A practical faith, a vigilant faith, one that throws us at the feet of Jesus in order to accomplish everything He may ask of us, for the glory of His Father.

It is then that Christ, as the Council of Trent said, *continually pours* into us His sanctifying power, as the head into its members, as the vine into its branches; for this salutary power always precedes, accompanies and follows our good actions.[6] It is through the grace of Christ that we become holy, pleasing to God His Father, in such a way that, also through Christ, all glory may return to the Father. Because He

---

[1] "He is not like those who perform their ministry by working externally, but as one who actually gives the increase from the inside": *Tract. in Johann.*, LXXX.

[2] John 6:57(56).   [3] Eph. 3:17 (Rheims).

[4] "Christ dwells in us through faith, as the third chapter of Ephesians says; and therefore the power of Christ is joined to us by faith": St Thomas, III, q. LXII, a. 5, ad 2.

[5] See translator's note on page 56.   [6] Council of Trent, sess. VI, cap. 16.

loves His Son, the Father has constituted Him head of the kingdom of the elect, and has put all things in His hands: "The Father loves the Son and has entrusted *everything* to Him."[1]

NOTE[2]

Here is a page of St. Thomas (Q.27 *De Veritate*, a.4) which sums up very well the doctrine expounded in this talk. We borrow the [French] translation of it by the Rev. Father Hugon, OP, in his work *La causalité instrumentale en théologie*. "The human nature of Our Lord," writes St. Thomas, "is an organ of the divinity, and that is why it was in communion with the operations of the divine power. Thus, when Christ cured a leper by touching him, this contact caused health instrumentally. Now, this instrumental efficacy that it had for bodily effects, the humanity of the Savior exercised also in the spiritual order; His blood shed for us has a sanctifying power to wash away our sins. The humanity of Jesus is thus the instrumental cause of justification, and the latter is applied to us *spiritually by faith, bodily by the sacraments*, because the humanity of Christ is soul and body. It is in this wise that we should receive within us the effect of the sanctification which is in Christ. Therefore, the most perfect of the sacraments is that which truly comprises Our Lord's body, that is to say, the Eucharist—end and consummation of all the others. As for the other sacraments, they receive something of that power by which the humanity of Christ is the instrument of justification—so that, according to the language of the Apostle (Hebr. 10), the Christian sanctified by baptism is also sanctified by the blood of Jesus Christ. The Savior's Passion, then, operates in the sacraments of the New Law; and these combine as instruments for the producing of grace."

[1] John 3:35 (Jerus.)   [2] By Marmion.

CHAPTER FIVE

THE CHURCH,
MYSTICAL BODY OF CHRIST

INTRODUCTION: The mystery of the *Church, inseparable* from the mystery *of Christ*: they are but one.

IN the preceding talks, I have endeavored to show you how Our Lord is our All. He has been chosen by His Father to be, in His state of Son of God and in His virtues, the one model of our holiness. He has merited for us, by His life, Passion and death, to be established for ever as the universal dispenser of all grace. It is from Him that all grace derives, that all divine life flows into our souls. St. Paul tells us that the Father has subjected all things under His (Christ's) feet, and has made Him head over all the Church, which is His body and His fullness, *plenitudo*.[1]

By these words when he speaks of the Church, the Apostle completes his indication of the Divine disposings of the mystery of Christ. Only by following St. Paul in his exposition of it shall we gain a real understanding of this mystery.

Christ, indeed, cannot be conceived without the Church. As the foundation of all His life, of all His actions, He had in view the glory

---

[1] Eph. 1:22-23.

of His Father; but the masterpiece by which He was to procure this glory was the Church. Christ came upon earth to create and set up the Church; this was the work to which all His existence led and which He affirmed by His Passion and death. Love for His Father took Christ Jesus to the mount of Calvary; but this was for the purpose of His forming the Church there and making her a spouse without stain, immaculate, by purifying her in His Divine blood through love: Christ "loved the Church, and delivered Himself up for her, that He might sanctify her...."[1]

That is what St. Paul says to us. Let us therefore look at what she is for the great apostle, this Church whose name returns beneath his pen so frequently as to be inseparable from the name of Christ.

We can consider the Church in *two ways*: as a visible and hierarchic society, founded by Christ to continue here below His sanctifying mission; she appears in that way as a living organism. But that point of view is not the only one. To have a complete idea of the Church, we must, besides this, regard her as the holy and invisible society of souls who participate, through grace, in the Divine Sonship of Christ and form the kingdom He has won by His blood. It is this that St. Paul calls the body of Christ—without doubt, not the physical body but His mystical body. It is particularly the second viewpoint that we shall dwell upon. However, we cannot pass over the first in silence.

It is true that the invisible Church, or the "soul" of the Church, is more important than the visible Church; but, in the normal Divine plan of Christianity, it is only through union with the visible society that souls enter into a participation in the good things and privileges of the invisible Kingdom of Christ.

---

[1] Eph. 5:25-26.

1. The Church, a *society* founded on the Apostles: depositary of the *doctrine* and *authority of Jesus*, dispenser of *His sacraments*, continuer of *His work of religion*. One does not come *to Christ* except *through the Church*.

I HAVE RELATED to you above the testimony that Peter, in the name of the other disciples, rendered to the divinity of Jesus: "You are the Christ, the Son of the living God." And Jesus said to him: "Blessed are you, Simon Bar-Jona: because flesh and blood has not revealed it to you"—it does not come from your natural intuition—"but my Father who is in heaven. And I say to you: That you are Peter, and upon this rock I will build my Church, and the gates of hell shall not prevail against it. And I will give to you the keys of the kingdom of heaven...."[1]

You will notice that this is still only a promise, a promise which rewarded the homage rendered by the apostle to the divinity of his Master. After the resurrection, Jesus, being again in the midst of His apostles, said to Peter: "Do you love me?" And the apostle replied: "Yes, Lord, I love you." And Our Lord said to him: "Feed my lambs." Christ repeats His question, asks it three times; and, at each protestation by Peter, He invests him—Peter and his successors—as visible leaders of all His flock, lambs and sheep.[2] This investiture takes place only after Peter, by a threefold act of love, has effaced his threefold denial.

Thus, Christ demanded a testimony of His divinity from His apostle before making and carrying out His promise of founding His Church upon him.

It is not necessary for me to expound to you how this society, established by Christ upon Peter and the Apostles to maintain supernatural life in souls, has been organized, has developed, has spread throughout the world.

What we should keep in mind is that she is the continuer,[3] here

---

[1] See Matt. 16:16-19.   [2] See John 21:15-17.

[3] [*Translator's note*: "*la continuatrice*," having the nuance of continuer, by His authority, of the work He began when on earth.]

below, of the mission of Jesus by her doctrine, by her jurisdiction, by the sacraments, by her worship.

By her doctrine, which she keeps intact and whole in a living and uninterrupted tradition. By her jurisdiction, in virtue of which she has authority to direct us in the name of Christ. By the sacraments, whereby she enables us to draw from the wellsprings of grace that her Divine Founder has created. By her worship, which she herself organizes in order to render all glory and all honor to Christ Jesus and to His Father.

How does the Church continue Christ by *her doctrine* and *her jurisdiction?*

After Christ had come into this world, the sole means of going to the Father was to submit oneself entirely to His Son Jesus: "This is my beloved Son ... hear Him."[1] At the beginning of the Savior's public life, the Eternal Father was presenting His Son to the Jews, and saying to them: "Listen to Him, because He is my only Son; I send you Him to reveal to you the secrets of my Divine life, and my will": "*Hear Him.*"

But since His ascension, Christ has left on earth His Church, and this Church is like the continuance of the Incarnation among us. She speaks to us, this Church—that is to say, the Sovereign Pontiff and the Bishops, with the pastors who are subject to them; she speaks to us with all the infallible authority of Christ Jesus Himself.

While He was on earth, Christ confined infallibility to Himself: "I am the truth"—"I am the way, and the truth, and the life";[2] "I am the light of the world. He who follows me does not walk in the darkness, but will have the light of life."[3] Before leaving us, He entrusted His powers to His Church: "As the Father has sent me, I also send you";[4] "He who listens to you, listens to me; he who despises you, despises me; and he who despises me, despises Him that sent me."[5] In the same way as I get my teaching from my Father, so with the teaching you give

---

[1] See Matt. 17:5; Mark 9:6; Luke 9:35.   [2] John 14:6.
[3] John 8:12.   [4] John 20:21.   [5] Luke 10:16 (Knox).

out. That teaching you get from me. Whoever receives this teaching, receives my teaching, which is that of my Father. Whoever despises it, to whatever degree and in whatever measure that may be, despises my teaching, despises me, despises my Father.

See, then, this Church which possesses all the power, all the infallible authority of Christ, and understand that the absolute submission of all your being, intellect, will and energies to this Church is the sole means of going to the Father.[1] Christianity, in its true expression, only exists by means of this absolute submission to the doctrine and the laws of the Church.

This submission to the Church is strictly speaking what distinguishes a Catholic from a Protestant. For example, the latter may believe in the Real Presence of Jesus in the Eucharist; but if he believes in it, it is because he has found this doctrine in the Scriptures and in Tradition, by his own efforts and his personal lights. The Catholic believes it because the Church, which stands in the place of Christ, teaches it to him. The two of them hold the same truth, but the manner of holding it is different. The Protestant does not submit to any authority,[2] he is dependent only on himself. The Catholic receives Christ, with all that He has taught and founded. Christianity is, in practice, submission to Christ in the person of the Sovereign Pontiff and the pastors united to him; submission of the intellect to their

[1] [*Translator's note*: So that this will not be misunderstood, see the note entitled "Salvation and those outside the Church" on pages 115-117.

[2] [*Translator's note*: In expressing it in this way, Marmion is being somewhat elliptical. A Protestant might, rightly, say that he believes it on the authority of Sacred Scripture. But if two Protestants read the Scriptural words on the Eucharist, and one of them genuinely finds in those words a teaching of the Real Presence in the full sense as believed by Catholics, and the other genuinely finds in them only a symbolic presence, what is it—in a person lacking belief in an authoritative and infallible teaching Church—that determines him upon the first interpretation and not the second, other than the authority of his own intellect as Marmion says?]

teachings, submission of the will to what they command. This way is sure, for Our Lord is with His Apostles "all days, even unto the consummation of the world,"[1] and He has prayed for Peter and Peter's successors that their faith "fail not."[2]

The voice of Christ in His teaching, the Church is also the living continuation of *His mediation.*

It is true, as I have told you,[3] that Christ, after His death, can no longer merit; but He "lives always to make intercession" to His Father for us.[4] I have also told you that it is above all by instituting the sacraments that He has willed to establish the means of applying His merits to us after His ascension, and of giving us His grace. But where does one find the sacraments? In the Church. It is to the Church that Our Lord has delivered them. At the time of His ascending to heaven, He said to His Apostles and to their successors: "Go and teach all nations, baptize them in the name of the Father, and of the Son, and of the Holy Spirit."[5] He communicates to them the power of forgiving or retaining sins: "Whose sins you shall forgive, they are forgiven them; and whose sins you shall retain, they are retained."[6] He commissions them to renew, in His name and in memory of Him, the Sacrifice of His body and blood.[7]

You want to enter into the family of God, to be admitted among His children, to be incorporated into Christ? Address yourself to the Church: it is her baptism, not any other, which is the door through which one must pass.[8] In the same way, to obtain pardon for our sins, it is to the Church that we must address ourselves.[9] If we wish to

---

[1] Matt. 28:20.   [2] Luke 22:32 (Rheims).   [3] See page 76 ff.
[4] Hebr. 7:25.   [5] See Matt. 28:19; Mark 16:15.   [6] John 20:23.
[7] Luke 22:19; 1 Cor. 11:23 ff.

[8] [*Translator's note*: But the Church recognizes the validity of baptisms performed, in a proper way and with proper intent, by other Christians.]

[9] Except, of course, in the case of material impossibility; in that case perfect contrition suffices. We are speaking of the rule and not of the exceptions, numerous

receive food for our souls, we have to attend on the priests who have received, through the sacrament of Holy Orders, the sacred powers of dispensing to us the Bread of Life. And, among those who are baptized, the union of man and woman is culpable unless the Church has consecrated it by her blessing.[1] So, then, the official means established by Jesus, the wellsprings of grace that He has caused to burst forth for us — the Church has them in her keeping; it is with her that they are to be found, because it is to her that Christ has delivered them.

Finally, Our Lord has entrusted into the hands of His Church the mission of continuing here below *His work of religion.*

On earth, Christ Jesus offered a perfect hymn of praise to His Father. His soul incessantly contemplated the Divine perfections; and born of that contemplation there was within His soul unending adoration, and an ceaseless hymn to the glory of the Father. By His incarnation Christ, in principle, associates the whole of humanity with the work of this praise. Upon leaving us, He gave to His Church the charge of perpetuating, in His name, this praise that returns to His Father. Around the Sacrifice of the Mass, the center of our whole religion, the Church organizes the public worship which she alone has the right to offer in the name of Christ, her Spouse. She establishes a whole ensemble of prayers, of formulas, of hymns, that enshrine her sacrifice. All year long, she arranges a celebration of the mysteries of her Divine Spouse, in such wise that her children shall be able, each year, to re-live these mysteries, to give thanks to Christ Jesus and His

---

as these can be. Besides, perfect contrition includes, at least implicitly, the resolution and the desire to address oneself to the Church.

[1] [*Translator's note:* As in the case of what he has just written in relation to forgiveness of sin through the Sacrament of Penance, Marmion here, though he says "among those who are baptized," has *Catholics* in mind (in the case of marriage, where both are Catholics or one of them is). As scarcely needs stating, the marriage of two *non-Catholics* is not "culpable" by reason of its taking place elsewhere than in a Catholic Church!]

Father for them, and to draw forth from them the divine life that these mysteries, lived in the first place by Jesus, have merited for us.

The whole of her worship comes back to Christ. It is in reliance on the infinite satisfactions of Jesus, in His capacity of universal and ever-living Mediator, that the Church concludes all her supplications: *"Through Our Lord Jesus Christ who, with Thee and the Holy Spirit, lives and reigns...."*; and, in the same way, it is by their passing through Christ that all the adoration and praise of the Church rises up to the Eternal Father and is accepted in the sanctuary of the Trinity: *"Through Him, with Him, in Him, all glory and honor are yours, God the Almighty Father, in the unity of the Holy Spirit."*[1]

Such, then, is the manner in which the Church, founded by Jesus, continues His Divine work here below. The Church is the authentic depositary of the doctrine and the law of Christ; the dispenser of His graces among men; and, finally, the spouse who, in the name of Christ, offers to God for all her children perfect praise.

And in this way the Church is so united to Christ, possesses such an abundance of His riches, that one can say that she is Christ living across the centuries. Christ came upon earth, not only for those who dwelt in Palestine at the time He lived there, but for all men of all times. When He deprived men of His tangible presence, He gave them the Church with her teaching, her jurisdiction, her sacraments, her worship, like another "Himself." It is in the Church that we shall find Christ. No one goes to the Father—and going to the Father is what salvation and holiness is all about; no one goes to the Father except through Christ: "No one comes to the Father but through me."[2] But remember well the following truth which is of no less capital importance. No one goes to Christ except through the Church; we only

---

[1] Ordinary of the Mass.   [2] John 14:6.

belong to Christ if we belong in fact or in desire[1] to the Church; we only live the life of Christ in the unity of the Church.

[1] See note below.

———∽∾∿∾∽———

TRANSLATOR'S NOTE: SALVATION AND THOSE OUTSIDE THE CHURCH

The *Catechism of the Catholic Church* (para. 846) asks how the affirmation "Outside the Church there is no salvation"—an affirmation "often repeated" by the early Christian Fathers — is to be understood. In its balanced answer, it first quotes Vatican II (*Lumen Gentium* 14):

> "Basing itself on Scripture [e.g. Mark 16:16] and Tradition, the Council (Vatican II) teaches that the Church, a pilgrim now on earth, is necessary for salvation: the one Christ is the mediator and the way of salvation; He is present to us in His body which is the Church. He Himself explicitly asserted the necessity of faith and Baptism, and thereby affirmed at the same time the necessity of the Church which men enter through Baptism as through a door. Hence they could not be saved who, **knowing that** the Catholic Church was founded as necessary by God through Christ [my emphasis], would refuse either to enter it, or to remain in it."

The two words I have emphasized above are important, for in its very next paragraph the Catechism makes a counterbalancing point: "This affirmation [that "outside the Church there is no salvation"] is not aimed at those who, *through no fault of their own*, do not know Christ and his Church" (para. 847; my italics). Having quoted *Lumen Gentium* 14, see above, it then quotes *Lumen Gentium* 16:

> "Those who, through no fault of their own, do not know the Gospel of Christ or His Church, but who nevertheless seek God with a sincere heart, and, moved by grace, try in their actions to do His will through the dictates of their conscience as they know it [i.e. as they know His will] — those too may achieve eternal salvation."

I now speculate on the extreme case of someone, in the wilds of the earth somewhere, who in the whole of his life has never heard the name of Christ, has never heard of Christ's Church. If such a person achieves salvation — as he may, if he lives according to his lights in the way *Lumen Gentium* 16 describes — it is **nonetheless through Christ and the Church** that he does so, as Marmion says. For it is through Christ and the Church that all grace and salvation comes.

There is a danger of speculation being rash when it concerns those who *have* heard of Christ and the Church, who know of Christ and the Church in differing degrees, but remain outside the Church. "All are *called* to the [full] Catholic unity of the people of God" (CCC, para. 836; my italics); but there are real, if "imperfect," relationships to the Church in the case of "the baptized who are honored by the name of Christian, but do not profess the Catholic faith in its entirety or have not preserved unity or communion under the successor of Peter" (CCC, para. 838).

Note also Marmion's phrase: "belong in fact or *desire* to the Church" (page 115). Marmion does not explore the concept of *implicit* desire (i.e. that if some specific person knew and believed the claims of the Catholic Church, he would enter and submit to her — and that God, who reads hearts, knows that).

All the above counterbalancing points, however, must themselves be counterbalanced in conclusion. After everything it has said as quoted in the earlier paragraphs of this note, and immediately after saying "Although in ways known to Himself God can lead those who, through no fault of their own, are ignorant of the Gospel, to that faith without which it is impossible to please Him," the Catechism adds: "*the Church still has the obligation and also the sacred right to evangelize all men*" (para. 848; my italics). Nothing in this translator's note is an invitation to espouse the idea that one religion is as good as another, or that membership of the visible Catholic Church is otherwise than a matter of huge moment. In his encyclical *Mystici Corporis*, Pius XII wrote about "those who do not belong to the visible Body of the Catholic Church," and he stressed that "even though by an unconscious desire and longing they have a certain *relationship* with the Mystical Body of the Redeemer, *they still remain deprived of those many heavenly gifts and helps which can only be enjoyed in the Catholic Church"* (para. 103, my italics). These last words are very important.

———

2. **A truth that puts into relief the particular characteristic of the** *visibility* **of the Church: it is** *through men* **that** *God* **wishes to lead us. Importance of this super-natural** *Divine disposing resulting from the Incarnation*; **it glorifies Jesus and exercises our faith.** *Our duties* **towards the Church.**

THIS CHURCH is *visible*, as you know.

She is, in her hierarchy, composed of the Sovereign Pontiff, successor of Peter, the bishops, and the pastors who, united to the Vicar of Christ and to the bishops, exercise their jurisdiction over us in the name of Christ. For it is through the intermediacy of men that Christ guides us and sanctifies us.

There is a profound truth here, on which we must now dwell.

Since the Incarnation, God, in His dealings with us, acts through men. I speak of the normal, regular, Divine disposings, and not of the exceptions by which God preserves intact His sovereign domain, here as in all things. For example, God could Himself have revealed to us directly what we must do in order to attain to Him. He does not do this, it is not His way; He refers us to a man—a man doubtless infallible in matters of faith but, still, a man like us, from whom we have to hold all doctrine. It is the same when someone has fallen into sin; that person prostrates himself before God, he is distressed, he rends himself with all sorts of penances. God says: "Very good, but if you want to obtain your pardon, you have to go down upon your knees before a priest, a man whom my Son has constituted His minister, and confess your sin to him." Without confession to this man, no pardon.[1] The most lively and deepest contrition, the most frightful penances, do not suffice to blot out a single mortal sin, if one has not the intention to submit to this humiliation of confessing one's sin to this man who stands in the place of Christ.

You see what God's super-natural disposings are. From all eternity, the Divine thought is fixed upon the Incarnation, and ever since His Son has been united to humanity and by becoming incarnate has saved the world, God wills that it shall be through the intermediacy of men like us, weak as we are, that grace shall be poured out upon the world. In that, there is a prolongment, an extension, of the Incarnation. God has drawn near to us in the person of His Son made man, and, since then, it is through the members of His Son that He continues to put Himself in communication with our souls. God wishes in that way to exalt His Son by, so to speak, making everything come down to His incarnation—by attaching to it, in such a visible way, all the Divine disposings of our salvation and sanctification, right up to the end of time.

---

[1] [*Translator's note*: As a description of Catholic doctrine this sentence is too starkly categoric, taken on its own. On pages 112-113, note 9, Marmion emphasized that he was "speaking of the rule and not of the exceptions, numerous as these can be." The Church teaches that where there is "*perfect* contrition" (that is, contrition arising "from a love by which God is loved above all else") such contrition itself obtains forgiveness of [even] mortal sins: CCC, para. 1452. However, in stating that, the Catechism attaches the condition: "if it includes the firm resolution to have recourse to sacramental confession as soon as possible." (To complete the picture, one should add that a contrition which is "imperfect," e.g. "born of the consideration of sin's ugliness or the fear of damnation, rather than the love of God" suffices *in sacramental confession*, notwithstanding its imperfection: CCC, para. 1453.)

Besides, both Marmion's words and the Catechism's condition precedent clearly have in mind Catholics, who therefore have sacramental confession available to them. It seems self-evident that non-use of a sacrament in which he or she does not believe will not bar a penitent non-Catholic from obtaining forgiveness. God is not bound by His own sacraments. Marmion has just said that he is here speaking of "the normal, regular Divine disposings" (*économie*) and that "God preserves intact His own domain, here as in all things."]

But, also, He has instituted those Divine disposings so as to make us live by faith. For there is in the Church a twofold element—a human element and a Divine element.

The human element is the frailty of the men to whom possession of Christ's power has been given, in order that they may direct us. Look at St. Peter, how frail he was! At the words of a servant-girl, he denies his Master, on the very day of his priestly ordination. Our Lord well knew of this frailty, since, after His resurrection, He exacts from His apostle a threefold protestation of love in memory of the threefold denial. And nevertheless, Christ founds His Church upon him: "Feed my lambs, feed my sheep."[1] Peter's successors are frail; the infallibility they possess in matters of faith does not give them the privilege of not sinning. Could Our Lord not have conferred impeccability upon them? Certainly; but He has not willed to do that: He has willed that our faith be able to be exercised. Why is that?

The faithful soul sees through the human element to the Divine element: the indefectibility of the doctrine, kept safe throughout all the ages and despite all the assaults of heresies and schisms; the unity of this same doctrine preserved by the infallible magisterium; the heroic and uninterrupted holiness manifested, in so many ways, in this Church; the unbroken succession by which, link by link, the Church of our day can be traced back to the foundations established by the Apostles; the force of universal expansion that characterizes it—so many certain signs by which we recognize that Our Lord is with His Church "to the end of time."[2]

Let us, then, have great trust in this Church that Jesus has left to us: it is another "Himself." We have the happiness of belonging to Christ in belonging to this community which is One, Catholic, Apostolic and Roman. We ought greatly to rejoice at that and render constant thanksgiving to God for "transferring us into the kingdom of His

[1] See John 21:15-17.   [2] Matt. 28:20 (Jerus.)

beloved Son."[1] Is it not a source of immense confidence to be able, through our incorporation into the Church, to draw upon grace and life at their authentic and official wellsprings?

Further, let us give to those who have jurisdiction over us the obedience which Christ demands of us. That submission of our intellect and will must be given to Christ in the person of a man; otherwise God does not accept it. Let us give to those who govern us—above all, to the Sovereign Pontiff, Vicar of Christ, to the bishops who are in union with him and who possess the lights of the Holy Spirit in order that they may guide us;[2] let us give them that interior submission, that filial reverence, that obedience in what we do, which makes us true children of the Church.

The Church is the Spouse of Christ. She is our Mother: we ought to love her, because she leads us to Christ and unites us to Him. We ought to love and revere her teaching, because it is the teaching of Christ Jesus, ought to love her prayer and associate ourselves with it, because it is the very prayer of the Spouse of Christ. There is nothing surer for us than that, nothing more pleasing to Our Lord. We ought, in a word, to be attached to the Church, to everything that comes to us from her, as we would have been attached to the person of Jesus Himself and to everything that would have come to us from Him, had we been able to follow Him during His life on earth.

Such is the Church as a visible society. St. Paul compares it to an edifice "built upon the foundation of the apostles ... with Christ Jesus Himself as the chief cornerstone."[3] We live in this house of God, "no longer aliens or foreign visitors: you are citizens like all the saints, and part of God's household."[4] It is in Christ that the whole well-ordered edifice rises, to form "a temple holy in the Lord."[5]

---

[1] Col. 1:13.

[2] "The Holy Spirit has placed you as bishops, to rule the Church of God": Acts 20:28.

[3] Eph. 2:20.   [4] Eph. 2:19 (Jerus.)   [5] Eph. 2:21.

3. The Church, *the mystical body. Christ* is its *head* because He *has all primacy.* Deepness of this union: "We are Christ," all "one in Christ." Dwelling *united to Jesus* and *one another* by charity.

ANOTHER IMAGE recurs more frequently in the writings of St. Paul, an image the more expressive because it is borrowed from life itself, and, above all, because it gives us a deeper conception of the Church by showing us the intimate relationship which exists between the Church and Christ. That relationship is summed up by this sentence taken from the Apostle: *The Church is a body of which Christ is the head.*[1]

When he speaks of the Church as a visible and hierarchic society, St. Paul tells us that Christ, who founded this society, has established some "as apostles, and some as prophets, others again as evangelists, and others as pastors and teachers."[2] And for what purpose? So that they may labor, he says, "for the perfecting of the saints, for the work of the ministry, for the edifying of the body of Christ"—and this, right up to the day when we all have arrived at unity of faith and knowledge of the Son of God, to the state of perfect man, "unto the measure of the age of the fullness of Christ."[3] What do these words mean?

We form, with Christ, a body which goes on developing and must attain to its full perfection. As you see, it is not here a question of the natural, physical, body of Christ, born of the Virgin Mary; that body attained its complete development long ago. From the time when He came out from the tomb, living and glorious, the body of Christ was no longer susceptible of growth; it possesses the fullness of perfection that had returned to it.

But, says St. Paul, there is another body which, over the course of the ages, Christ shapes as His. That body is the Church: it is the souls

---

[1] 1 Cor. 12:12 ff.; Col. 1:18. The Apostle uses still other expressions. He says that we are united to Christ like the branches to the trunk of a tree (Rom. 6:5 [Rheims: "planted"]), like the materials to a building (Eph. 2:21-22); but what he puts in especially high relief is the idea of a body united to the head.

[2] Eph. 4:11.   [3] Eph. 4:12-13 (Rheims).

who, through grace, live with the life of Christ. Together they make up, with Christ, one single body, one mystical[1] body of which Christ is the head. "Christ is formed in you,"[2] we must "grow up in Him."[3] This idea is very dear to the great apostle, who puts it in high relief by comparing the union of Christ and the Church to the union which exists in the human organism between the head and the body.[4] Listen to him: "For just as in one body we have many members ... so we, the many, are one body in Christ."[5] The Church is the body, and Christ is the head.[6] Elsewhere, he calls the Church "the fullness" of Christ,[7] as the members of a body are the fullness of the organism. And he concludes: "You are all *one* in Christ Jesus."[8]

The Church, then, makes up, with Christ, a single being. According to the beautiful saying of St. Augustine which faithfully echoes St. Paul, Christ cannot be understood fully without the Church: they are inseparable, as the head is inseparable from the body. Christ and His Church form one single collective being, *Totus Christus*, the whole Christ. "*The whole Christ* is head and body: the head the only-begotten Son of God, and the body His Church."[9]

Why is Christ the head, the chief one, of the Church? Because He has the primacy. First, a primacy of honor: God "has exalted Him, and has given Him a name which is above all names," that at the name of Jesus "every knee should bow."[10] A primacy of authority: "All authority

---

[1] "Mystical" is opposed, not to "real," but to "*physical*," as we have just seen. It is called *mystical*, not only to distinguish it from the natural body of Christ, but to indicate the character, at once super-natural and intimate, of the union of Christ with the Church, a union founded on and held together by *mysteries* perceptible to faith alone. The Church is a living organism; living, through the Spirit, by the grace of Christ.

[2] Gal. 4:19.   [3] Eph. 4:15 (Rheims).

[4] It is particularly in the First Letter to the Corinthians (12:12-30) that this idea is vividly expounded.   [5] Rom. 12:4-5.

[6] 1 Cor. 12:12; Col. 1:18.   [7] Eph. 1:23.   [8] Gal. 3:28.

[9] *De Unitate Ecclesiae*, 4. No one has expounded this doctrine better than St. Augustine: the Holy Doctor has developed it especially in *Enarr. in Psalmis*.

[10] Phil. 2:9-10 (Rheims).

in heaven and on earth has been given to me,"[1] given to me by my Father. But above all a primacy of life, of interior influence: God the Father "has subjected all things under His feet: and has made Him head over all the Church."[2]

We are all called to live with the life of Christ; but it is from Him that we all must receive it. Christ, as I have told you,[3] has by His death won this primacy, this supreme power of giving all grace to "every man who comes into the world."[4] He exercises a primacy of Divine influence, in being—for every soul, in diverse degrees—the one source of the grace that makes them live.[5] "Christ," says St. Thomas, "has received the plenitude of grace, not only in an individual capacity, but also as head of the Church."[6]

No doubt that Christ dispenses the treasures of His grace to souls unequally; but, adds St. Thomas, that is with the purpose that from this very gradation shall result the beauty and perfection of the Church, His mystical body.[7] That is the idea St. Paul has. After having said that grace has been granted to each "according to the measure of Christ's bestowal,"[8] the Apostle enumerates the different graces that adorn souls, and he concludes by saying that they are given "for building up the body of Christ."[9] There is diversity between the members, but this very variety contributes to a harmony of unity.

---

[1] Matt. 28:18 (Jerus.) [2] Eph. 1:22 (Rheims).
[3] See pages 69 ff. [4] John 1:9.
[5] This Divine and wholly interior influence of Christ within the souls who form His mystical body distinguishes this union from that—simply a moral one—which exists between the supreme authority of a human society and the members of that society. In the latter case, the influence of the authority is exterior and only goes to co-ordinating and maintaining the diverse energies of the members towards a common end. The action of Christ in the Church is more intimate, more penetrating; it attains to the very life of souls, and this is one of the reasons why "the *mystical body*" is not a fiction of our reasoning, but a reality of the profoundest kind.
[6] III, q. XLVIII, a. 1. [7] I-II, q. CXII, a. 4.
[8] Eph. 4:7. [9] Eph. 4:12.

Christ, then, is the chief one of us, and the Church forms with Him but one single mystical body, of which He is the head.[1] And this union between Christ and His members is such as to make for *oneness*. Touch the Church, touch the souls who, by baptism and their life of grace, are the members of the Church, and you touch Christ Himself. Look at St. Paul, when he was persecuting the Church and was riding towards the town of Damascus in order to imprison the Christians. On the road, he is thrown from his horse and he hears a voice that says to him: "Saul, Saul, why do you persecute me?" He replies: "Who are you, Lord?" And the Lord says to him: "I am Jesus, whom you are persecuting."[2] You will notice that Christ does not say: "Why do you persecute *my disciples?*"— something He could have said with just as much truth, since He Himself had already ascended into heaven and it was only the Christians that St. Paul was hunting down; but He says: "Why do you persecute *me?*"— "It is *I* whom you are persecuting." Why does Christ speak in this way? Because His disciples belong to Him as His very own; because the society composed of them forms His mystical body. To persecute the souls who believe in Jesus Christ is to persecute Christ Himself.

How well St. Paul understood this doctrine! With what force he expounded it, and how expressive he is! "No one," he said, "ever hated his own body; on the contrary he nourishes and cherishes it";[3] and Christ does same for the Church—because "we are members of His body," formed "from His flesh and from His bones."[4] And it is because we are so closely united to Christ, forming with Him one single and unique mystical body, that Christ has willed all His work to have been ours.

That is a profound truth we ought often to have before our eyes. Through Christ Jesus the Word incarnate, as I have told you, the

---

[1] "In the same way that a natural organism brings together the diversity of its members into its unity, so the Church, which is the mystical body of Christ, is considered as forming with its body but a single moral person": III, q. XLIX, a. 1.

[2] Acts 9:4-5.   [3] See Eph. 5:29.   [4] Eph. 5:30.

whole of humanity has recovered God's friendship in the person of Christ, constituted head of the human race. St. Thomas writes that, owing to the identification established by Christ between Himself and us from the time of the Incarnation, the fact that Christ has suffered voluntarily in our place and in our name constitutes so great a good that, for having found this good thing in human nature, God, being appeased, forgets all offenses among those who are united to Christ.[1] The satisfactions and merits of Christ have become ours.[2]

Since that time we are indissolubly associated with Christ Jesus.[3] We are one with Christ in the thought of our heavenly Father. "God," says St. Paul, "is rich in mercy"; for "even when we were dead by reason of our sins," He "brought us to life *together with Christ*"—raised us, *in Christ, with Christ*, from the dead, and seated *us too* in heaven, so that He "might show in the ages to come the overflowing riches of His grace, in kindness towards us in Christ Jesus."[4] In a word, He brings us to life *with* Christ and in Christ, so as to make us Christ's *co-heirs*. The Father, in His thoughts, does not separate us from His Christ. St. Thomas says that it is by one and the same eternal act of Divine wisdom that

---

[1] III, q. XLIX, a. 4.

[2] "The head and the members are as just as though one mystical person, and therefore the satisfaction of Christ extends to all the faithful as to His own members": III, q. XLVIII, a. 2, ad 1.

[3] In a book of his, of remarkable erudition, *Théologie de S. Paul*, Fr. Prat, SJ calls attention to "a long series of foreign words the majority of which cannot be rendered in another language except by a barbarism or a paraphrase. The Apostle has created or revived them to give graphic expression to the ineffable union of Christians with Christ and in Christ. These are: *to suffer with* Jesus Christ; *to be crucified with* Him; *to die with* Him; *to be brought to life* with Him; *to rise from the dead with* Him; *to live with* Him; *to share* His *likeness*; *to share* His *glory*; *to sit with* Him; *to reign with* Him; *to have part in* His *likeness*; *to have part in* His *life*; *to be* His *co-heir*. One can add to these: *co-sharing*; *co-corporal*; *co-built*, and some others still which do not directly express the union of Christians *with* Christ, but indicate the intimate union of Christians among themselves in Christ" (vol. 2, p. 52).

[4] Eph. 2:4-7; cf. Rom. 6:4; Col. 2:12-13.

Christ and we have been predestined:[1] the Father makes of all Christ's disciples, who believe in Him, who live by His grace, one and the same and the only object of His pleasure. It is Our Lord Himself who tells us: "The Father ... loves you *because* you have loved me" and have believed that I am God's Son.[2]

That, says St. Paul, is why Christ, whose will was so intimately united with that of His Father, delivered Himself up for His Church: Christ "loved the Church and sacrificed Himself for her."[3] Because the Church was to form with Him one single mystical body, He delivered Himself up for her, in order that this body should be "glorious," "not having spot, or wrinkle ... holy and without blemish."[4] And after having ransomed her, He has given her everything.

Oh! if we had faith in these truths! If we understood what it is for us to have entered, through baptism, into the Church; to be, through grace, members of the mystical body of Christ! "Let us congratulate ourselves, let us pour out thanksgiving," St. Augustine cries;[5] "*we have been made*, not only Christians but *Christ*. Do you understand, my brethren, the grace of God towards us? Let us marvel, let us thrill with joy, we have been made Christ: He the head, we the members — the whole man, He and us ... Who is the head, and who are the members? Christ and the Church." This, continues the great Doctor, would be "a pretension of insane pride, if Christ Himself had not deigned to promise us this glory when, by the mouth of His apostle Paul, He said: 'You are the body of Christ, member for member.'"[6]

---

[1] III, q. XXIV, a. 4.

[2] John 16:27.

[3] Eph. 5:25 (Jerus.)

[4] Eph. 5:27 (Rheims).

[5] *Tract. in Johann.*, XXI, 8-9. And elsewhere: "making us one man with Him, head and body": *Enarr. in Ps.* 85, c. 1. And again: "One man, head and body; one man, Christ and the Church, perfect man": *Enarr. in Ps.* 18, c. 10.

[6] 1 Cor. 12:27.

Yes, let us thank Christ Jesus for associating us so intimately with His life. We hold all in common with Him: merits, interests, possessions, beatitude, glory. That being so, let us be members who do not, by sin, condemn ourselves to become dead members. But rather, let us, through the grace that comes from Him, through our virtues modeled on His, through all of our holiness which is but a participation in His holiness, be members filled with life and super-natural beauty, members in whom Christ can glory, members who may fittingly be part of this society that He has willed to be without spot or wrinkle, holy and without blemish.

And, since we are "all one"[1] in Christ, since under one and the same head, Christ, we all live by the same life of grace, under the action of one and the same Spirit, even though all the members may each have a different function, let us remain united among ourselves; united also with all the holy souls who—in heaven as glorious members; in purgatory as suffering members—form with us one single body: "That they may be one."[2] This is the dogma, such a consoling one, of the *communion of saints.*

For St. Paul, the "saints" are those who belong to Christ—whether, having received the crown, they have already taken their place in the eternal kingdom, or whether they yet are fighting here below. But all these members belong to one single body, for the Church is one. They are bound up, one with another; everything is in common amongst them. If one member suffers anything, all the members suffer with it, or if one member receives honor, all the members share the joy of it.[3] The good of one member profits the entire body, and the glory of the body is reflected upon each of its members.[4] What profound perspectives on our

---

[1] See John 17:21-23.   [2] John 17:11.   [3] 1 Cor. 12:26.

[4] Just as in a natural body the operation of each member submits to the good of the whole body, so also in the spiritual body, namely the Church. Because all the faithful are one body, the good of one is communicated to another": St Thomas, *Opusc.*, VII, *Expositio Symboli*, c. XIII. Cf. I-II, q. XXI, a. 3.

responsibilities this thought opens! What a lively source of apostolate it is! Therefore St. Paul exhorts each one of us to labor until we all arrive at the unique perfection of the mystical body—at perfect manhood, "unto the measure of the age of the fullness of Christ."[1]

For that, it is necessary not only that we remain united to Christ who is the head, but that we are also "careful to preserve the unity of the Spirit"—who is the Spirit of Love—"in the bond of peace."[2]

This was the supreme wish of Christ, at the time of His reaching the end of His mission here below: "That they all may be one, as you, Father, in me, and I in you";[3] "so they may be perfectly made one."[4] For, says St. Paul, "you are all the children of God through faith in Christ Jesus";[5] "no longer is there Jew or Greek, no longer slave or free man,"[6] you are all *one* in Christ Jesus. Unity in God, in Christ and through Christ—there we have the end-point of the journey: "that God may be all in all."[7]

St. Paul, who has placed in such strong relief the union of Christ with His Church, could not fail to tell us something of the final glory of the mystical body of Jesus. Thus, he tells us[8] that on the day fixed by the Divine decrees, when this mystical body shall have arrived at the state of "fullness," in the measure of the perfect stature of Christ, then will dawn the day of triumph which is to consecrate for ever the union of the Church and her Head. Associated so intimately with the life of Jesus up to then, the Church, now complete, will share in His glory.[9] The resurrection triumphs over death, the last enemy that is to be conquered; then, the elect being all reunited under their Divine Head at

---

[1] Eph. 4:13 (Rheims). [*Translator's note*: The Knox version has: "that maturity which is proportioned to the completed growth of Christ."]

[2] Eph. 4:3.

[3] John 17:21 (Rheims).

[4] John 17:23 (Knox).

[5] Gal. 3:26.

[6] See Col. 3:11.

[7] 1 Cor. 15:28.

[8] 1 Cor. 15:24-28.

[9] 2 Tim. 2:12; Rom. 8:17.

last, Christ (these are the expressions of St. Paul) will present to His Father, so as to give Him homage thereby, this society—no longer imperfect, nor one still militant in the midst of troubles, temptations, struggles, or of failures when put to the test; no longer suffering the fires of expiation, but henceforth transfigured and glorious in all its members.

Oh! what an imposing spectacle it will be, to see Christ Jesus offer to the Eternal Father these glorious and unnumberable trophies that proclaim the power of His grace; this kingdom, conquered by His blood and which, in its entirety, will then be shining forth with a spotless splendor—fruit of the divine life that circulates, full and intoxicating, in each one of the saints!

We can well understand how St. John, having glimpsed something of these marvels and these joys, compared them in the Apocalypse, following Jesus Himself,[1] to a marriage-feast, the "marriage-feast of the Lamb."[2] Finally we can understand why, in order to conclude appropriately these mysterious descriptions of the heavenly Jerusalem, the same apostle makes us hear the ardent word of desire that Christ and the Church, the Bridegroom and the Bride, repeat, constantly, to each other *now*, in awaiting the hour of final consummation and perfect union: "Come!"[3]

---

[1] Matt. 22:2. [2] See Apoc. 19:9. [3] Apoc. 22:17.

CHAPTER SIX

THE HOLY SPIRIT,
SPIRIT OF JESUS

INTRODUCTION: The doctrine on the Holy Spirit completes the exposition of the Divine plan. Capital importance of this subject.

WE HAVE among our books of Sacred Scripture, under the title *Acts of the Apostles*, an account of the first days of the Church. This narration, owed to the pen of St. Luke, who has been a witness to many of the facts he reports, is full of charm and of life. We see from it how the Church, founded by Jesus upon the Apostles, develops at Jerusalem, then extends little by little outside Judea, thanks above all to the preaching of St. Paul. The greater part of the volume, indeed, is devoted to an account of the missions, labors and struggles of the great apostle. We are able to follow him in almost all the stages of his evangelical journeys. Those pages, all of them full of animation, reveal to us (taken as they are from real life) what unending tribulations St. Paul underwent, what numberless difficulties he came up against; the adventures that occurred, the sufferings endured in the course of his numerous travels undertaken in order to spread everywhere the name and the glory of Jesus.

It is related in these *Acts* that when, in the course of his missions, St. Paul arrived at Ephesus, he encountered some disciples there, and asked them: "Did you receive the Holy Spirit when you believed?" The disciples replied to him: "We have not so much as heard that there is a Holy Spirit."[1]

We ourselves certainly cannot be unaware of the existence of the Holy Spirit. But how many Christians there are today who are acquainted with Him by name only and know next to nothing of His workings in souls! And, yet, we cannot have a perfect conception of the Divine disposings without an idea, as clear as possible, of what the Holy Spirit is for us.

Look at how in almost all the passages where St. Paul expounds the eternal thoughts on our super-natural adoption, wherever it is a question of grace and of the Church, he speaks of "the Spirit of God," "the Spirit of Christ," "the Spirit of Jesus." "You have received the Spirit of adoption of sons, whereby we cry: Abba (Father)";[2] "God has sent the Spirit of His Son into our hearts," that we may call God our Father.[3] "Do you not know," he says elsewhere, "that you are"—through grace —"the temple of God and that the Spirit of God dwells in you?"[4] And again: "Your members are the temple of the Holy Spirit, who is in you."[5] It is in Christ, St. Paul says, that all the well-ordered building "grows into a temple holy in the Lord"; it is in Christ that "you too" are built together to be, *through the Holy Spirit*, a habitation where God dwells.[6] This in such fashion that as you form but one body in Christ, so are you all animated by one Spirit only: "One body and one Spirit."[7] The presence of this Spirit in our souls is so necessary that St. Paul says to us: "If anyone does not have the Spirit of Christ, he does not belong to Christ."[8]

---

[1] See Acts 19:2.

[2] Rom. 8:15 (Rheims). [*Translator's note*: Here my changing the Rheims's initial letter of "spirit" from small to large has the effect of making it accord with Marmion's interpretation of the verse.]   [3] Gal. 4:6.   [4] 1 Cor. 3:16.

[5] 1 Cor. 6:19.   [6] Eph. 2:21-22.   [7] Eph. 4:4.   [8] Rom. 8:9.

You now understand why the Apostle—to whose heart nothing was as dear as seeing Christ live in the souls of his disciples—asks them if they have received the Holy Spirit. It is because only those are children of God, in Jesus Christ, who are guided by the Holy Spirit: "whoever are led by the Spirit of God, they are the sons of God."[1]

We shall not, then, grasp perfectly the mystery of Christ and the Divine disposings of our sanctification unless we fix our gaze upon this Divine Spirit and upon His action within us. We have seen that the purpose of our whole life is to enter with great humility into the thoughts of God; to adapt ourselves to them as perfectly as possible, with the simplicity of a child. These thoughts being Divine, their efficacy is intrinsically absolute; they will infallibly produce their fruits of sanctification, if we accept them with faith and love. Now, to enter into the Divine plan, one must not only "receive Christ,"[2] but, as St. Paul indicates,[3] must "receive the Holy Spirit" and submit oneself to His action, in order to be "one with Christ."[4]

Look at Our Lord Himself. In that wonderful discourse after the Last Supper[5] when to those He calls His "friends" He reveals the secrets of the eternal life He is bringing them, He speaks to them, over and over again, of the Holy Spirit; almost as often as He does of His Father. He tells them that when He has ascended into heaven this Spirit will come among them in place of Him; that this Spirit will be their interior teacher—so necessary a teacher, that Jesus will ask the Father that He, the Spirit, shall be given to them and shall "abide with you, and shall be in you."[6]

Now, why should our Divine Savior have taken such great care to speak of the Holy Spirit, at so solemn an hour, in such pressing terms, if what He told us was meant to be something of a dead letter for us?

---

[1] Rom. 8:14.   [2] See John 1:12.   [3] Acts 19:2.
[4] See John 14:20; 15:4 ff.   [5] John 14.   [6] John 14:16 (Rheims).

Would it not be slighting Him, and causing very grave detriment to ourselves, if we passed over in silence a mystery so vital for us?[1]

I shall endeavor, then, to show you, as clearly as I am able, what the Holy Spirit is in Himself within the adorable Trinity; His action upon the sacred humanity of Christ; the ceaseless benefits He brings to the Church and to souls.

In that way we shall complete our account of the disposition of the Divine designs considered in itself.

There is no doubting that this subject is a lofty one, and that we ought only to treat it with profound reverence; but since Our Lord has revealed it to us, our faith ought also to consider it, with love and trust. Let us humbly ask the Holy Spirit Himself to enlighten our souls with a ray of His Divine light. Assuredly He will hear our prayer.

1. **The Holy Spirit *within the Trinity*: He proceeds from the Father and the Son through *love*. *Sanctification* is *appropriated* to Him because it is *a work of love*, of completion, of union.**

ABOUT THE HOLY SPIRIT we know only what Revelation tells us. Well, what does Revelation tell us about Him?

It belongs to God's infinite essence to be one God in three Persons, the Father, the Son and the Holy Spirit. That is the mystery of the

---

[1] In his encyclical on the Holy Spirit (*Divinum illus munus*, May 9, 1897), Leo XIII, of glorious memory, bitterly deplored that Christians should "have had but a very poor acquaintanceship with the Holy Spirit. They often make use of His name in their exercises of piety, but their faith is wrapped in thick darkness." Therefore the great Pontiff strongly insists that "all preachers and those having charge of souls regard it as a duty to teach people more carefully, and at greater length, *diligentius atque uberius*, that which treats of the Holy Spirit." There is no doubt that he wants them to "avoid all subtle controversy, all rash attempts to scan the deep nature of the mysteries," but he also wishes them "to recall, and luminously to expound, the numerous and remarkable benefits the Divine Donor has brought and does not cease to bring to our souls; for error or ignorance of these mysteries which are so great and so fruitful (error and ignorance unworthy of the sons of light) ought to disappear totally."

Blessed Trinity. Faith safeguards the truth that in God there is both Unity of nature and distinction between the Persons.[1]

The Father, in knowing Himself, declares—expresses—this knowledge in an infinite Utterance, the Word. This act is simple and eternal: and the Son, begotten of the Father, is like, and equal to, Him, because the Father communicates to the Son His own nature, His own life and perfections.

The Father and the Son are drawn to one another by a common and mutual love—the Father is of a perfection and beauty so absolute; the Son is so perfect an image of His Father! Therefore they give themselves each to the other, and this mutual love—which flows from the Father and the Son as from a single wellspring—is, in God, a subsistent Love, a *Person* called "the Holy Spirit," distinct from the other two Persons. This name is a mysterious one, but Revelation gives us no other.

The Holy Spirit, within the interior operations of the Divine life, is the ultimate completion, He "completes"—if in speaking of such mysteries one can stammer it out thus—the cycle of activity-of-heart within the Blessed Trinity. But, like the Father and the Son, He is God; like them and with them, He possesses the same, the unique, Divine nature, an equal knowledge, an equal power, an equal majesty, an equal goodness.

This Divine Spirit is called "Holy":[2] He is the Spirit of holiness. Holy in Himself, He sanctifies. In announcing the mystery of the Incarnation, the archangel Gabriel said to the Virgin Mary: "The Holy Spirit shall come upon you, and therefore also the Holy Being who shall be born of you shall be called the Son of God."[3] Works of sanctification are par-

---

[1] "The catholic faith ... is this: that we are to worship the One God in Three-ness of Persons, and worship the Threeness of Persons in One-ness—neither mingling together the Persons nor severing their Substance": Creed attributed to St. Athanasius.

[2] See what we have said above (page 17, n. 2) of holiness in the Trinity, and the reason why, according to St. Thomas, the Spirit is called *Holy*.

[3] See Luke 1:35.

ticularly attributed to the Holy Spirit. For an understanding of this, as for an understanding of all that will be said about the Holy Spirit, I must explain to you in a few words what in theology is called *appropriation*.

As you know, there is *in God* but one Mind,[1] one Will, one Power —because there is but one single Divine nature. But there is also a distinction of Persons. This distinction results from the mysterious *operations* that are accomplished *within the heart-life of God*, and from the mutual relationship that derives from these operations. The Father begets the Son, and the Holy Spirit proceeds from the Father and the Son. To "beget," to "be a Father," is the property exclusively of the First Person; to "be Son" is the property personally of the Son, just as "to proceed from the Father and the Son by way of love" is the property personally of the Holy Spirit. These personal properties establish between the Father, the Son and the Holy Spirit a mutual relationship from which the distinction [between the Persons] flows. But aside from these properties and this relationship, all is common to the three Persons and indivisible between them: the same Mind, the same Will, the same Wisdom, the same Power, the same Majesty—because the same indivisible Divine nature is common to the three Persons. That is what we are able to know of the inner operations within God.

As regards the "exterior" works, the actions that are accomplished *outside of God*, whether it be in the material world, like the action of directing every created thing towards its purposed end, or whether it be in the world of souls, like the action of producing grace—these actions are common to the three Divine Persons. Why is that? Because the source of these operations, of these works, of these actions, is the Divine nature, and this nature is, for the three Persons, one and indivisible; the Holy Trinity acts in the world as only one single and unique Cause. But God wills that men recognize and honor not only the Divine Unity, but also the Trinity of Persons. That is why the

[1] [*Translator's note*: French, "*intelligence*," referring to God's knowledge and understanding.]

Church, in the liturgy for example, attributes to one or other of the Divine Persons certain actions which are produced in the world and which, though common to the three Persons, have a special relation to, or a close affinity with, the place (if I can put it so) which that Person occupies within the Blessed Trinity; with the properties that are particular and exclusive to Him.

Thus, the Father being the source, the origin, the mainspring of the other two Persons (without this implying that there is in the Father either hierarchical superiority or priority of time), the works which are produced in the world and by which power is particularly manifested, or in which the character of *origin* reveals itself, are attributed to the Father. Creation, for example—by which God has drawn the universe out of nothing. We sing in the *Credo*: "We believe in God the Father Almighty, Creator of heaven and earth." Are we to suppose that the Father takes a greater part, manifests more power in this work than the Son and the Holy Spirit? No, to believe that would be an error: the Son and the Holy Spirit act just as much as the Father does in the work of creating; for God operates outwardly by the almighty power of God, and that almighty power is common to the three Persons. Why, then, does Holy Church speak in that way? Because *in the Blessed Trinity* the Father is the *First* Person, the mainspring without mainspring, from whom the other two Persons proceed. In that is to be found what is exclusively and personally proper to Him, the property which distinguishes Him from the Son and from the Holy Spirit; and it is so that we may not forget this property that the "exterior" actions which, by affinity of nature, put it into relief are attributed to the Father.

It is the same as that for the Person of the Son. He is, in the Blessed Trinity, the Word who proceeds from the Father by way of Mind; He is the infinite expression of the Divine Thought, and especially is He regarded as Eternal Wisdom. That is why those works in the effecting of which Wisdom especially shines forth are attributed to Him.

It is the same, finally, for the Holy Spirit. What is He within the Blessed Trinity? He is the final completion of the Divine operations, of the life of God in Himself. He closes (so to speak) the cycle of the Divine inner life: within love, He is the finishing perfection. It is His personal property to proceed from both the Father and the Son by way of love. That is why everything that is a work of completion, of perfection, everything that is a work of love, of union and consequently of holiness—for our holiness is measured by the degree of our union with God—is attributed to the Holy Spirit. Is it that He sanctifies more than the Father and the Son? No, the work of our sanctification is common to the three Divine Persons; but, once again, as the work of holiness in a soul is a work of perfecting, of completing, of union, it is attributed to the Holy Spirit, because in this way we more easily remember the personal properties of the Holy Spirit, so as to honor and adore Him in what distinguishes Him from the Father and the Son.

God wishes us, so to speak, to have it as much at heart to honor His Trinity of Persons as to adore His Unity of nature; and that is why He wishes the Church, even in her language, to remind her children, not only that there is but one God, but also that God is in three Persons.

That is what one calls in theology *appropriation*. It has its foundation in Revelation; it is employed by the Church;[1] its aim is to put into relief the attributes proper to each Divine Person. By so putting them into relief it makes us know these properties, it makes us love them more. St. Thomas says it is for the purpose of aiding our faith that the Church—following Revelation in that—adheres to this law of appropriation: "to the manifestation of faith."[2] Throughout the whole of eternity, our life, our beatitude, will be to contemplate God, to love Him, to joy in Him, as He truly is—that is to say, in the Unity of His nature and the Trinity of His Persons. What is there surprising in the

---

[1] In his encyclical letter of May 9, 1897, Leo XIII says that the Church makes use of this procedure *aptissime*: "with eminent aptness."

[2] I, q. XXXIX, a. 7.

fact that God, who predestines us for that life and prepares for us that beatitude, should wish us, even from our time here below, to keep in mind His Divine perfections—equally those of His nature and those of the properties that distinguish the Persons? God is infinite and worthy of praise in His Unity: He is equally so in His Trinity, and the Divine Persons are as wonderful in the Unity of nature they possess in an indivisible way as in the relationship they have among themselves, a relationship that is the basis of the distinction between them.

"Almighty God, eternal God, blessed God, I rejoice in your power, your eternity, your happiness. When shall I see you, O Mainspring who yourself have no mainspring? when shall I see issuing from your heart your Son who is equal to you? when shall I see your Holy Spirit proceeding from your union, perfecting the circle of your fecundity, completing your eternal action?"[1]

2. **Operations of the Holy Spirit** *in Christ.* **Jesus was conceived by the Holy Spirit. Sanctifying grace, virtues and gifts conferred by the Holy Spirit on the soul of Christ. Christ's** *human activity guided by the Holy Spirit.*

YOU WILL HAVE no trouble now in understanding the language of the Scriptures and of the Church when they make known the operations of the Holy Spirit.

To begin with, look at those operations within Our Lord. Let us approach, with reverence, the Divine Person of Christ Jesus, so as to contemplate something of the marvels realized in Him in the Incarnation and since the Incarnation.

As I have told you in explaining this mystery, the Blessed Trinity created a soul that it united with a human body to form thereby one human nature, and united that human nature to the Divine Person of

---

[1] Bossuet, *Preparation for death*, 4th prayer.

the Word. It was the three Divine Persons who combined together to do this ineffable work, though one should add immediately that the work had as its final end the Word alone: the Word—the Son—alone became incarnate.[1] This work, then, is due to the whole Trinity, but is especially attributed to the Holy Spirit; and that is what we say in the Creed: "I believe ... in Jesus Christ our Lord, who was conceived by the Holy Spirit." The Creed does no more than take up the angel's words to the Virgin Mary: "The Holy Spirit shall come upon you, and therefore the Holy Being who shall be born of you shall be called the Son of God."[2]

You will perhaps ask me: why this special attribution to the Holy Spirit? Because, among other reasons which St. Thomas gives,[3] the Holy Spirit is substantial Love, the love of the Father and the Son. Now, although the Redemption through the Incarnation is a work the effecting of which demanded an infinite wisdom, it nevertheless has its first cause in the love God bears for us: "God so loved the world that He gave His only-begotten Son."[4]

And look at how fruitful and wonderful the Holy Spirit's power in Christ is. Not only does the Holy Spirit unite the human nature to the Word, but it is to Him that there is attributed the effusion of sanctifying grace into Jesus's soul.

In Christ Jesus there are two distinct natures, both of them perfect, but united in the Person that embraces them: the Word. This is the "*Grace of union*" which makes the human nature subsist in the Divine Person of the Word. This grace is of an order altogether unique, transcendent and incommunicable. Through it, the humanity of Christ belongs to the Word; it has become the humanity of the true Son of God and the object of the infinite delight of the Eternal Father. But the human nature, though wholly thus united to the Word, is not annihilated and

---

[1] To employ an image given by certain Fathers of the Church: one person putting on his clothes is helped in that work by two other persons; all three combine for the work, for the sought end of the operation, but only one is apparelled. This image is necessarily an imperfect comparison only.

[2] See Luke 1:35.   [3] III, q. XXXII, a. 1.   [4] John 3:16.

does not remain in immobility: it keeps its essence, its integrity, as it does its energies and powers; it is capable of action. Now, it is "*sanctifying grace*" that elevates this human nature, in order that it may be able to act super-naturally.

To continue with the same idea in other terms: the "Grace of union"—hypostatic union—unites the human nature to the Person of the Word, and thus renders Divine the very depths of Christ: Christ *is*, through this Grace of union, a Divine "subject." The role of that "Grace of union," the character of which is unique, stops there. But it is still fitting for this human nature to be also adorned with "sanctifying grace" so as to *operate* divinely in each of its faculties. This sanctifying grace, which is "connatural" to the "Grace of union" (that is to say, derives from the Grace of union in a manner that in a sense is natural) puts the soul of Christ in a state befitting its union with the Word;[1] it sees to it that the human nature—which subsists in the Word by virtue of the "Grace of union"—shall be able to act as befits a soul raised to so eminent a dignity, and be able to produce Divine fruits.

And that is why this sanctifying grace has been given to the soul of Christ not in some measure only, as it is for the elect, but rather carried to its highest degree: "And we saw His glory ... *full of grace*."[2] Well, the effusion of this sanctifying grace into the soul of Christ is attributed to the Holy Spirit.[3]

[1] "The habitual grace of Christ is to be understood as consequent upon the hypostatic union, as splendor is consequent upon the sun": St Thomas, III, q. VII, a. 13.

[2] John 1:14.

[3] Thus, in Christ, the effect of the "Grace of union," which stops once the union of the human nature with the Person of the Word is constituted, is different from the effect of "sanctifying grace" which gives to the human nature—a nature which (even once the union with the Word has been accomplished) remains in its essence and faculties an integral human nature—gives to it the capacity to act supernaturally. It is therefore not a case of something having been employed in duplication, as may appear at first sight, and sanctifying grace in Christ is not superfluous (St Thomas, III, q. 7, a. 1 and 13). Cf. Schwalm, *Le Christ d'après S. Thomas d'Aquin*, ch. II, para. 6. It is to be noted, as well, that the "Grace of union" is met with only in

At the same time, the Holy Spirit diffused within the soul of Jesus the fullness of virtues[1] and the fullness of the Spirit's gifts: "And the Spirit of the Lord shall rest upon Him."[2] Listen to what Isaiah sang when speaking of the Virgin and of Christ who was to be born of her: "And there shall come forth a rod out of the root of Jesse (this rod is the Virgin), and a flower shall rise up out of his root (the flower, Christ). And the Spirit of the Lord shall rest upon Him: the spirit of wisdom and of understanding, the spirit of counsel, and of fortitude, the spirit of knowledge and of piety, and He shall be filled with the spirit of the fear of the Lord."[3]

In remarkable circumstances related by St. Luke, Our Lord applied to Himself [a similar] text from the prophet. You know that at the time of Christ the Jews used to gather in the synagogue on the day of the sabbath; a doctor of the Law, chosen from among those present, used to take the roll of the Scriptures so as to read from it the part of the sacred texts assigned to that day. St. Luke, then, recounts that one sabbath day, at the beginning of His public life, our Divine Savior went into the synagogue at Nazareth. Someone handed to Him the book of the prophet Isaiah, and having unrolled it He found the place where was written: "The Spirit of the Lord is upon me, wherefore He

---

Christ, whereas sanctifying grace is to be found also in the souls of the just. In Christ sanctifying grace is there in its fullness, and it is from this fullness that all receive it, in greater or lesser measure. But it should above all be noted that Christ is not the *adopted* son of God, such as we become through sanctifying grace; He is the Son of God by nature. In us, sanctifying grace sets up the Divine adoption. In Christ, the function of sanctifying grace is to operate in such a way that the human nature of Christ — once having been united to the Person of the Word by the Grace of union and having become, by this same Grace, the humanity of God's own Son — will be able to act in a super-natural manner.

[1] See above, page 50 ff.

[2] See Isa. 11:2. [*Translator's note*: My use of the large initial letter, "Spirit," in this one place, makes the quotation accord with Marmion's similar use in a Latin quotation he gives, and in his French.]   [3] Isa. 11:1-3.

has anointed me to preach the gospel to the poor, He has sent me to heal the contrite of heart, to preach deliverance to the captives ... to preach the acceptable year of the Lord."[1] Having rolled up the book, He gave it back, and sat down; and the eyes of all in the synagogue were fixed upon Him. Then He said to them: "This text is being fulfilled today even as you listen"[2]—you are seeing fulfilled the prediction that was spoken by the prophet. Our Lord made His own the words of Isaiah which compare the action of the Holy Spirit to an anointing.[3] The grace of the Holy Spirit has been poured forth upon Jesus like an oil of gladness that, first, has anointed Him Son of God and Messiah,[4] and then has filled Him with the plenitude of the Spirit's gifts and the abundance of the Divine treasures: God "has anointed you with the oil of gladness above your fellows."[5]

It was at the very moment of the Incarnation that this blest anointing occurred: and it was so as to signify this, to manifest it to the Jews, to proclaim that He is the Messiah, the "Christ" (which is to say, the anointed of the Lord) that the Holy Spirit, in the form of a dove, visibly descended upon Jesus on the day of His baptism, when the Word Incarnate was about to begin His public life. It was by this sign, indeed, that the Christ was meant to be recognized—as His precursor, St. John the Baptist, had declared. The Messiah would be the one "upon whom you will see the Spirit descending."[6]

From that time on, the Evangelists show us, the soul of Christ is in all things guided, and His activity inspired, by the Holy Spirit. It is the Holy Spirit who urges Him forward into the desert where He is to be tempted: "Then Jesus was led into the desert by the Spirit, to be

---

[1] Luke 4:18-19 (Rheims); Isa. 61:1-2.   [2] Luke 4:20-21 (Jerus.)

[3] In the liturgy (Hymn, *Veni Creator Spiritus*), the Holy Spirit is called *Spiritualis unctio*, Spiritual anointing.

[4] [*Translator's note*: As he says in the following paragraph, Marmion refers here to the moment of the Incarnation, when the eternal Son of God became man.]

[5] Ps. 44 (45):8, cf. Acts 10:38: "how God anointed Jesus of Nazareth with the Holy Spirit." Also Matt. 12:18; Jesus's quotation from Isa. 42:1.   [6] John 1:33.

tempted by the devil."[1] After His sojourn in the desert, it is "in the power of the Spirit"—moved by this same Spirit—that He returns to Galilee.[2] Through the action of this Spirit, He casts out devils from the bodies of those possessed;[3] it is under the action of the Holy Spirit that He thrills with joy when He thanks His Father for revealing the Divine secrets to little ones: "In that very hour He rejoiced in the Holy Spirit and said...."[4] Finally, St. Paul tells us that the crowning work of Christ, the one where His love for His Father and for us shone forth particularly, His bloody sacrifice upon the cross for the salvation of the world —it was through being moved by the Holy Spirit that Christ offered it: "who through the Holy Spirit offered Himself unblemished unto God."[5]

What do all these revelations show us? That in Christ, the human activity was guided by the Spirit of Love. The one *who* acts is Christ, the Word Incarnate; all His actions are actions of the unique Person of the Word, in whom the human nature subsists: but it was under the inspiration, by movement of the Holy Spirit that Christ was acting. The human soul of Jesus had, by the grace of the hypostatic union, become the soul of the Word; it was in addition filled with sanctifying grace; and, finally, it acted under the guidance of the Holy Spirit.

And that is why all the actions of Christ Jesus were holy. Certainly His soul is a created one, as everyone's soul is: but it is all-holy, first of all because it is united to the Word. It was thus, as from the first moment of the Incarnation, constituted in a state of union *with a Divine Person*—which makes it the soul, not merely of *a* holy person, but of *the* holy Person par excellence, the very Son of God: "The Holy Being who shall be born of you (said the angel to Mary) shall be called the Son of God."[6] That soul is holy, also, because it has been adorned with sanctifying grace, which makes it capable of acting super-naturally and in a manner worthy of the eminent union that constitutes its

---

[1] Matt. 4:1.   [2] Luke 4:14.   [3] Matt. 12:28.
[4] Luke 10:21.   [5] Heb. 9:14.   [6] Luke 1:35.

inalienable privilege. Finally, that soul is holy because all its actions, all its operations, though being and remaining actions of the one Incarnate Word, are carried out at the movement, under the inspiration, of the Holy Spirit, Spirit of love, Spirit of holiness.

Let us adore these marvels that are produced in Christ. The Holy Spirit renders holy Christ's being, renders holy His activity; and because, in Christ, this holiness attains the supreme degree, because all human holiness will be modeled upon it and must be a tributary-stream of it, the Church sings every day: "You alone are holy, Jesus Christ." You alone are holy, because you alone are by your incarnation the very Son of God. You alone are holy, because you possess sanctifying grace in its fullness, in order to distribute it to us. You alone are holy, because your soul was infinitely docile to the impetus of the Spirit of Love, who inspired and ruled all your movements, all your acts, and rendered them pleasing to your Father: "And the Spirit of the Lord shall rest upon Him."[1]

3. Operations of the Holy Spirit *in the Church.* The Holy Spirit, soul of the Church.

THESE MARVELS that operated in Christ under the inspiration of the Spirit are reproduced in us, at least in part, when we let ourselves be guided by this Divine Spirit. But do we possess this Spirit? Yes, without any doubt.

Before ascending to heaven, Jesus promised His disciples that He would pray His Father that the Holy Spirit be given to them. This gift of the Spirit to our souls He made the object of a special request: "And I will ask the Father and He will give you another Advocate ... the Spirit of truth."[2] And you know how this prayer of Jesus was granted,

---

[1] Isa. 11:2.   [1] John 14:16-17.

with what abundance the Holy Spirit was given to the apostles on the day of Pentecost. That marvel marked, so to speak, the Divine Spirit's taking possession of the Church, Christ's mystical body. We can say that if Christ is chief, is *head*, of the Church, the Holy Spirit is its soul. It is the Holy Spirit who guides and inspires this Church, keeping it, as Jesus said, in the truth of Christ and in the light that He has brought us: "He will teach you all things, and bring to your mind whatever I have said to you."[1]

This action of the Holy Spirit in the Church is diverse and multifarious. I have told you above that Christ was consecrated Messiah and High Priest, Bridge of man to God, by one ineffable anointing of the Holy Spirit. And all those whom Christ wills to make sharers of His priestly power, so as to continue here below His sanctifying mission, are made such by an anointing of the Holy Spirit. "Receive the Holy Spirit";[2] "The Holy Spirit has placed you as bishops, to rule the Church of God";[3] it is the Holy Spirit who speaks through their lips and gives value to their testimony.[4] In the same way the authentic means—the sacraments—that Christ has handed down to His priests in order to transmit life to souls, are never conferred without the Holy Spirit being invoked. It is the Holy Spirit who makes fruitful the waters of baptism:[5] "Unless a man be born again of water and the Spirit, he cannot enter into the kingdom of God";[6] God, says St. Paul, saves us "by means of the cleansing water of rebirth and by renewing us with the Holy Spirit."[7] In Confirmation the Holy Spirit is "given," to be the anointing that is to make the Christian a valiant soldier of Jesus Christ; the Spirit it is who gives us in this sacrament the fullness of the state of Christian, and invests us with the strength of Christ. To the Holy

---

[1] John 14:26. [2] John 20:22. [3] Acts 20:28.
[4] John 15:26; Acts 15:28; Acts 20:22-28.
[5] See, later on in this book, the talk on baptism. [6] John 3:5.
[7] Titus 3:5 (Jerus.)

Spirit—as the Eastern liturgy shows us especially—is attributed the changing of the bread and wine into the body and blood of Jesus Christ. Sins are forgiven, in the Sacrament of Penance, by the Holy Spirit.[1] In Extreme Unction He is entreated that His grace may cure the sick person of his debility and of his sins. In Matrimony, the Holy Spirit is invoked in order that the Christian spouses may be able, by their lives, to imitate the union which exists between Christ and the Church.

You see how lively, penetrating, incessant, the Holy Spirit's action in the Church is? Yes, He is indeed, as St. Paul said, "the Spirit of life"[2] —a truth the Church has taken up in her *Credo* when she sings of her faith in the life-giving Spirit: "I believe in the Holy Spirit, the Lord, *the Giver of life.*" He is truly the soul of the Church,[3] He is the vital principle that animates the super-natural body, that governs it, that unites all its members one with another and gives them vigor and super-natural beauty.

In the first days of the Church's existence this action was much more visible than in our own day. That was part of the designs of Providence, for the Church had to be able to establish herself solidly, by manifesting to the eyes of the pagan world the shining signs of her Founder's divinity, of her origin and her mission. These signs—fruits of the outpouring of the Holy Spirit—were wonderful; we are amazed when we read the account of the Church's beginnings. The Spirit descended upon those whom baptism made disciples of Christ, and filled them with charisms as numerous as they were astonishing: graces of miracles, gifts of prophecy, gifts of tongues, and so many other extraordinary favors accorded to the first Christians, in order that it

---

[1] John 20:22-23. "It is a property of the Holy Spirit that He be a gift of the Father and the Son; and, moreover, that the forgiveness of sins be effected by the Holy Spirit as by a gift of God": St Thomas, II, q. III, a. 8, ad 3. The Missal likewise says: "The Holy Spirit Himself is forgiveness of all our sins": Feria III, after Pentecost. See also the postcommunion of the prayer *pro petitione lacrymarum* (*Orationes diversae*).

[2] Rom. 8:2 (Rheims).   [3] See the note at the end of this talk (page 163).

might be recognized that the Church, adorned with such an abundance of gifts so remarkable, was truly the Church of Jesus.

Read St. Paul's first letter to the Corinthians, and see the delight with which the great apostle, who himself was a witness to these marvels, enumerates them. At almost every enumeration of these diverse gifts he adds that it is one and the same Spirit who is the source of them, because He is Love, and love is the mainspring of all the gifts. "In the same Spirit...."[1] It is the Spirit who makes fruitful this Church that Jesus has redeemed by His blood and has willed to be holy and without blemish.[2]

4. Action of the Holy Spirit *in the souls* He inhabits.

IF THE EXTRAORDINARY and visible character of the effects of the workings of the Holy Spirit has in large part disappeared, the action of this Divine Spirit ever continues in souls, and is no less wonderful for being mainly interior.

I have told you that holiness for us is nothing other than the complete flowering, the full development, of that first grace which is our Divine adoption, a grace which is given at baptism (as we shall see later) and by which we become children of God and brethren of Christ Jesus. To draw from this initial grace of adoption all the treasures and riches it contains and that God causes to flow from it, to draw them in order that they bear fruit—such is the very substance of all holiness. Christ, as I told you as well, is the model of our divine sonship; moreover He has merited that it be given us, and He Himself has established the means by which it comes to us.

But bringing that grace into being within us, now that Jesus has made it possible for us, is the work of the Blessed Trinity. It is, however,

---

[1] 1 Cor. 12:9.   [2] Eph. 5:25-27.

attributed especially to the Holy Spirit, and not without grounds. Why is that? Always for the same reason. This grace of adoption is purely gratuitous and has its source in *love*: "See how the Father has shown his love towards us; that we should be counted as God's sons, should be his sons."[1] Now, in the adorable Trinity, the Holy Spirit is substantial Love. That is why St. Paul tells us that the "charity of God"—he means the grace that makes us children of God—"is poured forth in our hearts by the Holy Spirit who has been given to us."[2]

And from the time that grace is infused in us by baptism, the Holy Spirit dwells in us with the Father and the Son. Our Lord says: "If any one love me ... my Father will love him, and we will come to him, and will make our *abode* with him."[3] Grace makes our soul a temple of the Blessed Trinity; our soul, adorned with grace, is truly an abode of God. He dwells in us not only as He does in all things, by His essence and His power whereby He sustains and preserves every created being in existence,[4] but in a way that is altogether particular and altogether intimate, as His being the object of super-natural knowledge and love. And because grace unites us to God in that way and is the mainspring and the measure of our charity, it is especially the Holy Spirit who is said to "dwell" in us[5]—not as if it were in a manner personal to Him to the exclusion of the Father and the Son, but because He proceeds from love and because it is He who unites the Father and the Son. He "shall abide with you, and shall be in you," says Our Lord.[6] Every individual, the sinner even, possesses in him still the vestiges of Divine power and wisdom. It is only the just, only those in a state of grace, who partake of the super-natural charity that is like an exclusive sign of the Holy Spirit. That is why St. Paul, speaking to the faithful, says to them: "Do

---

[1] 1 John 3:1 (Knox).　　　[2] Rom. 5:5.　　　[3] John 14:23 (Rheims).

[4] [*Translator's note*: See note 5 on page 287.]

[5] See the fine book by Fr. B. Froget, OP, *De l'habitation du Saint-Esprit dans les âmes justes, d'après la doctrine de S. Thomas.*　　　[6] John 14:17 (Rheims).

you not know that your members are the temple of the Holy Spirit, who is in you, whom you have from God?"[1]

And what is it that He does in our souls, this Divine Spirit? For, being God, being Love, He does not stay inactive. First of all, He gives testimony to us that we are children of God: "The Spirit Himself gives testimony to our spirit that we are sons of God";[2] He is the Spirit of love, the Spirit of holiness, who wishes—because He loves us—to make us have part in this holiness, so that we may be true and worthy children of God.

With sanctifying grace, which (so to speak) deifies our nature and makes it capable of acting super-naturally, the Holy Spirit puts within us strengths, "habits," which raise to the divine level the powers and faculties of our souls: these are the super-natural virtues—above all, the theological virtues of faith, hope and charity, which strictly are the virtues characteristic of, specific to, our status as children of God; and then, the infused moral virtues which aid us in the struggle against the obstacles, within us, that oppose themselves to the divine life.

Finally, there are the *gifts* of the Holy Spirit. Let us pause for a few moments to consider them. Our Divine Savior, who is our model, received them, as we have seen—but in an eminent and transcendent measure. The measure of the gifts within *us* is limited. And yet, that measure still remains so fruitful that it produces marvels of holiness in souls where these gifts abound. Why is that? Because it is above all through these gifts that our state of adoption is particularly perfected, as we are about to see.

What, then, are the gifts of the Holy Spirit? They are, as the name indicates, gratuitous benefits which the Holy Spirit distributes to us with sanctifying grace and the infused virtues. The Church in her liturgy tells us that the Holy Spirit is Himself the Gift par excellence: "best Gift of

[1] 1 Cor. 6:19.   [2] Rom. 8:16.

God above";[1] for He comes within us, as from the time of our baptism, to give Himself as an object of love. But this Gift is Divine and living: He is a guest who, full of munificence, wishes to enrich the soul that receives Him. Being Himself the uncreated Gift, He is the source of the created gifts, which, with sanctifying grace and the infused virtues, complete the putting of a soul into the state of living super-naturally in a perfect manner.

Even as armed with grace and virtues, our souls are not, in fact, re-established in that original integrity Adam was in before he sinned. Reason, itself subject to error, sees its sovereign power disputed by the lower appetites and the senses. The will is open to failures. From that state, what follows? That in the most important of all work, the work of our sanctification, we are in need of being aided constantly and directly by the Holy Spirit. He provides that aid by His inspirations, which all go to the finishing, the making perfect, the completing, of our holiness. And, so that His inspirations may be well received by us, He Himself puts into our souls dispositions that make us tractable and pliable: these are the gifts of the Holy Spirit.[2]

The "gifts" are not, then, the inspirations of the Holy Spirit themselves, but the dispositions that make us obey these inspirations promptly and easily.

By these gifts, the soul is rendered capable of being moved and steered in the direction of its super-natural perfection, in the direction of divine sonship. It possesses, as it were, a divine instinct of super-natural things. The soul which, by virtue of these dispositions, lets itself be guided by the Holy Spirit, acts in total sureness as befits a

---

[1] Hymn, *Veni Creator Spiritus*.

[2] In Christ Jesus, the presence of the gifts of the Holy Spirit does not flow from the necessity of aiding weakness of reason and will, Christ not being subject to any error, to any failing. These gifts have been bestowed on the soul of Jesus because they constitute a perfection and it is fitting that every perfection reside in Christ. We have seen above the influence the Holy Spirit exercised, by His gifts, in the soul of Jesus.

child of God. In all its spiritual life it thinks and acts *with a super-natural "precision,"* if I can thus express it.[1] The soul that is faithful to the inspirations of the Holy Spirit possesses a super-natural tact which makes it think and act with facility and promptitude as a child of God. You see at once, do you not, that the gifts place the soul, and dispose it to move, in an atmosphere where *everything* is super-natural, where nothing of the natural is mixed with it, so to speak. By the gifts, the Holy Spirit keeps, and reserves to Himself, the command of all our super-natural conduct.

And that is a most important point for our souls, our holiness being of an order that is essentially super-natural. By the virtues, the soul in a state of grace acts super-naturally, it is true; but it acts in a way conforming to its rational and human condition, as also of its own motion, on its own initiative. By the gifts, it is disposed to act directly and solely under Divine impetus (whilst keeping, of course, its liberty, manifested by acquiescence in the inspiration from on high), and this in a way which does not always square with its rational, natural, manner of seeing and viewing things. The influence of the gifts is, then, in a very real sense, superior to that of the virtues,[2] which doubtless they do not replace, but the operations of which they complement marvelously. For example, the gifts of understanding and of knowledge perfect the exercise of the virtue of faith; it is this that explains why simple souls, without education, but upright, docile to the inspirations of the Holy Spirit, have on spiritual matters a certainty, a comprehension, a penetration that are sometimes astonishing, have a spiritual instinct which warns them of error and makes them hold to revealed

---

[1] The gifts are, as it were, a person's perfections by which he is disposed to that which responds properly to the instigation of the Holy Spirit": St Thomas, I-II, q. LXVIII, a. 3.

[2] "The gifts are to be distinguished from the virtues in this: that, in relation to acts, it is in a human way that the virtues perfect; but the gifts do so in a way which is beyond the human": St Thomas, *Sent.* III, dist. XXXIV, q. 1, a. 1.

truth with a singular sureness that keeps them sheltered from all doubt. Where does that come from? From study? from profound examination of the truths of their faith? No—from the Holy Spirit, from the Spirit of Truth who, by the gift of understanding or of knowledge, perfects their virtue of faith.[1]

As you see, the gifts constitute for the soul a perfection of great price, because of their exclusively super-natural character. They complete the bringing to perfection of that wonderful, super-natural, organism by which God calls our souls to live by divine life. Accorded to every soul who is in a state of grace, in a measure greater or lesser in scope, the gifts remain there in a state of permanency, so long as we do not drive out, by mortal sin, the Divine Guest who is their source. Ever able to grow, they extend—spread out more—into the whole of our super-natural life, which they render extremely fruitful, because through them our souls find themselves under the direct action, and under the immediate influence, of the Holy Spirit. Now, the Holy Spirit, with the Father and the Son, is God; He loves us with an unutterable love; He wishes us to be holy; His inspirations, all with goodness and love as their origin, have no other object than to fashion us into the greatest possible resemblance to Jesus. And that is why, though it may not be their special and exclusive role, the gifts dispose us even to those heroic acts by which holiness is powerfully manifested.

How ineffably good is the goodness of our God, who equips us, so carefully and so richly, with everything necessary for us to arrive at Him! And is it not slighting the Divine Guest of our souls if we doubt His goodness and His love, if we lack confidence in His liberalities, His munificence, or show ourselves careless of profiting from them?

---

[1] "The special reason for the gifts is that through them a person may act in a way which is above the human": *Sent.* III, dist. XXXV, q. 2, a. 3.

5. The doctrine of the *gifts of the Holy Spirit*, in more detail.

LET US NOW say a word on each of the seven gifts. This number does not constitute a limit, for the action of God is infinite: but, rather, like many other biblical numbers, it signifies a plenitude. We shall simply follow the order indicated by Isaiah in his messianic prophecy. We shall not seek to establish any gradation or well-marked relationship between the gifts; we shall endeavor to say, in so far as we are able to, what it is special to each of them.

The first gift indicated is that of *wisdom*. What does "wisdom" signify here? It is a "flavorsome knowledge of spiritual things,"[1] a super-natural gift for knowing or esteeming Divine things through the *spiritual taste* with which the Holy Spirit inspires us in this matter. It is a flavorsome knowledge, intimate and profound, of the things of God. We ask for it in the prayer for the Feast of Pentecost itself: "Grant us in the same Spirit to relish what is right." *Sapere*, "to relish," is to have, not just the knowledge but the *taste* of heavenly and super-natural things. It is not—far from it—what one would call a devotion felt by the senses, but a spiritual *experience* of the Divine, that the Holy Spirit wills to produce in us. It is our response to "Taste, and see that the Lord is sweet."[2] This gift makes us prefer, without hesitation, the blessedness of serving God to all the joys of earth; it is this gift that makes the soul say: "How lovely are your tabernacles, O Lord of hosts! For better is one day in your courts," above thousands of years without you.[3] But in order to feel like that, one must carefully clear away all that draws us towards illicit delights of the senses.

The gift of *understanding* makes us get deeper into the truths of the faith. St. Paul tells us that "the Spirit searches all things, yes, the deep things of God,"[4] making them known to whomsoever He pleases.[5] Not

---

[1] [*Translator's note*: *Sapida cognitio*, a sapid knowledge: not one merely of the intellect, but one affecting a person's soul in a way that is analogous to good food satisfying the bodily taste-buds.]   [2] Ps. 33 (34):9.   [3] Ps. 83 (84), vv. 2, 11.
[4] 1 Cor. 2:10 (Rheims).   [5] John 3:8.

that this gift diminishes the incomprehensibility of the mysteries or does away with faith, but it gets us further into the mystery than does the simple acquiescence of faith; it bears upon the appropriateness or the grandeur of the mysteries, the relationship between them, their connections with our super-natural life. It has also as its object the truths contained in the sacred books, and it is this gift which seems to have been accorded in special measure to those who, in the Church, have shone out by the profundity of their doctrine and whom we call "Doctors of the Church." But every baptized soul possesses within itself this precious gift. You read a text of Holy Scripture; you may have read and re-read it many a time without its having really struck your mind: but one day, all of a sudden, a light flashes out, so to speak, illuminating to its very depths the truth stated in that text. That truth becomes then, for you, full of clarity—and often a mainspring of super-natural life and action. Is it through reflection on your part that you have arrived at this result? No, it is a light, an intuition from the Holy Spirit who, by the gift of understanding, makes you penetrate further into the inner and deep meaning of the revealed truths, so that you may hold fast to them more.

By the gift of *counsel*, the Holy Spirit answers this prayer of the soul: "Lord, what will you have me do?"[1] It saves us from all precipitancy, all want of taking serious thought, but especially from all presumption, something which is so dangerous on the spiritual road. A soul that wants simply to stand on its own, that worships its own personality—such a soul acts without consulting God through prayer, it acts in practice as though God were not its heavenly Father from whom all light comes: "Every ... perfect gift is from above, coming down from the Father of lights."[2] Look at our Divine Savior: He says that the Son—that is, He Himself—does nothing but what He may see being done by the Father: "The Son can do nothing of Himself, but only what He sees the Father doing."[3] The soul of Jesus gazed upon the

---

[1] Acts 9:6.　　　[2] James 1:17.　　　[3] John 5:19.

Father to see in Him the model for His own works, and it was the Spirit of Counsel who showed Him what the Father desired. That is why everything Our Lord did was pleasing to His Father: "I do always the things that are pleasing to Him."[1] That is the disposition whereby a child of God is in a position to judge things according to principles that are above human wisdom. Sometimes natural prudence, always limited, points to acting in such and such a way; but, by the gift of counsel, the Holy Spirit shows higher principles of conduct that ought to direct the actions of a child of God.

It is not always enough for us to *know* God's good pleasure. Because of our fallen nature, we often need strength to carry out what God requires of us. It is the Holy Spirit who, by the gift of *fortitude*, sustains us in moments that are particularly difficult. There are some pusillanimous souls who fear trials in the interior life. It is impossible that such trials will not make an appearance; they are deeper, even, the higher God calls us. But let us fear nothing, the Spirit of Fortitude is with us: "He shall abide with you, and shall be in you."[2] Like the Apostles on the day of Pentecost we shall, through the Holy Spirit, be clothed with strength from up above, "power from on high,"[3] to accomplish the Divine will generously, to "obey God rather than men" in the way the disciples did,[4] should the same choice fall to us; to bear valiantly the adversities we encounter in measure as we draw near to God. That is why St. Paul prayed so ardently for his dear flock, the faithful of Ephesus, that the Spirit might grant them the strength and the inner firmness they needed in order to advance in perfection.[5] The Holy Spirit says to one whom He fills with strength what God said to Moses when the latter took fright at the mission the Lord had entrusted to him, that of delivering the Hebrew people from the yoke of the Pharaohs: "*I will be with you*"[6]—"Do not be afraid, I will be with you." Such a one is strong with the very strength of God. It is this

---

[1] John 8:29.   [2] John 14:17 (Rheims).   [3] Luke 24:49.
[4] Acts 5:29.   [5] Eph. 3:16.   [6] Exod. 3:12.

strength that makes martyrs, sustains virgins. The world is astonished to see them so courageous because it imagines that they find their strength in themselves, whereas they draw it from God alone.

The gift of *knowledge* makes us see created things in a super-natural way, as only a child of God can see them. There are many ways of considering what is in us and around us. A non-believer and a holy soul contemplate nature, the creation, in ways that are quite different. The sceptic has only a purely natural knowledge, however extensive, however deep it may be. The child of God sees the creation in the light of the Holy Spirit; it appears to him as a work of God in which His eternal perfections are reflected. This gift makes us know the things of creation, and of ourselves, from God's point of view; it makes us know our super-natural end and the means of attaining it, but with intuitions that preserve us from the false maxims of the world and the suggestions of the spirit of darkness.

The gifts of piety and of fear complement each other. The gift of *piety* is one of the most precious of gifts, because it conduces directly to governing the attitude we ought to preserve in our relations with God; a mixture of adoration, respect, reverence towards a majesty that is Divine; love, trust, tenderness, perfect abandon, and holy liberty before Him who is our Father in heaven. Far from the one excluding the other, these two feelings, piety and fear, can be allied perfectly; but it is the Holy Spirit who will teach us in what measure the two feelings harmonize. Just as, in God, love and justice do not exclude each other, so in our attitude as children of God there is a mixture of unutterable reverence which makes us prostrate ourselves before Sovereign Majesty, and of loving tenderness that carries us in all fervor of heart towards the ineffable goodness of the heavenly Father. It is the Holy Spirit who governs these two feelings within us. The gift of piety bears another fruit: that of reassuring those timid souls (one does find them) who in their dealings with God are afraid of making mistakes in the "formulas" of their praying. That is a scruple the Holy Spirit dispels when one listens to His inspirations. He is "the Spirit of Truth";[1] and if the fact, as St. Paul says, is that "we do not know what we should pray for as we ought," the Spirit is within us, to help us; He prays in an ineffable manner which makes us cry out to and be heard by God.[2]

Finally, there is the gift of *fear*. It seems strange, does it not, to find the following words in the prophecy of Isaiah about the gifts of the Spirit poured upon the soul of Christ: "And He shall be filled with the spirit of the fear of the Lord"[3]—filled with the spirit of *fear*. How does that come into it? How can Christ, the Son of God, be filled with fear of God? It is because there are two kinds of fear of God: the fear which only considers the punishment due to sin—that is a servile fear, one that lacks nobility, though it is not always lacking in usefulness. Then there is the fear that makes us avoid sin because it offends God— that is filial fear: but it remains imperfect so long as the thought of punishment is mixed with it. It goes without saying that neither this imperfect fear nor servile fear found any place in the soul—the alto- gether holy soul—of Christ. Only perfect fear was there, reverential fear, the fear the angelic powers have before the infinite perfection of God—"*tremunt potestates*," "the angelic powers hold in awe";[4] that fear which expresses itself in adoration and is altogether holy: "The fear of the Lord is holy, enduring for ever and ever."[5] If we could have gazed upon the humanity of Jesus, we would have seen it lost in rever- ence before the Word to whom it is united. It is this reverence that the Holy Spirit puts in our souls; He keeps it there, but by mingling it, through the gift of piety, with that sentiment of love and filial tender- ness which results from our Divine adoption and which makes us cry out to God: "Father!" This gift of piety imprints in us, as in Jesus, that propensity to refer everything to our Father.

---

[1] John 16:13. [2] Rom. 8:26-27. [3] Isa. 11:3.
[4] Preface of the Mass. [5] Ps. 18 (19):10.

Such are the gifts of the Divine Spirit: I have already told you that they perfect the virtues, by disposing us to act with a super-natural sureness which constitutes in us, as it were, a divine instinct for heavenly things. By these gifts, which He himself puts in us to make us teachable, the Holy Spirit makes our status of child of God come to full bloom: "Whoever are led by the Spirit of God, they are the sons of God."[1]

Therefore, when we let ourselves be guided by movement of this Spirit of Love, when in measure with our weakness we are constantly faithful to His holy inspirations, to those inspirations which carry us towards God, towards what is pleasing to Him, the result is that our soul acts *fully* under a sense of its Divine adoption; and then the soul produces those fruits which at one and the same time are the achieved object of the Holy Spirit's action within us and also, by their sweetness, are for us like an advance reward of our fidelity to that action. These fruits, as listed by St. Paul, are: charity, joy, peace, patience, kindness, goodness, forbearance, gentleness, trust, modesty, continence and chastity.[2] These fruits, all worthy of the Spirit of love and holiness, are also worthy of our Heavenly Father, who finds in them His glory—"In this is my Father glorified; that you bring forth very much fruit";[3] and worthy, finally, of Christ Jesus who has merited them for us and to whom the Holy Spirit unites us: "he who abides in me, and I in him, he bears much fruit."[4]

At the Feast of the Tabernacles, one of the most glittering Jewish solemnities, Our Lord was in Jerusalem; and it was then, in the middle of the throng, that He cried: "If any man is thirsty, let him come to me! Let the man come and drink who believes in me! As scripture says,

[1] Rom. 8:14.

[2] Gal. 5:22-23. [*Translator's note*: Marmion gives a list of twelve fruits; other versions list nine. Knox's note is: "The Greek only mentions nine of the Twelve Fruits.... It is possible that the Latin version has accidentally included, in some cases, two renderings of the same Greek word."]   [3] John 15:8 (Rheims).   [4] John 15:5.

'From His breast shall flow fountains of living water.'"[1] And St. John adds: "He was speaking of the Spirit which those who believed in Him"—Christ—"were to receive."[2] The Holy Spirit, whom Christ has merited to send us, and whom He as the Word does indeed send us, is the wellspring, the source, within us of those rivers of living water, of the grace which irrigates us unto our life in eternity;[3] that is to say, which causes us to bear fruits of eternal life. Pending the supreme bliss, these waters make joyful the city of the souls they water: "The stream of the river makes the city of God joyful."[4] Whence St. Paul's comment that to all faithful souls, those who believe in Christ: "One Spirit was given to us all to drink."[5] That is why the liturgy, echoing the teaching of Jesus and of the apostle, makes us invoke the Holy Spirit—who is also the Spirit of Jesus—as a "fount of life": *Fons vivus*," "the living Spring."[6]

6. *Our devotion* to the Holy Spirit: invoking Him, being faithful to His inspirations.

SUCH, THEN, is the action of the Holy Spirit in the Church, in our souls. Like the Divine Source from which it emanates, this action is holy and it aims at making us holy. What will our devotion to this Spirit, who dwells in us since the time of our baptism and whose power within us is so deep and so efficacious of its nature, now be?

First of all, we ought often to *invoke* Him. Like the Father and the Son, the Holy Spirit is God: He, like them, wants us to be holy. Moreover, it is part of the Divine plan that we should address ourselves to the Holy Spirit just as much as we address ourselves to the Father and the

---

[1] John 7:37-38 (Jerus.)   [2] John 7:39 (Jerus.)   [3] "In this way, moreover, the streams are waters of life because they are in continuance of their source, that is to say, the indwelling Holy Spirit": St Thomas, *Tract. in Johann.*, VII, lect. 5.
[4] Ps. 45 (46):5.   [5] 1 Cor. 12:13 (Jerus.)   [6] Hymn, *Veni, Creator Spiritus.*

Son, to whom He, the Spirit, is equal in power and goodness. On this, the Church is our guide. She closes the cycle of solemnities in celebration of the mysteries of Christ with the feast of the sending of the Holy Spirit to us—Pentecost. She has wonderful prayers, aspirations full of ardor, such as the *Veni, Sancte Spiritus,* asking the Divine Spirit for grace. We ought often to have recourse to Him: "O Infinite Love, you who proceed from the Father and the Son, give me a spirit of adoption, teach me to act always as a true child of God. Dwell in me, make me dwell in you, so that I may love as you love. I am nothing without you:

> *If you take your grace away,*
> *Nothing pure in man will stay;*

I am worth nothing, but keep me united to you, fill me with your love, so that through you I may stay united to the Father and to the Son." Let us ask Him often for an ever-greater share in His gifts, the *Sacrum septenarium*, His "seven-fold grace." We ought also to *thank* Him, to render humble thanksgiving to Him. If Christ Jesus has merited all for us, it is through His Spirit that He guides and directs us,[1] it is from the magnificent liberality of His Spirit, that we receive those abundant graces that, little by little, make us resemble Jesus. How can we fail to show, often, our gratitude to this Guest whose presence within us—wholly one of efficacious love—showers benefits so rich upon us? *There* is the first homage we ought to render to this Spirit who, with the Father and the Son, is God—to believe, with a faith that is put into practice and makes us have recourse to Him, to believe in His divinity, His power, His goodness.

[1] When we say that Christ governs us *through* His Spirit, we are not saying that the Holy Spirit is an instrument—He is God, Cause of grace. What rather we are indicating thereby is that the Holy Spirit is the Wellspring (for us) of grace, He Himself proceeding from a Wellspring, from the Father and the Son. Jesus Christ, as the Word, sends us the Holy Spirit (St Thomas, I, q. XLV, a. 6, ad 2).

Next, let us see to it that we *do not impede His action* within us. "Do not extinguish the Spirit,"[1] says St. Paul; and again: "Do not grieve the Holy Spirit of God."[2] As I have told you, the action of the Spirit in a soul is delicate, because it is an action of completing, of perfecting; these are touches of an infinite delicacy. We must see to it that we do not impede the action of this Spirit by our want of serious thought, by our wilful distractions, by our heedlessness or intentional resistance, by an ungoverned attachment to our own way of thinking: "Be not wise in your own conceits."[3] In the things of God, do not trust in human wisdom, for then the Holy Spirit will leave you to this natural prudence; and you know what St. Paul says *that* is in the eyes of God: "foolishness."[4] This action of the Holy Spirit is perfectly compatible with those weaknesses that so often slip out from us before we know it, and that we then regret. It is compatible with our frailties, our human servitudes, our difficulties, our temptations. Our native poverty does not repel the Holy Spirit: He is *Pater Pauperum*, the "Father of the Poor," as the Church calls Him.[5]

What *is* incompatible with His action is intentional resistance to His inspirations, resistance coldly allowed in. Why is that? In the first place, because the Spirit proceeds from love, He is Love itself, but nonetheless, though His love for us is immeasurable, though His action is infinitely powerful, the Holy Spirit is a sovereign respecter of our liberty and in no way does violence to our will. We have the sad privilege of being able to resist Him, and nothing so thwarts His love as obstinate resistance to His advances. Next, it is above all by His gifts that the Holy Spirit guides us along the path of holiness and makes us live as children of God. Now, in the gifts, it is the Holy Spirit who urges and determines the soul to act: "In the gifts of the Holy Spirit, the human mind does not have power over itself as moving, but

---

[1] 1 Thess. 5:19. [2] Eph. 4:30. [3] Rom. 12:16. [4] 1 Cor. 3:19.
[5] Sequence, *Veni, Creator Spiritus.*

rather as moved,"[1] and yet the soul's part is doubtless not to remain entirely passive, but rather to dispose itself for the Divine inspiration, to listen to it, to be promptly faithful to it. Nothing so blunts the action of the Holy Spirit within us as our being rigid, unbending, towards those inner movements that bear us towards God, that urge us to the observance of His commandments, to the carrying out of His good pleasure, to charity, humility, trust. A "no," replied voluntarily, a deliberate "no"—even in little things—impedes the operation of the Holy Spirit within us; His action becomes less strong, rarer, and the soul then remains in an ordinary degree, at a mediocre level, of holiness; its super-natural life lacks intensity: "Do not grieve the Spirit of God."

And if those wilful, deliberate, resistances, coldly allowed in—if they multiply, become frequent, habitual, then the Holy Spirit is silent. The soul, left to itself then, without guide and without interior support on the path of salvation and perfection, is very near to becoming a prey of the prince of darkness; and that is the death of charity: "Do not extinguish the Spirit." Do not extinguish the Holy Spirit, for He is like a fire of love burning in our souls.[2]

Let us then, instead, in the measure of our weakness but with generosity, stay faithful to the "Spirit of truth"—who is also the Spirit of sanctification. Let us be souls who move promptly beneath the touch of this Spirit. If we let ourselves be guided by Him, He will cause there to come to full bloom in us that Divine grace of super-natural adoption which the Father has willed for us and the Son has merited for us. What profound joy, what interior liberty too, is experienced by a soul that is thus delivered up to the action of the Holy Spirit! This Divine Spirit will cause us to bear fruits of holiness, fruits pleasing to God. Divine Artist—"Finger of God's right hand," He will, with touches of infinite delicacy, complete within us the work of Jesus; or

---

[1] St Thomas, II-II, q. LII, a. 2, ad 1.

[2] "The Living Fire," hymn *Veni, Creator Spiritus*; "Come, O Holy Spirit, fill the hearts of thy faithful; and kindle in them the fire of thy love," Mass of Pentecost.

rather, He will form Jesus in us, as He formed the holy humanity of Jesus, in order that, through His working, we may reproduce in us, for the glory of the Eternal Father, the features of that divine sonship we have in Christ Jesus.[1]

NOTE[2]

The Holy Spirit is truly the soul of the Church[3]

When we say that the Holy Spirit is the soul of the Church, we obviously do not mean to say that He is the form of the Church as the soul is, in us, the form of the body. Taking things from that point of view, it would be more exact theologically to say that the soul of the Church is sanctifying grace (with the infused virtues which necessarily come in its train). Grace is, indeed, the wellspring of super-natural life, the wellspring that renders alive with divine life the members belonging to the body of the Church. However, even then, the analogy between grace and the [human] soul is only an imperfect one, but this is not the time to bring out the necessary distinctions.

When we say that the Holy Spirit, and not grace, is the soul of the Church, we take cause as effect. In other words, the Holy Spirit produces sanctifying grace, and we therefore wish by this expression (Holy Spirit = soul of the Church) to point to the influence—an interior, life-giving and "unifying" influence (if one can so express it)—that the Holy Spirit exercises in the Church. This way of speaking is perfectly legitimate; it has in its favor the opinions of several Fathers of the Church, such as St. Augustine: "That which is the soul in our body, the Holy Spirit is in the body of Christ, which is the Church" (*Sermo* CLXXXVII, *de tempore*). A good many modern theologians speak in the same way, and Leo XIII has hallowed this expression in his encyclical on the Holy Spirit. It is interesting to note that St. Thomas, in order to indicate the intimate influence of the Holy Spirit in the Church, compares it to the influence the heart exercises in the human organism (III, q. VIII, a. 1, ad 3).

[1] St Thomas, III, q. XXXII, a. 1.   [2] By Marmion.   [3] See page 146.

BOOK TWO

THE CHRISTIAN LIFE

CHAPTER ONE

FAITH IN JESUS CHRIST,
FOUNDATION OF THE CHRISTIAN LIFE

INTRODUCTION: Faith, *primary attitude* of the soul and *foundation* of the super-natural life.

IN the preceding talks, which constitute an overall account, I have endeavored to show you the dispensation of the Divine designs considered in itself.

We saw the eternal plan of our adoptive predestination in Jesus Christ; the carrying of that plan into effect by the Incarnation—Christ, Son of the Father, being at the same time our model, our redemption and our life; and, finally, the mission of the Church which, under the action of the Holy Spirit, continues here below the sanctifying work of the Savior.

The Divine figure of Christ dominates the whole of this plan: the eternal thoughts are fixed upon Him: He is the *Alpha*, He is the *Omega*, the first letter of the alphabet and the last. Before His coming, figures, symbols, rites and prophecies all lead towards Him. After, everything refers back and is related to Him; He is truly *at the center of the Divine plan*.

He is therefore also *at the center of the super-natural life*, as we have seen. That which is above the natural is first encountered in Him—the Man-God, a perfect humanity indissolubly united to a Divine Person; possessing the fullness of grace and of heavenly treasures, and meriting by His Passion and death to be the universal dispenser of these.

He is the Way, and the only way, of reaching the Eternal Father; outside that way one is off-course: "No one comes to the Father but through me."[1] Outside of that foundation pre-established by God, nothing is stable: "For other foundation no one can lay, but that which has been laid, which is Christ Jesus."[2] Outside of that Redeemer and of faith in His merits, there is no salvation at all, still less any holiness: "*Neither* is there salvation *in any other*. For there is no other name under heaven given to men by which we must be saved."[3] Christ Jesus is the one and only Way, the one and only Truth, the one and only Life. A person who does not follow that way is diverging from the truth and seeking life unavailingly: "He that has the Son, has life: he that has not the Son, has not life."[4]

For us all, to live super-naturally is to share in the plenitude of Divine life that is in Christ Jesus: "I came that they may have life";[5] "and of His fullness we have all received."[6] Our status of being adopted is something we have from Him. We are but children of God in the measure that we are conformed to Him who, alone, is the true and only Son of the Father by right, and who yet wishes to have with Him a multitude of brethren through sanctifying grace. The whole supernatural work, considered from God's viewpoint, comes down to this.

It was so as to turn this into reality that Christ came and gave Himself: "that we might receive the adoption of sons";[7] for this that He delivered all His treasures and all His powers to the Church, to whom He sent and continues to send "the Spirit of truth," the Spirit of sanctification, to direct her, to guide her and to perfect the work of holiness by His action in souls, right up to what the mystical body will be at the end of time, attained to her last perfection. Bliss itself, the final flowering of our super-natural adoption, is but an inheritance that Christ shares with us: "heirs indeed of God and joint heirs with Christ."[8]

---

[1] John 14:6.   [2] 1 Cor. 3:11.   [3] Acts 4:12.   [4] 1 John 5:12 (Rheims).
[5] John 10:10.   [6] John 1:16.   [7] Gal. 4:5.   [8] Rom. 8:17.

And this, in such a way that Christ is and remains the one object of the Divine delight. It is only in Him and because of Him that the elect, who form His kingdom, are enveloped with the same eternal gaze of love: "Jesus Christ yesterday, and today: and the same for ever."[1]

That is what we have seen so far. But it will avail us but little if we do nothing except look in an abstract and theoretical way at this Divine plan in which our God's wisdom and goodness shine out. We ought to *adapt ourselves in practice to this plan*, on pain of not being part of Christ's kingdom. That is what we shall see in the talks that are to follow. What I shall strive to show you is: grace taking possession of our souls at baptism; God's working being finely-wrought within us; and the condition of our personal action as free creatures in order that we be enabled to share the Divine life in largest possible measure.

We shall see that the foundation of the whole of this spiritual edifice is faith in the divinity of Our Lord, and see that baptism, the first of all the sacraments, marks the whole of our existence with a twofold character of death and of life, of "death to sin" and of "life for God."

In that wonderful discourse which He uttered at the Last Supper on the eve of His death, and in which He, as it were, lifted a corner of the veil that hides the secrets of the Divine life from us, Our Lord said: "In this is my Father glorified; that you bring forth very much fruit."[2] It is entering into the eternal thoughts, therefore, to seek to make our status as children of God come to flower within us, to the highest degree.

Let us ask Christ Jesus, the only Son of the Father and our model, to teach us in practice, not only how He lives in us, but also how we ought to live in Him. For that is the only way in which we shall bear much fruit, fruit that will make us be recognized by the Father as His beloved children: "He who abides in me, and I in him, he bears much fruit."[3]

---

[1] Hebr. 13:8 (Rheims).   [2] John 15:8 (Rheims).   [3] John 15:5.

As I have told you, all our holiness—and my greatest desire is that this truth be engraven in the depth of your souls—all holiness for us comes down to sharing in the holiness of Christ Jesus, Son of God.

But *how* does one share in it? By receiving Jesus Christ who is its only source. St. John, when speaking of the Incarnation, tells us: "To as many as received Him, He gave the power of becoming sons of God."[1] And how does one receive Christ, the Word Incarnate? By faith first and foremost: "To those who believe in his name...."[2]

St. John, therefore, tells us that it is faith in Jesus Christ that makes us children of God. That is likewise the thought of St. Paul: "You are all the children of God through faith in Christ Jesus."[3] This is because by faith in the divinity of Jesus Christ we identify ourselves with Him; we accept Him as what He is: Son of God and the Word Incarnate. Faith delivers us up to Christ; and Christ, introducing us into the supernatural domain, delivers us up to His Father. And the more perfect, deep, lively and constant our faith in the divinity of Christ is, the more do we, as children of God, have a right to the communication of the divine life. In receiving Christ by faith, we become by grace what He is by nature—children of God; and then our state calls forth from the Heavenly Father an influx of the divine life; our state as child of God is like a continuous prayer. O Father who art holy, give us this day our daily bread; that is to say, the Divine life of which your Son has the plenitude!

It is about this faith that I am going to talk to you. Faith constitutes the first of all attitudes we ought to have in our relations with God: "The first connection of man to God is through faith."[4] St. Augustine says the same: "Faith is the first thing that joins the soul to God."[5]

---

[1] John 1:12.   [2] *Ibid.*   [3] Gal. 3:26; cf. Rom. 3:22-26.

[4] St Thomas, IV *Sent.*, dist. 39, a. 6, ad 2. "First among the virtues is clearly that through which we have direct access to God. And our first access to God is through faith": II-II, q. CLXI, a. 5, ad 2. Cf. II-II, q. IV, a. 7 and q. XXIII, a. 8.

[5] *De agone Christiano*, 14.

Those who wish to approach God, says St. Paul, must begin by believing,[1] because "without faith it is impossible to please God,"[2] and (even more is it the case) impossible to attain to His friendship and become and remain His child.[3]

You will perceive at once that this subject is not only important, but vital. We shall understand nothing of the super-natural life, of the divine life in our souls, if we do not grasp that it is based entirely upon this faith—"*grounded*" in faith,[4] based upon this inner and deep conviction of the divinity of Jesus Christ. For, as the Council of Trent says, faith is the root and foundation of all justification,[5] and consequently of all holiness.

Let us, therefore, see what this faith is, what its object is, and how it is manifested.

1. Christ requires faith as a *prior condition* of union with Him.

LET US CONSIDER what happened when our Savior lived in Judea. When we go through the account of His life in the Gospels, we see that faith is what He demands first of all from those who address themselves to Him.

We read that one day two blind men followed Him crying out: "Son of David, have pity on us." Jesus lets them approach, and says to them: "Do you believe that I could cure you?" And they reply: "Yes, Lord." Then, He touches their eyes and gives them back their sight, saying: "According to your faith, be it done unto you."[6] Likewise, after His transfiguration, He finds, at the foot of Mount Tabor, a father who asks Him to cure his child who is possessed by a devil. And what does Jesus say to him? "If you can believe, all things are possible to him who

---

[1] Hebr. 11:6.   [2] *Ibid.*
[3] Council of Trent, Sess. 6, cap. 8.   [4] Col. 1:23 (Rheims).
[5] "Faith is the beginning, the foundation and the root of all justification": Sess. VI, cap. 8.   [6] See Matt. 9:27-30.

believes." And immediately the father of the child cries out: "I do believe, Lord; help my unbelief"—help the weakness of my faith. And Jesus delivers the child from the demon.[1]

When the ruler of the synagogue asks Him to restore his daughter to life, it is still the same reply that Jesus gives him: "Believe only, and she shall be safe."[2] Very many times does this saying return to His lips; very often, too, we hear Him say: "Go, your faith has made you safe"—your faith has cured you. He says it to the paralytic man, He says it to the woman who has been ill for twelve years and has been cured through having touched His cloak with faith.[3]

He makes faith in Him the indispensable condition of His miracles. Even from those He loves the most He demands this faith. Look at when Martha, the sister of Lazarus who was His friend and whom He would shortly raise from the dead—look at when Martha lets Him hear her say to Him that He would have been well able to prevent the death of her brother, had He been there. Our Lord tells her that Lazarus will be raised to life: but, before working this miracle, He wants Martha to make an act of faith in His Person: "I am the Resurrection and the Life ... do you believe this?"[4]

Wherever He does not encounter faith, He deliberately limits the effects of His power. The Gospel tells us expressly that "because of their unbelief," the unbelief of the inhabitants of Nazareth, "He did not work many miracles there."[5] It seems that lack of faith paralyzes (if I can so express it) the action of Christ.

But whenever He finds it, He can refuse nothing to it. He likes to give high public praise to it, effusive praise. One day when Jesus was at Capernaum, a pagan, an officer in command of a company of hundred men, approached Him and asked Him to cure one of his servants who was ill. Jesus said to him: "I will go and heal him." But the centurion

---

[1] See Mark 9:16-26; cf. Matt. 17:14-19; Luke 9:38-43.   [2] Luke 8:50 (Rheims).
[3] See Mark 5:25-34.   [4] John 11:21-26.   [5] Matt. 13:58.

straightaway replied to Him: "Lord, do not go to that trouble, for I am not worthy that you should enter beneath my roof; but simply say the word, and my servant will be healed. Look, I have soldiers under my orders; I say to one 'Go,' and he goes; to another 'Come,' and he comes; and to my servant 'Do this,' and he does it. In the same way, it will be enough for you to say one word, to command the illness and it will disappear." What faith this pagan had! Therefore, Christ Jesus, even before pronouncing the liberating word, shows what joy this faith gives Him: "Truly, I have not found such faith even amongst the sons of Israel. It is because of such faith that Gentiles will come and take their place at the feast of eternal life in the kingdom of heaven, while the sons of Israel, the first to be called to this banquet, will be rejected because of their unbelief." And, addressing Himself to the centurion, He says: "Go, and let it be done to you according to your faith."[1]

Faith is so pleasing to Jesus that it even ends up by obtaining from Him that which it was not His first intention to grant. We have a striking example of that in the cure asked of Him by a Canaan woman. Our Lord had arrived at the borders of Tyre and Sidon, a pagan region. A woman of those parts, having come to where He was, started crying out in a loud voice: "Have pity on me, Lord, Son of David; my daughter is grievously tormented by a devil." But Jesus answers her not a word. Then His disciples approach Him, and say to Him: "Do what she asks and then send her away, for she is annoying us with her cries." And Christ says to them: "My mission is to preach only to the Jews." He was leaving to His apostles the work of evangelizing the pagans. But see then how the woman comes and prostrates herself before Him: "Lord," she says, "help me!" And Jesus makes the same reply to her as to the apostles, but employing a proverbial way of speaking, in use at that time to distinguish Jews from pagans: "It is not good to take the bread of children, and to cast it to the dogs." And the woman,

---

[1] See Matt. 8:5-13.

animated by her faith, cries out: "That is true, Lord, but at least the little dogs eat the scraps that fall from their masters' tables." Jesus is so touched by this faith that He cannot prevent Himself from praising her and immediately granting her what she is begging of Him: "O woman, great is your faith; be it done to you according to your desire." And, at that same hour, her daughter was cured.[1]

No doubt in almost all these examples it is a matter of bodily cures; but it is also because of faith that Our Lord forgives sins and grants life eternal. Look, what is it He says to Mary Magdalene when this sinner comes and throws herself at His feet and waters them with her tears? "Your sins are forgiven you." The forgiveness of sins is certainly a grace of a purely spiritual order. Now, what was the reason why Christ gave back the life of grace to Mary Magdalene? It was because of her faith. Christ Jesus said exactly the same words to her as to those whom He cured of their bodily ills: "Go, your faith has made you safe again."[2]

Finally, look at Calvary. What a magnificent reward He gives to the good thief because of his faith! He was probably a brigand, was that thief: but, on the cross, when all the enemies of Jesus heap sarcasm and mockery upon Him—"If he is the Son of God, as he said, let him come down from the cross, and we will believe in him"[3]—that thief confesses his faith in the divinity of Christ, who is abandoned by His disciples and is dying upon a gibbet. For he speaks to Jesus of His "kingdom," at the time when Jesus is about to die. He asks Him for a place in that kingdom. What faith in the power of the expiring Christ was there! And how moved Jesus was by this faith! "Truly, you will be with me this very day in Paradise."[4] He forgives him all his sins because of this faith, and assures him of a place in His eternal kingdom.

[1] See Matt. 15:22-28.
[3] See Matt. 27:42.
[2] See Luke 7:37-50.
[4] See Luke 23:39-43.

So, then, faith is the first virtue that Our Lord requires of those who approach Him. And this conduct of Christ remains the same for all of us.

When, before ascending to heaven, He sends His apostles to continue His mission throughout the world, it is faith He calls for, and (so to speak) He gathers up in it all the bringing into being of the Christian life: "Go into the whole world and preach the gospel to every creature. He who believes and is baptized shall be saved, but he who does not believe shall be condemned."[1] Does that mean that faith alone suffices? No, the sacraments and observance of the commandments are necessary also; but a man who does not believe in Jesus Christ does not feel a need for His commandments and His sacraments. On the other hand, it is because we believe in the divinity of Jesus that we observe His precepts and approach the sacraments. Faith is, therefore, the basis of all our super-natural life.

God asks that, during the stage of our earthly life, we serve Him in faith; His glory wills it so. This is the homage that He expects from us and that constitutes our being put to the test before we can reach the eternal goal. One day, we shall see God without veil, and then His glory will consist in His communicating Himself fully in all the splendor and brightness of His eternal bliss. But so long as we are here below, it comes into the disposing of the Divine plan that God be for us a hidden God. Here below, God wishes to be known, adored and served in faith. And the wider, the livelier and the more practical this faith is, the more pleasing we are to God.

---

[1] Mark 16:15-16.

2. Nature of faith: assent to the *testimony of God proclaiming that Jesus is His Son.*

BUT, you will say to me, what *is* this "faith"? To speak in a general way, faith is the adhesion of our intellect to the word of another. When a man of integrity, a straightforward man, tells us something, we accept it, we have *faith* in his word. Giving one's word to someone is giving oneself.

Super-natural faith is the adhesion of our intellect, not to a man's word, but to God's. God can neither deceive us nor be deceived: faith is a homage rendered to God considered as supreme truth and supreme authority. In order that this homage be worthy of God, we ought to submit ourselves to the authority of His word, whatever difficulties our mind encounters. That Divine word affirms to us the existence of mysteries which go beyond our reason. Faith can be required of us in matters where our senses, our experience, seem to tell us the contrary of what God says; but God asks that our conviction of the authority of His revelation be so absolute that if the whole of creation were affirming the contrary to us, we would say to God in spite of everything: "My God, I believe it, because you tell me it."[1]

Believing, says St. Thomas, is giving to Divine truth the assent, the adhesion, of our intellect, under the sovereignty of the will moved by grace.[2] It is the mind that believes, but the heart is not absent from that; and in order that we may make this act of faith, God puts within us, at baptism, a power, a strength, a "habit": the virtue of faith, by

---

[1] This is not the place to enter into an examination of the numerous psychological and theological questions relating to the nature of the act of faith: the character of our present talks does not lend itself to that. We simply permit ourselves to refer readers who want to go more deeply into these questions to the very lucid work by Fr. Bainvel, SJ, *La foi et l'acte de foi* [tr. Sterck as *Faith and the Act of Faith*, St. Louis: Herder, 1926]. The account he gives of the thinking of Cardinal Billot on faith formed on authority is particularly worth dwelling upon. See also the remarkable study of Fr. Gardeil, OP, *La credibilité*.   [2] St Thomas, II-II, q. II, a. 9.

which our intellect is disposed to accept the testimony of God through love of His veracity. That is the very essence of faith, but this adhesion and this love naturally comprise an infinite number of degrees. When love, which brings us to believe, gives us up utterly to full acceptance of the testimony of God, in our mind and in our conduct, then our faith is perfect; it operates and expresses itself in charity.[1]

Now, what is this testimony of God that we ought to accept by faith? That testimony comes down to this: *That Christ Jesus is His own Son, sent for our salvation and given for our sanctification.*

The voice of the Father, you know, has made itself heard in the world three times only,[2] and each time it was to tell us that Christ is His Son, His only Son, worthy of all delight and all glory: "This is my beloved Son ... hear Him"—"*Listen to Him.*" There, according to the very words of Our Lord, is found God's testimony to the world when He gave it His Son: "The Father Himself, who has sent me, has borne witness to me."[3] And, to confirm this testimony, God gave His Son the power to work miracles; He raised Him from the dead. Our Lord has Himself told us that eternal life is bound up for us with full acceptance of this testimony: "This is the will of my Father who sent me, that whoever beholds the Son, and believes in Him, shall have everlasting life."[4] Christ Jesus emphasizes this point often: "Truly, truly, I say to you: he who hears my word, and believes Him who sent me, has life everlasting ... and has passed from death to life."[5]

St. John wrote the following words that we cannot meditate on too much: "God so loved the world that He gave his only-begotten Son." And why has He given Him? "That whosoever believes in Him, may

---

[1] "Faith, unless hope is added to it, and charity too, does not either unite one perfectly with Christ or make one a living member of His body": Council of Trent, Sess. VI, cap. 7.   [2] Matt. 17:5; Matt. 3:17; John 12:28.
[3] John 5:37; see the whole passage from v.31.   [4] John 6:40; cf. 17:21.   [5] John 5:24.

not perish, but may have life everlasting." And he adds in explanation: "For God did not send His Son into the world in order to judge the world, but that the world might be saved through Him. He who believes in Him is not judged; but he who does not believe is already judged, because he does not believe in the name of the only-begotten Son of God."[1] To "judge" has here the sense of "condemn": well then, St. John says that he who does not believe in Christ is already condemned. Take note of that expression: "is already condemned." What does it indicate? That he who has not faith in Jesus Christ attempts unavailingly to save himself: his cause is judged, right from the present time.[2] The Eternal Father makes faith in His Son, whom He has sent, the primary attitude our soul should have and the source of our salvation. "He who believes in the Son has everlasting life; he who is unbelieving towards the Son shall not see life, but the wrath of God rests upon him."[3] God sets so much store on our believing in His Son that His wrath "rests upon him"—note the present tense again; it rests already—upon him who does not believe in His Son. What does all that signify? That, according to the very mind of the Father, faith in the divinity of Jesus is the primary work to accomplish in order to share in the divine life. Believing in the divinity of Jesus Christ brings with it all the other revealed truths.

The whole of revelation, one might say, is contained in this supreme testimony God gives us that Jesus Christ is His Son. And, equally, the whole of faith is contained in the acceptance of this testimony. Indeed, if we believe in the divinity of Christ, then by that one same stroke we believe in all the revelation of the Old Testament,

---

[1] John 3:16-18.

[2] [*Translator's note*: For the Church's teaching on the position of those who do not believe in Christ, see note on pages 115-117. What is referred to in the scriptural texts quoted here is, not mere absence of belief in Christ (which may in no way be a person's fault) but what in the Rheims's note to John 3:18 is characterized as "obstinate unbelief." Marmion himself uses the phrase "refuses obstinately" in *Christ, the Ideal of the Priest*.]   [3] John 3:36.

which finds its realization in Christ; we believe in all the revelation of the New Testament; for the whole of what the Apostles and the Church teach us is but the development of the revealing of Christ.

One who accepts the divinity of Christ, then, embraces in the one stroke the totality of all revelation. Jesus is the Incarnate Word, and the Word says all that God is, all that God knows. This Word becomes incarnate and reveals God to men: "It is the only Son," in the heart's-embrace of the Father, "who has made Him known."[1] And when, by faith, we receive Christ, we receive all revelation.

Therefore, the inner conviction that Our Lord is truly God constitutes the primary foundation of all our super-natural life. If we have understood this truth and if we put it into practice, our interior life will be full of light and full of fruitfulness.

3. **Faith in the divinity of Jesus Christ is the *foundation of our interior life*. Christianity is the *acceptance of the divinity of Christ* in the Incarnation.**

SO MUCH IS THIS a truth of first importance, that I wish to dwell on it with you for several moments.

During the mortal life of Jesus, His divinity was hidden beneath the veil of His humanity. Even for those living in His company, His divinity was an object of faith.

There is no doubt that the Jews reported upon the sublimity of His doctrine: "Never," they repeated, "did man speak like this man."[2] They had witnessed works that God alone was able to do, they said.[3] But they saw also that Christ was a man. It is said that even His close relations, who had only known Him in the workshop at Nazareth, did not believe in Him, despite His miracles.[4]

[1] John 1:18 (Jerus.)   [2] John 7:46 (Rheims).
[3] "Rabbi... no one could perform the signs that you do unless God were with him": John 3:2 (Jerus.)   [4] John 7:5.

His apostles, even though they were His regular hearers, did not perceive His divinity. In that episode I have already related, in which we hear Our Lord ask His disciples: "Whom do you say that I am?" St. Peter answers: "You are Christ, the Son of the living God." But Our Lord immediately brings out the point that it is not that St. Peter has spoken in this way because he has natural evidence; it is solely as the result of a revelation the Eternal Father has made to him; and, because of this revelation, He declares His apostle to be blessed: "Blessed are you, Simon Bar-Jona, because flesh and blood has not revealed this to you, but my Father who is in heaven."[1]

More than once, also, we read in the Gospel that the Jews disputed amongst themselves on the subject of Christ. Thus, after Jesus had expounded the parable of the good shepherd who freely gives his life for his sheep, there was an argument among His hearers. Some said: "He is possessed by a devil; he is mad: why do you listen to him?" But others replied: "Look, are these the words of one who has a devil?" And alluding to the miracle of the man blind from birth who had been cured by Jesus a few days before, they added: "Can a devil open the eyes of a blind man?" Then, wishing to get to the heart of it, the Jews gathered around Jesus and said to Him: "How long are you going to keep our minds in suspense? If you are the Christ, tell us so plainly." And what did Our Lord say to them in reply? "I have said this to you, and you do not believe me; the works I do in the name of my Father give testimony of me"; and He adds: "But you do not believe me because you are not of my sheep. My sheep hear my voice; I know them and they follow me; I will give them life everlasting and they shall never perish, and no one shall rob me of them; no one shall rob them from the hand of my Father who has given them to me—for my Father and I are one." Then the Jews, taking Him for a blasphemer, because He called Himself the equal of God, gather up rocks to stone Him. And, as Jesus asks them why

[1] See Matt. 16:15-17.

they are doing this: "We are stoning you," they reply, "because of your blasphemy; because you, being a man, claim to be God." And what is the reply of Christ Jesus? Does He deny that of which they reproach Him? No, on the contrary; instead of that, He confirms it, it is just as they think—the equal of God. They have well understood His words, but He insists on affirming it afresh: He is the Son of God, since, He says, "I do the works of my Father, who has sent me," and since—by the Divine nature—"the Father is in me, and I in the Father."[1]

So then, you see that faith in the divinity of Christ Jesus constitutes the first step towards divine life—for us, as for the Jews of His day. Believing that Jesus is the Son of God, God Himself, is the primary condition for being counted among His sheep, for being pleasing to His Father. For that is exactly what the Father requires of us: "This is the work of God, that you believe in Him whom He has sent."[2] Christianity is nothing else than *acceptance—with all its remotest doctrinal and practical consequences—of the divinity of Christ in the Incarnation*. The reign of Christ, and through Him holiness, is established within us in the measure of the purity, the liveliness and the fullness of our faith in Jesus Christ.

You see, our holiness is the coming to blossom of our status as children of God. Now, it is in the first place by faith that we all awaken to that life of grace which makes us children of God: "Everyone who believes that Jesus is the Christ *is born of God*."[3] It is only if our life is based on this faith that we are truly children of God. The Father gives us His Son to be everything for us, our model, our satisfaction, our life. "Receive my Son, for in Him you have everything,[4] and in receiving Him you receive me myself; you become, through Him, in Him, my beloved sons." That is what Our Lord Himself said: "When someone believes in me, his faith does not stop at me; it goes right up to my Father who sent me."[5]

---

[1] See John 10:19-38.   [2] John 6:29.   [3] 1 John 5:1.
[4] "How has He not also, with Him, given us all things?": Rom. 8:32 (Rheims).
[5] See John 12:44.

St. John says that if we "receive the testimony of men"—if we reasonably believe what men affirm to us—the testimony of God is yet greater than human testimony.[1] And, once again, what is this testimony of God? It is the testimony God has rendered, that Christ is His Son. "He who believes in the Son of God has the testimony of God in himself. He who does not believe God, makes Him out to be a liar," since he does not believe the testimony God has rendered of His Son.[2] "He who believes in the Son of God has the testimony of God in himself"—these words contain a very profound truth. For in what does this testimony consist? That God, says St. John, "has given to us eternal life; and this life is in His Son. He that has the Son, has life: he that has not the Son, has not life."[3] What do these words signify?

To understand them we must, in the light of Revelation, take ourselves up to the very source of life in God. The Father's whole life in the Blessed Trinity is to "utter" His Son, His Word, to beget, by an act that is unique, simple, eternal, a Son who is like Himself, to whom He communicates the plenitude of His being and of His perfections. In this Word, infinite as He Himself is infinite, in this unique and eternal Utterance, the Father unendingly recognizes His Son, the image of Himself, "the brightness of His glory."[4] And everything God the Father says, every testimony He gives us exteriorly, as to Christ's divinity— such as the one that was given at the baptism of Jesus, "This is my beloved Son"—is but an echo, in the world of the senses, of that testimony the Father renders to Himself in the sanctuary of the Divinity, a testimony He expresses by an Utterance in which He puts the whole of Himself, and which is His inmost life. "You are my Son, this day have I begotten you."[5]

---

[1] 1 John 5:9.   [2] See 1 John 5:10.   [3] 1 John 5:11-12 (Rheims).   [4] Hebr. 1:3.
[5] Ps. 2:7; Acts 13:33; Hebr. 1:5, 5:5. [*Translator's note*: "today": "that is, in an eternal present" (Marmion): see Translator's Note, page xviii. Marmion uses that same phrase, "an eternal present," in the paragraph following this one. Note that on page 333 he sets "this day" in the context of the Incarnation and the mediating priesthood of the Word Incarnate.]

When, then, we accept this testimony of the Eternal Father, when we say to God: "This little child, sleeping in the crib, is your Son; I adore Him and deliver myself up to Him"; "this adolescent laboring in the workshop at Nazareth is your Son; I adore Him"; "this man crucified on Calvary is your Son; I adore Him"; "this fragment of bread is but the appearance under which your Son is hidden; I adore Him"; when we say to Jesus Himself: "You are Christ, the Son of the living God" and we prostrate ourselves before Him, delivering up our energies to serve Him; when all our actions accord with this faith and spring from the charity that makes faith perfect—then, the whole of our life becomes an echo of the life of the Father who eternally expresses His Son in one infinite Word; and since this action of life in God never ceases—embracing all time, being an eternal present—we associate ourselves, in that way, with the very life of God. That is what St. John says: "He who believes in the Son of God has the testimony of God in himself"—that testimony by which the Father "utters" His Son.

4. *Exercise* of the virtue of faith; *fruitfulness* of an interior life based upon faith.

IT IS IMPOSSIBLE to repeat too often these acts of faith in the divinity of Jesus Christ. This faith, we have received at baptism, but we should not leave it buried or asleep somewhere in the depths of our heart, we should ask God to increase it within us: "Lord, increase my faith"; we should, ourselves, exercise it through repetition of our acts of faith. And the more pure and living it is, the more will it envelop our whole existence: the more, also, will our spiritual life be solid, true, luminous, sure and fruitful. *For a deep conviction that Christ is God, and that He has been given to us, contains in it the whole of our spiritual life*; our holiness flows from this inner conviction as from its source. And when this faith is a living one, it breaks through the veil of the humanity that conceals Christ's divinity from our sight. The one whom it shows us in the crib, in the form of a little child; or in a laborer's workshop; as a prophet ceaselessly exposed to the contradictions of His enemies; in the ignominies of a shameful death; under the appearances of bread and wine—this one, faith tells us with ever equal certainty, is always the same Christ, true God as well as true man; equal to his Father and to the Holy Spirit in majesty, power, wisdom, love. And when this conviction is a deep one, it hurls us into an act of intense adoration, and of abandon to the will of Him who, though being a man, remains what He is—the Almighty, and Infinite Perfection.

If we have never done it, we should put ourselves at the feet of Christ and say to Him: "Lord Jesus, Word Incarnate, I believe that you are God, begotten of true God: 'true God from true God.'[1] I do not behold your divinity, but because your Father has told me 'This is my beloved Son,' I believe it, and because I believe it, I wish to submit myself to you, entirely—body, soul, judgement, will, heart, feelings, imagination, all my energies. I wish the words of your psalmist to become reality in me: 'Let everything be flung beneath your feet in homage.'[2] I wish you to be my leader, your Gospel to be my light, your will to be my guide. I wish to think of you alone, because you are Infallible Truth. I wish not to act outside of you, because you are the one way of going to the Father; not to seek my joy outside your will, because you are the very source of life. Possess me entirely, through your Spirit, for the glory of your Father!" By this act of faith, we lay the very foundation of our spiritual life: "For other foundation no one can lay, but that which has been laid, which is Christ Jesus."[3]

And if this act is renewed frequently, then Christ "dwells in our hearts," as St. Paul says: "that Christ may dwell by faith in your hearts."[4] In other words, He reigns in our souls in a lasting way, as Master, as King; and He becomes, through His Spirit, the wellspring within us of divine life.

[1] Nicene creed.
[2] "You have subjected all things under His feet": Ps. 8:8. See Hebr. 2:8 for this being applied to Christ.   [3] 1 Cor. 3:11; cf. Col. 2:6-7.   [4] Eph. 3:17 (Rheims).

Let us, then, renew often that act of faith in the divinity of Jesus, because every time we do so we make firm, we consolidate, the foundation of our spiritual life, and, little by little, we render it unshakable. When you go into a Church and you see the little lamp which, burning before the tabernacle, tells you of the presence of Christ Jesus, Son of God, let your genuflection not be a ceremony simply of convention, done as routine, but a homage of inner faith and profound adoration before Our Lord, as if you were seeing Him in all the brightness of His eternal glory. When you sing or recite, in the *Gloria* of the Mass, all those praises and all those supplications to Jesus Christ: "Lord God, Lamb of God, you are seated at the right hand of the Father, you alone are holy, you alone are Lord, you alone are the Most High, with the Holy Spirit, in the infinite glory of the Father," let these praises all come from your heart more than from your lips. When you read the Gospel, do so with this conviction: that it is the Word of God, it is Light, it is Infallible Truth that speaks to you and reveals to you the secrets of the Divinity. When you sing, in the *Credo*, of the eternal generation of the Word—the Word to whom the humanity was to be united: "God from God, Light from Light, true God from true God"— do not only be conscious of the meaning of the words or the beauty of the chant, but repeat them like an echo of the voice of the Father as He contemplates His Son and attests His equality to Himself: "You are my Son...." When you sing "And was made man," "*Et incarnatus est,*" let your whole being bow interiorly in an act of humbling yourself to nothingness before this God-made-man, in whom the Father has placed His delight. When you receive Jesus in the Eucharist, receive Him with a deep reverence as if you were seeing Him face to face.

Such acts are extremely pleasing to the Eternal Father, because all His demands—and they are infinite—come down to willing the glory of His Son.

And the more this Son veils His divinity, the more He abases Himself for love of us, the more profoundly too should we adore Him as the Son of God, the more should we exalt Him and give Him our homage. The supreme desire of God is to see His Son glorified: "I have both glorified it, and I will glorify it again"[1]—this is one of the three things the world has heard the Eternal Father say. He wills to glorify Christ Jesus, because Christ, His Son, is His equal; but He wills it also, says St. Paul, because His Son humbled Himself: He "emptied himself.... For *which cause* God also has exalted Him." Because of His Son's emptying of Himself, the Father "has exalted Him, and has given Him a name which is above all names," that at the name of Jesus "every knee should bow" and "every tongue should confess that the Lord Jesus Christ is in the glory of God the Father."[2]

That is why the more Christ abases Himself in making Himself a little child, hiding Himself at Nazareth, bearing those of our infirmities that are compatible with His dignity, submitting to death on a gibbet like one accursed (being "reputed with the wicked," as Isaiah says),[3] veiling Himself in the Eucharist; and the more His divinity is attacked and denied by the unbelieving, the more also should we place Him high in the glory of the Father and in our hearts, the more should we deliver ourselves up to Him in a spirit of intense reverence and complete submission to His Person, and the more should we work for the extension of His reign in souls.

---

[1] John 12:28. [*Translator's note*: In quoting John 12:28, doubtless from memory, Marmion treats it as the Father saying that He will glorify the Son's name. In fact, the context is that Christ says to the Father: "Father, glorify *your* name," and Father's reply, quoted by Marmion, is that He, the Father has glorified, and will glorify *His, the Father's name*, as the Son asks. But a connecting link between John 12:28 and the interpretation Marmion puts on it from memory may be found in John 13:31-32, where Christ says, of Himself: "Now is the Son of Man glorified, and God [the Father] is glorified in Him. If God is glorified in Him, God will also glorify Him [His Son, the Son of Man] in Himself." In all these words, no doubt, we catch a glimpse of the One-ness of the Trinity: the glory of one of the Persons reflects itself in the glory of all and each of the Three Persons.]

[2] Phil. 2:7-11 (Rheims).   [3] Isa. 53:12.

Such is true faith, perfect faith in the divinity of Jesus Christ—faith which, having its completion in love, delivers up our whole being and which, enveloping in practice all the acts, all the works of our spiritual life, constitutes the very *base* of all our super-natural edifice, of all our holiness. To be truly a *foundation*, faith must be the support of all the works we carry out, and become the basis of all our progress in the spiritual life.[1] "I have laid the foundation," says St. Paul, "as a wise architect," in making you know the Gospel of Christ (which you have received by faith); it is for each one now to see what he will make rise up on this foundation."[2]

This spiritual edifice is built of our works. St. Paul says, also, that "the just man lives by faith."[3] The "just man" is he who, through the justification received by baptism, is created in justice and possesses within him the grace of Christ, and, with it, the infused virtues of faith, hope and love. This just man *lives* by faith. To live is to have within one an inner mainspring which is the source of one's movements and operations. It remains true that the inner mainspring which should animate our acts in order that they may be acts of the super-natural life, proportioned to the final beatitude, is sanctifying grace; but it is faith that introduces every soul into the region of the super-natural. We do not partake of the Divine adoption except in receiving Christ, and we do not receive Christ except by faith: "To as many as received Him He gave the power of becoming sons of God; to those who believe in His name."[4] Faith in Jesus Christ leads us to life, conducts us to justification by grace;[5] that is why St. Paul says that the just live by faith.

---

[1] "Those who are justified ... in justice itself, received through the grace of Christ, *with the co-operation of faith*, grow in good works and are more greatly sanctified": Council of Trent, Sess. VI, cap. 10.   [2] See 1 Cor. 3:10.

[3] Rom. 1:17 (Rheims); Habac. 2:4. It is to be noted that St. Paul states this truth three times in his Epistles: cf. Gal. 3:11 and Hebr. 10:38.   [4] John 1:12.

[5] Gal. 3:11.

In the super-natural life, faith in Jesus Christ is a power that is more active the more deeply it is anchored in the soul. The soul first embraces with fervor the whole fullness of its object; and since, for this soul, all relates to Christ, it looks at all things in the divine light of Christ; and therefore this soul takes its course from that same Person of Jesus as regards all He has said, all He has done or carried out, all He has instituted—the Church, the sacraments, all that constitutes that super-natural organism established by Christ to make souls live by His divine life. More, the inner and deep conviction we have of the divinity of Jesus is what sets in motion all our activity so that we carry out all His commandments with generosity; so that we are made steadfast in temptation—"strong in faith,"[1] so that our hope and our love is sustained through every trial.

Oh, what intensity of super-natural life one finds in souls who possess an inner conviction that Christ is God! What an abundant source of interior life and untiring apostolate is this persuasion, rendered firmer each day, that Christ is all-Holiness, all-Wisdom, all-Power and all-Goodness!

"I believe, Lord Jesus, that you are the Son of the living God; I believe it, but I ask you to increase my faith!"

5. Why we should have a particularly *lively faith in the value*—the infinite value—*of the merits of Christ.* How faith is a source of joy.

THERE IS ONE point on which I want to dwell, and which should above all be made the explicit object of our faith if we wish to live the divine life fully. It is faith in the infinite value of the merits of Jesus Christ.

I have already touched on this truth in showing how Our Lord constituted the infinite price of our sanctification. But it is important to

---

[1] 1 Peter 5:9 (Rheims).

return to that here when speaking of faith, for it is faith that permits us to draw on those unfathomable riches that God has given us in His Christ: "the unfathomable riches of Christ."[1]

God has given us an immense gift in the Person of His Son Jesus. Christ is a tabernacle in which are hidden "all the treasures" that Divine Wisdom and Knowledge[2] can have stored up for us. Christ Himself, by His Passion and death, has merited to grant us communication of them, and He "lives always to make intercession for us" to His Father.[3] But we need to know the value of this Gift, and we need to know how to make use of it: "If you only knew what God is offering!"[4] Christ, with the plenitude of His holiness and the infinite value of His merits and credit, is this Gift. But this Gift is only of use to us in the measure of our faith. If our faith is large, lively, deep, rising to the height of this Gift so far as that is possible to a creature, there will then be no limit to the Divine communications made to our souls by the sacred humanity of Jesus. If we do not have a boundless regard for the infinite merits of Christ, it is because our faith in the divinity of Jesus is not intense enough; and those who doubt this divine efficacy do not know what the humanity is of one who is God.

We ought often to exercise that faith in the satisfactions and merits won by Jesus for our sanctification.

When we pray, let us present ourselves to the Eternal Father with an *unshakable confidence* in the merits of His Son. Our Lord has paid everything, settled everything, won everything; and He "lives always to make intercession *for us.*" That being so, let us say to God: "I know, O my God, that I am altogether a wretched person, that every day I only multiply my faults; I know that before your infinite holiness I am, of myself, like mire before the sun: but I prostrate myself before you. Through grace, I am a member of the mystical body of your Son: your

---

[1] Eph. 3:8.   [2] Col. 2:3.   [3] See Hebr. 7:25.   [4] John 4:10 (Jerus.)

Son has given me this grace, after having redeemed me by His blood. Now that I belong to Him, do not reject me from before your Divine Face." No, God cannot reject us when we rely in that way upon the credit of His Son, for the Son treats with Him as equal to equal. When we recognize this to be so—that of ourselves we are weak and wretched, that we can do nothing: "Without me you can do nothing,"[1] but that we wait on Christ for everything, for everything we need in order to live by divine life: "I can do all things in Him who strengthens me,"[2] then we recognize that this Son is our All; that He has been established as our head and our high priest, Bridge of man to God. And to do that, says St. John, is to render a homage very pleasing to the Father, who "loves the Son," who wishes everything to come to us through the Son, because He has given Him all power of life for souls—whereas the soul who does not have this *absolute* confidence in Jesus does not recognize Him fully for what He is, the beloved Son of the Father, and in consequence does not render the Father the honor He, the Father, has from infinity. "For the Father loves the Son ... all judgement He has given to the Son, that all men may honor the Son even as they honor the Father." Someone "who does not honor the Son, does not honor the Father who sent Him."[3]

In the same way, when we approach the Sacrament of Penance, let us have great faith in the Divine efficacy of the blood of Jesus. This blood it is which washes our souls clean of their sins at that time, which purifies them, renews their strength and gives them back their beauty. At the moment of absolution, the very blood of Christ is applied to us with His merits—that blood which Our Lord shed for us with incomparable love, those merits which are infinite but which He won at the price of unmeasurable sufferings and ignominies without name. "If you only knew what God is offering!"

---

[1] John 15:5.   [2] Phil. 4:13.   [3] John 5:20-23.

In the same way again, when you assist at Holy Mass, you are present at the Sacrifice which renews that of the cross. The Man-God offers Himself upon the altar for us as He did on Calvary, albeit that the manner of offering is different; but it is the same Christ, true God no less than He is true man, who immolates Himself upon the altar so as to make us share in His inexhaustible satisfactions. If only our faith were living and deep! With what reverence would we then assist at this Sacrifice, with what holy appetite would we go to the holy table every day, as our Mother the Church wishes, in order to unite ourselves with Christ. With what unshakable confidence would we receive Jesus at that moment when He gives Himself, with His humanity and His divinity, His treasures, His merits—He, the ransom of the world, and the Son in whom God places His delight! "If you only knew what God is offering!"

When we make, frequently, such acts of faith in the power of Jesus Christ, in the value of His merits, our life becomes, by that very fact, like a perpetual hymn of praise to the glory of this supreme High Priest; this universal Mediator who gives us every grace. And to do that is to enter deeply into the eternal thoughts, into the Divine plan; it is to adapt our soul to the sanctifying designs of God, and at the same time to associate ourselves with His will to glorify His beloved Son.

Let us go, then, to Our Lord; He alone brings us words of eternal life. In the first place, let us receive Him with a living faith, wherever He presents Himself—in the sacraments, in the Church, His mystical body, in our neighbor, in His providence which directs or permits all occurrences, even suffering. Let us receive Him, whatever be the form He assumes or the moment when He comes, with *a full adhesion to His Divine word and a complete abandon to His service.* All holiness comes down to this.

We have all read in the Gospel that episode, recounted by St. John with all its enjoyable detail, of the curing of the man blind from birth.[1] After having been cured by Jesus on the Sabbath Day the blind man is interrogated, a good many times, by the Pharisees, enemies of the Savior; they wish the blind man to admit that Christ is not a prophet because He does not observe the Sabbath rest prescribed by the Law of Moses. But the poor blind man doesn't know very much; he invariably replies that a man called Jesus has cured him by sending him to wash at the pool of Siloe: that is all he knows, and all he replies, to begin with. The Pharisees are not able to draw anything from him against Christ; and, finally, they cast him out of the synagogue because he will have it that a man opening the eyes of one born blind is something that has never been heard tell of, and that Jesus, therefore, must have been sent from God. Our Lord, knowing of his expulsion and having encountered him, says to him: "Do you believe in the Son of God?" The blind man replies: "Who is He, Lord, that I may believe in Him?" What promptitude of soul! Jesus says to him: "It is He who is talking with you." And, immediately, this poor blind man adheres to what Christ has said, cries "I believe, Lord," and in the intensity of his faith, "falling down, he adored Him." He embraced the feet of Christ and, in Christ, all Christ's works.

The man blind from birth is an image of our soul, cured by Jesus, delivered from eternal darkness and restored to the light by the grace of the Word Incarnate.[2] Therefore, wherever Christ presents Himself to the soul, the soul ought to say: "Who is He, Lord, that I may believe in Him?" And, immediately, it ought to deliver itself up completely to Christ, to His service, to the interests of His glory, which is also the glory of His Father. By doing so always we *live* by faith; Christ dwells and reigns in us, His divinity being, through this faith, the mainspring within us of our whole life.

---

[1] See John 9:1-38.   [2] Cf. St. Augustine, *Tract. in Johann.*, XLIV, 1.

FAITH: THE FOUNDATION 193

Finally, this faith, coming to completion and expressing itself by love, is for us a source of joy. Our Lord said: "Blessed are they who have not seen, and yet have believed."[1] He said these words, not for His disciples, but for us. And why is it, then, that Our Lord proclaims "blessed" those who believe in Him? Faith is a source of joy, because it makes us share in the knowledge of Christ; He is the Eternal Word who has told us the Divine secrets: "It is the only Son," in the heart's-embrace of the Father, "who has made Him known."[2] In believing what He tells us, we have the same knowledge as He. Faith is a source of joy because it is a source of light.

Also, faith is a source of joy because it puts us in radical possession of future good things, it is "the substance of things to be hoped for,"[3] eternal realities. Jesus Himself tells us: "He who believes in the Son has everlasting life."[4] Notice the present tense, "has." Christ does not speak of the future, "he will have." Instead He speaks as of a good thing the possession of which is assured already,[5] just as we have seen that one who does not believe *is* judged already. Faith is a seed, and every seed contains in germ the future harvest. Provided that we distance from it everything that can diminish it, tarnish it, weaken it, that we develop it by prayer and by exercising it, provided we constantly give it the occasion to manifest itself by love, then faith puts in our hands the substance of good things to come, and gives rise to unshakable hope: "Whosoever believes in Him shall not be confounded."[6]

Let us remain, as St. Paul says, "grounded" in faith[7]—founded upon Christ, and made firm in our faith in Him. "Therefore, as you have

---

[1] John 20:29.   [2] John 1:18 (Jerus.)   [3] Hebr. 11:1.   [4] John 3:36.

[5] "One is said already to have the end sought because of one's hope of obtaining that end": St Thomas, I-II, q. LXIX, a. 2; and the Angelic Doctor adds: "Whence the Apostle says: 'We are saved by hope'" (Rom. 8:24 [Rheims]). The whole of this article should be read.

[6] Rom. 9:33; 1 Peter 2:6 [both Rheims]; Isa. 28:16 ["the believer shall not stumble," Jerus.]   [7] Col. 1:23 (Rheims).

received Jesus Christ our Lord, so walk in Him; be rooted in Him and built up on Him, and strengthened in the faith, as you also have learnt."[1] Let us remain so strengthened—for that faith will be tried by this age of unbelief, of blasphemy, of scepticism, of naturalism, of human respect, that surrounds us with its unhealthy atmosphere. If we stay firm in this faith it will, says St. Peter, Prince of the Apostles (on whom Jesus founded His Church when Peter proclaimed that Christ was the Son of God) become a title to "praise and glory and honor" at the appearing of that Jesus whom you love though you have never seen Him, that Jesus in whom you believe though your eyes are not able to glimpse Him; but also that Jesus to believe in whom is to have an inexhaustible spring of ineffable joy opening in your hearts; it cannot be otherwise. For, St. Peter adds, the end and the assured reward of this faith is the salvation (and, it follows, the holiness) of your souls.[2]

[1] Col. 2:6-7.   [2] 1 Peter 1:7-9.

CHAPTER TWO

Baptism, Sacrament of Adoption
and Initiation, Death and Life

Introduction: Baptism, first of all the sacraments.

WE HAVE SEEN that faith is the soul's primary attitude in face of the revelation made to it of the Divine plan of our adoption in Jesus Christ. Faith is the root of all justification and the mainspring of Christian life. It holds fast, as to its primordial object, to the divinity of Jesus sent by the Eternal Father to effect our salvation: "Now this is everlasting life," that we "may know you, the only true God, and Him whom you have sent, Jesus Christ."[1]

From this principal object, faith radiates over everything that touches upon Christ—the sacraments, the Church, souls, the whole of revelation. And when it finds completion in love and adoration so as to deliver up our whole being to the full accomplishment of the will of Jesus and of His Father, it attains perfection.

But faith is not enough.

When Our Lord sent His apostles to continue on earth His sanctifying mission, He said that "he who does not believe shall be condemned."[2] He added nothing else for those who do not wish to believe—because,

[1] John 17:3. [2] Mark 16:16.

195

faith being the root of all justification, everything that is done without faith lacks value in the eyes of God: "Without faith it is impossible to please God."[1] But for those who do believe, Christ adds the reception of baptism as a condition of incorporation into His kingdom: "He who believes and is baptized shall be saved."[2] Likewise, St. Paul says that "all you who have been baptized into Christ, have put on Christ."[3] This sacrament, then, is the condition of our incorporation into Christ. Baptism is the first in date order of all the sacraments: the first infusion of Divine life into us takes place at baptism. All the Divine super-natural communications converge upon this sacrament or normally presuppose it. That is what gives it its value.

Let us pause to consider it; we shall find in it the origin of our title to super-natural nobility. For baptism is the sacrament of Divine adoption and of Christian initiation. At the same time we shall above all discover there, in germ as it were, the twofold aspect of "death to sin and life for God" that ought to characterize the whole existence of a disciple of Christ.

Let us ask the Holy Spirit, who by His Divine power has sanctified the baptismal waters in which we have been re-born—let us ask Him to make us understand the greatness of this sacrament and the commitments it brings with it. Its reception marked for us that ever-blessed moment when we became children of the Heavenly Father, brothers of Christ Jesus, and when our souls were consecrated like a temple to this Divine Spirit.

1. *Sacrament of our adoption by God.*

BAPTISM is the sacrament of our Divine adoption.

I have shown you that it is by Divine adoption that we become children of God. Baptism is like a spiritual birth in which the life of grace is conferred on us.

---

[1] Hebr. 11:6.   [2] Mark 16:16.   [3] Gal. 3:27.

We possess within us, to start with, a natural life—the one that we receive from our parents according to the flesh. By it, we enter into the human family. That life lasts for some years, and then ends in death.[1] If we had only *that* life, we should never see the face of God. It makes us sons of Adam and, by that very fact, beings that are marked with original sin from the time of our conception. Issuing from the race of Adam, we have received a life that is poisoned at its source; we share the disgrace of the head of our race; we are born, as St. Paul says, "children of wrath."[2] "When one is born, it is Adam who is born—one condemned *from* one condemned."[3] This natural life, the roots of which go down deep to sin, is, of itself, fruitless for heaven: "The flesh profits nothing."[4]

But this natural life—from the "will of man," the "will of the flesh"[5]—is not the only life. God, as I have told you, wishes to give us a higher life which, without destroying the natural life insofar as there is good in it, surpasses that natural life, raises it up and deifies it. God wishes to communicate His own life to us.

We receive this divine life by a new birth, a spiritual birth, which makes us be "born of God."[6] That life is a sharing in the life of God; it is, of its nature, immortal.[7] If we possess it here below, we hold the pledge of eternal bliss, we are "heirs indeed of God."[8] If we do not have it [at death], we are excluded for ever from the Divine society.

Now, the regular means, instituted by Christ, for being born into that life is baptism.

You know that episode of the conversation Nicodemus had with Our Lord, recounted by St. John.[9] This doctor of the Jewish law, a

---

[1] [*Translator's note*: By this, Marmion is *not* of course implying that on our death we do other than continue to exist for ever, for good or ill.]

[2] Eph. 2:3. [3] St. Augustine, *Enarr. in Ps.* 132. [4] John 6:64.

[5] John 1:13. [6] See John 1:13.

[7] "For you have been reborn, not from corruptible seed but from incorruptible, through the word of God who *lives* and abides for ever": 1 Peter 1:23.

[8] Rom. 8:17; Gal. 4:7. [9] See John 3:1 ff.

member of the Great Council, goes along to find Jesus, doubtless to become His disciple, for he regards Christ as a prophet. To his enquiry Our Lord replies: "Truly, truly I say to you: unless a man be born again, he cannot enter into the kingdom of God and its joy." Nicodemus, who does not understand, asks Christ: "How can a man who is already old be born? Can he enter a second time into his mother's womb and be born again?" What does Our Lord reply? What He has already said, but explaining it: "Truly, I say to you: unless a man be born again of water and the Holy Spirit, he cannot enter into the kingdom of God."[1] And Our Lord then contrasts the two lives, the natural and the super-natural: "That which is born of the flesh is flesh; and that which is born of the Spirit is spirit." And He repeats: "Do not wonder that I said to you 'You must be born again.'"

The Church, at the Council of Trent,[2] has laid down the interpretation of this passage: she applies it to baptism. The water regenerates the soul by the power of the Holy Spirit. The washing-clean by water, the perceptible element, and the pouring down of the Spirit, the Divine element, join together to produce the super-natural birth. That is what St. Paul has already said: God has saved us "not because of works of justice we ourselves have done, but because of His mercy, through the water of rebirth and through renewal by the Holy Spirit, the Spirit He has poured out upon us in abundance, through Jesus Christ our Lord; in order that, justified by His grace, we may become, already, heirs in hope of life eternal."[3]

So, you see, baptism constitutes the sacrament of adoption. Going down into the sacred waters, we are born there to divine life; that is why St. Paul describes as a "new man" one who is baptized.[4] God, in making

---

[1] "To be baptized, that is to say, to plunge into water, in order to be purified, was something well-known to the Jews. It only remained to explain to them that there might be a baptism where the Holy Spirit, joining Himself to the water, would renew a man's soul": Bossuet, *Meditations sur l'Évangile*, the Last Supper, 36th day.

[2] Sess. 7, *De baptismo*, can. 2.   [3] See Titus 3:5-7.   [4] Eph. 2:15; 4:24.

us share liberally in His nature, by a gift which infinitely surpasses what our requirements are, creates us afresh, so to say. We are—this is again an expression of the Apostle—a "new creature";[1] and because this life is divine, it is the undivided Trinity that makes the gift of it to us. At the beginning of time, the Trinity presided over the creation of man: "Let us make man to our image and likeness,"[2] and it is also in the name of the Father and of the Son and of the Holy Spirit that our new birth is effected. However, as the words of Jesus and of St. Paul indicate, that new birth is attributed especially to the Holy Spirit, because it is love, above all, that has brought God to adopt us: "See how the Father has shown His love towards us; that we should be counted as God's sons, should be His sons."[3]

This thought is put in high relief in the prayers by which, on Holy Saturday, the bishop blesses the baptismal waters that are to be put at the service of the sacrament. Listen to some of these prayers; they are very significant. "O Almighty and Eternal God ... send forth the Spirit of adoption to regenerate the new people whom the baptismal font will bring to birth for you"; "Look down, O Lord, on your Church and multiply in her your new generations." Then, the bishop calls upon the Divine Spirit to sanctify those waters: "May the Holy Spirit deign, by a secret impression of His divinity, to make fruitful this water prepared for the regeneration of men, so that, this divine font having conceived sanctification, we may see issuing from its immaculate womb a race that is altogether heavenly, creatures that are renewed." All the mysterious rites the Church multiplies at that time as though for the pleasure of it, all the invocations of that magnificent blessing, full of symbolism, are replete with this thought—that it is the Holy Spirit who sanctifies those waters, in order that they who go down into them may be born to divine life, after having been purified of all sin: "May the power of the Holy Spirit descend into all the water of this font ... and make it

---

[1] 2 Cor. 5:17; Gal. 6:15 (Rheims).   [2] Gen. 1:26.   [3] 1 John 3:1 (Knox).

fruitful for regeneration, so that all to whom this mystery of regeneration is applied may be born again, to the perfect innocence of a new childhood."

Such is the greatness of this sacrament; it is the efficacious sign of our Divine adoption. Through it we become truly children of God and we are incorporated into Christ. It then opens the door to all the heavenly graces. Hold on to this truth: that all the mercies of God in our regard, all His condescensions, derive from our adoption. When the eyes of our soul gaze into the depths of the Divinity, the first thing revealed to us about the Eternal purpose concerning us is the decree of our adoption in Jesus Christ. And all the favors God can shower upon a soul here below, right up to the day when, in the bliss of His Trinity, He communicates Himself without ending to that soul, have this initial grace of baptism as the first link to which the favors are attached. At that predestined moment, we have entered into the family of God, we have become members of a divine race, assured (in principle) of our eternal inheritance. At the time of our baptism, through which Christ prints an indelible character upon our soul, we receive the "pledge of the Spirit"[1]—the Divine Spirit—which renders us worthy of the Eternal Father's delight and, provided we are faithful in holding on to this pledge, makes us sure of all the favors that are granted to those whom God regards as His children.

That is why the saints, who have so clear a view of super-natural realities, have always held baptismal grace in such high esteem: the day of our baptism marked for us the dawning of God's liberalities and of our future glory.

[1] 2 Cor. 1:22; 5:5 (Rheims).

2. Sacrament of *Christian initiation*; the symbolism and grace of baptism explained by St. Paul.

BAPTISM will appear greater still to us if we consider it in its aspect of being the *sacrament of Christian initiation.*

As I have told you, our Divine adoption takes place in Jesus Christ. We only become children of God in order to be conformed, through grace, to the one Son of the Father. Never forget that it is only in His beloved Son that God predestined us to adoption: He "predestined us to be adopted through Jesus Christ"[1] as His children in order that He, His Son, might be "the firstborn among many brethren."[2] Moreover, it is the satisfactions of Christ that have merited this grace for us — as, again, it is Christ who remains our model when we desire to live as children of the Heavenly Father. We shall understand this perfectly if we recall the way in which Christian initiation was originally carried out.

In the first ages of the Church, as you know, baptism was ordinarily conferred only upon adults, after quite a long period of preparation during which the new convert was instructed in the truths he ought to believe. It was on Holy Saturday, or rather, the very night of Easter, that the sacrament was administered in the baptistery, a small building detached from the church, like the one to be seen in Italian cathedrals. The rites of the bishop's blessing of the baptismal font having been completed, the catechumen — that is, the one aspiring to be baptized — went down into the font. There, as the Greek word *baptizein* indicates, he was "plunged" into the water while the priest was pronouncing the sacramental words: "I baptize you in the name of the Father and of the Son and of the Holy Spirit." Thus, the catechumen was buried, as it were, beneath the waters — from which he then came out by the steps on the opposite side. There his godfather waited for him, dried off the holy water and re-clothed him.

---

[1] Eph. 1:5.   [2] Rom. 8:29.

When all the catechumens had been baptized, the bishop gave them a white robe, symbolizing the purity of their hearts; and then he marked the forehead of each of them with an unguent made of holy oil, saying: "May Almighty God, who has regenerated you by water and the Holy Spirit and has forgiven you all your sins, Himself anoint you unto life eternal." When all these rites were concluded, the procession went off back to the basilica. The newly baptized walked in front, clothed in white and carrying in their hands a lighted candle, to symbolize Christ, the Light of the world. Then began the Mass of the Resurrection, celebrating the triumph of Christ coming forth, victorious, from the tomb, alive with a new life which He communicates to all His elect. So happy was the Church at these new additions she had just brought to the flock of Christ, that for eight days they would have a separate place in the basilica, and the liturgy would be full of the thought of them during the whole of the Easter octave.[1]

So you see, these ceremonies are in the first place full of symbolism. They point, according to St. Paul himself, to the death and entombment, followed by the resurrection, of Jesus Christ, in all of which the Christian has a share.

But there is more than a symbol; there is grace produced. And if the ancient rites that pointed to the symbolism have been simplified since the practice of baptizing children was introduced, the power of the sacrament stays the same. The symbolism is only the outer skin; the

---

[1] Those catechumens prevented, by absence or insufficient preparation, from receiving baptism on Easter night received it on the night of Pentecost, within that solemnity which commemorates the visible coming of the Holy Spirit on the apostles and which at the same time closes the season of Easter. The same solemn rites, of the blessing of the fonts and the giving of the sacrament, were at that time repeated. To the symbolism of Easter, which remained in its entirety, there was added more explicitly at that time the thought of the Holy Spirit, who by His Divine power regenerates the soul in the baptismal water. Like the Masses of the Easter octave, those of the octave of Pentecost contain more than one allusion to those newly baptized.

rites have in substance remained, retaining with them the inner grace of the sacrament.

St. Paul explains, in a deep way, the original symbolism and the baptismal grace. Here, to begin with, is a summary of his thought which will make us better understand his words that follow.

The immersion in the waters of the font represents the death and burial of Christ: we share in it by burying within the holy waters sin and all attachment to sin, which we renounce. The "old" man,[1] sullied by Adam's fault, disappears beneath the waters and is buried, like a dead man (it is only the dead that we bury), as in a tomb. The coming forth from the baptismal font is the birth of the new man, purified from sin, regenerated by the water that has been made fruitful by the Holy Spirit. The soul is adorned with grace, which is the wellspring of divine life; is adorned with the infused virtues and the gifts of the Holy Spirit. It was a sinner who was plunged into the font; he leaves behind there all his sins and it is a just man who comes forth from it, imitating Christ coming forth from the tomb, and living with divine life.[2]

Such is the grace of baptism, indicated by the symbolism, a symbolism which appeared in fullest relief and all its significance when baptism was administered on Easter night.

Let us listen now to St. Paul himself: "Do you not know that all we who have been baptized into Christ Jesus"—in order to become members of the mystical body of Christ—"have been baptized into His death?"[3] In other words, the death of Jesus is for us the model and the meritorious cause of our death to sin in baptism. Why have we to "die"? Because

---

[1] St. Paul means by the "old" man the natural man—such as is born and lives, from the moral point of view, as a son of Adam, before being reborn in baptism through the grace of Jesus Christ.

[2] "... that by the mystery of one and the same element there may be both the end of vice and the beginning of virtue": Solemn blessing of the baptismal font on Holy Saturday.   [3] Rom. 6:3.

Christ, our model, is dead: we "have been *planted together* in the likeness of His death."[1] And what is it that dies? Tainted, corrupted, nature—the "old" man. "Our old self has been crucified *with Him*." And why? So that we may be free from sin: "that the body of sin may be destroyed, that we may no longer be slaves to sin."[2] For (continues St. Paul, explaining the symbolism) we have been "buried together with Him by baptism" in union with His death, in order that, just as Christ is risen from the dead by the glorious power of His Father, "so we also may walk in newness of life."[3]

There we have indicated to us the commitment to which we are held by baptismal grace: "to walk in newness of life"—that life which Christ, our Exemplar, shows us in His resurrection. Why is that? If it is the case that, through our union with Christ, we have reproduced the image of His death, we ought also to reproduce, by a life that is wholly spiritual, the image of His resurrected life. And our "old" man has indeed been crucified with Him, that is to say has been destroyed by the death of Christ, in order that we may no longer be in slavery to sin; for he that is dead is set free from sin.[4] So then, at baptism we have renounced sin for ever.

That is not enough; for we have, besides, received the seed-germ of divine life, and it is this germ that—"for ever," here also—must develop within us. That is what St. Paul adds: "But if we have died with Christ, we believe that we shall also live together with Christ";[5] and that,

---

[1] Rom. 6:5 (Rheims).   [2] Rom. 6:6.

[3] Rom. 6:4 (Rheims). "Just like one who is buried in the earth, so one who is baptized is immersed in the water. Wherefore in baptism also there is a threefold immersion, not only because of faith in the Trinity but also to represent the three days during which Christ was buried, and this is why it was on Holy Saturday that the Church celebrated solemn baptism": St Thomas, On the epistle to the Romans, c. VI, 1.i.

[4] "The sinful man," says St. Thomas, "is buried, by baptism, into the Passion and death of Christ; it is as if he himself suffered and died the Savior's suffering and death. And as the Passion and death of Christ has the power to satisfy for sin and for all the debts of sin, the soul that is associated through baptism with this satisfaction is free from all debt towards the justice of God": III, q. LXIX, a. 2.   [5] Rom. 6:8.

unceasingly. For Christ—who not only is our model but also infuses His grace into us—Christ, "having risen from the dead, dies now no more, death shall no longer have dominion over Him"; He died to sin once and for all, and His life is henceforth a life lived for God.[1]

St. Paul concludes his exposition with this application of it addressed to those who, through baptism, share in the death and the life of Christ, their model: "Let *you yourselves, also,* consider yourselves dead to sin, and alive for God, through Christ Jesus"[2]—Jesus, into whom you are incorporated through baptismal grace.

Such are the words of the great apostle. According to him, baptism represents the death and resurrection of Christ Jesus, and it produces that which it represents: it makes us *die to sin,* and grants us to *live in Jesus Christ.*

3. How *Christ's existence on earth encompasses the twofold aspect of "death" and "life"* that baptism reproduces in us.

IN ORDER THAT you may have a greater understanding of this profound doctrine, we must now highlight that twofold aspect of the life of Christ which is reproduced in us from the time of our baptism, and which ought to mark our entire existence.

As I have told you, the Divine plan of the super-natural adoption conferred on Adam was cut across by sin. The sin of the head of human-kind was transmitted to the whole of his race and excluded that race from the eternal kingdom. In order that heaven's doors might be re-opened, there needed to be reparation for the offense against God, an adequate and total satisfaction that would efface the infinite malice of the sin. And man, being simply a creature, was incapable of supplying it. The Word Incarnate, God-made-man, took that upon Himself; and because of this, His whole life, right up to the moment of the

---

[1] Rom. 6:9.   [2] See Rom. 6:11.

consummation of His sacrifice, was marked with a character of death. Of course, our Divine Savior had neither contracted the original fault nor committed personal sin, nor suffered those consequences of sin that were incompatible with His divinity, such as error, ignorance, illness. He is in everything like His brethren, save that He never at any time knew sin. Instead, He is the Lamb who takes away the sins of the world; His coming is for the purpose of saving sinners. But God has placed upon Him the iniquity of sinners: and (Christ having, from the time of His entry into this world, accepted the sacrifice His Father asked of Him) the whole of His existence, from the cradle to Calvary, bears a victim's mark.[1] Look at Him in His humiliations at Bethlehem; look at Him fleeing before Herod's anger, living a laborer's life in a workshop. Look at Him, during His public life, suffering the hate of His enemies. Look at Him during His sorrowful Passion—from the agony in the garden, which filled Him with grief and anguish, right up to His Father's abandonment of Him on the cross; at His being like a lamb led to the slaughter,[2] like a worm of the earth, cursed and trodden underfoot,[3] for He came "in the likeness of sinful flesh."[4] A propitiation for the crimes of the whole world, He paid off the universal debt only by dying upon a gibbet.

That death has earned eternal life for us. Jesus Christ slays, destroys, sin at the very time when death strikes Him—He, the innocent one, victim for all the sins of men:

> *Together Death and Life in a strange conflict strove:*
> *The Prince of Life who died now lives and reigns.*[5]

---

[1] Christ, however, cannot be said to be, in the strict sense of the word, a "penitent." A "penitent" has to pay off in justice a *personal* debt; and Christ is a high priest who is holy and "without sin" (Hebr. 4:15 [Rheims]). The debt He pays off is that of the whole human race, and He pays it off only because He has substituted Himself for us all, through love.   [2] Jerem. 11:19.   [3] Ps. 21 (22):7.

[4] Rom. 8:3.   [5] Sequence of the Mass of Easter Day.

Death and Life engage in strange combat. The Author of life dies, but, returned to life, He reigns. Of old, the prophet had exalted in advance this triumph of Christ: "O death, I will be your death."[1] To the question "O death, where is your victory?"[2] St. Paul gives answer: "Death is swallowed up in victory"[3]—the victory of Christ as He comes forth from the tomb. "By dying He destroyed our death, and by rising again He restored our life."[4]

For, once risen, Christ Jesus has returned to a life that is *new*. Christ "dies now no more, death shall no longer have dominion over him." He destroyed sin once and for all, and His life thenceforth is a life lived for God, a glorious life that would be crowned on the day of the Ascension.

You may say to me: has not Christ's life always been a life lived for God? Oh, certainly! Christ has lived only for His Father; in coming into the world He gave Himself up entirely to doing the will of His Father: "Behold, I come to do your will, O God."[5] That was His "food": "My food is to do the will of Him who sent me."[6] Even His Passion— He accepts it because He loves His Father: "that the world may know that I love the Father."[7] Despite the repugnance that He *feels*, He takes the chalice offered at the Agony, and only when He has accomplished everything does He expire. He can truly sum up the whole of His life by saying: "I do always the things that are pleasing to Him"[8]—for what He has always sought is the glory of His Father: "I honor my Father.... I do not seek my own glory."[9]

So therefore it is true that even before His resurrection Our Lord lived only for God, His life was devoted only to the interests and the

---

[1] Hos. 13:14.   [2] 1 Cor. 15:55.   [3] 1 Cor. 15:54.

[4] Preface of Easter time. [*Translator's note*: "destroyed our death." Before and after Christ's resurrection, the human soul was, and is, immortal. "Life" in this Preface refers to the super-natural life of grace, intended to culminate in eternal life with God in heaven. It is the absence of the possibility of that, owing to the Fall—such *absence* of super-natural life being given the opposite name, "death"—that Christ destroyed by His death on the cross.]   [5] Hebr. 10:9.   [6] John 4:34.

[7] John 14:31.   [8] John 8:29.   [9] John 8:49-50.

glory of His Father. But up to then He has—entirely also—been tinged with the character of a victim; whereas, once come forth from the tomb, free henceforth of every debt towards Divine Justice, Christ now lives for God alone. It is henceforth a perfect life, a life in all its fullness and splendor, without any bodily frailty, without there being ahead of Him a vista of expiation, of death, or even of suffering: "Death shall no longer have dominion over him." Everything in the risen Christ bears the character of life—glorious life in which wonderful prerogatives of liberty, of incorruptibility, in His body freed from all servitude are revealed to the dazzled sight of the apostles, even here below. A life that was an uninterrupted hymn of thanksgiving and praise, a life that would be exalted for ever on the day of the Ascension, when Christ would take permanent possession of the glory due to His humanity.

This twofold aspect of death and life, which characterizes the existence of the Incarnate Word among us, and which attains its highest intensity and splendor in His Passion and resurrection, ought to be reproduced by each Christian, by all those who are incorporated in Christ through baptism.

Having become disciples of Jesus in the sacred font, by an act which symbolizes both His death and His resurrection, we ought to reproduce that death and that resurrection throughout the days given us to spend here. This is what St. Augustine so well said: "Christ is our Way. Therefore, look upon Christ: He came in order to suffer, so as to merit glory; He came in order to court contempt, so as to be exalted; He came in order to die, but also to rise from the dead."[1] That is the very echo of the thought of St. Paul: "You also must consider yourselves to be dead to sin,"[2] as having renounced sin, so as now to live solely for God.

[1] *Sermo* LXII, c. 11.
[2] See Rom. 6:11. "Living to sin," "dying to sin" are familiar expressions with St. Paul; they signify "remaining in sin," "renouncing sin."

When we gaze upon Christ, what do we find in Him? A mystery of death and of life: He "was delivered up for our sins, and rose again for our justification."[1] The Christian takes and places in his own life that twofold element which makes him resemble Christ. St. Paul is very explicit about the above. He says: "Buried with Christ in baptism, you have, in that same baptism, been raised with Christ. You were dead (to eternal life) through your sins: He has given you back eternal life, pardoning you all your offenses."[2] Just as Christ has left in the tomb the winding-cloths which are an image of His state of death and of His life when it was subject to suffering, so we also have left all our sins behind in the baptismal waters. In the same way as Christ came forth, free and living, from the sepulchre, in that same way have we come forth from the holy font, not only purified from all sin but with our soul adorned, through the operation of the Spirit, with grace the wellspring of divine life—grace with its procession of virtues and gifts. The soul has become a temple where the Blessed Trinity dwells and an object of the Divine delight.

4. The whole of *the Christian life* is but the *development* in practice *of the twofold initial grace* given at baptism: *"death to sin"* and *"life for God."* Sentiments to which remembrance of baptism ought to give rise in us: *thanksgiving, joy* and *trust.*

THERE IS ONE TRUTH of which we must not lose sight, one of which St. Paul has already given us a hint. It is that this divine life that God gives us is only in the germ state; it has to increase and flower, just as our renunciation and our "death to sin" must constantly be renewed and sustained.

We lost everything at a stroke, by one single fault of Adam, but God does not give at one single time, at baptism, give us back the

[1] Rom. 4:25.   [2] See Col. 2:12-13.

Divine gift in its wholly unimpaired state. He leaves concupiscence[1] in us, to be a source of merits through the struggles to which it gives rise (concupiscence which is the seat of sin and conducive to the diminishing and destroying of the divine life). Which means that the task of the whole of our earthly existence is to bring about what baptism inaugurates. Through baptism, we are in communion with the mystery and Divine power of the death and resurrected life of Christ. "Death to sin" has been effected; but, because of the concupiscence that remains, we have to maintain that death by our continual renunciation of Satan, of his inspirations and works, of the enticements of the world and of the flesh. Grace, within us, is the source of life. But it is a germ which we have to develop, it is that kingdom of God within us that Our Lord Himself compares to a seed, to a grain of mustard that grows into a big tree. That is how it is with the divine life in us.

Look at how St. Paul expounds this truth to us. By being baptized, he says, you have stripped off the old self, with his works of death (the old self that descends from Adam), you have put on the new self created in justice and truth (the soul re-born in Jesus Christ through the Holy Spirit), the self constantly renewed in the image of its Creator.[2] Paul says the same thing to his dear flock the faithful of Ephesus;[3] he speaks of them being taught in Christ that, regard being had to their former manner of life, they are to put off the old self which is "being corrupted through its deceptive lusts"[4] and be renewed in the innermost part of the soul, putting on that new self which has been created conformably to God in true holiness and justice. Here below, then, for so long as we are on our earthly pilgrimage, we ought to pursue that twofold operation of death to sin and life for God: "Let you yourselves, also, consider yourselves dead to sin."[5]

In God's designs, that death to sin is something permanent, and that life is, of its nature, immortal; but we can lose that life and fall

---

[1] [*Translator's note*: concupiscence: "desire of the lower appetite contrary to reason": "the flesh lusts against the spirit": Gal. 5:17.]

[2] Col. 3:9-10.   [3] Eph. 4:20-24.   [4] Eph. 4:22.   [5] See Rom. 6:11.

into death again through sin. So it will be our task to preserve, to conserve and develop, that seed-germ until we arrive, on the Last Day, at the fullness of the age of Christ. The whole of Christian asceticism derives from baptismal grace and is simply directed to making there open out to flower, freed from every obstruction, that Divine seed-germ cast into the soul by the Church on the day of her children's initiation. *The Christian life is nothing other than the progressive and continued development, the application in practice, throughout the whole of our human existence, of the twofold initial act put into us in seed form at baptism, of the twofold super-natural result of "death" and of "life" produced by this sacrament.* In that is to be found the whole program of Christianity.

In the same way, too, our final beatitude is nothing other than total and permanent liberation from sin and death and suffering, and the glorious blossoming of that divine life planted in us along with the character of being baptized.

As you see, it is the very death and very life of Christ that are re-produced in our souls as from the moment of baptism; but the death is so that we may have the life. Oh, if we only understood St. Paul's words: "All you who have been baptized into Christ, have put on Christ."[1] Not simply clothed as with a garment we wear on the outside, but clothed interiorly.[2] We are "grafted" upon Him, in Him, says St. Paul[3]—for He is the vine, and we the branches[4]—and it is His divine life that, like the sap of a vine, flows within us,[5] in order that we may

---

[1] Gal. 3:27.

[2] This truth was signified by the white robe that clothed the new converts when they came out from the baptismal font. At the baptism of children nowadays, the priest, after the pouring of the water of re-birth, places a white veil upon the head of the one baptized.   [3] Rom. 11:17.   [4] John 15:5.

[5] "All the branches are holy if the root is holy." Like "shoots of wild olive, you have been grafted ... to share ... the rich sap provided by the olive tree itself": Rom. 11:16-17 (Jerus.). Here is a magnificent prayer of the Church, containing all this doctrine: note that it was said on Saturday the eve of Pentecost, a little before the solemn blessing of the baptismal fonts and the bestowal of baptism upon the

be "transformed into Him": "We are being transformed into his very image."[1] Through faith in Him, we have received Him at baptism: His death becomes *our* death to Satan and his works, to sin; His life becomes *our* life. That initial act which makes us children of God has rendered us brethren of Christ, we have been incorporated into Him, we have been made members of His Church, animated by His Spirit. Baptized into Christ, we are born, through grace, to the divine life in Christ. That is why, says St. Paul, we should "walk in newness of life."[2] Let us walk no longer in the sin that we have renounced, but in the light of faith, under the action of the Divine Spirit, who will grant us to produce many fruits of holiness through our good works,

Let us renew often the power of this sacrament of adoption and initiation, by renewing its promises—so that Christ, who that day was born in our souls by faith, may grow more and more in us *ad gloriam Patris*, to the glory of the Father. That is a pious practice which is very useful. Look at St. Paul: in his letter to his disciple Timothy he entreats him to stir up in his soul the grace of his priestly ordination.[3] I wish to say the same thing to you about baptismal grace. Make the grace received at baptism come alive in you, by renewing the vows you made then. When, with faith and love—for example, after receiving Holy Communion, while Our Lord is really present in our heart—we renew within us the dispositions of repentance, of renunciation of Satan, sin and the world, in order to attach ourselves to Christ alone—then, the grace of baptism shoots up, so to speak, from the depths of our soul

---

catechumens. "Almighty and Eternal God, who, through your only Son, have shown your Church that you are the Heavenly Husbandman, gently tending, so that they may bear abundant grapes, all the branches rendered fruitful in this same Christ your Son who is the true Vine: let not the thorns of sin over-run your faithful, whom you have caused to pass through the baptismal font like a vine transplanted from Egypt. Your Spirit of sanctification protecting them, let them be enriched by an unending harvest."   [1] 2 Cor. 3:18.

[2] Rom. 6:4.   [3] 2 Tim. 1:6.

where the baptized state remains graven indelibly; and this grace produces, by the power of Christ who dwells in us with His Spirit, what is like a new death to sin, like a new influx of divine life, like a new intensity of union with Jesus Christ.

In this way, although each day (as St. Paul says) the earthly man, the natural man, approaches nearer and nearer to death, yet the inner man—the one who has received divine life through the super-natural birth of baptism, the one who has been re-created in the justice of Christ, the "new" man—is renewed day by day. "Wherefore we do not lose heart. On the contrary, even though our outer man is decaying, yet our inner man *is being renewed day by day.*"[1]

And this renewal, inaugurated at baptism, continues throughout the whole of our Christian existence, remains, right up to what we come to in the glorious perfection of eternal immortality. "The things that are seen are temporal, but the things that are not seen are eternal."[2] On earth, St. Paul says again, this life is hidden in the depths of the soul. It expresses itself outwardly by our works, of course; but the mainspring of them is hidden within us. Here below "you have died and your life is hidden with Christ in God. When *Christ, your life*, shall appear, then you too will appear with Him in glory."[3]

In awaiting the coming of that blessed day when our interior renewal will shine forth in its eternal beauty, we ought often, from the depths of our hearts, to *thank* God for the Divine adoption given at baptism: it is the initial grace from which all the others flow for us. All our greatness has its source in baptism which has given us divine life. In the absence of this divine life, human life—as brilliant as it may be exteriorly, as full as it may appear—has no value for eternity; it is baptism that gives to our life the wellspring of its true fecundity. This thankfulness should show itself by a generous and constant fidelity to our baptismal promises. We ought so to be penetrated by a feeling of

[1] 2 Cor. 4:16.   [2] 2 Cor. 4:18.   [3] Col. 3:3-4.

our super-natural dignity in being a Christian, that we reject whatever can tarnish it and seek only for what is in conformity with it.[1]

Gratitude is the first feeling that baptismal grace should cause to arise in us. *Joy* is the second. We ought never to think of our baptism without a deep feeling of inner exhilaration. On the day of our baptism we were born, in principle, to eternal bliss. We hold the pledge of it, even, in that sanctifying grace we were then given. Having entered into the family of God, we have the right to share in the inheritance of the only Son. What greater motive for joy could there be for a soul, here below, than to reflect that on the day of our baptism the gaze of the Eternal Father rested upon it with love, and that the Father, by whispering the name of "child," called it to share in the blessings showered upon Christ?

Finally and above all, we should yield up our souls to great *confidence*. In our dealings with our Heavenly Father we should remember that we are His children, through participation in the Sonship of Christ Jesus, our elder brother. To doubt our adoption, and the rights it gives us, is to doubt Christ Himself. Never forget: we "put on" Christ on the day of our baptism; or, rather, we were incorporated into Him. We have, therefore, the right to present ourselves before the Eternal Father and say to Him: "I am your only-begotten one"—to speak in the name of His Son, to ask Him, with absolute confidence, for everything we need.

When the Trinity created us, it was to its own "image and likeness."[2] In conferring adoption on us at baptism, the Trinity imprinted on our souls the very features of Christ. And that is why, when seeing us clothed with sanctifying grace, which makes us resemble His Divine

---

[1] "O God ... grant to all admitted to those who profess Christianity that they may both reject those things which are opposed to that name and pursue those things which are appropriate to it": Prayer for the third Sunday after Easter.
[2] Gen. 1:26.

Son, the Eternal Father cannot but grant us what we are asking of Him not of ourselves but in reliance on the one in whom He places His delight.

Such is the grace and power that baptism brings us—of making us brethren of Christ by super-natural adoption, brethren capable, in all truth, of sharing His Divine life and His eternal inheritance: "You have put on Christ."

O Christian, when will you recognize your greatness and your dignity? When will you proclaim, through your works, that you are of a divine race? When will you live as a worthy disciple of Christ?

Twofold Aspect of the Christian Life:

Death to Sin, Life for God

DEATH TO SIN

CHAPTER THREE

"WHO CAN UNDERSTAND SIN?"

INTRODUCTION: *Death to sin* — first fruit of baptismal grace, *first aspect of the Christian life.*

BY ITS SYMBOLISM and by the grace it produces, baptism (as St. Paul shows us) stamps the whole of our Christian existence with the twofold character of "death to sin" and "life for God": "You also must consider yourselves dead to sin."[1] It is true that Christianity, properly speaking, is *life*: "Come to me that you may have life,"[2] says Our Lord — this is the divine life which, from the humanity of Christ where it is in its fullness, flows down on each of our souls. But that life does not open out to flower in us without effort. Its development remains conditioned upon the destruction of what is in opposition to it — that is to say, sin. Sin is, in a strict sense, the obstacle that prevents the divine life from developing and even from being maintained within us.

But, you may say to me, has not baptism destroyed sin in us? Certainly, it wipes out original sin and, when it is conferred on an adult, personal sins. It remits even the debt due because of sin. It produces in us "death to sin." In the designs of God, that death is permanent, definitive; we need not fall into sin again: "that we may no longer be slaves to sin."[3]

[1] See Rom. 6:11.   [2] John 5:40.   [3] Rom. 6:6.

However, baptism has not taken away concupiscence; this seat of sin remains in us. God has willed it so, He has willed that our liberty be exercised in the struggle, and thereby reap for us "a copious harvest of merits," says the Council of Trent.[1] This "death to sin" then, effected in principle at baptism, becomes for us a condition of our having life; we have to weaken the action of concupiscence within us, in the greatest measure possible. It is at such a price that the divine life will blossom out in our souls—blossom in the same degree as we renounce sin, and the habits of sin, and our attachments to it.

One of the means of arriving at this necessary destruction of sin is to have a hatred of it: one makes no pact at all with an enemy one hates. To have this hatred of sin, it would be necessary for us to know its deep malice and diabolical ugliness. But who can understand the malice of sin? To measure it, we would have had to understand God Himself whom it insults. And that is why the Psalmist cries out:[2] "Who has an understanding of sin?"[3]

Let us however, in the light of reason and above all of Revelation, try to get some idea of it. Let us suppose a baptized soul who, knowingly and voluntarily, commits a grave sin, deliberately violates, in a grave matter, one of the Divine commandments. What does that soul do? What does it become? We know that it scorns God, that it ranges itself among the enemies of Christ, to make Him die. And, lastly, it destroys the divine life within itself. *That* is the work of its sin.

---

[1] Catechism of the Council of Trent, c. XVI.   [2] Ps. 18 (19):13.

[3] [*Translator's note*: The Rheims has "Who can understand sins?," plural. But Marmion firmly (and surely very reasonably) interprets this as "Who can understand what sin is?" Some modern translations, influenced by the next succeeding words of that verse of the psalm, interpret its opening words along the lines of "Who can detect (or understand) one's own failings?"]

1. Mortal sin — basically a *scorning* of the rights and perfections *of God; a cause of the sufferings of Christ.*

SIN, it has been said, is "ill done to God."[1]

That term, as you know, is not strictly exact — it is only our way of speaking; for suffering is incompatible with Divinity. Sin is "ill done to God" because it is a denial, by a created being, of the existence of God, of His truth, His sovereignty, His holiness, His goodness. What does the soul of whom I spoke do when freely carrying out an action contrary to the law of God? That soul denies in practice that God is Sovereign Wisdom and that He has the power to lay down laws. That soul denies in practice God's holiness, and refuses to give Him the adoration He deserves. That soul denies in practice that God is the Almighty and has the right to demand obedience from beings who take their life from Him, denies that God is Supreme Goodness, worthy to be preferred to everything that is not that Goodness. Such a soul lowers God to a level below that of created beings. "I will not serve," "I do not recognize you, I will not serve you" — he repeats the words of Lucifer the rebel on the day of his revolt. Does that soul cry this with his mouth? No — not always at least; he would not like to, perhaps. But he cries it by his *act.* Sin is in practice a denying of the existence of the Divine perfections; it is in practice a scorning of the rights of God. In practice, if the thing were not rendered impossible by the nature of Divinity, that soul would do ill to Infinite Majesty and Infinite Goodness, would destroy God.

And is not this what in fact happened? When God took on human form, did not sin succeed in making Him die?

I have already said to you that the sufferings and Passion of Christ are a most shining revelation of God's love: "Greater love than this no one has."[2] Neither is there a deeper revelation of the immense malice of sin. Let us, with faith, contemplate for a few moments the sorrows the

---

[1] [*Translator's note*: Marmion's phrase is "*le mal de Dieu.*"]   [2] John 15:13.

Incarnate Word endured when the hour came for Him to expiate sin. We can scarcely form an idea of the depths of suffering and abasement to which sin made Him descend.

Christ Jesus is God's own and only Son; He is the object of the Father's delight; the Father's whole work is to glorify Him. For He is full of grace, grace superabounds in Him—this is an innocent high priest who, though He is like us, nevertheless knows no sin or imperfection. "Which of you," He said to the Jews, "can convict me of sin?"[1] "The prince of the world"—that is, Satan—"has no power over me."[2] So true is this, that it was unavailing for his bitterest enemies, the Pharisees, to comb through His life, examine His doctrine, keep their eyes upon all His actions and words, as hate knew how. They found no grounds on which to condemn Him: in order to find a pretext they had to have recourse to false witnesses. Jesus is purity itself, the reflection of the infinite perfections of His Father, the brightest splendor of the Father's glory.[3]

And see how the Father treated this Son when the time came for Jesus to pay off the debt due in justice for sins—pay it off in place of us. See how He was stricken, this Lamb of God[4] who was substituted for sinners. The Eternal Father willed, by that will which nothing can resist, to crush Him with suffering: "to bruise him in infirmity."[5] In the

---

[1] John 8:46.   [2] John 14:30 (Jerus.)   [3] Hebr. 1:3.   [4] John 1:29.

[5] Isa. 53:10. [*Translator's note*: In making his entirely valid point about the enormity of sin, Marmion pushes his own rhetoric—"See how the Father treated His Son"—to a point where it shocks. Here and later, such rhetoric almost presents Isaiah's references to the Son being stricken as though the Father positively wished to strike the Son. Of course, Marmion is actually saying no such appalling thing. ("*Supposed*," by us, to be stricken by God, but really stricken by our sins, says Isaiah.) "Our Divine Savior," wrote St. Francis de Sales, "was equally the beloved of His Father ... on Tabor where He was transfigured, and on Calvary where He was crucified." But on the cross, while truly being and remaining the Eternal Son incarnate, Christ was substituted for us and *represented sin and our sinfulness*—that is the point Marmion is making. "Christ accepted the taking of our sins upon Himself," wrote Marmion in an earlier chapter (page 67) "to the extent of His becoming upon the cross, in a way,

holy soul of Jesus, waves of sadness, worry, fear, weariness, pile up one upon the other, to the point where His immaculate body is bathed in a sweat of blood. So troubled and overwhelmed is He by our "torrents of iniquity,"[1] that in the repugnance experienced by His nature, a nature that feels things, He asks the Father that He may not drink the cup of bitterness that is presented to Him: "Father, if it is possible, let this cup pass away from me."[2] At the Last Supper on the eve of His Passion, He had not spoken in that way. "Father, I will...."[3] was what He said at *that* time to His Father, for He is the Father's equal. But now, the shame with which the sins of men cover Him—sins He had taken upon Himself—invades the whole of His soul, and He prays as if He were a criminal: "Father, if it is possible...." But the Father does not will it; this is the hour of justice, it is the hour when He wills to deliver up His Son, His own Son, like a plaything, to the power of darkness: "This is your hour; this is the reign of darkness."[4]

Betrayed by one of His apostles, abandoned by the others, denied by the leader of the apostles, Christ Jesus becomes an object of mockery and of outrages in the hands of a troop of lackeys. Look at Him— He, Almighty God—slapped in the face! That adorable face, which gives joy to the saints, now covered in spittle. They scourge Him, they hammer a crown of thorns on to His head; in derision they throw a purple robe over His shoulders, they put a reed into His hand. Then

---

universal sin, living sin." "He was wounded for our transgressions, bruised for our iniquities" (Isaiah). See Marmion's further explanation ("If we want to know ..."), albeit a disturbingly rhetorical one still, three paragraphs below the present one.

The Father's "sending" His Son (the word used by Christ in John 5:23 and elsewhere) in the knowledge that He would suffer at the hands of men should not be evaluated as if the "sending" were by you or me. It was because He "so loved the world" that He "*gave* His only-begotten Son" (John 3:16), but our human understanding cannot plumb the Divine, the Trinitarian, depths of it. Read again Marmion's words ("But, to make ...") on pages 67-68.]

[1] Ps. 17(18):5.   [2] Matt. 26:39; Mark 14:36; Luke 22:42.
[3] John 17:24.   [4] Luke 22:53 (Jerus.)

those lackeys bend the knee before Him with insolent mockery—what an abyss of ignominy for Him before whom the angels tremble! Gaze at Him—He, the Master of the Universe—treated as a malefactor, an imposter, put on a level with a notorious robber whom the crowd prefer to Him. Look at Him, cast outside the law, condemned, fastened to the cross between two thieves; enduring the pain of nails hammered into His hands and feet, enduring a thirst that tortures Him. He sees the people on whom He has showered benefits wag their heads as a sign of scorn. He hears the hateful sarcasm of His enemies: "He saved others, himself he cannot save," "let him come down now from the cross"—then, and only then, will we believe in him.[1] What humiliation and what obloquy!

Let us gaze at this startling spectacle of the sufferings of Christ, traced a very long time in advance by the prophet Isaiah. One cannot subtract a single feature of it; one must read it all, for all its features have a bearing. "Many were astonished at him—his appearance was so marred, beyond human semblance, and his form beyond that of the sons of men." He had no form or beauty to attract our eyes, no looks to make us be desirous of him. "He was despised and rejected by men; a man of sorrows" whom suffering has touched; "and as one from whom men hide their faces he was despised, and we esteemed him not." Truly he has borne our griefs and carried our sorrows; yet we regarded him as stricken by God and subjected to humiliation. "But he was wounded for our transgressions, he was bruised for our iniquities ... the Lord has laid on him the iniquity of us all." He was ill-used, yet he submitted to suffering, and "he opened not his mouth; like a lamb that is led to the slaughter, and like a sheep that before its shearers is dumb." He was put to death by an unjust condemnation; and who among his contemporaries thought that he was being cut off from the land of the living—that sorrow was

---

[1] Matt. 27:42; Mark 15:31-32.

striking him—*for the sins of his people?* For it was the Lord's will that he be broken by suffering.[1]

Does that suffice? No, not yet; our Divine Savior has not yet touched the lowest depth of sorrow. Look at Him, O my soul; look at your God hanging on the cross; He has no longer the look of what is human, even. He has become like something thrown away, scorned by the people: "I am a worm, and no man: the reproach of men, and the outcast of the people."[2] His body is one big wound; His soul is as though melted beneath suffering and derision. And at that moment, the Evangelist tells us, Jesus lets out a great cry: "My God, my God, why have you forsaken me?"[3] Jesus has been abandoned by His Father. We shall never know what an abyss of suffering that abandonment of Christ by His Father represents. That is a mystery of which no soul can sound the depths. Jesus abandoned by His Father! Yet, all His life, has He not done the will of His Father? Has He not fulfilled the mission He has received, of manifesting His Father's name to the world?—"I have manifested your name"[4] to men. Was it not from love that He delivered Himself up?—"that the world may know that I love the Father."[5] Oh, most certainly! Why, then, O Eternal Father, are you striking your beloved Son thus? *"For the wickedness of my people have I struck him."*[6] Because at that time Christ was delivered up for us so that He might give a full and entire satisfaction for sin, the Father no longer saw in His Son anything except the sin with which Christ was clothed, to the extent that sin seemed to consist in *Him*: "For our sake God made the sinless one into sin."[7] He had then, for our sake, "become a curse": "Christ redeemed us ... becoming a curse for us."[8] His Father abandoned Him; and even though, at the summit of His being, Christ still kept the

[1] Isa. 52:14; 53:2-10; Marmion used the translation into French of l'Abbé Crampon; the English direct quotations from Isaiah in this paragraph are taken from RSV, Cath. [2] Ps. 21 (22):7.
[3] Matt. 27:46; Mark 15:34; Ps. 21 (22):2. [4] John 17:6.
[5] John 14:31. [6] Isa. 53:8. [7] 2 Cor. 5:21 (Jerus.) [8] Gal. 3:13.

ineffable joy of the Beatific Vision, this abandonment plunged the soul of Jesus into a sorrow so deep that it wrung from Him that cry of infinite anguish: "My God, why have you forsaken me?" Divine Justice, giving itself free course in order to punish the sin of men, swept down like a raging torrent upon God's own Son: "He who has not spared even His own Son but has delivered Him for us all...."[1]

If we want to know what God thinks of sin, let us look at Jesus in His Passion. When we see God strike His Son (whom He loves infinitely) by the death of the cross, we understand a little what sin is in the sight of God. Oh, if in prayer we could understand that for three hours Jesus cried out to His Father "If it be possible, Father, let this chalice pass from me" and that the Father's reply was "No!"—that Jesus had to pay *our* debt to the last drop of His blood, that despite His anguished cries and tears[2] God did not spare Him. If we were able to understand that, we would have a horror—a *holy* horror—of sin. What a revelation of sin it is, that heap of obloquy, outrage and humiliation by which Christ was overwhelmed! How strong, therefore, God's hatred of sin had to be, for Him so to strike Jesus without measure, for Him to grind Jesus beneath suffering and ignominy!

The soul who, deliberately, commits sin bears his share of the sorrows and outrages that rested upon Christ. That soul has poured its bitterness into the chalice presented to Jesus during the Agony. That soul was with Judas to betray Jesus; with the soldiery to cover His Divine face with spittle, to blindfold Him and slap Him in the face. That soul was with Peter to deny Him; with Herod to make Him a laughing stock; with the crowd furiously to demand His death; with Pilate to condemn Him by a cowardly and iniquitous judgment. That soul was with the Pharisees who covered the dying Christ with the venom of their unassuaged hate; with the Jews to mock Him and overwhelm Him with sarcasm. And, at Jesus's final moments that soul offered Him gall and vinegar with which to quench His thirst.

[1] Rom. 8:32.   [2] Hebr. 5:7.

There you have the work of a soul who refuses to submit to the Divine Law. That soul causes the death of the only Son of God, of Christ Jesus. If, on one day only, we have had the misfortune to commit a single mortal sin, voluntarily, then we have been that soul. We can say: "The Passion of Jesus is *my* work. O Jesus, nailed to the cross, you are the holy and unsullied High Priest, Bridge of man to God, the Victim innocent and without stain. And I? I am a sinner!"

2. Mortal sin *destroys grace*, the wellspring of super-natural life.

NEXT, sin kills the divine life in the soul, it breaks the union God wishes to contract with us.

I have told you that God wishes to communicate Himself to us in a way that surpasses the demands of our nature. God wishes to give Himself as the object, not simply of contemplation but of union. He effects this union here below, in faith, through grace. God is Love; love aims at uniting itself with the object it loves, it requires that the loved object be but one with itself—and there you have Divine Love.

It is also *Christ's* love for us. His Father sends Him so that Christ may give Himself. "God so loved the world that He gave His only-begotten Son."[1] Christ came in order to give Himself, and to give Himself superabundantly, as is appropriate for one who is God: "I came that they may have life, and have it more abundantly."[2] He entreats His disciples to "abide in" Him: "Abide in me, and I in you."[3]

And in order to accomplish this union, no cost is too great for Him —neither the humiliations of the crib, nor the obscurity and abasement of His hidden life, nor the fatigue of His public life, nor the sorrows of the cross. To perfect this union, He institutes the sacraments, He establishes the Church, He gives us His Spirit. When the soul on its part contemplates all these Divine advances, it aims at responding to them in order to unite itself with Sovereign Good.

---

[1] John 3:16. [2] John 10:10. [3] John 15:4.

Now, [grave] sin constitutes, in itself, an insurmountable obstacle to this union.[1] Why is that? According to the definition of St. Thomas, sin consists in "turning away from God in order to turn towards a creature."[2] It is an act, known, willed, by which a man turns away from God, his Creator, his Redeemer, his Father, his Friend, his Final End, for some creature or other. In this act there is—more often implicitly, but always essentially—a choice. That creature[3] we turn to becomes our choice for the time being—in so far as "for the time being" depends on *us*; for death can make our choice permanent, for all eternity.

That, then, is what grave and deliberate sin is—a choice, made with eyes open. It is as though one were saying to God: "I know that you forbid such and such a thing, that by doing it I will lose your friendship, but I am going to do it just the same." You can see immediately how a mortal sin is, of its nature, opposed to union with God: one cannot, by the same act, both unite oneself to someone and turn away from him. "No servant can serve two masters," said Our Lord; for "he will hate the one and love the other."[4] The soul that opens its door to serious sin—that soul freely prefers the creature, and the gratification gained from the creature, to God and the law of God. Its union with God is completely broken off and its divine life destroyed. Such a soul becomes a slave of sin: "Truly, truly, I say to you, every one who commits sin is a slave to sin."[5] A slave of sin cannot be a servant of God. Between Belial and Jesus, between Lucifer and Christ, there is a radical and absolute incompatibility.[6]

As the source of our holiness is Christ Jesus, you can understand, too, that the soul who turns away from Him through mortal sin turns away from life. That soul, having super-natural life only through the grace of Christ, becomes, through sin, a dead branch not receiving the

---

[1] "Your iniquities have made a separation between you and your God": Isa. 59:2 (RSV, Cath.)   [2] St Thomas, I-II, q. LXXXVII, a. 4.
[3] [*Translator's note*: "creature" can mean thing as well as person: see note 2 on page 56.]   [4] Luke 16:13.   [5] John 8:34 (RSV, Cath.)   [6] 2 Cor. 6:14-16.

Divine sap; that is why the sin which totally breaks the union established by grace is called "mortal."[1] You can see that it is of harm to us, *the* harm opposed to our true beatitude. "He that loves iniquity hates his own soul."[2] The sin which destroys the life of grace in us makes us powerless to merit super-naturally. Such a soul cannot merit anything *de condigno*, by strict and rigorous right, like someone who possesses grace. That soul cannot even merit returning to God. If God gives contrition, it is through mercy, because He deigns to lean down towards the fallen creature. Everything in the activity of a soul in a state of mortal sin, as you know, is fruitless for heaven, however brilliant that activity may otherwise be in the eyes of the world, in the natural domain. A withered vine-shoot no longer receiving the divine sap of grace through its own fault, the soul that remains in this state is compared, by Christ Himself, to dead wood—branches that are "picked up and thrown into the fire, to burn there."[3]

---

[1] [*Translator's quotation*: CCC, paras. 1854-1857: "Sins are rightly evaluated according to their gravity. The distinction between mortal and venial sin, already evident in Scripture (cf. 1 John 5:16-17) became part of the tradition of the Church. It is corroborated by human experience. *Mortal sin* destroys charity [destroys sanctifying grace, the "state of grace"] in the heart of man by a grave violation of God's law; it turns man away from God, who is his ultimate end and his beatitude, by preferring an inferior good to Him. *Venial sin* [of smaller fault, not a grave violation of God's law] allows charity to subsist, even though it offends and wounds it. For a *sin* to be *mortal*, three conditions must together be met: 'Mortal sin is sin whose object is grave matter and which is also committed with full knowledge and deliberate consent.' Mortal sin, by attacking the vital principle within us—that is "charity"—necessitates a new initiative of God's mercy and a conversion of heart which is normally accomplished within the setting of the Sacrament of Reconciliation."]

[2] Ps. 10 (11):6. [*Translator's note*: This is the Douai's distinctive reading of this verse, a sense which Marmion follows.] [3] John 15:6 (Knox).

3. Mortal sin *exposes* the soul *to be eternally deprived of God.*

I HAVE TOLD YOU that Christ ever invokes His Father for His followers, that grace may abound in them: "He lives always to make intercession for them."[1] But the soul who remains in sin belongs to Christ no longer; he belongs to the devil. Satan replaces Christ in that soul. In opposition to Christ, the devil makes himself an accuser of that soul before God: "This soul is mine," he says to God. Day and night he demands that soul—he is "the accuser of our brethren ... who accused them before our God day and night."[2] Because that soul is indeed his.

And suppose death comes upon that soul unexpectedly, with no time for the soul to recognize it? There is nothing impossible about this supposition, since Our Lord Himself takes care to warn us: "I shall come to you like a thief, without telling you at what hour to expect me."[3] The state of aversion to God becomes then unchanging: the depraved disposition of the will, fixed as it was at the end of the soul's earthly life, is not able to suffer any change; the soul is no longer able to return to the ultimate good from which it is for ever separated:[4] eternity only ratifies and confirms the state of super-natural death freely chosen by the soul in turning away from God. It is no longer then the time of being put to the test and of mercy, it is the hour of the road's ending, and of justice: "O Lord, you God of vengeance!"[5]

And that justice is terrible, because it is then that God, with a strong hand, avenges His rights which have been wilfully ignored and obstinately scorned up to then, despite so many Divine advances and appeals. The Lord "is a strong avenger."[6]

For the good of our souls, Christ Jesus has willed to reveal this truth to us. God knows all things in their depths and in their essence and, that being the case, judges them infallibly, with infinite exactitude, and

---

[1] Hebr. 7:25.
[2] Apoc. 12:10.
[3] Apoc. 3:3 (Jerus.)
[4] St Thomas, IV, *Sentent.* L, q. II, a. 1, q. 1.
[5] Ps. 93 (94):1 (RSV, Cath.)
[6] See Jerem. 51:56.

without an atom of exaggeration being involved in His judgements: "Weight and balance are judgements of the Lord,"[1] for He judges calmly.[2]

God is Eternal Wisdom, deciding everything with true weight and measure. He is Supreme Goodness. He has accepted the abundant satisfactions given by Jesus on the cross for all the world's crimes. And yet, when the hour of eternity sounds, God pursues sin with hatred,[3] pursues it into torments without end, into that outer darkness where, in the very words of our Blessed Savior, there is only "weeping, and the gnashing of teeth,"[4] into that Gehenna where "the fire is not quenched,"[5] where Christ showed us the bad hard-hearted rich man, Dives, begging a poor man, Lazarus, to come and place upon his lips, consumed by the fire, a finger-end dipped in water, for "I am in anguish in this flame."[6] Such is the great horror which a "No" to His commandments, replied to Him by a creature deliberately and obstinately, inspires in God whose holiness and sovereignty are infinite. "And these will go into everlasting punishment," says Jesus Himself.[7]

Certainly this pain of "fire that is never quenched" is terrible: but what is comparable to the pain of being deprived for ever of God and of Christ? What is it to feel eternally drawn by all the natural energy of one's being towards Divine joy, and to see oneself eternally excluded from it? The essence of hell is this inextinguishable thirst for God which tortures a soul created by God and for God. Here below, the sinner can distract himself from God by occupying himself with creatures; but once in eternity, he finds himself face to face with God only. And that, so as to lose Him for ever. Only those who know what God's love is can understand what it is to lose the Infinite. To have a hunger and thirst for infinite beatitude, and never to possess it!

---

[1] Prov. 16:11. [2] Wisdom 12:18.
[3] This word "hatred" does not indicate a sentiment capable of existing in God, but rather the moral result which the presence of God produces in a creature who remains fixed for ever in a state of sin and rebellion against the Divine law. God's "hatred" is the exercise of His justice. It is the play of eternal laws which follow their free course.
[4] Matt. 22:13 [5] Mark 9:43. [6] Luke 16:24 (RSV, Cath.) [7] Matt. 25:46.

"Depart from me, accursed ones,"[1] says the Lord, "I do not know you";[2] I called you to share my glory and my beatitude, I wanted to bless you with every spiritual blessing;[3] for that I gave you my Son, I have filled Him with the fullness of grace so that it might overflow upon you. He was the Way that should have taken you to the Truth and led you to Life. He accepted to die for you, He gave you His merits and His satisfactions. He gave you the Church; He gave you His Spirit. With Him, what have I not given you, in order that one day you might share in the eternal banquet I have prepared to the glory of this beloved Son? You have had years to prepare for this, and you have not wished to do so; you have insolently scorned my merciful advances; you have rejected light and life. Now the hour has passed; go away, be accursed, for you do not resemble my Son. I do not know you, for you do not bear in you His features. In His kingdom there are only places for brethren who, through grace, are like Him. Go away; go to the eternal fire prepared for the devil and his angels; because you have chosen the devil, you bear in you the image of the devil, your father.[4] "*I do not know you*"—what a sentence! what torment to hear the Eternal Father speak those words: "Accursed ones, I do not know you."

At that, says Jesus, the sinners will cry out in despair: "Hills, fall on us; mountains, cover us!";[5] but all these damned souls, whom sin has separated from God for ever, are doomed, like living prey, to the gnawing worm of remorse that never dies, to the fire that is never extinguished, to the power of the devils who with rage and in total freedom now set upon their victims; to the bitterest and saddest despair. They are bound, despite themselves, to repeat these words of Scripture of which, in the light of eternity, they have received evidence that for themselves is so appalling: "You are just, O Lord: and your judgment is right,"[6] "The judgments of the Lord are true, justified in themselves"[7]—the

---

[1] Matt. 25:41.   [2] Matt. 25:12: "Truly, I say to you, I do not know you" (RSV, Cath.).
[3] Eph. 1:3.   [4] See John 8:44: "the father from whom you are is the devil"; 1 John 3:8.
[5] See Luke 23:30.   [6] Ps. 118 (119):137.   [7] Ps. 18 (19):10.

condemnation that weighs on us without ending is our own work, the result of our own will: "So it was we who strayed from the true way."[1]

What ill is there like that which, destroying divine life in the soul, amasses so much ruin there and threatens it with so great a punishment! If we have committed a deliberate mortal sin just once, we have deserved to have our choice made permanent for the whole of eternity, and we ought to say to God: "It is your mercy that has saved me"— that it is through His mercy "that we are not consumed."[2]

Sin is "ill" done to God, and it is because God is holy that He condemns it in this way for all eternity. If we truly loved God, we would feel as God does about sin: "You that love the Lord, hate evil."[3] It is written of Our Lord: "You have loved justice, and hated iniquity."[4] Ask Him, especially in prayer at the foot of the crucifix, to make us share this hatred of sin, the only real ill our soul can meet with.

Far be it from me to wish to found our spiritual life upon fear of eternal punishment. For, says St. Paul, we have not received the spirit of servile fear, the spirit of the slave who dreads punishment, but the spirit of Divine adoption.[5]

Nevertheless, do not forget that Our Lord—all of whose words, as He Himself says, are wellsprings of life for our souls[6]—advises us to fear, not punishment, but the Almighty who has power to discard us, body and soul; "has power to cast into hell."[7] And note that when Our Lord thus advises His disciples to have a fear of God, He does so because they are His friends: "But I say to you, *my friends*...."[8] This is evidence that He loves them when He makes arise in them this salutary fear.

Holy Scripture proclaims: "Blessed is the man who fears the Lord."[9] So many of the sacred pages are filled with such encomiums as that. God

---

[1] See Wisdom 5:6.   [2] Lam. 3:22; Marmion follows the Douai's reading of this verse.
[3] Ps. 96 (97):10.   [4] Ps. 44 (45):8.   [5] Rom. 8:15.
[6] John 6:64: "The words that I have spoken to you are spirit and life."
[7] Luke 12:5.   [8] Luke 12:4.   [9] Ps. 111 (112):1 (RSV, Cath.)

asks of us this homage of a holy, filial, fear that is full of reverence. There are some impious men whose hatred of God borders on madness, who would like to stand up to the Almighty. Who was that atheist who said: "If there is a God, I am sure I would put up with hell for all eternity, rather than bow down before him"? Insane! One who couldn't put his finger to the flame of a candle without at once withdrawing it!

See also how St. Paul, in addressing Christians, insisted that they should guard against all sin. He knew the incomparable riches of mercy that God gives us in Christ Jesus: "God, who is rich in mercy."[1] No one sang of those riches of mercy more than he; no one celebrated them more strongly or with more holy enthusiasm; no one knew as he did how to place alongside our weakness the power and triumph of the grace of Jesus. No one, again, knows as he does how to make such confidence in the superabundance of the merits and satisfactions of Christ arise in our souls. And yet, he speaks of the terror which on the Last Day grips a soul that has obstinately resisted the Divine law: "It is a fearful thing to fall into the hands of the living God."[2]

O Heavenly Father, deliver us from evil!

4. Danger from *venial sins*.

BUT, you may say to me, why are you talking to us like that? Have we not a horror of sin? Haven't we a gentle confidence of not finding ourselves in that state of turning away from God?

That is true; and since your conscience gives you this inner testimony, oh! address abundant thanksgiving to the Father who has "rescued us from the power of darkness and transferred us into the kingdom of His beloved Son,"[3] who has made us worthy to share the inheritance of the saints in eternal light.[4] Rejoice also at this: that Jesus has "delivered us from the wrath to come";[5] for, by grace, says St. Paul,

---

[1] Eph. 2:4.   [2] Hebr. 10:31.   [3] Col. 1:13.   [4] Col. 1:12.   [5] 1 Thess. 1:10.

you are already saved "in hope";[1] you hold, even, a "promise" of the life of bliss.[2]

Nevertheless, in awaiting the resounding of those words from Jesus, "Come, blessed of my Father"[3]—the happy sentence that will fix your dwelling in God for ever, remember that we carry this Divine treasure of grace in fragile vessels.[4] Our Lord Himself tells us to "watch and pray," for "the spirit indeed is willing, but the flesh is weak."[5] There are not only *mortal* falls, there is also—and here I touch on a very important point—the danger from venial sins.

It is true that, even when they are repeated, venial sins do not, in themselves, prevent the radical and essential union with God. However, they diminish the fervor of that union, because they constitute a beginning of a turning away from God, deriving from pleasure taken in creatures, from a failure of the will, from a slackening in intensity of our love for God.

In this matter, we must make a necessary distinction. There are venial sins which slip out from us by surprise, which often result from our temperament, which we regret, which we seek to avoid. These are miseries that in no way prevent the soul from being in a high degree of union with God; they are wiped out by acts of charity, by a good Communion;[6] and, further, they keep us humble.

But what we must sovereignly fear are those venial sins which are habitual, or are fully deliberate. These are a real peril for the soul; they are a step, and too often a real step, towards a complete break with God. When—in practice, if not by word of mouth—a soul is in the

---

[1] Rom. 8:24. [2] 1 Tim. 4:8; Rom. 8:1. [3] Matt. 25:34.
[4] 2 Cor. 4:7. [5] Matt. 26:41; Mark 14:38.

[6] "It cannot be doubted that the Eucharist remits and pardons the small sins that are commonly called venial. All that a soul carried away by concupiscence in the heat of the moment has lost of the life of grace by committing small faults, the sacrament gives back to him by wiping out these little faults.... However, that only applies to sins the feeling and attraction of which are no longer moving the soul": Catechism of the Council of Trent, c. XX, 1.

habit of responding with a *deliberate* "No" to the will of God (in a small matter, since we are talking about venial sins), it cannot aspire to safe-guarding the Divine union in that soul for long. Why is that? Because such sins, coldly allowed in, tranquilly carried out, turning (in the absence of the soul feeling remorse) into a habit not fought against, necessarily result in a diminution of super-natural docility, a diminution of watch-fulness, a diminution of our strength to resist temptation.[1] Experience shows that from a succession of willed negligences in little things, we slide imperceptibly, but nearly always fatally, into grave sins.[2]

I will go even further. Imagine a soul that sincerely seeks God in all things, that truly loves Him, and suppose it happens that that soul, through weakness, voluntarily consents to a grave sin. That sort of thing occurs — there are, in the world of souls, abysses of failings. It is for that soul a huge calamity, for the Divine union is broken. But that grave sin, being transient, is much less dangerous and above all much less baneful for that soul than are, for someone else, venial sins that are habitual or are fully deliberate. Why so? The first soul humbles itself, gets up again and, in the memory of the sin it was able to com-mit, it will find an excellent motive for keeping and anchoring itself in humility, a powerful stimulus to a more generous love and a fidelity that is greater than ever.[3] Whereas, with that other soul, the venial

---

[1] We do not say a diminution of the grace itself — if that were so, grace would end up by disappearing with an ever increasing number of venial sins; we mean a diminution in the fervor of our charity. That diminution, however, can produce in the soul such a super-natural torpor that the soul finds itself helpless before grave temptation and succumbs to evil.

[2] St Thomas, I-II, q. LXXXVIII, a. 3, "Whether venial sin may dispose towards mortal sin."

[3] "The holy ones of the Lord," writes St. Ambrose, giving the example of David, "burn with impatience to arrive at the end-point of a pious struggle and to reach the finishing-line of salvation. If it happens to them (as it happens to all men) that they fall, carried away more by the frailty of their nature than by a desire to sin, they then pick themselves up again, more ardent for the race ahead, and, under spur of

sins, frequently allowed in and without remorse, set it up in a *state* in which the super-natural action of God is constantly impeded. Such a soul can in no way aspire to a high degree of union with God. Very much the contrary: the Divine action grows dim within that soul; the Holy Spirit is silent; and that soul, almost infallibly, will before long fall into graver sins. Doubtless, like the first soul, it will immediately seek to return to grace with God, but it will return to that grace, not so much because it loves God as because it fears punishment; and then the memory of its sin will not for it—as it will for the first soul—constitute a point of departure for a new surge of heart towards God. Not having any intensity of love for God, it will continue to live a mediocre super-natural life, exposed always to the slightest blows of the enemy and to new falls. One cannot vouch for the salvation, still less the perfection, of such a soul that constantly puts obstacles in the way of the Divine action and does not make serious efforts to get out of its state of lukewarmness.[1]

It can happen that, through weakness, through being swept along, through surprise, we fall into a grave sin. But, at least, let us never return a deliberate "No" to the Divine will. Let us never say, even by a single act of ours: "Lord, I *know* that such and such a thing—even a very little thing—displeases you; but I *want* to do it." As soon as God asks us for anything, whatever it may be, even if it is our very life-blood, we must say: "Yes, Lord, here I am":[2] otherwise we come to a halt on the road of union. And to halt is often to go backwards; it is nearly always to lay oneself open to grave falls.

---

their shame, battle on even harder. Far from being an obstacle to them, therefore, their fall can be regarded as a stimulus that increases their speed": *De apologia David*, I, c. 2.

[1] "Granted that a man who is cold is worse than one who is lukewarm, yet the state of a lukewarm man is worse: because a lukewarm man is in greater danger of falling without hope of rising": Cornelius a Lapide, *In Apoc.*, III, 16.

[2] See Acts 9:10.

5. Overcoming *temptation* through watchfulness, prayer and trust
    in Jesus Christ.

THOSE HABITS of deliberate sin, even if the sin is simply venial, are not
created all on their own. They are, you know, established in us bit by
bit. "Watch and pray," then, as Our Lord says, "that you may not enter
into temptation."[1]

Temptation is inevitable. We are surrounded by enemies; the devil
prowls around us like "a roaring lion";[2] the world envelops us with its
corrupting attractions, or with its spirit that is so opposed to the super-
natural life. That is why it is not in our power to avoid all temptation;
it is, even, often independent of our will. Of course, temptation is a
trial, a very painful one sometimes, especially when it is accompanied
by spiritual darkness. We are then inclined to call souls happy only if
they are never tempted. But God, through the mouth of the sacred
writer, declares, on the contrary, that those who endure temptation
without having laid themselves open to it are blessed—"Blessed is the
man who endures temptation."[3] Why is that? Because, says the Lord,
such persons, after having been put to the test, "will receive the crown
of life which God has promised to those who love Him."[4] Let us, then,
never be discouraged by reason of the frequency or the extent of temptation; let us (there is no doubt we have to) watch over the treasure of
grace with the greatest care, avoid dangerous occasions, but let us
always retain full trust also. Temptation, however violent and prolonged it may be, is not a sin. The waters of temptation may invade the
soul, like a frightful quagmire;[5] but we can be reassured so long as the
fine point of the soul, which is the will, emerges above them. That fine
point—the "mind's apex"—is the only one God looks at.

Moreover, St. Paul tells us, God "will not permit you to be tempted
beyond your strength,"[6] but with the temptation will, through His grace,

---

[1] Matt. 26:41; Mark 14:38.   [2] 1 Peter 5:8.   [3] James 1:12.
[4] *Ibid.*   [5] Ps. 68 (69):2-3.   [6] 1 Cor. 10:13.

arrange a happy outcome[1] by giving you the power to endure it. The great apostle is himself an example of this. He tells us that "lest the greatness of the revelations should puff me up," God put what he calls "a thorn" in his flesh—a figurative phrase for temptation. He was given "a messenger of Satan to buffet me." "Concerning this," he says, "I thrice besought the Lord that it might leave me," but the Lord replied: "My grace is sufficient for you, because it is in the weakness of man (that is to say, in making the weakness triumph through my grace) that my power is revealed."[2]

Divine grace is, indeed, the aid that is to help us overcome temptation; but we should ask for it. "Watch *and pray....*" In the prayer that Christ taught us, He makes us beg our Heavenly Father to "lead us not into temptation, but deliver us from evil." Let us repeat that prayer often, since Jesus willed to put it on our lips. Let us repeat it, relying upon the merits of the Passion of our Savior.

Nothing is more efficacious against temptation than to remember the cross of Jesus. What did Christ come here below to do if not, in short, to "destroy the works of the devil"?[3] And how *has* He destroyed them, how has He (as He himself says) "cast out" the devil,[4] if not by His death upon the cross? During His mortal life, Our Lord drove out demons from the bodies of the possessed; He also expelled them from souls when He forgave the sins of Mary Magdalene, of the paralytic man and so many others. But, as you know, it is above all by His blessed Passion that He shattered the devil's sway. At the precise moment when the devil thought he had triumphed for ever by making Christ die at the hands of the Jews, he himself, the devil, received the mortal blow. For the death of Christ destroyed sin and gave to all the baptized, as of right, the grace of dying to sin.

---

[1] [*Translator's note*: "A happy outcome" ("*une heureuse issue*") is Marmion's interpretation of a phrase in 1 Cor. 10:13, and it strikes me as being, in itself, at least no less apposite than that of the Cfy and other versions which have "issue" in the sense of "a way out," an exit.]   [2] See 2 Cor. 12:7-9.

[3] 1 John 3:8.   [4] John 12:31.

Let us, then, through faith, rely upon the cross of Christ Jesus; its power has not run dry. Our condition as children of God and our status as baptized persons give us the right to do so. By baptism, we have been marked with the sign of the cross, we have become members of Christ, illumined by His light, sharing in His life and in the salvation He brings us. Therefore, what can we fear, united to Him? "The Lord is my light and my salvation; whom shall I fear?"[1] Let us say to ourselves: "God has commanded His angels to guard you in all your ways so that you do not stumble,"[2] and also: "A thousand enemies may fall on your left, and ten thousand on your right, and *you* will not be hit."[3] "Because he cleaves to me, I will deliver him," says the Lord; "I will protect him, because he knows my name. He shall cry to me, and I will hear him: I will be with him in tribulation, I will deliver him and I will glorify him; I will satisfy him with happiness of days, and shall make him see my salvation."[4]

Let us, therefore, pray Christ to be our support in the struggle against the devil, against the world, which is the devil's accomplice, against the concupiscence that is in us. Like the apostles buffeted by the tempest, let us cry out to Him: "Lord help us, for without you we perish."[5] And stretching out His hand, Christ will save us. Like Christ who, for our example and to merit for us the grace to resist, willed to be tempted, even though by reason of His divinity that temptation would have been purely exterior—like Christ, let us force Satan to withdraw, by saying to him as soon as he presents himself: "There is only one Lord I wish to adore and serve. On the day of my baptism I chose Christ; He is the one I wish to listen to."[6]

---

[1] Ps. 26 (27):1 (RSV, Cath.)   [2] See Ps. 90 (91):11-12.   [3] See Ps. 90 (91):7.
[4] See Ps. 90 (91):14-16.   [5] See Matt. 8:25.
[6] Look at the terms in which St. Gregory Nazianzen wanted every baptized person to repulse Satan—terms full of super-natural assurance: "Strong in the sign of the cross that has marked you, say (to the devil): 'I, too, am the image of God,

With Christ Jesus, our head, we shall be conquerors of the power of darkness. Christ is within us since our baptism; and St. John says: "Greater is He who is in you"—greater, beyond comparison, is Christ—"than he who is in the world,"[1] that is, Satan. The devil has not conquered Christ. The prince of this world, said Christ, has nothing of me that belongs to him.[2] Hence, the devil will not be able to conquer us either, he will for ever lack the ability to make us fall into sin if, watching over ourselves, we stay united to Jesus and rely upon His words and His merits: "Take courage, I have overcome the world."[3] A soul who seeks to stay united to Christ by faith is on top of his own passions, on top of the world and the demons. Everything in and around can rise up, but Christ, by His Divine strength, will keep that soul above every assault.

Christ is called in the Apocalypse "the lion of the tribe of Juda"[4] who "went forth victorious to conquer again,"[5] because by His own victory He won for those who take sides with Him the power to conquer in their turn. That is why St. Paul, after having reminded us that death, the fruit of sin, has been destroyed by Christ Jesus who brings us immortal life, cries out: "Thanks be to God who has given us the victory"—victory over the devil, father of sin; victory over sin, source of death; victory, in short, over death itself—through Jesus Christ. "The sting of death is sin.... But thanks be to God, who has given us the victory through our Lord Jesus Christ."[6]

---

and I have not, as you have, been thrown out of heaven by reason of my pride. I am clothed with Christ; through baptism Christ has become my good. It is for you to bend the knee before me'": *Orat. 40 in sanct. baptismate*, c. 10.

[1] 1 John 4:4.   [2] See John 14:30.   [3] John 16:33.   [4] Apoc. 5:5.
[5] See Apoc. 6:2; Cfy has: "went forth as a conqueror to conquer."   [6] 1 Cor. 15:56-57.

CHAPTER FOUR

THE SACRAMENT AND THE VIRTUE OF PENANCE

INTRODUCTION.

IN EXPLAINING the symbolism of baptism to the first Christians, St. Paul writes to them that they ought no longer, by sin, to destroy within them the divine life received from Christ: "no longer be slaves to sin."[1] The Council of Trent says that "if our gratitude to God, who has made us His children through baptism, were commensurate with this ineffable gift, we would keep intact and without blemish the grace received in that first sacrament."[2]

There are privileged souls, truly blessed, who preserve the divine life without ever losing it. But for the others—those who give way to sin—is there a means of getting grace back again, of reviving anew the life brought by Christ? Yes; such means exist: Christ Jesus, Man-God, has made such means a sacrament, the Sacrament of Penance. It is a wonderful monument to Divine Wisdom and Divine Mercy, one in which God is able to harmonize two things—His finding His glory in it, and His giving us our pardon.

---

[1] Rom. 6:6. [2] Sess. XIV, cap. 1.

1. How, *through pardoning* sins, *God shows His mercy.*

YOU KNOW THAT magnificent prayer which the Church, guided by the Holy Spirit, puts on our lips in the Mass of the Tenth Sunday after Pentecost: "O God, it is above all in pardoning us, in having pity on us, that you make your omnipotence shine forth: shed that mercy upon us in abundance."

That is a revelation which God makes to us through the mouth of the Church. It is in pardoning us, in having pity on us, that God "above all," "*maxime*," gives us a sign of His power. In another of its prayers, the Church says that it is one of God's most exclusive attributes to have pity always and to pardon.[1]

Pardon presupposes offenses, debts to remit. Pity and mercy can only exist where there are miseries. What, indeed, *is* being merciful? It is taking the misery of others into one's own heart, in some way—the Latin word is *misericordia*.[2] Well, God is Goodness itself, Infinite Love. "God is Love";[3] and goodness and love become mercy in the presence of wretchedness—which is why we say to God: "You are God, my defense: *my God, my mercy*."[4] In the prayer I have just quoted, the Church asks God to "shed that mercy upon us in abundance." Why is that? Because our miseries are immense, and it is of these miseries that one has to say: "Deep calls to deep."[5] The deep abyss of our wretchedness, of our faults, of our sins, calls upon the abyss of Divine Mercy.

All of us, indeed, are in misery; we are all sinners, some more than others, it is only a question of degree. "In many things we all offend," says the apostle James,[6] and St. John says: "If we say that we have no sin, we deceive ourselves, and the truth is not in us."[7] He goes even

---

[1] Collect for the Rogation Days: "O God, to whom alone it belongs always to have pity and to pardon, favorably receive our prayer that we and all your servants bound by the chains of sin may receive clemency and be delivered from those chains through your merciful goodness."

[2] "A person is said to be merciful when he has a heart that feels for the miseries of others": St Thomas, I, q. XXI, a. 3.   [3] 1 John 4:8.   [4] Ps. 58 (59):18.

[5] Ps. 41 (42):8.   [6] James 3:2.   [7] 1 John 1:8.

further when he adds that saying we have no sin "makes God a liar."[1] Why? Because God requires us all to say: "Forgive us our trespasses," forgive us our *debita*, debts. God would not require us to ask for this if we did not have debts. We are all sinners; the Council of Trent was so right when it condemned those who say that it is possible to avoid all sins, even venial ones, without a special privilege from God such as was accorded to the blessed Virgin Mary.[2] We are all sinners, and in that is our misery.

But that misery ought not to discourage us. It is known to God, and that is why He has pity on us, "as a father has compassion on his children."[3] For He knows that we are not merely drawn out of nothing, we are molded from mud. He "knows what we are made of; He remembers we are dust."[4] He knows this accumulation of flesh and blood, of muscles and nerves, of miseries and weaknesses, which constitutes a human being, and which makes sin and return to God possible, not once but (as Our Lord says) "seventy times seven"[5]—that is, an indefinite number of times.

God places His glory in relieving our misery, in forgiving our sins. God wills to be glorified by showing His mercy towards us, because of the satisfactions of His beloved Son. In eternity, says St. John, we shall sing a hymn to God and to the Lamb. And what will that hymn be? Will it be the *Holy, Holy, Holy* of the angels? God did not spare one faction of His pure spirits: after their first revolt He struck them down for ever—because they had not those weaknesses, those miseries, that are our lot. The *faithful* angels sing of the holiness of God—that holiness which could not have suffered the defection of the rebels for one instant.

But we—what will *our* hymn be? One that sings of mercy: "The mercies of the Lord I will sing for ever."[6] That verse of the Psalmist will be like a refrain of the hymn of love we shall sing to God. We shall

---

[1] See 1 John 1:10.   [2] Sess. VI, can. 22.   [3] Ps. 102 (103):13.
[4] Ps. 102 (103):14 (Jerus.)   [5] Matt. 18:22.   [6] Ps. 88 (89):2.

sing it also to the Lamb. And what is it that we shall sing to Him? "You have redeemed us, Lord, by your blood"[1]—you have redeemed us by your precious blood, you have had such pity on us that you shed your blood to save us from our miseries, to free us from our sins; it is what here below, in the Mass, is said every day in your name: "This is the chalice of my blood which has been shed for the remission of sins."[2]

Yes, immense glory returns to God from this mercy He exercises towards sinners who claim upon the satisfactions of His Son Jesus. Whence, it can be understood that one of the greatest affronts that could be made to God is doubting His mercy and the pardon He gives us in Jesus Christ.

Nevertheless, subsequent to our baptism, this pardon is only accorded us if we bear "the acceptable fruit of repentance."[3] There is, says the Council of Trent, a big difference on that point between baptism and the Sacrament of Penance. It is true, so far as an adult is concerned, that baptism requires a detestation of sin and a resolution to shun it: but there is no special satisfaction, no special reparation, the person is asked to make. Read the rites of the conferring of baptism, and you will find there no mention of any work of penance to perform; it is a total and absolute remission of sins committed and of the penalty incurred by those sins. Why? Because baptism, the first sacrament in order of being received, constitutes the first-fruits of the blood of Jesus given to the soul.

But (continues the Council) if, after baptism, after we have been grafted upon Christ Jesus, after having been "delivered from the slavery of sin and of the devil and become temples of the Holy Spirit"—if we then of our own free will fall again into sin, we can only regain grace and life on condition of doing penance. That is what Divine Justice has laid down, and not inappropriately."[4]

---

[1] See Apoc. 5:9.
[2] Words of Consecration.
[3] Luke 3:8 (Knox).
[4] Sess. XIV, cap. 2 and 8.

Now, penance can be considered as a *sacrament*, and as a *virtue* which shows itself by the acts that are proper to it.

A few words, now, on the one and on the other.

2. *The Sacrament* of Penance; its elements. *Contrition*, its particular efficacy in the sacrament. *Confession* of sins constitutes a *homage to the humanity of Christ. Satisfaction* has no value except in union with the expiation of Jesus.

THE SACRAMENT has been instituted by Jesus Christ for the forgiveness of sins, for giving us back the life of grace when we have lost it subsequent to baptism. It contains in itself a limitless grace of pardon. But, for it to act within a soul, this soul has to remove every obstacle that stands in the way of the action of the sacrament. Now, what is the obstacle here? Sin, and attachment to sin.

The sinner has to make avowal of his sins—as regards *mortal* sins, every one of them. Then, he has to destroy his attachment to sin, by contrition and acceptance of the satisfaction that is imposed.

As you know, of all these essential elements regarding the penitent, *contrition* is the most important. Even if self-accusation of sins has been rendered materially impossible, the necessity for contrition remains. Why is that? Because, through sin, the soul has turned away from God, to take pleasure in a created entity. If it wishes God to communicate Himself anew to it and restore life to it, it has to repudiate its attachment to the created entity in order to turn to God. This act comprises detestation of sin and the firm intention of not committing it any more—otherwise, the detestation is not sincere. That is what contrition is.[1] As the word indicates, it is a feeling of sorrow which crushes a soul enlightened about its unhappy state and the offense against God, and makes it turn again to God.

---

[1] "Contrition is the soul's sorrow for, and detestation of, sin committed, together with the intention of not sinning any more": Council of Trent, Sess. XIV, cap. 4.

The contrition is *perfect* when the soul is sad at having insulted Sovereign Good and Infinite Goodness: this perfection comes from the *motive*, which is the highest there can be: the Divine Majesty. But it goes without saying that this contrition, perfect in nature, admits of a whole series of levels of *intensity*. This intensity varies according to the degree of each soul's fervor. Whatever this degree of intensity may be, an act of contrition perfect in its motive wipes out mortal sin from the moment the soul produces that act. But in the existent Divine plan, by virtue of the positive precept laid down by Christ, self-accusation of mortal sins remains obligatory, when it is possible.

Imperfect contrition—that which comes from the shame experienced because of the sin, from the punishment the sin deserves, from the loss of eternal happiness—has not, in itself, the effect of wiping out mortal sin; but it is suffices with absolution given by the priest.

Those are truths that I need simply to recall to you. But there is one important point to which I want to draw your attention.

Outside of confession, contrition already places a soul in opposition to sin. The hatred of sin to which it gives rise constitutes a commencement of the destruction of sin: this act is, in itself, pleasing to God.

In the Sacrament of Penance, contrition (like, moreover, the other acts of the penitent—self-accusation of sins, and satisfaction) takes on a sacramental character. What does that mean? In every sacrament, the infinite merits won for us by Christ are applied to the soul in order to produce the special grace contained in the sacrament. The grace of the Sacrament of Penance is to destroy sin in the soul, to weaken the remnants of sin, to give back life or, if there are only venial sins, to forgive them and to increase grace. In this sacrament, the hatred of sin that Christ experienced in His agony and on the cross—"You have loved justice, and hated iniquity"[1]—passes into our soul so as to produce there the destruction of sin. The downfall of sin, effected by Christ

[1] Ps. 44 (45):8.

substituting Himself for us in His Passion, is reproduced in the penitent. The contrition remains what it is, even outside the sacrament: an instrument of death to sin; but in the sacrament the merits of Christ raise this instrument higher—infinitely, so to say—and give it a sovereign efficacy. It is with His Divine blood that Christ washes our souls at this time: He has "washed us from our sins in His own blood."[1]

Never forget, then: every time you receive this sacrament worthily, with devotion, even if there are only venial sins to confess, the blood of Christ flows in abundance upon your soul, so as to vivify it, make it strong against temptation, render it generous in the struggle against attachment to sin; and so as to destroy in it the roots and the effects of sin. The soul finds in this sacrament a special grace for uprooting vices and purifying itself more and more; for regaining the life of grace or increasing that life within itself.

Before confession, then, let us always renew our faith in the infinite value of the expiation made by Jesus Christ. He has borne the weight of all our sins,[2] He has been offered for each one of us: He "loved me and gave Himself up for me."[3] His satisfactions are more than superabundant; He has won the right to pardon us; there is no sin that cannot be wiped out by His Divine blood. Let us arouse our faith and our confidence in His inexhaustible merits, the fruits of His Passion. As I have told you, when He was journeying through Palestine and someone came to Him to be delivered from the devil, Christ Jesus demanded faith in His divinity. It was only in response to faith that He granted a cure or the forgiveness of sins: "Your sins are forgiven you.... Your faith has made you safe, go in peace."[4] It is faith which, above all, must accompany us to this tribunal of mercy, faith in the sacramental character of all our acts;[5] faith especially in the superabundance of the satisfactions given for us by Jesus to His Father.

---

[1] Apoc. 1:5. [2] Isa. 53:11. [3] Gal. 2:20; cf. Eph. 5:2.
[4] See Luke 7:48-50. [5] [*Translator's note*: i.e., acts of contrition, confession and satisfaction: see next paragraph.]

Of course, our acts (contrition, confession and satisfaction) do not produce the grace of the sacrament: yet, quite apart from their being first necessary in order that the grace of the sacrament may be applied to us, since they are "the matter, as it were" of the sacrament,[1] the *degree* of this grace, in point of fact, is measured in accordance with the dispositions of our soul.

That is why it is an eminently useful practice to beg God for the grace of contrition on the morning of the day of our confession, while present at the Holy Sacrifice of the Mass. Why is that? On the altar, as you know, the immolation of Calvary is renewed. The holy Council of Trent declares that: "the Lord, placated by this oblation, grants the grace and gift of repentance, and, by reason thereof, forgives crimes and sins, however enormous they may be."[2] Is it that the Mass forgives sins directly? No, that belongs only to perfect contrition and the Sacrament of Penance; but when we assist devoutly at this Sacrifice, which reproduces the oblation of the cross, when we unite ourselves to the Divine Victim, God gives us (if we ask with faith for this) those feelings of repentance, of good intention, of humility, of trust, that lead us to contrition and make us capable of receiving fruitfully the forgiveness of our sins, won by Jesus at the cost of His Divine blood.

---

[1] The holy Council of Trent says "the matter, as it were"—*"quasi materia"* (Sess. XIV, cap. 3). The Catechism of the Council of Trent (cap. XXI, 3) gives the following explanation: "It must be pointed out to the faithful that the big difference between this sacrament and the others is that the matter of those other sacraments is always some natural or artificial thing, whereas the acts of the penitent—contrition, confession and satisfaction—are, as the Council of Trent says, 'the matter, as it were' of this sacrament. And these acts are necessary on the part of the penitent—for the sacrament as a whole and the forgiveness of sins in its entirety. That is of Divine institution. Equally, the acts of which we speak are regarded as very parts of the penance. And though the holy Council simply said that the acts of the penitent are 'the matter, as it were' of the sacrament, this is not to say that they are not the true matter of it. It is rather that they are not of the same kind as the matter of the other sacraments, which matter is taken from outside, like the water in baptism, and the holy oil in confirmation." [2] Sess. XXII, cap. 2.

Contrition should be followed by *confession*.

The Sacrament of Penance has been instituted in the form of judge-ment: "Whatever you shall bind or loose upon earth, shall be bound or loosed in heaven also"[1]—where you, the Church, forgive someone's sins, those sins shall be forgiven in heaven. But it is for the guilty person to accuse himself to the judge who has to give him his sentence. And who is this judge? Avowal of my sins is something owed to God alone; no one, neither angel nor man nor devil, has the right to pene-trate into the sanctuary of my conscience, into the tabernacle of my soul. God alone deserves such a tribute and He demands it, in this sacrament, for the glory of His Son Jesus.

In speaking of the Church I told you that, since the Incarnation, God wills, in the ordinary disposings of His Providence, to guide us by men who stand here before us in place of His Son. This is like an extension of the Incarnation, and at the same time is a tribute rendered to the holy humanity of Christ. Why is that?

In order to redeem us from sin and give us back divine life, Christ, the Word Incarnate, descended into abysses of humiliation. It was as man that He reduced Himself to nothing, that He suffered, that He died, that He expiated. And because He thus abased Himself to save the world, Christ has been exalted by His Father. The Son "emptied Himself ... even to the death of the cross. For which cause"—*therefore*—"God also has exalted Him":[2] the Father wills to glorify His Son as man. And what is the glory that He gives Him? He makes Him sit at His right hand, in highest heaven; He wishes "every knee to bend before Him and every tongue to proclaim that Jesus is the only Savior";[3] for the Father has given Him "all power in heaven and on earth."[4] And among the attributes of that power is the one of judging every soul. The Father—it is Jesus Himself who tells us—does not judge anyone; "all judgment He has given to the Son, that"—*so that*—"all men may

---

[1] See Matt. 18:18.   [2] Phil. 2:7-9 (Rheims).
[3] See Phil. 2:10:11.   [4] Matt. 28:18.

honor the Son."[1] The Father has given Him the power to render judgement "because He is the Son of Man"[2]—because His Son, in His humanity, has won the right to be Redeemer of the world. Christ has been established, by His Father, as judge of heaven and of earth. Here below, He is a merciful judge. On the last day—Our Lord declared this at the time of His Passion—"they will see the Son of Man coming in the clouds" with all majesty and glory,[3] to "judge the living and the dead."[4]

Such is the glory the Father wills to give to His Son, and it is this glory that He wants *us* to give to His Son in this sacrament. Suppose someone has committed a mortal sin; he comes before God, he feels sorry for the sin he has committed, he afflicts his body with scourgings, he offers to accept all the expiations. God says to him: "That is good, but I want you to recognize, to declare, the power of my Son Jesus, by submitting yourself to Him in the person of one who represents Him in your presence—and that means one who has received, on the day of his priestly ordination, a communication of the judicial power of my Son." If the sinner does not want to give that homage to the sacred humanity of Jesus, God refuses to hear him;[5] but if he submits himself with faith to that condition, then there are no transgressions, no sins, no crimes, no heinous offenses, that God does not pardon—and pardon again, as often as the repentant and contrite sinner desires it.

This avowal of one's sins must be made from a heart moved by repentance. Confession is not a narrative, it is an accusation. One must go there like a criminal before his judge. There are two enemies of such a simple and humble confession, namely routine and scruples. Mechanical routine stems almost always from habit, and the best way to do away with it is to re-arouse our faith in the greatness of this

---

[1] John 5:22-23.
[2] John 5:27 (Rheims).
[3] Mark 13:26 (Jerus.)
[4] 2 Tim. 4:1; 1 Peter 4:5.
[5] [*Translator's note*: Marmion clearly has in mind the Catholic, who, therefore, both accepts the claims of Christ and is aware that the Sacrament of Penance is the mode of forgiveness established by Him.]

sacrament. As I have told you, every time we go to confession, even if we only accuse ourselves of venial sins, the blood of Jesus is offered to His Father, to obtain pardon for us.

Scruples consist in taking the accidental for the essential, in dwelling without reason on details or circumstances which add nothing to the substance of the sin, if indeed it *is* a sin. In confession, one has to have the desire to tell everything one has on one's mind. That becomes an easy thing to do when one has the excellent habit of examining, every evening, the actions of that day. If there is a doubt and this doubt weighs upon us, we should accept as part of the penance the worry that often results from this, and should tell only what we know. God does not want confession to become a torture for the soul: on the contrary, He wants it to give the soul peace.[1] Look at the prodigal son: when he returns to his father does he dwell upon fine distinctions, and distinctions about it that go on for ever? One cannot imagine him doing so. No, he throws himself at the feet of his father, and says to him: "I'm a shabby man, I am not worthy to speak to you, but I am going to tell you what I have done." And immediately his father lifts him up, holds him tight in his arms: he pardons everything, he forgets everything, he prepares a feast to celebrate the return of his son.

And so it is with our Heavenly Father. God finds His glory in pardoning us, because all pardon is granted by virtue of the satisfactions of Jesus Christ, His beloved Son. The precious blood of Jesus has been shed to the last drop for the remission of sins: the expiation Christ offered to the justice, to the holiness, to the majesty of His Father is of infinite value. Well, every time God pardons us, every time the priest gives us absolution, it is as if all the sufferings, all the merits, all the

---

[1] "Without any doubt, the object and the effect of this sacrament, so far as its power and efficacy is concerned, is reconciliation with God; and its ordinary consequence on the occasions when it is received, in those who are pious and receive this sacrament with devotion, is a peace and serenity of conscience accompanied by strong spiritual comfort": Council of Trent, Sess. XIV, cap. 3.

love, all the blood of Jesus were being presented to His Father and applied to our souls, so to give those souls life again, or to increase the life where the sins were only venial. "(He instituted) the Sacrament of Penance by which those who have fallen after baptism receive the benefit of the death of Christ."[1] "May Jesus Christ absolve you," says the priest, "and I, by virtue of His authority, absolve you from your sins." Can someone pardon an offense committed against someone else? No. And yet, the priest says: "*I* absolve you." Why can he say that? Because it is Christ who speaks through his mouth.

At every confession, we seem to hear Jesus say to His Father: "O Father, I offer you, for this soul, the satisfactions and the merits of my Passion; I offer you the chalice of my blood which has been shed for the remission of sins." Then, in exactly the same way as Christ ratifies the judgment and the pardon given by the priest, the Father in His turn confirms the judgment rendered and the pardon granted by the Son. He says to us: "I, too, pardon you."

Those are words which establish the soul in peace. Think of what it is to receive from God an assurance of pardon. If I have insulted an upright man, and he, holding out his hand to me, says: "I've forgotten all about it," I do not doubt his forgiveness. In the Sacrament of Penance, it is Christ, the Man-God, Truth in person, who says to us: "I pardon you"—and are we to doubt His forgiveness? No, one cannot doubt it; this pardon is absolute, irrevocable. God says to us: "If your sins are as glaring as scarlet, I will so wash your soul that they will be as resplendent as snow."[2] He says again: "I have made your iniquities vanish like a cloud, your sins like a mist."[3] God's pardon is worthy of Him. What a king does is kingly; what God does is Divine. Let us believe in His love, His words, His forgiveness. Such an act of faith and of trust is extremely pleasing to God and to Jesus, for it is a homage given to the infinite value of the merits of Christ. It is declaring

---

[1] Council of Trent, Sess. XIV, cap. 1.   [2] See Isa. 1:18.   [3] See Isa. 44:22.

that the fullness and the universality of the pardon God accords to men here below is one of the triumphs of the blood of Jesus.

To contrition of the heart, to confession of the lips, must finally be joined a humble acceptance of the *satisfaction* due. This acceptance is an essential element of the sacrament. In times past, the work of satisfaction a person had to carry out was considerable. Nowadays the satisfaction imposed by the confessor as the punishment for sin is reduced to some prayers, or a giving to the poor, or a practice of mortification. Of course, Our Lord has superabundantly satisfied for us; but, says the Council of Trent,[1] equity and justice require that, having sinned after baptism, we bring our own share of expiation in settlement of the debt resulting from our sins.

This satisfaction being sacramental, Christ Jesus, by the mouth of the priest who takes His place, unites it to His own satisfactions. That is why it is of great efficacy for producing in the soul "death to sin." By making this satisfaction for our sins, says the holy Council of Trent, we conform ourselves to Jesus Christ who has given to His Father an infinite expiation for our sins. The Council notes that these works of satisfaction, whilst being performed by ourselves, nevertheless derive their value only from our union with Jesus Christ. Without Him, indeed, we can do nothing; but, strengthened by His grace, we are in a position to suffer all things. And thus, all our glory is in belonging to this Christ, in whom we live, *in whom we make satisfaction* when, in order to expiate our sins, we perform worthy fruits of penance. *It is in Him that these acts of satisfaction draw their merit; it is by Him that they are offered to the Father, and it is because of Him that the Father accepts them.*[2]

---

[1] Sess. XIV, cap. 8.

[2] Let us look at the exact words of this very beautiful passage from the Council: "Whenever we suffer in order to expiate our sins, we become conformed to Jesus Christ who has made satisfaction for our sins, and from whom all our assurance comes, and we have thereby a sure pledge of being glorified with Him if we suffer

You see what a wonderful sacrament the wisdom, power and goodness of God has established for our salvation. God finds in it His glory and that of His Son; for it is by virtue of the infinite merits of Jesus that pardon is there granted us, that divine life is there restored to us or increased. Let us, as from here and now, join together in that hymn the elect sing to the Lamb: "O Christ Jesus, immolated for us, you have redeemed us by your precious blood; may all praise, all power, all glory, all honor be rendered you for ever!"

3. *The virtue* of penance *necessary in order to maintain* in us *the fruits of the sacrament.* The nature of this virtue.

EVEN WHEN God has pardoned us, there remain in us the remnants of sin—bad roots that are always ready to shoot up and produce bad fruits. Neither baptism nor the Sacrament of Penance remove concupiscence totally. If, therefore, we wish to attain to a high degree of union with God, if we wish the divine life to develop powerfully in our souls, we must ceaselessly labor to diminish these remnants, to weaken these roots of sin that disfigure our souls in the sight of God.

There exists, outside the action of the Sacrament of Penance, an efficacious means of removing those scars of sin, scars which do not permit God to communicate His life to us in abundance.

This means is the *virtue* of penance. What is that virtue? A habit which, when it is a well-rooted and lively one, disposes us continually towards expiation for sin, and towards destruction of the results of sin. This virtue, as we shall see, must doubtless manifest itself by acts

---

with Him. *And yet, the work of satisfaction that we perform on account of our sins does not take place without Christ.* Indeed, although of ourselves we can do nothing, we can do all things with the support of Him who strengthens us. Thus, man has nothing with which to glorify himself, but all our glorying is in Christ, in whom we live, we move, *we make satisfaction*, in performing worthy fruits of penance *which draw their power from Him, which are offered to the Father by Him, and which the Father accepts from Him*": Council of Trent, Sess. XIV, cap. 8.

proper to it, but it is above all an habitual attitude of the soul that keeps alive in us a regret at having offended God and a desire to make amends for our sins. It is this, as an habitual feeling, that ought to prompt our acts of penance.

By those acts, a man is in mutiny against himself so as to avenge the rights of God that he has trampled underfoot. By his sins, he has risen up against God, he has opposed his own will to the all-holy will of God: by his acts of penance, he is now going to unite himself to God in His hatred of sin and in His justice that demands expiation for sin. The soul at that time looks at sin by faith, through the eyes of God. "I have sinned," the soul says, "I have done an act the full malice of which I cannot measure, but which is so terrible, which so violates the rights of God, of His justice, of His holiness, of His love, that only the death of the Man-God was able to expiate it." The soul is moved then, and says to God: "O my God, I detest my sin, I wish to avenge your rights through penance, I would rather die than offend you again." There you have the *spirit* of penance which drives the soul and disposes it to perform *acts* of penance.

You will understand that this attitude of soul is necessary in all those who have not lived in perfect innocence. When it is motivated by fear of hell it is good, the Council of Trent says;[1] God accepts it. But when it is motivated by love, it is excellent and perfect. The more one's love of God increases, the more also does one feel the need to offer God the sacrifice of a heart that is humbled and contrite—"A contrite and humbled heart, O God, you will not despise";[2] and the need to say often to Him, with the Publican in the Gospel: "O God, be merciful to me, a sinner."[3] Such a feeling of compunction, when it is habitual, maintains that soul in great peace, keeps it humble. It also becomes a powerful instrument of purification, it helps us to mortify those unruly instincts, those perverse tendencies—in a word, everything that might

---

[1] Sess. XIV, cap. 4.   [2] Ps. 50 (51):19.   [3] Luke 18:13 (Rheims).

lead us into new wrongdoing. When one has this virtue, one is attentive to employ all means arising for making amends for sin.[1]

That virtue, as far as we are concerned, is the greatest possible
assurance of perseverance in the way of perfection—because it is,
when one really looks it, one of the purest forms of love. One loves
God so much, one regrets so profoundly having offended Him, that
one wants to make amends, to expiate. That is the source of a life of
generosity and forgetfulness of self. "Holiness," says Father Faber, "has
lost its principle of growth when it is separated from abiding sorrow
for sin. For the principle of growth is not love only, but love born of
forgiveness."[2]

Certain souls, even pious ones, on hearing this word "penance"—like
the word "mortification" which expresses the same idea—sometimes
experience a feeling of repugnance. Where does this repugnance come
from? It ought to be no surprise, for it has a psychological basis.

Our will necessarily seeks good; good in general—happiness, or
what seems to be such. Now, mortification, which curbs certain of the
tendencies we feel, certain of our most natural desires, appears to these
souls to be opposed to happiness. Hence this instinctive repugnance in
the presence of all that constitutes the practice of self-renunciation.

Moreover, we too often see mortification as an end, whereas we
should see it only as a means—a necessary means doubtless, an indispensable means, but a means all the same. We do not detract from
Christianity by restricting self-renunciation to the role of means.

Christianity is a mystery of death and of life, but the death only
exists to safeguard the divine life within us: "He is not the God of the

[1] In another series of talks we shall deal at greater length with the foremost role
of compunction of the heart in order to make progress in one's interior life.
[*Translator's note*: For this, see *Christ, the Ideal of the Monk*, VIII. That book is not to be
confused with *Christ, the Ideal of the Priest*.]

[2] *Growth in Holiness*, Ch. XIX.

dead, but of the living."[1] "By dying He destroyed our death, by rising He restored our life."[2] The essential work of Christianity—like the final end at which, of its nature, it aims—is a work of life. Christianity is the reproducing of the life of Christ in the soul. Now, as I have said to you, Christ's existence on earth can be summed up from this two-fold point of view: He "was delivered up for our sins, and rose again for our justification"[3]—rose again so that we might have the life of grace. The Christian dies to everything that is sin, the better to live the life of God. Penance, then, first and foremost, serves but as a means of arriving at this sought end—*life.*

That is what St. Paul has well noted. He speaks of our "always bearing about in our body the dying of Jesus, so that the life also of Jesus may be made manifest" in us.[4] May the life of Christ, which has its source in grace and its perfection in love, blossom forth within us. That is the end sought, there is no other. In order to arrive at this end, mortification is necessary: that is why St. Paul says that "they who belong to Christ"—and we belong to Christ through our baptism—"have crucified their flesh" with its vices and evil desires, its concupiscences.[5] And elsewhere he says, even more explicitly: "If you live according to the instincts of the flesh, you will put to death the life of grace within you. But if you mortify the depraved tendencies of the flesh, then you will live by divine life."[6]

---

[1] Matt. 22:33.   [2] Preface of the Mass for Easter (see also, now, the second acclamation in Eucharistic Prayer III).   [3] Rom. 4:25.
[4] 2 Cor. 4:10.   [5] Gal. 5:24.   [6] See Rom. 8:13.

4. The purpose of the virtue: *to re-establish order* and *to make ourselves like Jesus crucified*. General principle and *diverse applications* of its exercise.

LET US SEE how this is brought about, let us see in more detail why and how we must "die" in order to "live"; why and how we must, as Our Lord Himself said, lose ourselves in order to keep ourselves.[1]

The first man had rectitude as God created him: "God made man upright."[2] In Adam, the lower faculties of the senses were entirely ruled by reason, and his reason was perfectly submissive to God. With sin, this harmonious order disappeared: the lower appetites have become rebels, and the flesh fights against the spirit. "Unhappy man that I am!"[3] cries St. Paul, for "I do not do the good I want, but the evil I do *not* want is what I do."[4] It is concupiscence, a movement of the lower appetites, that inclines us to disorder and urges us to sin. Now, this concupiscence, "the lust of the flesh, and the lust of the eyes, and the pride of life,"[5] tends to increase, tends to bear sin and super-natural death as its fruits. Hence, in order that the life of grace may be maintained within us and may be developed there, it is necessary to mortify —that is to say, reduce to the extent of rendering powerless, "do to death"—not our nature itself, but that in our nature which is a source of disorder and of sin: the unruly instincts of the senses, the flights of imagination, the perverse inclinations.

It is from this that the primary necessity for penance is drawn; it is so as to re-establish order in us, to give back to reason (reason itself submissive to God) an empire over the lower powers; so as to permit

---

[1] "If it (the grain of wheat) die, it brings forth much fruit. He who loves his life, loses it; and he who hates his life in this world, keeps it unto life everlasting": John 12:25.

[2] Ecclesiastes, 7:29 (30) (RSV, Cath.)   [3] Rom. 7:24.   [4] Rom. 7:19 (RSV, Cath.)

[5] 1 John 2:16. [*Translator's note*: The Jerusalem's phrase for "the pride of life" is "pride in possessions" (it adds the note: "Lit. 'the ostentation of living'"). The Knox has: "the empty pomp of living."]

the will to deliver itself wholly up to God. In *that* is to be found life. Never forget: Christianity only asks for mortification in the first place in order to immolate within us what is opposed to life. The Christian labors, by renunciation, to eliminate from his soul every element of spiritual death, with the object of allowing the divine life to blossom forth within him with greater freedom, ease and fullness.

From that point of view, mortification is a strict consequence of our baptism, of our Christian initiation. St. Paul tells us that the new convert, on being plunged into the sacred font, dies to sin there, and begins to live for God. As we have seen, that is the twofold formula to which all Christian conduct comes down. One cannot be a Christian unless, by renunciation of sin, one first reproduces in oneself Christ's death: "Consider yourselves also as dead to sin."[1]

You will ask me what this death to sin consists of, how far it extends, what must be the application within ourselves of this law of renunciation.

That application can vary infinitely, of course. States of soul are not the same for everyone, and the stages that one and the same soul goes through are diverse.

St. Gregory the Great[2] lays down in principle that the more that super-natural order has been disturbed by the predominance of the lower appetites, the longer should renunciation be exercised. There are souls who have been more deeply impaired by sin. In them, the roots of sin are more hardy, the sources of spiritual disorder more active, the life of grace more exposed to danger. For these souls, mortification must be more vigilant, more vigorous, more unremitting. In other souls—for example those who are no longer at the start of the spiritual life—the roots of sin are more slender, diminished, weakened; grace finds a more "generous," more productive, soil—one that is more fertile. For these souls, the

---

[1] Rom. 6:11.   [2] *Homil. in Evang.*, XX, c. 8. See also *Reg. pastor*, III, c. 29.

necessity of penance, *in so far as it has for its object the doing to death of sin*, will be less pressing a requirement, the obligation of renunciation less wide-ranging. But, for these faithful souls, in whom grace abounds, another motive then arises (one we shall touch on later)—that of more closely imitating Christ, our leader and the head of a mystical body to which all the members are bound together in solidarity. And the field which opens up to these generous souls is unlimited.

The above is the general principle; but whatever the measure of its application may be, there are some works that every Christian is obliged to fulfill: exact observance of the commandments of God, of the rules decreed by the Church (observance of Lent, vigils and ember days);[1] daily fidelity to the duties of one's state, to the law of work; watchfulness so as constantly to avoid occasions of sin, which are so numerous. All this often demands renunciation and sacrifices for which nature pays dearly.

Then there is the struggle against one's special faults, those that dominate us and weaken the divine life. With one soul, it is self-love; with another, a want of seriousness; with another, jealousy or anger; with another, sensuality or sloth. These faults, not fought against, are the source of a thousand sins and voluntary infidelities that hinder God's action within us. However small these vices may appear, Our Lord expects us to take the trouble of seeing them, of working generously to extirpate them, through a constant watchfulness over ourselves, through careful examination of what we have done each day, through mortification of the body as well as through interior renunciation. He expects us to have no truce with them until their roots be so weakened that they are unable to produce fruit. For the more these roots are diminished, the stronger is the divine life within us, because the greater is its freedom to flower.

---

[1] [*Translator's note*: This is a reference to laws of the Church, requiring fasting and abstinence from meat, which today have been much mitigated (but which in relation to Ash Wednesday and Good Friday remain in force).]

Finally, there are the renunciations that, under the guidance of Providence, determine the course of one's life, and which we should accept as true followers of Christ Jesus. These are: suffering; illness; the loss of beings who are dear to us; reverses and adversities; opposition and annoyances that cut across the achieving of what we have planned; failure of our enterprises; our disappointments; moments of weariness, hours of sadness; that "day's heaviness" which of old weighed down St. Paul so greatly,[1] to a point where, as he himself says, he was "weary even of life"[2]—all the misfortunes that do not detach us from ourselves and from creatures except by *mortifying* our nature and by "making us die" bit by bit: "I die daily."[3]

5. How, *in Christ, value is drawn*—along with consolation—*from our acts* of renunciation.

IT WAS St. Paul's phrase, but if he "died daily," it was so as—"daily" also—to live more, with the life of Christ. And, in speaking about his sufferings, he wrote the following words which seem strange but are very profound. He says that he fills up "what is lacking of the sufferings of Christ," and that he fills it up "for His body," His mystical body "which is the Church."[4] Is something, then, lacking in the sufferings, in the satisfactions, of Christ? Certainly not. As I have told you, their value is infinite; Christ's sufferings are the sufferings of one who is God-Man and who substituted Himself for us. Nothing is lacking in the perfection and the plenitude of these sufferings, they have been more than sufficient to redeem us all: "*He* is a propitiation for our sins … those of the *whole* world."[5] Then why does St. Paul speak of a "filling-up" that he, Paul, brings to these sufferings?

St. Augustine gives us the answer, and it is a magnificent one. The whole Christ, he says, is made up of the Church united to its leader—

---

[1] See Rom. 9:2.   [2] 2 Cor. 1:8.   [3] 1 Cor. 15:31.   [4] Col. 1:24.   [5] 1 John 2:2.

made up of the members (which we are) united to the head (who is Christ). The head of this mystical body, Christ, has suffered; the large expiation is that of Jesus. The members, if they wish to remain worthy of the head, should in their turn bring *their* share of suffering and renunciation: "All the sufferings are complete—but in the head. There still remain *the sufferings of Christ in His body.* Now, you are the body and the members."[1]

Contemplate Christ Jesus, making His way to Calvary, weighed down by His cross; He falls beneath the heaviness of this burden. Had He wished, His divinity would have supported His humanity; but that was not what He wanted. Why? Because He wished, in order to expiate sin, to experience in His innocent flesh the crushing weight caused by sin. But the Jews[2] feared that Jesus would not live to reach the place of crucifixion; so they then made Simon of Cyrene help Christ carry His cross, and Jesus accepted this help.

In this, Simon represents us all. Members of the mystical body of Christ, we should help Jesus carry His cross. It is a sure sign that we belong to Him if, following Him, we renounce ourselves and carry our cross: "If anyone wishes to come after me, let him deny himself, and take up his cross daily, and follow me."[3] The secret of those voluntary mortifications carried out by faithful souls, privileged souls, holy souls —mortifications which afflict and rend the body, as well as those which repress the desires, even the legitimate desires, of the spirit—is to be found in that. These souls have doubtless expiated their own sins: but love urges them to expiate for those members of the body of Christ who insult their head; in order that the vigor, the beauty and splendor of the divine life may not be diminished in the mystical body. If we truly love Christ, then, following the counsel of a prudent spiritual director, we will generously take our share of these voluntary mortifications

[1] *Enarr. in Ps.* 87, c. 5.   [2] [*Translator's note*: It was in fact the Roman soldiers (Matt. 27:27-32; Mark 15:16-21). Marmion seems to follow a purely grammatical attribution in Luke 23:17-26.]   [3] Luke 9:23.

that will make us less unworthy disciples of a crucified head. Was it not this that St. Paul was seeking? Did he not write[1] that he wished to renounce everything, so as to be admitted to the fellowship of His sufferings — "that I may know Him ... and may share His sufferings, becoming like Him in His death"?[2]

If our nature experiences some revulsion, let us ask Our Lord to give us the strength to imitate Him in following Him all the way to Calvary. According to the beautiful thought of St. Augustine, the innocent Christ, like a compassionate physician, kept for Himself the dregs[3] of the cup of suffering and renunciation — the cup from which we must drink a few drops: "You cannot be cured unless you drink from the bitter cup. The physician, who is in good health, has drunk from it first, in order that the sick man may drink from it without hesitation."[4] For Christ, says St. Paul, knows from personal experience what sacrifice is. The High Priest who came to save us is not of the number of those unable to sympathize with our weakness. In order to be like us, He has experienced everything.[5] I have told you the extent to which Our Lord shared our sufferings. Well, never forget that in thus sharing our sorrows and all those of our miseries that were compatible with His divinity, Christ sanctified our sufferings, our debilities, our expiations. In so doing, He merited for us that we have the strength to bear them in our turn, and to see them accepted by His Father.

But, for that to be so, we must unite ourselves to Our Lord by faith, by love, and agree to carry our cross after Him. It is from this union that our sufferings and sacrifices draw the whole of their value. In themselves, they have no value for heaven, but united with those of Christ they become extremely acceptable to God and very salutary for our souls.[6]

---

[1] Phil. 3:7-10.
[2] Phil. 3:10 (RSV, Cath.)
[3] [Translator's note: the sediment, the worst part.]
[4] De verbis Domini, Serm. XVIII, c. 7 and 8.
[5] Hebr. 4:15 [the foremost exception being that He never sinned, ibid.]
[6] See the passage from the Council of Trent given above, pages 254-255, n. 2.

That uniting of our will to Our Lord in suffering becomes for us a source of solace, too. When we suffer, whenever we are in pain, in sadness, in a state of worry, in adversity, in difficulties, and we come to Christ Jesus, we are—not delivered from our cross, for the servant is not above his Master,[1] but comforted. It is Christ Himself who tells us this. He wishes us to carry our cross—that is an indispensable condition for becoming His true disciple, but He promises also to give solace to those who come to Him in order to find in Him a balm for their sufferings. And He Himself invites us to do so: "Come to me, all you that labor, and are burdened, and I will refresh you."[2] What He says is infallible: if you go to Him with trust, be assured that He will bend down towards you, because, according to that word the Gospel uses about Him, He will be moved by "*pity*": "He had pity on her."[3] Has He not been crushed beneath a weight of suffering to the point of crying out: "Father, let this bitter cup pass from me"?[4] St. Paul expressly tells us that one of the reasons Christ wanted to feel sorrow was to experience it in order that He could give solace to those who would come to Him.[5]

He is the Good Samaritan who bends down over suffering humanity and, along with salvation, brings to it the consolation of the Spirit of Love. It is from Christ that all true consolation for our soul arises. St. Paul repeats this to us: "For as the sufferings of Christ abound in us, so also *through Christ* does our comfort abound."[6] You see how he identifies his tribulations with those of Jesus, since he is a member of the mystical body of Christ: and how it is from Christ, too, that he receives consolation.

And how those words are borne out in him! How great is the share he takes of the sorrows of Christ! Read that pen-picture, so lively and gripping, of the considerable difficulties that assailed the great apostle

---

[1] Luke 6:40.   [2] Matt. 11:28 (Rheims).
[3] Luke 7:13 (Knox).   [4] See Matt. 26:39; Mark 14:36; Luke 22:42.
[5] Hebr. 4:15, and 2:16-18: "He had to be made like His brethren in every respect, *so that* He might become a merciful ... high priest" (RSV, Cath., v. 17).   [6] 2 Cor. 1:5.

during his apostolic journeys: "Often have I seen death near to me; five times I received lashes; three times was I beaten with rods; once I suffered stoning; three times I was shipwrecked; I spent a day and a night adrift upon the depths of the sea. And my numberless journeyings, full of perils: perils on rivers, perils from brigands, perils from people of my own nation, perils from unbelievers, perils in towns, perils in deserts, upon the sea; perils from false brethren: my labors and my hardships, my numerous sleepless nights, sufferings of hunger and thirst; my frequent fasts; cold, nakedness: and, to leave out as many other things, I will recall only my daily cares, my solicitude for all the churches I have founded."[1]

What a picture! How buffeted the soul of the great apostle must have been by so many woes, constantly recurring! And yet, in all his tribulations, he "*overflows with joy*": "I overflow with joy in all our troubles."[2] What is the secret of this joy? It is the love he has for Christ who has been delivered up for him: "Christ's love impels us."[3] It is through Christ that his comfort "abounds": "For as the sufferings of Christ abound in us, so also through Christ does our *comfort abound*."[4] Because he is united to Christ through love, he stays unshakable in the midst of all his woes and all the renunciations to which he is subject. "Who shall separate me from the love of Christ? Shall tribulation, or distress, or persecution, or hunger, or danger, or the sword? Even as it is written: 'For your sake, Lord, we face death all the day long; we are regarded as sheep marked down for the slaughter'; but," he adds, "we are more than conquerors through Him who has loved us."[5]

Such is the cry of a soul who has understood the immense love of Christ upon the cross, and who, as a true disciple, wants to walk in His footsteps all the way to Calvary, by taking his share of the sufferings of his Divine Master, taking that share through love.[6] For, as I have told you, it is from Calvary, it is from the Passion of Christ Jesus, that our sufferings,

[1] See 2 Cor. 11:23-28.   [2] 2 Cor. 7:4.   [3] See 2 Cor. 5:14.
[4] 2 Cor. 1:5.   [5] See Rom. 8:35-37; Ps. 43 (44):22 (23).   [6] 2 Cor. 5:14.

our sacrifices, our acts of renunciation and mortification, draw the whole of their super-natural value, so as to destroy sin and let the divine life unfold within us. We ought, by deliberate intention, to relate them to the Sacrament of Penance which applies to us the merits of the sufferings of Christ, having as our object to make ourselves die to sin. If we do that, the efficacy of the Sacrament of Penance extends, as it were, to all acts of the *virtue* of penance, so as to make their fruitfulness increase.

6. **According to the mind of the Church,** *relating acts of the virtue* **of penance** *to the sacrament.*

MOREOVER, that is very much the thinking of the Church. Look at what the priest does after he, the minister of Christ, has imposed on us the necessary satisfaction and, by the absolution, has washed clean our soul in the divine blood. He recites over us these words: "May whatever of good you do, whatever of ill you suffer, serve for you towards the remission of your sins, an increase of grace and the reward of life eternal." This prayer is not essential to the sacrament, but as it is the Church that has laid the saying of it down, as well as the teaching it contains—a teaching she assuredly wants to see us put into practice, it has the value of a sacramental.[1]

By this prayer, the priest gives to our sufferings, to our acts of satisfaction, of expiation, mortification, reparation and patience (which in that way he relates and links to the sacrament) a particular efficacy that our faith cannot fail to highlight.

"For the remission of your sins." The Council of Trent teaches a very consoling truth on this subject. It tells us that God is so munificent in His mercy that, not only the works of expiation which the priest imposes

---

[1] [*Translator's quotation*: "Holy Mother Church has ... instituted sacramentals. These are sacred signs which bear a resemblance to the sacraments. They signify effects, particularly of a spiritual nature, which are obtained through the intercession of the Church": *Sacrosanctum Concilium*, 60. See further CCC, paras. 1667-1673.]

on us, or which we choose ourselves, but, as well, all the afflictions inherent in our condition here below, all the temporal adversities which God sends or permits, and which we bear with patience, serve, through the merits of Jesus Christ, as satisfactions before the Eternal Father.[1] That is why—I cannot recommend it to you too much—it is an excellent and very fruitful practice, when about to present ourselves before the priest (or rather before Jesus Christ) for the purpose of accusing ourselves of the faults we have committed, that we accept, in expiation of our sins, all the afflictions, all the annoyances, all the contradictions, which may arise subsequently; and, more still, that we decide at the same time upon this or that special act of mortification, however slight, that we will carry out between our present and our next confession.

Fidelity to this practice, which enters so well into the mind of the Church, is something that bears very great fruit. First of all, it does away with the danger of routine. A soul that, through faith, thus re-immerses itself in a consideration of the greatness of this sacrament in which the blood of Jesus is applied to us; a soul that, by an intention full of love, offers also to bear with patience, in union with Christ on the cross, everything of the hard, the difficult, the painful, the annoying, that may arise—such a soul is resistant to the rust that, in the case of many people, attaches to frequent confession. Next, this practice constitutes an act of love extremely pleasing to Our Lord because it indicates that we are willing to share in the sufferings of His Passion, the holiest of His mysteries. Finally, when frequently renewed, it helps us to acquire bit by bit that true spirit of penance that is so necessary if we are to become like Jesus, our head and our model.

---

[1] "In addition, this holy Council teaches that so great is the Divine munificence, that not only penances voluntarily undertaken by ourselves for the purpose of atoning for sin, or those imposed at the discretion of the priest, or even (which is the greatest proof of love) by earthly sufferings inflicted by God and borne patiently by us, we may make satisfaction before God through Jesus Christ": Sess. XIV, cap. 9.

And the priest adds: "serve *for an increase of grace*"—"May whatever you bear or suffer serve for an increase of the divine life within you." As I have said to you, death is here the prelude to life. The grain of wheat, Our Lord Himself said, must first die in the ground before it puts forth shoots and gives the ears of corn which the father of the family will pack into his granaries.[1] This life can become more fruitful, grace can be more abundant, the more that renunciation has reduced, weakened and diminished the obstacles standing in the way of its free upward growth. For—always hold on to this central truth—our holiness is of an essentially super-natural order, and it is God who is the source of it. The more the soul, by mortification and detachment, frees itself from sin and becomes empty both of itself and of creatures, the more powerful is God's action within it. It is Christ who says this: He tells us, even, that His Father employs suffering in order to make the life of the soul more fruitful: "I am the true vine, and my Father is the vine-dresser," "you are the branches." And every branch that bears fruit, my Father "prunes, *that*"—in order that—"it may bear more fruit.... By this my Father is glorified, that you bear much fruit."[2]

When the Eternal Father sees that a soul, united already to His Son by grace, has a resolute desire to give itself fully to Christ, He wills to make the life in that soul be abundant, wills to increase the soul's capacity. To this end, He Himself enters into the work of renunciation and detachment, because that is the prerequisite of our fruitfulness. He prunes away everything that prevents the life of Christ from producing all its effects, everything that is an obstacle to the action of the Divine sap. Our corrupted nature contains roots tending to produce bad fruits. By the sufferings—increased in number and deep—which He permits or sends, by the humiliations and the contradictions, God purifies the soul, hollows it out, ploughs it so to speak, detaches it from creatures,

[1] See John 12:24-25.
[2] John 15:1-8 (RSV, Cath.) [*Translator's note*: For "prune," other versions have "cleanse," "purge," "trim clean."]

empties it of itself, with the object of making it bear numerous fruits of life and of holiness. He purifies it, so that it bears more fruit.

Finally, the priest's words end with: "your reward in life eternal": "May all things serve for you to become the reward of life eternal." After having re-established order, here below, so as to allow the life of Christ to grow and increase within us, our sufferings, our acts of expiation, our efforts to do good, assure our soul of a share in the heavenly glory. Remember the conversation that two disciples had, when they were going to Emmaus the day after Christ's Passion. Disconcerted by the death of the Divine Master, which seemed to put an end to their hopes of a messianic reign, not yet knowing of the resurrection of Jesus, they share with each other their profound disappointment. Christ joins them, in the shape of a stranger, and asks them what they were talking about. And, after hearing the expression of their discouragement—"We had hoped...," He immediately reproaches them: "O foolish ones! O hearts slow to believe! Was it not *fitting* that the Christ should suffer all these things *and so* enter into his glory?"[1] It is the same for us; we must take our share of the sufferings of Christ in order to share His glory.

This glory and this bliss will be immense. "Do not lose heart" in the midst of your tribulations, writes St. Paul. "On the contrary, even though our outer man is decaying"—will constantly get weaker—"yet our inner man is being renewed day by day. For our present light affliction, which is for the moment, prepares for us an eternal weight of glory that is beyond all measure."[2] Similarly, he writes elsewhere: "If we are sons, we are heirs also: heirs indeed of God and joint heirs with Christ," provided, however, that we "suffer with Him that we may also be glorified with Him." And he adds: "For I reckon that the sufferings of

---

[1] See Luke 24:13-26. St. Paul echoed these words of the Divine Master when he wrote to the Hebrews that we saw Jesus "crowned with glory and honor *because* of His having suffered death": Hebr. 2:9; cf. Phil. 2:7-9.   [2] 2 Cor. 4:17.

the present time are not worthy to be compared with the glory to come that will be revealed in us."[1] That is why, in the same measure as we "are partakers of the sufferings of Christ," we should rejoice, for when the glory of Christ is manifested on the Last Day, we also will be in "exultation."[2]

"Courage, then!" I repeat to you with St. Paul. Look, he says, making allusion to the public games that took place in his time; look at what a severe regime they submit to, those who want to take part in the races in the arena in order to carry off the prize. And what prize? A crown of one day! Whereas we—it is for an imperishable crown that we impose renunciation upon ourselves[3]—and this crown is the crown of sharing for ever in the glory and the bliss of Jesus our head.

Here below—now—says Christ Jesus, you are in affliction: the world, which does not know me, lives in pleasure, whilst you, in the exercise of a life of faith, share with me the burden of the cross. "You shall weep and lament, but the world shall rejoice; and you shall be sorrowful." *But* "your sorrow shall be turned into joy."[4] "I will see you again"—on the Last Day—"and your heart shall abound with joy, *and that joy, no one shall take away from you.*"[5]

---

[1] Rom. 8:17-18. [2] 1 Peter 4:13.
[3] See 1 Cor. 9:24-25. [4] John 16:20. [5] See John 16:22.

Twofold Aspect of the Christian Life:

Death to Sin, Life for God

LIFE FOR GOD

CHAPTER FIVE

"TRUTH IN CHARITY"

INTRODUCTION: Christianity, *the religion of life.*

CHRISTIANITY is a mystery of death and of life, but it is above all a mystery of life. Death, you know, was not included in the Divine plan. It was man's sin that introduced it on earth; and that which sin is — a "No" to God — produced the refusal "No" to life, which is death.[1] If, then, Christianity calls for renunciation, it is so as to immolate within us that which is adverse to life. We have to remove the obstacles because they are opposed to the free blossoming within us of the divine life Christ brings to us. He is the great agent of our sanctification, without whom we can do nothing. It is therefore not a question of seeking out or practicing mortification for its own sake, but first and wholly with a view to facilitating the development of the divine wheat-germ put in us at baptism. When St. Paul tells the new converts that they should "die to sin," he does not confine the whole practice of Christianity to that single formula; he adds that they should also be "alive for God in Christ Jesus."[2] As we shall see in the course of the following talks, that expression — one so rich in meaning — sums up the second work the soul has to do.

[1] "Through one man sin entered into the world and through sin death, and thus death has passed into all men": Rom. 5:12. [2] Rom. 6:11 (Jerus.)

Like all life, the super-natural life has laws that are special to it, laws to which it must submit if it is to be maintained. In the two preceding talks I have shown you the elements constituting "death to sin." Let us now consider what the elements are of "life for God in Christ Jesus."

It is necessary first to establish the *fundamental principle* which rules all Christian activity, and on which its value in the eyes of God depends. Let us see what this due order is—an essential and general one that in the super-natural domain ought to govern the infinite variety of actions of which the ordinary fabric of our lives is woven.

1. *Primary character* of our works: *truth.* Works *conforming to our nature as reasonable beings.* Harmony of grace and nature. Works conforming *to our individuality, to our special vocation.*

YOU KNOW that passage of St. Paul, in his letter to the Ephesians, in which he says that we are to "practice the truth in charity."[1] I would like to pause with you there for a few moments, and you will see how by these words the Apostle lays down the fundamental law that governs our super-natural activity in the domain of grace.

"Practice the truth in charity." What that comes down to saying is that super-natural life has to be maintained in us by human acts animated by sanctifying grace, acts having relation to God through *caritas*, charity.

The word "practice" points to the necessity of works. I need not insist much on that point. All life must express itself by acts. Without works, faith, which is the foundation of super-natural life, is a dead faith: "Faith by itself, if it has no works, is dead." It was the apostle St. James who wrote that.[2] And St. Paul, who never ceases showing us the riches we have in Our Lord, is not afraid to tell us that Christ is only a

---

[1] See Eph. 4:15.   [2] James 2:17 (RSV, Cath.)

cause of salvation and of eternal life for those who obey Him: "He became, to all *who obey Him*, the cause of eternal salvation."[1] If our desire to be pleasing to God is sincere, let us listen to what Christ Jesus says: "If you love me, keep my commandments"[2]—for it is not those who merely say with their lips "Lord, Lord" that enter into the kingdom of heaven, but "those who do the will of my Father."[3] It is to this that Christ wishes to bring us. He redeems us, purifies us, in order that, living by His life and animated by His Spirit, we may do good works worthy of Him and of His Father.[4] That is what He expects of us.

But what works have we to perform? What is their nature and character? "Practice the truth"... *true* works. What does St. Paul mean by that? To speak the truth is to express something that accords with our thought. An object is "true" when there is an accord between what it ought to be, considering its nature, and what it really is. Gold is said to be *true* when it possesses all the properties we know to belong to the nature of that metal. Gold is *false* when it has the appearance, but not the properties, of gold. Between what it appears to be and what (considering the elements we know are constituents of its nature) it ought to be, there is no accord.

A human action is *true* if in reality it answers to our human nature as created beings endowed with reason, will and freedom. We ought, says St. Paul, to perform true works, that is, those which are in conformity with our human nature. Every act that is the opposite, which does not answer to our nature as reasonable beings, is a *false* act. We are not statues any more than we are automatons. Nor are we angels. We are men; and the character our actions ought first to manifest—and the character God wishes to find in them—is that of human works, performed by a free creature, one endowed with a will enlightened by reason.

---

[1] Hebr. 5:9.   [2] John 14:15.   [3] See Matt. 7:21.

[4] He "gave Himself for us that He might redeem us from all iniquity and cleanse for Himself an acceptable people, pursuing good works": Titus 2:14.

Look at the universe around you. God finds His glory in all creatures, but only when they conform to the laws that govern their nature.

The stars in the heavens silently praise God by their harmonious courses in immeasurable space: "The heavens declare the glory of God." [1] The waters of the sea do so in not crossing the limits God assigns to them: "You have set a bound which they shall not pass over";[2] the earth, in keeping the laws of its stability: "You have founded the earth, and it continues";[3] the bushes, in giving flowers and fruits after their kind and according to the seasons; the animals, in following the instincts the Creator has put within them. Each order of beings has special laws which govern their existence and which, manifesting the power and the wisdom of God, constitute a hymn of praise to His glory: "O Lord, our Lord, how majestic is your name in all the earth!"[4] Finally, man—whom the Lord has established as king of creation: "You have subjected all things under his feet"[5]—has laws which are conditions governing his nature and his activity as a reasonable creature. Like all created beings, man has been made to glorify God; but he can only glorify Him by giving first place to those acts which are in conformity with his nature. In that way man answers to the ideal God formed in creating him, and, by doing so, he glorifies Him and is pleasing to Him.

Now, man is, of his nature, a reasonable being; he cannot, like an animal lacking reason, act only by instinct. What distinguishes him from all the other beings of the earthly creation is his having been endowed with reason and freedom. Reason, therefore, ought to be sovereign in man; but, reason being a created thing, it ought itself to be subject to the Divine will upon which it depends and which is manifested by the natural law and the positive laws.[6]

[1] Ps. 18 (19):2 (Jerus.)

[2] Ps. 103 (104):9. The whole of this psalm, which is a magnificent hymn to the Creator, indicates the different operations proper to the three kingdoms, mineral, vegetable and animal.   [3] Ps. 118 (119):90.   [4] Ps. 8:9 (RSV, Cath.)

[5] Ps 8:8 (RSV, Cath.); other versions have various numberings of the verse.

[6] [*Translator's note*: "Positive" laws in the sense of laws (here, Divine laws) explicitly laid down.]

To be "true," which is the first requisite condition for being pleasing to God, every human action should therefore be in conformity with our state of existence as free and reasonable created beings subject to the Divine will. Otherwise it does not answer to our nature, to the resultant properties of that nature, to the laws that govern it: it is *false*.

Do not forget that the natural law is something essential in the order of religion. God need not have created me: but having been created, I am and remain a created being; and the relationship that for me is based upon that status is unchangeable. One cannot, for example, conceive that any man could be created for whom it would be permissible that he should blaspheme his Creator.

It is this feature of human acts fully free but in accord with our nature and the final end of our creation, and morally good in consequence, which ought to be the primary mark of our works in the sight of God. "He who says that he knows Him, and does not keep His commandments, is a liar and the truth is not in him."[1]

To act as Christians, we ought first to act as men. And this is not unimportant. Doubtless a perfect Christian will necessarily fulfill his duties as a man, for the law of the Gospel includes and perfects the natural law. But one meets with Christian souls, or rather those who call themselves Christians—and not only among the simple faithful, but among men and women in religious orders, among priests—who are exact to the point of scrupulosity in the pious practices they have chosen, but who set little store by certain precepts of the natural law. These souls will have at heart their not missing their devotional exercises, and that is excellent. But, for example, they will not refrain from attacking their neighbor's reputation; from stooping to untruths; from not keeping their word when they have given it; from misrepresenting an author's thinking; from failing to respect the laws of literary or artistic copyright; from deferring the payment of debts, sometimes to

[1] 1 John 2:4.

the detriment of justice; from not observing precisely the terms of a contract.

These souls "whose religion spoils their morality" (to borrow the remark of a celebrated English statesman, Gladstone)[1] have not understood St. Paul's precept: "Practice truth." There is illogicality in their spiritual life, there is "falsity." With many souls, that "falsity" is perhaps unconscious, but it is no less harmful, because God does not find in them that order He wishes to see reigning in all His works.

So then, we ought to be "true"; that is the primary foundation on which grace works. As you know, grace does not destroy nature. Even though we may, by being Divinely adopted, have received new being as it were—a "new creature"[2]—yet grace (which ought to become in us the source and the mainspring of new and super-natural operations) presupposes nature and the proper resultant operations of nature. Far from clashing, grace and nature—in what is good and pure in the latter—harmonize, by each of the two keeping its own character and its own beauty.

---

[1] "There is one proposition which the experience of life burns into my soul: it is this, that man should beware of letting his religion spoil his morality. In a thousand ways, some great, some small, but all subtle, we are daily tempted to the great sin": Sir John Morley, *Life of Gladstone*, II, 185. Comparable with this thought are the following words of Bossuet. "This and that person is uneasy if he has not said his rosary and his other regular prayers; or if he has missed out some 'Hail Marys' in a decade. I do not blame him—God forbid! I have nothing but praise for religious exactitude in exercises of piety. But who could approve of his tearing off from the Ten Commandments four or five of the precepts they give for our observance— doing this daily and no trouble about doing it; who could approve his trampling underfoot without any scruple the holiest duties of Christianity? Strange illusion, fostered to bewitch us by the enemy of the human race! He cannot tear from the heart of man the principle of religion that he sees is too deeply graven there; he gives to it, not its legitimate use but a dangerous amusement, with the object that, deceived by this appearance, *we may think we have satisfied by our little attentions the serious obligations religion imposes on us.* Undeceive yourselves, Christians! ... In doing works which go beyond those that duty requires, take care not to forget those which are of necessity": *Sermon for the Feast of the Conception of the Virgin*, 1669; the whole of the ending of this sermon deserves to be read.   [2] 2 Cor. 5:17.

Think of what happened within Christ Jesus, for He is always the one we should look at, in all things. Is He not the model of all holiness? He is God and man. His state of Son of God is the source from which flows the Divine value of all His acts; but He is man also: *Perfectus homo*, perfect man. Even though united in an ineffable manner to the Divine Person of the Word, His human nature lost nothing of the activity proper to that nature, its special mode of acting; that nature was the source of perfectly authentic human actions. Christ Jesus prayed, worked, took nourishment, suffered, gave Himself up to rest: these were human actions which showed that Our Savior was truly man. I would even dare to say that no one has ever been as much man as He, for His human nature was of an incomparable perfection. Only in Him did the human nature subsist in the divinity.

Something analogous takes place in us. Grace does not suppress or overturn nature—neither the essence of nature nor its good qualities. There is no doubt that grace constitutes a new state added over-and-above, one infinitely superior to our natural state. From the point of view of our goal, which has become a super-natural one—and from the point of view of the strengths serving to attain that goal—it has brought about in us a profound modification; but our nature is neither disturbed nor lessened.[1] It is by exercising our own faculties—intellect, will, affections of heart, feelings, imagination—that our human nature, even as adorned with grace, must carry out its operations: but these acts deriving from nature are elevated by grace to the point of being worthy of God.

We ought first of all to remain ourselves; to live in a manner that conforms to our nature as free and reasonable created beings. That is the primary element of the "truth" of our actions. I will add that we ought to live in a way *that corresponds to our individuality.*

[1] It goes without saying that the super-natural state aims at excluding what is depraved in our nature owing to original sin; what ascetical writers call the "natural" life, as opposed to the "super-natural" life. We have seen, above, that mortification consists precisely of destroying that "natural" life.

In our super-natural life we ought still to keep our personality as regards those things in it that are good. This is part of that "truth," of that "sincerity," which the life of grace requires. Holiness is not a single mold in which the natural qualities that characterize the personality special to each person must disappear so as to represent after that but one uniform type. Far from it! In creating us, God has endowed each one of us with gifts, talents, privileges. Each soul has its particular natural beauty: one soul shines through the profundity of its intellect, another is distinguished by the firmness of its will; a third attracts by the wideness of its charity. Grace will respect that beauty, as it respects the nature on which it is based; it will simply add to the native splendor a divine brilliance that lifts and transfigures it. In His sanctifying operations, God respects His work of creation, for it is He who has willed that diversity: each soul, by expressing one of the Divine thoughts, has its particular place in the heart of God.

Finally, we ought to be "true" in being *in accord with the vocation* to which God has called us. We are not simply isolated individuals; we are part of a society that embraces different states of life. It is clear that, to "be in truth," we must observe the duties proper to us, the duties created for each of us by the special state in which Providence has enlisted us; grace cannot be in contradiction to this. It would be a "falsity" for the mother of a family to remain for long hours in church when her presence is required at home for the running of her household;[1] it would be a "falsity" if someone in a religious order, through devotion, were to spend an hour in meditation in preference to the work prescribed by obedience, no matter how trivial that work was. Such acts are not entirely "true."

"Father," said Jesus, praying for his disciples at the Last Supper, "sanctify them in the truth."[2]

---

[1] Cf. 1 Tim. 5, vv. 4, 8.   [2] John 17:17.

2. Carrying out our works *in charity*, in a state of grace. *Necessity and fruitfulness of grace* for the super-natural life.

Is it enough that our acts are "true," that they are in conformity with our condition as reasonable created beings subject to God, that they are freely carried out and are in conformity with our state of life—is all this enough for them to be acts of super-natural life?

No, that is not enough; they must, as well (and this is the chief point) proceed from grace—be carried out by a soul adorned with sanctifying grace. That is what St. Paul means by his phrase "in charity."

"*In charity*"—which is to say: first and foremost, in that fundamental, essential, charity which makes us relate entirely to God, finding in Him the Supreme Good we prefer to every other good; this is a description of the fruit of the grace which makes us pleasing to God to the point of being His children. It is true that super-natural charity is not grace; but the two always go together: "The charity of God is poured forth in our hearts by the Holy Spirit who has been given to us."[1] Grace elevates our *being*; charity transforms our *activity*. Grace and charity are always united—the degree of the one marks the degree of the other; and every grave sin, of whatever nature it be, kills within us grace and charity at the same time.

Sanctifying grace should be the source at which all human activity feeds. Without it, we cannot produce any super-natural acts, acts that will have some meritorious proportion to the bliss of eternal life. God first establishes within us a state, the state of grace: that is what matters in the very first place. A being only carries out actions by reason of its nature: *we* only perform *human* actions if we possess in the first place a

[1] Rom. 5:5. "Sanctifying grace and Divine Charity are the outpouring of Christ's Spirit, the Paraclete. For habitual grace and the supernatural spiritual endowment of charity are only distinguishable from one another as the sun's light is distinguished from the sun. Sanctifying grace is the life of the soul; charity is that same living force ready to burst forth into all the operations of the supernatural life, and chiefly into actual love of the Source of all its life and beauty": Hedley, *Retreat*, pp. 302-303.

human nature. In the same way, we cannot talk of someone performing acts of super-natural life unless that person, through grace, possesses in the first place a new nature as it were: *Nova creatura*, a "new creature."

Look at that man stretched out on the earth, there beneath your eyes. He might only be sleeping; he might also be a corpse. If he is only sleeping, he is going to awake in a short while; the whole of his body is going to start moving, his natural energies are going to show themselves. Why? Because he still retains within himself the source from which his animating energies issue—that is, the soul. But if the soul is absent, the body will not move: try as you may to shake it, it will remain in its cold inertness as a corpse. From now on, no activity will spring forth from this dead body; the vital principle from which its energies derive has left it.

And so it is with the super-natural life. Sanctifying grace is its inner mainspring from which all super-natural activity emanates. If a soul possesses this grace, it can produce acts of life, acts that are super-naturally meritorious. If not, that soul in the sight of God is a dead soul.[1]

Christ Jesus has given a comparison which makes one have a real understanding of this role of grace within us. Our Lord liked to make use of images that made the truth easy to grasp. It is after the Last Supper. Our Divine Savior leaves the supper-room, with His disciples, to betake Himself to the Mount of Olives. On His way, in going out of the city, He passes a hill covered with vineyards.[2] This sight inspires

---

[1] Of course, this is no more than a comparison serving to show us the necessity of grace as a super-natural vital principle; for a soul in a state of mortal sin is able, through the Sacrament of Penance, to come alive again by getting grace back. Further, the soul has to prepare for and have recourse to the sacrament by free acts that are super-natural (that is to say, carried out under the impulse of *actual* super-natural helps given by God), acts of fear, hope, love, contrition. Cf. note 2 on page 288.

[2] Fouard, *Vie de Notre-Seigneur Jésus-Christ*, Book VI, ch. V on the subject of Jesus's discourse on His way to Gethsemane.

Christ Jesus to make His final discourse. "You see these vines?" He says to His apostles, "well, I am the True Vine, and you are the branches. He who abides in me, and I in him, bears much fruit: for without me you can do nothing."[1] Just as the vine-shoot cannot bear fruit if it does not stay united to the trunk, so it is with you, if you do not remain united to me by grace.

Grace is the sap that rises from the root into the branches. What bears fruit is neither the root nor the trunk, it is the branch—but the branch united, through the trunk, with the root, and drawing from the root the nutritive sap. Break off the branch, separate it from the trunk, and, no longer receiving the sap, it dries up and becomes dead wood incapable of producing the smallest fruit. It is the same as this with the soul that does not possess grace: it is not united to Christ, it does not draw from Him that sap of super-natural grace which would make it super-naturally alive and fruitful. Do not forget that Christ alone is the source of super-natural life: all our activity, the whole of our existence, have no value for life eternal except insofar as we are united to Christ through grace. If we are not, we can bustle about as much as we like, we can spend ourselves, perform actions of the most brilliant kind in the eyes of men, but before God all that activity is without super-natural fruitfulness, without merit for life eternal.

You may say to me: "Are these actions, then, bad ones?" No, not necessarily. If the actions are honest actions, they do not fail to be pleasing still to God, who, sometimes, rewards those actions with temporal favors; they give the person performing them a certain merit in a very wide sense of that word; or rather, there is some suitability in God's not leaving them without some reward. But, as sanctifying grace is missing, there is not the necessary proportion between those actions

[1] See John 15:1-5.

and the eternal inheritance God has promised only to those who are His children through grace—"*if* we are children we are heirs as well."[1] God cannot recognize in these actions the requisite super-natural character for them to count with Him for eternity.

Look at those two men giving alms to a poor person; one of these men, through grace, is in the holy friendship of God, he gives the alms at the prompting of divine charity; the other lacks sanctifying grace in his soul. Outwardly, the two of them perform the same action; but in the sight of God, what a difference! The alms of the first earn for him an increase of infinite and eternal happiness; it is of him that Our Lord has said that whoever gives a cup of cold water to drink "because he is a disciple of mine ... shall not miss his reward."[2] The alms of the second are without merit in regard to that same beatitude—even if he should give gold in handfuls. That which flows only from nature has no value for life eternal.

Doubtless God, who is Goodness itself, will not look without kindliness upon the honest acts performed by a sinner, especially when they are acts of charity towards neighbor, done, not through human ostentation but through the impulse of compassion towards the unfortunate. Often, even (and this is a great cause for confidence) God's mercy inclines Him to grant to souls who devote themselves to such charitable actions graces of conversion that finally give back to them the supreme good of the Divine friendship. But only sanctifying grace gives to our lives their true significance and their fundamental value.

So much is this so, that when a sinner returns to a state of grace, even *then* these actions that were performed without grace—however numerous and however excellent they may have been naturally—remain without value from the point of view of super-natural merit and the beatitude that rewards it; they are lost beyond recall.

---

[1] Rom. 8:17 (Jerus.)   [2] Matt. 10:42 (Knox).

St. Paul has shed much light on this truth. Listen to what he says. "If I should speak with the tongues of men and of angels, but do not have charity, I have become as sounding brass or a tinkling cymbal. And if I have prophecy and know all mysteries and all knowledge, and if I have all faith so as to remove mountains, yet do not have charity, I am nothing. And if I distribute all my goods to feed the poor, and if I deliver my body to be burned, yet do not have charity, it profits me nothing."[1] In other words, the most extraordinary gifts, the most excellent talents, the most generous enterprises, the most brilliant actions, the greatest efforts, the most profound sufferings, have no merit for life eternal without charity—that is to say, without that sovereign love of the soul for God considered as He is in Himself, without that super-natural love which arises from sanctifying grace like a flower from its stem.

Let us, then, refer the whole of our life to God, our last end and eternal beatitude. The charity of God that we possess with sanctifying grace ought to be the motive-power of all our activity. When we possess divine grace within us, we are carrying out the wishes of Our Lord, we are "abiding in Him"—"Abide in me"; and He abides in us—"and I in you."[2] He abides in us along with the Father and the Holy Spirit: "We will come to him, and will make our abode with him."[3] The Holy Trinity, truly living in us as in a temple, does not stay inactive there, but abides in us to sustain us constantly, in order that our soul can exercise its super-natural activity: "My Father goes on working, and so do I."[4]

You know that in the natural order God, by His action, sustains us ceaselessly in existence[5] and in the exercise of our acts: this is called

---

[1] 1 Cor. 13:1-3.   [2] John 15:4.   [3] John 14:23 (Rheims).   [4] John 5:17 (Jerus.)

[5] [*Translator's quotation*: F.J. Sheed, *Theology and Sanity*: "Consider what the Church (sees) when She looks at the universe. For one thing She sees all things whatsoever held in existence from moment to moment by nothing but the continuing will of God that they should not cease to be. When She sees anything at all, in that same act She sees God holding it in existence. Do we? If we do not, we are not living mentally in the same world as the Church. What is more, we are not seeing things as they are, for that *is* how they are."]

the "Divine concourse." This Divine concourse exists also in the super-natural order; we are never able to act super-naturally unless God gives us the grace to act. This grace, by reason of its transitory effect, is called *actual*[1] (as distinct, in our way of expressing it, from *sanctifying* grace—which, being of its nature permanent, is called *habitual* grace). Along with sanctifying grace and the infused virtues and the gifts of the Holy Spirit, it—actual grace—is part of that wonderful whole which constitutes the super-natural order. In the ordinary exercise of the super-natural life, it is nothing else than the Divine concourse applied to the super-natural order. But on special occasions resulting from the state of our soul since original sin—the darkness of our intellect; the weakness of our will that is turned aside from the seeking of true infinite good by concupiscence, by the devil and the world—this Divine concourse expresses and manifests itself in a manner that is likewise special: a particular illumination of the intellect, a greater strength given to the will in order to resist a grave temptation or carry out an arduous work. Without this particular help, which God grants in response to prayer, we would not be able to attain to our supreme end; we would not be able, as the Council of Trent puts it, to "perse-vere in justice."[2]

This, then, in broad outline, is the basic law of the exercise of our spiritual life. Without changing anything of what is essential to our nature, of what is good in our individuality, of what is required by our particular state of life, we ought to live by the grace of Christ, referring,

---

[1] [*Translator's note*: The relevance of this comes out better in the French, in which language "*actuel*" has the meaning of "current," "of the present time."]

[2] Sess. IV, can. 18; cf. can. 13. However, it is very evident that a soul in the state of mortal sin can receive *actual* super-natural graces which enlighten his intellect and strengthen his will in the work of his conversion; but with such a soul these graces do not attach—as they do for the soul who possesses sanctifying grace—to that "Divine concourse" of which we have been speaking and which preserves sanc-tifying grace in the souls of the just. The Holy Spirit *moves* the sinner towards conversion; He does not *dwell in* his soul.

through charity, the whole of our activity to the glory of His Father. Grace is grafted upon nature, upon our native energies, and envelops the operations peculiar to nature. Such is the primary source of that diversity we find in the saints.

3. Marvelous *variety of the fruits of grace* in souls. There is one single source of those fruits, however.

Moreover, the degree of grace itself varies in souls. It is true, as I have told you, that there is but one single model of holiness, as there is but one source of grace and life—Christ Jesus. Justification and eternal bliss are specifically, in their basis and their substance, the same for all: "One Lord, one faith, one baptism," says St. Paul.[1]

But in the same way that all those who possess human nature vary in their qualities, so also does God distribute His super-natural gifts freely, following the designs of His wisdom: "To each one of us grace was given according to the measure of Christ's bestowal."[2] In Christ's flock, every sheep has its "name" of grace: the Good Shepherd, says Jesus, "calls His own sheep by name,"[3] just as the Creator knows the multitude of the stars and "calls them all by their names,"[4] for every one has its own form and perfection. Every soul receives different gifts from the same Spirit, says St. Paul;[5] the operations of God in souls are many and various, but it is the same God who operates in us all. To one is given wisdom; to another, a very high gift of faith; to this one, the gift of healing; to that one, the power to work miracles. One is an evangelist, another a prophet, a third a teacher. But it is one and the same Holy Spirit who produces of all these gifts for us, distributing them to each in particular as He pleases.

---

[1] Eph. 4:5 (Rheims).   [2] Eph. 4:7.   [3] John 10:3.
[4] Ps. 146 (147):4. Cf. Baruch 3:34-35: "The stars shine joyfully at their set times: when He calls them, they answer, 'Here we are'; they gladly shine for their Creator" (Jerus.)   [5] 1 Cor. 12:4-11.

And each soul responds to the Divine idea in a way that is special to that soul. Each soul turns to account the talents entrusted to its freedom, makes real within itself the features of Christ, through a co-operation that has its own particular character.

Thus, under the infinitely delicate and finely-shaded action of the Holy Spirit each soul, in its individual activity that is raised higher and transformed by grace, ought to aim at representing the Divine Model—which is how that harmonious variety which makes God "wonderful in His saints"[1] comes about. He finds His glory in all of them, but one can say (as the Church does)[2] of *each of them*: "There was not found the like of him in glory, who kept the law of the Most High."[3] The radiance of holiness of a St. Francis de Sales is not the same as that of a St. Francis of Assisi. The splendor that in heaven adorns the soul of a St. Gertrude or a St. Teresa of Avila is very different from that of a St. Mary Magdalene.

In each of the saints, the Divine Spirit has respected nature with the particular features which creation has put there. Grace has transfigured those features, has added to them its special gifts of a super-natural order. The soul, guided by the one whom the Church calls the "Finger of the Father's right hand,"[4] has responded to these gifts, and in this way has achieved its holiness. There will most certainly be a real delight for us in contemplating in heaven the marvels which Christ's grace has caused to shine forth upon a foundation as varied as that of our human nature.

Great as the saints are, high as they be in super-natural union with God, the primary wellspring of all their holiness is to be found in the grace of the Divine adoption. I have said to you, but I want to repeat it: all the graces, all the gifts God gives us have *as their first link in the chain* that Divine gaze which has predestined us to be children of God

---

[1] Ps. 67 (68):36.
[2] Office of Confessors.
[3] Ecclesiasticus (Sirach) 44:20.
[4] Hymn, *Veni Creator*.

through the grace of Christ Jesus. That is the dawn of all the mercies of God in our regard. To that grace of adoption which was brought to us by Jesus, and which we received at baptism, are attached all the kind attentions, all the courtesies, of God towards each one of us. Oh, if you only knew what God is offering! If we only knew the worth of that grace which, without changing our nature, makes us children of God and grants us to live as children of God while awaiting the eternal inheritance! Without it, as you have seen, natural life—be it the richest in gifts, the most brilliant in works, the most dazzling in genius—is barren for celestial bliss.

That is why St. Thomas could write that "the perfection which results for one single soul from the gift of grace surpasses all the good things spread throughout the universe."[1] Is not that what Our Lord Himself declared? "What does it profit a man," Jesus asked, "if he gains the whole world"—if he wins the world's esteem—"but suffers the loss of his own soul?"[2]—if, not possessing my grace, he is excluded for ever from my kingdom? Grace is the wellspring of our true life, the seed of future glory, the true budding of a blest eternity.

That being so, we can understand what an inestimable jewel sanctifying grace is for a soul. It is a precious pearl, all the luster of which is due to the blood of Jesus. We can understand why our Divine Savior should have been brought to utter such terrible anathemas against anyone who, through his scandal, leads a soul into sin and makes that soul lose the life of grace: "It were better for him if a millstone were hung about his neck and he were thrown into the sea."[3] We can understand, too, why those holy souls who lead a life of labor, prayer or expiation for the conversion of sinners, for the benefit of grace to be restored to them, are so pleasing to Christ Jesus. Our Divine Master would one day show St. Catherine of Siena a soul that had obtained salvation through

---

[1] "The good of one grace is greater than the [natural] good of the entire universe": I-II, q. CXIII, a. 9, ad 2.　　　[2] See Matt. 16:26.　　　[3] Luke 17:2.

her prayer and her patience. "The beauty of that soul was such," the Saint told Blessed Raymond, her confessor, "that no words would be able to express it."[1] And yet, that soul had still not been clothed in the glory of the beatific vision; it had only the radiance given by the grace of baptism. "See," said Our Lord to the Saint, "see how, through you, I have recovered this soul previously lost"; and then He added: "Does this soul not seem to you very charming, very beautiful? Who, then, would not accept whatever pain it might be, in order to gain so wonderful a creature? ... That I have shown you this soul is so as to make you more ardent to obtain the salvation of all, and so that you may lead others to do this work, according to the grace that will be given you."

Let us, then, be on guard to preserve jealously the divine grace within us; let us carefully keep away from it whatever is able so to weaken it as to leave it without defense against the mortal blows of the devil, those deliberate resistances to the action of the Holy Spirit who dwells in us and who, ceaselessly, wishes to orientate our activity towards the glory of God. May our soul be "rooted and grounded" in charity, as St. Paul puts it.[2] By its possessing within it this divine "root" of sanctifying grace and of charity, the fruits the soul produces will be fruits of life. Through grace and charity, let us remain united to Christ Jesus like the vine-shoot to the Vine: "Be rooted in Him," says the Apostle in another place.[3] Baptism has "grafted" us on Christ,[4] and thenceforth we have in us the divine sap of His grace. It is thus that we are able to perform all our actions divinely, because their inner mainspring is divine.

And when this mainspring is powerful to the point of becoming the one and only mainspring, to the point where all our activity proceeds from it, then we have made real the words of St. Paul: "And I live, now

---

[1] Life of St. Catherine by Blessed Raymond of Capua.   [2] Eph. 3:17.
[3] Col. 2:7.   [4] Rom. 11:17.

not I; but Christ lives in me."[1] "I live"—that is, I exercise my human and personal activity. "Now not I"—meaning "or rather no, it is not I who live," it is Christ who lives in me. It is Christ who lives, because the basis upon which all my own activity, all my personal life, is founded is the grace of Christ. Everything comes from Him through grace, everything returns to His Father through love. "I" live for God, in Christ Jesus—"alive for God in Christ Jesus."[2]

NOTE[3]

Can we know whether we are in a state of grace, in God's friendship? As a matter of absolute knowledge which excludes even the shadow of a doubt, no. But we can—we even ought to—hope that we possess grace if we are not conscious of any mortal sin and if we sincerely seek to serve God with steadfast goodwill. That last indication is one given by St. Mary Magdalene de Pazzi somewhere in her writings. In the case of generous souls who are docile to inspirations from on high, the Holy Spirit often adds His testimony: "The Spirit Himself gives testimony to our spirit that we are sons of God."[4] There is, then, a practical certainty—one which, while it does not exclude fear, ought to be sufficient for us to live, with confidence, the divine life to which God calls us, and to taste the profound joy arising in the soul from the thought of being, in Jesus, an object of the Heavenly Father's delight.

---

[1] Gal. 2:20 (Rheims).   [2] Rom. 6:11 (Jerus.)   [3] By Marmion.   [4] Rom. 8:16.

CHAPTER SIX

Our Super-natural
Growth in Christ

Introduction: The super-natural life is subject to a *law of progress.*

ALL LIFE TENDS, not only to being manifested by acts which are proper to it and which emanate from its inner mainspring, but as well as this, to grow, to progress, to bloom, to become more perfect. The child that first sees the light of day does not stay always a child; the law of nature is that it attain the age of manhood.

The super-natural life is not exempt from this law. Had He wished, Our Lord could in an instant, after one act of adhesion of our will, have placed us permanently in the degree of holiness and glory He destined for our souls, as occurred with the angels. He has not so wished. He has laid it down that, although His merits are the cause of all holiness, and His grace the wellspring of the whole of our super-natural life, we are all the time to bring our own share of the work of our perfection and our spiritual progress. The time we spend here below in faith is granted us to that end. As we have seen, we ought first to clear aside all the obstacles that stand in the way of the divine life within us, and at the same time carry out the acts meant to develop that super-natural life, right up to what it be when, at the moment of our death, it is fixed permanently at the ending of the journey. That is what St. Paul calls coming "to the mature measure of the fullness of Christ."[1]

[1] Eph. 4:13.

294

The same apostle takes care to indicate the necessity of this growth, this progress, and in what ordered way it is to be achieved. After having told us to practice the truth in charity, he immediately adds: "and so grow up in all things in Him who is the head, Christ."[1]

In the preceding talk we have seen what St. Paul means by living in truth and charity. I showed you that these words contain the *fundamental* principle by which we ought to act in order to live super-naturally, namely to stay united to Christ Jesus through sanctifying grace and, through love, to refer all our human actions to the glory of His Father. Such is the primordial law which presides over the divine life within us.

Let us now see how this life of which we received the seed-germ at baptism ought—in so far as this depends on us—to develop and blossom.

This is an important subject. Look at Christ Jesus: the whole of His life is consecrated to the glory of His Father, whose will He carries out always: "I seek not my own will, but the will of Him who sent me."[2] The will of His Father—He seeks only that. At the time when He is concluding His earthly existence, He says to His Father that He has "accomplished the work that you have given me to do," which is that of giving Him glory: "I have glorified you on earth."[3] The desire of His Divine heart is that we too should follow His example and seek the glory of His Father. Well now, what does that mean for us?

Our Lord tells us. "That we should bear much fruit"—that our perfection shall not remain mediocre, but that our super-natural life be intense: "In this is my Father glorified; that you bring forth *very much* fruit."[4] Is it not for this, moreover, that Jesus came? is it not for this that He gave His life-blood, that He makes us partakers of His infinite merits? "I came that they may have life, and have it *more abundantly*."[5] Like the woman of Samaria[6] to whom He had revealed the greatness

---

[1] Eph. 4:15. [2] John 5:30; 6:38. [3] John 17:4.
[4] John 15:8 (Rheims). [5] John 10:10. [6] John 4:5-15.

of the "divine gift," that of "giving us living water,"[1] let us ask Him to teach us, through His Church, what are the springs to which we should go and draw so as to find an abundance of these waters. For they make us produce many fruits of life and of holiness pleasing to His Father; they continuously slake our thirst until we come to life eternal.

The sacraments are the principal sources of growth of the divine life within us. They act in our souls by the efficacy of their very operation, *ex opere operato*, as the sun produces light and heat; it is necessary only that within us no obstacle stand in the way of their operation. Of all the sacraments, the Eucharist is the one which most increases the divine life in us, because in its case we receive Christ in Person, we drink at the very source of the living waters. That is why—because of the greatness of this sacrament—I shall expound to you later, in a special talk, the nature and conditions of its action within us.

What I want to show you now are the general laws by virtue of which we can increase the life of grace within us, outside of the reception of the sacraments.

1. Outside of the sacraments, the super-natural life becomes more perfect *through the exercise of the virtues.*

THIS IS HOW the Council of Trent expounds the doctrine on this subject: "Once we have been purified and become friends of God and members of His race [by sanctifying grace],[2] we are renewed day by day (as St. Paul says),[3] going on 'from virtue to virtue'[4].... Through observance of the commandments of God and of the Church, we grow in the state of justice in which we have been placed through the grace of Jesus Christ. Faith and our good works co-operate, and in that way we advance in

---

[1] See John 4:10.

[2] Marmion's explanatory insertion, as are the words in square brackets later in the passage.   [3] 2 Cor. 4:16.

[4] Ps. 83 (84):7. [*Translator's note*: The RSV (Cath.) has "from strength to strength"; Knox, "at each stage refreshed."]

the grace that makes us just in the sight of God. For it is written: 'He that is just [that is, he who possesses, through sanctifying grace, the friendship of God], let him be just still.'" "And again: 'Be not afraid to be justified even until death.'[1] It is this increase of grace that the Church asks for when she says to God (on the Thirteenth Sunday after Pentecost): 'Give us an increase of faith, hope and charity.'"[2]

Along with our works, the Holy Council, as you see, indicates to us *practice of the virtues*—principally the theological virtues—as the source of our progress, of our growth in the spiritual life of which grace is the wellspring.

How does that growth come about? First, through good works. I have told you that every good work done in a state of grace, under the urging of divine charity, is meritorious; and every meritorious work is a source of increase of grace in us: "A meritorious act"—whatever it may be—"merits for a person an increase of grace."[3] The good actions of a soul in a state of grace are not only fruits or manifestations of our status as children of God; they are, besides that, says the Council of Trent, a cause of increase of that justification which makes us pleasing to God.[4] In measure, then, as our good works multiply, grace increases. It becomes stronger, more powerful, and charity with it. And with it, as well, comes an increase of future glory—glory which is but the flowering, in heaven, of our degree of grace here below.[5] That is why the holy

---

[1] Apoc. 22:11; Ecclesiasticus (Sirach) 18:22. [*Translator's note*: Marmion's version or interpretation of these verses of Scripture is "... let him become ever more just" and "Progress [or advance] in justice until death"; thus underlining the Council of Trent's point that it is a matter not just of preserving but of increasing.]

[2] Sess. VI, cap. 10.   [3] St Thomas, I-II, q. CXIV, a. 8.

[4] "If anyone says that justification received is not preserved *and even increased* in the sight of God through good works, but maintains that these works are only the fruit and the signs of justification received, and not *a cause of the increase itself*, let him be anathema": Sess. VI, can. 24.

[5] "If anyone says ... that a man justified by good works, which are his through the grace of God and the merits of Jesus Christ of whom he is a living member, has

Council[1] repeats to us the words of St. Paul: "Be steadfast and immovable, always abounding in the work of the Lord, knowing that your labor is not in vain in the Lord."[2]

But above all it is through practice of the virtues that the life of grace increases.

In man, as you know, nature makes spring forth from his depths certain faculties—intellect, will, feelings, imagination—which are sources of action, powers of operation, within us; faculties that allow us to act fully as men. Without them, a man is not perfect in his concrete reality of man.

Something analogous is found in the super-natural life. Sanctifying grace informs[3] our soul, and, making us a "new creature,"[4] giving us a new *being* as it were, it renders us children of God. But God who does all things with wisdom and who pours forth His gifts on us with munificence—has given to this being faculties which, proportioned to the person's new condition, give him the capacity to *act* in pursuance of the super-natural goal to be attained, that is to say, as a child of God who awaits the inheritance of Christ in eternal bliss. These faculties are the infused super-natural virtues.

They are called *virtues* (from the Latin word *virtus*, strength) because they are capacities for action, mainsprings of operation, energies that remain in us in the state of firm habits, and which, exercised at the required moment, make us produce, with promptitude, ease and joy, works pleasing to God. As these powers of operation do not have their

---

not truly merited an increase of grace, eternal life, an increase of the same eternal life (provided he dies in a state of grace), and even a consequential increase of glory, let him be anathema": Sess. VI, can. 32.

[1] Sess. VI, cap. 16.

[2] 1 Cor. 15:58. [*Translator's note*: "abounding": Marmion's version is: "*de plus en plus*," "more and more."]

[3] [*Translator's note*: "inform" in the sense of "animate" or "actuate by vital powers," powers of life.]

[4] 2 Cor. 5:17 ("If then any man is in Christ, he is a new creature"); Gal. 6:15.

source in us, and since they are aimed at making us act with a view to an end that goes beyond the demands and exceeds the strength of our nature, they are called *super-natural*. Finally, the word *infused* indicates that God Himself, directly, puts them in us, along with sanctifying grace on the day of our baptism.

By grace, we *are* children of God. By the infused super-natural virtues we *are able to act* as children of God, to produce acts that are worthy of our super-natural end.

We must distinguish infused virtues from natural virtues. The latter are qualities, "habits," which a man, even an unbeliever, acquires and develops in himself by his personal efforts and his repeated acts: such as courage, strength, prudence, justice, gentleness, loyalty, sincerity. These are natural dispositions which we have cultivated and which, through exercise on our part, have arrived at the state of acquired habits. They perfect and embellish our *natural* being in the intellectual or simply moral domain.[1]

A comparison will make you grasp the nature of a natural acquired virtue. You possess an understanding of several foreign languages; this knowledge you did not receive at birth, you have *acquired* it by exercise and repeated effort. Once acquired, it is in you in the state of a habit, a power, ready to make itself available at the smallest command of your will. When you want to, you will speak those languages without any difficulty. It is the same with one who has acquired the art of music; he can be prevented from exercising this art at every moment, but the art remains in him in the state of a habit. When the artist wants to, he will take his bow or sit himself down at the piano, and will play as easily as others open their eyes, walk etc. Equally, as you will understand, an acquired natural virtue, like every acquired habit, must be maintained and cultivated if it is not to be lost—and this, on the very principle that made it arise, namely by practice.

[1] Cf. St Thomas, I-II, q. CX, a 3.

Of a different essence are the infused super-natural virtues. To begin with, they lift us above our nature. We exercise them no doubt by the faculties with which nature has endowed us (intellect and will), but these faculties are heightened, raised right up to the divine level, if I may so express it; in such a way that the acts of these virtues reach the proportions requisite for attaining to our super-natural end. Then also, it is not by our personal efforts that we acquire them; their seed-germ is liberally put within us by God, along with the grace in train of which they come; they are "poured forth together."

2. The *theological virtues.* Nature of these virtues; how they are specific to the state of child of God.

WHAT ARE THEY, these virtues? As I have told you, they are powers of acting super-naturally, they are strengths that make us capable of living as children of God and reaching our heavenly beatitude.

The Council of Trent, when it speaks of the increase of the divine life in us, singles out faith, hope and charity above all. They are called *theological*, because they have God as their immediate object.[1] By them, we can know God, hope in Him, love Him in a super-natural way worthy of our vocation to future glory and of our condition as children of God. These in a strict sense are the virtues of the super-natural order—whence their primacy and their prominence.

And see how well they answer to our Divine vocation. What, indeed, is needed in order to possess God?

One needs, first, to *know* Him. In the life above we shall see Him face to face, and this is why "we shall be like to Him: because we shall see Him as He is."[2] But here below we do not see Him; it is by *faith* in

---

[1] St Thomas (I-II, q. LXII, a. 1) indicates two other reasons for this term "*theological* virtues": that those virtues are given by God alone; and, further, that Divine revelation—it alone also—makes them known to us.   [2] 1 John 3:2 (Rheims).

Him, in His Son, that we believe in His word, that we know Him; it is knowledge in obscurity. But what He tells us about Himself, about His nature, His life, His designs of redemption through His Son, we nevertheless know with certainty. The Word, who is everlastingly in the heart of the Father, tells us what He sees, and we know it because we believe what He says. "No one has ever seen God; it is the only Son," in the heart's-embrace of the Father, "who has made Him known."[1] This knowledge of faith is therefore a Divine knowledge, and that is why Our Lord has said that it is a knowledge which brings eternal life: "Now this is eternal life: that they may *know* you, the only true God, and Jesus Christ, whom you have sent."[2]

In this light of faith we know where our beatitude is; we know what "eye has not seen nor ear heard, nor has it entered into the heart of man" to conceive, namely the beauty and greatness of the glory that "God has prepared for those who love Him."[3] But this ineffable beatitude is beyond the strength of our nature—shall we be able to arrive at it? Yes, without any doubt. God even places in our soul this feeling that we are assured of reaching that supreme goal with His grace, fruit of the merits of Jesus, and despite the obstacles standing in the way of doing so. We can say with St. Peter: "Blessed be the God and Father of our Lord Jesus Christ, who according to His great mercy has regenerated us" (in baptism) and given us this "lively *hope*" of an incorruptible inheritance that is reserved in heaven for us.[4]

Finally, *charity*, love, brings about our drawing closer to God, here below, whilst waiting to possess Him on high. Charity completes and perfects faith and hope; it makes us experience a real taking of pleasure in God, we prefer God to everything and we seek to manifest to God this taking of pleasure and this preference, by doing His will. "The companion of faith," says St. Augustine, "is hope; hope is necessary because we do not see what we believe. With it, we do not fall faint in

[1] John 1:18 (Jerus.)
[2] John 17:3 (Rheims).
[3] 1 Cor. 2:9; Isa. 64:4.
[4] 1 Peter 1:3-4 (Rheims); cf. 2 Cor. 1:3.

the waiting; indeed, charity comes and puts into our heart a hunger and thirst for God, imparts to our soul an impetus towards Him."[1] For the Holy Spirit has shed in our hearts the charity which makes us cry out to God "Father! Father!"[2] It is a super-natural faculty which makes us adhere to God as the infinite goodness we love more than anything else: "Who shall separate us from the love of Christ?"[3]

Such are the theological virtues: wonderful mainsprings, marvelous powers for living the divine life while we are here below. To *know* God as He is revealed to be by Our Lord; to *hope* in Him and in that bliss He promises as a result of the merits of His Son Jesus; to *love* Him above all things—there is nothing better we can do to make real our status as children of God and to stretch forward towards that eternal inheritance we are called to share with Christ, who has become our elder brother.

God has put these powers in us liberally. But let us not forget that though they have been given to us without our concurrence, they are neither maintained nor progressed without our efforts.

It is of the nature of a power, and it is its perfection, to accomplish the act that is its correlative.[4] A power which stayed inert—for example, an intellect that never produced an act of thought—would never arrive at the end, and consequently the perfection, that is its due. Faculties are only given in order that we put them into play.

Infused though they be, the theological virtues are no exception to this law of perfecting. If they remain unused, that will be to the great detriment of the perfection of our super-natural life. It is true that practicing them does not make them arise—otherwise they would no longer be infused; and for the same reason it is God alone who, Himself, increases them in us. Therefore the holy Council of Trent tells us to

---

[1] *Sermo* LIII.
[2] Rom. 8:15: "Abba! Father!"
[3] Rom. 8:35.
[4] St Thomas, II-II, q. LVI, a. 2; I-II, q. LV, a. 2.

beseech from God an increase of these virtues.[1] Look in the Gospels: the apostles ask Our Lord: "Increase our faith."[2] To the faithful at Rome St. Paul writes that he is asking God to make them "abound in hope";[3] and likewise he begs the Lord to kindle charity in the hearts of his dear Philippians.[4]

To prayer, to reception of the sacraments, must be joined exercise of these virtues. Though God is the *efficient* cause of an increase of them in us, our own acts, done in a state of grace, are the *meritorious* cause of that increase. By our acts, we merit that God increase in our souls these virtues that are so vital. Further, exercise of them produces in us the *facility* of carrying out such acts. And that is a very important point, since these virtues are proper to our state as children of God.

Let us, then, often ask our Heavenly Father to increase them within us. Let us say to Him, especially when going to the sacraments, in prayer, in temptation: "O Lord, I believe in you, but, I beg you, increase my faith. You alone are my hope, but strengthen my trust in you. I love you above all things, but increase that love, so that I seek nothing but your holy will!"

3. Why *pre-eminence* should be given to *charity*.

WE OUGHT to practice *charity* in particular. When we come to the close of our earthly life, faith and hope will disappear; faith will give place to sight, and hope to possession; and from that clear sight, from that assured possession, will radiate the love that never ends. That is why St. Paul says that charity is the greatest of the three theological virtues; it alone lasts for ever: "The greatest of these is charity."[5]

That place of honor, charity already holds here below. And this is a central truth I want to dwell on with you now.

[1] Sess. X, cap. 10.   [2] Luke 17:5.   [3] Rom. 15:13.   [4] Phil. 1:9.   [5] 1 Cor. 13:13.

You know that when it accompanies the exercise of the other virtues, charity adds a new luster to them. It confers on them a new efficacy, it is the source of a new merit. You undergo and accept from the heart some humiliation—that is an act of the virtue of humility. You freely renounce a permitted pleasure—that is an act of the virtue of temperance. You honor God by singing His praises—that is an act of the virtue of religion. Each of these acts, performed by a soul in a state of grace, has its own value, its particular merit, its special splendor. But if in addition each of those acts is performed with love of God as an explicit intention, this last-mentioned motive "colors"—if I may so express it—the acts of the other virtues and, without removing anything from their particular merit, adds a new merit to it.[1]

What follows from that? This consequence—one that completes the putting into relief of charity as holding the highest place. Namely, that our super-natural life and our holiness grow and advance in exact ratio to the degree of love with which we perform our actions. The more that in the performance of an act (provided of course the act, as we have seen, is super-natural, is in accordance with Divine order; an exercise, say, of piety, of justice, of religion, of humility, of obedience, of patience)—the more, I repeat, that our love of God is perfect, pure, disinterested, intense; that is to say, the more the motivation of the actions is drawn from our love of God, our love of His interests and His glory, the higher too is the degree of merit of that action; and hence the more rapid the increase of grace and divine life within us.

Listen to what was said by St. Francis de Sales, that eminent teacher on the interior life who spoke so well on these matters: "If our heart's tenderness is ardent, strong and excellent, it will enrich and perfect all the works of virtue that proceed from it. As St. Paul presupposes,[2] one can suffer death and flame without having charity; and there is even stronger reason to say that one can suffer it and have

---

[1] St Thomas, II-II, q. XXIII, a. 8.   [2] 1 Cor. 13:3.

little charity. Now, Theotimus, I say that it might well be that a very small amount of virtue would have greater value in a soul where a holy love reigns ardently than even martyrdom in a soul where holy love is languid, weak and slow…. In that way, the little simplicities of life, the abjections and humiliations in which the great saints took such pleasure in order to hide themselves and make their heart a shelter against vainglory, these having been done with a great excellence in the art and ardor of heavenly love, have been found more pleasing in the sight of God than the large and famous pieces of work of a number of others which were done with little charity or devotion."[1]

In the same passage, St. Francis de Sales gives us as an example Our Lord Jesus Christ. And with how much reason for doing so!

Let us think for a moment of our Divine Savior, for example in the workshop at Nazareth. Up to the age of thirty years His life was one of labor and obscurity, so much so that when He began His preaching and worked His first miracles His fellow countrymen were astonished at His doing this to the point of being scandalized: "Is not this the carpenter's son?"—someone we have known. "Then where did he get all this?"[2] And indeed, Our Lord during those years had done nothing extraordinary that might have brought Him to people's notice; His life had been one of labor, very simple labor too. And yet that labor was infinitely pleasing to His Father. Why is that? For two reasons: first, because the one who was laboring was the very Son of God; at each moment of that obscure life the Father was able to say: "This is my beloved Son, in whom I am well pleased."[3] Furthermore, Christ Jesus not only brought to His labor a great material perfection, He did everything solely for the glory of His Father: "I seek not my own will, but the will of Him who sent me,"[4] the will of the Father. In this is to be found the sole motivation of all His actions, of all His life: "I do always

---

[1] *Treatise on the Love of God*, XI, c. 5.   [2] Matt. 13:55.
[3] Matt. 3:17; 17:5; Mark 1:11; Luke 3:22; 2 Peter 1:17.   [4] John 5:30.

the things that are pleasing to Him."[1] Our Lord did everything with an incomparable perfection of inner love towards His Father.

Such is the twofold reason why the works of Jesus, commonplace as they may have appeared on the outside, were so pleasing to the Father and redeemed the world.

Are we able to imitate Christ Jesus in this? Yes. What, in us, corresponds to the hypostatic union that makes Jesus God's own Son is *the state of grace*. That grace makes us children of God: the Father can say, in looking at one who possesses sanctifying grace: "This is my beloved child." Our Lord said: "Is it not written in your Law, 'I said you are gods'?"[2]—that is, you are like God (even though it is true that Christ is not an adopted son like us, but the Son by nature). The second reason for the value of our works is (as with Christ) not only the *motive* of charity but also the *interior perfection* of the charity with which we perform them, the degree of love that envelops those acts and determines, by the same token, our growth in the divine life.

That is very important if we wish, not just to content ourself with what is strictly required in order that our actions shall be meritorious, but to increase the degree of this merit and to advance rapidly in union with God. Look around you; you will come across two pious persons, in a state of grace, who side by side lead an identical existence. On the outside, the two perform the same material actions; and yet there could be—there often is, even—an enormous difference between them in God's sight. The one moves his feet on the same piece of ground, is at a virtual standstill; the other advances with great strides in the life of grace, perfection and holiness. In what is the difference between them to be found? In the state of grace? No, since we are supposing both these persons to be in possession of God's friendship. In the special excellence of the actions of one of them? No, since we are supposing also that those material actions are substantially the same. Perhaps

---

[1] John 8:29.   [2] John 10:34; Ps. 81 (82):6.

from the care taken in the material performance of those actions? No, again, for though that may of course come into it, the supposition is that such wholly exterior perfection is equal as between the two of them.

Where, then, is the difference to be found? In the interior perfection, the intensity of love, the degree of charity with which each of them performs his actions. One of them, attentive to God, acts with a love that is elevated, mighty; that soul acts only in order to please God. Inside, it stays bowed down before the Lord in a spirit of adoration. At root, its activity proceeds only from God, and that is why each of its actions brings it closer to God; it advances rapidly in Divine union.

The other person performs the same job of work, but in that person faith is asleep; that soul is not thinking of the interests of God. Its love is not very ardent, is ordinary to a degree, mediocre. Doubtless its actions are not without merit, but the measure of that merit is low and can be diminished yet more by its distractions, self-love, vanity, and so many other human motivations that this soul, through negligence or lack of serious reflection, will allow to creep in to its actions.

That is the secret of the considerable difference that sometimes exists in the sight of God between certain souls living alongside each other and leading an outwardly identical existence.[1]

Such is the pre-eminence of the virtue of charity. It is this virtue that, properly speaking, governs the measure of the divine life in us.

Let us, then, be watchful to see that in all things we act only to imitate Our Lord, so as to bring glory to His Father. Let us, in our intimate conversations with Him, ask Christ Jesus, often, that all our activity may spring forth from love, as did His. Let us ask Him to grant us

---

[1] I have said "in the sight of God," for the human eye cannot always perceive that difference. It may even be that *outwardly* one of them is more "correct" and less open to the criticism of men; whereas with the other — in reality more advanced in union with God — defects of temperament, independent of the person's will, may obstruct the *outward* blossoming of grace.

part in that love He had for His Father, a love that made Him do everything with perfection, because "I love the Father."[1] Our Divine Savior cannot fail to hear our prayer fully.

4. Need for the *moral virtues*, acquired and infused.

But, you may say to me, if that is how it is, will it not be enough to hold on to charity? Does not charity make the other virtues useless? No, it would be a grave error to believe that. Why so? Because charity, love, is a treasure which is more exposed than the other virtues are.

You know that faith and hope are only destroyed in us by grave faults directly contrary to their object, for example, heresy or despair. Whereas charity is destroyed, like the grace that is its root, by every mortal fault of whatever nature. *All* grave sin is a mortal enemy to charity. By grave sin, indeed, the soul turns completely away from God so as to turn towards a created being; and that is the exact opposite of super-natural charity. The latter is a pearl of great price and an inestimable treasure, but it is exposed to being lost by no matter what grave fault. This is why one must protect it on all sides; and that is the role of the *moral virtues*. Those virtues are like guards of love; through them the soul keeps away the deliberate venial sins and the grave sins that threaten charity.

Here I must say a few words to you about the moral virtues. The framework and the character of our talks do not permit me to give you a very extensive account of them. I hope, however, to show you sufficiently the necessity of these virtues and the place they hold in our super-natural life.

As their name indicates, the moral virtues are those which regulate our morals, that is say, the actions we must freely carry out in order to make our conduct accord with the Divine law (commandments of

[1] John 14:31.

God, precepts of the Church, duties to the State), and thus to attain our last end. The immediate object of these virtues, you will understand, is not God in Himself as with the theological virtues. The moral virtues are very numerous: patience, obedience, humility, self-denial, mortification, piety and so many others; but they all come down, or are related, to the four great virtues called "cardinal"[1] (fundamental) virtues: prudence, fortitude, justice and temperance. There are both natural (acquired) and super-natural (infused) "cardinal virtues," the ones having their corresponding virtues in the other. There is an acquired temperance and an infused temperance, an acquired fortitude and an infused fortitude, and so on. What is their mutual relationship? They have the same field of action, and the concurrent operation of the acquired moral virtues is necessary for the full flowering of the infused moral virtues. Why is that?

Since original sin, our nature is tainted; there are in us depraved tendencies that result from ancient heredity,[2] from temperament, and also from the bad habits we contract—all the above are obstacles to the perfect accomplishment of the Divine will. What will remove these obstacles? The infused moral virtues that God puts in us along with grace? No, they have not, by themselves, that privilege. Without doubt, they are wonderful mainsprings of operation; but it is a psychological law that the destruction of vicious habits and the correcting of bad tendencies can only be effected through the contrary habits, and these good habits themselves result only from the repetition of acts—which brings us to the *acquired* moral virtues. It is for them to destroy our bad habits and to cause a facility for good to arise in us. That facility is something the acquired moral virtues will bring, as a concourse[3] with

---

[1] From the Latin *cardo*, "pivot, hinge." These four virtues constitute, as it were, the pivot upon which the whole of our moral life rests and depends.

[2] [*Translator's note*: Marmion's word is *l'atavisme*, "atavism."]

[3] [*Translator's note*: This word in its literal sense can mean a confluence, as when two running waters have met and now run together.]

the infused moral virtues. The latter capitalize[1] on this in-flow—very humble as it is, but necessary—and, in return, they raise the acts of the virtue to a new level and grant them a meritorious value. I want you to keep hold of this truth, indeed: that no natural virtue, however powerful it be, has the strength on its own to lift itself up to the super-natural level. That belongs only to the infused moral virtues, and this is what constitutes the superiority and pre-eminence of the latter.

An example will make the account of this doctrine clearer. Since original sin, we carry within us a leaning towards the pleasures of the senses. A man is able to force himself to abstain from dissoluteness and the abuse of these pleasures in order to obey his natural reason, and by frequent repetition of acts of temperance he *acquires* a certain facility, a certain habit which constitutes for that man a strength (*virtus*) of resistance. This acquired facility is of a purely natural order; if that man does not possess sanctifying grace, those acts of temperance are not meritorious for eternal life. But let grace, with the infused virtues, supervene. If in that man there had not already been a certain facility of temperance as a result of the *acquired* moral virtue, the *infused* moral virtue (of temperance) would have found difficulty in developing, because of the obstacles which result from our bad tendencies, obstacles that have not been removed by the contrary good habits. But the infused moral virtue, finding a certain facility for good, makes use of it so as to exert itself with more ease. Then, not only will it urge that man on further and make him advance to a higher degree of virtue, to the point of making him despise even permitted pleasures so as more closely to imitate Jesus crucified, but, as well as this, grace (without which there is no infused virtue) will give to the acts of acquired moral virtue a super-natural and meritorious value to which those acts will never attain by themselves.

When the two virtues (acquired and infused) meet, a necessary exchange is therefore established between them. The natural or acquired virtue clears away the obstacle and creates the facility for good; the

---

[1] [*Translator's note*: Marmion's words *captent à leur profit* are ones sometimes used of the "harnessing" of a river, to advantage.]

infused or super-natural virtue seizes upon this facility in order that it may expand more freely itself, but in order, also, to raise this good habit in value, to bring to it an increase of strength, to extend its field of operation and make it super-naturally deserving of eternal beatitude.

5. The moral virtues *safeguard charity*, which in return holds sway over and crowns them.

A SIMILAR EXCHANGE of services exists between the moral virtues (acquired and infused) and charity. I told you that the latter is a treasure exposed to be lost through every grave fault: it is for the moral virtues to protect it. They are the guards of love. Through these virtues, the soul keeps away the mortal faults that threaten the existence of charity, and the venial faults that lead to grave sin.

That is especially true of souls who are not yet very advanced in the interior life, and with whom love has not yet reached that high degree which makes it strong and stable. One of these souls receives Our Lord in Holy Communion; the communion is a fervent one, and at that moment the soul is full of love. But if, during the day, this soul is enticed by a temptation of the senses, it is necessary for the moral virtue of temperance to tilt him towards resistance; otherwise the soul will consent, and love will suffer shipwreck. In the same way, if a soul is tempted by anger, it is necessary for the moral virtue of patience, of forbearance, to rise up at that time so as to urge that soul to accept a humiliation: if not, the soul will allow itself to yield to anger, to vengeance, at the risk of losing sanctifying grace, and, with it, charity.

It is not only mortal sin that threatens charity: every habitual *venial* fault that is not fought against becomes a danger for it, as I have told you above,[1] because these faults expose the soul to grave falls. Now, in order to fight against these venial faults—deliberate ones or faults of habit—it is necessary to exercise the moral virtues, which make us resist the numerous enticements of concupiscence. Our will is weak-

---

[1] Section 4, page 234 ff.

ened since original sin, it has great pliability and leans easily towards evil. For it to lean towards good, a strength is necessary. That strength is the virtue; it is a "habit" which constantly tilts the soul towards good. It is a fact of experience that we act almost always, if not always, in the direction to which our habits incline us. From a bad habit, especially one not fought against, sparks fly out ceaselessly, as from a blazing hearth-fire. A soul that has the vice of pride, if it does not fight against it, will constantly commit acts of pride and vanity. It is the same with the virtues; they are habits from which acts corresponding to them ceaselessly arise.

The moral virtues (acquired and infused) serve, then, principally to thrust aside from the soul all the obstacles that halt us on our march forward to God. They help us to make use of the means that are necessary for fulfilling the diverse obligations of the moral life, and thus they safeguard within us the existence of charity. Such is the service the moral virtues have to render to charity.

In return, charity—especially when it is strong and ardent—crowns, as I have said, the other virtues by giving them particular luster and adding to them a new merit.

The influence of charity goes even further. It can so command our actions as a whole that, at need, it leads the soul to call the acquired moral virtues into being, so to speak. Urged on by charity the soul performs, bit by bit, acts the repetition of which produce the acquired moral virtues. The *motive* at that time comes from charity; but charity cannot practice all the acts of all the virtues: it is down to each faculty to have its own role and its special way of being practiced.

That is what happens with souls advanced in the divine life. In these souls, charity has attained a great perfection. Not only is it on their lips and in their heart, it expresses itself in their works. If we truly love God, we will keep His commandments.[1]

---

[1] John 14:15.

Affective love, love which stirs the emotions, is necessary for the perfection, the completion of charity. When we love someone, we praise, we extol that person, we rejoice in the qualities that person possesses. The soul that loves God takes pleasure in His infinite perfections, it repeats constantly as the Psalmist did: "Who is like you, O God?"[1] "O Lord, how worthy of admiration is your name, writ upon all your works!"[2] That soul ardently gives itself up to singing of the glory of God. From its heart, praises rise to its lips: "Singing is the mark of a lover."[3] It was because they loved that St. Francis of Assisi composed his wonderful *Canticles*, and St. Teresa of Avila her burning *Exclamations*.

But does that suffice? No. In order to be perfect, love has to express itself in its acts: affective love has to extend to *effective* love that embraces the Divine good pleasure and gives itself up to *that*, whole and entire. That is the true sign of love.[4] And when this love is ardent, when it is well anchored in the soul, it then commands all the other virtues, all the good works; it is sovereign. Because it is powerful, it ceaselessly inclines the will towards good, towards God.[5] It expresses itself by a constant fidelity to the Divine good pleasure, to the inspirations of the Holy Spirit. It was to these souls full of love that St. Augustine was able to say: "Love, and do what you will,"[6] because no longer were such souls willing to let in at the door anything other than what pleases God. Following the example of Christ Jesus, such souls are able to say: "I do always the things that are pleasing to Him"[7]—that please my Heavenly Father. That is perfection.

[1] "What great god is there like our God?": Ps. 76 (77):14 (St P.)

[2] "How admirable is your name in the whole earth!": Ps. 8:2.

[3] St. Augustine, *Sermo* 336, c. 1: *"cantare amantis est."*

[4] "We have two principal exercises of our love of God: one affective, the other effective. By the former, we have an attachment-of-heart to God and to everything God is attached to. By the latter, we serve God and do what He commands us to do. The one makes us take pleasure in God, the other makes us please God": St. Francis de Sales, *Treatise on the Love of God*, VI, c. 1.   [5] Cf. St. Francis de Sales, *ibid.*, XI, c. 8.

[6] *Tract. in Epistol. Johann.*, VII, c. 4.   [7] John 8:29.

6. Aiming at perfect charity through *purity of intention.*

WELL, how does one acquire it, this perfect love? How increase it in such a way that one really lives it? For, when it is a true love, it contains the seed of all the virtues. It sets them all in motion—each at the required moment, of course—as a captain his soldiers.[1] Charity "believes all things, hopes all things, endures all things."[2] Each step taken in love is a step in holiness, in being united with God. How shall we be able to arrive at this perfection of holiness? How maintain within us an intensity of love?

It is above all through the sacrament of the Eucharist, the sacrament of union, that this love increases. We shall shortly look at that point in detail. Here, we shall consider the question outside of the action of the sacraments, in the domain of our co-operation.

Charity is maintained in us, and its intensity increased in us, especially through the renewal of the intention in view of which we act. As the Fathers of the Church say so well when they comment on a saying of Our Lord: intention is the soul's "eye"[3] which orientates its whole

---

[1] St. Francis de Sales, *Introduction to the Devout Life*, III, c. 1. This is what St. Jeanne de Chantal wrote about this Saint: "Divine Goodness had put in this holy soul a perfect charity. For (to use his own words) when charity enters into a soul, it gives lodging there, along with itself, to a whole train of virtues. Certainly it had placed and ranged them in his heart in admirable order. Each held there the rank and authority that belonged to it; the one undertook nothing without the others, for he saw clearly what was advisable for each and the degrees of their perfection; and all produced their actions according to the occasions that presented themselves and, as charity prompted, gently and without making any fuss": Letter to Fr. Jean de St. François, *Abrégé de l'esprit intérieur ... de la Visitation*, Rouen, Cabut, 1744, p. 95.

[2] 1 Cor. 13:7.

[3] "By the 'eye' we must understand here the intention by virtue of which we do everything we do. If it is pure and right, and has its gaze on what it ought to, then all the good actions we perform by virtue of this intention are necessarily good": St. Augustine, Book II on the later part of Our Lord's sermon on the mount, c. XIII, n. 45. "What does the 'eye' signify if not the heart's intention which precedes action? Before proceeding to the act, this intention already looks at what it desires. And

being towards God. If this eye is pure,[1] does not give a dazzling blur through any human, any created, obstacle, then all the soul's activity will relate to God.

Is it necessary that this intention to act from love of God—that is, in order to give Him glory by carrying out His will—shall always be present? No, that is neither requisite nor even possible. But the experience and the knowledge of the saints has shown how well-founded and super-naturally expedient is the practice of frequently renewing our intention in order to advance, to progress, in the love of God and in the divine life.[2] Why is that? Because purity of intention keeps our soul in the presence of God and spurs it on to seek in all things only Him. It prevents curiosity, lack of seriousness, vanity, self-love, pride, ambition from creeping in to, infiltrating, our actions so as thereby to diminish their merit. A pure intention frequently renewed, surrenders the soul to God in its being and in its activity; it constantly rekindles in the soul, and there keeps alive, the hearth-fire of divine love; and in this way, by each good work that it causes to be executed and referred to God, it increases the life of the soul.

"To make excellent progress in devotion," says St. Francis de Sales, "one must offer all one's actions to God every day, for by this daily renewal of our oblation we pour out upon our actions the vigor and virtue of tender love through a new application of our heart to the Divine glory; by means of which that heart of ours is ever more sanctified.

---

what does the 'body' represent if not every action that follows upon the intention, as though upon the gazing of an eye? Thus, 'the lamp of the body is the eye' [Matt. 6:22], for the lamp-ray of a good intention lights up the merits of the action": St. Gregory, *Moralia*, Book XXVIII, c. XI, n. 30. Cf. the Venerable Bede on the Gospel of St. Luke, Book IV, c. XI; St Thomas, I-II, q. XII, a. 1, on 1 and 2.

[1] Matt. 6:22.

[2] We are not talking here of what is strictly requisite for an act to be meritorious; we are talking, rather, of increase of perfection. "Our intentions," Bossuet says somewhere, "are of their nature subject to being extinguished if one does not revive them." In practice, the intention is renewed by a sign of the cross, an ejaculatory prayer, a surge of the heart up to God.

Besides that, let us turn to Divine Love, hundreds and hundreds of times a day, through the practice of ejaculatory prayers, liftings-up of the heart and spiritual retreats [recollections by the soul]; for these holy exercises, continuously throwing, flinging, our minds up to God, carry there all our actions in their train. And how could it be other-wise, I ask you, than that a soul which, every moment, rushes towards Divine Goodness and incessantly sighs out words of tenderness in order to keep its heart close to the heart of this Heavenly Father—how should this soul not have been deemed to have been doing all its actions in God and for God?"[1]

Take care, then, habitually to act only for the glory of God, in order to please Him, to be acceptable to Him, in order that, in accordance with the very prayer of Christ, "the name of our Father in heaven be hallowed, His kingdom be extended in hearts and His will be done." A soul that is thus orientated towards God is a soul overcome by love more and more. For, at each step, that soul advances more deeply into love of God by ever renewing its acts of love. Love becomes then a weighty thing that, with ever increasing momentum, bears the soul along to generosity and fidelity in God's service: "My love, that weight of mine," said St. Augustine.[2] And from this comes that promptitude of the soul to devote itself to the service of God, to seek the interests of His glory. That is true devotion. What is the meaning of the word "devotion"? The Latin word *devovere* indicates the meaning; it is to be consecrated, vowed to the service of God and to carry out that service readily. Devotion is not simply having been consecrated to Christ in baptism; it is to vow with readiness and promptitude all one's energies, all one's works, to the service of Christ and the glory of His Father.[3] This is what the Church asks often for us: "Grant us, O Lord, ever to

---

[1] *Treatise on the Love of God*, XII, c. 9; Marmion's insertion in square brackets.

[2] *Confessions*, XIII, c. 9. [*Translator's quotation*: "Our love is our weight, as St. Austin observes; by which we are carried whithersoever we are carried": James Archer, *Sermons*.]

[3] "Devotion is some act of the will aimed at this: that one readily surrenders one-self to obedience of God": St Thomas, II-II, q. LXXXII, a. 3.

have a will devoted to thee, and to serve thy majesty with a sincere heart."[1] Elsewhere, she makes us ask to be devoted to God in a way that will bring glory to His name through our good works: "devoted in good works to the glory of thy name."[2]

Not, in the exercise of our activity, to have any other mainspring than grace, any other goal than the accomplishment of the will of God who has made us His children, any other supreme driving-force than love of this God and the interests of His glory—this, as St. Paul says, is to "walk worthily of God and please Him in all things, bearing fruit in every good work and growing in the knowledge of God."[3]

May that ideal be ours. We shall then make real that precept which Jesus gave us, and which is the greatest precept of all, the one that best sums up the super-natural life: "Love the Lord your God with your whole heart, and with your whole soul, and with your whole mind, and with your whole strength."[4]

7. Charity can envelop *all human actions.* Sublimity and simplicity of the Christian life.

ST. PAUL has just told us that, in order to fulfill this precept, we should please God "in all things." He employs the same expression when it is a question of increase of the divine life within us: that we may "grow up in all things."[5] The phrase returns more than once in the writings of the apostle, and it is full of meaning. What does St. Paul mean by "growing up *in all things*"? That, from the moment it is "true" (in the sense in which we used that word), no action is excluded from the domain of grace, of charity, of merit; that there is no action which may not serve to increase the life of God within us. In his first letter to the Corinthians,

---

[1] Prayer for the Sunday in the octave of the Ascension.
[2] Prayer for the 21st Sunday after Pentecost.   [3] Col. 1:10.
[4] Mark 12:30; Deut. 6:5.   [5] Eph. 4:15.

St. Paul has himself gone into detail to explain that phrase "in all things": "Whether you eat or drink, or do anything else, do all for the glory of God."[1] And, in his letter to the Colossians: "Whatever you do in word or in work, do all in the name of the Lord Jesus, giving thanks to God the Father through Him."[2]

So you see: it is not only such actions as of their nature are related directly to God, like pious "exercises," going to Mass, Holy Communion and reception of the other sacraments, works of spiritual and corporal charity. As well as these, it is the most ordinary and mundane actions, the most commonplace incidents of our everyday life—like taking food; attending to our daily concerns or our work; fulfilling in society as man or citizen our various duties, necessary or useful; relaxing; giving oneself up to rest. All these actions which are repeated each day and which, in monotonous and routine succession, literally weave the thread of our entire life, can be transformed, through grace and love, into acts that are very pleasing to God and rich in merits. It is like a grain of incense; a bit of dust with no solidity, but when it is thrown into the fire it becomes a pleasing perfume. When grace and love seize hold of everything in our life, then every bit of our existence is like a perpetual hymn to the glory of the Heavenly Father. Through our union with Christ, our life becomes for the Father like a censer from which rise perfumes that rejoice Him: "We are the fragrance of Christ *for God*."[3] Each act of virtue gives immense joy to the heart of God, because it is a flower and a fruit of grace, and because grace has been won by the merits of Jesus: "Unto the praise of the glory of His grace."[4]

---

[1] 1 Cor. 10:31.   [2] Col. 3:17.   [3] 2 Cor. 2:15.

[4] Eph. 1:6. "These little everyday charities—that headache, that toothache, that bad cold, that breaking of a glass, that sneer or that pout at one—in short, all these little sufferings, when taken or embraced with love, very much please Divine Goodness, who for a single cup of water has promised a sea of bliss to all his faithful.... Great occasions of serving God rarely present themselves, but the small occasions are common ... therefore do all things in the name of God, and all things done will be well done": St. Francis de Sales, *Introduction to the Devout Life*, III, c. 35.

No good action, then, is excepted: no effort, no labor, no work done, no renunciation, no suffering, no pain, not a tear but comes under this salutary influence of grace and charity, if we wish it so. Oh! how simple and sublime the Christian life is! Sublime, because it is the very life of God, going forth from God, coming into us through the grace of Christ and leading to God: "O Christian, recognize your worth."[1] Simple, because this divine life is grafted upon human life—however low, humble, infirm, poor, ordinary, that human life may in itself be. For us to be His children, for us to become co-heirs with His Son, God does not ask us to perform numerous heroic acts, He does not ask us to "cross the seas"[2] or "scale heaven"[3] No, it is within us that the kingdom of God is to be found; within us that it is built, beautified and perfected: "The kingdom of God is within you."[4] The super-natural life is an inner life, the wellspring of which is hidden with Christ in God and within the soul: "Your life is hidden with Christ in God."[5]

We do not have to change nature, but to redress what is defective in it. We do not have to use long formulas; a single glance of the heart can hold an intensity of love. It suffices for us to remain in sanctifying grace, to refer all to God and His glory through a pure intention, and consequently to live our human lives, in the place Providence has assigned to us, by carrying out the Divine will, by fulfilling the duties of the present moment, and this, simply, quietly, calmly, unfeverishly, with that deep interior confidence—composed of liberty of soul and inner joy—of the child who knows he is loved by his Father and, to the best of his weak ability, returns that love.

In the eyes of the world, this life animated by grace and filled with love is not always apparent. Doubtless every tree, as Our Lord says,[6] is recognized by its fruit. The Holy Spirit who dwells in the soul makes it produce these fruits of charity, of kindness, that betray, on the outside, the

---

[1] St. Leo, *Sermo* I on the Nativity of the Lord.   [2] Deut. 30:13 (Jerus.)
[3] Deut. 30:12 (Knox).   [4] Luke 17:21.   [5] Col. 3:3.   [6] Matt. 12:33.

power of His action. But the mainspring of this action is entirely intimate, its substantial splendor is wholly interior: "All the glory of the king's daughter is within";[1] her super-natural splendor is often veiled beneath the outward coarse-weave of her daily existence.

How careless we are, then, in neglecting so often to profit from such benefits brought within our reach every day, in being attached to deceptive trifles, "the bewitching of vanity."[2] What would we say of poor folk to whom a splendid prince offered his treasures and who, instead of dipping into them with wide-open hands to make themselves rich, passed by, indifferent to these riches? We would call them mad. Let us not be those poor madmen. As I have told you, we can do nothing of ourselves, Our Lord wants us never to forget that— "Without me you can do nothing,"[3] but when we possess His grace in us it should, along with love, become the mainspring of a life that is wholly divine.

We ought, with the grace of Christ, to do everything with the object of pleasing His Father. "I can," says St. Paul, "do all things in Him who strengthens me."[4] Let us make all our actions—the smallest like the biggest, the lowliest like the most brilliant—serve to take us forward in the divine life with great strides, through the intense love with which we perform those actions.

Then it is that God will look on us with pleasure, because He will find in us the image of His Son, an image that will become more and more perfect. With an increase of grace, of charity, and of the other virtues, the features of Christ are reproduced in us with greater accuracy, for the glory of God and the joy of our soul.

---

[1] Ps. 44 (45):14.   [2] Wisdom 4:12.   [3] John 15:5.   [4] Phil. 4:13.

8. The *fruit of charity*, and of the virtues charity commands:
making us grow in Christ **in order to perfect His mystical body.**

IT IS INDEED so as to become conformed to Christ Jesus that we should
in this way live in all things by charity. We should "grow up in all
things *in Him who is the head, Christ*."[1] For each one of us, the goal of
this development of the super-natural life is to attain "unto the measure of the age of the fullness of Christ."[2]

In speaking of the Church, I told you that Christ in His personal
and physical reality is perfect, but that He forms with His Church a
mystical body which has not yet attained its complete perfection. This
perfection comes into being in souls little by little, over the course of
centuries, "according to the measure of Christ's grace given to each
one of us";[3] for in a body there are many members, and not all have
the same function or the same nobility. This mystical body is but one
with Christ Jesus who is its head. Through grace, we make up part of
this body, but we ought to become perfect members who are worthy of
their Divine leader; that is what we aim at in our super-natural
progress.

And because He is the head, Christ is the primary source of this
progress. Never forget this: that Christ, after having taken our nature,
has sanctified all our actions, all our feelings. His human life has been
like our life, and His Divine Heart is the blazing hearth-fire of all the
virtues. Christ Jesus has practiced all forms of human activity; we
must not imagine that Our Lord was held motionless in ecstasy. On
the contrary, He found in the beatific vision of His Father's perfections
the driving-force of His activity; He willed to glorify His Father by
sanctifying, in His own Person, the forms of activity we ourselves have
to practice. We pray: He spent nights in prayer. We work: He toiled
in labor up to the age of thirty years. We eat: He was seated at table
with His disciples. We suffer annoyances from people: He knew such

---

[1] Eph. 4:15.   [2] Eph. 4:13 (Rheims).   [3] See Eph. 4:7.

annoyances—did the Pharisees ever leave Him in peace? We suffer: He shed tears. Before we suffered, He suffered for us, both in His body and in His soul, and as no one else has ever suffered. We experience joy: His sacred soul felt ineffable joys. We give ourselves up to rest: sleep closed His eyelids too. In short, He has done all these things that we do. And why did He do all that? Not only to set us an example since He is our leader but, as well, so as by all His actions to merit for us the power to sanctify all our own acts, so as to give us that grace which renders our actions pleasing to His Father. That grace unites us to Him, we are made members of His mystical body; and in order to grow in Him, to arrive at our perfection as members, we have only to let this grace invade not just our being, but all our activity.

Christ dwells in us with all His merits, so as to give life to all our actions. When therefore, through a right and pure intention, frequently renewed, we unite all our everyday acts with the same human actions that Jesus carried out here below, the Divine power of His grace has a constant influence on us. If we do all things united to Him through love, it is certain that we shall go forward very speedily. Listen to those magnificent words of Our Lord. My Father, He says, "has not left me alone, because I do always the things that are pleasing to Him."[1] Each of us should do likewise: "O Heavenly Father, it is solely to please you, solely for your glory, for the glory of your Son, that I do this action. Christ Jesus, it is in union with you that I wish to perform this act, so that you may sanctify it through your infinite merits."

The love for His Father that filled the heart of Christ should become the driving-force for His members' actions, as it was for His own. The glory of His Father was the first and last thought of all the works of Christ; may it also be that for *our* actions, through our continuous union with the grace and charity of Christ. That is why Holy Church makes us ask God to render our actions conformable to His good

[1] John 8:29.

pleasure. In staying united to the "Son of His tenderness," we shall merit to abound in good works.[1] "Walk in charity after the example of Christ," says St. Paul;[2] you will thereby be fully in accord with your leader—"Have this mind in you which was also in Christ Jesus."[3] In that way we shall "go from virtue to virtue,"[4] we shall thereby stretch out towards the perfection of our model by an uninterrupted growth, for Christ dwells in us, with His Father by whom we are loved—"If any one love me ... my Father will love him,"[5] with the Holy Spirit who guides us by His inspirations. There we have the source of an unceasing progress, one fruitful for heaven. In that way we shall achieve the solid perfection which is born of a plenitude of works entirely conformed to the Divine will: "that you may *stand perfect* and *full* in all the will of God."[6]

9. **Super-natural** *progress* **can be** *continued* **right up to death:** "*until we all meet ... unto the measure of the age of the fullness of Christ.*"

As long as we are here below, we can all the time increase in grace. The river of divine life began in us on the day of baptism as a spring, but it can continually get bigger, to the joy of our soul that it waters and makes fruitful, until it hurls itself into the Divine Ocean: "The stream of the river makes the city of God joyful."[7]

Do not tell me that that is a mercenary thought. It is true that it is in our interest to make the divine life expand within us; for the more we advance in grace and charity, the more our merits grow and the greater and wider will be our future glory and our eternal bliss. But in His generosity God Himself has willed it so. If it is a matter of our joy

---

[1] "Almighty and everlasting God, direct our actions according to your good pleasure; that in the name of the Son of your tenderness—*dilecti Filii*—we may deserve to abound in good works": Prayer for the Sunday in the octave of the Nativity.

[2] See Eph. 5:2.   [3] Phil. 2:5.   [4] Ps. 83 (84):8.
[5] John 14:23 (Rheims).   [6] Col. 4:12 (Rheims).   [7] Ps. 45 (46):5.

for all eternity, it is also a matter of the will of God, of the glory brought to our Heavenly Father by the accomplishing of that will.[1]

In this, St. Paul is an admirable model. He has come to the end of his life's course; he has but little time to live, for he awaits death in the prisons of Rome. He has preached Christ with indefatigable perseverance, he has sought to reproduce in himself the Divine traits of that Christ whom he loves so much. And this is what he writes to his dear Christians at Philippi, after so many labors undertaken for Jesus, after so many struggles suffered for His glory, and so many tribulations borne with that ardent love that nothing was able to lessen: "I have not yet attained perfection, but I pursue my inner course towards it so as to strive to lay hold of it, seeing that Christ has laid hold of me. I do not think I have already laid hold of it, but there is one thing only I do. Forgetting what is behind me, I take myself on with the whole of my being towards what is before. I go straight on to my goal, so as to win the prize to which God has called me from on high, in Jesus Christ."[2] Why does St. Paul stretch forward towards his goal with all the energy of his great soul? Doubtless, in order to "win the prize"—but in order to win the prize "to which God has called him from on high, in Jesus Christ." I told you, when I began this, that it is the Eternal Father's glory that we bear much fruit. Our Lord Himself has assured us of that. It is so that the divine life may abound in us that God has given us His Son, that His Son has given us the Church, His Spirit, and all His merits.

That is why St. Paul so much exhorted the Christians of his day to progress in the Christian life. "Therefore," he said to them, "as you have received Jesus Christ our Lord, so walk in Him; be rooted in Him and built up on Him," "strengthened in the faith" and making progress in it—"rendering thanks abundantly."[3] From his prison again, he wrote

---

[1] "A soul that loves God ought sincerely to wish to assemble within itself all the perfections in which God takes pleasure and to possess them in a measure conformed to His will": St. Mary Magdalene de Pazzi, *Life* by Fr. Cepari.

[2] See Phil. 3:12-14.   [3] Col. 2:6-7.

to the Philippians: "And this I ask of God, that your charity may more and more abound ... that you may be pure and blameless for the day when Christ is to appear to us, that you be filled with the fruit of justice, through Jesus Christ, to the glory and praise of God."[1] And with more insistence still: "May the Lord ... strengthen your hearts," making them "blameless in holiness before God our Father, at the coming of our Lord Jesus Christ, with all his saints."[2] "Brethren, I beseech and exhort you in the Lord Jesus; you have learnt from us how one must behave in order to please God—walk, then, from progress to progress. You know, indeed, the precepts I have given you on behalf of the Lord Jesus. What God wants is that you be holy."[3]

Let us, then, seek to carry out this will of our Heavenly Father. Our Lord asks that the splendor of our works be such as to bring those who are witness of them to glorify His Father.[4] Let us fear neither temptation (when we resist it, God will make profit come out of it for us,[5] because it is the occasion of a victory which strengthens us in the love of God); nor trials either. We can go through great difficulties, suffer grave contradictions, endure deep sufferings, but from the moment that we set ourselves to serve God through love, those difficulties, those contradictions, those sufferings, serve as the food of love. When one loves God, one can still feel the cross; God will even make us feel it more in the measure that we advance, because the cross establishes in us a greater likeness to Christ: but one loves then, if not the cross itself, at least the hand of Jesus that places the cross on our shoulders. For this hand gives us also the unguent of grace for bearing our burden. Love is a powerful weapon against temptation and an invincible force in adversity.

---

[1] See Phil. 1:9-11.   [2] 1 Thess. 3:12-13.   [3] See 1 Thess. 4:1-3.

[4] "So let your light shine before men, that they may see your good works, and glorify your Father who is in heaven": Matt. 5:16 (Rheims).

[5] 1 Cor. 10:13 (Rheims). [*Translator's note*: As to Marmion's interpretation of the verse in this sense, rather than as "letting us escape from it," see note 1 on page 239.]

Let us no longer be disheartened by our miseries, by the imperfections we deplore. They do not impede the flowering of grace, for God knows of what mud we are formed, He "knows what we are made of,"[1] and our miseries and imperfections are the price to be paid for our human nature and are a fruitful root of humility. Let us have patience with ourselves in this search for perfection, unending though it be. The Christian life has about it nothing of the fretful or the anxious; its development within us is perfectly reconcilable with our miseries, our servitudes, our weaknesses. For it is in the midst of those weaknesses that we feel dwelling within us the triumphant strength of Christ: *"that the power of Christ may dwell in me."*[2]

It is God, indeed, who is the first and principal author of our sanctification, as of our salvation.[3] Let us never forget that. The Council of Trent said: "Let us not glory, as if we did everything ourselves; but God is so rich in mercy that He wishes to reward the gifts that He Himself puts in us."[4] It is, said St. Paul, "by the grace of God (that) I am what I am"; and he adds: "and His grace in me has not been fruitless"—I have not let His grace be inactive in me. "In fact," he says, "I have labored more than any of them, *yet not I*"—not I alone—"but the grace of God with me."[5] He further says that for God to give increase, one must plant and water: "I have planted ... but God has given the growth."[6]

Let us aim, then, with all the energy of our being, through the meritorious exercise of the virtues, especially the theological virtues, and

---

[1] Ps. 102 (103):14 (Jerus.)   [2] 2 Cor. 12:9 (Rheims).

[3] "May the God of peace," wrote St. Paul, "make you capable of every good work for the accomplishment of His will, by working within us what is pleasing in His sight, through Jesus Christ, to whom be glory for ever and ever": see Hebr. 13:20-21.

[4] "Let no Christian trust in or glory in himself, rather than in God—God whose goodness to men is so great that He wishes what are *His own gifts* to be *merits for them*": Sess. VI, cap. 16. This is something that a prayer on Holy Saturday (after the 12th Old Testament prophecy) states very well: "Almighty, eternal God, sole hope of the world ... mercifully increase the devotion of your people, for in none of your faithful can any virtues increase but by your inspiration."   [5] 1 Cor. 15:10.   [6] 1 Cor. 3:6.

with that basic disposition of doing everything for the glory of our Heavenly Father—let us aim, I say, at letting the action of the Father and of the Holy Spirit blossom out in us with the greatest possible liberty. It is by doing this that we shall "grow up" in Christ who is our head.[1] Let us set our sights on this, because we have been called to it by Christ: "Christ Jesus has laid hold on me."[2] For a soul to come to a halt on the road of sanctification is for that soul to go backwards. On the other hand, for so long as we are here below we can always advance. As Our Lord said of Himself: "I must carry out the work of the one who sent me; the night will soon be here when no one can work."[3] Death alone, indeed, will bring to an end the heart's effecting its "ascent by steps"[4] in this vale of tears.

May we be able, by that hour of our death, to have reached the age of perfection in Christ—the fullness of life and bliss that God has willed for each one of us by predestining us in His beloved Son: "Until we all attain ... unto the measure of the age of the fullness of Christ."

NOTE[5]

We thought it would be useful to end this talk with a very quick glance at the super-natural organism as a whole. This broad synthetic view will have the effect of indicating the order of the different elements that constitute the life of a child of God. With that as our aim we cannot do better than look for a few moments at the very person of Our Lord, since He is our model.

By virtue of the grace of hypostatic union, Christ Jesus is, by nature, God's own Son (pp. 49 and 139-140 above); we become children of God through the grace of adoption (pp. 20-21). In

---

[1] Eph. 4:15.　　　　[2] Phil. 3:12.　　　　[3] John 9:4 (Jerus.)

[4] "Blessed is the man whose help is from you: in his heart he has disposed to ascend by steps": Ps. 83 (84):6 (Douai). [*Translator's note*: Other English translations (vv. 7 or 8) have going "from strength to strength" or "from height to height."]

[5] By Marmion. Page references as indicated by him (or his editor, Thibaut).

Christ, sanctifying grace exists in its fullness (pp. 139-140); we share in this fullness in a measure more or less abundant, according to the gift of it Christ has made to us (p. 27): "according to the measure of Christ's bestowal."[1] Sanctifying grace brings in its train the infused virtues, theological and moral. Strictly speaking, Our Lord did not have faith. He had hope, up to a certain point; He carried charity to its highest degree (p. 50-53). Faith, hope and charity dwell in us, while we are here below, in greater or lesser degree (pp. 300-302). Christ Jesus possessed the infused cardinal virtues and the other moral virtues compatible with His divinity (pp. 52-53), but in Him, they blossomed freely, without hindrance and without effort because, Our Lord having a perfect human nature exempt from sin and the results of sin, these virtues met no obstacle at all to their exercise. In us, as a result of the consequences of original sin, the flowering of the infused moral virtues is hindered and calls for the concurrent operation of the acquired moral virtues (p. 308 ff). Finally, the Holy Spirit has effused into the soul of Jesus the fullness of His gifts (pp. 141-143); He gives to us a participation in them which, though it is limited, produces wonderful fruits (pp. 149-159).

Let us add that the theological virtues and the gifts of the Holy Spirit take us to wholly special ground, which does not necessitate the direct help of the natural virtues at all (pp. 149-150, and 299-300) whereas the infused moral virtues, for their full flowering, call for the concurrent operation of the corresponding natural moral virtues, a concurrent operation they elevate in their use of it. Only charity renders the other virtues super-naturally alive: that is why it has primacy among the virtues.

Such, in a line or two, is the marvelous super-natural organism that the infinite goodness and sovereign wisdom of God has established in order to bring about our holiness.

[1] Eph. 4:7.

CHAPTER SEVEN

THE EUCHARISTIC SACRIFICE

INTRODUCTION: The Eucharist, source of divine life.

IN ALL the preceding pages, I have endeavored to show you how God wishes us to make us partakers of His life, how the grace of Christ, rendering us children of God, is the wellspring of divine life in us. Baptism has given us this grace: it is super-natural life at its dawning, it is the divine river at its beginning. Obstacles stand in the way of that life's opening to resplendence, of the development of that river; I have told you how they should be cleared away. In the last two talks I showed you finally what the general laws are which determine the preservation of that life in our souls and the measure of its growth: staying united to Christ through sanctifying grace, relating every one of our actions to the glory of His Father with a pure intention and the intense impelling of charity. That law extends to all our activity, it embraces all our works, of whatever nature they may be.

When a soul has understood the greatness of that life, when it has grasped that the wellspring of it is to be found in union with Christ through faith and charity, it aspires to the perfection of that union; it seeks the fullness of the life that it should, in accordance with the thought of God, possess within itself. That union—might it be just a dream, the soul asks itself? No, it is not a dream; it can—it should—become a reality, sublime as that may be. What seems impossible to men is easy for God: "With men this is impossible, but with God all things are possible."[1]

It is indeed true that all the efforts of human nature, left to itself, at a distance from Christ, are not able to advance us one step in the achieving of that union, in the birth and development of the life it brings forth. It is God alone who gives us the seed-germ and the growth; we care for the plant, we water it: that is necessary, indispensable, says St. Paul;[2] but the fruits of life are produced only because God causes the sap of His grace to rise within us.

God gives us incomparable means of keeping alive this sap within us. For if it is infinite and sovereignly efficacious Goodness who wishes to make us sharers of His nature and of His bliss, God is also Eternal Wisdom who proportions the means to the end, with a strength unequaled except by the gentleness with which He acts: Wisdom "reaches ... from end to end mightily, and orders all things sweetly."[3]

Now, if after having seen how at baptism God gives us the seed of this life and the first-fruits of this union, and if, having seen to what general law their growth is subject, we then wish to know in particular the means that God gives us, we shall see that they come down principally to prayer and to reception of the Sacrament of the Eucharist.

God has made a promise in regard to the soul that addresses itself to Him: "If you ask the Father anything in my name," said Jesus, "He will give it to you"; and that is why Jesus adds that you should "ask, and you shall receive, that your joy may be full."[4] That joy is the joy of Christ: "that they may have my joy made full in themselves";[5] the joy of His grace, the joy of His life, which, like a divine river, flows from Him into us, to rejoice us: "The stream of the river makes the city of God joyful."[6]

---

[1] Matt. 19:26.   [2] 1 Cor. 3:6.   [3] Wisdom 8:1.
[4] John 16:23-24.   [5] John 17:13.   [6] Ps. 45 (46):5.

The Eucharist is another means, but more powerful. When we pray, God communicates His gifts, under certain conditions. In the Sacrament of the Eucharist, it is God, it is Christ Himself who gives Himself to us; the Eucharist is specifically the sacrament of union which nourishes the divine life and keeps it within us. It is of the Eucharist that Our Lord was able to say very particularly: "I came that they may have life, and have it more abundantly."[1] By receiving Christ in Holy Communion, we unite ourselves to Life itself.

But before giving Himself as food for the soul, Christ has first been immolated; it is only in the Sacrifice of the Mass that He renders Himself present under the sacramental species. That is why I must first speak to you of the oblation of the altar, postponing until my following address my talking to you about Eucharistic Communion.

Let us, then, say what the Sacrifice of the Mass is, and what power of transformation into Jesus it contains for our souls.

This subject is an ineffable one. Even the priest, who makes the Eucharistic Sacrifice the center and sun of his life, is powerless to put into words the marvels Christ Jesus's love has amassed there. Everything that a man, a created being, is able to say of this mystery which has issued from the heart of one who is God remains so much short of its reality, that when someone has said everything he knows about it, it seems as if he had said nothing about it at all. There is no subject of which the priest loves more to speak, and of which he altogether dreads to speak, so holy and so high is this mystery.

Let us ask faith to enlighten us; the Eucharistic Sacrifice is, par excellence, a mystery of faith, *Mysterium fidei*. In order to understand anything about it, one must go to Christ, by repeating to Him the words of St. Peter when Jesus announced this mystery to the Jews, and even some of His disciples were scandalized and left Him: "To whom shall we go, O Divine Master? you are the only one who utters words that

---

[1] John 10:10.

lead us to eternal life."[1] And above all let us, as St. John said, believe in love, "know and believe the love God has for us."[2] Our Lord willed to institute this sacrament at the very time when He was about to give us the greatest testimony of His love for us, by His Passion, and He willed that it be perpetuated among us "in remembrance of" Him. It was like the last thought, the last testament of His sacred heart: "Do this ... in remembrance of me."[3]

1. The Eucharist considered as *Sacrifice*. Transcendence of *Christ's* priesthood.

THE COUNCIL OF TRENT, as you know, has defined that the Mass is "a true sacrifice," which "recalls and renews the immolation of Christ on Calvary. The Mass is offered as a true sacrifice, properly so called."[4] "In this Divine Sacrifice which is accomplished in the Mass there is contained and there is immolated in an unbloody manner the same Christ who, on the altar of the cross, offered Himself in a bloody manner. There is but one single Victim; and the same Christ who offered Himself upon the cross now offers Himself through the ministry of the priests; the manner of the offering of Himself is the only difference."[5] Thus, the Sacrifice of the altar essentially renews that of Golgotha; the difference resides only in the mode of oblation. If, then, we want to understand the greatness of the Sacrifice offered at the altar, we must consider for a moment what it is that constitutes the value of the immolation of the cross. That value derives from the dignity of the High Priest and of the Victim. Let us, therefore, say a word about the priesthood and the sacrifice of Christ.

Every true sacrifice supposes a priesthood, that is, the establishment of a minister charged with offering the sacrifice in the name of all. Under

---

[1] See John 6:69.   [2] 1 John 4:16 (RSV, Cath.)   [3] 1 Cor. 11:24.
[4] Sess. XXII, can. 1.   [5] Sess. XXII, cap. 2.

the Jewish law, the priest was chosen by God from the tribe of Aaron and consecrated to the service of the temple by a special anointing. But, with Christ, the priesthood is transcendent; the anointing that consecrates Him as supreme High Priest, Bridge of man to God, is altogether singular: it is that Grace of Union which, at the moment of the Incarnation, united to the Person of the Word the humanity He had chosen to be united to Himself. The Word Incarnate is "Christ"—which signifies one "who is anointed"; but not by an exterior anointing like that which served to consecrate the kings, prophets and priests of the Old Testament. *He* is anointed by the Divinity out-poured on His Humanity as though it were a delightsome oil: "God, your God, has anointed you with the oil of gladness above your fellow kings."[1] It is by the grace which makes Him "Man-God, Son of God,"[2] and it is at the very moment of this union, that Jesus is "anointed," consecrated, constituted priest and High Priest—Mediator, that is to say, between God and men; and it is His Father who thus establishes Him as Supreme High Priest. Listen to what St. Paul says: "Christ did not raise Himself to the dignity of the High Priesthood; it was the Father who raised Him to it"—on the day of the Incarnation—"when He said, 'You are my Son, this day have I begotten you'"—called Him to establish Him Priest of the Most High.[3]

Thus, it is because He is God's own Son that Christ will be able to offer the only Sacrifice worthy of God. And we hear the Eternal Father ratifying, by the oath He swore, this condition and dignity of High Priest: "You are a priest for ever, according to the order of Melchizedek."[4] Why is Christ an eternal priest? Because the union of the Divinity and the Humanity in the Incarnation, a union which consecrates Him

---

[1] Ps. 44 (45):8 (St P.)

[2] [*Translator's note*: Marmion refers, of course, to the Incarnation of the Eternal Son of God, the Word, in Mary's womb.]

[3] See Hebr. 5:5; Ps. 2:7. Cf. Hebr. 5:6; 7:1.   [4] Ps. 109 (110):4.

as High Priest, is indissoluble. Christ, St. Paul says, "because He continues forever, has an everlasting priesthood."[1]

And this priesthood is "according to the order of" (that is, one that resembles) the priesthood "of Melchizedek." St. Paul recalls this mysterious personage of the Old Testament, who prefigures, by his name and his offering of bread and wine, the Priesthood and the Sacrifice of Christ. "Melchizedek" signifies "king of justice," and Holy Scripture tells us that he was "king of Salem"[2]—which signifies "king of peace." Jesus is King; at the time of His Passion He affirmed His royalty before Pilate: "'You are then a king?' Jesus answered, 'You say it; I am a king.'"[3] He is King of Justice, for He will accomplish all justice; He is "King of Peace": *Princeps Pacis*.[4] He comes to re-establish peace here below between God and men; and it is in His Sacrifice that justice, satisfied at last, and peace, regained at last, will receive the kiss of reconciliation: "Justice and peace have kissed."[5]

So you see: Jesus, the Incarnate Son of God is the supreme and eternal High Priest, the sovereign Mediator between men and His Father: He is the "Christ," the High Priest par excellence: "God, your God, has anointed you … above your fellow kings." That is why His Sacrifice bears, as His Priesthood does, the character of unique perfection and infinite value.

---

[1] Hebr. 7:24; 7:3.   [2] Gen. 14:18; Hebr. 7:1.
[3] John 18:37.   [4] See Isa. 9:6.   [5] Ps. 84 (85):11.

2. Nature of sacrifice. How *the old sacrifices* were only *figures*; the immolation of Calvary *the sole reality*. The *infinite value* of this oblation.

CHRIST BEGAN the work of His priesthood immediately on His incarnation. "Every high priest," indeed, "is appointed ... that he may offer gifts and sacrifices";[1] that is why it was necessary that Christ, supreme High Priest, Bridge of man to God—that He also should have had something to offer. And what was He going to offer? What would be the subject of His Sacrifice? Let us see what was being offered before He came.

Sacrifice belongs to the very essence of religion; it is as old as religion itself.

From the time that there are created beings in existence, it is equitable and just that they should recognize the Divine sovereignty. That is one of the elements of the virtue of religion, which is itself a form of the virtue of justice. God is the being subsistent of Himself; He contains in Himself the whole raison d'être of His existence; He is the necessary being, independent of every other being. Whereas the essence of a created being is dependence on God. For a created being to exist, for it to be drawn into being out of nothingness and be preserved in existence, for it to be able to engage in activity, the concourse of God is needed. Therefore, to be *in the truth* of its nature, the created being must avow and recognize this dependence: and this avowal, this recognition, is adoration. To adore is to recognize the sovereignty of God by one's own abasement: *Venite adoremus*, "Come, let us adore, and fall down before God,"[2] since "He made us, and not we ourselves."[3] As a matter of fact, in the presence of God our abasement would have to go as far as annihilation; that would be the supreme homage—even though *that* could not testify with sufficient truth to our condition as pure creatures and to the infinite transcendence of Divine Being. But as God has given us existence, we do not have the right to destroy

---

[1] Hebr. 5:1.   [2] See Ps. 94 (95):6.   [3] Ps. 99 (100):3.

ourselves by the immolation of ourselves, by the sacrifice of our life. That being the case, man substitutes created things in place of himself, principally those that serve to sustain his existence, like bread, wine, fruit, animals.[1] By the offering, immolation or destruction of these things, man recognizes the infinite majesty of the Supreme Being: that is sacrifice. After sin, an expiatory character came to be added to the other notions of sacrifice.

The first men offered fruits and immolated the best of what they had in their flocks, in order thus to testify that God is the sovereign master of all things.

Later, God Himself laid down the forms of sacrifice in the Mosaic law. There were first of all holocausts, sacrifices of adoration; the victim was entirely consumed. There were pacifying sacrifices of thanksgiving or petition; part of the victim was burned, another part reserved for the priests, and a third assigned to those for whom the sacrifice was offered. Finally, most important of all, there were expiatory sacrifices for sin.

All these sacrifices, says St. Paul, were only figures: "All these things happened to them in figure,"[2] as poor "elemental things":[3] they were only pleasing to God because they represented the sacrifice to come, the only Sacrifice that could be worthy of Him—the Sacrifice of the Man-God on the cross.[4]

Of all these symbols, the most expressive was the sacrifice of expiation that was offered once a year by the high priest in the name of the whole

---

[1] "O God, our God, who *principally from these created things which you have established in support of our weakness,* have likewise commanded gifts to be set apart and dedicated to your name, grant we beseech you, that they may produce for us both help in this present life and an eternal sacrament": Prayer of the Mass of the Thursday after Passion Sunday.

[2] 1 Cor. 10:11 (Rheims).   [3] Gal. 4:9 (Jerus.)

[4] "O God, who ratified the various sacrifices of the Old Law by one perfect Sacrifice...": Prayer of the Mass of the 7th Sunday after Pentecost.

people of Israel, and in which the victim was substituted for the people.[1] What, indeed, do we see? A victim[2] presented to God by the high priest. The latter, wearing priestly habits, first placed his hands upon the victim, during which time the multitude of the people were prostrate in an attitude of adoration. What did this symbolic rite signify? That the victim was substituted for the faithful; it represented them before God, laden, so to speak, with all the sins of the people.[3] Then, the victim was immolated by the high priest, and this death-blow, this immolation, to all intents and purposes was a blow struck at the multitude who recognized and deplored their crimes before God, sovereign master of life and of death. After that, the victim, placed upon the pyre, was burned and went up before the throne of God "in an odor of sweetness," symbolic of that offering of themselves that the people ought to make to Him who was not only their *first beginning*, but also their *last end*. The high priest, having sprinkled the blood of the victim upon the corners of the altar, went into the Holy of Holies to pour it also upon the Ark of the Covenant. In consequence of this sacrifice, God renewed the compact of friendship made with His people.

All that, as I have told you, was only symbol. Where, then, is the reality? In the immolation of Christ by the shedding of His blood on Calvary. Jesus, says St. Paul, offered Himself up for us to God as an oblation and a Sacrifice "to ascend in fragrant odor."[4] It is Christ whom God has shown to men as the propitiating Victim: "whom God has set forth as a propitiation by His blood through faith."[5]

But note well that on the cross Christ Jesus *completed* His sacrifice. It was immediately on His incarnation that He inaugurated it, by accepting to offer Himself for the human race. As you know, the smallest

---

[1] Levit. 16, vv. 9, 16.   [2] [*Translator's note*: An animal, such as a lamb.]
[3] God Himself, in Leviticus, had declared that He was the author of this substitution: Levit. 17:11.   [4] Eph. 5:2.   [5] Rom. 3:25.

suffering of Christ, considered in itself, would have been enough to save humanity. Christ being God, the least of His actions possessed an infinite value because of the dignity of the Divine Person. But the Eternal Father willed, in His incomprehensible wisdom, that Christ should buy us back through a death by bloodshed upon the cross.[1] Well, St. Paul tells us expressly that Christ accepted that decree of the adorable will of His Father on His very entry into this world. Christ Jesus, at the moment of the Incarnation, embraced in a single glance everything He was to suffer for the salvation of the human race, from the cradle to the cross, and He devoted Himself, from then on, to the full accomplishment of the eternal decree. At that moment Jesus made a voluntary offering of His own body to be immolated. Listen to St. Paul: "Christ, coming into the world, said to his Father: 'You have, till now, accepted neither sacrifice nor oblation, but you have formed a body for me. You have accepted neither holocaust nor sacrifice for sin. Then I said: Behold ... I come to do your will, O God.'"[2]

And having thus begun the work of His Priesthood by the perfect acceptance of everything willed by His Father and the oblation of Himself, Christ consummated His Sacrifice by a death of bloodshed on the cross. He inaugurated His Passion by renewing the total gift He had made at the moment of the Incarnation. "Father," He says when He sees the cup of sorrows He is presented with, "let your will be done, not mine";[3] and His last words before expiring will be to say that He has accomplished it all: "It is consummated!"[4]

Consider this Sacrifice for a little while, and you will see that Christ has carried out the sublimest of acts and rendered the most perfect homage to God His Father. The High Priest, Bridge of man to God—it is He, the Man-God, the beloved Son. True, it is in his human nature that He offered this Sacrifice, since only a man is able to die. True,

---

[1] See last paragraph of translator's note on pages 222-223. [2] See Hebr. 10:5-9.
[3] Luke 22:42 (Jerus.); Matt. 26:39; Mark 14:36. [4] John 19:30.

also, that this oblation was limited to its historical duration. But the High Priest who offers it is a Divine Person, and this dignity imparts to the immolation an infinite value. The Victim is holy, pure, without stain, for it is Christ Himself, it is He, the unblemished Lamb, who washes away the sins of the world with His own blood, shed to the last drop as in the holocausts. Christ was immolated in our stead, He substituted Himself for us. Laden with all our iniquities, He became a victim for our sins: "the Lord has laid on Him the iniquity of us all."[1] Lastly, Christ had accepted and on Calvary offered this Sacrifice with a liberty full of love. Only because He so willed it did they take away His life: "No one takes it from me, but I lay it down of myself."[2] And He willed it solely because He loved His Father: "that the world may know that I love the Father."[3]

Therefore this immolation of one who is God, an immolation voluntary and full of love, has effected the salvation of the human race. The death of Jesus ransoms us, reconciles us with God, re-establishes the covenant from which every good thing flows for us, re-opens for us the gates of heaven, restores to us the inheritance of eternal life. This Sacrifice thenceforth suffices for everything: that is why, when Christ dies, the veil of the temple of Israel is rent in twain, to show us that the former sacrifices are abolished for ever and replaced by the one-and-only Sacrifice worthy of God. From this time forward there is salvation and justification only in participation in the Sacrifice of the cross, the fruits of which are inexhaustible. By this "*one* oblation," says St. Paul, Christ has brought perfection "*for ever*" to those who are sanctified.[4]

---

[1] Isa. 53:6.   [2] John 10:18.   [3] John 14:31.   [4] Hebr. 10:14 (Rheims).

3. The immolation of Calvary is *reproduced and renewed by* the Sacrifice of *the Mass.*

DO NOT be surprised that I have spoken at such length about the Sacrifice of Calvary; this immolation is reproduced at the altar: the Sacrifice of the Mass is the same as that of the Cross. There cannot, indeed, be any other Sacrifice than that of Calvary. That oblation is unique, says St. Paul, it fully suffices; but Our Lord willed that it should continue here below so as to apply its fruits to the souls of all.

How has Christ turned that will into reality, seeing that He has gone back up to heaven? It is true that He remains eternally the High Priest par excellence, Bridge of man to God. But, through the sacrament of Holy Orders, He chooses certain men whom He makes sharers in His priesthood. When the bishop, on the day of ordination, extends his hands to consecrate priests, the voices of angels repeat over each of them: "You are a priest for ever; the sacerdotal character you bear will never be taken away from you: but it is from the hands of Christ that you receive it, it is His Spirit that fills you so as to make you a minister of Christ." Christ will renew His sacrifice through the intermediacy of men.

Look at what happens at the altar. What do we see there? After some preparatory prayers and some readings, the priest offers the bread and wine. That is the "offering" or "offertory." Those elements, the bread and wine, will soon be changed into the body and blood of Our Lord. Next, the priest invites the faithful and the heavenly spirits to surround the altar which is going to become a new Calvary, and to accompany the holy action with praise and homage. After which, he enters silently into more intimate communication with God; the moment of the Consecration arrives; he extends his hands over the offerings, as the high priest did in times past over the victim to be immolated; he recalls all the gestures and all the words of Christ at the Last Supper at the time He instituted this Sacrifice: "On the day before He suffered...." Then, identifying himself with Christ, he pronounces the ritual words: "*This is my body*," "*This is my blood*".... These words effect the changing of the bread and wine into the body and blood of Jesus Christ. Through the carrying out of His express will and what He formally instituted, Christ makes Himself present, really and substantially, with His divinity and His humanity, beneath the appearances which remain and hide Him from our eyes.

But, as you know, that formula has a wider efficacy: by those words, the *Sacrifice* is accomplished. By virtue of the words *This is my body*, Christ, through the priest as intermediary, puts His flesh beneath the appearances of bread. By the words *This is my blood*, He puts His blood beneath the appearances of wine. He thus separates mystically His flesh and His blood, which on the cross were physically separated and the separation of which brought death. After His resurrection, Christ Jesus cannot die any more: "death shall no longer have dominion over Him";[1] the separation of His body and His blood that takes place at the altar is a mystical one. The same Christ who was immolated on the cross is immolated on the altar, though in a different way; and this immolation, accompanied by the offering, constitutes a true Sacrifice. "In the Divine Sacrifice accomplished at Mass, that same Christ is contained, that same Christ is immolated, who offered Himself, bloodily, upon the altar of the cross."[2]

The Communion brings the Sacrifice to an end: it is the last important act of the Mass. The rite of manducation[3] of the Victim completes the expression of the idea of substitution and especially of union which is found in every sacrifice. By uniting himself so intimately with the victim who has been substituted for him, a man (so to speak) immolates himself the more. By eating the offered victim, become holy and sacred, one takes to oneself in some way the Divine power resulting from that consecration.

In the Mass, the victim is Christ Himself, Man-God: that is why Holy Communion is the act par excellence of union with the Divinity.

---

[1] Rom. 6:9.   [2] Council of Trent, Sess. XXII, cap. 2.

[3] [*Translator's note*: "manducation": eating with the mouth and teeth; it is what Christ enjoined expressly: "*Take and eat*; this is my body" (Matt. 26:26).]

It is the best and the most intimate sharing in those fruits of uniting and divine life that the immolation of Christ earns for us.

So then, the Mass is not just a simple *representation* of the Sacrifice of the cross; it has not just the value of a simple remembrance. It is a true Sacrifice, the same as the Sacrifice of Calvary, which it reproduces and continues and the fruits of which it applies.

4. Inexhaustible *fruits* of the sacrifice of the altar. Homage of a *perfect adoration.* Sacrifice of *full propitiation. The only thanks-giving* worthy of God. Sacrifice of *powerful entreaty.*

THE *fruits* of the Mass are inexhaustible, because they are the very fruits of the Sacrifice of the cross.

It is the same Christ Jesus who offers Himself for us to His Father. Doubtless He can no longer merit since His resurrection, but He offers the infinite merits won by His Passion. The merits and satisfactions of Jesus always retain their value, just as Christ keeps for ever, with His character of supreme High Priest and universal Mediator, the Divine reality of His Priesthood. Now, next to the sacraments, says the Council of Trent, it is at Mass that these merits are applied to us individually in most abundance: "The fruits of that offering which was bloody are gathered *most abundantly* by means of this unbloody sacrifice."[1] That is why every priest offers each Mass not for himself only, but "for all here present, as also for all faithful Christians, both living and dead."[2] So extensive and immense are the fruits of this Sacrifice, so sublime is the glory that returns to God from it!

When, therefore, we feel the desire to recognize the infinite greatness

[1] Council of Trent, Sess. XXII, cap. 2.

[2] "Accept, O Holy Father Almighty ... this immaculate Host ... for all here present, as also for all faithful Christians, both living and dead, that it may be profitable for my own and for their salvation unto life eternal."

of God and, in spite of our poverty as created beings, to offer Him a homage that will be pleasing to His majesty, a homage that assuredly will be accepted at His hands, let us offer or otherwise assist at the Holy Sacrifice, and present the Divine Victim to God. The Eternal Father receives from Him, as at Calvary, a *homage of infinite value*, a homage perfectly worthy of His ineffable perfections.

It is indeed through Jesus Christ, Man-God, His beloved Son, immolated on the altar, that all glory and all honor are rendered to the Father; "through Him, with Him, in Him ... all glory and honor is yours, almighty Father."[1] There is not, in the whole of religion, an action which is so satisfying to a soul that is convinced of its own nothingness and yet is eager to render to God a homage that shall not be unworthy of the Divine greatness. All the combined homage of creation and of the world of the elect does not render to the Eternal Father the glory He receives from the offering of His Son. It needs faith in order to understand the value of the Mass, that faith which is like a participation in the knowledge that God has of Himself and of Divine things. In the light of faith, we are able to look at the altar in the way the Heavenly Father looks at it. What does the Eternal Father see on the altar where the Holy Sacrifice is being offered? He sees "the Son of His love,"[2] the Son well-pleasing to Him, present, in all truth and reality—*Vere et realiter*—and renewing the Sacrifice of the cross. God measures all things by the glory He receives from them. And, in this Sacrifice, as on Calvary, an infinite glory is rendered to Him by His beloved Son; God cannot find homage more perfect than that; it contains and surpasses all other homage.

The Holy Sacrifice is, as well, *a source of confidence and pardon.*

When we are overwhelmed by remembrance of our sins and when we look for a way of making amends for our offenses and of satisfying Divine Justice more fully, in order that the penalty for our sins may be

---

[1] Ordinary of the Mass.　　　　[2] Col. 1:13 (Rheims).

remitted, we cannot find a more efficacious and more reassuring means than the Mass. Listen to what the Council of Trent says: "By this oblation of the Mass, God, appeased, grants grace and the gift of repentance; He remits offenses, even enormous sins."[1] Is it that the Mass directly remits sins? No, that is reserved to the Sacrament of Penance and to perfect contrition; but the Mass contains abundant and powerful graces which enlighten the sinner and cause him to make acts of repentance and contrition that lead him to Penance and, through that Penance, give him back the friendship of God.[2] If this is true of the sinner not yet absolved by the hand of the priest, it will be especially true of souls who are justified but who seek as full a satisfaction for their sins as possible, and in the hope of its fulfilling their desire for reparation. Why is that? Because the Mass is not only a sacrifice of praise, or simply a remembrance of that of the cross; it is a *true sacrifice of propitiation*, instituted by Christ in order to "apply to us every day" the redemptive power of the immolation of the cross.[3] That is why we see the priest, who already possesses the friendship of God, offer this Sacrifice for his "innumerable sins, offenses and negligences." The Divine Victim *appeases God and makes Him favorable to us*. Therefore when remembrance of our sins troubles us, let us offer this Sacrifice. It is Christ who is offered for us, "the Lamb of God who takes away the sins of the world,"[4] and who renews "the work of our redemption" every time He is offered: "*As often* as the commemoration of this Victim is celebrated, the work of our redemption is carried into effect."[5]

---

[1] Sess. XXII, cap. 2.

[2] If we can thus put it, the Eucharist as a sacrament procures (or, if you like, has for its primary object) grace *in recto* (directly, formally), and the glory of God *in obliquo* (indirectly). The Holy Sacrifice procures *in recto* the glory of God and *in obliquo* the grace of repentance and of contrition through the feelings of compunction it excites in the soul.

[3] "So that the saving power of that sacrifice when His blood was shed may be applied to the forgiveness of those sins that are daily committed by us": Council of Trent, Sess. XXII, cap. 1.

[4] From the Mass; taken from John 1:29.   [5] Prayer for ninth Sunday after Pentecost.

What confidence we should we have in this Sacrifice of expiation! Whatever our offenses and our ingratitude may be, a Mass gives more glory to God than all our insults can have taken away from Him, so to say. "O Eternal Father, look upon this altar, look upon your Son who loved me and delivered Himself up for me on Calvary; who now, for me, presents His infinite satisfactions to you. 'Look upon the face of your anointed',[1] and forget those faults I have committed against your goodness. I offer you this oblation in which you are well-pleased; I offer it in reparation for all the insults given to your Divine majesty." A prayer such as this cannot but be heard by God, because it relies upon the merits of the Beloved Son, who, by His Passion, has expiated everything.

At other times, what comes over us is a remembrance of the mercies of the Lord: the benefit of the Christian faith which has opened for us the way of salvation and made us sharers in all the mysteries of Christ while awaiting the inheritance of eternal bliss; a multitude of graces that, since baptism, have been placed in position along the roadway of our entire life. When it looks back, the soul is almost overwhelmed at the sight of the innumerable graces God has shed upon it open-handedly. Then, lost in wonder at being an object of God's delight, it cries out: "Lord, what can I, a poor created being, render you in return for so many benefits? What could I give you that would not be unworthy of you? Even though you have 'no need of my goods',[2] it is only fair, nonetheless, that I recognize your infinite goodness towards me. I feel this need from the depths of my being; how does one satisfy it in a way that will be worthy both of your greatness and of your benefits, O my God?"—"What shall I render to the Lord, for all the things that He has rendered to me?"[3] This is the cry of the priest after receiving the

[1] Ps. 83 (84):10 (St P.)
[2] Ps. 15 (16):2 [*Translator's note*: a distinctive interpretation of the Rheims.]
[3] Ps. 115 (116):12.

Sacred Host at Communion-time.[1] And what reply does the Church put on his lips? "I will take the chalice of salvation...."[2] The Mass is the *thanksgiving* par excellence, the most perfect and the most pleasing we could ever render to God. The Gospels tell us[3] that before He instituted this Sacrifice Our Lord gave "thanks" to His Father: "*eucharistesas.*" St. Paul employs the same expression[4] and the Church has kept this term in preference to all others — although it does not exclude the other characteristics of the Mass — to refer to the oblation of the altar. "*Eucharistic* sacrifice," that is, sacrifice of thanksgiving. See: at each Mass, after the offertory and before proceeding to the Consecration, the priest, following the example of Jesus, sings a hymn of thanksgiving: "It is truly meet and just, right and salutary, that we should always and in all places give thanks to you, O holy Lord, Father Almighty, Eternal God ... through Christ our Lord: *Per Christum Dominum nostrum.*[5] Then he immolates the holy Victim: it is this Victim who gives thanks for us, who acknowledges worthily — for Jesus is God — all the benefits that have come down on us from on high, from the heart of the Father of lights: "Every good endowment and every perfect gift is from above, coming down from the Father of lights."[6] It is through Christ Jesus that they have come to us, and it is through Him also that all the soul's gratitude ascends in return, to the very throne of God.

Finally, the Mass is a *petition or supplication.*

Our poverty is immense; we have incessant need of light, of strength, of consolation. We shall find such help in the Mass. There, indeed, is truly He who has said: "I am the Light of the world; I am the Way, I am the Truth, I give Life. Come to me, all you who are weighed-down, and I will comfort you. If anyone comes to me, I will not turn

---

[1] [*Translator's note*: The allusion is to the prayer said by the celebrant in the Tridentine Mass just after receiving the Host and before receiving the Precious Blood.]

[2] Ps. 115 (116):13.   [3] Matt. 26:27; Mark 14:23; Luke 22:19.

[4] 1 Cor. 11:24.   [5] Preface of the Mass.   [6] James 1:17 (RSV, Cath.)

him away from my door."[1] This is the same Jesus who "went about doing good";[2] who pardoned the Samaritan woman and Mary Magdalene and the good thief upon the cross; who freed those possessed, cured the sick, restored sight to the blind and the power of movement to paralytics; the same Jesus who allowed St. John to rest his head upon His sacred heart. But note well that He is there, on the altar, by a special right. He is there as holy Victim who offers Himself at this time to His Father, and offers Himself for us. He is there, immolated, and yet living and praying for us: ever living "to make intercession for us."[3] He offers His infinite satisfactions to obtain for us the graces of life which are necessary for us. He supports from His merits what we ask and beg for: we cannot be more assured of obtaining the graces we need than at this favorable time. The altar where Christ offers and immolates Himself is truly (as St. Paul said, when speaking precisely of the great High Priest "who has passed into the heavens" for us and who is full of "compassion" for those whom He deigns to call His brethren)—that altar, I repeat, is truly "the throne of grace"[4] which we should approach "with confidence" so as to find grace when we are in need of help.

Keep in mind those words of St. Paul: "with confidence." That is the condition for being heard. We should offer or assist at the Holy Sacrifice with faith and confidence. This Sacrifice does not act within us *ex opere operato*, as the sacraments do. Its fruits are inexhaustible, but they are measured in great part according to our interior dispositions. There are for us infinite possibilities of perfection and holiness in every Mass, but the measure of the graces we receive there is the measure of our faith and of our love. You will have noticed that when, before the Consecration, the priest lists those whom he wishes to recommend to God, he ends the list by speaking of all those present, but by indicating

---

[1] See John 8:12; 14:6; Matt. 11:28; John 6:37.
[2] Acts 10:38.
[3] Hebr. 7:25 (Rheims).
[4] Hebr. 4:14-16.

the dispositions of their hearts: "Be mindful, O Lord of ... all here present, whose faith and devotion are known to you." These words indicate to us that the graces which flow from the Mass are given to us in the measure of the liveliness of our faith and the sincerity of our devotion. I have told you what faith is: but this *"nota devotia,"* "devotion known to you"—what is that? It is the prompt and complete giving of the whole of ourselves to God, to everything He wills, to His service. God, who alone reads the depths of our hearts, sees if our desire, if our will to be faithful to Him, to be wholly His, is sincere. If it is so with us, then we are among those "whose faith and devotion are known to you," for whom the priest prays specially, and who will draw in great measure upon the treasure of the infinite merits of Christ who is offered for them.

If, then, we have a profound conviction that everything comes to us from our Father in heaven through Christ Jesus; that God has deposited in Christ all the treasures of holiness that men can desire; that this Jesus is there upon the altar with these treasures, and not only present but offering Himself for us to the glory of His Father, rendering Him at that time the most perfect homage that could be pleasing to Him; renewing the Sacrifice of the cross so as to continue it and apply to us its sovereign efficacy—if we have, I say, this profound conviction, there will be no grace that we cannot ask for and obtain. For at that time it is as though we were with the Virgin, St. John and St. Mary Magdalene at the foot of the cross, at the very source of all salvation and all redemption. Oh, if we only knew what God is offering—if we knew what treasures we can draw upon, for ourselves, for the entire Church!

5. Intimate *participation* in the oblation of the altar *through
identification* of ourselves *with Christ, High Priest and Victim.*

HOWEVER, we ought not to leave it at that, if we want to penetrate fully
into the intentions which Jesus Christ had in instituting the Holy Sacrifice, and which the Church, His Spouse, expresses in the ceremonies
and the words of the oblation. Through this Divine Sacrifice, as I have
just said, we can present to God a perfect homage, beg that all our
transgressions be fully forgotten, render to Him a worthy thanksgiving, and obtain the light and the strength that are necessary. But all
these attitudes and all these acts of the soul, excellent as they are, cannot but be and remain the acts and attitudes of a simple spectator who
assists in the holy action with piety, but from the outside as it were.

There is a more intimate participation we ought to seek to achieve.
What is that participation? It is to identify ourselves, as fully as
possible, with Jesus Christ in His twofold capacity of High Priest and
Victim, in order to be transformed into Him.[1] Is that possible?

---

[1] [*Translator's note*: "transformed into Him." In order that Marmion shall not be
misunderstood, it is necessary to emphasize what this is *not*. It is not a loss of one's
own "personality," taking that word in the sense of one's individual, substantial
personhood. We are not substantially submerged into God, in the sense of losing
our own identity and personhood. Recall Marmion's words (page 55): "It goes without saying that, in the order of *being*, we always keep our personality; we always stay,
by nature, purely human creatures."

But, that caveat made, Marmion then moves from "the order of being" (as in the
above paragraph of this note) to "the order of activity." "Our union with God through
grace ... is so much greater when the autonomy of our personality, in the order of
activity, further effaces itself before Divinity." That is what he means by "transformation into Christ." Marmion sums up the two aspects by saying: "We should, then, not
annihilate our personality—*that is neither possible nor wished by God*—but rather bring
it (if I may use the phrase) to a complete capitulation before God." We should "strip
ourselves of our personality *in so far as it constitutes an obstacle to perfect union with God*.
It places such an obstacle when our own judgement, our self-will, our self-love, our
susceptibilities, makes us think and act otherwise than in accordance with the
desires of our Heavenly Father." In a later passage (page 212) Marmion equates
"transformed into Him" (Christ) with "transformed *into His very image*."]

I have told you that it was at the moment of the Incarnation that Jesus was consecrated High Priest, Bridge of man to God, and that it was as man that He was able to offer Himself to God as a Victim. Now (here there is a truth I have expounded to you at length, and one I desire you never to forget): in His incarnation, the Word associated all of humanity with His mysteries and His Person, by a mystical union. The whole of humanity constitutes a mystical body of which Christ is the head, a society of which He is leader and we are the members.[1] In principle, the members can neither separate themselves from the head nor remain strangers to His action. The action par excellence of Jesus, the one that sums up His life and succeeds in giving it all its value, is His Sacrifice. Just as He has taken our human nature into Himself, sin excepted, so does He wish us to participate in the foremost mystery of life. No doubt we were not present bodily on Calvary when He was immolated for us, after being substituted for us: but He willed, says the Council of Trent, that His sacrifice be perpetuated, with its inexhaust-

---

[1] [*Translator's note*: This sentence might be thought to pose a difficulty (is it not *the Church*, rather than the whole of humanity, which is "the mystical body of Christ"?). But the difficulty is more verbal than one of substance. As Marmion rightly states, Christ's "headship" extends to all the redeemed, that is, to all members of the human race—who as long as they are on earth are sharers, actual or at least potential sharers, in Divine grace (grace which, whether this is known to them or not, comes from Christ and the Church). Later (pages 452-453) Marmion writes: "Since the Incarnation, and through the Incarnation, all men are *by right, if not in fact* [my italics] united to Christ as the members are united to the head in the one same body. The damned alone are cut off for ever from that union."

However, the phrase—and the concept of—"the mystical body of Christ" has traditionally been used of *the Church*, and it is firmly in that sense that it is used in Pius XII's encyclical *Mystici Corporis* (which appeared two decades after Marmion's death). Marmion, too, normally uses it in that sense, though without derogating from his words in this paragraph. In the chapter of the present book entitled *The Church, the Mystical Body of Christ*, he unequivocally identifies "the mystical body" with the Church. And even when, earlier, he speaks of Christ's merits becoming ours because Christ has become the head of all humanity, he adds (page 70, n. 2): "It goes without saying that Christ's merits have to be applied to us in order that we

ible power, in the hands of His Church and its ministers: "[He gave] Himself to be sacrificed by the Church, under perceptible signs, through the ministry of priests."[1]

It is true that only priests, who participate, through the sacrament of Holy Orders, in the Priesthood of Christ—only they have the power to offer officially the body and blood of Jesus Christ. But nevertheless, all the faithful can, in a real way—though by a lesser right—offer the Sacred Host. Through our baptism, we participate in some way in the Priesthood of Christ, because we participate in the Divine being of Christ, in His qualities, in His states. He is King; we are that with Him. He is Priest, we are that also. Listen to what St. Peter says to those who are baptized: that they are a chosen race, a race that is royal and priestly, a holy nation, a people whom God has won: "You, however, are a chosen race, a royal priesthood, a holy nation, a purchased people."[2] The faithful, then, can offer the Sacred Host in union with the priest.

The prayers with which the Church accompanies this Divine Sacrifice make us clearly understand that that oblation belongs also to those who are present at it. For, look, what does the priest say, after the offertory, when turning for the last time towards the people, before singing the Preface? "Pray, brethren, that my sacrifice *and yours* may be acceptable to God the Father Almighty." Just as, in the prayer that precedes the Consecration, the priest asks God to remember the faithful

---

may experience their efficacy." He goes on: "Baptism inaugurates this application of them to us. By baptism we become living members of His mystical body...." Thus, when Marmion refers to the whole of humanity as "a mystical body," he is using this phrase in a different sense to that in which he generally uses it; an extended sense which emphasizes the fact that all are *called* to grace and glory. See further translator's notes on pages 23-24 and 115-117.]

[1] Sess. XXII, cap. 1.

[2] 1 Peter 2:9. Cf. Apoc. 1:5-6: "To Him who has loved us, and washed us from our sins in His own blood, and made us to be a kingdom, and priests to God His Father—to Him belong glory and dominion."

who are present: "Be mindful, Lord, of your servants ... all here present, for whom we offer to you, or who offer to you, this sacrifice of praise for themselves and all those belonging to them." And then, extending his hands over the oblation, he prays God to accept it as the sacrifice of the whole spiritual family gathered around the altar: "We beseech you, therefore, O Lord, to receive favorably this oblation of our service and that also of all your family." You see: it is indeed the faithful united with the priest, and, through him united to Jesus Christ, who offer this sacrifice. Christ is the supreme and principal High Priest; the priest is His minister, chosen by Him. Finally, the faithful, at their level, participate in this Sacred Priesthood and in all the acts of Christ.

"Let us be attentive; let us follow the priest who acts in our name, who speaks for us. Let us call to mind the former custom of each offering his own bread and wine, of furnishing the material of this Heavenly Sacrifice. The ceremony has changed, but the spirit of it remains: we all offer with the priest; we consent to all he does, all he says.... Let us offer ... with him; let us offer Jesus Christ. Let us offer ourselves with all His Catholic Church, spread throughout all the earth."[1]

Our likeness to Christ Jesus does not stop there. He is High Priest, but He is also Victim, and the desire of His sacred heart is that we share that status also. It is through this, above all, that our souls are transformed in holiness.

Let us consider for a moment the material of the Sacrifice, the bread and wine which will be changed into the body and blood of Jesus Christ. The Fathers of the Church insisted upon the symbolism of these two elements. The bread is formed from grains of wheat, ground and united together to form but one substance; the wine comes from the bunches of grapes which have been gathered together and pressed so as to make there flow out from the wine-press but one single liquid

---

[1] Bossuet, *Meditations upon the Gospel: The Last Supper*, 63rd day.

to drink. This is an image of the union of the faithful with Christ, and of all the faithful among themselves.

In the Greek rite, the union of the faithful with Christ in His Sacrifice is expressed with all the liveliness of oriental ideas. At the beginning of the Mass the priest, with a lancet of gold, divides the bread into several fragments and assigns to each of them, by a special prayer, the role of representing the personages, or the categories of personage, in honor of whom or for whom the Sacrifice is about to be offered. The first fragment represents Christ; another, the Virgin Mary, co-redemptrix; then the others, the martyrs, the virgins, the saint of the day, the whole procession of the Church Triumphant. Next come the fragments reserved for the Church Suffering, the Church Militant; the Sovereign Pontiff, the bishops, the faithful who are present. This function completed, the priest puts all the fragments upon the paten and offers them to God, for all of them will soon be transformed into the body of Jesus Christ. This ceremony indicates how great our union with Christ in His Sacrifice must be.

The Latin liturgy is more sober, but no less categoric. It possesses a ceremony—one of its most ancient ones—which the priest cannot omit without grave fault, and which shows well that we ought to be inseparable from Christ in His immolation. At the moment of the offertory, the priest pours a drop of water into the chalice which already contains the wine. What does that ceremony signify? It is explained by the prayer which accompanies it: "O God, who in creating human nature didst wonderfully dignify it, and"—by the Incarnation— "has still more wonderfully renewed it: grant that *by the mystery of this water and wine, we may be partakers of His divinity, who vouchsafed to become a partaker of our humanity,* Jesus Christ, your Son our Lord: who lives and reigns with you in the unity of the Holy Spirit, God, for ever and ever. Amen." Then the priest offers the chalice, that it may be accepted by God *"in odorem suavitatis,"* "with an odor of sweetness." In this way, then, the mystery symbolized by this mixing of the water with the wine is, in the first place, the union of the divinity and the humanity in Christ; and from this mystery there derives another—one also indicated by this prayer: our union with Christ in His sacrifice. The wine represents Christ, the water represents the people, exactly as St. John said in the Apocalypse, and the Council of Trent has confirmed: "The waters ... are all the peoples."[1]

We ought to be united with Christ in His immolation, to offer ourselves with Him. Then He takes us with Him, He immolates us with Himself, He bears us before His Father "with an odor of sweetness." It is *we ourselves* that we ought to offer with Jesus Christ. If the faithful share in the Priesthood of Christ, through baptism, it is, says St. Peter, in order "to offer spiritual sacrifices acceptable to God through Jesus Christ."[2] So true is this, that in more than one prayer following the offering she has just made to God, when awaiting the time of the Consecration, the Church draws attention to this union of our sacrifice with that of her Spouse. "Be pleased, Lord, to sanctify these gifts, we beseech you; and, receiving the offering of this unworldly Sacrifice, make *ourselves* an eternal oblation to you—to your glory—"through Jesus Christ our Lord."[3]

But in order that we may be thus acceptable to God, the offering of ourselves must be united to that which Christ made in His own person upon the cross and which He renews upon the altar. Our Lord substituted Himself for us in His immolation; He took the place of us all, and that is why the blow which struck Him has made us in principle die with Him: "If one man died on behalf of all, then all thereby became dead men."[4] As far as we ourselves are concerned, it is only by uniting ourselves with His Sacrifice at the altar that we die with Him. And

---

[1] Apoc. 17:15 (Jerus.) "By this mixing is represented the union of the faithful people itself with its head, Christ": Council of Trent, Sess. XXII, cap. 7.　　　[2] 1 Peter 2:5.

[3] Mass of Pentecost Sunday. A similar prayer (the *secretum*) can be found in the Mass of the Feast of the Holy Trinity.　　　[4] 2 Cor. 5:14 (Knox).

how *do* we unite ourselves as victims with Christ Jesus? By delivering ourselves up, as He did, to the complete accomplishment of the Divine good pleasure.

God has to have at His full disposal the victim that is offered to Him; we have to be in that basic attitude of giving *everything* to God, of carrying out our acts of renunciation and mortification, of accepting the sufferings, the trials and the troubles of each day for love of Him, in such a way that we can say, as Christ Jesus did at the time of His Passion: "That the world may know that I love the Father" I do this.[1] That is what offering oneself with Jesus is. When we offer His Divine Son to the Eternal Father, and when we offer ourselves along with "the holy Victim" with the same dispositions as those which animated the sacred heart of Christ on the cross: intense love of His Father and of our brethren, ardent desire for the salvation of souls, full abandon to all things willed from on high, especially in regard to whatever they contain which is painful or annoying for our nature, we then offer to God the most pleasing homage He could receive from us.

We also find there the most assured means of being transformed into Jesus, especially if we unite ourselves with Him in Holy Communion, which is the most fruitful participation in the Sacrifice of the altar. For Christ, finding us united to Him, immolates us with Him, renders us pleasing to His Father, makes us, through His grace, more and more like Himself.

That truth is signified by this mysterious prayer which the priest recites after the Consecration: "We humbly beseech you, Almighty God; command these things to be carried by the hands of your holy angel to your altar on high, in the sight of your Divine Majesty; that all of us who, by participation at this altar, shall receive the most holy body and blood of your Son, may be filled with every heavenly blessing and grace."

[1] John 14:31 (Rheims).

A very excellent way of assisting at the Holy Sacrifice, therefore, is to follow with one's eyes, mind and heart what is happening at the altar, to associate oneself with the prayers which the Church puts on the lips of her ministers at such a holy time. When we thus unite ourselves to Christ, High Priest and Victim of His sacrifice—unite ourselves through a deep reverence, a lively faith, an ardent love, a true contrition for our sins[1]—then Christ, who lives in us, takes all our intentions into His heart and presents to His Father for us a perfect adoration, a full satisfaction; He renders to Him a worthy thanksgiving, and His prayer is all-powerful. All these acts of the eternal High Priest, who renews upon the altar His immolation on Calvary, become ours.

At the same time as we give to God, through Christ, all honor and all glory—*Omnis honor et gloria*,[2] abundant graces of light and of life are poured within us and into all the Church: "Fruits are received most abundantly."[3] Each Mass, indeed, contains all the fruits of the Sacrifice of the cross. But, in order to gather them, our soul must enter into the dispositions of Christ at the time when He was about to offer Himself on Calvary. When we enter into the feelings of the heart of Jesus— "Have this mind in you which was also in Christ Jesus"[4]—the Eternal High Priest brings us with Him into the Holy of Holies, before the throne of the Divine Majesty, to the very source of all grace, of all life and all bliss.

"If you only knew what God is offering!"

---

[1] "This holy Council teaches ... that if we come to God with a sincere heart and an upright faith, with fear and respect, then through this Sacrifice we shall obtain mercy and shall find the grace of opportune help": Council of Trent, Sess. XXII, cap. 2.   [2] Prayer of the Mass, after the Consecration.

[3] Council of Trent, Sess. XXII, cap. 2.   [4] Phil. 2:5.

CHAPTER EIGHT

THE BREAD OF LIFE:
PANIS VITAE

INTRODUCTION: The Eucharistic *Communion*, the *most assured means* of maintaining divine life within us.

"WE HUMBLY beseech you, O Almighty God ... that all of us who shall receive the most holy body and blood of your Son, by this participation at the altar"—partaking of the Victim at this altar—"may be filled with all heavenly blessing and grace."

These words serve as the conclusion of one of the prayers which, in the Holy Sacrifice of the Mass, follow the august rite of the Consecration. As you know, Our Lord makes Himself present on the altar, not only to give a perfect homage to His Father through a mystical immolation which renews His oblation on Calvary, but in addition to this, to make Himself the food of our souls, under the sacramental species.

At the time He instituted this Sacrifice, Christ Jesus Himself manifested to us this intention of His sacred heart: "Take and eat; this is my body";[1] "Drink of this; for this is my blood."[2] If Our Lord willed to make Himself present under the appearances of bread and wine, it is in order that we might eat of Him. Now, if we seek to understand why Christ willed to institute this sacrament in the form of nourishment, we shall see that it is, first, in order to maintain the divine life within

[1] Matt. 26:26.   [2] Matt. 26:27.

us; and then so that, receiving this super-natural life from Him, we might remain united to Him. Sacramental Communion, fruit of the Eucharistic Sacrifice, constitutes for the soul the most assured means of staying united to Jesus.

It is in this union with Christ, as I have told you, that the true life of the soul, super-natural holiness, is to be found. Jesus is the Vine, we are the branches, grace is the sap which goes up into the branches so as to make them bear fruit. Well, it is above all through the gift of Himself in the Eucharist that Christ makes grace abound in us.

Let us contemplate with faith and reverence, with love and confidence, this mystery of life, in which we unite ourselves to Him who is at the same time our Divine model, our infinite satisfaction and the very source of all our holiness.[1] We shall see in what follows what are the dispositions with which we ought to receive Him in order to arrive at the perfection of union that Christ wishes to effect in us by giving Himself to us.

1. Communion is the banquet in which Christ gives Himself as Bread of Life.

WHEN, in prayer, we ask Our Lord to tell us why, in His eternal wisdom, He has willed to establish this ineffable sacrament, what does He say to us in reply?

To begin with, He speaks to us those words He made us hear, for the first time, when He announced to the Jews the institution of the Eucharist: "As the living Father sent me, and I live because of the Father, so he who eats me will live because of me."[2] It is as if He were saying: "My desire is to communicate my Divine life to you. I myself take my being, my life, everything, from my Father: and because I receive everything from Him, I live only for Him; I have but one intense desire—that you also, receiving everything from me, shall live only for me.

---

[1] Catechism of the Council of Trent, cf. XX, para. 1.   [2] John 6:57 (58) (RSV, Cath.)

Your bodily life is sustained and developed through nourishment; I wish to be the food of your soul, in order to maintain and develop its life, which is myself.[1] One who eats me, lives by my life. I possess the plenitude of grace, and I cause to share in that plenitude those to whom I give myself as food. The Father has life in Himself, but He has given to the Son also to have life in Himself.[2] And because I possess this life, I have come but to give it—life full and abundant.[3] I make you live because I give myself as food. I am the living bread, the bread of life come down from heaven so as to bring you divine life; that bread which gives the life of heaven—life eternal, of which grace is the dawn.[4] The Jews in the desert ate manna, a corruptible food. But I—I am the bread that is ever-living, and ever-necessary for your souls, for if you do not eat it you will condemn yourselves to perish: "Unless you eat the flesh of the Son of Man ... you shall not have life in you."[5]

Such are very words of Jesus. It is not only in order that we may adore Him, that we may offer Him to His Father as an infinite satisfaction, that Christ makes Himself present on the altar; it is not only in order to *visit* us that He comes. It is in order that we may eat of Him as food of the soul and that, eating of Him, we may have life, the life of grace here below, the life of glory on high.

"The Son of God being Life in its essence, it is for Him to promise life; it is for Him to give it. The holy humanity He deigned to take in the fullness of time (a humanity touching Life so closely) so much takes its power from Life, that there flows out therefrom an inexhaustible source of living water.... Is not this the bread of life, or rather is it not a living bread that we eat in order to have life? For this sacred

---

[1] "He willed that this sacrament be taken as the spiritual food of souls, to nourish and comfort those who live by the life of Him who said: 'He who eats me will live because of me'": Council of Trent, Sess. XIII, cap. 2.

[2] John 5:26.

[3] John 10:10: "I came that they may have life, and have it more abundantly."

[4] "I am the bread of life" (John 6:35; 6:48), "I am the living bread that has come down from heaven" (John 6:51).   [5] John 6:54.

bread is the holy flesh of Jesus, that living flesh, that flesh conjoined to life, that flesh wholly filled and wholly penetrated by a life-giving spirit. If ordinary bread, not itself having life, preserves the life of our bodies, with what wonderful life shall we not live, we who eat a living bread, who eat Life itself at the table of the living God? Who has ever heard tell of such a marvelous thing, that one should be able to eat Life? It belongs only to Jesus to give us a foodstuff like that. He is Life by nature: to eat Him is to eat Life. O delicious banquet of the children of God!"[1] That is why the priest, when he distributes Holy Communion, says to each one: "May the body of our Lord Jesus Christ preserve your soul to life everlasting"!

I have told you that the sacraments produce the grace that they signify. In the natural order, food preserves and sustains the life of the body, gives it growth, restores it and causes it to mature.[2] It is so with this heavenly bread; it is the food of the soul, that *maintains, mends, increases* and *gladdens* the life of grace in the soul, because it gives to it the very Author of grace. The divine life can enter into us by other doors, but it is by Holy Communion that it inundates our souls like a river in flood. Holy Communion is so much a sacrament of life, that of itself it forgives and wipes out venial sins to which we are no longer attached;[3] it acts in such a way that the divine life in the soul, recovering its vigor and its beauty, grows, develops and bears abundant fruit. O sacred feast where the soul receives Christ: "O sacred banquet in which Christ is the food ... the soul is filled with grace."[4] O Christ Jesus, Word Incarnate, you in whom "dwells all the fullness of the Godhead bodily,"[5] come into me, so as to make me share in that fullness. That is life for me; because to receive you is to become a child of

---

[1] Bossuet, Sermon for Holy Saturday, *Oeuvres oratoires*, ed. Lebarq, vol 1, pp. 121-122.

[2] These, following St Thomas (III, q. LXXIX, a. 1) are the four effects of nourishment; the holy doctor applies them to the Eucharist, food of the soul.

[3] See above, page 235, n. 6, the words of the Catechism of the Council of Trent.

[4] Magnificat antiphon of the Second Vespers of Corpus Christi.   [5] Col. 2:9.

God,[1] it is to partake of the life which you have received from your Father and by which you live for your Father; that life which, from your humanity, overflows upon all your brethren through grace. Come, that I may eat of you, in order to live with your life: "He who eats me will live because of me."[2]

2. Through Holy Communion, Christ *dwells in us* and we in Him.

ONE of the intentions of the heart of Christ Jesus in instituting the Eucharistic Sacrifice is, then, that He be the heavenly Bread which maintains and increases the divine life within us. But there is another end which Our Lord has willed and which completes the first: "He who eats my flesh and drinks my blood abides in me, and I in him."[3] What is the meaning of the word "abide" here?

When we read St. John's Gospel—St. John who reports to us the words of Jesus—we see that he almost always employs this term when he wishes to express perfect union. There is no greater union than that of the Father and the Son in the Blessed Trinity, since these two Persons, with the Holy Spirit, possess the same unique Divine nature. St. John says that the Father "abides" in the Son.[4]

To "abide in Christ" is, first of all, to share through grace His Divine Sonship: it is to be one with Him, in being, like Him—albeit by a different title of right to His—a child of God. That is the basic and fundamental union, the one that Christ Himself indicated in His parable of the vine: "I am the vine, you are the branches. He who *abides* in me, and I in him, he bears much fruit."[5]

---

[1] John 1:12: "To as many as received Him He gave the power of becoming sons of God."

[2] John 6:57 (RSV, Cath.); in other translations, v. 58.

[3] John 6:56 (RSV, Cath.); in other translations, v. 57.

[4] John 14:10 (Rheims). [*Translator's note*: St. John records Christ's words: "The Father who abides in me...."]   [5] John 15:5.

That union is not the only one. To "abide" in Christ is to identify oneself with Him in everything that concerns our intellect, our will, our activity. We abide in Christ *through the intellect* in accepting, by an act of faith, simple, pure and entire, everything that Christ tells us. The Word is eternally close to the Father's heart; He sees the Divine secrets and He makes us share in what He sees: "It is the only Son," in the heart's-embrace of the Father, "who has made Him known."[1] By faith, we say "Yes," *Amen*, to everything the Incarnate Word tells us; we accept what He says; and in this way we identify ourselves with Christ in our intellect. Holy Communion makes us abide in Christ by faith; we can only receive Him if we accept by faith everything He says and everything He is. Look at when Our Lord announced to the Jews the institution of the Eucharist. He said to them: "I am the bread of life: he who comes to me shall never hunger, and he who believes in me shall never thirst."[2] And as the Jews murmured in their incredulity, He repeats to them what He has said: "Truly, truly, I say to you, he who believes in me has life everlasting."[3] It is in faith that Our Lord gives Himself to us as food; and to unite oneself with Him is to accept, through the adhesion of our intellect to His words, everything that He reveals to us. In bringing all truth to us, Christ is the food of our intellect.

To abide in Him is also to submit *our will* to Him. It is to make the whole of our super-natural activity depend upon His grace—in other words, we abide in His love by agreeing to do His will: "If you keep my commandments *you will abide in my love*, as I also have kept my Father's commandments, and abide in His love."[4] It is to prefer His desires to ours, it is to espouse His interests, it is to deliver ourselves up to Him, whole and entire, without measuring out what we give, without reserving anything or taking anything back. For one cannot *abide* if one is not firm and stable, with that absolute confidence a wife has in her husband. A wife is never more pleasing to her husband than when she relies solely on his wisdom, his power, his strength, his love.

[1] John 1:18 (Jerus.)   [2] See John 6:35.   [3] John 6:47.   [4] John 15:10.

By thus giving nourishment to love, this Heavenly Bread maintains the life of our will.

That is the divine state Christ Jesus wants to set up in the soul that receives Him. Christ Jesus comes into the soul so that she may "abide in" Him—in other words, that having full confidence in what He says, she abandons herself to Him so as to carry out His Divine good pleasure and to have no other driving-power for the whole of her activity than the action of His Spirit: "Anyone who is joined to the Lord is one spirit with Him."[1]

For, Our Lord—He too abides in the soul. One who "abides in me *and I in him*," He said, that soul bears much fruit.[2] Look at what took place in the Incarnate Word. There was in Him a natural activity—human, very intense; but the Word, to which the humanity was indissolubly united, was the deep hearth-fire where all His activity was fed and radiated forth.

The desire of Christ in giving Himself to the soul is to produce in her something analogous to this. Without establishing a union as close as that of the Word with the sacred humanity, Christ in giving Himself to the soul wishes to be—by His grace and the action of His Spirit—the mainspring within her of all her interior activity. "... *and I in*" the soul; He is in the soul, He abides in her, but He is not inactive; He wishes to work within her.[3] And when the soul stays, "abides," delivered up to Him, to His will in everything, then the action of Christ becomes so powerful that this soul will infallibly be carried to the highest perfection, in accordance with God's designs for her. For Christ comes within her with His divinity, His merits, His riches, in order to be her light, her way, her truth, her wisdom, her justice, her redemption: "Christ Jesus ... has become for us God-given wisdom, and justice, and sanctification, and redemption";[4] in a word, to be the

---

[1] 1 Cor. 6:17 (Jerus.)   [2] John 15:5.
[3] "My Father goes on working, and so do I": John 5:17 (Jerus.)   [4] 1 Cor. 1:30.

life of the soul, Himself to live in the soul—"I live, now not I; but Christ lives in me."[1] It is the soul's dream to be but one with Him she loves. Holy Communion, in which the soul receives Christ as food, realizes this dream by transforming the soul, little by little, into Christ.

3. Difference between the effects of bodily food and the fruits of taking and eating the Eucharist. How *Christ transforms us* into Himself. Influence of this marvelous food upon the body.

THE FATHERS of the Church, indeed, have brought out a profound difference between the action of food which serves to nourish our bodily life, and the effect produced in the soul by the Eucharistic Bread.

When we assimilate the food of the body, we convert it into our own substance, whereas it is so as to transform us into Him that Christ gives Himself to us as food. St. Leo writes these remarkable words: "Sharing in the body and blood of Christ produces in us an effect which is none other than that of making us be changed into that which we take."[2] St. Augustine is yet more explicit; he makes Christ say: "I am the nourishment of the strong; have faith and eat me. But you will not change me into yourself; it is you who will be transformed into me."[3] And St. Thomas, with his habitual clarity, has laid down this doctrine in a few lines: "The principle for arriving at a right understanding of the distinctive effect of a sacrament is to consider it by analogy with the matter of the sacrament.... The matter of the Eucharist is a food. It must, then, be that its distinctive effect is analogous to that of nourishment. One who assimilates bodily nourishment transforms it into himself; that conversion makes good the losses of the organism and gives it its proper growth. But the Eucharistic nourishment, instead of being transformed into the one who takes it, transforms that person into Itself.

---

[1] Gal. 2:20 (Rheims). The Knox version has: "I am alive; or rather, not I; it is Christ that lives in me."

[2] *Sermo* 63 on the Passion, 12, c. 7.   [3] *Confessions*, VII, c. 4.

It follows that the distinctive effect of this sacrament is such a transformation of the person into Christ that that person can truly say: 'I live, now not I; but Christ lives in me.'"[1]

How does this spiritual transformation operate? In receiving Jesus Christ, we receive Him whole and entire: His body, His blood, His soul, His humanity, His divinity. Christ makes us enter into His thoughts, share His feelings; He communicates His virtues to us, but above all He enkindles in us that "fire" He came to cast upon the earth,[2] the fire of love, of charity; *that* is the purpose of this transformation produced by the Eucharist. "The efficacy of this sacrament," writes St. Thomas, "is to work a certain transformation into Christ by means of charity. And that is its distinctive fruit.... The property of charity is to transform him who loves into the object of his love." In other words, the coming of Christ into us tends, of its nature, to establish between His thoughts and our thoughts, between His feelings and our feelings, between His will and our will, such an exchange, such a correspondence, such a likeness, that we have no other thoughts, no other feelings, no other wishes, than those of Christ: "Have this mind in you which was also in Christ Jesus."[3] And that, through love: love delivers up the will to Christ and, through the will, all our being, all our energies. And because it thus delivers up the whole man, love is the means of our super-natural transformation and our super-natural growth. St. John has very well said: "He who abides in love abides in God, and God in him."[4]

Without that, there is no true "communion."[5] We receive Christ with our lips; but at the same time we should also unite ourselves to

---

[1] In IV *Sentent.*, dist. 12, q. 2, a. 1.   [2] Luke 12:49.

[3] Phil. 2:5. [*Translator's note*: This section, and this sentence in particular, makes even clearer the sense in which Marmion uses the phrase "transformation into Christ."]   [4] 1 John 4:16.

[5] [*Translator's note*: Observe Marmion's own inverted commas around this word. He has in mind the literal derivation of the word "communion"—*one*-ness of spirit between the communicant and Christ.]

Him with our mind, our heart, our will, with the whole of our soul, so as to share His Divine life (to the extent that that is possible here below); in such a way that, through the faith we have in Him, through the love we bear Him, it may truly be His life, and no longer our "Me," that is the mainspring of our life. This is something indicated very well by a prayer the Church makes the priest recite after Communion: "Lord, make our soul and our body entirely submissive to the operation of your heavenly gift, in such a way that it may no longer be our own human judgments, but the effect of this sacrament that ever rules within us."[1]

That prayer of the Church lets us understand that the Eucharistic action overflows from the soul upon the body itself. True, it is to the soul that Christ unites Himself immediately; it is the deification of the soul that He comes first of all to assure and confirm: "that we may be numbered among the members of Him of whose body and blood we have communicated."[2] But the union of the body and the soul is so basic and so close that in increasing the life of the soul, in leading the soul strongly towards the delights of heaven, the Eucharist tempers the heat of the passions and brings peace to the whole of our being.

The Fathers of the Church[3] even speak of an influence more direct still. What further amazing thing is that? When Christ was living on the earth, mere contact with His sacred humanity was enough to heal bodies. Is this curative power likely to have become less because Christ veils Himself beneath the sacramental species? "Do you think, daughters," asked St. Teresa of Avila, "that this most holy food may not sustain the body also, and not be a remedy for its ills? Speaking for myself, I am well aware that it has this power. I know a person"—the Saint is doubtless referring to herself—"who, in addition to her big infirmities, often

---

[1] Postcommunion of the Fifteenth Sunday after Pentecost.

[2] Postcommunion of the Saturday of the third week in Lent.

[3] St. Justinus, *Apolog. ad Anton. Pium.*, n. 66; St. Irenaeus, *Contra haereses*, V, c. 2; St. Cyril of Jerusalem, *Catech.* XXII (*Mystag.* IV), n. 3; *Catech.* XXIII (*Mystag.* V), n. 15.

experienced very sharp pains at the time of going to Communion, and who no sooner received the Bread of Life than she felt all these ills disappear, as if someone's hand had removed them from her.... Certainly, our adorable Master is not accustomed to pay badly for His stay in the hostelry of our soul when He receives a good welcome there."[1]

Before the Communion, the priest asks Christ that the receiving of His sacred flesh may become a help for the body as for the soul: "May the receiving of your body, Lord Jesus Christ ... be a safeguard and healing remedy for my soul and body." The Church makes us repeat the same prayer in more than one of her postcommunions, at the time of rendering thanks to God for the Divine gift: "Purify our souls, O Lord, renew them with your heavenly sacraments, so that *our bodies* themselves may experience the help of your almighty power *in this world* as in the next."[2]

Let us not forget that Christ is ever living, ever acting. In coming to us He unites our organs with His own; He purifies, He uplifts, He sanctifies, He (so to say) transforms all our faculties, in such a way that—to borrow the beautiful thought of an ancient author—we love God through the heart of Christ, we praise God through the lips of Christ, we live with His life. The Divine presence of Jesus and His sanctifying power permeate all our being so intimately that, body and soul with all their powers, we become "other Christs."

Such is the truly sublime expression for that union with Christ in the Eucharist, a union which each Holy Communion tends to bring about ever more perfectly. If we only knew what God is offering! For, those who draw at this spring of the waters of grace no longer ever thirst. They are refreshed; one "who drinks of the water that I shall give him shall never thirst."[3] They find at that spring every good thing:

[1] St. Teresa of Avila, *The Way of Perfection*, Ch. XXXIV. The Saint is more explicit still in Chapter XXX of her *Life, written by herself.*

[2] Postcommunion of the 16th Sunday after Pentecost. See also: "May the heavenly mystery be to us, O Lord, the *reparation* of mind *and body*": Postcommunion of the Eighth Sunday after Pentecost.   [3] John 4:13.

"How has He not also, with Him, given us all things?"[1] From the altar every blessing and every grace flow down to us: "that all of us who shall receive the most holy body and blood of your Son may be filled with every heavenly blessing and grace."[2]

4. *Need for a preparation* in order in order to assimilate the fruits of the Communion.

EFFECTS SO MARVELOUS do not operate in the soul unless the soul is prepared for the pouring-down of so many good things. It is true, as I have told you, that the sacraments produce of themselves the fruit for which they have been instituted; but on condition that no obstacle stands in the way of their action: *non ponentibus obicem*. Well, what *is* an obstacle here?

Naturally there cannot be one on the part of Christ: in whom are "all the treasures" of "the fullness of the Godhead,"[3] and He has an infinite desire to communicate them to us in giving Himself to us. He brings no parsimony into this, for He comes to give us life, He wishes to give us it in abundance: "that they may ... have it more abundantly."[4] He repeats to each one of us what He said to the apostles on the eve of the institution of this sacrament: "With desire"—with an intense desire—"I have desired to eat this pasch with you."[5]

Let us not lose sight of the fact that Holy Communion is not of human devising, but a Divine sacrament established by Eternal Wisdom. Now, it belongs to wisdom to proportion the means to the end. If, then, our Divine Savior has instituted the Eucharist in order to unite Himself with us and to make us live with His life, let us be assured that this

---

[1] Rom. 8:32 (Rheims). [*Translator's note*: The "with Him" of the text that Marmion quotes follows on the previous wording of the verse, 32; i.e. when the Father has given His own Son for us, how has He not also given us all things along with that gift?]

[2] Canon of the Mass, after the Consecration.   [3] Col. 2, vv. 3, 9.

[4] John 10:10.   [5] Luke 22:15 (Rheims).

sacrament contains everything needed to bring about this union and to carry it to its highest degree. He hides Himself within this marvelous devising of potentialities that are efficacious beyond compare for producing in us a Divine transformation.

The obstacle, then, is in *us*. What is it?

To know what it is, we have only to consider the very nature of the sacrament. It is a food which is meant to *maintain the life* of the soul and to *cement the union.*

Everything, then, that stands in the way of super-natural life and of union is an obstacle to the reception and to the fruit of the Eucharist. Grave sin that gives death to the soul is an absolute obstacle. As food is only given to the living, so the Eucharist is only given to those who already possess the life of grace. This is the primary condition. Along with the "right intention," that condition suffices for every one of the faithful to be able to approach Christ and receive the Bread of Life. That is what that great Pope, Pius X, laid down in a memorable document.[1] The sacrament acts *ex opere operato*: of itself. The Eucharist nourishes the soul and increases grace, and at the same time the habit of charity. This is the first and essential fruit of the sacrament.

There are still other fruits—secondary ones, it is true, but nevertheless so great that they deserve to be brought out. These are the actual graces of union that put charity into action; that stir up our fervor to render love for love, to carry out the Divine pleasure, to avoid sin; that fill the soul with joy. "The delightsomeness of this heavenly Bread that is full of sweetness" communicates itself to the soul to quicken its devotion in the service of the Lord and to make it strong against sin and temptation.[2]

---

[1] Decree of December 20th 1905. The Sovereign Pontiff explains "right intention" in this way: "It consists in approaching the holy table, not through habit, or through vanity or for human reasons, but in order to fulfill what God wishes, to unite oneself with Him more intimately through love, and, thanks to this Divine remedy, to fight against one's faults and failings."

[2] See Catechism of the Council of Trent, ch. XX, para. 1.

Now, these secondary effects can be more abundant or less; and, in practice, they depend in large measure upon our dispositions,[1] especially when love, the mainspring of union, is the motive-power that impels us to prepare for Our Lord a dwelling less unworthy of His divinity, and to render to Him, with the greatest possible affection, the homage He deserves in coming to us.

Doubtless Christ Jesus, being sovereignly free and infinitely good, grants His gifts to whomsoever He pleases; but, besides the fact that His infinite majesty (for He always remains God) requires us, in the measure of our weakness, to prepare a dwelling for Him within our heart, can we doubt for one single moment that He looks with extreme kindness upon the efforts of a soul who desires to receive Him with faith and love?[2]

Look at how, in the Gospel, He rewarded the desires and efforts of Zaccheus. This leading publican only wanted to see Jesus; and Our Lord, meeting him, anticipates his desires and tells him that He wishes to go down to his home. And His visit earned for that man pardon and salvation.[3] Look, as well, at when Our Lord was received by Simon the Pharisee. During the meal a woman, Mary Magdalene, comes into the room, approaches Jesus and proceeds to spread perfumes upon His feet and to kiss them. But the onlookers have immediately recognized that this woman is a sinner. And Simon the Pharisee is indignant within himself: "If only Jesus knew who this woman is!" Christ knows these secret thoughts, and He defends Mary Magdalene. He contrasts what she does in order to please Him with what the Pharisee has omitted in

---

[1] D. Coghlan, *De SS. Eucharistia*, p. 368.

[2] Although the sacraments of the New Law produce their effect *ex opere operato* (of themselves), nonetheless this effect is the greater as the dispositions of those who receive the sacrament are more perfect. We should therefore make sure that a diligent preparation precedes Holy Communion, and that it is followed by a suitable thanksgiving": Pius X, Decree of December 20th 1905 on daily Communion.

[3] Luke 19:2-10. [*Translator's note*: Zaccheus also had to "go down," from a tree. Being small of stature, he had climbed it, to see Our Lord.]

the exercise of his hospitality towards Christ: "You see this woman?" says Jesus to Simon. "I came into your house, and you gave me no water to wash my feet: but she has wet them with her tears and dried them with her hair. You gave me no welcoming kiss; but she, from the time she came in, has not stopped kissing my feet. You did not anoint my head with oil; but she has spread perfumes on my feet. That is why I tell you that her many sins are pardoned her because she has loved much." Then He says to the woman: "Your sins are forgiven you, your faith has made you safe; go in peace."[1]

You see, then, that Our Lord is attentive to the dispositions, to the signs of love, with which we receive Him. The Eucharist is the sacrament of union, and the less that Christ meets with obstacles to the perfection of this union, the more the grace of His sacrament acts within us. The Catechism of the Council of Trent tells us that "we receive all the abundance of the gifts of God when we partake of the Eucharist with a heart that is well disposed and perfectly prepared."[2]

5. Remote dispositions: *complete gift of oneself* to Christ; *orientating all our actions towards Holy Communion.*

NOW, there is one very important *general disposition* which derives from the nature of union and which serves admirably as habitual preparation for our union with Jesus Christ, and especially for the perfection of that union. It is *the total gift*, frequently renewed, *of oneself to Christ Jesus.*

This gift of ourselves to the Word Incarnate started at baptism — baptism that was the first taking of possession of our soul by Christ. At that time we began, through grace, to assimilate ourselves to God, to remain united to Him. Now, the more we remain in that basic disposition which baptism inaugurated, of death to sin and life for God, the

---

[1] See Luke 7:36-39; 44-50. [2] Ch. XX, para. 3.

better prepared are we, from afar,[1] to receive the abundance of Eucharistic grace. To stay attached to venial sin, to deliberate imperfections, to intentional negligences, to willed infidelities—all these things cannot but affront Our Lord when He comes to us. If we desire the perfection of this union, we must not "bargain" with Christ over our heart's liberty. We must not reserve in that heart a place, however small it be, for creatures[2] loved for their own sake. We must empty ourselves from ourselves, disengage ourselves from creatures, aspire to a complete accession of the reign of Christ within us by the submission of the whole of our being to His Gospel and to the action of His Spirit.

That is a disposition of the most excellent kind. What is it that prevents Christ from identifying us perfectly with Himself when He comes within us? Is it our infirmities of body or mind, the miseries inherent in our condition of being exiles, the servitudes of our human nature? Certainly not; these imperfections, and even those faults which slip out from us and which we deplore and work to destroy—these do not stop Christ. Quite the reverse, He comes within us in order to help us to destroy those faults and to bear with those weaknesses patiently; for He is a compassionate High Priest who "remembers that we are dust,"[3] and who takes upon Himself all our miseries. Truly "He has borne our infirmities."[4]

What prevents the perfection of the union are those bad habits, known and not disavowed, that for lack of generosity we are afraid to touch; the attachments, retained voluntarily, to ourselves or to creatures. To the extent that we do not work to uproot these bad habits and sever these attachments, through vigilance over ourselves and through

---

[1] [*Translator's note*: By "from afar," "*de loin*," Marmion refers to "remote" preparation for the Eucharist: see the title to this section. "Remote" preparation contrasts with preparation *near to* Communion, a short time before one receives the Eucharist; such preparation is dealt with in section 6 below.]

[2] [*Translator's note*: See note 2 on page 56.]   [3] Ps. 102 (103):14 (RSV, Cath.)
[4] Isa. 53:4.

mortification, Christ will not be able to make us share in the abundance of His grace.

And that is especially true of deliberate or habitual faults against charity towards our neighbor. I shall develop this point when I expound to you the motives we have for loving one another. But I must say a word about it here. Our Lord is one with His mystical body; all Christians are, through grace, its members. And when we go to Communion, we must do so to the whole Christ; in other words, unite ourselves, through charity, to Christ in His physical being *and* to Christ's members—we cannot separate them. Our Lord willed, the Council of Trent says, "to leave us this sacrament as a symbol of the inner unity of this mystical body of which He is the head."[1] There is "one bread" only, says St. Paul in speaking of the Eucharist. In the same way, although we may be numerous we are one single body, all "who partake of the one bread."[2]

Listen to what Christ Himself tells us: "If at the time you present your offering at the altar you remember that your brother has something against you, go first to reconcile yourself with him; only then come and present your offering."[3] That is why the least intentional coldness, the least resentment harbored in the soul in relation to our neighbor, constitutes a great obstacle to the perfection of that union Our Lord wishes to have with us in the Eucharist.

If, then, we discover in our heart any voluntary attachment to our own judgement or to our self-love or, above all, to habits contrary to charity, we may be certain that to the extent that we accommodate ourselves to this state of things, the abundance of the fruits of the sacrament will remain limited. But if a soul makes a resolution to

---

[1] [He wished this sacrament to be] "a symbol of that one body, of which He is the head and we are, as it were, the members. He wished us to be drawn together, tied close by the bonds of faith, hope and charity, so that all of us might say: 'There are no schisms among us'": Sess. XIII, cap. 2.

[2] 1 Cor. 10:17.

[3] See Matt. 5:23-24.

correct itself of the bad habits it notes in itself; if it makes serious efforts to destroy them; if it approaches Christ in Holy Communion in order to draw from Him the necessary strength, it can be assured that Our Lord will look upon it with kindness, will bless its efforts and reward it abundantly.

Once again, it is wholly correct to say that our dispositions do not cause the grace of the sacrament. All they do is give it free rein, by removing the obstacles; but we ought to open our hearts as widely as possible to the pouring down of the Divine gift. It is, then, an excellent disposition to seek to refuse nothing to Christ. A soul that remains habitually in that disposition of clearing away from itself all that can affront the gaze of the Divine Guest, and of always holding itself ready to carry out His Divine will, is admirably "adapted" to the sacramental action.

And what is the reason for that? The Eucharist is the sacrament of *union*, as is indicated by the word "communion"; it is in order to unite Himself with us that Our Lord comes within us. To "unite" is to make two things into one thing only. But we unite ourselves to Christ as He is. Now, every Communion presupposes the Sacrifice of the altar, and, consequently, the immolation of the cross. In the offering of Holy Mass, Christ associates us with His state of High Priest, Bridge be tween man and God. In Holy Communion, He causes us to share in His condition of Victim. The Holy Sacrifice presupposes, as I have told you, that full and inner oblation which Our Lord made to the will of His Father on coming into the world, an oblation He renewed often during His life, and which He completed by His death through the shedding of His blood upon Calvary. All that, says St. Paul, is recalled to us by Holy Communion: "*As often* as you shall eat this bread and drink the cup, you proclaim the death of the Lord, until He comes."[1] Christ Jesus gives Himself to us, but after having died for us. He gives

---

[1] 1 Cor. 11:26.

Himself as food, but after having offered Himself as Victim. In the Eucharist, Victim and food are sacrifice and sacrament—two inseparable features. And this is why that habitual disposition of making a total gift of oneself is so important. Christ gives Himself to us in the measure that we give ourselves to Him, to His Father, to our brethren who are the members of His mystical body. That basic disposition assimilates us to Christ, but to Christ the Victim; it establishes a sympathy between those at both ends of the union.

When Our Lord finds a soul thus disposed, delivered up fully and without reserve to His action, He acts in it with that Divine power which, because it meets with no obstacle, brings about marvels of holiness. The absence of this disposition of union, *dispositio unionis*, also explains why quite a few souls advance so little in perfection, despite frequent Communions. Christ does not find in these souls the super-natural pliability that will allow Him to act freely in them. They are *divided* by voluntary attachments, not disavowed, which hold them to creatures, hold them to their own conceit, self-admiration, touchiness, selfishness, jealousy, sensuality, and which prevent the *union* between themselves and Christ becoming of that intensity, that fullness, by which transformation of the soul is brought about and completed.

Let us ask Our Lord Himself to help us acquire little by little that fundamental disposition: it is extremely precious, because it adapts our soul marvelously to the action of the sacrament of divine union.

To this disposition of union, which serves excellently as habitual preparation, we can add another, a remote preparation just as that one is, but rather one of each present moment—a preparation that consists of, every day, *orientating all our actions towards Holy Communion* by an explicit act, in such a way that our union with Christ in the Eucharist may truly be the sun that lights our life. At the time of his priestly ordination, St. Francis de Sales resolved to make every moment of the day a preparation for the Eucharistic Sacrifice of the day after, in such wise that if someone asked him the reason for his behavior he could truthfully reply, "I am preparing to celebrate Mass."[1] That is an excellent practice.

But if it is true that without Christ Jesus we "can do nothing,"[2] how much more will that be found true when it is a matter of our carrying out the action which is the holiest one of each day! To unite oneself sacramentally to Christ Jesus in the Eucharist is, for a created being, the highest act there can be. All human wisdom, whatever heights it may reach, is nothing in comparison with that act. We are incapable of adequately disposing ourselves in this without the help of Christ Himself. Our prayers show the reverence we have for Him, but it is He Himself who must prepare a dwelling for Himself within us. As the psalmist says: "The Most High has sanctified His own tabernacle."[3] Let that be something we ask of Our Lord by going to visit the Sacrament of the Altar in the afternoon.[4] "O Christ Jesus, Word Incarnate, I want to prepare for you a dwelling within me, but I am incapable of that work. O Eternal Wisdom, I ask you to dispose my soul to become your temple through your infinite merits; make me be attached to you alone. I offer you my actions and my sufferings of this day, in order that you may make them pleasing to your Divine gaze, and that tomorrow I do not come before you with empty hands." Such a prayer is excellent; the day is thus directed towards union with Christ. Love, the mainspring of union, envelops our acts; and, far from murmuring at what happens to us that is disagreeable, tiresome, we offer it to Christ by a movement of tender love, and thus the soul will find itself prepared, wholly naturally as it were, when the moment of receiving its God comes.

---

[1] Hamon, *Vie de S. François de Sales*, Vol. I, Book II, ch. 1.   [2] John 15:5.
[3] Ps. 45 (46):5.   [4] [*Translator's note*: In Marmion's time Mass was said in the morning only. The afternoon visit he speaks of would be in preparation for Mass the following day.]

6. Dispositions *near to the time of Communion*: faith, trust and love. How Our Lord rewards these dispositions. *Communion* constitutes the *deepest participation in the Divine Sonship of Jesus.* Variety of the "formulas" and the attitudes of immediate preparation.

AFTER THAT, the time of Communion come, there will only remain the *immediate preparation* required by the infinite dignity of Him who comes to us. And, though this preparation draws its value and its power from that fundamental disposition about which I have spoken to you, it may be not without use for me to say a few words about it.

One of the most important immediate dispositions is *faith*. The Eucharist is essentially a "mystery of faith": *Mysterium fidei*.[1] Are not all the mysteries of Christ, then, mysteries of faith? Certainly, but faith is nowhere as useful and as fruitful as in this mystery. Why is that? Because neither reason nor the senses perceive anything of Christ. Look at the crib; Christ is a little child, but the angels sing His coming so as to manifest His divinity and His mission as Savior of men. During His public life, His miracles and the sublimity of His doctrine give testimony that He is the Son of God. On Tabor, His humanity is transfigured in His divinity. On the cross, even, the divinity does not disappear entirely: nature, by the upheaval it undergoes, proclaims that this Crucified One is the creator of the world.[2] But on the altar, neither the humanity nor the divinity shows itself: "Here thy manhood lieth hidden too."[3] To the senses, to sight, taste and touch, there is nothing but bread and wine. To pierce through these appearances, to penetrate these veils in order to reach the Divine realities, the eye of faith is needed. Faith is what is needed first and foremost here.

[1] Words contained in the formula of the consecration of the Precious Blood.
[2] Luke 23:44.
[3] "On the cross was hid thy Godhead's splendor,/ Here thy manhood lieth hidden too": Hymn, *Adoro te devote.*

That is so clearly apparent when we read the chapter where St. John recounts how Christ announced to the Jews the mystery of the Eucharist.[1] Just the evening before, the Savior had shown His goodness and His power by feeding thousands of people with a few loaves of bread. Following this striking miracle, the Jews cried out: "This is indeed the Prophet who is to come into the world."[2] And, proceeding from wonderment to action, they tried to take Him by force, to make Him king. But see how Jesus reveals to them a mystery much more astonishing than the marvel of the multiplication of the loaves of bread: "I am the bread of life," "I am the bread that has come down from heaven."[3] At once these words, these words alone, stir up murmurings among the Jews: "Is this not Jesus the son of Joseph, whose father and mother we know? How, then, does he say, 'I have come down from heaven'?" And Jesus replies to them: "Do not murmur among yourselves…. I am the bread of life. Your fathers ate the manna in the desert, and have died. This is the bread that comes down from heaven, so that if anyone eat of it he will not die…. If anyone eat of this bread he shall live for ever; and the bread that I will give is my flesh for the life of the world."[4]

Thereupon, the Jews, becoming more incredulous, go on to argue among themselves: "How can this man give us his flesh to eat?" But Christ does not withdraw any of the things He has asserted. On the contrary, He makes them more formal: "Truly, truly, I say to you, unless you eat the flesh of the Son of Man, and drink His blood, you shall not have life in you. He who eats my flesh and drinks my blood has everlasting life…. For my flesh is food indeed, and my blood is drink indeed." Incredulity overcomes the disciples, even, at this time. Some among them protest: "This is a hard saying. Who can listen to it?" And from then on, adds St. John, "many of His disciples," no longer believing in Jesus, abandoned Him "and no longer went about with Him." After they had gone, Our Lord turned to His twelve apostles and said to

---

[1] John 6:30-70.   [2] John 6:14.   [3] John 6, vv. 35, 41, 52.   [4] John 6:41-52.

them: "Do you also wish to go away?" Then Peter spoke, and said to Him: "Lord, to whom shall we go? You have words of eternal life, and we have come to believe and to know that you are the Christ, the Son of God."[1]

And we too—let us believe, with Peter and the apostles who stayed faithful. Let our faith make up for what our senses lack.[2] Christ said: "This is my body, this is my blood; take, eat, and you will have life." You have said this, Lord, and that is enough for me; I believe it. This Bread you give us is Yourself, Christ, the beloved Son of the Father. It is You yourself—you who became incarnate and was delivered up for me; who were born at Bethlehem, lived at Nazareth, healed the sick, restored sight to the blind; you who pardoned Mary Magdalene and the good thief; who, at the Last Supper, allowed St. John to rest his head upon your heart; you who are the Way, the Truth and the Life; you who died for love of me; who ascended to heaven, and who now, at the right hand of your Father, reign and continuously intercede for us. O Jesus, Eternal Truth, you affirm that you are present there on the altar, really and substantially, with your humanity and all the treasures of your divinity. I believe it, and because I believe it, I prostrate myself before you to adore you. Receive, as my God and my All, this homage of my adoration." Such an act of faith is the sublimest we could make, and the most complete homage our intellect could give to Christ.

It is equally an act of *trust*. For Christ as presented to us by faith comes to us as our head and our elder brother. We ought to quicken our desires: "O Lord Jesus," we ought to say with the priest at the time of Holy Communion, "do not look upon my sins, which I detest, but upon the faith of your Church, which tells me you are here present, veiled by the Host, in order to come to me. You have the power, O Christ Jesus, to draw me wholly to yourself, in order to transform me

---

[1] See John 6:53-70.

[2] *"Praestet fides supplementum sensuum defectui"* (Hymn, *Pange lingua*).

into you. I give myself up to you, whole and entire, so that you may make yourself the Master of the whole of my being and the whole of my activity, so that I now may only live by you, through you, for you." If we ask for this grace, we may be certain that Christ will grant it to us; that is why we ought to go so far as to beg Him for it persistently, setting no bounds to our holy desires.

If we took account of the riches this Sacrament possesses—and they are infinite, seeing that it consists of Christ Himself,[1] if we knew all the fruits that the coming of Christ can produce in us, we would have a huge desire to see them become reality in us. All the fruits of the Redemption are included in that coming so as to become ours: "That we may ever perceive within us the fruit of your redemption."[2] Our Lord wants, has an intense wish, to make us partake of it; but He asks that we dilate our hearts through desire and trust. "God knows certainly what we are in need of," says St. Augustine, "but He wants our desire to be set aflame in prayer, in order to make us more capable of receiving what He prepares for us. We shall have a greater capacity to receive the Bread of Life to the extent that our faith in that Life becomes greater, our trust firmer, our desire more ardent."[3] "Open your mouth wide, and I will fill it," Christ says to us, as God said of old to the psalmist.[4] "Open up yourself by faith, by trust, by love, by holy desires, by abandonment to me, and I will fill you." "With what, Lord?" "With myself. I will give myself to you, whole and entire, with my humanity

---

[1] "The utility of this sacrament is great and universal ... for, being the sacrament of the Passion of the Lord, it consists indeed of Christ who has suffered; and from this it follows that everything that is the effect of the Lord's Passion is likewise entirely the effect of this sacrament": St Thomas, *In Johann. Evang.*, c. VI, lect. 6. And again: "The effect which the Passion of Christ has produced in the world, this sacrament produces in man": III, q. LXXIX, a. 1.

[2] Prayer for the Feast of Corpus Christi.

[3] *Epist.* CXXX, c. 8. St. Augustine says that of life eternal, but one can apply it perfectly to the Eucharist which is the very pledge of that life: "is given to us as a pledge of future glory" (Antiphon of Vespers for the Feast of Corpus Christi).

[4] Ps. 80 (81):11.

and my divinity, with the fruit of my mysteries, the merit of my labors, the satisfaction of my sufferings and the price of my Passion. I will come down within you, as of old I came down upon the earth, to "destroy the works of the devil" there;[1] to render there, with you, a divine homage to my Father. I will make you partake of the treasures of my divinity, of the eternal life which I have from my Father, and which my Father wants me to communicate to you in order that you may resemble me. I will shower my grace upon you so as to become, myself, your wisdom, your sanctification, your way, your truth, your life. You shall become another "Myself," and—like me, and because of me—be the object of my Father's delight. "Open your mouth wide, and I will fill it."

What more is needed than these words to make us deliver ourselves up to Christ so that His grace may invade us, and that He may accomplish in us everything He wills? And see how great a return Christ Jesus makes to us for what we give to Him, how He increases in us the faith, the trust, the love, that we bring in order to receive Him. He is the Word, the Eternal Utterance, who repeats the Divine secrets to us in the depths of our hearts and who floods us with His light, for He "enlightens every man who comes into the world."[2] He is also the one who came down upon the earth for our salvation and who, in this Eucharistic uniting, will apply to us the infinite merits of His death. What invincible assurance and what peace Jesus brings to the soul by coming to her! Not content with applying His satisfactions to her, He gives her the pledge of future life: "a pledge of future glory." Finally, He vivifies love. Love lives by union. This is truly the sacrament of super-natural life and growth. Each Communion well made brings us closer and closer to our Model. Especially does it make us enter more deeply into the knowledge, love and practice of the mystery of our

[1] 1 John 3:8.   [2] John 1:9.

predestination and adoption in Christ Jesus, our elder brother. It perfects in us the grace of Divine sonship.

So important is this point, that I want to insist on it. All our holiness comes down to participating, through grace, in the Divine Sonship of Christ Jesus; to being, through super-natural adoption, what Christ is by nature. The wider this participation is, the higher is our holiness. Now, what is it that gives us this participation, what is it that makes us children of God? St. John tells us: it is the faith with which we receive Christ, wellspring and source of all grace: "To as many as received Him He gave the power of becoming sons of God; to those who believe in His name."[1] Therefore, the deeper our faith is when we receive Christ, the more Christ communicates to us what of His is higher— His state of Son of God, and consequently the greater is the measure of our participation in His Divine Sonship.

Now, there is no action where our faith can be exercised with more intensity than in Holy Communion; there is no homage of faith more sublime than that of believing in Christ whose divinity and humanity are hidden beneath the appearances of the Host. When the Jews saw Christ working miracles of a striking kind, for example multiplying loaves of bread in the desert, they were inclined, through the extraordinary character of these events, to admit the divinity of Jesus. That was an act of faith, but of an ordinary degree. When Our Lord said to the Jews: "I am the bread of life, the bread come down from heaven," faith in these words was already a higher one: and indeed we see a good many of His hearers no longer being capable of such an act, and leaving Our Lord for ever. But when Christ Jesus, holding out a bit of bread, a little wine, says to us: "This is my body," "This is my blood," and our intellect, putting aside all the senses tell it, accepts that word of Christ and our will leads us to the holy table with reverence and

---

[1] John 1:12.

love in order to put that adhesion into practice, we perform the deepest and most absolute act of faith there can be.

Thus, to receive Christ in the Eucharist is to make a statement of faith of the largest kind, and consequently it is to share in highest possible measure in the Divine Sonship of Christ. And that is why each Communion well made is for us so vital and so fruitful: not only because it is Christ Himself we receive; but, also, because faith, which is the only thing that permits us to receive Christ, finds nowhere to manifest itself with greater scope or liveliness. For it is not only the intellect that, here, makes an act of faith; it is our whole being that translates this act into practice by our approaching the altar.

Eucharistic Communion is therefore *the most perfect act of our Divine adoption.* There is no time when we can be more justly entitled to say to our Father in heaven: "O Heavenly Father, I abide in your Son Jesus, and your Son abides in me. Your Son, proceeding from you, receives communication of your Divine life, in its fullness. I have received your Son with faith. At that time, faith tells me, I am with Him. And since I share in His life, look at me in Him, through Him, with Him, as the Son in whom you are well pleased." What graces, what lights, what strengths will such a prayer not bring to a child of God! What superabundance of the Divine life, what closeness of union, what depth of adoption does such a faith not communicate to us! We are touching here the culminating point, on earth, of the Divine adoption.

As for the "formulas" that help us towards the immediate preparation for this union with Jesus, one cannot lay down any of these to the exclusion of others. The needs, like the aptitudes, of souls vary infinitely.

Some are attached to following the prayers and the gestures of the priest who offers the Holy Sacrifice, before they approach the holy table at Communion time during the Mass. That, when it is possible, is the best way to dispose oneself immediately for the reception of Christ.

The prayers which our mother, Holy Church, puts on the priest's lips so that he may prepare himself to receive Christ—why should they not be good for the simple faithful? By preparing oneself in that way, one unites oneself more directly with Christ's Sacrifice and with the intentions of His sacred heart. The Missal, moreover, contains—for example, in the *Gloria*—wonderful expressions of faith, of trust, of love. "We praise you, we bless you, we adore you, we glorify you, we give you thanks ... Lord Jesus Christ"; "Lamb of God ... you who take away the sins of the world, have mercy on us ... receive our prayer"; "You who are seated at the right hand of the Father, have mercy on us." What an act of faith! This fragment of bread I am about to receive consists of Him who is seated on the right hand of the Heavenly Father, in eternal glory with the Father and the Holy Spirit: "you only are holy ... you only are the most high, O Jesus Christ, with the Holy Spirit, in the glory of God the Father."

Other people re-read the sixth chapter of St. John's Gospel, intermingling with it aspirations of faith, hope and charity—that chapter where the apostle relates the Eucharistic promises. People can also nourish their devotion from the fourth book of *The Imitation of Christ* which is specially devoted to the mystery of the altar; or, again, make use of formulas contained in approved works of piety.[1]

In this, everyone can follow the inclination of their own preferences. From the time when mind and heart join together in the words the lips express; from the time, above all, when the soul dilates its capacity for union by a living faith, a deep reverence, an absolute trust, an ardent desire and love, and especially a generous abandonment to the will of Christ Jesus—from *then*, all is well. The only thing remaining is to receive the Divine gift.

---

[1] [*Translator's note*: All this was written at a time when for the persons in the pew there were lengthy periods of silence which gave each the space to lift up mind and heart individually. Modern liturgists stress the community aspect of doing the same things together.]

7. *Thanksgiving* after Holy Communion: *"All things that are mine are yours, and yours are mine."*

I WILL LEAVE the same latitude for *thanksgiving*. Some, in silence, adore the Divine Word within them. The humanity we receive is the humanity of the Eternal Word: through that humanity we enter into communion with the Word who, from the heart's-embrace of the Father, has come down into us. The Word, by essence, belongs entirely to His Father; He has everything from Him, without on that account being less than His Father. But He relates everything back to His Father: "I ... draw life from the Father";[1] His essence is to live by the Father. When we are united in that way with Him and we deliver ourselves up to Him, then, through the faith we have in Him, He carries us to the very Holy of Holies: "reaching even behind the veil."[2] There, we can unite ourselves with those acts of intense adoration which the sacred humanity of Christ renders to the Trinity. We are so united to Christ at that time, that we are able to make our own the actions of His sacred humanity, and to render to the Eternal Father, in union with the Holy Spirit, acts of homage that are extremely pleasing. Christ becomes, Himself, our thanksgiving, our *Eucharist*: He it is (let us never forget) who supplies for all our weaknesses, all our infirmities, all our miseries. What limitless confidence should this presence of Christ in the soul not engender!

Again, we can lend our lips to sing the hymn of creation; creation that gets its life from the Word, so that all the beings that have been made by the Word—"It was through Him that all things came into being, and without Him came nothing that has come to be"[3]—shall, in and through the Word, sing of the glory of God. That is what the priest does when he comes down from the altar. The Church, the spouse of Christ, who knows better than anyone the secrets of her Divine Spouse, makes the priest sing an inner hymn of thanksgiving[4]

---

[1] John 6:57 (Jerus.)   [2] Hebr. 6:19.   [3] John 1:3 (Knox).
[4] [*Translator's note*: The reference here is to a passage from the third chapter of the Book of Daniel which appears in the Office of Lauds. See vv. 57-87.]

in the sanctuary of his soul where the Word is dwelling. The soul brings the whole of creation to the feet of its Lord and God, so that He may receive the homage of every being, living or inanimate: "All you works of the Lord, bless the Lord: praise and exalt him above all for ever. Angels of the Lord, bless the Lord; you heavens, bless the Lord. Sun and moon, stars of the sky, bless the Lord. Rains and dews, winds and tempests, fire and flame, cold and heat, dew and rime, frost and chill, ice and snow, O bless the Lord. Night and day, light and dark, lightning and black clouds, O bless Him." After that, the priest invites the earth, the mountains and the hills, the plants, the seas and the rivers; the fish, the birds, the wild beasts; men, priests, the humble of heart, the holy—invites them to give glory to the Trinity, to whom all honor is rendered by the sacred humanity of Jesus. What a wonderful hymn is that of the entire creation sung in this way by the priest, at that time when he is united to the Eternal High Priest, to the one and only Mediator, to the Divine Word by whom everything has been created!

Others, like Mary Magdalene seated at the feet of Jesus, converse familiarly with Him, listening to what He says in the depths of the soul, wholly prepared to give Him what He asks. For, at this time when the Divine light is within us, Jesus often shows the generous soul what He requires of her. St. Teresa of Avila says: "It is a sovereignly precious time, this hour that follows Holy Communion; at that time the Divine Master is pleased to instruct us; so let us lend an ear, and, in gratitude for His deigning to teach us His lessons, let us kiss His feet and entreat Him not to go away from us."[1]

One can also read again, slowly, as if one were listening to Christ, the magnificent discourse after the Last Supper, at which Jesus had instituted this sacrament: "Do you not believe"—do you not believe on my word—"that I am in the Father and the Father in me?" ... "He who keeps my commandments, he it is who loves me." And: "he who loves

---

[1] *The Way of Perfection*, Ch. XXV.

me will be loved by my Father, and I will love him and manifest myself to him." ... "As the Father has loved me, I also have loved you. Abide in my love." ... "These things I have spoken to you that my joy may be in you, and that your joy may be made full." ... "I have called you "friends" because all things that I have heard from my Father I have made known to you." ... "The Father Himself loves you, because you have loved me and have believed that I came from the Father." ... "These things I have spoken to you that in me you may have peace. In the world you will have affliction. But take courage"—have trust in me—"I have overcome the world."[1]

Or again, we can mentally converse with Our Lord, as if we were at the foot of the cross; or pray vocally by reciting psalms that relate to the Eucharist. "The Lord is my shepherd; I shall not want. In verdant pastures He gives me repose. Beside restful waters He leads me; He refreshes my soul.... Even though I walk in the dark valley"—in the midst of the shadow of death—I shall "fear no evil," for you, Lord, "are at my side."[2]

All these attitudes of soul are excellent; the inspiration of the Holy Spirit varies endlessly. The main thing is that we recognize the greatness of the Divine gift declared by St. Paul to be "inexpressible";[3] that, for our own needs and the needs of all our brethren, the needs of the whole Church, we draw upon the treasures of this infinite gift. For "the Father loves the Son, and has given all things into His hand,"[4] to be communicated to us. Christ gives everything by giving Himself. We too—we ought to give everything, by repeating to Him, from the depths of our heart, the words He Himself said: "I do always the things that are pleasing to Him,"[5] by ourselves saying: "I wish always to do what is pleasing to you": or again those words spoken by Jesus to His Father at the Last Supper, words that are the very expression of perfect union: "All things that are mine are yours, and yours are mine."[6]

---

[1] John chs. 14 (vv. 10, 21); 15 (vv. 9, 11, 15), all Cfy; 16 (vv. 27, RSV, Cath., 33, Cfy).
[2] Ps. 22 (23):1-4 (St P.) [3] 2 Cor. 9:15 (Jerus.) [4] John 3:35.
[5] John 8:29. [6] John 17:10.

That indeed, I repeat, is the distinctive fruit of the Eucharist: the identification of ourselves with Christ, through faith and love. If you receive the body of Christ well, St. Augustine so admirably says, you are what you receive.[1]

No doubt, the act itself of Holy Communion is transitory and passing; but the effect it produces—the union with Christ, the Life of the soul—is, of its nature, permanent; it continues as long as, and in the measure that, we wish. The Eucharist is the sacrament of life only because it is the sacrament of union; it is necessary that we "*abide* in Jesus, and Jesus *abide* in us."[2] Let us, then, not allow the fruit of the Eucharistic reception and union to diminish in the course of the day, through our lack of serious thought, our distractions, our curiosity, our vanity, our pursuit of self-love. It is a Living Bread we have received, a Bread of Life, a Bread that makes us live. It is works of life, works of a child of God, that we must do each day after having been nourished by this Divine Bread in order to be transformed into Him. For "he who says that he abides in Christ ought to live as Christ Himself lived."[3]

And let us not say, through lack of generosity, in order to excuse our sloth—let us not say that we are weak. That is true, more true even than we think. But beside that abyss (and it is an abyss) of our weakness, which moreover is perfectly compatible with good will and which Our Lord knows better than we do, there is another abyss—that of the merits and treasures of Christ. And, through Holy Communion, this Christ is ours.

---

[1] "The distinctive power here understood is that of producing unity, in such a way that as we are drawn into His body and are made His members, we are what we receive": *Sermo* LVII, c. 7.   [2] See John 15:5.

[3] See 1 John 2:6. This is what the Church makes us ask, in the Mass of the Second Sunday after Pentecost: "May the offering to be dedicated to your name"—may this oblation of your Divine Son—"purify us, O Lord, and carry us on, from day to day"—raise us, daily—"to the practice of a heavenly life."

CHAPTER NINE

THE VOICE OF THE SPOUSE:
VOX SPONSAE

INTRODUCTION: *Divine Praise* **forms an essential part of the sanctifying mission entrusted by Christ to the Church.**

AS WE HAVE SEEN, the Holy Sacrifice in which the soul participates through sacramental Communion forms the center of our religion. It consists, in one and the same act, of the remembrance, the renewal and the application of the immolation of Calvary.

But the Mass does not on its own replace all the religious acts we ought to carry out. Although it is the most perfect homage we could render to God, and although it contains in itself the substance and the power of every homage there is, it is nevertheless not the only homage. What else do we owe to God? The homage of prayer, at one time public, at another personal. In the talk that follows this one I will speak to you about private prayer, about praying. Let us see, in the present talk, what the homage of *public* prayer consists of.

If you read the letters of St. Paul, you will see that he exhorts us to it on more than one occasion. "Under the inspiration of grace," he writes to the Colossians, "may your hearts be poured out to God in psalms, hymns and spiritual songs."[1] And again: "Join together in psalms, hymns

---

[1] See Col. 3:16.

and spiritual songs, singing and chanting from the depths of your hearts in honor of the Lord, constantly giving thanks for all things to God the Father, in the name of our Lord Jesus Christ."[1] He himself, in prison, with his companion Silas, "broke the silence of the night by offering to God, with a happy heart, praises for their torments, thanksgiving for their wounds."[2] "At midnight Paul and Silas were praying, singing the praises of God."[3]

This divine praise is intimately linked with the Holy Sacrifice and we see that Our Lord wished to show us that by His own example. The Gospel writers tell us, indeed, that Christ did not leave the supperroom after the institution of the Eucharist without having recited a hymn of praise: "After reciting a hymn...."[4] Public prayer totally revolves around the Sacrifice of the Altar; it is there that it finds its best support; from there that it draws its greatest worth in the sight of God, because it is presented to Him by the Church, in the name of her Spouse the eternal High Priest, Bridge between man and God—the High Priest who by His Sacrifice, ceaselessly renewed, has merited that all glory and honor shall return to the Father in the unity of the Holy Spirit: "Through Him, and with Him, and in Him, is to you ... all honor and glory."[5]

Let us, then, see what it consists of, this homage of the official prayer of the Church; and how, besides constituting a work very pleasing to God, it becomes for us a pure and abundant wellspring of union with Christ and of eternal life.

---

[1] See Eph. 5:19-20.   [2] Bossuet, *Panégyrique de S. Paul.*   [3] Acts 16:25.
[4] Matt. 26:30; Mark 14:26.   [5] Canon of the Mass.

1. **The Eternal** *Word — Divine Hymn.* **The Incarnation** *associates humanity* **with this Hymn.**

BEFORE ASCENDING into heaven, Christ Jesus bequeathed to His Church its greatest treasure: the mission of continuing His work here below.[1] That work, you know, is a twofold one: it is a work of praise in regard to the Eternal Father, a work of salvation in regard to men. It was for us that the Word became flesh: "For us men and for our salvation He came down from heaven."[2] This is true; and yet that very work of our redemption is a work that Christ accomplishes only because He loves His Father: "That the world may know that I love the Father...."[3]

That is the mission the Church receives from Christ. She receives the sacraments and the privilege of infallibility so as to sanctify men; but she also participates in the religion[4] of Christ towards His Father so as to continue here below the homage of praise that Christ, in His sacred humanity, offered to His Father.

Christ Jesus, in this as in everything, is our model. Let us contemplate for a moment the Word Incarnate. Christ is, first of all, the one and only Son of the Father, the Eternal Word. In the adorable Trinity He is the Utterance by which the Father eternally tells of all that He, the Father, is. The Word is the living expression of all the perfections of the Father, "the very stamp of His nature,"[5] says St. Paul, and "the brightness of His glory."[6] The Father contemplates His Word, His Son; He sees in Him the perfect, substantial and living image of Himself. Such is the essential glory the Father receives. If God had created

---

[1] See, above, the talk on *The Church* (page 107).

[2] Nicene Creed.   [3] John 14:31.

[4] [*Translator's note*: "religion": Marmion, who was a Latinist, has not far from his mind the derivation of this word from "*ligo*," to bind — here, a binding of heart, a "reverence for, and desire to please" His Father (Oxford English Dictionary). It is in accordance with this that Marmion's French word "*religion*," in relation to Christ and His Father, is hereafter reproduced in translation.]

[5] Hebr. 1:3 (RSV, Cath.)   [6] Hebr. 1:3.

nothing, had left all things in a state of possibility, He would nonetheless have had His essential and infinite glory. The eternal Utterance,
the Word—simply in being what He is—is like a Divine Hymn, a
living Hymn, who sings the praise of the Father by expressing the
plenitude of the Father's perfections. He is the Infinite Hymn, ceaselessly sounding in the heart's-embrace of the Father.

In taking human nature, the Word remains what He was: "That
which He was, He remained";[1] He does not cease to be the only Son,
the complete image of the perfections of the Father; He does not cease
to be, in Himself, the living glorification of His Father. The Infinite
Hymn, as sung from all eternity, began to be sung on earth when the
Word became incarnate. By the Incarnation, humanity is, as it were,
carried along by the Word into this work of glorification. That Hymn
sung in the sanctuary of the Divinity is prolonged by the Incarnate
Word in His humanity.

Upon the lips of Christ Jesus, true man as well as true God, this
Hymn takes on a human expression, human accents; as also a character
of adoration that the Word, equal to the Father, could not, *as* the
Word, render to Him. However, if the expression of this Hymn is
human, its perfection is altogether holy and of Divine price; it has an
infinite value. Who among us could assess the majesty of what bound
Christ to His Father, of what He rendered to Him? Who could recount
anything of the hymn of praise that Jesus sang within Him, in His
thrice-holy soul, to the glory of His Father? The soul of Christ contemplated the Divine perfections in a continuous vision, and from this contemplation was born a plenitude of reverent love and a perfect adoration; from this contemplation sprang forth sublime praise. At the end
of His life on earth Christ Jesus addresses His Father: He declares that
everything He has done has been to glorify Him; that is the foremost
work of His life, and He has perfectly fulfilled it: Father, "I have glori-

[1] Antiphon of the Feast of the Circumcision.

fied you on earth; I have accomplished the work that you have given me to do."[1]

But note well that in personally uniting our nature to Himself, the Word has (so to say) incorporated into Himself the whole of humanity. He has associated all of humanity, as a matter of right and in principle, with the perfect praise He gives to His Father. Here again, we have received of the fullness of Christ. And this in such a way that, in Christ and through Christ, every Christian soul, united to Him by grace, ought to sing the Divine praises. Christ is our head, all the baptized are the members of His mystical body: in Him, and through Him, we should render to God all glory and honor.

Christ has left us a share of praise to carry out, just as He has given us a share of suffering to bear. Do our adoration and praise add anything to the merit and perfection of Christ's adoration and praise? Certainly not. But Christ has willed that, through the Incarnation, the whole of humanity, of which He stands in the place, should as a matter of right be indissolubly united with all His circumstances and all His mysteries. Never forget: He makes Himself but one with us; His adoration and praise He renders to His Father in our favor, but also in our name. And that is why the Church, which is His mystical body, has to associate herself here below with this work of reverent love, and of praise, that the humanity of Christ renders His Father *in splendoribus sanctorum*, "in the brightness of the saints."[2] The Church, following the example of her Spouse, must offer what St. Paul calls the "sacrifice of praise"[3] which the infinite perfections of the Eternal Father deserve.

---

[1] John 17:4.   [2] Ps. 109 (110):3.   [3] Hebr. 13:15.

2. *The Church charged with organizing the public worship of her*
   Spouse under the guidance of the Holy Spirit. The use she has
   made of the *psalms* in that. How those inspired hymns *exalt the*
   Divine perfections, express our needs, speak to us of Christ.

LET US SEE how the Church, guided in this by the Holy Spirit, carries
out her mission.

At the center of her religion she places the Holy Sacrifice of the
Mass, a true sacrifice which renews the work of our redemption on
Calvary and applies its fruits. She accompanies this oblation with
sacred ceremonies which she carefully regulates and which are like the
protocol of the court of the King of kings; she surrounds it with a
collection of readings, hymns, psalms, that serve as preparation or as
thanksgiving for the Eucharistic immolation.

This collection constitutes "the Divine Office." As you know, the
Church imposes the reciting of it as a grave obligation on those whom
Christ, by the sacrament of Holy Orders, has made official partici-
pants in His eternal priesthood. As for the elements, the "formulas," of
her praise, the Church herself puts them together: such as hymns from
the pen of Doctors of the Church, who are also admirable saints—St.
Ambrose for instance; but above all she borrows them from the books
of sacred scripture, from the books inspired by God Himself. St. Paul
tells us that we do not know how we ought to pray;[1] but, he says, the
Holy Spirit "Himself expresses our plea in a way that could never be
put into words."[2] That is to say, only God knows how we ought to
make our prayer to Him. This is true of prayer that asks for something; but above all it is true of prayer of praise and thanksgiving.
Only God knows how He should be praised. The most magnificent

---

[1] [*Translator's note*: This is how some versions of the biblical text have it, and
Marmion himself. Other versions have "*When* we do not know how to pray...."]

[2] Rom. 8:26 (Jerus.) [*Translator's note*: RSV Cath. has the lovely, but perhaps
slightly ambiguous, wording "with sighs too deep for words"—this, surely, much
better than the "unutterable groanings" of other versions.]

conceptions of God that come from our intellects are human conceptions. To praise God fittingly, God Himself must compose the terms of
these praises. And that is why the Church puts those psalms on our lips
as the most perfect praise, after the Holy Sacrifice, that we are able to
offer to God.[1]

Read those sacred pages, and you will see how these hymns,
inspired by the Holy Spirit, *recount, proclaim, exalt all the Divine
perfections*.[2] The hymn of the Eternal Word in the Blessed Trinity is
simple, and yet infinite; but on the lips of us creatures, incapable of
comprehending the infinite, the praises are multiplied and repeated.
With a wonderful richness and a great variety of expression, the psalms
sing, by turns, of the power, magnificence, holiness, justice, goodness,
mercy, beauty, of God. "Whatever He wills, He does."[3] "For He spoke,
and they were made; He commanded and they were created...."[4] "O
Lord, our Lord, how glorious is your name over all the earth!"[5] "You
have made all things in wisdom...."[6] "High above all nations is the
Lord."[7] "All nations are before Him as if they had no being at all."[8]
"Above the heavens is His glory. Who is like the Lord, our God?"[9]
"The mountains melt like wax before the Lord.... The heavens
proclaim His justice, and all peoples see His glory."[10] "May the glory
of the Lord endure for ever: the Lord shall rejoice in His works. He
looks upon the earth, and makes it tremble: He touches the mountains, and they smoke"[11]—like incense.

---

[1] "So that He may be praised properly, God has praised Himself; and because
He has deigned to praise Himself, man has discovered how to praise Him": St. Augustine, *Enarr. in Ps.* 144.

[2] See the excellent little volume *Le livre des psaumes*, a translation of the Book of
Psalms by the Abbé Crampon (Tournai, Desclée). It contains, moreover, translations
of the principal inspired *Hymns* of which the Church makes use. There are some
good tables at the end of it.

[3] Ps. 113(B) (115):3 [11] (St P.); cf. Ps. 134 (135):6; Ecclesiastes 8:3.

[4] Ps. 32 (33):9; 148:5.   [5] Ps. 8:1 (St P.)   [6] Ps. 103 (104):24.

[7] Ps. 112 (113):4 (St P.)   [8] Isa. 40:17; cf. Ps. 61 (62):9 (10).   [9] Ps. 112 (113):4-5 (St P.)

[10] Ps. 96 (97):5-6 (St P.)   [11] Ps. 103 (104):31-32.

And see in what terms the psalms speak to us of the goodness, of the mercy, of the Lord. The Lord "is faithful in all His words,"[1] is "merciful and gracious,"[2] is "good to all and compassionate toward all His works."[3] "The Lord is near to all who call upon Him, to all who call upon Him in truth"[4]—with a sincere heart. "He fulfills the desire of those who fear Him, He hears their cry and saves them. The Lord keeps all who love Him...."[5] "Let all that is within me bless His holy name,"[6] "for His mercy endures for ever."[7]

Those are some of the accents the Holy Spirit Himself puts on our lips. Let us love to make use of those inspired accents in order to praise God; let us say again with the psalmist: "I will praise the Lord all my life; I will sing praise to my God while I live"[8]—until my last breath. A soul who loves God experiences, indeed, a need to praise Him, to bless Him, to exalt His perfections. Such a soul takes pleasure in those perfections, wishes to extol them as they deserve.[9] It is a torment for that soul to feel powerless to extol them, and that is why so often in the psalms we invite all things created to praise God with us. "Let the heavens declare His power, let the works of His hands manifest His greatness";[10] "Praise the Lord, all you nations; glorify Him, all you peoples,"[11] because He is "the Lord of lords."[12] For the soul, these are so many acts of perfect love, of pure delight in Him, that are extremely pleasing to God.

At the same time as they extol the Divine perfections, the psalms *express wonderfully the feelings and needs of our souls.* The psalms can

---

[1] Ps. 144 (145):13.   [2] Ps. 102 (103):8 (St P.)   [3] Ps. 144 (145):9 (St P.)
[4] Ps. 144 (145):18 (St P.)   [5] Ps. 144 (145):19-20 (St P.)   [6] Ps. 102 (103):1.
[7] Ps. 117 (118):1-4; Ps. 135 (136), passim (St P.)   [8] Ps. 145 (146):2 (St P.)
[9] Cf. *Treatise on the Love of God,* by St. Francis de Sales, Book V, chs. 7, 8 and 9.
[10] See Ps. 18 (19):2. [*Translator's note*: Marmion seems clearly to have this psalm and verse in mind, even though it is not an exhortation as he expresses it, but a statement: "The heavens declare the glory of God...."]
[11] Ps. 116 (117):1 (St P.)   [12] Ps. 135 (136):3.

weep and rejoice; can desire and beg.[1] There is no inner disposition of our soul that they could not express. The Church well knows our needs, and that is why, like an attentive mother, she puts on our lips all those aspirations, so deep and ardent, of repentance, trust, joy, love, delight, that are inspired by the Holy Spirit Himself. "Have mercy on me, O God, in your goodness; in the greatness of your compassion," for "against you only have I sinned."[2] "My soul has hoped in the Lord … because with the Lord there is mercy: and with Him plentiful redemption."[3] "O God, come to my assistance; O Lord make haste to help me. Let them be confounded and ashamed"—reduced to silence—those "that seek my soul,"[4] my enemies. "You are my strength and my refuge";[5] "Hide me under the shelter of your wings."[6] "For though I should walk in the midst of the shadow of death, I will fear no evils, for you are with me."[7] "You are with me"—what an act of confidence!

Sometimes, too, we feel a need to tell God how much we thirst for Him, and how we wish to seek but Him alone. Here, again, we find in the psalms the most appropriate expression of our feelings. O God, you are "my salvation and my glory."[8] "Whom have I in heaven but you? And there is nothing upon earth that I desire besides you."[9] "You are the God of my heart, and the God that is my portion"—my inheritance— "for ever."[10] "With my whole heart have I sought after you";[11] "I will love you, O Lord, my strength."[12] You shall make me "joyful in gladness with your countenance,"[13] for "at your right hand are delights," for evermore.[14] "As the hind longs for the running waters, so my soul longs for you, O God.... When shall I go and behold the face of God?"[15] "*Satiabor cum apparuerit gloria tua*"—"I shall be satisfied

---

[1] St. Augustine, *Enarr. in Ps.* 30; *sermo* III, n. 1.   [2] Ps. 50 (51), vv. 1, 6 (St P.)
[3] Ps. 129 (130): 5-7.   [4] Ps. 69 (70):2-3.   [5] Ps. 30 (31):4.
[6] Ps. 16 (17):8 (Knox).   [7] Ps. 22 (23):4.   [8] Ps. 61 (62):8.
[9] Ps. 72 (73):25 (RSV, Cath.)   [10] Ps. 72 (73):26.
[11] Ps. 118 (119):10; cf. Ps. 9 (9-10):2; Ps. 110 (111):1; Ps. 137 (138):1.
[12] Ps. 17 (18):1.   [13] Ps. 20 (21):7.   [14] Ps. 15 (16):11.   [15] Ps. 41 (42):2-3 (St P.)

when your glory shall appear."[1] Where else can one find accents as profound for telling God the ardent desires of our souls?

Finally—and this is the highest motive the Church has for choosing them—the psalms, like all the inspired books, *speak to us of Christ.* To employ the beautiful expression of an author of early times, the Law— which is to say the Old Testament—"was bearing Christ in its womb."[2] I showed you this in speaking of the Eucharist. Everything was symbol and figure for the Jews, says St. Paul;[3] the reality announced by the prophets, prefigured by the sacrifices, symbolized by so many rites, was the Word Incarnate and His work of redemption. And that is especially true of the psalms. You know that David, to whom a number of the sacred hymns refer, was a figure of the Messiah, just as Jerusalem, which is so often mentioned in the psalms, is a type of the Church. Our Lord said to His apostles: "Everything written about me in ... the psalms must be fulfilled."[4] They are full of Christ; His divinity, His humanity, a good few of the circumstances of His life, and details of His death, are indicated with sure strokes. "The Lord has said to me: 'You are my Son, this day have I begotten you.'"[5] "Before the day-star I begot you."[6] "With your comeliness and your beauty ... reign. Because of truth, and meekness, and justice...."[7] "The kings of the Arabians and of Saba shall bring gifts: and all kings of the earth shall adore Him."[8] "God, your God, has anointed you with the oil of gladness."[9] "You are a priest for ever, according to the order of Melchizedek."[10] "He will have pity on the poor and needy,"[11] be "the rescuer of the afflicted man from those too strong for him."[12]

---

[1] Ps. 16 (17):15.
[2] Those words are found in a sermon attributed to St. Augustine (*Œuvres*, Appx., CXCVI); but the substance of this sermon is from Faustus of Riez.   [3] E.g. Hebr. 9:9.
[4] Luke 24:44 (RSV, Cath.)   [5] Ps. 2:7.   [6] Ps. 109 (110):3.
[7] Ps. 44 (45):5.   [8] Ps. 71 (72):10-11.   [9] Ps. 44 (45):8.
[10] Ps. 109 (110):4.   [11] See Ps. 71 (72):12-13.   [12] Ps. 34 (35):10 (St P.)

Listen to the voice of Christ in the accents that follow—Christ Himself who speaks to us of His sorrows and His humiliations: "Zeal for your house consumes me, and the insults of those who blaspheme you fall upon me."[1] "They have pierced my hands and my feet."[2] "They gave me gall for my food, and in my thirst they gave me vinegar to drink."[3] "They divide my garments among them, and for my vesture they cast lots."[4]

Then, we hear the psalmist extol the triumph of Christ the conqueror: "The stone which the builders rejected has become the cornerstone."[5] "Nor will you suffer your faithful one"—you will not allow the flesh of Christ—"to undergo corruption."[6] "You have ascended on high, you have led captivity captive"[7]—ascended with victorious captives tied to His chariot. "Lift up your gates, O you princes, and be lifted up, O eternal gates: and the King of Glory shall enter in"[8]—enter into heaven, where He will be seated at the right hand of the Lord, for ever: "The Lord said to my Lord: 'Sit at my right hand.'"[9] "Let His name be blessed for evermore: His name continues before the sun"—shall remain as long as the sun shall shine forth. "And in Him shall all the tribes of the earth be blessed: all nations shall magnify Him"[10]—hold in high honor His perfections.

You see how all these features apply wonderfully to Christ Jesus. During His mortal life He most certainly recited or sang these hymns composed by the Holy Spirit. Indeed, He alone was able to sing them with all the truth they contained about His own Divine Person.

And now that Christ, having accomplished all, is ascended into His glory, the Church has gathered up these hymns so as through them to offer daily praise to her Divine Spouse and to the Blessed Trinity: "Holy Church, throughout all the world, acknowledges you."[11] For the

---

[1] Ps. 68 (69):10 (St P.) [2] Ps. 21 (22):17 (St P.) [3] Ps. 68 (69):22.
[4] Ps. 21 (22):19 (St P.) [5] Ps. 117 (118):22 (St P.) [6] Ps. 15 (16):10 (St P.)
[7] Ps. 67 (68):19. [8] Ps. 23 (24):7. [9] Ps. 109 (110):1 (St P.)
[10] Ps. 71 (72):17. [11] Hymn, *Te Deum.*

Church concludes all the psalms with the same chant: "Glory be to the Father, and to the Son, and to the Holy Spirit"—or according to another formula: "Glory be to the Father, through the Son, in the Holy Spirit"—"as it was in the beginning, is now and ever shall be, world without end, Amen."[1] The Church wishes to refer all glory to the Blessed Trinity, first beginning and last end of all that exists; she associates herself, through faith and love, with the eternal praise the Word renders to His Father in being the Pattern of all creation.

3.   Great *power of intercession* of this praise on the lips of the Church, the spouse.

BUT IT IS ON CHRIST that the Church leans. All her prayers end by recalling entitlements from her Spouse: "Through Our Lord Jesus Christ." It is on Him, seated now at the right hand of His Father and reigning with the Father and the Holy Spirit, that the Church rests her appeal: Our Lord Jesus Christ, "who with you lives and reigns...." Christ is the Bridegroom and the Church is the Bride, as St. Paul says. What here is the Bride's dowry? It is her woes, her weaknesses, but also her heart to love with, and her mouth with which to praise. And what does the Bridegroom bring? His satisfactions, His merits, His Precious Blood, all his riches. Christ, being united with the Church, gives to her His power of adoring and praising God. The Church joins herself to Jesus and leans upon Him for support. In seeing her, the angels ask themselves: "Who is this that comes up from the desert"—from the desert, but "flowing with delights, leaning upon her beloved?"[2] It is the Church, who, from the desert of her native poverty, goes up towards God, adorned like a virgin with the glorious riches her Spouse gives her. And in the name of Christ, with Him, she offers the adoration and

---

[1] Cf. St. Leo, *Sermo* I on the Nativity of the Lord: "Let us give thanks to God the Father through His Son in the Holy Spirit."   [2] Song of Songs 8:5.

praise of all her children to the Heavenly Father. This praise is "*Vox Sponsae*," the voice of the Bride—the voice that delights the Bridegroom. It is the hymn of praise sung by the Church in union with Christ, and that is why, when we unite ourselves with it in faith and trust, it is so pleasing to Christ Jesus: "Your voice is sweet,"[1] its value surpasses that of all our private prayers in God's sight. See her there, this spouse, proud of her position and station, assured of rights which are eternal and have been sovereignly won by her Divine Spouse—see her boldly enter into the sanctuary of the Divinity, where Christ her Head and Spouse, ever living, prays for us. Between the two of them there is the distance from earth to heaven, but the Church crosses that distance through faith, and she blends her voice with that of Christ in the heart's-embrace of the Father, *in sinu Patris*. It is one and the same prayer, this prayer of Jesus united to His mystical body and rendering, with her, one and the same homage to the Adorable Trinity. How could such a prayer *not* be pleasing to God, seeing that He receives it from Christ? What power will it not have over the heart of God? How could such praise not be a source of graces for the Church and for all her children? It is Christ who prays, and Christ ever has the right to have His prayer granted: "I knew that you always hear me."[2]

Look how already, in the Old Testament, the prayer of the leader of the people of Israel was all-powerful over the heart of God; and yet, that chosen people of God was only a figure, only a shadow of the Church. An important war was being conducted between the Hebrews and their enemies, the Amalekites.[3] The fight had been going on for some time, and with differing results by turns. At one time the Israelites yielded, at another they had the upper hand. Finally, the victory remained won by the Hebrews. Now, what was the event, what fact was it, that decided this victory? Suppose for a moment that those who were conducting the battle had left detailed reports on the twists and

---

[1] Song of Songs, 2:14.   [2] John 11:42.   [3] Exod. 17:8-16.

turns of the fight, and that those documents were submitted to a general of modern times, to know what he felt. This general would find that such and such a fault of tactics had been committed, that such and such a measure of strategy had not been effected, that such and such a maneuver had failed, such an attack been badly supported. He would give all the reasons—except the true one. And what was it? The reason for the differing results, now this way, now that, the reason for the happy issue to the war, God Himself has made known to us. It was that on a nearby mountain Moses, the leader of Israel, was praying for his people, arms raised up. Every time Moses, tired, let his arms drop, the Amalekites prevailed; every time Moses lifted up suppliant hands again, the victory tilted towards the Israelites. In the end, Aaron and his companion held Moses's arms up, until the victory was won by Israel. What an imposing scene, that of this leader obtaining victory for his people from the God of Hosts through his prayer! If we ourselves were to advance this explanation, many thinkers would smile with pity; but it is God in person who has given the explanation to us, the God of Hosts, He whose chosen people Israel was, and to whom Moses was friend.[1]

Doubtless this teaching is applicable to all prayer, but how much more true it is of the prayer of Christ, Head of the Church, praying, through the voice of the Church, for His mystical body which fights here below against "the prince of this world"[2] and of "darkness";[3] renewing every day upon the altar the prayer He made for us, arms extended, upon the mount of Calvary, and offering to His Father the infinite merits of His Passion and death: He "was heard because of His reverent submission."[4]

---

[1] "Arms lifted up to God break through more battalions that those that strike the blows": Bossuet, *Funeral oration of Marie-Thérèse of Austria*.

[2] John 12:31 (Rheims).   [3] Eph. 6:12.   [4] Hebr. 5:7.

4. Numerous *fruits of sanctification*. The prayer of the Church,
   source of light; it makes us *share the feelings* of the soul *of Christ*.

THIS PRAISE, that the Church addresses to God in the Holy Sacrifice and
in the "canonical hours" which revolve around the Mass, possesses not
only a power of intercession, but also a great *sanctifying value*. How is
that?

Through the way the Church has arranged the liturgical cycle, the
public prayer becomes for our mind a source of light, of union with the
feelings of the soul of Christ and with the mysteries of His life. See,
indeed, how the Church has arranged the cycle of feasts during which
she presents herself before God so as officially to sing His praises and
give Him homage.

As you know, this cycle can be divided into two sections. The one
runs from Advent, a time of preparation for Christmas, until Pentecost;
the other comprises the string of Sundays after Pentecost.

The basis of the first part is essentially constituted by the mysteries
of Christ. The Church remembers, in broad outline, the principal
stages of the earthly life of her Spouse. During Advent, the preparation
for Him under the Old Testament. At Christmas, His birth at Bethlehem; His epiphany, that is to say His manifestation to the Gentiles in
the persons of the Magi; His presentation in the temple. And then, during Lent, His fasting in the desert. She celebrates after that, during
Holy Week, His Passion and death; she sings of His resurrection at
Easter; His ascension; the sending of the Holy Spirit to the apostles
and the founding of the Church.

Like a bride who has nothing more dear to her than her bridegroom, the Church unfolds before the eyes of her children all the
events of the life of Jesus in their actual succession; and sometimes
following a detailed chronology, as in the period from Holy Week to
Pentecost.

If our soul is attentive, this representation will be for it *an abundant source of light*. We derive from this vivid reproduction, renewed each year, a sure and thorough knowledge of the mysteries of Christ.

Furthermore, this representation is not a simple and dry reproduction. The Church, through the choice, through the setting in due order, of these bits and longer extracts taken from the sacred books, *makes us enter into the very feelings that animated the heart of Christ Jesus*. How is that?

You will have already noticed that, even in the important events of the life of Christ, the Gospel writers often give no more than a purely historical account, with nothing or almost nothing added about the feelings that filled the soul of Jesus. For instance, during the Passion, the writer of the Gospel recounts the crucifixion of Jesus: "And they (the soldiers) took Jesus, and led Him forth ... to that place which is called Calvary ... where they crucified Him."[1] That is a simple attestation of fact, nothing more. But who will tells us of the feelings with which the soul of Jesus was overflowing? It is true that we are here on the threshold of a sanctuary of which only God knows the sacred depths. Nevertheless, we would like to know something of those feelings, for having that knowledge would bring us closer to our Divine Model. The Church, our mother, will lift for us a corner of the veil.

You know that Christ, hanging on the cross, uttered these words: "My God, my God, why have you forsaken me?"[2] These words form the first verse of a messianic psalm, which could only apply to Jesus, and in which not merely the circumstances of His crucifixion, but the feelings which would at that time have filled His sacred soul are expressed in a wonderful manner.[3] St. Augustine says explicitly that Christ on the cross recited this psalm which is "a gospel before

---

[1] John 19:16-18 (Rheims).   [2] Matt. 27:46; Mark 15:34.
[3] Ps. 21(22):7-9, 13-15, 20-22 (St P.)

it happened."[1] Read it, and you will hear Our Lord, crushed beneath the blows of Divine Justice, revealing His anguish, His inner feelings. "I am a worm, not a man: the scorn of men, despised by the people. All they who see me scoff at me; they mock me with parted lips, they wag their heads," saying: "'He relied on the Lord; let Him deliver him, let Him rescue him, if He loves him!'" ... "Many bullocks"—raging bullocks—"surround me.... I am like water poured out; all my bones are racked. My heart has become like wax melting away within my bosom." ... "But you, O Lord, be not far from me; O my help, hasten to aid me ... save me from the lion's mouth!"[2] These words are a revelation of the feelings of the heart of Christ during His Passion. The Church knows this well: guided by the Holy Spirit, she causes us to recite this psalm during Holy Week, so as to make our souls share in the feelings of the heart of Christ.

And so it is for the other mysteries. At the same time as the Church relates the narrative of the mystery, brings it forward again beneath the eyes of her children, you will see her intermingle with it those psalms, those prophecies, those passages in the letters of St. Paul, in which there is an indication of the feelings of Jesus.

In that way, the Church not only gives us, each year, a living and spirited representation of the life of her Spouse; she makes us enter—in so far as created beings can there enter—into the soul of Christ, in order that, reading there His inner dispositions, we may share them and be more intimately united with our Divine leader. With profound art and admirable ease, she makes us carry out the precept of St. Paul: "Have this mind in you which was also in Christ Jesus."[3] Is not that a turning into reality of the very formula of our predestination?

---

[1] "He wished to make His own the words of the psalm, while He was hanging on the cross": *Enarr. in Ps.* 85, c. 1. "The Passion of Christ, of course, is there recounted, like a Gospel": *Enarr. in Ps.* 21.   [2] Ps. 21(22), vv. 7-9, 13-15, 20-22 (St P.)   [3] Phil. 2:5.

5. **Again, the Church makes us** *participate in His mysteries,* **a sure and infallible way to** *make ourselves resemble Jesus.*

THAT is not all. These mysteries of Christ that the Church makes us celebrate each year are *mysteries which are still living ones.*

Put a believer and an unbeliever in front of the representation of the Passion that unfolds at Oberammergau or at Nancy. The unbeliever would be able to appreciate the beautiful development of the drama, the play of the scenery; he might draw aesthetic emotions from it. Its influence upon the believer would be yet more marked. Why? Because, even when he was not gripped by the artistic side of the representation, the scenes he has before his eyes recall events that touch his faith very closely. But, even so far as he is concerned, that influence is produced by an exterior cause only: the spectacle at which he is present. The representation does not contain any interior, intrinsic, power which could, of itself, touch his soul super-naturally. That is something which belongs only to the mysteries of Jesus celebrated by the Church. Not that they contain grace like the sacraments, but these mysteries are living ones, they are sources of life for the soul.

Each mystery of Christ is not only an object of contemplation for the mind, a memory that we invoke in order to praise God, to thank Him for what He has done for us. It is something more. *Each of these mysteries constitutes,* for the soul that has faith, *a participation in the various circumstances of the Incarnate Word.*

And this is very important. The mysteries of Christ have in the first place been lived by Him—but in order that we, in our turn, may live them in union with Him. How do we do that? By breathing in their spirit, by making the power of them our own, with the object that we, living by them, may make ourselves resemble Christ.

It is true that Christ Jesus is now glorious in heaven. His life on earth, in its physical duration and exterior form, lasted only thirty-three years; but the power of each of His mysteries is infinite and remains inexhaustible. When we celebrate them in the sacred liturgy, we receive therefrom, according to the measure of our faith, the same graces as if we had lived at the time of Our Lord and had been present at all of His mysteries.[1] These mysteries had as their author the Incarnate Word. As I have told you, Christ through the Incarnation has associated the whole of humanity with His Divine mysteries and has merited, for all His brethren, the grace He has willed to attach to them. And it is in their celebration by the Church—which He has given the task of continuing His mission here below—that Christ, throughout the ages, has caused faithful souls to share in the grace those mysteries enclose. They are, as St. Augustine says,[2] the type of the Christian life we ought to lead in our capacity of disciples of Jesus.

See how this applies to the Nativity. "When we adore the birth of our Savior," says St. Leo, "what occurs is that we celebrate our own origin. This generation of Christ in the sphere of time is indeed the source from which the Christian people sprang, and the birth of our head is at the same time the birth of His mystical body. Every person, in whatever part of the world he lives, finds through this mystery a new birth in Christ."[3] Indeed, Christmas each year brings to the soul that celebrates this mystery with faith (for it is through faith in the first place, through Eucharistic Communion later, that we enter into contact with the mysteries of Christ)—brings to the soul a grace of interior renewal that increases the degree of its participation in Divine Sonship in Christ Jesus.

And so it goes on with the other mysteries. The celebration of Lent, of the Passion and Death of Jesus during Holy Week, brings with it a

---

[1] See above, page 99 ff.

[2] "Everything that took place at the cross of Christ, in the sepulchre, on His resurrection on the third day, on His ascension into heaven, on His being seated at the right hand of the Father, took place in order that the Christian life one leads here below might be conformed to those things which have not only been said in a mystical sense but have, also, actually taken place": St. Augustine, *Enchiridion*, c. LIII.

[3] *Sermo* IV on the Lord's Nativity.

grace of "death to sin" which helps us more and more to destroy in us sin, attachment to sin, attachment to creatures. For, St. Paul says explicitly, Christ has made us die with Him and we have been buried with Him: "Since one died for all, therefore all died."[1] And "*con*sepulti sumus," "we were buried *with Him* by means of Baptism into death."[2] This, for everyone—by right and in principle: but its application over the ages to the individual soul takes place through our participating in the death of Christ, especially during the season when the Church brings its memory to our minds.

It is the same at Easter, when we sing the glory of Christ coming forth from the tomb, victorious over death. Participating in this mystery, we draw from it a grace of spiritual life and liberty. St. Paul says that God raises us up *with Christ*: He has brought us to life again "together with Christ."[3] And again, in speaking of the grace proper to this mystery, he says: "If you have risen *with Christ*"—"*con*surrexistis cum Christo"—"seek the things that are above ... not the things that are on earth."[4] In other words: "If you have been raised up *with Christ*, seek and savor, not what is of the earth—that which, being created, contains the germ of corruption and death—but rather what is on high, that which will lead you to eternal life: "*Just as Christ* has arisen from the dead through the glory of the Father, *so we also* may walk in newness of life."[5]

After having associated us with His resurrected life, Christ has made us participate in the mystery of His ascension. And what is the special grace of that mystery? St. Paul gives us the answer: "God ... gave us a place *with Him* in heaven,"—"fecit *con*sedere in caelestibus"—in Christ Jesus."[6] The great apostle, who, by all these examples, illustrates admirably the explanation, so dear to him, of our union with Christ as

---

[1] 2 Cor. 5:14. [*Translator's note*: The Jerusalem translates as: "then all men *should* be dead" [to sin]: my italics.]   [2] Rom. 6:4.   [3] Eph. 2:6.

[4] Col. 3:1-2.   [5] Rom. 6:4.   [6] Eph. 2:4-6 (Jerus.)

members of His mystical body—the apostle tells us in very explicit terms that God has made us sit *with Christ* in the kingdom of heaven. Whence, an ancient author wrote: "Let us, while we are here below, follow Christ to heaven by faith and love, with the object of following Him there in body on the day appointed by His eternal promises."[1] Is not that what the Church makes us ask in the prayer for the feast of Ascension Day? "Grant ... that we who believe that ... our Redeemer ascended this day into heaven, may ourselves also in mind dwell in heavenly things"—through our desires, dwell already in heaven.

In this way, from year to year, the Church puts before our eyes a representation of the events that marked the earthly life of her Spouse. First of all, she makes us contemplate these mysteries, and each year it is a new illumination that enlightens us. She reveals to us the feelings of the heart of Christ, and, each year, we enter further into the inner states of mind of Jesus; she makes us re-live within us these mysteries of our Divine head. She supports our prayers that ask that we may obtain the special grace proper to each of these mysteries lived by Christ, and in this way we advance, by faith and love, by the imitation of our Divine Model ceaselessly put before our eyes, into that supernatural transformation which is the journey's-end of our union with Jesus: "I live, now not I; but Christ lives in me."[2] Is not all our holiness to be found in that, and the very shape of our Divine predestination— to become so like the Beloved Son that His life becomes ours?

Let us, then, be guided by the Church, our Mother, in that primordial devotion which is meant to make us share in Christ's heart-ties to His

---

[1] "In the meantime let us ascend with Christ in heart. When His promised day comes, we shall follow in body too. If, then, rightly, faithfully, in holiness and piety we celebrate the Ascension of Our Lord, we may ascend with Him and have our hearts above with Him." This sermon, of which an extract may be read in the Breviary, in the second nocturn of the Sunday in the Octave of the Ascension, has been wrongly attributed to St. Augustine. The substance of it, however, is borrowed from the works of the great Doctor.   [2] Gal. 2:20 (Rheims).

Father. Christ has put the celebration of these mysteries into the hands of His spouse. The prayer laid down by the Church is a true and authentic expression of homage worthy of God. When the Church, who knows the secrets of Jesus sets herself, and us with her, to celebrate the mysteries of Christ, it seems as if these words of the Song of Songs reach our ears from heaven: "Let me hear your voice; for your voice is sweet and your face is beautiful"[1]—your voice full of charm and your face resplendent with beauty. The Church is adorned with the riches of her Divine Spouse, she has the right to speak in His name; and that is why the homage of adoration and praise that she puts on the lips of her children is extremely pleasing to Christ and to His Father.

This prayer of the Church also constitutes a sure way for us; we could not seize on anything that would lead us more directly to Christ and assimilate us more to His life. The Church, as though taking us by the hand, conducts us straight to Him. If it is an act of humility and obedience to let oneself be guided by her, for she has received all from Christ—"He who hears you, hears me; and he who rejects you, rejects me,"[2] it is also for us a means of arriving infallibly at knowing Christ, of entering deeper into the meaning of His mysteries, and of staying united with Him so as to find in Him, not only a model but the well-spring of the eternal life which, through the abundance of His merits, He has made to flow forth: "The sacrifice of praise shall glorify me: and there is *the way* by which I will show him the salvation of God."[3]

---

[1] Song of Songs 2:14 (Jerus.)   [2] Luke 10:16.   [3] Ps. 49 (50):23.

6. Why and how *the Church celebrates the saints.*

BESIDES THE MYSTERIES of Christ, the Church celebrates also *the feasts of the saints.*

What is it that has led the Church to celebrate the saints? That principle, ever fruitful, of the union that exists since the Incarnation, between Christ and His members. The saints are the glorious members of Christ's mystical body; Christ is already "formed in them"; they have "attained their fullness"; and, in praising them it is Christ whom one glorifies in them. "Praise me for being the crown of all the saints," said Christ to St. Mechtilde. And the nun saw that the whole beauty of the elect was being nourished by the blood of Christ, that it shone with the virtues practiced by Him: and, responding to the Divine appeal, she praised with all her strength the Most Blessed and Adorable Trinity "for deigning to be for the saints their diadem and their wonderful dignity."[1]

It is indeed to the Trinity, as you know, that the Church is still offering her praises when she keeps the feasts of the saints. Each saint is a manifestation of Christ; each bears in his or her self the features of the Divine Model, but in a way that is special and distinct.[2] This is a fruit of Christ's grace, and it is to the glory of that grace that the Church delights to exalt her triumphant children: "Unto the praise of the glory of His grace."[3]

Such is the form of the Church's loving reverence towards the saints — taking pleasure in them. She is proud of these legions of the elect, who are the fruits of her union with Christ and who already, in the splendors of heaven, are part of the kingdom of her Spouse. She celebrates Christ in them: "O Lord, our Lord, how admirable is your name in the whole earth!.... You have crowned him with glory and honor."[4]

---

[1] *Livre de la grace spéciale*, I, c. 31.   [2] See above, pages 289-290.
[3] Eph. 1:6. See the development of this idea in the talk "Christ, the crown of all the saints," in our book *Christ in His Mysteries*.   [4] Ps. 8:2-6.

She renews in them the memory of the joy that flooded into their souls when they entered heaven: "Good and faithful servant ... enter into the joy of your Lord...."[1] Come, bride of Christ, "receive the crown the Lord has prepared for you from all eternity."[2] She exalts the virtues and merits of her apostles, her martyrs, her pontiffs, her confessors, her virgins; she rejoices in their glory, she puts them forward as examples, if not always for the imitation, at least for the praise of their brethren here below: "If it is not in your power to follow the martyrs in fact, then follow them in feeling. If it is not in your power to follow them in glory, follow them through your joy: if not in your merits, then in your desires; if not through your excellence, then through your ties with them."[3]

And after having praised them, she commends herself to their intercessory prayers. Does she thereby detract from the infinite power of Christ, without whom we can do nothing? Certainly not. Christ, not in order to diminish His action but to extend it, is delighted to listen to the saints, who are the princes of His heavenly court, and to give us, through them, the graces we entreat.[4] Thus is there established a supernatural flow of exchanges between all the members of His mystical body.

Lastly, not being able to celebrate all of them in particular, the Church joins them together at the end of the liturgical cycle in one solemn Feast, that of All Saints, where (so to say) she uses up her most triumphant praises. Transporting us into heaven, following the apostle St. John, she shows us that glorious portion of her Spouse's kingdom, those innumerable legions of the elect—that "great multitude" of the

---

[1] Matt. 25, vv. 21, 23 (Rheims).

[2] See Matt. 25:34.   [3] St. Augustine, *Sermo* 280, c. 6.

[4] "This, indeed, is our connection with the Saints: we express to them our happiness for them, and they show compassion for us and fight for us through their loving intercession": St. Bernard, *Sermo* 5 on the Feast of All Saints.

saints "which no man could number," standing before the throne of God, "clothed in white robes, and with palms in their hands:"[1] and from their ranks rises up a mighty acclamation: "Glory to God, glory to the Lamb who was slain for us, who by His blood has ransomed us from every tribe, and tongue, and people, and nation."[2] At this glorious vision, the Church feels a thrill of gladness. Hear how she calls out to her triumphant children: "Bless the Lord, all you His elect, keep high festival and sing His praises. For singing is the portion all His saints.... This glory belongs to all his saints."[3]

We, too—we are called to share this triumph, to form the court of Christ *in splendoribus sanctorum*, in the splendors of the saints; to share the glory of the Son in the heart's-embrace of the Father, after having shared in His mysteries here below. Let us give prelude to this praise in heaven, where resounds an eternal *Alleluia*, by joining in it as much as is possible here below, with great faith and with an ardent love—joining in the prayer of the Church, spouse of Christ and mother of us.

---

[1] Apoc. 7:9-10.   [2] See Apoc. 7:10; 5:9.
[3] See Antiphons of Vespers for All Saints. Cf. Tob. 13:10; Ps. 148 (149):14; 149 (150):9.

CHAPTER TEN

Prayer

INTRODUCTION: **Importance of prayer. The prayer-life is transforming.**

OUR LORD'S DESIRE to give Himself to us is so great that He has multiplied the means of His doing so. Along with the different sacraments, He has indicated prayer to us as a source of grace. It is true—as I have said to you often in the course of these talks—that the sacraments produce grace through the very fact of their being applied to a soul who does not place any obstacle in the way of their action.

Prayer has not, in itself, an efficacy as intrinsic as that which the sacraments have. It is, though, of a no less great necessity to us for obtaining Divine help. We see Christ Jesus, during His public life, grant miracles in answer to prayer. A leper comes up to Him: "Lord, have pity on me"—and He cures him.[1] Someone brings a blind man to Him: "Lord," he says to Him, "make me see"—Our Lord gives him back his sight.[2] Martha and Magdalene say to Him: "Lord, if you had been here, our brother would not have died." It was a prayer of entreaty, to which Our Lord replied by the resurrection of Lazarus.[3]

[1] See Matt. 8:2-3; Mark 1:40-42.   [2] See Mark 8:22-25.   [3] John 11:17-44.

These were temporal favors; but grace itself is granted to prayer. "Sir," says the Samaritan woman to Him, "give me this water"; this living water, of which you are the source, water "springing up unto life everlasting"—and Christ reveals Himself to her as the Messiah, brings her to confess her sins, so that He may give her remission of them.[1] On the cross, the good thief asks Him to "remember him" when He comes into His kingdom—and He grants him full pardon: "This day you shall be with me in paradise."[2]

Our Lord has elsewhere urged us to make entreaty of that sort: "Ask, and it shall be given you; seek, and you shall find; knock, and it shall be opened to you."[3] "If you ask the Father anything"—anything good for us to be granted—"in my name" (that is to say, by claiming upon me) "He will give it to you."[4] St. Paul, as well, exhorts us to "use every kind of prayer and supplication; pray at all times through the Spirit."[5] As you can see, the vocal prayer of entreaty is a powerful means of drawing down to us the gifts of God.

It is about mental prayer, about praying, that I want to talk to you especially. That subject is a very important one.

Praying is one of the most necessary means of bringing about, here below, our union with God and our imitation of Christ Jesus. Frequent contact of the soul with God in faith, through prayer and the prayer-life, is a powerful aid to the transformation of our soul from the supernatural point of view. Prayer well made, the life of prayer, is transforming.[6]

Besides, union with God in prayer makes us begin to participate more fruitfully in the other means Christ has established for communicating Himself to us and making us resemble Him. Why is that, then?

---

[1] John 4:13-26.   [2] Luke 23:42-43.   [3] Matt. 7:7.   [4] John 16:23.
[5] See Eph. 6:18.   [6] "A soul cannot flatter itself that it is an interior image of Jesus if it is not what is called a soul of prayer. The form matters little, but the thing itself is indispensable": Msgr. Gay, *Instructions en forme de retraite*, ch. XIII.

Could prayer be higher, more efficacious, than the Holy Sacrifice, than the reception of the sacraments which are authentic channels of grace? Certainly not! Every time we approach these wellsprings, we draw from them an increase of grace, a growing in divine life. But that growing depends, at least in part, on our dispositions.

Now prayer—the life of prayer—maintains, stimulates, quickens and perfects those feelings of faith, humility, trust and love which together constitute the best predisposition of the soul to receive an abundance of divine grace. A soul to whom prayer is a familiar thing profits more from the sacraments and other means of salvation than does another in whom prayer, intermittent prayer, is disconnected and without vigor. A soul that is not faithfully devoted to praying can recite the Divine Office, assist at Holy Mass, receive the sacraments, hear the word of God, but its progress will often be mediocre. Why is that? Because the principal author of our perfection and of our holiness is God Himself, and prayer keeps the soul in frequent contact with God; it establishes, and having established keeps going, a fire-hearth in the soul, as it were—one where, even if it is not in action all the time, love's fire is all the time smouldering, at least. And as soon as that soul is put into direct communication with the Divine life (for instance in the sacraments) this is like a strong breath of air that sets the soul ablaze, stirs it up, fills it with a marvelous superabundance. A soul's super-natural life is measured by its union with God through Christ in faith and love. This love has to produce acts: but those acts, if they are to be produced in a regular and intense way, require a life of prayer. It can be established that, so far as its ordinary paths are concerned, progression-forward in our love of God depends in practice on our life of prayer.

Let me, then, put into words what prayer is—that is to say, what its nature is; what are its degrees; and then the dispositions one has to bring to it in order that it bear fruit.

I need hardly say that I do not intend to give here a whole treatise on prayer; there are excellent ones in existence. I wish simply to touch upon some essential points in relation to the central idea of these talks: our super-natural adoption in Christ Jesus which makes us live by His grace and His Spirit.

1. *Nature* of prayer: *conversation of a child of God with its Father in heaven under the action of the Holy Spirit.*

WHAT IS PRAYER?

We will define it as *a conversation of a child of God with its heavenly Father.* You will note the words "conversation of a child of God." I have put that in by design. One sometimes comes across men who do not believe in the divinity of Christ, such as certain deists of the eighteenth century, such as those who instituted the cult of the Supreme Being at the time of the French Revolution and who invented prayers to "the Divinity," thinking perhaps to dazzle God thereby. But those prayers were only the futile games of a purely human spirit which God could not find pleasing.

That is not what prayer is with us. It is not a conversation of a man, a simple created being, with the Divinity. It is a conversation of a child of God with its Heavenly Father, to adore Him, to praise Him, to say "I love you" to Him, to learn to know His will and to obtain from Him the help that is necessary to do that will.

In prayer, we appear before God in our status as children, a status that in essence establishes our soul in the super-natural order. Of course, we ought never to forget our condition of being creatures—of having been created from nothing, that is to say. But the point of departure or (to speak more accurately) the ground on which we ought to place ourselves in our conversations with God is the super-natural ground. In other words, it is our divine sonship, daughtership, our status as children of God through the grace of Christ, which ought to condition our fundamental attitude and serve, so to say, as a conductor-wire in prayer.

See how St. Paul throws light on this point. "We do not know," he says, "what we should pray for as we ought"—how to pray according to our needs—"but the Spirit Himself pleads for us,"[1] comes to the help of our weakness—"expresses our plea in a way that could never be put into words."[2] Now, says St. Paul in the same passage, this Spirit who has to pray for us, within us, is the Spirit "of adoption," the Spirit who "gives testimony to our spirit that we are sons of God" and God's "heirs"; who causes us to cry out to God: "Abba," "Father."[3] This Spirit was given to us when, "the fullness of time" being come, "God sent his Son" so as to confer on us "the adoption of sons."[4] Because the grace of Christ makes us God's children, God "has sent the Spirit of His Son into our hearts," the Spirit who makes us pray to God as a Father.[5] We are, indeed, "no longer strangers," no longer guests of passage, but members of God's family, of that dwelling-place of which Christ Jesus is "the chief cornerstone."[6]

So, then, it is the Spirit we have received at baptism, in the sacrament of our Divine adoption, who makes us cry out to God: "You are our Father." What does that mean if not that, in consequence of our having been thus adopted, we have henceforth the right and the duty to present ourselves before God as His children?

Let us listen to Our Lord Himself. He came in order to be "the light of the world," and His words, "full of truth,"[7] show us the way: "I am the light of the world,"[8] "I am the way, and the truth."[9]

Seated on the edge of Jacob's well, He converses with the Samaritan woman.[10] This woman has just recognized that He who is talking to her is a prophet, one sent from God. Straight away, she asks Him (it was a subject of strong dispute between her compatriots and the Jews) whether one ought to worship God on the mountains of Samaria or at

---

[1] Rom. 8:26.   [2] Rom. 8:26 (Jerus.)   [3] Rom. 8:15-17.   [4] Gal. 4:4-5.
[5] Gal. 4:6; cf. Rom. 8:15; 2 Cor. 1:22.   [6] Eph. 2:19-20.   [7] See John 1:14.
[8] John 8:12.   [9] John 14:6.   [10] John 4:5 ff.

Jerusalem. And what does Christ reply to her? "Woman, believe me, the hour is coming when neither on this mountain nor in Jerusalem will you worship the Father.... But the hour is coming, and is now here"— is already here—"when the true worshippers will worship the Father in spirit and in truth. For the Father ... seeks such to worship Him."[1] Notice how Our Lord puts into relief this name of "Father." In Samaria, as you know, they worshipped false gods, and this is why Christ says that one must worship "in truth," that is to say, worship the true God. At Jeru-salem they worshipped the true God, but not "in spirit"; the religion of the Jews was quite a material one in its expression and its object. The hour *"is now here"*—it is the Word Incarnate who inaugurates the new religion, that of the true God worshipped in spirit, in the spirit of a Divine, super-natural, spiritual adoption which makes us children of God; and that is why Our Lord insists on this term "Father": "the *true worshippers* will worship *the Father* in spirit and in truth."

There is no doubt that as we are *adopted* children and God in making us His children diminishes nothing of His Divine majesty or absolute sovereignty, we ought to worship Him, to abase ourselves before Him. But we ought to worship Him in truth and in spirit, that is to say, in the truth and spirit of that super-natural order through which we are His children.

Elsewhere, Our Lord is more explicit still. With the Samaritan woman, He has (so to say) laid down the principle. With the apostles, He gives the example. One day, says St. Luke, He was praying, and when He had finished, one of his disciples said to Him: "Lord, teach us to pray." And what reply did Christ make? "When you pray, pray thus: 'Our Father, who art in heaven, hallowed be thy name....'"[2] Do not forget this: Our Lord is God; as the Word He is always in the heart's-embrace of the Father; no one knows God if the Son does not. Christ, then, knows perfectly what we ought to say to God, or ask of Him, in

---

[1] John 4:21-24.　　　　　[2] See Luke 11:1 ff.

order to be those "true worshippers" whom God "seeks." He also knows perfectly what attitude we ought to have in appearing before God in order to converse with Him, in order to be pleasing to Him. What He teaches us, He tells us because He can but reveal what He has seen: "The only-begotten Son ... He has revealed Him."[1] And what He tells us we can, we must, listen to. He is the Way, to be followed without fear: anyone who takes that Way "does not walk in darkness."[2] Well, what does Jesus say, when He wants us to learn this science of prayer which He has declared to be so necessary that one must apply oneself to it always: "we ought always to pray"?[3]

He begins by indicating the title we ought to give to God before offering Him our homage, that title which is like a signpost; or (shall we say?) something indicating the color that ought to be given to the ensuing conversation, something on which one will be basing the requests that are to follow; the title which dictates our soul's attitude before God. And what is that title? "Our Father...."

We thus obtain from the very lips of Christ, from the beloved Son in whom God has placed His delight, this precious indication that the first and fundamental disposition we ought to have in our relations with God is that of a child in the presence of its Father. There is no doubt, yet again—this point is of no less importance—that such a child will never forget its original condition of a creature fallen into sin and retaining within itself a seat of sin that is capable of separating that creature from God. For He who is our Father dwells in heaven; He is, as well as our Father, our *God*. Christ said, on leaving His apostles: "I ascend to my Father and your Father, to my God and your God."[4] That is why a deep reverence and a great humility will ever accompany the child of God; he will ask that his trespasses be forgiven, that he shall not give way to temptation, that he be delivered from evil, but he will crown this humility and this reverence with an

---

[1] John 1:18.   [2] John 8:12.   [3] Luke 18:1 (Rheims).   [4] John 20:17.

inexhaustible confidence (for "every perfect gift is from above, coming down from the Father of Lights"),[1] and with it a tender love, the love of a son for his Father, for the Father who loves him.

Prayer, then, is like the expression of our intimate life as children of God, like the fruit of our divine sonship in Christ, like the spontaneous flowering of the gifts of the Holy Spirit. And that is why it is so vital; so fruitful too. A soul devoted regularly to prayer draws from it ineffable graces that transform that soul, little by little, into an image of Jesus, the only Son of the Heavenly Father. "The door," says St. Teresa of Avila, "through which graces of a choice kind enter into the soul (like those God has given me) is prayer. Once that door closes, I do not know how He would be able to grant them to us."[2] The soul also draws from it joys that give it something like a foretaste of union in heaven, of that eternal inheritance which awaits us. Truly, said Christ Jesus every-thing—everything which is good to be granted us—that you ask the Father for in my name, He will give you—"that your joy may be full."[3]

Such is mental prayer: a heart-to-heart between God and the soul: "a conversation, person to person, with God, to express our love to Him who we know loves us."[4]

And this conversation of the child of God with its Heavenly Father is carried out *under the action of the Holy Spirit*. God, indeed, through the prophet Zachariah, has promised that, under the new covenant, He will pour into souls, "pour … upon the inhabitants of Jerusalem the spirit of grace and of prayers."[5] That spirit is the Holy Spirit, the Spirit

---

[1] James 1:17. "Borne as if on [the] two wings [of faith and hope], the soul flies up towards heaven and mounts right up to God.... With an ardent *piety* and a deep *reverence*, the soul, in complete trust, talks to Him of all its needs—*like the trust an only son would have in the most loved of fathers*": Catechism of the Council of Trent, 4th part, ch. I, para. 3. "What God ordains is that you come before Him, not under constraint and trembling, like a slave before his master, but taking refuge close to Him *in total liberty and in perfect trust like a child close to its father*": *Ibid.*, 4th part, ch. II, para. 2.

[2] *Life, written by herself*, ch. VIII.　　　　　　　　　　[3] John 16:23-24.

[4] St. Teresa, *op. cit.*　　　　　　　　　　　　　　　　[5] Zach. 12:10.

of adoption, whom God has sent into the hearts of those He predestines to be His children in Christ Jesus. The gifts that this Divine Spirit confers on our souls on the day of our baptism, by infusing our souls with grace—those gifts aid us in our relations with our Heavenly Father. The gift of fear fills us with reverence before Divine Majesty; the gift of piety[1] harmonizes with fear the tenderness of a child towards its Father. The gift of knowledge presents to the soul the truths of the natural order in a new light; the gift of understanding makes it penetrate the hidden depths of the mysteries of faith; the gift of wisdom gives it the savor, the emotional knowledge, of revealed truths. The gifts of the Holy Spirit are dispositions, very real ones, that we do not take into consideration enough; it is by these gifts that the Holy Spirit, dwelling in the soul of a baptized person as in a temple, aids and guides that soul in its conversations with the Heavenly Father: "The Spirit... comes to help us in our weakness... the Spirit *Himself* expresses our plea in a way that could never be put into words."[2]

The essential element of prayer is the super-natural contact of the soul with God, in which the soul draws upon that Divine life which is the source of all holiness. This contact occurs when the soul, lifted up by faith and love, with Jesus Christ as its support, delivers itself up to God, to His will, through a prompting by the Holy Spirit: "The wise man... will give his heart to resort early to the Lord that made him, and he will pray in the sight of the Most High."[3] No reasoning, no purely natural effort, can produce this contact: "No one can say 'Jesus is Lord,' except in the Holy Spirit."[4] This contact occurs in the darkness of faith, but it fills the soul with light and life.

Prayer is therefore the flowering, under the action of the gifts of the Holy Spirit, of the feelings that result from our divine adoption in

---

[1] [*Translator's note*: "*piété*," piety—earlier translated as "loving reverence." Marmion explicitly calls it here "the tenderness of a child towards its Father."]

[2] Rom. 8:26 (Jerus.) "The Holy Spirit is the very soul of our prayers; He inspires them in us and makes them always acceptable": Catechism of the Council of Trent, 4th part, ch. I, para. 7.   [3] Ecclesiasticus (Sirach) 39:1,6.   [4] 1 Cor. 12:3.

Jesus Christ; and that is why it has to be accessible to every baptized soul of good will. Moreover, Christ Jesus invites all His disciples to aim at perfection, and this, in order that they may be worthy children of the Heavenly Father: "You, therefore, must be perfect, as your heavenly Father is perfect."[1] Now, perfection is in practice only possible if the soul lives by prayer. That being so, is it not evident that Christ did not wish that the manner of treating with Him in prayer should be difficult, or beyond the capacity of the most simple of souls who seek Him sincerely? That is why I have said that prayer can be defined as a conversation of a child of God with its Heavenly Father: "When you pray, say 'Our Father, who art in heaven.'"[2]

2. **Twofold element that ought to determine the course of the conversation. First, *the measure of the grace of Christ*.[3] The great discreetness to be preserved on this subject. Teaching of the principal masters of the spiritual life. The method is not the prayer.**

IN a conversation, one listens and one speaks: the soul delivers itself up to God, and God communicates Himself to the soul.

In order to listen to God, in order to receive His light, it is enough that the heart be filled with feelings of faith, reverence, humility, ardent trust, generous love.

In order to speak to Him, one must have something to say to Him. What will be the subject of the conversation? That depends principally on two elements: *the measure of grace* that Christ Jesus gives to the soul; and *the state of the soul* itself.

The first element to be taken into account is the measure of the gifts of grace communicated by Christ: "according to the measure of Christ's bestowal."[4] Christ Jesus, being God, is absolute master of His

---

[1] Matt. 5:48 (RSV, Cath.). [2] See Matt. 6:9; Luke 11:2.
[3] [*Translator's note*: The *second* factor of Marmion's "twofold element" is the state of the soul: see section 3, page 428.] [4] Eph. 4:7.

gifts; He dispenses His grace to the soul as He sees fit; He sheds His light into the soul as it pleases His sovereign majesty. Through His Spirit, Christ guides and draws us towards His Father. If you read the masters of the spiritual life, you will see that they always hold in holy respect this sovereignty of Christ in His dispensing to us His favors and lights. It is this that explains their extreme reserve when they have to intervene in the soul's relations with its God.

St. Benedict, who was a great contemplative favored with extraordinary graces of prayer, and who was a past master in the knowledge of souls, exhorts his followers to "give themselves up frequently to prayer";[1] he makes us clearly understand that the life of prayer is absolutely necessary for finding God. But when it is a question of regulating the *way* of giving oneself up to prayer, he becomes singularly circumspect. He naturally supposes that one has already acquired a certain habitual knowledge of Divine things, through assiduous reading of Holy Scripture and the works of the Fathers of the Church. For prayer, he contents himself with indicating at the start the attitude a soul ought to have towards God at the time of approaching Him: profound reverence and humility.[2] He wants the soul to remain in the presence of God in a spirit of great compunction and perfect simplicity; that attitude is the best one for listening to the voice of God fruitfully.

As for the conversation itself, beyond linking it very definitely to the chanting of the psalms (of which it is, so to speak, but an interior prolongation), St. Benedict makes it consist of surges of the heart, brief and fervent, towards God. "The soul," he says, taking up the very advice Christ gave,[3] "should avoid a multiplicity of words. It should prolong the exercise of prayer only if it is urged to do so by the prompting of the Holy Spirit who dwells in it through grace." Other than that, nothing

[1] *Rule*, ch. IV.

[2] It is worthy of note that the patriarch of monks entitles the chapter on prayer: *De reverentia orationis*, "On the reverence one ought to preserve in prayer": *Rule*, ch. XX.

[3] Matt. 6:7: "in praying, do not multiply words."

explicit on this subject is to be found in what the legislator for the monastic life wrote.

Another great master of the spiritual life, one arrived at a high degree of contemplation and filled with the lights of grace and of experience, St. Ignatius of Loyola, wrote some words the deep wisdom of which one cannot overestimate. "For each person," he writes to St. Francis Borgia, "the best meditation is that in which God communicates Himself more to him. For God sees and knows what is more suited to us, and, knowing all, He Himself shows us the way to follow. But in order to find it, we must grope our way forward before we can encounter the path that will lead us to the life without end, where we shall joy in God's holiest gifts."[1] The Saint teaches, therefore, that one must leave to God the job of indicating to each soul what is the best way of conversing with Him.

St. Teresa of Avila, in different passages in her *Works*, enunciates the same thought: "Whether a soul practices prayer much or little, it is of extreme importance neither to force it too much nor, so to speak, to chain it up in a corner."[2]

St. Francis de Sales is no less reserved. Listen to what he says; the quotation is a bit long, but it well characterizes the nature of prayer as fruit of the gifts of the Holy Spirit, and the circumspection one must bring to regulating it: "Do not think, daughters, that prayer can be a work of the human mind; it is a wholly particular gift of the Holy Spirit, who raises the soul's powers above their natural strength, so that it may be united to God through feelings and communications that all the words and wisdom of men are unable to effect without

---

[1] *Études*, 1905, I, pp. 567-568.

[2] *The Interior Castle*, First mansion, ch. II. See also *Life, written by herself*, the beginning of ch. XII to ch. XIII [Marmion's reference is to the French edition of the *Works*, translated by the Carmelites of Paris]. In ch. XXII she writes: "God leads souls by many roads, many different paths." See also chs. XVIII and XXVII, where she shows what an excellent prayer it is to keep company with Our Lord in His different mysteries and to talk with Him in simple conversations.

Him. The ways in which He guides the saints in this exercise (which is the most Divine employment of a reasonable creature) are marvelous in their diversity, and one has to esteem them all, since they take us to God, and that under the guidance of one who is God: but it is not necessary to go to the trouble of following them all, or even of choosing any one of them of our own accord. The important point is to recognize the pull of grace on us and to make ourselves faithful to it."[1]

One could multiply similar testimonies, but those I have given will suffice to show you that as much as the masters of the spiritual life bid souls to give themselves up to prayer, since prayer is a vital element for spiritual perfection, as much also do they take care not to impose one way rather than another on all souls indiscriminately. We say "impose"; they advocate or commend certain ways; they suggest or propose particular methods; all have their value which needs to be known, all have their usefulness which can be put to the test. But to wish to impose an exclusive method on all souls without discrimination would be to take into account neither the Divine liberty with which Christ Jesus distributes His grace nor the attractions His Spirit causes to arise in us.

In the matter of method, what helps one soul can hinder another. Experience shows that many souls who have the facility of conversing, habitually and simply, with God and of gaining fruit from those conversations, would be hindered if one sought to tie them down to this or that method. It is up to each soul, then, to examine itself in the first place, before settling on the way of conversing with God that will be best for it. It should, on the one hand, consider its aptitudes, its dispositions, its tastes, its aspirations, its way of life. It should seek to know the way the Holy Spirit is attracting it, to take account also of its progress on the spiritual paths. At the same time, it should be generously docile to the grace of Christ and the action of the Holy Spirit.

[1] *Abrégé de l'esprit intérieur des religieuses de la Visitation*, expounded by St. Francis de Sales and collected by Msgr. Maupas, Rouen, Cabut, 1744, pp. 68-69.

Once the best path is found, after some feeling of its way that is inevitable at the start, the soul should faithfully keep to that path, until the Holy Spirit attracts it to another path. That, for it, is a condition of fruitfulness.

Another point which I consider to be important, and which ties up very closely with the preceding one, is that we should not fail to distinguish between the essence of prayer and the methods — whatever they be, moreover — that help or serve to bring prayer about. There are some souls who believe that unless they are employing this or that method, they are not praying. There is in that a confusion which cannot be without danger in its consequences. Because they have linked the essence of prayer to the use of such and such a method, these souls do not dare to change the method, even when they have recognized that it is for them an obstacle or has become something that is useless. Or more than that (what happens most often), finding the method wearisome, they give it up and at a stroke give up prayer itself with it — and that, to their great detriment. Method is one thing, prayer another. The method should vary according to the aptitudes and needs of souls, whereas prayer (I speak of ordinary prayer) stays always, basically, the same for all souls: a conversation in which the heart of a child of God pours itself out before its Heavenly Father and listens to Him in order to please Him. The method, by giving support to the mind, helps the soul in its union with God; it is a means, but it should neither be nor become an obstacle. If such and such a method enlightens the intellect, stirs the will into flame, brings the soul to deliver itself up to Divine guidance and outpour itself interiorly to God, then that method is good: but it ought to be given up when really it hinders the attraction of the soul, constrains it, does not help it to make progress along the spiritual path; or, on the other hand, when it has become useless in consequence of the progress the soul has in fact made.

3. Second element: *the state of the soul.* The different stages on the way of perfection characterize, in a general way, *the different degrees* of the life of prayer. *Discursive toil* at the beginning.

THE SECOND ELEMENT that must, indeed, be taken into consideration in order to settle upon the habitual subjects of our conversations with God is the *state of the soul.*

The soul is not always in the same state. As you know, ascetic tradition distinguishes three stages or states of perfection: the purgative way, in which beginners are involved; the illuminative way, in which the fervent progress; and the unitive way, proper to perfect souls. Those states are thus named according as this or that characteristic has ascendancy, albeit not exclusively—in the one case, the labor of the soul's purification, in the other its illumination; and finally its state of union with God. It goes without saying that the habitual nature of the soul's conversations varies according to the state in which the soul finds itself.[1]

Due reserve made, then, for the attracting of the Holy Spirit[2] and the aptitudes of the soul, a person just starting out on the spiritual paths has to make real efforts to acquire by himself the habit of prayer. Although the Holy Spirit gives us powerful help in our relations with our Heavenly Father, His action does not take place in the soul independently of certain conditions that result from our nature. The Holy Spirit leads us on according to our nature; we are intellect and will, but we only will the good that we know; affection only flies towards the good the intellect shows. We ought, then, in order to attach ourselves to God fully— and is not that the best fruit of prayer?—we ought to know God as

---

[1] We shall go back over this point at greater length in another series of talks [see *Christ, the Ideal of the Monk*, VII, iii and XVI, iii]. The little we say about it here, however, will be enough to make our thinking understood.

[2] It is recounted in the life of St. Teresa of Avila that so much did divine grace precede a young novice, that from the first days of her religious life she received the gift of contemplation: *Histoire de Ste Thérèse*, according to the Bollandists, vol. 2, p. 70.

perfectly as possible. That is why, says St. Thomas, "everything that renders faith real is directed towards charity."[1]

At the beginning of its search for God, then, the soul ought to amass intellectual data and understandings of faith. Why? Because without that it will not know what to say, and the conversation will degenerate into a vague reverie, without depth and without fruit, or become so much an exercise filled with boredom that the soul will soon abandon it. Those understandings ought to be amassed at the beginning; and then, afterwards, be maintained, renewed, increased. How can one set about it? One should give oneself over for some time, with the help of a book, to a prolonged reflection on some point or other of Revelation. The soul devotes a period—longer or shorter according to its aptitudes—to considering in that way the principal articles of its faith, so as to see them in detail. The result is that in these successive reflections, the soul derives the necessary understandings which are to serve as its point of departure for prayer.

This labor, purely discursive, ought not to be mistaken for prayer itself. It is only a preamble—useful and necessary, in order to enlighten, guide, make manageable or give support to the intellect, but a preamble all the same. Prayer does not really commence until the time when the will, stirred into flame, makes super-natural contact with Divine Good through affection and abandons itself to Him through love, so as to please Him, so as to carry out His precepts and His desires. It is in the heart that prayer essentially resides. It is said of the Virgin Mary that she kept the words of Jesus "in her heart";[2] it is there, indeed—never forget it—that prayer fundamentally has its lodging-place. When Our Lord taught His apostles to pray, He did not say: "Engage in this or that reasoning," but "Express the affection of your hearts as children": "In this manner ... shall you pray: 'Our Father... hallowed be thy name.'"[3] "The petitions Christ has taught us to make,"

---

[1] *On St. Paul's First Epistle to Timothy*, ch. 2, lect. 2a.   [2] Luke 2:51.   [3] Matt. 6:9.

says St. Augustine, "are the model for the desires of our heart."[1] A soul—we are here only making a supposition—who regularly confined his labors to intellectual reasoning, even on matters of faith, would not be engaging in prayer.[2]

That is why one encounters souls, even amongst those who are beginners, who gain more fruit from a simple reading, interspersed with affections and aspirations of the heart, than they would from an exercise where reason came almost exclusively into play. In this, one cannot, at the beginning, avoid a certain, repeated, "feeling of the way forward." In order to be wary of the delusions of sloth, the soul must necessarily seek the help of an enlightened director.

---

[1] *Sermo* LVI, 3, c.

[2] This is what the Abbé Saudreau, whose ascetical works may be familiar to you, says (the insertion in square brackets is ours): "Let us note well: petition is the central part of prayer; or, to put it better, prayer does not commence without it. During the time when the soul is not turning to God to speak to Him [to praise, bless, glorify Him, to take pleasure in His perfections, to address its supplications to Him, to deliver itself up to where He leads], the soul can meditate, it is true; but it does not pray, it is not saying its prayers. One sees people who misunderstand this and, in an exercise of half an hour, spend *all* their time in *reflecting*, without saying anything to God. Even if they have added holy desires and generous resolutions to their reflections, that still is not saying their prayers. Doubtless the mind has not been alone in acting, the heart has been set afire, has been disposed to good with ardor, but it has not poured itself out into the heart of God. Meditations of such a kind are a little bit near to being sterile; very quickly they engender fatigue, and very often also discouragement and the abandoning of this holy exercise": *Les degrés de la vie spirituelle*, vol. 1, i.II, ch. 3, a. 2. Cf. also Rev. Fr. Schrijvers, CSSR, *La bonne volonté*, Part II, ch. 1, *L'oraison*.

4. In the illuminative way, how important *contemplation of the mysteries of Christ* is. *The state* of prayer.

NONETHELESS, it is a fact of experience that the more a soul advances along the spiritual paths, the more the discursive labor of reasoning is going to diminish. Why is that? Because the soul, at that time it has reached, is filled with Christian truths; it no longer needs to amass understandings of faith; those understandings henceforth *are* amassed, the soul possesses them. The only thing for it to do will be to maintain and renew them by holy reading.

Hence, long considerations are much less necessary to this soul, wholly permeated as it is, wholly laden with Divine truths. The soul has within it all the material elements of prayer; it can now enter into contact with God without the discursive toil imposed in a regular way on those who do not yet possess those understandings. This law of experience naturally involves exceptions which have to be carefully respected. There are souls very advanced on the spiritual paths who can never enter into prayer without the help of a book. Reading a book helps them to start up, so to speak: it would be a mistake for them to do without it. There are others who can only converse with God by praying vocally: to urge them to go down another path would be to hinder them. However, in a general way, it remains true that in measure as a soul progresses in the light of faith and in fidelity, the Holy Spirit's action increases in that soul; it feels less and less the necessity of having recourse to reasoning in order to find God.

This is especially true, as experience also shows, of those who have a deeper and more extensive understanding of the mysteries of Christ.

Listen to what St. Paul wrote to the early Christians: "Let the word of Christ dwell in you abundantly."[1] The great apostle desires this in order that the faithful may "in all wisdom teach and admonish one

---

[1] Col. 3:16.

another." But that exhortation is of value also for our conversations with God. How is that?

The word of Christ is contained in the Gospels, which are principally, along with the letters of St. Paul and St. John, the most supernatural (because the inspired) exposition of the mysteries of Christ. The child of God finds there the best title to his divine adoption and the most direct example for his conduct. Christ Jesus shows Himself to us there in His earthly existence, in His doctrine, in His love. We find there the best source for knowing God, His nature, His perfections, His works: He "has shone in our hearts ... in the face of Christ Jesus."[1] Christ is the great revelation of God to the world; God says to us: "This is my beloved Son ... hear Him."[2] It is as if God were saying to us: "If you wish to be pleasing to me, look at my Son, imitate Him; I ask for nothing else, for in that is your predestination—that you be conformed to my Son."

Looking at Our Lord and contemplating His actions is the most direct road to knowing God. To see Him is to see His Father; He is but one with His Father; He does only what is pleasing to His Father; every one of His actions is the object of His Father's delight and deserves to be the object of our contemplation. "Though you may have been at the very summit of contemplation," writes St. Teresa of Avila, "take no other road than that of looking upon the sacred Humanity of Jesus. Upon that road one walks with assurance. Our Lord is for us the source of all good; He Himself will teach you. Look at His life; there is no better model." And the Saint adds: "That we of ourselves, designedly and sedulously, instead of forming the habit of having (in prayer) this holy Humanity always present (and please God that it may indeed have been "always"!)—that we of ourselves may be doing precisely the contrary, is something, again, of which I disapprove. To act thus is to walk on empty air, as they say. And in fact, however full of God a soul

---

[1] Cor. 4:6 (Rheims).   [2] Matt. 17:5; Mark 9:6; Luke 9:35.

may think itself to be, it lacks a base on which to stand. We being men, it is very advantageous for us, all through our present life, to consider God made man."[1]

But Christ did not merely act, He also spoke: "... all that Jesus began to do *and teach*."[2] All His words reveal to us Divine secrets; all He speaks of, He sees. And His words, as He Himself tells us, are "spirit and life";[3] they contain the soul's life—not in the way the sacraments do, but they, His words, carry with them the light that enlightens and the strength that sustains. The actions and the words of Jesus are for us motives for trust and love, and mainsprings of action.

That is why the words of Christ must "abide in" us—so that they may become for us sources of life. That is also why, for the soul who desires to live by prayer, it is so useful constantly to re-read the Gospels, to follow the Church, our Mother, when she re-presents to us the actions and recalls to us the words of Jesus in the course of the liturgical cycle. In making all the stages of the life of Christ—her Spouse, our elder Brother—pass before our eyes, the Church thereby furnishes for us an abundant source where the soul can find food for prayer. A soul that follows Our Lord step by step in this way possesses, as presented to it by the Church, the material elements necessary to that soul for prayer. It is there that the faithful soul finds above all the "Word of God," and, by uniting itself to Him through faith, is made super-naturally fruitful. For the least word of Christ Jesus is for the soul a light, a source of life and of peace.

It is the Holy Spirit who makes us understand these words in all their fruitfulness for us. What did Jesus say to His disciples before ascending to heaven? "The Holy Spirit, whom the Father will send in my name, will teach you everything and remind you of all I have said

[1] *Life, written by herself*, ch. XXII. One should read this magnificent chapter in its entirety, and hear in what bitter terms the great contemplative deplores her having, for a whole period, put aside contemplation of the humanity of Christ Jesus in her prayers.   [2] Acts 1:1 (RSV, Cath.)   [3] John 6:64.

to you."[1] That is not a promise without effect—for Christ's words do not pass away. Christ, the Incarnate Word, gave us His Spirit on the day of our baptism; He and the Father sent Him within us, because baptism made us children of the Heavenly Father and brethren of Christ Jesus. This Spirit dwells within us: "He will dwell with you, and be in you."[2] And what does He do within us, this Divine Spirit? Our Lord Himself declares it: the Spirit of Truth will "bring to mind" the words of Jesus. What does that signify? When we contemplate the actions of Christ Jesus, His mysteries, whether by reading the Gospels, or by going through some Life of Our Lord, or under the guidance of the Church in the course of the liturgical year, it happens that such and such a saying, that we have read and re-read many a time, maybe without its having particularly struck us, all of a sudden stands out in a super-natural relief such as we did not know before. That is a shaft of light which the Holy Spirit unexpectedly causes to flash into the depths of the soul. It is like the sudden revelation of a source of life unsuspected before then. It is like a new horizon, a wider one, that opens before our eyes. It is like a hidden world that the Spirit reveals to us. The Holy Spirit, whom the liturgy calls *Digitus Dei*, "Finger of God's right hand,"[3] engraves this Divine saying, etches it, into the soul; and there it ever remains, to be a light and a mainspring of action. If the soul is humble and attentive, that Divine saying will do its work there—silent, but fruitful.

When we are faithful in devoting a time every day, more long or less long, according to our aptitudes and the duties of our state of life, for conversing with our Heavenly Father and for garnering those inspirations and listening to those "reminders" of the Spirit, then the sayings of Christ—the *Verba Verbi*, the "words of the Word," as St. Augustine calls them—will multiply, flooding the soul with Divine light,

---

[1] John 14:26 (Jerus.)   [2] John 14:17.   [3] Hymn, *Veni Creator*.

and opening wellsprings of life within her at which she, the soul, can ever refresh herself. In this way the promise of Christ Jesus is fulfilled: "If anyone thirst, let him come to me and drink. He who believes in me, as the Scripture says, 'From within him there shall flow rivers of living water.'" And St. John adds: "He said this ... of the Spirit whom they who believed in Him were to receive."[1]

The soul, in return, constantly translates its feelings into acts of faith, of repentance, of compunction, of trust, of love, of taking pleasure [in God], of *abandon* to the will of the Heavenly Father. It moves as in an atmosphere that keeps it, more and more, in union with God; prayer becomes as it were its breath, its life; it is filled with the spirit of prayer. Prayer becomes then a *state*, and the soul can find its God whenever it wishes, even in the midst of all its occupations.

Those times of the day that a soul devotes exclusively to the formal *exercise* of prayer are but an intensification of this state, in which the soul stays, habitually but sweetly, united to God in order to speak to Him from its inner self, and in turn to listen to the voice from on high.

This state is more than the simple presence of God; it is an inner conversation, full of love, in which the soul speaks to God—sometimes with the lips, but more often it is the heart that speaks—and in which the soul stays intimately united with Him, despite the labors and the occupations of the day. There are many simple and upright souls who, faithful to the attracting of the Holy Spirit, arrive at this state that is so desirable.

Lord, teach us to pray![2]

---

[1] John 7:37-39.   [2] Luke 11:1.

5. The prayer *of faith*. *Extraordinary* prayer.

SOON, however, in measure as the soul comes closer to the Sovereign Good, it shares in the Divine simplicity more. In meditation we form for ourselves a conception of God, by means of the gift of reason, and that of Revelation. In measure as we advance in the super-natural life, the conceptions we have of God simplify, but those *conceptions* are not God. Where is God to be found as He is? In pure faith. Faith is for our soul, during the present life, what the beatific vision will be in heaven, where we shall see God face to face, as He is.

Faith reveals to us the incomprehensibility of God. When we have come to see that God infinitely surpasses all our conceptions, we have then come to that point where we start to understand what God is. The conceptions we have of God, analogous though they be, nevertheless show us something of the Divine *perfections* and *attributes*. In *the prayer of faith*, the soul understands that the Divine *essence*, as it is in itself, in its transcendent simplicity, is not at all what is represented to us by the intellect—even the intellect aided by Revelation.[1] The soul has removed from its sight everything that the senses, the imagination, the intellect even, up to a certain point, has presented to it—the soul has done that in order to rest where God is shown by pure faith. It has progressed, it has successively passed through the spheres of the senses and the imagination, of intellectual understandings, of revealed symbols; it has arrived at the veil of the Holy of holies. It knows that God is hidden behind this veil, as in darkness; it almost touches Him, but it does not see Him. In this state of the prayer of faith, the soul stays recollected in God, with whom it feels itself united, notwithstanding the darkness which the beatific light—that alone—will cause to disappear. Without greatly varying its affections, the soul tastes the happiness of staying there before God: "I sat in the shadow of the one I had desired, and His fruit was sweet to my taste."[2] That is a beginning of *the prayer of quiet*. One can affirm that many souls, faithful to grace,

---

[1] St Thomas, I, q. XIII, a. 2, ad 3.   [2] See Song of Songs 2:3.

arrive there. When prayer of that kind asserts and strengthens itself in the soul, the soul finds in this very simple adhesion of faith, in this embrace of love, the courage, the inner elevation, the liberty of heart, the humility before God, the *abandon*, which are so necessary for it in that long pilgrimage towards the holy mountain, towards the plenitude of God: "An abundance of words," says St. Augustine, "is one thing; a lasting affection quite another."[1]

Then, if it pleases the Supreme Goodness, God will lead the soul on beyond the common frontiers of the super-natural, in order to give Himself to her in mysterious communications, where the natural faculties, upraised by the Divine action, receive, under the influence of the gifts of the Holy Spirit (notably, understanding and wisdom) a higher mode of operation. Writers on mysticism describe the different degrees of these Divine operations which are sometimes accompanied by extraordinary phenomena, like ecstasies.[2]

There is no way at all in which we can arrive by our own efforts at such degrees of prayer and of union with God; they are solely dependent on the free and sovereign will of God. May one, however, desire them?

The answer is no, if it is a question of the accidental phenomena that accompany prayer, such as ecstasy, revelations, stigmata; there would be presumption and temerity in desiring them.

But if it is a question of the very substance of prayer, that is to say, of the knowledge of Himself and His perfections—most pure, simple and perfect knowledge—which God gives us in prayer; of the very intense love derived therefrom in the soul, then I will say to you: Desire with

---

[1] *Epist.* CXXX, c. 19.

[2] Our readers will be acquainted with the recent excellent works with the following titles: *L'état mystique*, by the Abbé Saudreau; *Les graces d'oraison*, by Rev. Fr. Poulain, SJ; *La contemplation ou les principes de théologie mystique*, by Rev. Fr. Lamballe; *Des voies de l'oraison mentale*, by Dom Lehody.

all your strength to possess a high degree of prayer, to enjoy perfect contemplation. For God is the principal author of our holiness; He acts powerfully in these communications, and not to desire them would be not to desire to "love the Lord your God with all your heart, and with all your soul, and with all your mind, and with all your strength."[1] And then, what is it which gives our life all its value, which—on our part and making due allowance for the Divine action—determines the degree of our holiness? It is, as I have told you, the purity and the intensity of the love with which we go through life, perform the actions of our life. Now, outside of the direct action of the sacraments, this purity and this intensity of charity are drawn forth abundantly in prayer; and that is why prayer is so useful for us. That is also why we can legitimately desire to possess a high degree of prayer.

It is clear, at the same time, that we must subordinate this desire to the will of God; He alone knows what best suits our souls; and while we should spare neither our efforts to stay generously and humbly faithful to present grace, nor our ardent aspirations towards a higher perfection, it is nevertheless important that we remain constantly at peace, assured as we are of the goodness and wisdom of God in regard to each one of us.

6. *The dispositions* required in order to make prayer fruitful: purity of heart, recollection of mind, *abandon*, humility and reverence.

RETURNING to ordinary prayer, it remains for me to come back to the *dispositions* of heart we should bring to it in order to make it fruitful.

In order to converse with God, we must first of all *detach ourselves from created persons and things*; we cannot worthily speak to our Heavenly Father if created beings occupy the imagination, the mind and, above all, the heart. Purity of soul is extremely necessary: it is an indispensable remote preparation.

---

[1] Mark 12:30 (RSV, Cath.)

Further, we should *be recollected*. Souls who are light-minded, lacking concentration, habitually inattentive, and who make no serious effort to repress the wanderings of a vagabond imagination, will never be souls of prayer. During the prayer itself, we should not trouble ourselves about the distractions that occur, but should remain faithful and bring the mind back gently, without violence, to the subject that should be occupying us—if need be, with the aid of a book.

Why is this solitude, physical solitude even, and this interior detachment of the soul—why are they necessary for prayer? Because, as I have told you following St. Paul, it is the Holy Spirit who prays in us, for us. Now, His action in the soul is extremely delicate; we ought to do nothing to impede that action—nothing that will "grieve the Holy Spirit," as St. Paul puts it";[1] otherwise this Divine Spirit will end up being silent. But, in abandoning ourselves to Him, we ought to clear away all the obstacles that stand in the way of the liberty of His operations. We ought to say: "Speak, Lord, for your servant hears"[2]—"speak, O Divine Master! speak to my soul; and may my soul listen to you." But that voice we shall only hear properly in the silence of the soul.

We ought especially to be in that general and basic disposition of which I have spoken to you in regard to preparation for Holy Communion; the disposition of refusing nothing of what God asks of us, of being ready, following the example of Our Lord, to do everything that is pleasing to His Father: "I do always the things that are pleasing to Him."[3] This disposition is excellent, because it delivers up the soul to the accomplishment of the Divine wishes. When we say to God in prayer: "Lord, you are infinitely good and perfect, you alone are worthy of all love and all glory; I give myself to you, and because I love you, I embrace your holy will," then the Divine Spirit shows us an imperfection to correct, a sacrifice to make, a good work to carry out; and our love leads us to eradicate everything displeasing to the sight of our Heavenly Father, brings us to accomplish His good pleasure.

[1] Eph. 4:30.   [2] 1 Kings (1 Samuel) 3:10.   [3] John 8:29.

For that we ought also to enter into prayer with a disposition of deep reverence before the majesty of our Father: the Father "of an infinite majesty."[1] We are *adopted* children; fundamentally we remain created beings. God, even when He communicates Himself intimately to the soul, remains God—that is to say, the infinitely sovereign Being, "Lord of all things."[2] Adoration is an essential reaction of the soul before God: "Such the Father seeks to worship Him"—those "who worship Him ... in spirit and truth."[3] Note the combination of those two words "Father" and "worship." We become children of God, but we stay created beings.

God, moreover, wishes that, by that humble and deep reverence, we recognize our powerlessness. In prayer, He makes the conferment of His gifts subject to this avowal which constitutes a homage at the same time to His power and to His goodness: "God resists the proud, but gives grace to the humble."[4] And you know how, in the parable of the Pharisee and the Publican, Our Lord put this truth into high relief.[5]

This humility ought to be the greater in the soul who has offended God by sin. The attitude of the soul ought then to reveal that interior compunction which makes us regret our wrongdoings and prostrates us at the feet of the Lord, like Mary Magdalene the sinner.

However, despite our past sins and our present miseries, we can approach very close to God. How so? Through Our Lord. "God is so great, so holy, so perfect," you say to me? That is true. Of ourselves, we are far distant from God. But Christ Jesus has brought us near to God: "You, who were once afar off, have been brought near through the blood of Christ."[6] "I am so shabby!" you say? Admittedly—but Christ gives us His riches in order that we may present ourselves before His Father. "My soul has been so soiled!" But the blood of Jesus has washed it and given it back all its beauty. It is Christ, indeed, who has

---

[1] Hymn, *Te Deum*.   [2] 2 Mach. 14:35.   [3] John 4:23-24 (RSV, Cath.)
[4] James 4:6.   [3] Luke 18:9-14.   [6] Eph. 2:13.

made up for our distance from God, for our misery, our unworthiness. It is on Him that we ought to lean in prayer. Through His Incarnation He has closed the gap which separates man from God.

7. Only *union with Christ Jesus by faith* is able to make *the life of prayer fruitful.* The joy arising for the soul from that union.

THIS POINT I have been making is of such great importance for all souls aspiring to a life of prayer, that I want to insist on it.

As you know, the abyss between God and us, between Creator and creature, is infinite. God alone is able to say: "I am the Being subsistent of myself": "I AM who AM."[1] Every other being is drawn from nothingness. Who will throw a bridge across that abyss? Christ Jesus. He is, par excellence, the Mediator, the High Priest, Bridge between man and God. It is only through Christ Jesus that we can rise up to God. What the Word Incarnate says on that is decisive: "No one comes to the Father but through me."[2] It is as if He were saying: "You will only arrive at the divinity by going through my humanity." He is, you should never forget, the Way, the one and only Way. Christ alone, God and Man, lifts us up to His Father. From this, we see how much it matters to have a living faith in Christ Jesus. If we have this faith in the power of His humanity, as being the humanity of one who is God, we shall be assured that Christ can make us enter into contact with God. For, as I have said to you often, the Word, by uniting Himself with human nature, has, in principle, united us all with Him. Christ carries us, united with Him through grace, into that sanctuary of the divinity where, as the Word, He is before all ages: "and the Word was with God."[3] He admits us with Him into the Holy of holies, as St. Paul says.[4]

---

[1] Exod. 3:14.   [2] John 14:6.
[3] John 1:1: "In the beginning was the Word, and the Word was with God, and the Word was God."   [4] Hebr. 9:12.

It is through Christ that we have become children of God: "God sent his Son ... that we might receive the adoption of sons."[1] It is, therefore, also through Christ and united with Him that we shall *act* as children of God, that we shall fulfill the duties which flow from our divine adoption. Consequently, if it is in our capacity of children of God that we ought to present ourselves to God in prayer, we have also to do that presenting with Christ and through Christ. We ought never to begin our prayer without uniting ourselves, in intention and from the heart, with Our Lord, asking Him to admit us to the Father's presence. We have to unite our prayers to those He made here below on earth, to that sublime prayer which, in His capacity of Mediator and High Priest, He continues in heaven for us, incessantly: "always living to make intercession for us."[2]

See how Our Lord has sanctified our prayers by His example: "all night He continued in prayer to God."[3] St. Paul tells us that this Divine High Priest, in the days of His life on earth, "offered up prayers and supplications, with loud cries and tears."[4] "O Christian," says St. Ambrose in speaking of the prayer of Christ, "an image has been given you, a model has been presented to you, that you ought to imitate."[5] Jesus prayed for Himself when He asked His Father to glorify Him: "And now, Father, glorify me."[6] He prayed for His disciples: "I pray for them ... because they are yours"—because they belong, through me, to the Father; "I do not pray that you take them out of the world, but that you keep them from evil."[7] He prayed for all of us who believe in Him: "And not for them only [the disciples] do I pray, but for them also who through their word shall believe in me."[8]

Moreover, Christ Jesus has given us a wonderful formula of praying, in that prayer in which is found everything a child of God can ask of

---

[1] Gal. 4:4-5.   [2] Hebr. 7:25 (Rheims).   [3] Luke 6:12 (RSV, Cath.)
[4] Hebr. 5:7 (RSV, Cath.)   [5] *Exposit. Evangel. in Luc.*, V, c. 6.   [6] John 17:5.
[7] John 17, vv. 9, 15.   [8] John 17:20 (Rheims).

its Heavenly Father. "*Our Father ... hallowed be thy name*"—may I act in everything for your glory, may that be the prime motive-power of all my actions. "*Thy kingdom come*"—in me, in all those you have created; may you truly be the Master and Sovereign of my heart. In all things, pleasant or painful, "*thy will be done*"! May I be able to say, like your Son, that I live for you. All our prayers, says St. Augustine, ought to come down, basically, to those acts of love, those aspirations, those most pure desires, which Christ Jesus, the Beloved Son, has placed upon our lips, and which His Spirit, the Spirit of adoption, re-echoes within our hearts.[1] The "Our Father" is the prayer par excellence of a child of God.

Not only has Our Lord sanctified our prayers by His example; not only has He thereby given us a model, but, also, He supports them by His credit, a Divine and infallible credit. For our High Priest, Bridge of man to God, has always the right to be heard: He "was heard because of His reverent submission."[2] He Himself has told us that everything—everything which is for our good—that we ask the Father for "in my name" (claiming upon Him, that is to say) will be given to us.[3]

When, therefore, we present ourselves before God, let us be mistrustful of ourselves certainly, but let us especially quicken our faith in the power that Christ, our head and elder brother has, of bringing us into the close presence of His Father, who is our Father also: "I ascend to my Father and your Father."[4] For if that faith is a living one, we

---

[1] "The words our Lord Jesus Christ has taught us for praying are the ideal of our desires; you have no right to ask for anything except what is to be found written there": St. Augustine, *Sermo* LVI, c. 3. "For, whatever other words we say, which the disposition of the person praying either conceives and says by way of preface to clarify it, or directs attention to at the end so as to strengthen it, we say nothing more than what is already contained in this Lord's Prayer, assuming we pray properly, in the way it ought to be prayed. In praying, one is free to use other words, provided they express the same thing, but one should not be free to say something else": St. Augustine, *Epist.* CXXX, c. 12.   [2] Hebr. 5:7.

[3] John 15:16.   [4] John 20:17.

unite ourselves firmly to Christ; and Christ who is "dwelling through faith in your hearts"[1] takes us with Him. "Father, I will that where I am, they also whom you have given me may be with me."[2] And where *is* He? *In sinu Patris*—we, through faith, are where He is in reality: in the heart's-embrace of the Father.[3] In Christ, says St. Paul, "we have assurance and confident access through faith in Him."[4]

It is there that the conversation begins. Christ, through His Spirit, prays with us, for us, "always living to make intercession for us." What a motive for our having immense confidence when coming before God! Presented by Christ who has merited for us our divine sonship, we "are now no longer strangers and foreigners," but children—"members of God's household";[5] we can be unconstrained in a tender love allied perfectly with a deep reverence. The Holy Spirit, who is the Spirit of Jesus, harmonizes in us, by His gifts of fear and piety,[6] those feelings of limitless adoration and boundless trust which at first sight seem so contrary to each other, and He gives to our inner attitude just the right note that is fitting for such a conversation.

Let us, therefore, lean upon Christ. "Whatever you ask in my name, I will do it, that the Father may be glorified in the Son."[7] "Hitherto (He further said to His apostles) you have not asked anything in my name. Ask, and you shall receive, that your joy may be full."[8] Asking in the name of Jesus is asking for what conforms to our salvation, by being united to Him through faith and love, as living members of His mystical body. Christ "prays *for* us as High Priest; He prays *in* us as our head," says St. Augustine.[9] That is why, he adds, the Eternal Father cannot separate us from Christ, any more than the body is separated from the head. In seeing us, He sees His Son, for we make but one with His Son.

---

[1] Eph. 3:17.   [2] John 17:24.   [3] See John 1:18 [Jerus.]   [4] Eph. 3:12.   [5] Eph. 2:19.
[6] [*Translator's note*: "piety": see note 1 on page 422.]   [7] John 14:13 (RSV, Cath.)
[8] John 16:24.   [9] *Enarr. in Ps.* XLXXV, c. 1.

And that, also, is why, in granting us what His Son asks of Him in us, the Father is "glorified in the Son"; for He finds His glory in loving His Son and placing His delight in Him. "God," says St. Teresa of Avila, "is extremely pleased to see a soul humbly placing His Divine Son as an intermediary between that soul and Him."[1] Is this not what the Church, Bride of Christ, herself does when she ends her prayers with the name of her Divine Bridegroom: "who, with the Father and the Holy Spirit, lives and reigns...."?

And, at the same time, our joy is full. Not here below, of course, where we still have to struggle, and where we cannot always obtain at once what we desire—for, according to the thought of St. Augustine, "the man that sows today cannot hope to reap as soon as tomorrow";[2] but it becomes fuller little by little, this inner joy of being a child of God, and we have confidence that one day it will come to full flower in heaven's bliss. For the soul that faithfully devotes itself to prayer disengages itself more and more from what is created, in order to enter more deeply into the life of God.

Let us, then, seek to be souls who remain united to God through a life of prayer. Let us ask Our Lord to grant us this infinitely precious gift, itself the source of excellent graces. Let us ask for this gift in the measure that is fitting for each one of us according to the Divine plan. If we are faithful in entreating this and, on the other hand, in responding, in the measure of our weakness, to the graces God gives us in Christ, we may be assured that we shall live more and more according to the spirit of our adoption; and our status as children of God, as brethren of Jesus Christ, is going to be strengthened more and more, to the glory of our Heavenly Father and to the plenitude of our joy: "that the Father may be glorified in the Son," "that your joy may be full."

---

[1] *Œuvres*, vol. 1, p. 281.   [2] Cf. *Tract. in Johann.*, LXXIII, n. 4.

CHAPTER ELEVEN

"Love One Another"

INTRODUCTION.

In all the preceding pages, we have seen how faith in Jesus Christ, Son of God—a living practical faith which, under the influence of love, finds expression in works of life and is nourished by the Eucharist and by prayer—brings us by degrees to intimate union with Christ, to the point of transforming us into Him.

But if we want this transformation of our life into that of Christ Jesus to be complete and real, to encounter no obstacle to its perfection, then the love that we have for Our Lord must radiate around us and shine out upon everyone. That is what St. John indicates to us when he sums up the whole of Christian life in these words: "And this is His commandment, that we should believe in the name of His Son Jesus Christ, and love one another."[1]

I have shown you, up to now, how faith in Our Lord is put into practice. It remains for me now to tell you how we shall carry out His precept of mutual love. Let us therefore see why Christ has made this precept of charity in regard to His members the completion, as it were, of the love we ought to have for His Divine Person; and what are the characteristics this charity entails.

[1] 1 John 3:23.

1. Fraternal charity — *new commandment* and *distinctive sign* of souls who belong to Christ. Why love towards one's neighbor is the *manifestation of love towards God.*

WHEN did St. John hear this commandment that he makes known to us? At the Last Supper. The day so ardently desired by Our Lord has arrived: "With desire I have desired....";[1] He has eaten the paschal meal with His disciples, but He has replaced figures and symbols by a Divine reality; He has just instituted the Sacrament of union, and given His apostles the power of perpetuating it. And now it is that, before going to suffer death, he opens His sacred heart so as thereby to reveal its secrets to His "friends"; it is like the will and testament of Christ. His words are: "A new commandment I give unto you: That you love one another, as I have loved you":[2] and at the end of His discourse He renews His precept: "This is my commandment, that you love one another."[3]

Our Lord begins by saying that the love we ought to have for one another constitutes "a new commandment." Why that expression?

Our Lord calls "new" the precept of *Christian* charity, because the latter had not been explicitly promulgated, at least in its universal acceptation, in the Old Testament. The precept of the love of God had indeed been explicitly given in the Pentateuch, and love of God includes *implicitly* love of neighbor. Some great saints of the Old Testament had, by the light of grace, understood that the duty of fraternal affection extended to the whole human race. But in no part of the Old Law does one find an *explicit* precept to love *everyone*. The precept "You shall not bear hatred for *your brother* ... cherish no grudge against *your fellow-countrymen.* You shall love your *neighbor* as yourself"[4] was understood by the Israelites, not of everyone, but of one's neighbor in a restricted sense (the Hebrew word indicates that "neighbor" means: those of your race, a "compatriot," "one like you"). Besides, God Himself

---

[1] Luke 22:15 (Rheims).   [2] John 13:34 (Rheims).
[3] John 15:12.   [4] Levit. 19:17-18 (St P.)

having forbidden His people to have any connection with certain races, having even ordered them to be exterminated (the Canaans),[1] the Jews had added a false interpretation, which did not come from God: "You shall love your neighbor and hate your enemy." The *explicit* precept to love everyone, including one's enemies, had not been affirmed and promulgated before the time of Jesus Christ. That is why He calls it a "new" precept and "His" precept.

And so much does He care about the observation of His new commandment, that He asks His Father to bring about this mutual tenderness of heart: "Holy Father, keep them in your name whom you have given me … that they may be one, as we also are one … I in them, and you in me: that they may be made perfect in one."[2]

Note well that this prayer is one that Jesus made not only for His apostles, but for all of us: "Not for them only do I pray, but for them also who through their word shall believe in me: that they all may be one, as you, Father, in me, and I in you: that they also may be one in us."[3]

So, it is the supreme wish of Christ, this commandment of love for our brethren. So much is it His desire, that He makes it, not a counsel but a commandment — *His* commandment, and gives the accomplishment of it as the infallible sign by which one will recognize His disciples: "By this all men will know that you are my disciples, if you have love for one another."[4] It is a sign within reach of all, He has not given us any other: "By this *all men* will know …," it is an unmistakable sign: the super-natural love that you will have for one another will be unequivocal proof that you truly belong to me, Christ. And in fact, in the early centuries the pagans used to recognize Christians by this sign: "Just see," they would say, "how they love each other!"[5]

---

[1] One can understand this severity of Jehovah in regard to populations sunk in the worst idolatries and immoralities: contact with them would inevitably have been fatal to the Israelites.   [2] John 17, vv. 11 and 22-23 (Rheims).   [3] John 17:20-21 (Rheims).
[4] John 13:35 (RSV, Cath.)   [5] Tertullian, *Apolog.*, c. 39.

For Our Lord Himself, this will be the sign of which He will make use on Judgement Day to distinguish the elect from the reprobate; it is He who tells us that. Let us listen to Him, for He is infallible Truth.

After the resurrection of the dead, the Son of Man will be seated on His throne of glory; the nations will be assembled before Him: He will place the good on His right hand and the wicked on His left. And, addressing the good: "Come, blessed of my Father, take possession of the kingdom prepared for you from the foundation of the world." And what reason for this will He give? "I was hungry and you gave me to eat; I was thirsty and you gave me to drink; I was a stranger and you took me in; naked and you covered me; sick and you visited me; I was in prison and you came to me."[1] And the just will be astonished, for they have never seen Christ in these necessities. But He will reply to them: "Truly I say to you, as long as you did it to one of these, my least brethren, you did it to me"[2]—"*You did it to me.*" He will then speak in the same way in addressing the wicked, He will separate them from Himself for ever; He will curse them—"Depart from me, accursed ones." Why? Because these ones have not loved Him in the persons of His brethren.[3]

So, from the very mouth of Jesus, we know that the sentence that will decide our eternal fate will be founded on the love we have had for Jesus Christ in the persons of our brethren. When we appear before Christ on the Last Day, He will not ask us if we have fasted much, if we have lived a life of penance, if we have passed numerous hours in prayer—no, but if we have loved and helped our brethren. Then is it that the other commandments are left on one side? Certainly not; but fulfilling them will have served for nothing if we have not observed this precept—so dear to Our Lord, since it is *His* commandment—of loving one another.

[1] Matt. 25:31-36.   [2] Matt. 25:40 (Rheims).   [3] Matt. 25:41-45.

On the other hand, it is impossible for a soul to be perfect in the love of neighbor without that soul possessing within itself a love of God; a love which at the same time embraces the full extent of the Divine will. Why is that?

The reason is that charity—whether it has God for its object or is exercised in regard to one's neighbor—is *one* in the super-natural *motive* for it, namely the infinite perfection of God.[1] This, therefore, is why if you truly love God you will necessarily love your neighbor. "Having perfect love towards neighbor," said the Eternal Father to St. Catherine of Siena, "depends essentially on having perfect love for me. The same measure of perfection or imperfection that the soul puts into its love for me is found also in the love it bears to creatures."[2] From another standpoint, there are so many things which cause us to be distanced from our neighbor: selfishness, conflicts of interest, differences of character, injuries received, that if you truly and super-naturally love your neighbor it cannot but be that the love of God is reigning in your soul, and, with the love of God, the other virtues He commands. If you do not love God, your love of neighbor will not for long resist the difficulties it will meet in being exercised.

It is, therefore, not without reason that Our Lord gives this "charity" as the distinctive sign by which, infallibly, one will recognize His disciples: "By this all men will know...." And so St. Paul writes that all the commandments are "summed up in these words 'You shall love your neighbor as yourself.'"[3] And again, in a more explicit way: "The *whole* of the law is summed up in *one* phrase, 'You shall love your neighbor as yourself.'"[4]

---

[1] Cf. St Thomas, II-II, q. XXV, a. 1.

[2] *Dialogue* (in the Hurtaud translation, II, p. 199).

[3] See Rom. 13:9. [*Translator's note*: To quote v. 9 precisely, St. Paul instances the commandments against committing adultery, killing, stealing and coveting, and continues: "and if there is any other commandment, it is summed up," etc.]

[4] Gal. 5:14 (Knox).

It is what St. John said so well: "If we love one another, God abides in us and His love is perfected in us."[1] Echoing Christ whose last words he heard, St. John says that charity is the mark of children of God. "We *know*"—note the sovereign certainty expressed by this way of putting it: we *know*—"that we have passed from death to life (supernatural and divine life) if we love our brethren. He who does not love, abides in death."[2] St. Augustine says: "Do you want to know whether you live the life of grace, whether God is giving you His friendship, whether you truly are numbered among Christ's disciples, whether you live by His Spirit? Examine yourselves; see whether you love your fellow-men, all of them, whether you love them for God, and you will have your answer. And that answer is one which does not deceive."[3]

Listen to what St. Teresa of Avila likewise says on this subject; the passage is a bit long, but it is very explicit. "God asks of you two things only: one is that you love Him; and the other is that you love your neighbor. That, therefore, is what we have to work at; by accomplishing the two things faithfully we shall do His will and be united with Him." She states our goal there; how shall we be sure of reaching it? "The most certain indication by which to know whether we practice those two things faithfully," continues the Saint, "is, to my mind, the indication that we have a sincere and real love for our neighbor. For we cannot with certainty know how far our love for God goes, even though there may be large signs for judging of that; but we see much more clearly in what concerns love of neighbor. It is therefore extremely important for us to consider well what our disposition of soul is, and what our outward conduct is, in regard to our neighbor. If everything is perfect in the one and in the other, then we can be reassured, for, considering the depravity of our nature, we could never

[1] 1 John 4:12.　　　　　　　　　　　　　　　　[2] See 1 John 3:14.

[3] "Do you want to know whether you have received the (Holy) Spirit? Question your heart, and if you find love of your brother there, be reassured. There is no love possible without the Spirit of God": *Tract in Epistol. Johann.*, VI, c. 3.

love our neighbor perfectly if there were not within us a great love of God."[1]

In this, the great Saint is only echoing the teaching of St. John. That apostle, who is the herald of love, treats as "a liar" one who says "I love God," and hates his brother, for (St. John asks): "How can he who does not love his brother, whom he sees, love God, whom he does not see?"[2] What do these words signify?

We ought to love God *totaliter et totum*, entirely and entire.

To love God *totaliter*, "entirely," is to love God with all our soul, and all our mind, and all our heart, and all our strength:[3] it is to love God by accepting, to its full extent, what His holy will prescribes.

To love God *totum*, "entire," is to love God and all that God associates with Himself. Now, what *does* God associate with Himself? First of all, He associates with Himself the humanity of Christ, in the Person of the Word. And that is why we cannot love God without loving Christ Jesus at the same time. When we tell God that we want to love Him, God asks us first of all to accept this humanity united personally with His Word: "This is my beloved Son ... hear Him."[4] But the Word, by uniting Himself to human nature, has, in principle, united the whole of humanity in a mystical fashion: Christ is but the eldest-born of a multitude of brethren, brethren whom God makes partakers of His nature, and with whom He wishes to share His divine life, His own beatitude. So united with Him are they, that Our Lord Himself declares that they are like "gods," that is to say, similar to God.[5] They are through grace what Jesus is by nature: the beloved sons of God. We touch here upon the inner reason for the precept that Jesus calls "His" commandment, upon the deep reason why it is of such vital importance. Since the Incarnation and through the Incarnation, all men are

---

[1] *The Interior Castle*, Fifth mansion, c. 3.   [2] 1 John 4:20.
[3] Deut. 6:5; Mark 12:30; Luke 10:27.   [4] Matt. 17:5; Mark 9:6; Luke 9:35.
[5] "Jesus answered them: Is it not written in your law: '*I said, you are gods*'?" (John 10:34, Rheims); Jesus quoting Ps. 81 (82):6.

by right, if not in fact, united to Christ as the members are united to the head in the one same body. The damned, alone, are cut off for ever from that union.

There are souls who seek God in Christ Jesus, who accept the humanity of Christ, but who stop there. That is not enough; we should accept the Incarnation with all the consequences it imposes; we should not let the gift of ourselves stop at Christ's own humanity, but should extend it to His mystical body. That is why—never forget this, for I touch here on one of the most important points of the super-natural life—to abandon the least one of our brethren is to abandon Christ Himself; to bring relief to one of these is to bring relief to Christ in person. When someone hits a part of your body—hits your eye or your arm—it is you yourself on whom the blow lands. In the same way, to strike a blow at our neighbor, whosoever it may be, is to strike a blow at one of the members of the body of Christ; it is to lay hands on Christ Himself.

And that is why Our Lord tells us that whatever we do, of good or of bad, to the least of His brethren, it is to Him that we do it.

Our Lord is Truth itself; what He teaches us cannot be other than based on a super-natural reality. Well, in this, the super-natural reality that faith makes us discover is that Christ, by becoming incarnate, united Himself mystically to the whole of humanity. Not to accept and not to love all those who belong, or can belong, to Christ through grace is not to accept and not to love Christ Himself.

We find a remarkable confirmation of this truth in the account of the conversion of St. Paul. Filled with hate against the Christians, he heads for the town of Damascus in order to imprison the disciples of Christ. And then, on the way there, he is thrown to the ground by the Lord, and he hears a voice cry out to him: "Why do you persecute me?"—why do you persecute *me?* "Who are you, Lord?" Paul asks. And the reply comes: "I am Jesus, whom you are persecuting." Christ does not say: "Why do you persecute my disciples?" No, He identifies Himself with them, and the blows the persecutor is dealing at the Christians are landing on Christ Himself: "I am Jesus, whom you are persecuting."[1]

The lives of the saints abound in touches of this kind. Look at St. Martin: he was a soldier, not yet baptized, and what happened was that on the road he was taking he encountered a poor man. Moved with compassion, he divides his cloak with him. The following night, Christ Jesus appears to Him, clothed in the part of the cloak that had been given to the poor man, and Martin, enraptured, hears these words: "It was you who clothed me in this habit."

Look at St. Elizabeth of Hungary. One day, in the absence of her husband, the duke, she encounters a little leper-boy, abandoned by everyone. She takes him and carries him to her own couch. The duke, on his return, hears the news and, wholly incensed, wants to drive the poor leper away. But, on approaching the bed, he sees the figure of Christ crucified.[2]

Likewise, we read in the Life of St. Catherine of Siena that one day she was in the church of the Dominican Friars when a poor man came up to her and asked her for alms for the love of God. She had nothing to give him, for she was unaccustomed to carry either gold or silver on her. She therefore asked the man who was begging to wait while she returned to her house, promising him she would then, gladly and unstintingly, give him as alms all she had been able to find at home. But the poor man insisted: "If you have something available, I ask that you give it to me here, for I cannot wait as long as that." Catherine, anxious, sought for what she might give him to relieve his necessity; she ended by finding on her a little silver cross, and, at once, she gave it joyfully to the poor man, who went away content. The following night, Our Lord appeared to the Saint; He had in His hand the little cross, adorned with precious stones. "Do you recognize this cross, dear child?" "Certainly, I recognize it," replies the Saint, "but it was not as beautiful as that when I had it." The Lord resumes: "You gave it me

---

[1] Acts 9:1-5 (RSV, Cath.)   [2] Montalembert, *Ste Élisabeth de Hongrie*, ch. 8.

yesterday, through love of the virtue of charity; it is this love that is signified by the precious stones. I promise you that on the day of judgement, before the whole assembly of angels and men, I shall present this cross to you, as you now see it, so that your joy may be overflowing. On that day, when I shall solemnly manifest the mercy and the justice of my Father, I shall not allow to be unknown this act of mercy you did to me."[1]

Christ has become our neighbor; or rather, our neighbor is Christ who presents Himself to us in this or that form: He presents Himself to us, suffering in those who are sick, destitute in those in want, a prisoner in those who are captives, sad in those who mourn. But it is faith that shows Him to us thus in His members; and if we do not see Him in them, it is because our faith is weak, our love imperfect. That is why St. John says that if we do not love our neighbor whom we see, how can we love God whom we do not see? If we do not love God under the visible form in which He presents Himself to us, that is to say in our neighbor, how can we say that we love Him in Himself, in His divinity?[2]

2. *Principle of this Divine disposing*; extension of the Incarnation. *Christ is one*: someone cannot separate himself from the mystical body without separating himself from Christ Himself

I HAVE told you already, when speaking of the Church, that there is something remarkable in the Divine disposing as revealed to us since the Incarnation, and that is the considerable place taken by men— persons with whom we live—as instruments of the conferring of grace.

If we want to know the authentic doctrine of Christ, we do not have to address ourselves to God directly or search in the inspired books ourselves, interpreting them through our own judgment; we

---

[1] *Life of St. Catherine*, by Blessed Raymond of Capua, II, ch. 3.
[2] Cf. St Thomas, II-II, q. XXIV, a. 2, ad 1.

have rather to ask the shepherds who have been constituted to govern the Church. "But are these not men," you will say to me, "men like us?" That does not matter; it is to them we must go, they represent Christ; it is Christ we must see in them: "He who hears you, hears me; and he who rejects you, rejects me."[1]

It is the same for receiving the sacraments: we have to receive them from the hands of men established by Christ. Baptism, forgiveness of our sins—it is Christ who confers them on us, but through the intermediacy of a man.

It is the same, also, for charity. Do you want to love God, do you want to love Christ Jesus?—and we have to, since this is "the greatest and the first commandment."[2] Then love your neighbor, love the persons with whom you live; love them because God purposes for them all (as He does for you) the same eternal beatitude, merited by Christ, our one and only head;[3] because it is in the form of our neighbor that God presents Himself to us here below.

So true is this, that God's conduct in regard to us is governed by what our own conduct is in regard to our neighbor: God acts towards us as we act towards our brethren. Here are Our Lord's own words: "The judgements you give are the judgements you will get, and the amount you measure out is the amount you will be given."[4] And see how He takes care to go into detail: your Heavenly Father will only forgive your offenses if you forgive those that are committed against you. If you do not show mercy, a judgement without mercy will be reserved for you. Do you want neither to be judged nor condemned? Then, do not yourselves either judge or condemn: "Do not judge, and you shall not be judged; do not condemn, and you shall not be condemned."[5] And if you want God to exercise kindness towards you,

---

[1] Luke 10:16.   [2] Matt. 22:38.

[3] "God is loved as being the cause of our beatitude; whereas our neighbor is loved as a sharer with us of the beatitude that comes from God": St Thomas, II-II, q. XXVI, a. 2.

[4] Matt. 7:2 (Jerus.)   [5] Luke 6:37.

exercise kindness in the same way in regard to men, your brethren. "Give," He says again, "and it shall be given to you," there will be poured into your heart a "good measure, pressed down, shaken together, running over."[1] And why so much insistence? Once again it is because, since the Incarnation, Christ is so united to humanity that the whole of the love we show super-naturally to men rebounds on to Christ.

Many souls, I am sure, will find here the reason for the difficulties, the bleakness, the slightness of the flowering of their interior life; they do not give themselves enough to Christ in the persons of His members; they hold themselves back too much. Let them give and it will be given to them, and given abundantly; for Christ Jesus does not let Himself be outdone in love. Let them rise above their selfishness, let them deliver themselves up to their neighbor with generosity, for God; and then Christ will deliver Himself up to them in plenitude. Because they forget self, Christ will take special care of them—and who better than He can lead us to beatitude?

It is no small thing to love our neighbor always and unfailingly; to do that needs a love that is strong and generous. Although love of God may in itself, because of the transcendence of its object, be more perfect than love of neighbor, nevertheless, as the motive should be the same in the love which we bear for God and in that which we bear for our neighbor,[2] often an act of love towards one's neighbor requires more intensity and gains more merit. Why is that? Because, God being beauty itself and goodness itself and He having shown us an infinite love, grace prompts us to love Him: whereas, in the case of our neighbor we are not without the possibility of encountering in him—or in us—obstacles resulting from different interests that surface between

[1] Luke 6:38.

[2] "God being the formal reason for the love we should have for our neighbor (for we should love our neighbor only for God), it is clear that the act by which we love God is specifically the same as that by which we love our neighbor": St Thomas, II-II, q. XXV, a. 1.

our neighbor and ourselves. These difficulties demand from the soul more fervor, more generosity, more forgetfulness of self and of the soul's own feelings and personal wishes; and that is why love of neighbor, if it is to be maintained, requires more effort.

In this there occurs something of what happens when a soul is in interior dryness; the soul then needs more generosity in order to remain faithful than when it abounds in consolations. It is the same when one is in suffering; God often makes use of it in the spiritual life so as to develop our love, because at such times the soul has to overcome itself more, and that is a sign of the firmness of its charity. Look at Our Lord; no loving action of His was more intense than at the time when, in the agony in the garden, He accepted the cup of bitterness held out to Him, and when, in abandonment by His Father, He carried out to the end His sacrifice upon the cross.

In a similar way, a super-natural love exercised towards one's neighbor despite repugnance, antipathy or natural differences of opinion shows, in the soul who possesses it, a greater intensity of divine life. I do not fear to say that a soul that delivers itself up super-naturally, unreservedly, to Christ in the person of its neighbor—I do not fear to say that such a soul has a great love of Christ and is infinitely loved by Him. That soul will make great progress towards oneness with Our Lord. Whereas if you meet someone who devotes himself to frequent prayer and, despite that, voluntarily closes his heart to the necessities of his neighbor, you may take it for certain that a large degree of illusion is entering his prayer-life. For prayer has as its object simply the yielding up of the soul to the Divine will. Now, in closing his heart to his neighbor, such a soul closes his heart to Christ, to the most sacred desire of Christ: "That they may be one ... that they may be made perfect in one."[1] True holiness shines forth through charity and the entire gift of oneself.

[1] John 17:22-23 (Rheims).

If, then, we want to remain united to Our Lord, it is extremely important to see whether we are united to the members of His mystical body. Let us be on our guard. The smallest intentional coldness, deliberately retained, against one of our brethren will constitute an obstacle —more or less grave, according to degree—to our union with Christ. That is why Christ tells us that if, at the time of presenting our gift at the altar, we remember that our brother has something against us, we should leave our gift before the altar and "go first to be reconciled to your brother, and then come and offer your gift" to the Lord.[1] When we go to Communion, we receive the substance of the physical body of Christ; we ought also to receive, accept, His mystical body. It is impossible for Christ to come down within us and be there a principle of union, if we maintain resentment against one of His members. St. Thomas styles a sacrilegious Communion "a lie."[2] Why is that? Because by approaching Christ to receive Him in Holy Communion, one affirms, by that very fact, that one is united to Him. If one is in a state of grave sin, that is to say if one has turned away from Christ, approaching Him constitutes a lie. In the same way (always keeping proportion in the matter),[3] to approach Christ, to want to be united with Him, when we exclude from our love a single one of His members, is to commit a lie; it is wanting to divide Christ. We ought to communicate with what St. Augustine calls "the whole Christ."[4]

[1] Matt. 5:23-24.

[2] "Since sinners who communicate in this sacrament in a state of mortal sin give it to be understood that they are united with Christ through a really living faith [*per fidem formatum*], they perpetuate a lie in thus going to Communion": St Thomas, III, q. LXXX, a. 4, conclusion.

[3] [*Translator's note*: I think these words of Marmion's are important for avoiding scruples about going to Communion. His references to refraining from Communion do not apply to every little tiff with a neighbor, but to *grave matters and mortal sin*, for that is how the Church interprets the intent of Christ's words. See further Marmion's exposition on pages 373-374. Nevertheless, even venial sins against our neighbor, though not a bar to going to Communion, are defects in our "union" with Christ— obstacles to union (i.e. to a *full* one-ness with Christ) being "more *or less* grave," in Marmion's words.]   [4] St. Augustine, *De unitate Ecclesiae*, 4. See the passages from the same Saint quoted above, page 126.

Listen to what St. Paul says on this subject: "The cup of blessing that we bless,"—that is, the Eucharistic chalice—"is it not the sharing of the blood of Christ? And the bread that we break, is it not the partaking of the body of the Lord?" "Because the bread is one," he adds, we "though many, are one body," for we "partake of the one bread"[1]— the same heavenly bread.

Thus, the great apostle, who understood the doctrine of the mystical body so well, and who expounded it in such a lively way, held in horror the discords and dissensions that reigned among Christians. "I beseech you, brethren, by the name of our Lord Jesus Christ, that you all use the same language; and that there be no dissensions among you, but that you be perfectly united in the same mind and the same feelings."[2] And what reason does he give for that? "As the body is one, and has many members, and as all the members of the body, though they are many, form but a single body, so it is with Christ. All of you, indeed, whether you be Jews or Greeks, slaves or free, have been baptized in the same Spirit; you are the body of Christ and you are its members,"[3] "individually members of it."[4]

3. *Practice and diverse forms* of charity; it should be modeled upon that of Christ Jesus. How St. Paul exhorts us on this: "That they may be made perfect in one."

IT IS from so elevated a principle that charity draws its innermost reason; and it is also in accordance with this principle that we are able to establish *what qualities it should have in practice.*

Seeing that we all form but one single body, our charity ought to be universal. Charity, in principle, does not positively exclude anyone, for Christ died for all, and all are called to share in His kingdom. Charity embraces even sinners, because, for them, the possibility remains of

[1] 1 Cor. 10: 16-17. [2] See 1 Cor. 1:10.
[3] See 1 Cor. 12:12-14. [4] 1 Cor. 12:27 (RSV, Cath.)

their becoming again *living* members of the body of Christ.[1] The only ones excluded from charity are the souls whom the sentence of damnation has separated for ever from the mystical body.

But this love has to take on different forms, according to the state in which our neighbor is to be found. Our love, indeed, has to be, not a platonic love—one of pure theory, exercised upon abstractions, that is to say—but, rather, a love that expresses itself by appropriate acts.

The blessed in heaven are the glorious members of the body of Christ; they have arrived at the fulfillment of their union with God. Our love in their regard takes one of the most perfect of its forms, that of delight and thanksgiving; it will consist of congratulating them on their glory, of rejoicing with them, of thanking God with them for the place He accords them in the kingdom of His Son. Towards the souls that are completing their purification in purgatory, our love will become one of pity: our compassion should bring us to aid them through our intercessory prayer, and above all through the Holy Sacrifice of the Mass.

Here below, on earth, Christ presents Himself to us in the person of our neighbor under very many diverse forms that furnish our charity with varying modes of its being exercised. Doubtless there are degrees and an order to be observed. Our "neighbors" are, first of all, those who are most closely united to us by the ties of blood; nor does grace upset here the order established by nature. Charity on the part of a superior will not have the same "tonality" as on the part of one subject to him or her. In the same way, the exercise of charity in the material sphere requires to be reconciled with the super-natural virtue of prudence: the father of a family cannot divest himself of all his fortune in favor of the poor but to the detriment of his own children. True though it is that the super-natural virtue of justice can and should demand repentance and expiation from a delinquent before he is

---

[1] [*Translator's note*: By "sinners" here, Marmion clearly means those in mortal sin.]

forgiven, what is not at all permitted is hate—that is to say, to will or wish evil for evil; what is not permitted is positively excluding someone from one's prayers: such an exclusion goes directly against charity. Often there is scarcely a better proof of forgiveness we could give than to pray for those who have wronged us. Indeed, to love your neighbor super-naturally is to love him in view of God, for the purpose of obtaining for him, or of preserving within him, the grace of God that brings him to the eternal beatitude.[1] To love is to "wish good" to someone, says St. Thomas;[2] but every specific good is subordinated to the supreme good. That is why giving God, the Infinite Good, to those who do not know Him, by instructing them, is so pleasing to God.

It is the same with praying for the conversion of unbelievers, of sinners, that they may arrive at faith or recover divine grace. When, in prayer, we commend to God the needs of souls, or when in the Mass we sing the *Kyrie Eleison*, the "Lord, have mercy," for all the souls who await the light of the Gospel or the strength of grace in temptation, when we pray for the work of missionaries, we perform acts of true charity extremely pleasing to Our Lord. If Christ promised to give a reward for one glass of water offered to someone in His name,[3] what will He not give for a life of prayer or of expiation devoted to obtaining the spreading of His reign?

There are yet other necessities. There is a poor man who needs to be helped; a sick man who needs to be solaced, nursed or visited; there is a sad soul needing to be comforted by kind words; a soul brimming with joy who is asking for someone to share it. "Rejoice with those who rejoice; weep with those who weep."[4] Charity, says St. Paul, becomes "all things to all men."[5] See how Christ Jesus made a reality of this formula for charity, so as to be our model.

---

[1] "The reason for loving our neighbor is God. Indeed, what we should love in our neighbor is his potential of being in God": St Thomas, II-II, q. XXV, a. 1, and q. XXVI.

[2] "To love is nothing other than to wish good to someone": St Thomas, I, q. XX, a. 2. Cf. also I-II, q. XXVIII, a. 1.   [3] Matt. 10:42; Mark 9:40.

[4] Rom. 12:15.   [5] 1 Cor. 9:22.

Christ loved to give pleasure. The first miracle of His public life was to change water into wine at the wedding-feast at Cana, in order to avoid embarrassment to His hosts who had just run out of wine.[1] We hear Him promise: "Come to me, all you who labor and are burdened, and I will give you rest."[2] And how He fulfilled that promise! The writers of the Gospels often bring out the fact that He performed His miracles because He was moved with "compassion";[3] that is His motive when He cures lepers, when He raises to life the son of the widow of Naim. It is because "I feel sorry for all these people"—the crowd who have untiringly followed Him for three days and are now hungry—that He multiples the loaves.[4] Zaccheus, a leader of the Publicans, of that class of the Jews who were regarded by the Pharisees as sinners, desires ardently to see Christ. But, because of his smallness of stature, he cannot reach Him, for the crowd surrounds Jesus on every side: so then he climbs up a tree at the side of the road along which Jesus must pass; and Our Lord anticipates the desire of this Publican. Having come close to where he is, He tells him: "Zaccheus, make haste and come down; for I must stay at your house today."[5] Zaccheus, full of joy at how his wishes have been fully granted, receives Him into his house.

Again, see how for His friends He puts His power at the service of His love. Martha and Magdalene are mourning in His presence their brother Lazarus, who is already in the tomb. Jesus is moved; and tears —real human tears, but they are the tears of one who is God—flow from His eyes: "Jesus wept."[6] "Where have you laid him?" He asks immediately, for His love cannot stay inactive, and He goes to raise His friend from the dead. And the Jews, witnesses of His tears, said: "See how he loved him."[7]

Christ, says St. Paul, who is fond of using this phrase, is the very "goodness and kindness of God," appeared upon the earth.[8] He is a

---

[1] John 2:1-11.   [2] Matt. 11:28.   [3] E.g. Luke 7:13.   [4] Mark 8:2 (Jerus.)
[5] Luke 19:5 (RSV, Cath.)   [6] John 11:35.   [7] John 11:34.   [8] Titus 3:4.

King, but a King full of meekness,[1] who bids us forgive and declares "blessed" those who, following His example, are merciful.[2] St. Peter, who had lived three years with Him, says that wherever He went He spread kindnesses: He "went about doing good."[3] Like the good Samaritan whose charitable action He Himself so well described, Christ has taken humanity into His arms, He has taken its sorrows into His soul. Truly, "He has borne our infirmities, and carried our sorrows."[4] He comes "for the destruction of sin,"[5] sin which is the height of all evils, the only real evil. He drives out the devil from the bodies of those possessed; but above all He drives him out from souls, by giving His own life for each one of us: He "loved me and gave Himself up for me."[6] What greater indication of love is there than that? There is none: "Greater love than this no one has, that one lay down his life for his friends."[7]

Well, the love of Jesus for men is the example that ought to rule our own love. "Love one another, *as I have loved you*."[8] What is the deep reason why Christ loved His disciples, and us included in them?

Because they belonged to His Father: "I pray ... for those whom you have given me, because they are yours."[9] It is because souls belong to God and to Christ that we ought to love them. Our love ought to be super-natural; true charity is a love of God which encompasses, in one and the same embrace, God and all who are united to Him. We ought to love every soul as Christ does, to the furthest degree of the gift of ourselves—*in finem*, to the end.

See how St. Paul, so alive with the spirit of Christ—see how filled he was with charity towards the Christians: "Who is weak, without my being weak too? Who suffers harm in his soul without I myself suffering it, like something that burns me?"[10] What a charitable soul this was who could say, "I will most gladly spend and be spent myself"[11]—*most gladly*

---

[1] Matt. 21:5.   [2] Matt. 5:7.   [3] Acts 10:38.   [4] Isa. 53:4.
[5] Hebr. 9:26.   [6] Gal. 2:20.   [7] John 15:13.   [8] See John 13:34.
[9] John 17:9.   [10] See 2 Cor. 11:29.   [11] 2 Cor. 12:15.

do this for his brethren! The Apostle goes so far as to be willing to be under "anathema" for solacing his brethren.[1] In the midst of his continual journeys, he works with his own hands so as not to be a burden on the Christian communities that receive him.[2] And you know his short letter—it is such a touching one—to his friend Philemon, in which he asks a favor concerning a slave, Onesimus. This slave had fled from his master's house so as to escape a punishment. He had taken refuge with St. Paul, who converted him and to whom he rendered much service. But the great apostle, not wanting to infringe Philemon's rights under the laws then in force, sends the slave back to his friend. To prepare a favorable reception for him, he writes a few lines to Philemon (who has power of life and death over the fugitive). This note —as St. Paul says himself—is one written, in his own hand, in the prison at Rome. He expresses in it everything charity can find to say that is most pressing and most delicate: "Writing as who I am—Paul, who have already turned the corner into old age and, what is more, am at present a prisoner for Jesus Christ—I, Paul, plead with you for my spiritual son whom I engendered while in my chains.... I send him back to you: welcome him, this object of my tenderness, as you would welcome myself. And if he has done you any injury, or if he owes you anything, put that to my account.... Yes, let me obtain from you this satisfaction in the Lord; set my mind at rest in Christ...."[3]

We understand, after that, how the Apostle could have written so magnificent a hymn in praise of charity: "Charity is patient, is kind; it is not envious, or thoughtless; it is not puffed up with pride; not self-seeking; it does not get annoyed; it thinks no evil; it does not rejoice at wickedness, but rejoices in the truth. Ready to excuse all things, it believes all things, hopes all things, endures all things."[4]

But all these acts, which are so diverse, spring from one and the same source: Christ seen in our neighbor, through faith.

---

[1] Rom. 9:3.
[3] See Philem. 8 ff.

[2] 2 Thess. 3:8; cf. 2 Cor. 12:16.
[4] See 1 Cor. 13:4-7.

Let us, then, endeavor first of all to love God by staying united to Our Lord. From this divine love (as from a blazing hearth-fire out of which dart out a thousand rays, lighting and warming) our charity will spread forth around us, and spread so much the farther as the fire of it blazes up the more. Our charity towards our brethren ought to be the radiation of our love for God. So, then, I say to you with St. Paul: "Love one another ... each seeking to be the first to give honor to the other.... Rejoice with those who rejoice; weep with those who weep. Have the same feelings, one with the other.... If it be possible, so far as it depends on you, be at peace with all."[1] And, to sum up his doctrine: "I beg you earnestly: bear with one another with charity, striving to preserve the unity of the Spirit in the bond of peace; for there is but one body and one Spirit, and it is to one and the same hope that we have been called."[2]

Let us never forget the principle that has to guide us along our way: we are *all one in Christ*, and it is charity that preserves this unity. We can only go to the Father through Christ: but we have to accept Christ as a whole—Christ Himself and Christ in His members. In that is to be found the secret of true divine life within us.

That is why Our Lord has made mutual charity *His* commandment and the object of His last prayer: "That they may *become perfectly one*."[3] In the measure of what is possible, let us strive to make a reality of this supreme wish of the heart of Christ. Love is a source of life, and if we draw upon this love in God so that it may radiate unfailingly upon all the members of the body of Christ, life will be superabundant in our souls, because Christ Jesus, according to His own words, will, in return for forgetfulness of ourselves, pour into us grace in "good measure, pressed down, shaken together, running over."[4]

---

[1] See Rom. 12, vv. 10, 15-16, 18.　　　　[2] See Eph. 4:1-5.
[3] See John 17:21 (RSV, Cath.)　　　　[4] Luke 6:38.

CHAPTER TWELVE

The Mother of the
Incarnate Word

Introduction: The place devotion to the Virgin Mary holds in our spiritual life: a follower of Christ has to be, like Jesus, a *son of Mary*.

In the course of these talks, I have said to you often that the whole of our sanctity consists in imitating Christ Jesus, in conforming the whole of ourselves to the Son of God, in participating in His Divine Sonship. To be through grace what Jesus is by nature is the end-purpose of our predestination and the norm of our holiness: God foreknew us and predestined us "to become conformed to the image of His Son."[1]

Now, there are in Our Lord some essential features and some accidental ones. Christ was born at Bethlehem, fled into Egypt, spent His childhood at Nazareth, died "under Pontius Pilate"; these diverse circumstances of place and time are only accidental features of Christ's existence. Other features are so essential to Him that without them Christ would no longer be Christ. He is God and man, Son of God and Son of Man, true God and true man: *those* are constitutive, inviolable titles.

There is in the Scriptures an astonishing saying applied to Eternal Wisdom, to the Word of God: "My delight is to be with the sons of

[1] Rom. 8:29.

467

men."[1] Who would have believed that? The Word is God:[2] in the heart's-embrace of His Father He lives in infinite light; He possesses all the riches of the Divine perfections, He enjoys the fullness of all life and all beatitude. And yet He declares, through the mouth of the sacred writer, that He finds His joy in living among men.

That marvel came to pass; for "the Word was made flesh, and dwelt among us."[3] The Word desired to be one of us. In an ineffable way He effected this Divine desire, and His effecting it seems (so to say) to have fulfilled all He wished. When we read the Gospels we see, as a matter of fact, that Christ affirms His divinity often, as when He speaks of His eternal relationship to His Father: "My Father and I are one,"[4] or on the occasions of His confirming a profession of faith from His hearers. "Blessed are you, Simon Bar-Jona," He said to Peter who had just proclaimed the divinity of his Master, "blessed are you ... it is my Father in heaven who has revealed this to you."[5] Yet we do not see Him give Himself the title "Son of God" in so many words.

How many times, on the contrary, do we not hear Him call Himself the "Son of Man." One might say that Christ is proud of this title that He is fond of giving Himself. But He is careful never to separate it from His Divine Sonship or from the privileges of His divinity. He tells us that "the Son of Man has power on earth to forgive sins"[6]—a power belonging to God alone. We see that immediately after Peter proclaims Him "the Christ, the Son of the living God,"[7] He tells His disciples that He, the "Son of Man," must suffer and be put to death, but after three days rise again.[8]

Perhaps nowhere in His words has our Divine Savior more strongly and clearly linked the fact of His being man with that of His being God than in the days of His Passion. See Him brought before the

---

[1] See Prov. 8:31.

[2] "In the beginning was the Word, and the Word was with God; and the Word was God": John 1:1.   [3] John 1:14.   [4] John 10:30 (Knox).   [5] See Matt. 16:17.

[6] Mark 2:10.   [7] Matt. 16:16; cf. Mark 8:29; Luke 9:20.   [8] Luke 9:22; Mark 8:31.

tribunal of the Jewish high priest, Caiphas. The latter, in the midst of the assembly, formally requires Jesus to say whether He is the Son of God. Jesus replies: "You have said it";[1] I am He. "And moreover, I tell you, you will see the Son of Man seated at the right hand of the Almighty and coming on the clouds of heaven."[2] Note that Jesus does not say (as we might have expected, since the question was simply one about His divinity): "You will see the Son of God come as eternal and sovereign judge on the clouds of heaven," but "You will see the Son of Man...." In the presence of the supreme tribunal He joins this latter title to that of His divinity. For Him, the two titles are inseparable, just as the two natures on which they are based are indissolubly united and inseparable. Someone is no less in error if he rejects the humanity of Christ than if he denies His divinity.

Now, if Christ Jesus is the Son of God by eternal and ineffable birth, in the heart's-embrace of the Father—"You are my Son...,"[3] He is the "Son *of Man*" by His birth in the sphere of time, in the womb of a woman: "God sent His Son, born of a woman...."[4]

That woman is Mary, but that woman is also a virgin. It is from her, and from her alone, that Christ takes His human nature. It is to her that He owes His being the "Son of Man"; she is truly *"mother of God."* Therefore, in actual fact, Mary occupies in Christianity a place which is unique, transcendent, essential. Just as the fact of His being "Son of Man" cannot in Christ be separated from the fact of His being "Son of God," in that same way is Mary united to Jesus. In actual fact, the Virgin Mary enters into the mystery of the Incarnation by a title that is due to the very essence of the mystery.

That is why we must pause a few moments to contemplate a marvel —that a merely created being, Mary, has been associated, by ties so close,

---

[1] Matt. 26:64. [*Translator's note*: Were the English not so impossibly slangy, one could accurately translate this as "You've said it!"]

[2] See Matt. 26:64; cf. John 1:51; John 3:13.   [3] Acts 13:33; Ps. 2:7.   [4] Gal. 4:4.

with the plan of the fundamental mystery of Christianity and consequently with our super-natural life; with that divine life which comes
to us from Christ, the Man-God (and which, as I have told you, Christ
as God gives us, but by making use of His humanity[1]). We must be,
like Jesus, *Son of God* and *Son of Mary*. He is completely the former
and completely the latter. If, therefore, we wish to reproduce His image in us, we must bear within us that twofold quality.

A soul's loving devotion would not be truly Christian if it did not
include within its object the mother of the Incarnate Word. Devotion
towards the Virgin Mary is not only important but necessary, if we
wish to draw abundantly from the source of life. To separate Christ
from His mother in our loving devotion is to divide Christ; it is to lose
from sight the essential role of His sacred humanity in the conferment
of Divine grace. When one forsakes the Mother, one no longer understands the Son. Is not this what has happened to the Protestant
nations? In having rejected devotion to Mary, on the plea of not derogating from the dignity of the one and only Mediator, have they not
even ended up by losing faith in the divinity of Christ Himself? If
Christ Jesus is our Savior, our Mediator, our elder brother, because He
has taken to Himself a human nature, how can we truly love Him,
how can we resemble Him perfectly, without having a special devotion
to her who is precisely she from whom He takes this human nature?

But this devotion ought to be an enlightened one. Let us, then, say
in a few words what Mary has given to Jesus, and what Christ has
done for His mother. We shall thereupon see what the Virgin ought to
be for us; and, finally, see the super-natural fruitfulness of which the
devotion we show to the Mother of Christ is the source.

---

[1] Book One, Chapter Four, above, page 83: *Christ, Efficient Cause of all Grace.*

1. **What Mary has given to Jesus.** By her "Fiat," the Virgin agreed
to *give to the Word a human nature*; she is the *Mother of Christ*;
and, by title of this, she enters essentially into the life-giving
mystery of Christianity.

WHAT HAS MARY given to Jesus?

She has, while still remaining a virgin, given Him a human nature.
That is a unique privilege, one which Mary shares with no one else:
"Before her, none has been seen like her, nor shall there be any like her
hereafter."[1] The Word could have appeared here below by taking a
human nature created *ex nihilo*—drawn from nothing—and already
constituted in the completeness of its bodily organism, as Adam was
formed in the earthly paradise. For Infinite Wisdom's own motives, He
did not do that. In uniting Himself to humanity, the Word willed to go
through—in order to sanctify them—*all the stages of human growth*.
He willed to be born of a woman.

But a wonderful thing about this birth is that the Word made it
subject (so to say) to this woman's consent.

Let us transport ourselves in spirit to Nazareth, to gaze on that
ineffable scene. The angel appears to the young virgin. After greeting
her, he makes known to her his message: "Behold, you will conceive in
your womb and bear a son; and you shall call His name Jesus. He will
be great, and will be called the Son of the Most High ... and of His
kingdom there will be no end."[2] Mary asks the angel how this may be
done, seeing that she is a virgin: "How shall this happen, since I do not
know man?"[3] Gabriel replies to her: "The Holy Spirit will come upon
you, and the power of the Most High will overshadow you; that is why
the Holy One who will be born of you will be called the Son of God."[4]
Then, mentioning the example of Elizabeth, who had conceived in
spite of her barrenness, because it had pleased the Lord that this

---

[1] Antiphon of the Lauds of Christmas.   [2] Luke 1:31-33 (RSV, Cath.)
[3] Luke 1:34.   [4] See Luke 1:35.

should happen, the angel adds: "Nothing is impossible to God"[1]—when He wills to, He can suspend the laws of nature.

God proposes the mystery of the Incarnation, which will only be fulfilled within the Virgin when she has given her consent. The fulfillment of the mystery remains in suspense until Mary's free acquiescence is given. At the moment of her acquiescence she represented in her person all of us, St. Thomas says. It was as if God was awaiting the response of the humanity to which He desired to unite Himself: "At the Annunciation, the Virgin's consent on behalf of the whole of human nature was awaited."[2] What a solemn moment that was! For it was at this moment that the life-giving mystery of Christianity was about to be decided upon. St. Bernard, in one of his most beautiful homilies on the Annunciation, shows us the whole of the human race, which for thousands of years had been hoping for salvation, shows us the angelic choirs and God Himself as if in suspense, awaiting the acceptance of the young Virgin.[3]

And see how Mary gives her response. Full of faith in the words from heaven, wholly submissive to the Divine will that has just been manifested to her, the Virgin replies with an *abandon* entire and absolute: "Behold the handmaid of the Lord; be it done unto me according to your word."[4] That "Be it done unto me ..." is Mary's consent to the Divine plan of the Redemption, an account of which has just been given to her. That *Fiat* is like an echo of the *Fiat* of creation, but it is a new world, an infinitely higher world, a world of grace, that God Himself is about to bring into existence in train of this acquiescence. For at that moment the Divine Word, the Second Person of the Blessed Trinity, becomes incarnate within Mary: "*And the Word was made flesh.*"[5]

Without doubt (we have just heard it from the mouth of the angel) no human assistance will intervene—for everything must be holy in

---

[1] Luke 1:37 (Jerus.)   [2] St Thomas, III, q. XXX, a. 1.
[3] Homily IV on the *Missus est*.   [4] Luke 1:38.   [5] John 1:14.

the conception and the birth of Christ, and it is from *her* most pure blood that Mary conceives through the operation of the Holy Spirit; it is from her womb that the Man-God will come forth. When Jesus is born at Bethlehem, who is it that lies there on the straw? It is the Child-God, it is the Word, who, while remaining a Divine Person— "What He has been, He remains"[1]—has united a human nature to Himself in the womb of the Virgin. There are in this Child two quite distinct natures, but one Person only—the Divine Person. The end, the purpose, of this virgin birth is the Man-God: "The Holy One who will be born of you will be called the Son of God"; this Man-God, this God-made-man, is the Son of Mary. That is what Elizabeth, "filled with the Holy Spirit," said: "Why is this granted me, that the mother of my Lord should come to me?"[2]

Mary is the mother of Christ, for, like all other mothers for their sons, she formed and nourished the body of Jesus from her substance most pure. Christ, says St. Paul, was "formed of a woman."[3] That is a dogma of faith. If, by His *eternal* birth in holy splendor[4] Christ is truly Son of God—"God from God,"[5] He is truly Son of Mary by His birth in the sphere of time. The only Son of God is also the only Son of the Virgin.

Such is the ineffable union that exists between Jesus and Mary: she is His mother, He her Son. This union is indissoluble; and as Jesus is at the same time the Son of God, come to save the world, Mary is, in actual fact, associated intimately with the life-giving mystery of the whole of Christianity. The foundation of all her greatness is this special privilege of her being Mother of God.

---

[1] Antiphon of the Office of the Circumcision.   [2] Luke 1:43 (RSV, Cath.)
[3] See Gal. 4:4. [*Translator's note*: Some biblical translations have simply "born of a woman," but the Rheims has "made of a woman."]
[4] Ps. 109 (110):3 (St P.)   [5] Nicene Creed.

2. **What Jesus has given to His mother.** He has *chosen* her among
all women; He has *loved* her and *obeyed* her. He has *associated*
her, in an altogether intimate way, *with His mysteries*, principally
with that of the Redemption.

BEING Mother of God is not her only privilege. A whole crown of
graces adorns the virgin mother of Christ, even though all of them
draw their raison d'être from her being thereby mother of God. Jesus,
as man, depends on Mary, but, as the Eternal Word, He exists before
Mary did. Let us see what He has done for her from whom He was to
take a human nature. Being God—that is to say, Almighty and Infinite
Wisdom, He was to adorn this creature with [spiritual] jewels beyond
price.

First of all, He has, with the Father and the Holy Spirit, *chosen* her
above all others. So as to indicate how high above all others, the Church
on feast-days of the Virgin applies to her a passage of Scripture that, in
certain features, can only relate to Eternal Wisdom: "The Lord possessed
me in the beginning of His ways, before He made anything.... I was
established from eternity, before the earth was made. The depths were
not as yet, and I was already formed.... Before the mountains had
firmed, before the hills, was I brought forth":[1] *"Before the hills, was I
brought forth."* What do those words show? The special predestination
of Mary in the Divine plan. The Eternal Father, in His Divine thoughts,
does not separate her from Christ. In the same act of love by which He
places His delight in the humanity of His Son, is embraced the Virgin,
who will be the mother of Christ.[2] This singular predestination is for
Mary the source of unique graces.

[1] See Prov. 8:22-25.

[2] "The same words by which the Holy Scriptures speak of Uncreated Wisdom
and depict His lineage from all eternity ... the Church has been accustomed to apply
to the beginnings of the Virgin, which were predetermined by the same decree as
was the Incarnation of Divine Wisdom": Pius IX, Bull, *Ineffabilis Deus*, written for the
definition of the Immaculate Conception.

The Virgin Mary is *immaculate*. All the children of Adam are born soiled with original sin, slaves of the devil, enemies of God.[1] That is the law which God laid down for the whole race of sinful Adam. Alone among all creatures, Mary would escape this law. The Eternal Word would make one exception to this universal law, one exception only — for her in whom He was to become incarnate. Not for a single instant would Mary's soul belong to the devil; she would be radiant with purity; and that is why, from the very morrow of the fall of our first parents, God established an absolute enmity between the devil and the chosen Virgin: it was she who, with her heel, would crush the hellish serpent.[2] With the Church, we often recall to Mary that privilege, which she is the only one to possess, of being without stain. We love to say to her: "You are all-beautiful, Mary, and the stain of original sin is not in you."[3] "Your vesture is white as snow, and your face as resplendent as the sun: wherefore the King of Glory has ardently desired you."[4]

Not only is Mary born immaculate; *grace abounds in her*. When the angel greets her, he declares her "full of grace"; for "the Lord is with you"[5] — the Lord, the Source of all grace. Next, in the conception and the birth of Jesus, *Mary keeps her virginity intact*. She gives birth, while remaining a virgin. In Mary, as the Church sings,[6] are combined the glory so pure of virginity with the joys of fruitful motherhood; she having "the joys of a mother with the honor of a virgin."

Then, there are the graces which her hidden life with Jesus brings to Mary; there are the graces of her unity with her Son in the mysteries of His public life and His Passion; and, for full measure, there is the *Assumption into heaven*. Mary's virginal body, from which Christ has drawn the substance of His human nature, is not to know any corruption; on her head is to be placed a crown of inestimable price; she is to

[1] See note 1 on page 24.   [2] Gen. 3:15.
[3] Antiphon of Vespers for the Feast of the Immaculate Conception.
[4] *Ibid.*   [5] Luke 1:28.   [6] Antiphon for the Lauds of Christmas.

reign as queen at her Son's right hand, adorned with the vesture of glory that all these privileges have woven for her: "At your right hand stands the queen, in Ophir gold arrayed."[1]

Now, whence do they derive for Mary, all these signal graces, all these remarkable privileges, which make her a creature above every other creature, "blessed among women"?[2] From the eternal choice that God has made of Mary to be the mother of His Son. If she is "blessed among women"—blessed among all women; if God, for her, over-turned so many laws that He Himself had established, it is because she was to be the mother of His Son. If you take away that dignity from Mary, all those prerogatives no longer have any raison d'être or significance. For all those privileges prepare or accompany Mary in her position of being Mother of God.

But what is incomprehensible is the love which decided that singular choice the Word made of this young virgin, in order that He take on a human nature from her.

Christ *loved* His mother. Never has God so loved one who is simply a creature; never son loved his mother as Christ Jesus does. He has loved men so much, as He Himself has said, that He died for them and could not have given them more evidence of His love than that: "Greater love than this no one has, that one lay down his life for his friends."[3] But never forget this truth: that Christ died above all for His mother, to pay for her privileges. The unique graces that Mary has received are the first fruits of the Passion of Jesus. The most holy Virgin would not have enjoyed any prerogative without the merits of her Son; she is the greatest glory of Christ, because it is she who has received the most from Him.

The Church makes us understand this doctrine very clearly when she celebrates the Immaculate Conception—the first, in time order, of the graces received by the Virgin. Read the collect prescribed for the

----

[1] Ps. 44(45):10 (Knox).   [2] Luke 1:28.   [3] John 15:13.

Feast, and you will see that this singular privilege is granted to the Virgin because the death of Jesus, foreseen in the eternal decrees, has paid the price of it in advance: "O God, who, by the Immaculate Conception of the Virgin, prepared a worthy habitation for your Son, we beseech you that, as by the *foreseen* death of that same Son, you preserved her from all stain...."[1] We can say that, out of all humanity, Mary was the first object of the love of Christ, even of the suffering Christ. It was above all for her, in order that grace might abound in her in unique measure, that Christ shed His precious blood.

Finally, Jesus *obeyed* His mother. As you will know from your reading, the only things the Gospel writers tell us about the hidden life of Christ at Nazareth are that "Jesus advanced in wisdom and age," and that He was "subject to" Mary and Joseph.[2] Is there anything incompatible with divinity there? No, certainly not. The Word was made flesh, He so far abased Himself as to take a nature like ours, sin excepted; He came, He said, "not to be served but to serve,"[3] to make Himself "obedient unto death."[4] That is why He wished to obey His mother. At Nazareth He obeyed Mary and Joseph, the two privileged creatures whom God had put close to Him. In a way, Mary shares in the Eternal Father's authority over the humanity of His Son. Jesus could have said of His mother what He said of His Heavenly Father: "I do always the things that are pleasing to *her*."

Not only has the Word predestined Mary to be His mother so far as His humanity is concerned; not only has He, by filling her with graces, rendered her the honor this dignity brings with it. He has *associated her with His mysteries.*

We see in the Gospels that Jesus and Mary are inseparable in the mysteries of Christ. After the angels announce to them that they will find a Savior, who is Christ the Lord, wrapped in swaddling clothes in

---

[1] Collect for the Feast. [*Translator's note*: Marmion's italics.]   [2] Luke 2:51-52.
[3] Matt. 20:28 (RSV, Cath.)   [4] Phil. 2:8 (Rheims).

the cave at Bethlehem, the shepherds go there and find "Mary and Joseph, and the babe" lying in the manger;[1] it is Mary who presents Jesus in the temple and who by that offering preludes the sacrifice of Calvary.[2] As I have just said to you, all the hidden life at Nazareth takes place under Mary's authority; it is at her behest that Jesus, at the start of His public life, reveals Himself by His first miracle at Cana;[3] the Gospel writers tell us that she followed Christ in more than one of His apostolic journeys.

But note well that in all this it is not a question of a simply material unity. It is with heart and soul that the Virgin Mary enters into the mysteries of her Son. St. Luke tells us that the mother of Jesus "kept in mind all these words"—the words of her Son—"pondering them in her heart."[4] The words of Jesus were for her sources of contemplation: may we not say the same of the *mysteries* of Jesus? Assuredly Christ, when He was living these mysteries, illumined the soul of His mother with light upon each one of them. She understood them; she associated herself with them; everything Our Lord said and did was—for her He loved among all women—a source of graces. Jesus, so to say, gave back to His mother in *divine* life (of which He is the source) what He had received from her in human life. That is why Christ and the Virgin are so indissolubly united in all the mysteries; and it is also why Mary has united us all, in her heart, with her Divine Son.

Now, the work par excellence of Jesus, the holy of holies of His mysteries, is His Passion. It is by His bloody sacrifice on the cross that He completes His restoring of divine life to men, that He reinstates them in their dignity of children of God. Christ Jesus willed to make His mother enter into that mystery in a capacity so special, and Mary united herself with the will of her Son the Redeemer in that mystery so

---

[1] Luke 2:8-16. [*Translator's note*: Marmion, speaking from memory, wrongly quoted the angels as saying "You will find the babe and His mother..." It was St. Luke's phrase referring to Mary that was at the back of his mind.]

[2] Luke 2:22-39.   [3] John 2:1-11.   [4] Luke 2:19.

fully, that, while keeping her rank as simply a creature, she truly shares with Him the glory of having at that time brought us to birth in the life of grace.

Let us go to Calvary, at that moment when Christ Jesus was about to accomplish fully the work His Father had given Him to carry out here below. Our Lord has arrived at the end of His apostolic mission on earth; He is about to reconcile the whole of humanity with His Father. Who is to be found at the foot of the cross at that supreme moment? Mary, the mother of Jesus, with John the beloved disciple and some other women: *Stabat mater eius*, "Now there were standing by the cross of Jesus His mother...."[1] She is there, standing erect; she has just renewed the offering of her Son that she made long before when she presented Him in the temple. At this moment she offers to the Eternal Father as ransom for the world "the blessed fruit of her womb." He, her Jesus, has only a few minutes to live; then the sacrifice will be accomplished and Divine grace restored to men. He wills to give us Mary as our mother. That is one of the forms taken by the following truth—that in the Incarnation the Word is united with the whole of humanity; the elect constitute the mystical body of Christ, from which no one can separate them. Christ will give us His mother to be our mother also, in the spiritual order. Mary will not draw a dividing line between ourselves and Jesus, her Son, our head.

Thus, before expiring and completing, as St. Paul says, the conquest of a nation of souls that He willed to make His glorious kingdom,[2] Jesus saw at the foot of the cross His mother, submerged in such deep sorrow, and His disciple John whom He loved so much—that John who heard His last words and has recounted them to us. "Jesus said to His mother: 'Woman, this is your son.' Then to the disciple He said:

[1] John 19:25.
[2] Christ "loved the Church, and delivered Himself up for her ... in order that He might present to Himself the Church in all her glory, not having spot or wrinkle": Eph. 5:25-27.

'This is your mother.'"[1] Here St. John represented us all; it is to *us* that Jesus, when dying, bequeathed His mother. Is He not our "elder brother"? Are we not predestined to be like Him, so that He may be "the firstborn among many brethren"?[2] Well, if Christ has become our elder brother, by taking a nature like ours from Mary, a nature which made Him a sharer of our race, why is it astonishing that when dying He should have given to us, as our mother in the order of grace, her who was His mother according to human nature?

And as what He said, being a saying of the Word, is all-powerful and of Divine efficacy, it created in the heart of St. John filial sentiments worthy of Mary—exactly as in the Virgin's heart it caused to be born a special tenderness for those whom grace makes brethren of Jesus Christ. Can we doubt for a moment that, on her part, the Virgin would have responded, as at Nazareth, with a "Fiat"—a "Let it be done to me according to thy word," silent this time, but no less full of love, humility and obedience, in which the fullness of *her* will flowed into the river-course of that of Jesus, so as to bring about her Son's last wish?

St. Gertrude recounts that, hearing one day in the singing of the Divine Office these words in the Gospel: "*First-born Son of the Virgin Mary*" referring to Christ, she said to herself: "The title '*only* Son' would seem to fit Jesus much better than the title 'first born.'" While she was dwelling on this thought, the Virgin Mary appeared to her. "No," she said to the great nun, "it is not at all 'only Son,' it is 'first-born Son' which fits best; for, after Jesus, my very dear Son—or, more exactly, in Him and through Him—I have become mother of all of you in the womb of my charity, and you have become my children, the brethren of Jesus."[3]

---

[1] John 19:25-27 (Jerus.)   [2] Rom. 8:29.   [3] *Le héraut de l'amour divin*, IV, c. 3.

3. The *homage* we owe Mary: extolling her privileges, after the example of the Church in its liturgy.

TO ACKNOWLEDGE the unique place Jesus has willed to give to Mary in His mysteries, and the Virgin's love of us, we ought to render her the honor, love and trust due to her as mother of Jesus and our mother.

How can we *not* love her, if we love Our Lord? If, as I have told you, Christ Jesus wishes us to love all the members of His mystical body, then how can we not love first among them her who gave Him that human nature through which He has become our head, gave Him that humanity of His which serves Him as instrument for communicating grace to us? We cannot doubt that the love we show to the mother of Jesus is extremely pleasing to Christ. If we wish to love Christ, if we wish Him to be all in all to us, we ought to have a really special love for His mother.

In what way shall we manifest this love? Jesus loved His mother by —as God—showering sublime privileges upon her. And we, we shall show our love by extolling those privileges. If we want to be very pleasing to Our Lord, let us admire those wonders with which, from love, He has adorned the soul of His mother. He wants us to give, with her, an incessant thanksgiving to the Blessed Trinity; He wants us to praise the Virgin herself for having been chosen from among all women to give the Savior to the world. By doing that, we shall truly enter into the sentiments felt by Jesus about her to whom He owes it that He is Son of Man. "Yes," let us sing to her, "'you alone have ravished the heart of your God,'[1] you have been pleasing to God as no one else has. May you be blest among all creatures—blest because you believed the Divine word, and because in you the eternal promises are fulfilled."

To help us in this devotion, we have only to look at what the Church does. See how this Spouse of Christ, the Church, has multiplied

---

[1] Antiphon of the Benedictus of the office of the Blessed Virgin *in Sabbato*.

here below her testimonies in honor of Mary, and see what the Church's practice is concerning this veneration—special because it transcends that given to all the other saints; this veneration called *hyperdulia*.[1]

The Church devotes numerous feasts to the Mother of God, celebrating in turn her Immaculate Conception, her Nativity, her Presentation in the Temple, the Annunciation, the Visitation, the Purification, the Assumption.

See also how, in each of the principal seasons of the liturgical cycle, she devotes to the Virgin a special "antiphon" which she prescribes to be recited by her ministers every day at the end of the canonical hours. You will note that in each of these antiphons the Church delights in recalling the privilege of being Mother of God which is the foundation of the other greatnesses of Mary. *"Fruitful mother of the Redeemer,"*[2] we sing during Advent and the Christmas season, "you have, to the great astonishment of nature, given birth to your Creator. A virgin in conceiving Him, you have remained a virgin after giving birth to Him; *Mother of God*, intercede for us." During Lent, we greet her as "the root from which sprang the flower that is Christ," as "the gate through which light has arisen upon the world." At Eastertime, it is a hymn of elation; we felicitate Mary on the triumph of her Son, we renew in her soul the joy that flooded into her at the day-break of that glory: "Queen of Heaven, rejoice: He is risen, *He whom you bore in your womb*—yes, rejoice and exult, O Virgin, because Christ the Lord has truly come forth, glorious and living, out of the tomb." Then, during the time after Pentecost which symbolizes the period of our pilgrimage here below, it is the *Salve Regina*, full of trust: "Mother of mercy," our hope and our safety, "to thee do we send up our sighs, mourning and

---

[1] To all the saints, we owe the homage of *dulia*—a Greek word that signifies "service." Because of the eminent dignity of her position, the mother of the Incarnate Word deserves an entirely special homage—that which is expressed by the word *hyperdulia*.   [2] [*Translator's note*: The italicizations in this paragraph are Marmion's.]

weeping in this vale of tears.... After this our exile, show unto us *the blessed fruit of thy womb*, Jesus. Pray for us, O *holy Mother of God*, that we may be made worthy of the promises of Christ." Thus, there is not a day when the voice of the Church is not lifted up to felicitate Mary on her graces and to remind her that we are her children.

Is that the whole of it? No. Every day as well, after Vespers, the Church sings the *Magnificat*; she unites with the Virgin herself in praising God for His goodness to the mother of His Son. Let us say often, after her and with the Church: "My soul magnifies the Lord, and my spirit rejoices in God my Savior; because He has regarded the lowliness of His handmaid...." Yes, henceforth, Mary, all generations will call you blessed; because He who is mighty has "done great things" to you.[1] When we sing these words, it is a hymn of thanks we are offering to the Blessed Trinity for the privileges of Mary, as though these privileges were ours.

Next, there is the "Little Office" of the Blessed Virgin; there is the Rosary, which is so pleasing to Mary because it is always as joined with her Divine Son that we praise her, by constantly repeating, with love, the praise the heavenly messenger addressed to her on the day of the Incarnation: "Hail Mary, full of grace." It is an excellent "practice" to recite the rosary every day with devotion—in that way, to contemplate Christ in His mysteries in order to unite ourselves with Him; to felicitate the Virgin on having been so intimately associated with those mysteries, and to give thanks to the Blessed Trinity for Mary's privileges. Then, if every day we have said often to the Virgin: "Mother of God, pray for us ... now and at the hour of our death," we may be sure that the Virgin will not abandon us when that moment comes at which "now" and "the hour of our death" are one and the same time. There are, as well, the Litanies; there is the *Angelus*, by which we renew in the heart of the Virgin the ineffable joy she must have felt at the time of the Incarnation, and so many other forms of devotion.

[1] Luke 1:46-49.

It is not necessary to weigh oneself down with "practices." One should choose some; but stay faithful to what has been chosen, once the choice has been made. Such daily homage given to His mother will be one that could not be more pleasing to Our Lord.

4. **Fruitfulness which devotion to the Virgin brings to a soul. Mary *inseparable from Jesus* in the Divine plan. Her all-powerful *credit*; her grace of *spiritual motherhood*. Asking Mary to "form" Jesus within us.**

BESIDES being extremely pleasing to Jesus, devotion to the Blessed Virgin is something of *very great fruitfulness* for us. And that, for three reasons you will already have foreseen.

First because, in God's plan, *Mary is inseparable from Jesus*, and because our holiness consists in entering to the utmost of our ability into the Divine disposing. In the eternal thoughts, Mary belongs in fact to the very essence of the mystery of Christ. As mother of Jesus, she is the mother of Him in whom we find everything. In accordance with the Divine plan, life is only given to men through Christ, Man-God: "Nobody can come to the Father, except through me."[1] But Christ has only been given to the world through Mary: "For us men and for our salvation, He came down from heaven: by the power of the Holy Spirit He became incarnate from the Virgin Mary."[2] That is how it was ordained by God. And that ordaining is not subject to change. Note, indeed, that it is something that does not only avail for the day on which the Incarnation itself was effected; it still continues in force for applying the fruits of the Incarnation to souls. Why is that? Because the source of grace is Christ, the Incarnate Word, but His *being* the Christ, His *being* the Mediator, remains inseparable from His human nature, the nature He got from the Virgin.[3]

[1] John 14:6 (Knox).   [2] Nicene Creed.   [3] "God having once willed to give us Christ through the holy Virgin, the gifts of God are not repented of, and

The second reason for its continued applicability, a reason belonging very close to the preceding one, is that no one more than the Mother of God has *credit before Him, her Son, for obtaining grace for us*. As a result of the Incarnation, God—not so as to derogate from His Son's power of mediation, but on the contrary so as to extend and exalt that power—is pleased to recognize the credit of those who are united to Jesus, head of the mystical body. This credit is the more powerful in measure as the union of the saints with Christ is the more intimate.

"The closer something is to its source," says St. Thomas, "the more it experiences the effects produced by this source. The closer you get to the fire on the hearth, the more you feel the heat that radiates from it." Well, the holy doctor adds, "Christ is the source of grace, seeing that He is the Author of it as God, and the instrument of it as man; and as the Virgin has been the creature closest to the humanity of Christ (it being from her that Christ has taken that human nature), the Virgin has received from Christ a higher grace than that of any other creature."

"But (it is still St. Thomas speaking) every person receives from God grace proportioned to that person's providential destination. As *man*, Christ was predestined and chosen in order that, being the Son of God,

---

this ordaining is not subject to any more change. It is and will always be true that, after having through her charity received the universal Source of all grace, it is still through her intermediacy that we shall receive the diverse applications of grace in all the different states that make up the Christian life. Her maternal charity having so much contributed to our salvation in the mystery of the Incarnation which is the universal source of all grace, she will contribute to it eternally in all the other operations that are but dependent on the Incarnation": Bossuet, *Sermon pour la fête de la Conception*, 1669, *Œuvres oratoires*, ed. Lebarq, vol. V, p. 609.

Let us quote also these words of Pope Leo XIII: "Of the magnificent treasury of graces brought by Christ, nothing, *according to the Divine thoughts*, is to be dispensed to us, if not through Mary. That being so, it is by addressing ourselves to her that we should go to Christ—a little like the way in which we approach our Heavenly Father through Christ": Encyclical on the Rosary, September 22, 1891.

He might have the power to sanctify all men.[1] Consequently, He was to possess—He alone possessed—a fullness such as could overflow on to every soul: 'Of his fullness we have all received.'[2] The fullness of grace the Blessed Virgin received had as its purpose to make her the creature closest to the Author of grace; so close, indeed, that the Virgin contained within her womb Him who is full of grace, and in giving Him to the world by childbirth she, so to speak, gave the world grace itself, because she gave to the world the Source of grace."[3] In forming Jesus in her womb so pure, the Virgin has given us the very Author of life. At Christmastide, when celebrating Christ's birth, the Church sings of this in the prayer of an antiphon to the Virgin—sings of her "through whom we have been made worthy to receive the Author of life." The Church invites the nations to sing of the life that has been brought to them by this virginal motherhood:

> *Life, through the Virgin has been giv'n —*
> *Ransomed nations, shout and sing!*

If, therefore, you wish to draw in large measure from the wellspring of Divine life, go to Mary; ask her to lead you to that wellspring. She, indeed, is the one who, more than any other creature, will bring you near to Jesus. That is why we call her, and with good reason, *Mother of Divine Grace*. That, too, is why the Church applies to her this passage from Scripture: "He that shall find me, shall find life, and shall have salvation from the Lord."[4] Salvation, the life of our souls, comes only from the Lord Jesus—"from the Lord"; He is the one and only Mediator. But who will lead us to Him more surely than Mary? who has as much power to make Him propitious to us as His mother has?

She has, moreover, received from Jesus Himself, in regard to His mystical body, a *special grace of motherhood*. That is the final reason for the super-natural fruitfulness of devotion to the Blessed Virgin.

---

[1] Hebr. 13:12.   [2] John 1:16.
[3] St Thomas, III, q. XXVII, a. 5.   [4] Prov. 8:35.

Christ, after having received a human nature from Mary, has, as I told you, associated His mother with all His mysteries, from the offering in the temple, right up to His immolation on Calvary. Now, what is the end-purpose of all the mysteries of Christ? That of making Him the Exemplar of our super-natural life, the price paid for our sanctification, and the source of all our holiness; that of creating for Him an eternal and glorious company of brethren who shall resemble Him. That is why Mary is associated with the new Adam as a new Eve; but much more than Eve was, is she "the mother of all the living";[1] the mother of those who live by the grace of her Son.

Indeed, as I said to you earlier, this association is not merely an outward one. Christ—who is God, who is the Almighty Word—created in the soul of His mother the feelings she was to have about those whom He, by being born of her and living His mysteries in her, wished to constitute His brethren. The Virgin, for her part, enlightened by the grace that abounded in her, responded to this appeal of Jesus by a *Fiat*, a "Let it be done to me," in which the whole of her soul poured itself out with submission and in oneness of mind with her Divine Son. By giving her consent to the Divine proposing of the Incarnation, she agreed to enter into the plan of the Redemption in a unique capacity; she agreed not only to be the mother of Jesus but to associate herself with the whole of His mission as Redeemer. To each one of the mysteries of Jesus she was to renew this *Fiat* that was so full of love, right up to the moment when, after having offered on Calvary for the salvation of the world this Jesus, this Son, this body she had formed, this blood that had been her own, she was able to say "All is consummated." At that blessed hour, Mary had entered so far into the feelings of Jesus that she can be called "Co-redemptrix." Like Jesus, she at that time, by an act of love, completed the bringing of us forth to the life of grace.[2]

[1] Gen. 3:20.

[2] "She co-operated through charity in the faithful being born in the Church": St. Augustine, *De sancta Virginitate*, n. 6.

According to the thought St. Augustine expressed, she, mother of our head, by having borne Jesus in her womb became, through her soul, will and heart, the mother of all the members of the Divine head: "In body, mother of our head; in spirit, mother of His members."[1]

And because here below she was associated with all the mysteries of our redemption, Jesus has crowned her not only with glory but with power; He has placed His mother at His right hand, in order that, by a title that is unique, as her title "Mother of God" is unique, she may give out the treasures of eternal life: "At your right hand stands the queen."[2] This is what Christian piety is referring to when it proclaims the mother of Jesus *Omnipotenta supplex*, "all-powerful suppliant."

Oh! let us therefore say to her, as the Church does and filled with trust: "Show yourself a mother"—mother of Jesus, through your credit with Him; our mother through your mercy towards us. May Christ receive our prayers through you—this Christ who, born of you so as to bring us life, willed to be your Son."

> *Show thyself a Mother;*
> *Offer Him our sighs*
> *Who for us incarnate*
> *Did not thee despise.*

Who, indeed, knows the heart of her Son better than she? We find in the Gospel[3] a magnificent example of her trust in Jesus. It was at the wedding-feast at Cana; she was present at it with Jesus, and she was not so sunk in contemplation as to know nothing of what was going on around her. What happened was that the bride and groom began to run out of wine. Mary saw their confusion; she said to Jesus: "They have no wine." We recognize here the heart of a mother. How about those "mystical" souls who, if they had been there, would not have

---

[1] *Ibid.*   [2] Ps. 44 (45):10 (Knox).   [3] John 2:1 ff.

wanted to think about the wine! And yet, what are they alongside the Blessed Virgin? Driven by her kindness, she asks her Son to help those whose embarrassment she sees. Our Lord looks at her, and does not seem to pay any attention to what she says: "What is that to you and to me, woman?"[1] But she knew her Jesus. So certain is she of Him even, that she says, straight away, to the servants: "Do whatever He tells you." And, sure enough, the vessels into which water was poured are found to have become filled with excellent wine.

What shall we ask of the Mother of Jesus, if not—before every-thing and above everything—that she will form Jesus in us, by commu-nicating to us her faith and her love?

The whole of the Christian life consists in "carrying Christ to birth" within us, and in having Him live there. That is an idea of St. Paul's.[2] Now, where was Christ first formed? In the womb of the Virgin, through the operation of the Holy Spirit. But, say the Fathers of the Church, Mary first carried Christ within her by faith and love, when by saying "Let it be done to me" she gave her awaited consent. "She first conceived in her mind, before conceiving in her body."[3] Let us ask her to obtain for us that faith which brings Christ into being within us—Christ "dwelling in your hearts through faith";[4] to obtain for us

---

[1] See John 2:4. [*Translator's note*: "What is that to you and to me?" is a literal trans-lation of the Vulgate's "*quid mihi et tibi est?*" quoted by Marmion. But the Jerusalem and the Knox have slightly different interpretations, both based upon a certain idiomatic phrase in Hebrew [Jerusalem: "why turn to me?"; Knox: "why do you trouble me with that?"], and those interpretations fit in well with Christ's immediately next words: "*My time has not come yet*" [i.e., my time for working miracles]. As to "woman" as a form of address, Knox says in a note to his translation: "'Woman' was an address used in the ancient world without any suggestion of disrespect." Christ used it again when, on the cross, He entrusted Our Lady to St. John: "Woman, this is your son...." Some commentators see the word as an echo of Genesis 3:15: "I will put enmities between thee [the devil] and the woman...."]   [2] Gal. 4:19: "until Christ is formed in you."

[3] St. Augustine, *De virginitate*, c. 3; *Sermo* CCXV, n. 4; St. Leo, *Sermo I de nativitate Domini*, c. 1; St. Bernard, *Sermo I de vigilia nativitatis*.   [4] See Eph. 3:17.

that love which makes us live with the life of Jesus. Let us ask her that we become like her Son; there is no greater favor we could beg her for, neither would she wish to grant us anything beyond that. For she knows, she sees, that her Son cannot be separated from His mystical body; she remains so united in soul and in heart to her Divine Son, that now, in glory, she desires but one thing—that the Church, the kingdom of the elect, bought at the price of Jesus's blood, shall appear before Him "glorious, with no spot or wrinkle or anything like that, but holy and immaculate."[1]

Therefore, when we address ourselves to the Blessed Virgin, let us join her with Jesus, and say: "O mother of the Incarnate Word, your Son has said that 'whatever you do to the least of my brethren, you do to me';[2] I am one of those 'least' among the members of your Son Jesus, and it is in His name that I come before you to implore your help." If Mary refused a petition presented in that way, she would be refusing something to Jesus!

Let us go to her, then, but let us go with confidence. There are souls who go to her as to a mother, confiding their concerns to her, disclosing to her their troubles, their difficulties, having recourse to her when in need, when in temptation—for there are everlasting "enmities" between the Virgin and the devil: with her heel, Mary crushes the head of the hellish serpent.[3] On every occasion, their dealings with the Blessed Virgin are like a child's with its mother; some of them go before a statue of the Virgin in order to disclose to her their desires and their wishes. Childishness, all this, you will say. Perhaps; but you know what Christ said, don't you? "Unless you ... become like little children, you will not enter into the kingdom of heaven."[4]

Let us ask of the Virgin that grace will flow down to us in abundance from the humanity of her Jesus who possesses the fullness of it,

[1] See Eph. 5:27.
[2] See Matt. 25:40.
[3] Gen. 3:15.
[4] Matt. 18:3.

so that we may more and more be conformed, through love, to this beloved Son of the Father, who is also her Son. That is the best request we could possibly make to her. At the Last Supper, Our Lord said to His apostles: "My Father loves you because you have loved me and have believed that I came forth from Him."[1] He could say the same thing to us of Mary: "My mother loves you, because you love me and believe that I was born of her." Nothing is more pleasing to Mary than hearing it proclaimed that Jesus is her Son, and seeing Him loved by all creatures.

The Gospel, as you know, has preserved for us only a very few sayings of the Virgin. I have just recalled one to you: what she said to the servants at the wedding-feast at Cana—"Do whatever He tells you."[2] These words are like an echo of the words of the Eternal Father: "This is my beloved Son, in whom I am well pleased; *hear Him*."[3] We can apply to ourselves that saying of Mary: "Do everything my Son tells you to." That will be the best fruit of this talk, that will be the best form of our devotion to the Mother of Jesus. The Virgin Mary has no greater wish than to see her Divine Son obeyed, loved, glorified, exalted. As is so with the Eternal Father, Jesus is the object of all her delight.

---

[1] See John 16:27.   [2] John 2:5.   [3] Matt. 17:5; Mark 9:6; Luke 9:35.

CHAPTER THIRTEEN

"Co-Heirs with Christ"

Introduction: The heavenly inheritance, final objective of our adoptive predestination.

"Father, I have glorified you on earth; I have accomplished the work you have given me to do. And now, Father, glorify me in your own presence, with the glory I had with you before the world was made ... Father, I will that those you have given me may be with me where I am, to behold my glory, the glory you have given me...."[1]

These words form the beginning and the ending of the ineffable prayer Jesus addressed to His Father at the Last Supper, at the time when, by His redeeming sacrifice, He was crowning His mission of salvation here below.

[In this prayer] Christ Jesus asks first of all that His holy humanity enter into a sharing of that glory which the Word possesses from all eternity. Then, since Christ never separates Himself from His mystical body, He asks that His disciples and those who shall believe in Him be associated with this glory along with Him. He wants us to be "where He is." And where is that? "In the glory of God His Father."[2] *There* is the final objective of our predestination, the consummation of our adoption, the culmination that makes our perfection complete, the fullness of our life.

[1] See John 17, vv. 4, 24.   [2] See Phil. 2:11.

Let us hear how the apostle St. Paul shows us this truth. After having said that God, who wants us to be holy, has predestined us to be conformed to the image of His Divine Son, so that His Son may be the firstborn of a great many brethren, He immediately adds: "And those whom He predestined He also called; and those whom He called He also justified; and those whom He justified He also glorified."[1] These words indicate the successive phases of the work of our sanctification: our predestination and our being called in Christ Jesus, our justification by grace which makes us children of God, and our final glorification which assures us of life eternal.

We have seen what God's plan for us is; how baptism is the sign of our super-natural calling, the sacrament of our Christian initiation; how we are justified—that is to say, made just—by the grace of Christ. This justification can go on being constantly made more perfect, according to the degree of our union with Christ Jesus, until it finds its ultimate completion in glory: "those whom He justified He also glorified." Glory is that divine inheritance which is restored to us as children of God: "If sons, heirs also: heirs, indeed, of God";[2] the inheritance that Christ has merited to give us, the inheritance of which He Himself is in possession and which He wants to share with us: "*joint* heirs with Christ."[3] The inheritance Christ has, the inheritance that is to become ours; these are one and the same—eternal life, eternal glory, eternal beatitude, in our possession of God. The end-of-journey of the divine life within us is not to be found here below, but, as Jesus said, in the Father's own presence—"in the glory of God the Father."[4]

It is fitting, therefore, that in concluding these talks on the life of Christ within us, we should rest our gaze upon that eternal inheritance Our Lord asked His Father to give us. We ought to think about it often, for it is the final goal of all the work of Christ.

---

[1] Rom. 8:30 (RSV, Cath.)   [2] Rom. 8:17 (Rheims).   [3] *Ibid.*   [4] Phil. 2:11.

"I came"—I came here below—"that they may have life";[1] but that life is not truly life unless it is eternal. All our knowledge and love of the Father and of His Son Jesus ought to lead to an eternity of that life which makes us children of God. "This is *everlasting life*: that they may know you, the only true God, and Him whom you have sent, Jesus Christ."[2] Here below, we can always lose the divine life that Christ gives us through grace; only death "in the Lord"[3] makes that life permanent, assures it within us in a way that is unchangeable. The Church indicates this truth by giving the name "day of birth" to the day on which a saint enters into eternal possession of that life.[4] Here below, the life of Christ within us is only a dawn; it does not attain its noonday—a noonday, though, which has no decline—unless it comes to its fullness in glory. Baptism is the wellspring from which the divine river spouts forth, but the river's-end "which makes joyful the city of God"[5]—the city of souls—is the ocean of eternity. That is why we would have only an incomplete idea of the life of Christ in our souls if we did not contemplate the river's-end to which, of its nature, the life should flow.

You know how earnestly St. Paul prayed for the faithful of Ephesus that they might understand the mystery of Christ: "I fall on my knees to the Father," he said, that it might be given to them to comprehend the "breadth and length and height and depth" of this mystery;[6] but the great apostle is careful also to show them that this mystery has its crowning only in eternity, and that is why he ardently desires that this thought shall occupy the minds of his dear Christians. "I do not cease to remember you in my prayers," he writes to them, "that the God of our Lord Jesus Christ, the Father of glory, may enlighten the eyes of your mind, so that you may know what is the hope to which He has

---

[1] John 10:10.   [2] John 17:3.

[3] [*Translator's note*: i.e. being in a state of grace at the time of death.]

[4] For instance, in a prayer prescribed for the feast-day of St. Prisca (January 18th).

[5] See Ps. 45 (46):5.   [6] Eph. 3, vv. 14, 18 (Knox).

called you, what are the riches of the glory of the inheritance He has reserved for those that are holy."[1]

Let us, therefore, look at what this "hope" is, what are "the riches" St. Paul had so keen a desire to see known. But has not he himself said that we cannot surmise "what things God has prepared for those who love Him"; that "eye has not seen nor ear heard, nor has it entered into the heart of man"[2] to know what these marvels are? That is true; everything we say about these "riches of the glory of our inheritance" will fall short of the reality. Let us listen, however, to what Revelation tells us on the subject. We can understand it if we have the Spirit of Jesus, for St. Paul says in the same passage: "The Spirit fathoms everything, even the deep things of God ... and we have received (at baptism) that Spirit who is from God, that we may know the marvels God has given us,"[3] given us through His grace which is the dawn of glory. Let us listen to Revelation, then—but let us listen with faith, not with the senses; for everything it will tell us is super-natural.

1. Eternal *beatitude* consists in *seeing* God face-to-face, changeless *love* and perfect *joy*.

SPEAKING OF THE theological virtues which come in the train of sanctifying grace and which are like springs from which super-natural activity on the part of a child of God flows, St. Paul says that in our present state here below "there abide faith, hope and charity, these three"; but, he adds, "the greatest of these is charity."[4] And what is the reason for that? It is because in heaven, which is the completion of our adoption, faith in God gives place to vision of God, hope vanishes in our possession of God, but love remains and unites us to God for ever.

This is what it consists in, the glorification which awaits us and which will be ours: we shall see God, we shall love God, and we shall

---

[1] See Eph. 1:15-18.   [2] 1 Cor. 2:9; Isa. 64:4.   [3] See 1 Cor. 2:10-12.   [4] 1 Cor. 13:13.

joy in God; those acts constitute eternal *life*, an assured and full participation in the very life of God; and hence, beatitude of the soul, a beatitude in which the body is to share after the resurrection.[1]

In heaven, we shall *see* God. To see God as He sees Himself is the first element of this participation in the Divine nature which constitutes the *life* of blessedness; it is the first vital[2] act in glory. Here below, says St. Paul, we only know God by faith, in an obscure manner, but then we shall see Him face-to-face. Today, he says, I only know God imperfectly, but then I shall know Him "even as I am known" by Him.[3] What it is in itself, this "seeing," we cannot know now. But the soul will be given strength by "the light of glory," which is nothing else but grace itself reaching its full resplendence in heaven. We shall see God with all His perfections: or rather, we shall see that all His perfections come down to one infinite perfection which is Divinity; we shall contemplate the inner life of God; we shall enter, as St. John says, into "fellowship" with the Holy and Blessed Trinity, Father, Son and Holy Spirit;[4] we shall contemplate the fullness of Being, the fullness of all truth, all holiness, all beauty, all goodness. We shall contemplate, and for ever, the humanity of the Word Incarnate; we shall see Christ Jesus, in whom the Father is infinitely well-pleased; we shall see Him who has willed to become our "elder brother"; we shall contemplate the Divine features, henceforth glorious, of Him who has delivered us from death by the bloodshed of His Passion, who has given us the ability to

---

[1] [*Translator's note*: The judgement of each individual (the "particular judgement") takes place immediately on death, and this judgement determines the eternal destination of that soul: "it is appointed unto men once to die, and after this the judgement" (Hebr. 9:27, Rheims). The Last Judgement—of everyone—will take place at the end of the world, at the coming of Christ in glory. It "will reveal even to its furthest consequences the good each person has done or failed to do during his earthly life": CCC, para. 1039. Preceding the Last Judgement, the mortal bodies of everyone will be brought to life again (Rom. 8:11) and joined again to the individual souls ("the resurrection of the body"): CCC, paras. 998-1001.]

[2] [*Translator's note*: Marmion uses this word, derived from the Latin *vita*, in the sense of "pertaining to life."]   [3] 1 Cor. 13:12 (Rheims).   [4] 1 John 1:3.

live this immortal life. It is to Him that we shall sing a hymn of thanksgiving: "You it is who have ransomed us, O Lord, by your blood; who have established us in your kingdom. To you, praise and glory!"[1] We shall see the Virgin Mary, the choirs of angels, all that multitude of the elect which St. John declares "no man could number" and whom he shows surrounding the throne of God.[2]

This, that we see God without veil, without obscurity, without intermediary, is our future inheritance, is the consummation of our Divine adoption. "The adoption of sons of God," says St. Thomas,[3] "comes about through a certain conformity of likeness to Him who is His Son by nature."[4] This is brought about in a twofold fashion: here below, by grace (*per gratiam viae*, through grace for the journey) which is an imperfect conformity; in heaven, by glory (*per gloriam patriae*, through the glory of our homeland), which will be a perfect conformity, as St. John said: "My dearly beloved, we are now already children of God; but what we shall one day be has not yet been revealed. However, we know that on the day when God appears in His glory, we shall be like Him, for we shall see him just as He is."[5]

Here below, then, our resemblance to God is not complete; but in heaven it will appear in its perfection. Here below, we have to labor, in the obscure light of faith, to make ourselves resemble God, to "destroy the old self," to let the "new self," created in the image of Jesus Christ, come to its maturity.[6] We have to renew ourselves, perfect ourselves, ceaselessly in order to come near to the Divine model. In heaven, our resemblance to God will be one that has been made complete; we shall see that we are truly children of God.

But this "seeing God" will not put us in the position of an immobile statue, which would prevent our doing anything at all. Contemplation

---

[1] See Apoc. 5:9-13.   [2] Apoc. 7:9.   [3] III, q. XLV, a. 4.
[4] "He predestined us to become conformed to the image of His Son": see Rom. 8:29.
[5] See 1 John 3:2.   [6] See Col. 3:9-10; cf. Eph. 4:22-24.

of God will not be the annihilation of our activity. For all that the soul will not cease for a moment to contemplate the Divinity, it will keep free play of all its faculties. Look at our Lord Jesus Christ. Here on earth, His holy soul continuously enjoyed the beatific vision; and yet His human activity was not absorbed by this continuing contemplation; it remained intact, it was manifested by His apostolic journeys, His preaching and miracles. The perfection of heaven would not be perfection if it had to annihilate the activity of the elect.

We shall see God. Is that the whole of it? No: seeing God is the first element of eternal life, the primary source of beatitude; but if the intellect is divinely satisfied by Eternal Truth, must not the will be so too, by Infinite Goodness? We shall *love* God.[1] Charity, says St. Paul, "never ends."[2] We shall love God, not with a love that is weak, vacillating, so often distracted by created persons and things, exposed to ruin, but instead a powerful love, a pure love, a perfect and eternal love. If, in this vale of tears where, to preserve the life of Christ within us, we have to weep and struggle, if here below love is already so strong in certain souls that it rends out of them cries that move us to our depths: "Who shall separate me from the love of Christ? Neither persecution, nor death, nor any creature will be able to separate me from God"[3]— what will this love be when it embraces Infinite Good, never to lose it? Fervor of soul for God—we gaze and are never sated! Held secure by Love—ever we are at peace! And this love that has no end will be expressed in acts of adoration, of delight, of thanksgiving. St. John shows us the saints prostrated before God and making heaven ring

---

[1] According to St Thomas (I-II, q. III, a. 4), beatitude consists essentially in the possession of God, gazed on face-to-face. This beatific vision is above all an act of the intellect; from this possession through the intellect there flows, as a property of it, beatitude of the will which finds its satisfaction and its repose in possession of the beloved object made present through the intellect.

[2] 1 Cor. 13:8 (RSV, Cath.)   [3] See Rom. 8:35-39.

with their praise: "Glory and honor and power to you, Lord, forever and ever!"[1] That is an expression of their love.

Finally, we shall *joy in* God. You have read in the Gospel that Our Lord Himself compares the kingdom of heaven to a banquet which God has prepared in order to honor His Son: "He will gird himself, and have them sit at table, and He will come and serve them."[2] What does this signify if not that God will Himself be our joy? "O Lord," cries the psalmist, the elect "shall be inebriated with the plenty of your house; and you shall make them drink of the torrent of your pleasure. For with you is the *fountain of life*"[3]—the very source of life. God says to the soul that seeks Him: "It is I—I myself—who will be your great reward."[4] It is as if He were saying: "I have loved you so much that I have not wished to give you a natural bliss, a natural happiness; I have wished to take you into my own house, to adopt you as my child, in order that you might have a share of my beatitude. I wish you to live by my very life; I wish my own beatitude to become your beatitude. I gave you my own Son on earth. Become mortal by His humanity,[5] He was delivered up for you to merit the grace of your being and remaining my child; He has given Himself to you in the Eucharist under the veil of faith. Now it is I myself in glory who give myself to you, so as to make you a sharer of my life; to be your beatitude without end." The Father "will give Himself because His Son gave Himself; He will give Himself immortal to immortals because His Son gave Himself mortal to mortals."[6] Grace here below, glory above; but it is the same God who gives us them: and glory is but the coming into flower of grace. It is the Divine adoption, hidden and imperfect here below, revealed and complete in heaven.

---

[1] See Apoc. 7:12.   [2] Luke 12:37 (RSV, Cath.)

[3] Ps. 35 (36):9-10.   [4] See Gen. 15:1.

[5] [*Translator's note*: This is the correct translation; the words are predicated, of course, of the Son. I regret that my rendering in *Barb of Fire* (2001) was a mistranslation.]

[6] St. Augustine, *Enarr. in Ps.* XLII, 2.

That is why the psalmist so much sighed after this possession of God: "As the hind longs for running waters, so my soul longs for you, O God."[1] "My soul thirsts for God, for the *living* God."[2] "I shall be satisfied when your glory shall appear"[3]—I shall be satisfied only when your glory, a glory full of delights, shall appear to me.

For that matter, Our Lord Himself when speaking of this beatitude tells us that God causes the faithful servant to "enter into the joy" of his Lord.[4] This joy is the joy of God Himself, the joy God possesses in the knowledge of His infinite perfections, the beatitude God feels in the ineffable fellowship of the Three Persons; the infinite repose and contentment in which God dwells. His joy will be our joy: "that they may have my joy made full in themselves";[5] His beatitude and repose, *our* beatitude and repose; His life, our life; a perfect life, in which all our faculties will be fully contented.

In this will be found "that full participation in unchangeable good," as St. Augustine excellently calls it.[6] To such an extent has God loved us. Oh! if we knew what God has in store for those who love Him!

And because this beatitude and this life are those of God Himself, they will be, for us, eternal. They will have no end, no termination. "Death shall be no more," says St. John, "neither shall there be mourning, nor cries of pain, nor suffering"; "God will wipe away every tear from the eyes of those who enter into His joy."[7] There will be no sin any more, nor death, nor fear of death: nothing will rob us of this joy. It is *for always* that we shall be with the Lord: "we shall be with the Lord for ever."[8] Where He is, there shall we be.

---

[1] Ps. 41 (42):2 (1) (St P.)   [2] Ps. 41 (42):2 (3) (RSV, Cath.)   [3] Ps. 16 (17):15.
[4] Matt. 25:21; Marmion alludes to words of Christ referring to it in parable.
[5] John 17:13.   [6] *Epist. ad Honorat.* CXI, 31.
[7] See Apoc. 21:4.   [8] 1 Thess. 4:16 (Knox).

Hear in what strong terms Jesus has given us this assurance: "I give my sheep everlasting life, and they shall never perish, and no one shall snatch them out of my hand. My Father, who has given them to me, is greater than all, and no one will be able to snatch them out of my Father's hand. My Father and I are one."[1] What assurance Christ Jesus gives us! We shall be with Him for ever, with nothing thenceforth being able to separate us from Him; and in Him we shall savor an infinite joy that no one can ever take away from us, because it is the very joy of God and His Christ. "You now," said Jesus to His disciples, "have sorrow"—here below—"but I will see you again, and your heart shall rejoice; and your joy no man shall take from you."[2] Like the Samaritan woman,[3] let us say to Him: "O Lord Jesus, Divine Master, Redeemer of our souls, elder Brother, give us this divine water, that we may never thirst; this water that will make us live. Grant us, here below, to stay united to you through grace, so that one day—as you have prayed your Father for us[4]—we may see for ever the glory of your humanity, and rejoice in you, for ever, in your kingdom!"

2. *The bodies* of the just are to share, *after the resurrection*, **in this beatitude. The glory of** *this resurrection* **already** *come to reality in Christ*, **head of His mystical body.**

As you know, this life of blessedness becomes the portion of every soul as soon as it goes forth from this world, if it is, through grace, a child of God, and if there no longer remains anything of the penalty of sin for it to expiate in Purgatory. However, this is not all: God still reserves something more for us. What? Is not the soul completely full of joy? Certainly, but God wishes also to give the body its beatitude, when the end of time brings the general resurrection.

---

[1] See John 10:27-30.   [2] John 16:22 (Rheims).   [3] See John 4:15.   [4] John 17:24-26.

It is a dogma of faith, this resurrection of the dead: "I believe in ... the resurrection of the body ... life everlasting."[1] Our Lord has promised it us: "He who eats my flesh and drinks my blood ... I will raise him up on the last day."[2]

What is more, Christ has already made, in Himself, a reality of this resurrection, by coming forth, victorious and living, from the tomb. Now, by rising from the dead, Christ has raised us, with Him, from the dead. I have said to you often: by becoming incarnate, the Word has united Himself mystically with the whole of human nature and forms, with His elect, a body of which He is the head. If our head is risen, then not only shall we be raised with Him one day, but on the day of His triumph He raised—already, in principle and by entitlement—all those who believe in Him. Hear with what clarity St. Paul expounds this doctrine:[3] God, who is rich in mercy, by reason of the immense love He bears for us, has already brought us to life "together *with Christ*"[4]—in Jesus Christ and through Jesus Christ. He has raised us all up *with* Him, and seated us in heaven *with* Him—because He does not separate us from Him. See how great is the mercy! that so much does God love us in His Son Jesus that He does not wish to separate us from Jesus, that He wishes us to resemble Jesus and to share Jesus's glory, not only so far as the soul is concerned, but in the body.

How right the great apostle is to say that God is rich in mercy and that He loves us with an immense love! It is not enough for God to satisfy our soul with eternal happiness; He desires that our flesh share in this endless beatitude, after the example of the flesh of His Son. He desires to adorn it with those glorious prerogatives of immortality, agility,[5] spirituality, with which the humanity of Jesus was resplendent when He came forth from the tomb. Yes, the day will arrive when we shall all be raised, all "in their proper order."[6] Christ is the first to have

---

[1] The Apostles' Creed.   [2] John 6:55; cf. John 11:23-25.   [3] Eph. 2:4-6.   [4] Eph. 2:5.
[5] [*Translator's note*: *Agilité*, agility, quickness of motion.]   [6] 1 Cor. 15:23 (Jerus.)

been raised, as being the head of the elect and the "first-fruits" of a harvest;[1] and, after this, there will rise all those who belong to Christ by grace.[2] "As in Adam all die, so also in Christ all shall be made alive."[3] "Then comes the end," when Christ "delivers the kingdom to God the Father,"[4] the kingdom won by His blood. For Christ "must reign, until 'He has put all His enemies under His feet.' And the last enemy to be destroyed will be death."[5] And "when all things have been made subject to Him," made subject to Christ by the Father, then the Son Himself, in His humanity, will give homage to Him who has subjected all things to Him, that thus "God may be all in all."[6] Christ Jesus conquered death on the day of His resurrection: "O death, where is your victory?"[7] He will conquer it in His elect as well, at the final resurrection.

Then His work as leader and head of the Church will have been completed, entirely consummated; Christ will possess this Church He has loved, and for which He delivered Himself up so that it would be glorious, "having no spot or wrinkle" or any such thing, but pure and "without blemish."[8] The mystical body will have fully arrived at "that maturity which is proportioned to the completed growth of Christ."[9] Then, Christ Jesus will present to His Father that multitude of the elect whose elder brother He is. Oh! what a glorious sight it will be to see this kingdom that is subject to Jesus; to contemplate the work of His blood and of His grace, offered by Christ Himself, King of glory, to His Father! What ineffable beatitude to be part of that, with the Virgin, the angels, the elect; with those blessed souls we have known here below, with whom we have been united by the bonds of blood or by holy affection! Then it is that Jesus will be able to repeat in all truth:

---

[1] 1 Cor. 15:23 (Jerus.)   [2] The damned will be raised as well, but without the glorious prerogatives of the elect; their bodies will for ever be subject to eternal agonies. [Marmion's note.]   [3] 1 Cor. 15:22 (Rheims).   [4] 1 Cor. 15:24.
[5] 1 Cor. 15:24-26; Ps. 109 (110):1.   [6] See 1 Cor. 15:28.   [7] 1 Cor. 15:55.
[8] See Eph. 5:27.   [9] Eph. 4:13 (Knox).

"Father, I have finished the work you gave me to do";[1] then it is that the wish His sacred heart made heard at the Last Supper will have been fulfilled: "Father, I pray to you for those you have given me; that they may have my joy made full in themselves; that where I am, they also may be, so that they may behold my glory; and that the love with which you have loved me may be in them."[2] The wishes of Christ will be accomplished; the Church Triumphant will gaze upon the glory of its Leader; it will itself be filled with that "fullness of joy," streaming down upon it from Him. Divine life, eternal life, will overflow upon each one of us, and we shall reign for ever with Christ.

St. John, in his Apocalypse, has described something of the glory of this kingdom. "I heard what was like the voice of a great crowd, and as the voice of many waters, and as the voice of mighty thunders, saying, 'Alleluia! for the Lord, our God, the Almighty, reigns! Let us rejoice and thrill with gladness, let us give Him glory; for the hour of the marriage of the Lamb has come' (the Lamb is Christ), 'and his Bride has made herself ready' (the Bride is the Church, triumphant henceforth). 'And it has been granted her to clothe herself in fine linen, shining and pure.'" The "fine linen," adds St. John, is the virtues of the saints. "And an angel said to me: 'Write: Happy are those who are called to the marriage-feast of the Lamb.'"[3]

Those words are but a shadow of the divine reality, of the beatitude that awaits us. At baptism, we received the seed-germ of it. But this seed-germ needed to grow, to develop, to be protected against the briars and the stones. We have cleared away from it, by Penance, what was able to destroy it or lessen its growth; we have maintained it by the Sacrament of Life, by our practice of the virtues. At present, this divine life that Christ communicates to us remains hidden within us: "your life is hidden with Christ in God,"[4] but in heaven it will reveal itself, its

---

[1] See John 17:4.
[3] See Apoc. 19:6-9.
[2] See John 17, vv. 6, 9, 13, 24, 26.
[4] Col. 3:3.

splendor will appear, its beauty will become manifest. And never forget that, once arrived at this flowering-forth, it will know no more increase, its splendor will grow no greater, its beauty become no more perfect. Faith tells us that the place for labor and merit is here below; that heaven is journey's-end. There, no more increase is possible: it is reward after the fight. "Merit is amassed by one who believes; the reward is given to one who sees."[1]

3. The *degree of our beatitude* is determined here below in the measure of our grace. How St. Paul exhorted the faithful to *progress* in the exercise of the super-natural life "unto the day of Christ."

THERE IS still more. We shall joy in God in the same measure that grace has attained in us at the time of our departure from this world.[2]

Let us not lose sight of this truth: the degree of our eternal beatitude is determined by—and for ever and ever will remain as—the degree of charity we have attained, with the grace of Christ, when God calls us to Him. Each moment of our life is therefore infinitely precious, since it suffices to advance us by one degree in the love of God, to lift us up further in the beatitude of life eternal.

And let us not say that one degree more, or one degree less, is of small importance. What is of *small* importance when it is a question of God—of a beatitude, and a life without end, of which God is the very source? If, according to the parable spoken by Our Lord in person, we have received five talents, it is not for the purpose of our burying them, but in order that we shall make them bear fruit.[3] And if God measures our reward by the efforts we have made to live by His grace, to in-crease that grace within us, will you then call it a small thing to yield

[1] St. Augustine, *Tract. in Johann.*, LXVIII, 3.
[2] "Each shall receive his wages according to his labor" (1 Cor. 3:8, RSV, Cath.)
[3] Matt. 25:14-30.

the Heavenly Father merely a harvest "such as it is"? Jesus has Himself told us: "By this my Father is glorified, that you bear much fruit,"[1] that is: "My Heavenly Father finds His glory in seeing you abound, through my grace, in fruits of holiness that, for you in heaven, will be fruits of beatitude." So true is this, that Christ compares His Father to a vine-dresser who prunes us, by our sufferings, with the object of our bearing more fruit—"that it," the branch, "may bear more fruit."[2] Anyway, is our love of Christ Jesus so weak that we count it a small matter to be, in the Heavenly Jerusalem, a more resplendent or a less resplendent member of His mystical body? The holier we become, the more we shall glorify God throughout all eternity, and the greater will be our share in that hymn of thanksgiving the elect sing to Christ the Redeemer: "You have ransomed us, O Lord."[3]

Let us, then, be watchful always to clear away the obstacles that can lessen our union with Jesus Christ; to let the Divine action penetrate us so deeply, to let the grace of Jesus act so freely within us, that it makes us reach "that maturity which is proportioned to the completed growth of Christ." Listen to the pressing exhortations that St. Paul, who had been "caught up to the third heaven,"[4] gave to his dear Philippians: "For you," he said, "whom I love with all tenderness in the heart of Jesus Christ, I am praying to God, that your charity may abound more and more ... so that you may be pure and blameless for the day of Christ, filled with the fruits of justice through Jesus Christ, to the glory and praise of God."[5]

And see especially how St. Paul himself set a wonderful example of the carrying out of this precept. The great apostle has come to the final days of his life; the captivity he is now enduring at Rome has

---

[1] John 15:8 (RSV, Cath.)   [2] John 15:2.   [3] See Apoc. 5:9.

[4] 2 Cor. 12:2. [*Translator's note:* "the third heaven," i.e. the highest heaven. St. Paul "is using the language of some astronomical system he had heard of (there were many). He certainly means ... the place where God dwells." (*A Catholic Commentary on Holy Scripture*).]   [5] See Phil. 1:8-11.

suspended the course of the numerous journeys he undertook so as to spread the good news of Christ. He is close to the end of his struggles and his labors. The mystery of Christ, that he has revealed to so many souls, is one he has lived so deeply that he can say to those same Philippians: "Christ is my life, and death to me is henceforth gain."[1]

"Nevertheless," he continues, "if by living longer here below I am to reap fruit thereby, I would not know which to choose. I am pressed from both sides; I have a desire to die and be for ever with Christ — which is much the better thing of the two; but it is more necessary that I still remain on earth, because of yourselves ... for your progress and joy in the faith."[2] The apostle then recalls to them[3] how he has spurned the advantages of Judaism in order to attach himself solely to Jesus Christ, in whom he has found everything, for nothing thenceforth can separate him from Christ. And yet, listen to the words he writes: "It is not that I have already laid hold of this" — the prize, the crown given to the victor after the race, "or that I have already attained perfection.... I do only one thing. Forgetting all I have accomplished up to now, putting the whole of myself into pressing ahead, I run straight for the finishing-line in order to carry off the prize to which God has called me from on high in Jesus Christ."[4] So St. Paul wanted to forget all the progress of his past life, in order to stretch forward with more energy than ever towards his eternal goal.

Then, see how he exhorts his faithful[5] to follow him: "You also, brethren — be imitators of me, as I am of Christ."[6] "Our homeland is in heaven, and we await the coming from there of our Savior, Jesus Christ, who will transform our poor bodies by making them resemble His own glorious body, through the mighty power by which He subjects all things to Himself." And the Apostle, so full of charity, prisoner though he be, finally concludes with this emotional and pressing

---

[1] See Phil. 1:21.   [2] See Phil. 1:22-25.   [3] Phil. 3:4-11.   [4] See Phil. 3:12-14.
[5] [*Translator's note*: i.e. the faithful, at Corinth and Philippi, to whom he is writing.]
[6] See 1 Cor. 11:1.

salutation: "So therefore, my dear and beloved brethren, my joy and my crown, stand fast thus in the Lord."[1]

And you also, I say to you in concluding these talks—you also stand fast in faith in Christ Jesus; retain an invincible hope in His merits, live in His love. For so long as you are still here below, "exiled from the Lord" as St. Paul says,[2] never stop increasing—through an ardent faith, through holy desires, through a charity that unreservedly delivers you up to the generous and faithful accomplishment of the Divine good pleasure—your capacity to see and love God, to joy in Him in the eternal beatitude, to live by His own life. The day will arrive when faith will give place to sight, when hope will be succeeded by blessed reality, when love will come to full flower in God, in an embrace that is eternal. It sometimes seems to us that this beatitude is so far away. But no, each day, each hour, each minute, brings us closer to it.

With St. Paul, I say to you again: "Seek the things that are above, where Christ is seated at the right hand of God." Place your affection in "the things that are above, not the things that are on earth," like wealth, honors, pleasures. For "you have died"—to the attraction of all these things (which are fleeting), and your life—your true life, that of grace, pledge of eternal beatitude—"is hidden with Christ in God." But "when Christ your Life," your head, "shall appear"—triumphant on the Last Day—"then you too will appear with Him in glory,"[3] the glory you will share with Him, because you are His members.

Therefore, let no pain, no suffering, cast you down; for all "our present light affliction, which is for the moment, prepares for us an eternal weight of glory that is beyond all measure."[4] Let no temptation bring you to a halt; for if in the time of trial you are found faithful, the hour will come when you receive that crown which is to mark your entry into the true life, "the crown of life which God has promised to

---

[1] See Phil. 3:20-4:1.   [2] 2 Cor. 5:6.   [3] Col. 3:1-4.   [4] 2 Cor. 4:17.

those who love Him."[1] Let no insane joy seduce you; for "the things which are seen are temporal"—they last only for a time—"but the things which are not seen are eternal."[2] "The time is short," and "this world ... is passing away."[3] What never passes are the words of Jesus Christ: "my words will not pass away."[4] Those words are for us sources of eternal life: "The words that I have spoken to you are spirit and life."[5]

As I have endeavored to show you in the course of these talks, the divine life within us is but a participation, through grace, in that fullness of life which is in the humanity of Christ Jesus and which flows down into each of our souls in order to make them children of God: "Of his fullness we have all received."[6] The source of our holiness is there, and not elsewhere. That holiness, as I have said to you often, and wish to repeat to you in concluding, is of an essentially supernatural order; we shall only find it in being united with Jesus Christ: "Without me you can do nothing."[7] All the treasures of grace and of holiness that God destines for souls are to be found stored up in Christ Jesus; He came here below simply in order to make us partakers of them in superabundance: "I came that they may have life, and have it more abundantly."[8] The Eternal Father gives us His Son simply in order that He may be "*our* redemption, *our* wisdom, *our* sanctification, *our* justification,"[9] *our* life.

Which means that, though without Him we can do nothing, *in* Him we become rich and do not lack anything: "nothing is wanting to you in any grace."[10] These riches are "so much greater than we can understand,"[11]

---

[1] James 1:12.
[2] 2 Cor. 4:18 (Rheims); cf. Rom. 8:18: "the sufferings of the present time are not worthy to be compared with the glory to come that will be revealed in us" (Cfy).
[3] 1 Cor. 7:29-31.   [4] Luke 21:33.   [5] John 6:64.
[6] John 1:16.   [7] John 15:5.   [8] John 10:10.
[9] See 1 Cor. 1:30. [*Translator's note*: Marmion's italics.]
[10] 1 Cor. 1:7 (Rheims).   [11] Phil. 4:7 (Jerus.)

says St. Paul; because they are Divine. But, if we wish, they can become ours, we can take them to ourselves. What is needed for that? That we remove the obstacles—sin, attachment to sin, attachment to created persons and things, attachment to ourselves; obstacles that can impede the action of Jesus Christ and of His Spirit within us. That we deliver ourselves up to Christ with all the energies of our body and our soul, in order, like Him, to seek to be pleasing to our Heavenly Father through love.

And then our Heavenly Father will recognize in us the features of His beloved Son. Because of Christ Jesus, He will place His delight in us, He will shower His gifts upon us as we await the coming of that thrice-blessed day when we shall all, together and for ever, be with the Lord, Christ Jesus our Life: "When *Christ*, *your Life*, shall appear, then *you too* will appear *with Him* in glory."[1]

O Christ Jesus, Incarnate Word, Son of Mary, come and live in your servants, with your spirit of holiness, the fullness of your power, the reality of your virtues, the perfection of your ways, the communication of your mysteries; and overcome all the power of the enemy through your Spirit, to the glory of the Father! Amen.

'CHRIST, GOD, IS THE HOMELAND TO WHICH WE GO.

CHRIST, MAN, IS THE ROAD BY WHICH WE GO THERE.'

St. Augustine, *Sermo* 123, c. 3.

---

[1] Col. 3:4. [Marmion's italics.]

AFTER THE BEATIFICATION...

EXTRACTS FROM TWO TALKS BY DOM MARK TIERNEY ON
BLESSED COLUMBA'S CAUSE FOR CANONIZATION

The favors of the Lord are not all past,
His kindnesses are not exhausted;
Every morning they are renewed;
Great is His faithfulness

Lamentations, 3:22-23

WE ARE GATHERED here this evening, to give thanks to God for the life
and work of Blessed Columba Marmion.[1] We also give thanks to Pope
John Paul II, for having beatified Columba Marmion just two weeks
ago in Rome. But we must also express our thanks to those many
faithful disciples of Marmion who down the years have prayed for his
beatification. And surely this parish of Dundrum must rank first
among these faithful disciples who have helped to perpetuate his name
and his reputation for sanctity in this city of Dublin. I could think of
no more deserving place for us to meet and to express our gratitude
than here in this church. For it was here that the young Father
Marmion celebrated Mass and exercised his priestly ministry during
the years 1881 and 1882....

Already, at this early stage of his life, he had discovered the secret
of communicating with people. Above all, he had discovered the joy of
caring for people and leading them to God. Today, the Marmion
Society carries on this work of helping and caring for the people of
Dundrum parish. It is a blessed task, one which I know continues to
bring joy, comfort and grace, to the hundreds of people who use the

[1] Excerpts from a homily preached by Dom Mark Tierney in Dundrum Church,
Dublin, Ireland, September 17, 2000.

Dom Marmion House. May God and the Blessed Columba Marmion smile on your work and give you the strength to carry on.

One of the highlights of the Beatification ceremony in Rome on September 3, was the homily of His Holiness, John Paul II. When he came to speak of Columba Marmion, he did so in English. Let me quote just one sentence from his homily : "Dom Columba Marmion, in his writings, teaches a simple yet demanding way of holiness for all the faithful, 'whom God has destined in love to be his adopted children through Jesus Christ.' A simple, yet demanding way of holiness!" The key word is "holiness." It is interesting to note that the Vatican daily newspaper *l'Osservatore Romano*, when reporting the Beatification of Pius IX, John XXIII, Tommaso Reggio, William Chaminade and Columba Marmion, put as the main heading of their leading article "Five Men linked by a desire for Holiness." The actual words used by the Pope, who was speaking in Italian at that point, were these: "Five different personalities, each with his own features and his own mission, all linked by a longing for holiness." To "long for" something is a little stronger than just to "desire" it. From the beginning of his priestly life, Marmion had already made his own the opening lines of the psalm : "As the hind longs for the running waters, so my soul longs for you, O God." Longing and yearning for God was the one goal of his life, a goal he also set for all his spiritual sons and daughters.

What of "the life of the soul" of Columba Marmion? We only have to peruse his own writings : *Christ, the Life of the Soul*; *Christ in His Mysteries*; *Christ, the Ideal of the Monk*, to recognize the story of his own spiritual ascent and realize that Marmion became indeed one of those chosen souls who are "clothed with God as with a garment." He wrote, not only from his own *conviction* but from his own *experience*; he had found God, before he attempted to speak of God to others. And having found God, he set himself as his life-long mission: "to bring God to people and to bring people to God."

One of the principal symbols employed by Marmion to bring people to God, was the Cross, the Cross as the sign of the triumph of

Christ over Satan. The Cross as a sign of Victory, not defeat. Here we are, gathered in this church dedicated to the Holy Cross. It was no mere chance that Marmion spent many happy years in Holy Cross College, Clonliffe and then later, one happy year laboring on the mission in Dundrum, in this church of the Holy Cross.

I am certain that this persisting experience in the two Holy Crosses, had an indelible effect upon him.

It is said that he made the Stations of the Cross everyday of his priestly life. He saw the Cross as more than a mere sign or symbol, but rather as the key to the understanding of the human condition. From Baptism, when we are first signed with the Cross, up to the moment of our death, when we give our last loving look at the crucifix, the Cross is never far from our lives. Marmion composed a very moving commentary on the Stations of the Cross, which is printed in Chapter XIV of *Christ in his Mysteries*. In one of his reflections, he says: "The more we enter into these dispositions that filled the heart of Jesus as he made his sorrowful way to Calvary, the more our souls will receive graces and lights, because the Father will behold in us a more perfect image of His Divine Son."

I don't want you to go away from this church thinking that Marmion was one of those people who lock themselves away in their monastic cells, kill-joys, who never make a joke or give a good laugh. On the contrary Marmion was full of fun, a wonderful friend. He had many, many friends, from every walk of life, rich and poor, young and old. Let me tell you the story of one of his correspondents, a young lady, who wanted to become a religious sister. She wrote asking his advice, and he recommended the Dominicans. However, after a few months in the convent she left, and again sought his advice. This time he suggested the Carmelites, so she offered herself to the local Carmelite convent, and was accepted. But this did not work out either. Yet, she still persisted. Marmion never lost patience with her, though at this stage he began addressing her as "My Dear Mousie." He thought of her as a Mouse, going in and out of a hole in a room. She never took offense. In the end, she did find a convent, the Poor Clares, that suited her. In all his letters thereafter, he still addressed her as "My dear Mousie." When the monks of Maredsous began studying Marmion's letters, they were baffled by the series of "Dear Mousie" ones. They looked up every English dictionary of names, and found "Mickey Mouse" and even "Minnie Mouse," but no "Mousie." So, they simply put a capital "M," and the letters were headed "My dear M...." They had missed the nuance, and had also missed out on Marmion's sense of humor.

The lives of the saints are meant to inspire us to seek a similar holiness. Saints are, above all, people of prayer. Marmion never tired of saying that "Prayer is the only sure path to holiness." I will leave you with the quotation from the Book of Lamentations, which I gave at the beginning:

> *The favors of the Lord are not all past,*
> *His kindnesses are not exhausted;*
> *Every morning they are renewed;*
> *Great is His faithfulness. Amen*

IT SHOULD BE recorded that a number of factors occurred in the 1980s and 1990s, which helped to stir up interest in the Cause of Dom Columba Marmion.[1] One such factor, was the lobbying of the Roman authorities by cardinals, archbishops, bishops, religious leaders and lay people from all over the world, in the form of postulatory letters, requesting the Canonization of Marmion. Among those who wrote a postulatory letter to Rome was the future Pope John Paul I, then Monsignor Albino Luciani, Archbishop of Venice. Many of the writers referred to Marmion's "heroic sanctity" and "noble virtues," and urged that his Cause be advanced as soon as possible. Another factor was the renewed interest in Marmion's spirituality, which was noticeable in the aftermath of Vatican Council II. In fact, his name had come up on several occasions in the discussions of the Council Fathers. Marmion's doctrine is recognizable in several articles of the Constitution on the

---

[1] Excerpts from a talk given by Dom Mark Tierney in Dom Marmion House, Dublin, Ireland, October 11, 2003.

Church, the Sacred Liturgy, and the Church in the Modem World. It was Marmion who first coined the phrase "The Liturgical Movement."

And then there was the visit by Pope John Paul II to Belgium in 1985, when the papal helicopter flew over Maredsous on the way from Brussels to Beauraing. We have it on good authority that the Holy Father, at this moment, confided to one of his aides: "I owe more to Columba Marmion for initiating me into things spiritual than to any other spiritual writer." And on his return to Rome, he asked about the actual state of the Process for the Cause of Marmion's Beatification. As a result of this Papal intervention, and also his saying later "I hope to beatify Abbot Columba Marmion before I die," the monks of Maredsous were urged to make some more significant move to have Marmion's Cause advanced in Rome. I was given the job, because I am a historian.

I have often told the story of my first visit to the Congregation for the Causes of the Saints. I made an appointment with a certain sub-sub-Secretary, who, it turned out had never heard of either myself or Columba Marmion. He looked up Marmion in the file-names beginning with M., but could find no reference to any Marmion. Then he looked under C. for Columba, and drew a blank. I had only one card left and suggested he should look under J, as Marmion's baptismal name was Joseph. But no sign of it there. At this stage I felt quite a fool, as the good sub-sub-Secretary made it quite clear that I was wasting his time. However, at that moment I got a brainwave, and suggested that the good man look up under the I's, as Joseph in Latin is Ioseph. And sure enough, there was the vital evidence on the index-card, which was entitled "De Canonisatione Servi Dei Iosephi Columbae MARMION." The good sub-sub-Secretary did not quite embrace me, but at least I was accepted as a legitimate person, chosen to work on the Cause of Columba Marmion. He did, however, point out to me that Marmion had been given the number Prot. 948, and that I should not be too optimistic about his Cause reaching any conclusion in my life-time. He assured me that Marmion would have to wait in line, until the other 947 candidates had been dealt with.

I spent the next five years working on the biography, in Maredsous, Rome and Glenstal. The work was eventually published in 1994 by the Vatican Press, and given the very interesting title: *Canonisationis Servi Dei Josephi Columba Marmion Sac. Prof. OSB (1858-1923).* This seemed to imply that Marmion was up for Canonization, though it was clear that he had first of all to be beatified. The truth of the matter is that anyone who has been beatified—as is the case with Marmion— is also a worthy candidate for canonization.

All this became very clear to me, less that a week after Marmion's beatification on September 3, 2000, when I was approached by the Congregation for the Causes of the Saints, and invited to work on the process for his Canonization. It was also indicated to me that they hoped one day to declare Marmion a Doctor of the Church—The Doctor of Divine Adoption.

At this very moment, we are about half-way towards that goal. There are three steps on the way to Canonization. The first is the publication of the Complete Correspondence of Blessed Columba Marmion. There are about 2000 extant letters written by him, covering all of his adult life. The majority of these are kept in the archives of the Abbey of Maredsous, in Belgium, although there are a number still in private hands. I have spent the last three years preparing these for publication. The letters will be published in three volumes, under the title: *Blessed Columba Marmion: Self-portrait in his Letters.* It will then be studied by the people in the Congregation for the Causes of the Saints. I should add that the majority of these letters are in French, and the first edition will be a French-language version. However, I will have them translated into English, as soon as possible, in order to have them available in the English-speaking countries of the world.

The second requirement for the Canonization process is a new and lengthy study of Marmion's writings, stressing his importance in the history of Catholic spirituality, and showing how he is worthy of being declared a Doctor of the Church. This is a big challenge, but the work is progressing satisfactorily....

The third factor, which forms part of the on-going process for Canonization, is a *miracle*. Rome is usually looking for a miracle in the form of a cure from a serious or terminal illness. It must be a cure which medical science cannot explain, being outside the experience of ordinary medical practice. We had such a miracle in the process for the Beatification of Blessed Columba. The person in question was cured of terminal cancer. Her doctors proclaimed that they could not explain her condition "by medical science alone." She visited the tomb of Blessed Columba in Maredsous in 1966, prayed for a miracle, and has been cancer-free ever since. She is still living, in good health, and of course so grateful to Blessed Columba. I should add that she is a woman of strong faith, the mother of seven children and innumerable grandchildren. Marmion has certainly changed her life.

We have, I think, to pray that the Lord will grant another miracle through Blessed Columba. Many people write to me to say that they have received "favors." In the Abbey of Maredsous, over the years, thousands of such letters have been received, from all over the world. People pray to Marmion especially for help in family matters. For example, married couples who seem to be unable to have children pray to him, and their prayers have been heard. People pray to him to deepen their spiritual life, or help in times of despair and doubt.

Let me conclude by quoting the words of Pope John Paul II, which he used in Rome, on September 3rd, 2000, when beatifying Columba Marmion: "May a widespread rediscovery of the spiritual writings of Blessed Columba Marmion help priests, religious and laity to grow in union with Christ, and bear faithful witness to him through ardent love of God and generous service of their brothers and sisters."

APPENDIX B

A Chronology of the Life of
Blessed Columba Marmion

1858	April 1	Joseph Marmion born at 57 Queen Street, Dublin, the seventh of nine children.
	April 6	Baptized in St. Paul's Church, Arran Quay, Dublin.
1864	May	First Holy Communion in St. Paul's Church.
1868		First formal education, St. Laurence O'Toole's School, Dublin.
1869	January 11	Enters Belvedere College.
1873	December 18	Leaves Belvedere, having completed his secondary education, winning a scholarship to Clonliffe.
1874	January 11	Enters Holy Cross College, Clonliffe.
	October 3	Begins his studies in philosophy at the Catholic University, Dublin.
1877	October	Bachelor of Arts Degree.
1879	March 13	Promise made, with two other Clonliffe students. As well as daily prayer, it bound them (following St. John Berchmans) to acts for three intentions: tender devotion to the Mother of God, profound humility, and ardent love for souls.
	December 24	Arrives in Rome to complete his theological studies.
1880	September	Visit to Monte Cassino and first call to the Benedictine way of life.
1881	February 27	Receives minor orders.
	March 12	Ordained Subdeacon.
	April 15	Ordained Deacon.
	May	Awarded Gold Medal and declared "Student of the Year" at Propaganda Fide College, Rome.

	June 16	Ordination to the Priesthood.
	June 17	First Mass.
	July 23-24	First visit to Maredsous Abbey, Belgium.
	September 14	Appointed Curate in Dundrum, Dublin.
	November	Serious illness.
1882	September 1	Appointed chaplain to the Redemptoristines, Drumcondra, Dublin.
	September 15	Professor of Metaphysics and French at Holy Cross College, Clonliffe.
1885	April 29	Marmion finally decides to become a monk in Maredsous.
	September	Archbishop Walsh, of Dublin, asks Marmion to postpone his departure for Maredsous for a year.
1886	June 26	Relinquishes his chaplaincy to the Redemptoristines and is appointed chaplain to Mountjoy Prison, Dublin.
	October 25	Obtains permission from Archbishop Walsh to join the Benedictine Order.
	November 18	Departure from Dublin for Maredsous, arriving on November 21.
	November 24	Receives the monastic habit, as a Postulant.
1887	January	Begins keeping his Diary or *Private Notes*.
	February 10	Begins his Novitiate, and receives the name *Columba*.
1888	February 10	Makes First monastic Profession.
	March	Appointed Professor of English in Abbey School.
1889	February 5	Marmion's timely action saves the monastery from being burned down.
	September	Appointed Professor of Philosophy to junior monks of Maredsous.

1891	February 10	Makes Solemn Profession in Maredsous.
	February 15	Begins his active ministry, preaching at Graux.
1893	October 2	Appointed Assistant Novice-Master.
1894	September	Writes his first article for the *Revue Bénédictine*.
1895	June 10 - July 4	Journey to Ireland for Centenary celebrations at Maynooth College.
1897	September 29	Appointed Prefect of Clerics in Maredsous
	November	Begins his monthly conferences to the diocesan clergy of Dinant.
1898	Nov. 30 - Dec. 8	Gives his first retreat in Maredret.
1899	January	Notified of his appointment as Sub-Prior and Prefect of Clerics in new foundation in Louvain.
	February 12	Nominated Confessor to the Carmelite Convent of Louvain.
	April 13	Arrival at Mont César, Louvain, to start foundation.
	June	External Examiner in Theology at Catholic University of Louvain.
	July 11	Appointed Prior of Mont César.
1900	September	Retreat to the monks of Maredsous.
		(Gives Retreats, between 1901 and 1915, at Douai (France). Erdington, Ampleforth, Douai Abbey, nr. Reading (England), Haywards Heath, Westminster Diocese, Ramsgate, Ware, Stanbrook, Nottingham, Cork, Mount Melleray, Paris and other places; and engages in much spiritual correspondence. Is zealous to share the Catholic Faith with individual non-Catholics.)
1908	December 21	Marmion's Prayer of Consecration to the Trinity.
1909	September 28	Elected as Abbot of Maredsous.

1913	Feb. onwards	Helps the monks of Caldey, Wales, in their journey from Anglicanism to Rome.
1914	August	Outbreak of war. Marmion's Council at Maredsous decides to relocate part of the Community in England or Ireland.
	September 14	Marmion leaves for England, via Holland, in disguise, so as to find a suitable property, following which, one at Edermine, Co. Wexford, Ireland, is bought for him. Gives a series of retreats in England.
1916	March 23	Following serious illness in London, convalesces in the Isle of Wight.
	April 11	Despite advice that he might now be treated as a spy in Belgium and shot, Marmion returns to Maredsous, via Holland, arriving on May 19.
1917	December 8	*Christ, the Life of the Soul* is published.
1918-1922		Marmion involved in the delicate question of which Benedictines should be responsible for the Dormition Abbey in Jerusalem following the end of the War, and in the formation of a new Belgian Benedictine Congregation.
1919	March 25	*Christ in His Mysteries* is published.
	April 4-23	Seriously ill, in St. Vincent's Hospital, Dublin.
1922	July 5	*Christ, the Ideal of the Monk* is published
1923	January 25	Offers his last Mass.
	January 30	Marmion dies, at Maredsous, of bronchial pneumonia, and is buried on February 3rd.

For a detailed account of Marmion's life, see *Dom Columba Marmion: A Biography* by Dom Mark Tierney, OSB (1994, The Columba Press, Blackrock, Dublin).

INTRODUCTORY MATERIAL FROM PRIOR EDITIONS OF
CHRIST, THE LIFE OF THE SOUL

LETTER OF HIS HOLINESS BENEDICT XV

TO THE AUTHOR

To Our beloved Son
Columba Marmion, OSB,
Abbot of Maredsous

Beloved Son, health and the Apostolic Benediction.

Having recently perused, as far as Our occupations permitted, the two books: *Christ, the Life of the Soul* and *Christ in His Mysteries*, which you have kindly sent Us, We readily appreciate their praiseworthiness as being singularly conducive to excite and maintain the flame of Divine love in the soul. For although these pages do not contain the whole of the discourses you have made to your spiritual sons concerning Jesus Christ, the Exemplar and Cause of all sanctity, nevertheless these commentaries, so to speak, on the matter of your teaching, show clearly how this doctrine is capable of fostering the desire to imitate Christ and to live by Him "Who of God is made unto us wisdom, and justice, and sanctification, and redemption."

It was therefore a most happy inspiration to publish these works so that not only your own spiritual children but many others should be helped in the way of perfection. We are told that these works are already in the hands of many even among the laity. Therefore thanking you, We at the same time congratulate you and, as a pledge of heavenly reward, We impart to you, beloved Son, the Apostolic Benediction.

Given at Rome, near St. Peter's, October 10, 1919, the sixth year of Our Pontificate.

BENEDICT XV, Pope.

"RECEIVED in private audience at the Vatican [the year after the Pope wrote this letter] Dom Marmion had the joy of hearing the Sovereign Pontiff say, as he showed him *Christ, the Life of the Soul* on a shelf of his household volumes: 'I make use of it for my spiritual life.'

When, subsequently, the Vicar of Christ was receiving in audience Msgr. Szepticky, Archbishop of Lemberg, he recommended to him the works of Dom Marmion. 'Read this,' he said, 'it is the pure doctrine of the Church.'" (Dom Raymond Thibaut)

Preface[1]

by

Blessed Columba Marmion

THE CONFERENCES that make up the present work are the fruit of several years of reflection and prayer. They have been given in very varied circumstances; but the author, not having had the intention of publishing them, had never committed them to writing. A number of people who had heard them, believing they might do good to souls, had taken abundant notes and had begged the author to allow them to be published. In the form in which the talks had been delivered, with all the imperfections of something spoken to suit a particular occasion[2] in a language other than the author's mother tongue, it would not have been possible to present them to the public.

But a devoted collaborator [Dom Raymond Thibaut] took on the difficult and delicate task of bringing together those numerous notes, of arranging them and of preparing them for the printers.[3] Throughout the entire course of his labor he strove to preserve the author's own

---

[1] To the first (French-language) edition of *Christ, the Life of the Soul*.

[2] "When preaching, Dom Marmion never used his notes; always, even during retreats comprising a large number of conferences, he spoke from the abundance of his heart, not confining himself to the notes which he had prepared." (Dom Matthew Dillon)

[3] But: "There is not a single page which was not submitted to him (Marmion), not a page that was not revised by him, pen in hand, making a correction here and there and adding an occasional text from the Scriptures, the Fathers or the Liturgy,

manner, and this same concern for fidelity impelled him to retain as much as possible of the direct style and the simple tone in which the conferences were delivered. The author is convinced that this collaborator has succeeded in his task: he wishes to acknowledge the latter's devotion and to testify to his own great gratitude to him, as also to all who, in whatever way, have helped him in his labor.

The arrangement of the different conferences is due to that collaborator, and it will be enough to cast a glance at the index placed at the front of the volume to appreciate the simplicity of the plan adopted.

The first part comprises an overall account of the scheme of the divine designs. The endeavor is to show there the plan pursued by God, Father, Son and Holy Spirit, in order that we, in Jesus Christ, may share in the Divine life.

The second part shows how the soul can and should adapt itself to God's plan so as to take to its own self the divine life brought by Christ. Faith in the divinity of Jesus is the first attitude of the soul, and baptism the first sacrament. Here one borrows from St. Paul the fundamental doctrine according to which that sacrament of Christian initiation imprints upon the whole life of the disciple of Christ a double direction to go in, namely "Death to Sin" and "Life for God." Next is set forth in some detail how this twofold character ought to be re-encountered in the whole development of one's Christian life.

The majority of the conferences contain the material for several talks; hence the length of some of them. Rather than multiply the chapters, our collaborator has preferred to group around one subject everything that relates to it, so as to safeguard the homogeneity of the ideas.

With a view to facilitating the use of the book for prayer, there have been placed at the beginning of each conference some short

---

the better to illustrate his thought. This constant and exhaustive revision not only served to guarantee the editor against all danger of error, but enabled Dom Marmion to give his work the hall-mark of absolute authenticity." (Dom Matthew Dillon)

Summaries in which the numbers (which are then repeated in the body of the conference) indicate the principal divisions.[1] The words in italics show the main ideas. The reader who desires to have a more detailed recapitulation of the contents of the conferences will wish to refer to the tables.[2]

May these pages be of help to all souls who are eager for interior life! The book has been written merely as a commentary on the words of Christ Jesus: Come to me; I am the Life of your souls; you will find this Life only in me, but you will find it in abundance:

> *I came that they may have life,*
> *and have it more abundantly.*

---

[1] In the present edition the summaries, instead of being grouped together at the beginning of a chapter, have been placed at the head of the section to which they refer.

[2] Detailed summaries at the conclusion of the first and subsequent editions.

PREFACE

by

Désiré-Joseph Cardinal Mercier
Archbishop of Malines[1]

These pages will do much good. They are restful for the soul. They simplify Christian life.

The chief object of the author who has received the confidences of many restless souls, embarrassed by the complications of their personal methods, is, if I am not mistaken, to enlarge these souls, to free them from their self-bondage, to facilitate for them, by rendering it more attractive, their ascension towards God. He leads them, in each of his conferences, to Him Who is "the Way, the Truth and the Life."[2]

He shows them, by turns, Divine Providence enveloping, in the same design of predestination, Christ, the Word made Man and ourselves (Book One, first chapter); then, on the lines laid down by St. Thomas Aquinas,[3] he describes the mediation of Christ, the Sanctifier of our souls (Book One, second and third chapters), he shows in Him, true God and true Man, the one and universal Exemplar of all holiness; the meritorious and satisfactory Cause who has paid the price of our salvation to Divine justice, according to these words of the apostle St. Paul: "And being consummated, He became, to all that obey Him, the cause of eternal salvation: called by God a high priest, according to

---

[1] One of the leaders of the 20th-century Thomistic revival, the Belgian churchman (1851-1926) was named a Cardinal in 1907. This piece appeared in the French-language edition of *Christ, the Life of the Soul*. The translation is from an early English edition.

[2] John 14:6.   [3] St Thomas, III, q. XXIV, a. 3.

527

the order of Melchizedek";[1] and lastly, the realizer, the efficient Cause of our holiness, for, always following the doctrine of the apostle St. Paul whom the author is never tired of quoting: We have our divine origin in Christ: God has willed He should be "made unto us wisdom, and justice, and sanctification, and redemption."[2]

The office of Christ being thus shown under all its aspects, the Benedictine theologian next considers the realization of the Divine plan in souls: Christ forms His mystical body, the visible and invisible Church; but the Holy Ghost formed Christ[3]—at least it is so expressed by theology in its language of "appropriation"—and, as the "Spirit of Jesus," He consummates the work of our sanctification (Book One, fifth and sixth chapters).

Thus is completed the picture of the work of Christ conceived eternally in the designs of the Heavenly Father and realized by Christ the Mediator and by His sanctifying Spirit.

Christ is the center of the plan and of the work of God: as Man-God He sums up all: *Tu solus sanctus, tu solus Dominus, Jesu Christe*; You alone are holy, you alone are Lord, Jesus Christ.

The Blessed Albert the Great, the master of St. Thomas Aquinas, in that substantial and delightful opuscule entitled: *De adhaerendo Deo* "Of the adherence of the soul to God," invites us to enter into Christ, from man to God, to pass through the open Wounds of the suffering and dying Humanity of Christ so as to penetrate into the secrets of His Divinity: "Nor, I say, should one concentrate in one's mind on any other object than the wounded Jesus Christ alone, and so direct one's attention continually and earnestly through Him at Him, that is to say, through man at God, through the wounds of His humanity at the innermost nature of His divinity."[4]

---

[1] Hebr. 5:9.   [2] 1 Cor. 1:30.

[3] [Mercier refers to the Incarnation of the Eternal Son of God, the Word, in Mary's womb.]

[4] "Nec aliud, inquam, objectum quis mente attendat quam solum Jesum Christum vulneratum, sicque per eum in eum, id est, per hominem in Deum, per vulnera

All the substance of the spirituality of the Gospel lies in this formula. Hence the Right Reverend Abbot Columba says wisely: "For certain souls, the life of Christ Jesus is one subject of meditation among many others; this is not enough. Christ is not *one* of the means of spiritual life; He is *all* our spiritual life" (page 83).

The second part of the volume is consecrated to showing forth the work of the soul that wills to receive abundantly the Divine life of which Christ is the source.

Faith in the Divinity of Jesus Christ constitutes the first step towards this life. Baptism, the first of all the sacraments, renders the one on whom it is conferred a disciple of Christ. The work of baptism is double, although simultaneous: it takes away sin, the germ of death, and gives grace, the source of life. By this sacrament of adoption and initiation, the Christian becomes a partaker of the death and glorious life of his Divine Head. These two aspects of spiritual life, so clearly pointed out by St. Paul, ought to envelop the whole existence of every Christian.

The author next shows in detail how we "die to sin" and how we "live for God." He develops the laws to which the practice and growth of this life for God are subject, and the sources whence it is especially nourished: the Eucharist, Sacrifice and Sacrament; prayer, whether it be the prayer of the Church in her liturgy "which makes us one with Christ," or mental prayer, "the blossoming of the gifts of the Holy Ghost." The love of a soul for Christ will necessarily overflow on all who compose the mystical body of Christ; and in the first place ranks the Virgin Mary who, by her Divine Maternity, enters into the very essence of the mystery of the Incarnation. The last chapter shows how "the fullness of the mystical body of Christ" is only attained in the beatitude of eternal life; that is the final term of our predestination, the consummation of our adoption in Christ Jesus.

---

humanitatis ad intima divinitatis suae sedulo et obnixe intendat." B. Alberti Magni, *De adhaerendo Deo*, cap. 2.

Thus end these conferences which place the mystery of Jesus in high relief. They refer everything to Christ the source of all grace, of all life, of all holiness. This leading idea, full of significance, give the work its unity as well as its strength.

The table of contents marks out with much clearness the continuity of this idea in its different stages and renders it superfluous for us to attempt here any detailed exposition. Besides this book is not one to be subjected to a dry analysis. It must be read and meditated with the heart as well as with the head, as it was with all his apostolic soul that the author delivered the conferences of which the book is composed.

There are perhaps some souls who will wonder at this simplification of spirituality; they cannot accustom themselves to the idea that it is not necessary to seek difficulties where none exist, in order to arrive at perfection.

However, it is Christ and His Gospel that are right. And is it not written in the Gospel: "Unless you become as little children, you shall not enter the Kingdom of Heaven"? And did not our Divine Jesus say in a moment of holy exultation—*Exsultavit Spiritu Sancto*[1]—"I confess to Thee, O Father ... because Thou hast hidden these things from (those the world esteems) the wise and prudent, and hast revealed them to little ones"?

The perfume of Holy Scripture, to be breathed in at each page of this volume, gives the impression that it was conceived and prepared during prayer, at the foot of the altar, before being given to the public.

Souls desirous of living the inner life will gratefully welcome this work. The religious communities above all, to whom these conferences were preached, will recall the communicative accents they heard whilst listening to the solid and clear doctrine now left to them as a guide, and they will ask the Holy Spirit, as we do, to grant this inspiring book, *Christ, the Life of the Soul*, the full success it merits.

---

[1] "He exulted in the Holy Spirit," Luke 10:21.

PREFACE

by

Francis Cardinal Bourne
Archbishop of Westminster[1]

CHRIST, THE LIFE OF THE SOUL has received in its original forms such ample commendation both from our Holy Father the Pope and from the learned and much venerated Cardinal Archbishop of Malines that any further praise seems almost out of place. Yet very willingly indeed I add my less authoritative tribute to the more important words that they have written, and I very gladly advise all those who seek in the English language a work that will surely help and guide them on the path of closer union with their Maker, to read and study this translation of the extremely valuable treatise which is the outcome of long thought and labor on the part of the Abbot of Maredsous. Those who have been privileged to make retreats under his guidance will know what to expect from his pen, and they will not suffer disappointment. And by his written work and its translation into English his teaching will reach a far wider and more permanent diffusion.

Such solid teaching is much needed at the present time. The number of souls seeking more intimate union with God is rapidly increasing.

---

[1] Born in 1861, he was appointed Archbishop of Westminster in 1903, named Cardinal in 1911, and remained head of the Catholic Church in England and Wales until his death in 1935. This piece was written for the first English-language edition.

But many are held back by the want of simplicity, the discouraging complexity, and the exaggerated refinement and multiplication of detail, which have lessened the value of so many modern spiritual books. The main object of striving has been obscured by too great insistence on the methods of attaining, and the freedom of the soul under the guidance of the Holy Ghost has been impaired. Abbot Marmion carries us back to a wider and more wholesome tradition, and many will rise up to bless him, as they find in his teaching new strength, and fresh vigor in their striving after God.

To the Clergy both in the world and in the cloister, to the religious communities of women, active as well as contemplative, and to the devout laity I very earnestly commend this book.

Feast of Saint Michael the Archangel

Zaccheus Press

Zaccheus Press is a small Catholic press devoted to publishing fine books for all readers seeking a deeper understanding of the Catholic faith.

To learn more about Zaccheus Press, please visit our webpage. We welcome your comments, questions, and suggestions.

www.zaccheuspress.com

A nd behold, there was a rich man named Zaccheus, who was the chief among the tax collectors. And he sought to see Jesus, but could not because of the crowd, for he was short of stature. So he ran ahead and climbed up into a sycamore tree to see Him, for He was going to pass that way.

—Luke 19:2-4